PRACTICAL GUIDE TO U.S. TAXATION OF INTERNATIONAL TRANSACTIONS

EIGHTH EDITION

ROBERT J. MISEY, JR.
MICHAEL S. SCHADEWALD

.CCH
a Wolters Kluwer business

Editorial Staff

Production . . . . Jennifer Schencker

Index . . . . Deanna Leach

This publication is designed to provide accurate and authoritative information in regard to the subject matter covered. It is sold with the understanding that the publisher is not engaged in rendering legal, accounting, or other professional service and that the authors are not offering such advice in this publication. If legal advice or other expert assistance is required, the services of a competent professional person should be sought.

ISBN 978-0-8080-2682-2

Printed in the United States of America

SUSTAINABLE FORESTRY INITIATIVE

Certified Sourcing

www.sfiprogram.org

SFI-01028

To Monica.

To my sons, Doug and Tom.

Robert J. Misey, Jr.

Michael S. Schadewald

Preface

This book provides the reader with a practical command of the tax issues raised by international transactions and how those issues are resolved by U.S. tax laws. The book emphasizes those areas generally accepted to be essential to tax practice. The book is written primarily as a desk reference for tax practitioners and is organized into four parts. Part I provides an overview of the U.S. system for taxing international transactions, and also discusses the U.S. jurisdictional rules and source-of-income rules. Part II explains how the United States taxes the foreign activities of U.S. persons, and includes chapters on the foreign tax credit, anti-deferral provisions, foreign currency translation and transactions, export tax benefits, and planning for foreign operations. Part III describes how the United States taxes the U.S. activities of foreign persons, including the taxation of U.S.-source investment income and U.S. trade or business activities, as well as planning for foreign-owned U.S. operations. Finally, Part IV covers issues common to both outbound and inbound activities, including transfer pricing, tax treaties, cross-border mergers and acquisitions, state taxation of international operations, and international tax practice and procedure.

Robert J. Misey, Jr.

Michael S. Schadewald

July 2011

About the Authors

Robert J. Misey, Jr., J.D., M.B.A., LL.M., is a shareholder with the law firm of Reinhart Boerner Van Deuren s.c. in Milwaukee, Wisconsin and chair of the firm's International Department. Mr. Misey concentrates his practice in the areas of international taxation, transfer pricing, and tax controversies. He previously worked as an attorney with the IRS Chief Counsel (International) in Washington, D.C. and as a large-case attorney in the Western and Southeast Regions. He also led a region of Deloitte & Touche's International Tax Services Group and has tried 23 cases before the U.S. Tax Court.

Mr. Misey received his Master of Laws degree, with high distinction, from Georgetown University, where he was the graduate student editor of *The Tax Lawyer,* and received his Juris Doctor and Master of Business Administration degrees from Vanderbilt University. He also studied international law at Emmanuel College in Cambridge, England. He is a member of the Tax Section of the District of Columbia, Wisconsin, and California bars.

Mr. Misey has written numerous articles and spoken on international taxation, transfer pricing, and tax controversies at continuing education programs in many states and foreign countries. He also teaches a course on International Taxation in the Master of Taxation program at the University of Wisconsin-Milwaukee.

Michael S. Schadewald, Ph.D., CPA, is on the faculty of the University of Wisconsin-Milwaukee, where he teaches graduate and undergraduate courses in business taxation. A graduate of the University of Minnesota, Professor Schadewald also co-authors the *Multistate Corporate Tax Guide* and writes a column for the *Journal of State Taxation,* both of which are published by CCH, a Wolters Kluwer business. He has also published over 40 articles in academic and professional journals, including *Journal of Accounting Research, The Accounting Review, Contemporary Accounting Research, Journal of the American Taxation Association, Journal of Taxation, Tax Adviser, CPA Journal, Issues in Accounting Education, Journal of Accounting Education, International Tax Journal, Tax Notes International, Journal of International Accounting, Auditing and Taxation, Journal of State Taxation, State Tax Notes, TAXES-The Tax Magazine,* and *Advances in Taxation.* Professor Schadewald has served on the editorial boards of *Journal of the American Taxation Association, International Tax Journal, International Journal of Accounting, Journal of State Taxation, Advances in Accounting Education, Issues in Accounting Education,* and *Journal of Accounting Education.* Prior to entering academics, he worked in the Milwaukee office of Arthur Young (now Ernst & Young).

Acknowledgments

I would like to acknowledge the assistance of my father and mentor, Robert J. Misey, Sr., Esq., who provided organizational and, as always, motivational input with respect to various aspects of this work. I would also like to acknowledge the assistance of several attorneys at Reinhart Boerner Van Deuren s.c.—Adam R. Konrad and Amy E. Arndt—as well as Jennifer E. Weigel, CPA, who all provided thoughtful comments on previous drafts of several chapters of this book. Finally, I would like to acknowledge the assistance of my legal secretary, the incomparable Donna Simon.

Robert J. Misey, Jr.

I would like to acknowledge the support and encouragement of my colleagues, past and present, at the University of Minnesota, the University of Texas, and the University of Wisconsin-Milwaukee.

Michael S. Schadewald

Table of Contents

Chapter 5: Anti-Deferral Provisions

Chapter 14: Section 367—Outbound, Inbound and Foreign-to-Foreign Transfers

List of Appendices

Chapter 1

Overview of U.S. Taxation of International Transactions

¶ 101 BASIC PRINCIPLES

.01 Tax Jurisdiction

In designing a system to tax international transactions, a government must determine which "persons" to tax as well as what "income" to tax. One basis upon which countries assert tax jurisdiction is a personal relationship between the taxpayer and the country. For example, a country may wish to tax any individual who is either a citizen or a resident of the country, or a corporation that is created or organized in the country. A second basis upon which countries assert tax jurisdiction is an economic relationship between the taxpayer and the country. An economic relationship exists whenever a person derives income from property or activities that are located within a country's borders.

A double taxation problem may arise when a taxpayer who has a personal relationship with one country (the home country) derives income from sources within another country (the host country). The host country usually asserts jurisdiction on the basis of its economic relationship with the taxpayer. The home country also may assert jurisdiction over the income on the basis of its personal relationship with the taxpayer. Traditionally, it has been up to the home country to solve the double taxation problem of its citizens and residents, either by allowing them to exclude foreign-source income from taxation, or by taxing foreign-source income but allowing a credit for any foreign taxes paid on that income.

The United States employs a credit system. Therefore, the United States taxes U.S. persons on their worldwide income.[1] U.S. persons include U.S. citizens, resident alien individuals, and domestic corporations (i.e., corporations organized under U.S. law). An alien is considered a U.S. resident if he or she meets either the green card test (i.e., lawful permanent immigrant status) or the substantial presence test.[2] To mitigate double taxation, a U.S. person can claim a credit for the foreign income taxes imposed on foreign-source income.[3] A key feature of the U.S.

---

[1] Code Sec. 61.
[2] Code Sec. 7701(b).

[3] Code Sec. 901.

credit system is the foreign tax credit limitation, which restricts the credit to the portion of the pre-credit U.S. tax that is attributable to foreign-source income.[4]

One major exception to the U.S. credit system is the deferral privilege, whereby the United States does not tax foreign-source income earned by a U.S. person through a foreign corporation until those profits are repatriated by the domestic shareholder through a dividend distribution. The policy rationale for deferral is that it allows U.S. companies to compete in foreign markets on a tax parity with their foreign competitors. A second major exception to the U.S. credit system is the foreign earned income exclusion, under which a U.S. citizen or resident alien who lives and works abroad for extended periods of time may exclude from U.S. taxation a limited amount of foreign earned income plus a housing cost amount.[5]

U.S. tax law contains a two-pronged system for taxing the U.S.-source income of foreign persons, including nonresident aliens and foreign corporations (i.e., corporations organized under the laws of a foreign country). The United States taxes foreign persons at graduated rates on the net amount of income effectively connected with the conduct of a trade or business within the United States.[6] The United States also taxes the gross amount of a foreign person's U.S.-source investment-type income at a flat rate of 30%.[7] The U.S. person controlling the payment of U.S.-source investment income must withhold the 30% tax.[8] Income tax treaties usually reduce the withholding tax rate on interest, dividend, and royalty income to 15% or less.[9] In addition, the United States provides a broad statutory exemption for portfolio interest income.[10] Capital gains from sales of stocks or bonds also are generally exempt from U.S. taxation.[11] Special rules apply to gains from the sale of U.S. real property, which are taxed in the same manner as income effectively connected with the conduct of a U.S. trade or business.[12]

.02 Source of Income Rules

The source of income rules play an important role in the computation of a U.S. person's foreign tax credit limitation, which equals the portion of a taxpayer's pre-credit U.S. tax attributable to foreign-source income.[13] Foreign taxes in excess of the foreign tax credit limitation are referred to as "excess credits." One strategy for eliminating excess credits is to increase the foreign tax credit limitation by increasing the percentage of the taxpayer's total taxable income that is classified as foreign-source for U.S. tax purposes. The source rules play a more prominent role in the taxation of foreign persons, since the United States generally taxes foreign persons only on their U.S.-source income.

The source rules for gross income are organized by categories of income. Under the general rules, interest income is U.S.-source if the payer is a domestic

---

[4] Code Sec. 904.

[5] Code Sec. 911.

[6] Code Secs. 871(b) and 882.

[7] Code Secs. 871(a) and 881.

[8] Code Secs. 1441 and 1442.

[9] Articles 10, 11 and 12 of the United States Model Income Tax Convention of November 16, 2006 ("U.S. Model Treaty").

[10] Code Secs. 871(h) and 881(c).

[11] Reg. § 1.1441-2(b)(2).

[12] Code Sec. 897.

[13] Code Sec. 904.

corporation or a U.S. resident, and foreign-source if the payer is a foreign corporation or nonresident. Dividend income is U.S.-source if the payer is a domestic corporation and foreign-source if the payer is a foreign corporation. Personal services income is U.S.-source if the services are performed in the United States, and foreign-source if the services are performed abroad. Rental and royalty income is U.S.-source if the property is used in the United States and foreign-source if the property is used abroad. A gain on the sale of a U.S. real property interest is U.S.-source income, whereas a gain on the sale of real property located abroad is foreign-source income.[14]

As a general rule, gains on the sale of personal property are U.S.-source income if the taxpayer is a U.S. resident and foreign-source income if the taxpayer is a nonresident. There are exceptions, however, for inventories, depreciable property, intangibles, and stock of a foreign affiliate. As a consequence, the residence-of-seller source rule applies primarily to sales of stocks or bonds.[15]

Gross income from the sale of inventory that the taxpayer purchased for resale is sourced based of where the sale occurs.[16] The place of sale is determined solely by where title to the goods passes from the seller to the buyer.[17] Therefore, such income is U.S.-source income if title passes in the United States, and foreign-source income if title passes abroad. On the other hand, income from the sale of inventory manufactured by the taxpayer generally is allocated between U.S.-source and foreign-source income using the 50-50 method. Under the 50-50 method, a U.S. manufacturer apportions 50% of the gross profit from export sales based on the percentage of export sales for which title passes abroad, and the other 50% based on the percentage of production assets located abroad.[18]

If the operative tax attribute is the net amount of U.S.-source or foreign-source income, the taxpayer allocates and apportions its deductions between U.S.-source and foreign-source gross income. Deductions are allocated to a related class of gross income, and are then apportioned between U.S.-source and foreign-source gross income using an apportionment base that reflects the factual relationship between the deduction and the gross income.[19]

Special source of income rules apply to currency exchange gains and losses, insurance underwriting income, international communications income, space and ocean activities income, and transportation income. In addition, special allocation and apportionment rules apply to interest expense and research and experimentation expenditures.

¶ 102 TAXATION OF U.S. PERSON'S FOREIGN ACTIVITIES

.01 Foreign Tax Credit

A U.S. citizen, resident alien, or domestic corporation may claim a credit for foreign income taxes paid or incurred.[20] The credit is limited, however, to the

---

[14] Code Secs. 861 and 862.
[15] Code Sec. 865.
[16] Code Secs. 861(a)(6) and 862(a)(6).
[17] Reg. § 1.861-7(c).

[18] Reg. § 1.863-3.
[19] Reg. § 1.861-8.
[20] Code Sec. 901.

portion of the taxpayer's pre-credit U.S. tax that is attributable to foreign-source income.[21] This limitation prevents U.S. persons operating in high-tax foreign countries from offsetting those higher foreign taxes against the U.S. tax on U.S.-source income, and thereby confines the effects of the foreign tax credit to mitigating double taxation of foreign-source income. Foreign income taxes that exceed the limitation can be carried back one year and forward up to ten years and taken as a credit in a year that the limitation exceeds the amount of creditable foreign taxes.[22]

The relation of U.S. and foreign tax rates is a major determinant of whether a taxpayer is in an excess limitation or an excess credit position. In general, taxpayers will be in an excess limitation position when the foreign tax rate is lower than the U.S. rate and in an excess credit position when the foreign tax rate is higher than the U.S. rate. When a taxpayer is in an excess credit position, the non-creditable foreign income taxes increase the total tax burden on foreign-source income beyond what it would have been if only the United States had taxed that income.

One strategy for eliminating excess credits is to increase the limitation by increasing the percentage of the taxpayer's total taxable income that is classified as foreign-source for U.S. tax purposes. For example, the title-passage rule for sourcing income from inventory sales provides U.S. companies with a significant opportunity to increase foreign-source income. By arranging for the passage of title in the importing country rather than the United States, export sales will generate foreign-source income.

Another strategy for eliminating excess credits is cross-crediting. If a taxpayer can blend low-tax and high-tax foreign-source income within a single foreign tax credit limitation, then the excess limitation on the low-tax income will soak up the excess credits on the high-tax income. This averaging process produces an excess credit only when the average foreign tax rate on all of the items of foreign-source income within a single limitation is higher than the U.S. rate.

The current foreign tax credit limitation system is found in Code Sec. 904(d), and is designed to prevent cross-crediting between lightly taxed passive foreign investment income and more heavily taxed active foreign business profits. Cross-crediting is still allowed, however, with respect to active business profits derived from different foreign countries or passive investment income derived from different foreign countries.

There are currently two separate limitations, one for passive category income and the other for general category income. Passive income primarily includes dividends, interest, rents, and royalties, and net gains from dispositions of property that produces such income. General limitation income is a residual category, and includes most of the income from active foreign business operations, such as manufacturing, distribution, and service operations. Special look-through rules apply to dividends, interest, rents, and royalties received by a U.S. shareholder from a controlled foreign corporation (CFC), as well as dividends received by a domestic corporation from a non-controlled Code Sec. 902 corporation. For exam-

---

[21] Code Sec. 904(a).   [22] Code Sec. 904(c).

¶102.01

ple, a dividend received from a CFC that earns only manufacturing income is treated as general category income, not passive income.[23]

.02 Deemed Paid Foreign Tax Credit

A domestic corporation generally cannot claim a dividends-received deduction for a dividend from a foreign corporation. As a result, dividends from foreign subsidiaries are included in a domestic parent corporation's U.S. taxable income. However, the domestic parent may claim a foreign tax credit for any foreign withholding taxes paid on the dividend, as well as a deemed paid foreign tax credit for the foreign income taxes paid by a 10%-or-more-owned foreign corporation.[24] Congress enacted the deemed paid credit to protect domestic corporations with foreign subsidiaries against double taxation, as well as to better equate the tax treatment of U.S. companies with foreign subsidiaries to those with foreign branches.

A domestic corporation that receives a dividend from a 10%-or-more-owned foreign corporation is deemed to have paid an amount of foreign income taxes equal to the foreign corporation's post-1986 foreign income taxes multiplied by the ratio of the dividend to the foreign corporation's post-1986 undistributed earnings. Post-1986 undistributed earnings equal the cumulative amount of the foreign corporation's undistributed earnings and profits, reduced by actual and deemed dividend distributions in prior years. Post-1986 foreign income taxes equal the cumulative amount of the foreign corporation's foreign income taxes, reduced by the amount of foreign income taxes related to prior-year actual or deemed dividend distributions. A domestic corporation that operates abroad through multiple tiers of foreign corporations may also be eligible to claim deemed paid credits for taxes paid by second-tier through sixth-tier foreign corporations.[25] Only a domestic corporation may claim a deemed paid foreign tax credit. U.S. citizens and resident aliens are not eligible, nor are S corporations.[26]

Because the amount of dividend income recognized by a domestic parent corporation is net of any foreign income taxes paid by a foreign subsidiary, the domestic corporation is implicitly allowed a deduction for those foreign taxes. To prevent a double tax benefit, the domestic corporation must gross up its dividend income by the amount of the deemed paid foreign taxes, which offsets the implicit deduction.[27]

The U.S. tax consequences of dividend repatriations depend on whether the foreign corporation is operating in a low-tax or high-tax foreign jurisdiction. No U.S. tax is due on a dividend from a foreign corporation operating in a high-tax foreign jurisdiction because the available deemed paid foreign tax credits exceed the pre-credit U.S. tax, whereas a dividend from a foreign corporation operating in a low-tax foreign jurisdiction results in a residual U.S. tax. Through cross-crediting, the excess credits on dividends from high-tax foreign subsidiaries can be used to offset

---

[23] Code Sec. 904(d). In 2010, Congress enacted Code Sec. 904(d)(6), which creates a special basket for items of income re-sourced by treaty.

[24] Code Sec. 902.

[25] Code Sec. 902.

[26] Reg. § 1.902-1(a)(1).

[27] Code Sec. 78.

the residual U.S. tax due on dividends from low-tax foreign subsidiaries. The CFC look-through rule makes cross-crediting possible with respect to dividends from CFCs located in low-tax and high-tax foreign jurisdictions, as long as the underlying earnings of both types of CFCs are assigned to the limitation for general category income.

Foreign withholding taxes can exacerbate the excess credit problems associated with dividends from high-tax foreign subsidiaries. However, income tax treaties usually reduce the statutory withholding tax rate on dividends to 15% or less. Therefore, a domestic parent corporation may be able to use tax treaties to reduce foreign withholding taxes by, for example, owning foreign operating subsidiaries through a foreign holding company located in a country with a favorable treaty network that contains lenient limitation of benefits articles.

Finally, it may be advantageous for a domestic parent corporation to repatriate the earnings of a foreign subsidiary through interest and royalty payments rather than dividend distributions. A foreign corporation usually can claim a foreign tax deduction for interest and royalties paid to its U.S. parent, whereas dividend distributions typically are not deductible. On the other hand, only a dividend distribution can provide the domestic parent corporation with a deemed paid credit. If the foreign corporation is operating in a high-tax foreign jurisdiction, the benefits of a deduction at the foreign subsidiary level may exceed the cost of losing the deemed paid credit at the domestic parent level.

.03 Anti-Deferral Provisions

The United States generally does not tax a U.S. multinational corporation's foreign-source income earned through a foreign subsidiary until the subsidiary repatriates those earnings through a dividend. This policy, known as "deferral," creates an opportunity to avoid U.S. taxes on portable income which is easily shifted to a foreign corporation located in a tax haven country. In 1962, Congress attempted to close this perceived loophole by enacting Subpart F (Code Secs. 951– 965), which denies deferral to certain types of tainted income earned through a foreign corporation.

Subpart F requires a U.S. shareholder of a "controlled foreign corporation" (CFC) to include in income a deemed dividend equal to a pro rata share of the CFC's Subpart F income.[28] A foreign corporation is a CFC if U.S. shareholders own more than 50% of the stock of the foreign corporation, by vote or value. Examples of Subpart F income include foreign personal holding company income, and foreign base company sales income. Foreign personal holding company income includes dividends, interest, rents, and royalties, whereas foreign base company sales income includes income from the sale of goods which the CFC buys from or sells to a related person, and are neither manufactured nor sold for use in the CFC's country of incorporation.[29] Subpart F also requires a U.S. shareholder of a CFC to recognize a deemed dividend equal to a pro rata share of the CFC's earnings invested in U.S.

---

[28] Code Sec. 951.

[29] Code Sec. 954.

property. This rule reflects the reality that a CFC's investment in U.S. property often is substantially equivalent to distributing a dividend to its U.S. shareholders.[30]

Consistent with the notion that a Subpart F inclusion represents a deemed dividend, a domestic corporation which directly owns 10% or more of a CFC's voting stock can claim a deemed paid foreign tax credit for the CFC's foreign income taxes attributable to a deemed dividend.[31] In addition, to prevent a second layer of U.S. tax on the CFC's earnings, a U.S. shareholder can exclude from income the receipt of an actual distribution of a CFC's earnings that were taxed to the U.S. shareholder in a prior tax year by reason of a Subpart F inclusion.[32] Finally, to prevent the conversion of ordinary income into capital gains, a U.S. shareholder must treat the gain on the sale of the stock of a CFC as a dividend to the extent of the shareholder's pro rata share of the CFC's post-1962 (non-Subpart F) earnings and profits.[33]

Congress enacted the passive foreign investment company (PFIC) regime to expand the reach of U.S. taxing authority with respect to passive investment income earned by U.S. persons through a foreign corporation. Congress enacted the PFIC provisions to deal with perceived abuses by U.S. investors in foreign mutual funds, but the regime applies to any foreign corporation which qualifies as a PFIC. A foreign corporation is a PFIC if either 75% or more of the corporation's gross income is passive income, or 50% or more of the corporation's assets (by value) are passive assets.[34]

A PFIC's undistributed earnings are subject to U.S. taxation under one of three methods, each of which eliminates the benefits of deferral. Under the qualified electing fund (QEF) method, U.S. investors who can obtain the necessary information can elect to be taxed currently on their pro rata share of the PFIC's earnings and profits.[35] A U.S. investor who does not make a QEF election is not taxed on the PFIC's earnings until the PFIC makes an excess distribution, which is taxed as if it had been realized pro rata over the holding period for the PFIC's stock. Thus, the tax due on an excess distribution is the sum of the deferred yearly tax amounts, increased by interest charges.[36] Finally, a U.S. shareholder of a PFIC may make a mark-to-market election with respect to the stock of the PFIC if such stock is marketable.[37]

.04 Foreign Currency Translation and Transactions

The foreign branches and subsidiaries of domestic corporations often conduct business and maintain their books and records in the currency of the host country. This creates a currency translation problem for the U.S. parent, which must translate into U.S. dollars the income and earnings remittances of a foreign branch, as well as actual and deemed distributions from a foreign subsidiary. In addition, a domestic corporation may realize currency exchange gains and losses when it engages in transactions denominated in a foreign currency, or when a foreign

---

[30] Code Secs. 951 and 956.
[31] Code Sec. 960.
[32] Code Sec. 959.
[33] Code Sec. 1248.

[34] Code Sec. 1297.
[35] Code Sec. 1293.
[36] Code Sec. 1291.
[37] Code Sec. 1296.

¶102.04

branch or subsidiary repatriates earnings that were previously taxed to the U.S. parent. Finally, foreign income taxes are paid in the local currency, and must be translated in U.S. dollars.

A domestic corporation must make all of its U.S. tax determinations in its functional currency, which is the U.S. dollar. However, a separate qualified business unit (QBU) of the domestic corporation may have a non-dollar functional currency if that QBU conducts a significant part of its activities in an economic environment in which a foreign currency is used and maintains its books and records in that foreign currency. A foreign subsidiary corporation is automatically a QBU, and a foreign branch qualifies as a QBU if it is a separate and clearly identified unit of a trade or business of the corporation for which separate books and records are maintained.[38]

If a foreign branch qualifies as a QBU and has a functional currency other than the U.S. dollar, the taxable income of the branch is computed in its functional currency and then translated into dollars using the average exchange rate for the branch's tax year. When the branch remits its earnings to the U.S. home office, the domestic corporation recognizes a currency exchange gain or loss equal to the difference between the dollar value of the remittance (determined using the spot rate) and the taxpayer's basis in the distributed earnings (determined by the dollar amount at which the earnings were previously included in U.S. taxable income). Any foreign income taxes paid on branch income generally are translated into U.S. dollars at the average exchange rate for the tax year to which the taxes relate.[39]

If a foreign corporation pays a dividend in a foreign currency, the domestic parent corporation translates the dividend into U.S. dollars using the spot rate. A deemed dividend of Subpart F income is translated into dollars using the average exchange rate for the CFC's tax year, and a deemed dividend for a CFC's investment in U.S. property is translated into dollars using the spot rate on the last day of the CFC's tax year. If a domestic parent corporation receives a distribution of previously taxed income, it recognizes a currency exchange gain or loss equal to the difference between the dollar value of the distribution (determined using the spot rate) and the taxpayer's basis in the distribution (determined by the dollar amount at which the earnings were previously included in U.S. taxable income). For purposes of computing the deemed paid foreign income taxes attributable to an actual or deemed dividend distribution, the foreign corporation's pool of post-1986 foreign income taxes are translated into dollars using the average exchange rate for the year, whereas the dividend distribution and post-1986 undistributed earnings are maintained in the foreign corporation's functional currency.[40]

Finally, Code Sec. 988 provides rules for determining the amount, timing, character, and source of currency exchange gains and losses associated with the following foreign currency transactions: (i) dispositions of a nonfunctional currency, (ii) acquisition or issuance of a debt obligation denominated in a nonfunctional currency, (iii) accruing an item of income or expense denominated in a

---

[38] Code Secs. 985 and 989.
[39] Code Secs. 987 and 989.

[40] Code Secs. 986 and 989.

¶102.04

nonfunctional currency, and (iv) acquiring or entering into a forward contract, futures contract, option, or similar instrument involving a nonfunctional currency.

¶ 103 TAXATION OF FOREIGN PERSON'S U.S. ACTIVITIES

.01 Foreign Persons Investing in the United States

U.S. tax law contains a two-pronged system for taxing the U.S.-source income of foreign persons, including nonresident aliens and foreign corporations. The United States taxes foreign persons at graduated rates on the net amount of income effectively connected with the conduct of a trade or business within the United States.[41] The United States also taxes the gross amount of a foreign person's U.S.-source investment-type income at a flat rate of 30%.[42] The U.S. person controlling the payment of the U.S.-source investment income must withhold the 30% tax.[43] Income tax treaties usually reduce the withholding tax rate on interest, dividend, and royalty income to 15% or less.[44] In addition, the United States provides a broad statutory exemption for portfolio interest income.[45] Capital gains from sales of stocks or bonds also are generally exempt from U.S. taxation.[46]

Withholding is required because it is the only sure way to collect taxes from passive offshore investors. Once the appropriate amount of U.S. tax is withheld, the foreign recipient of U.S. source investment-type income generally has no further U.S. tax obligations. The withholding tax agent is any person having control, receipt, custody, disposal, or payment of an item of U.S.-source investment-type income to a foreign person.[47] Examples include corporations distributing dividends, debtors paying interest, and licensees paying royalties. A withholding agent who fails to withhold is liable for the uncollected tax.[48]

Special rules apply to gains from the sale of U.S. real property. Under Code Sec. 897, gains or losses realized by foreign persons from dispositions of a U.S. real property interest are taxed in the same manner as income effectively connected with the conduct of a U.S. trade or business. A U.S. real property interest includes stock of a domestic corporation which is a U.S. real property holding corporation. A domestic corporation is a U.S. real property holding corporation if the market value of its U.S. real property interests equals 50% or more of the net fair market value of the sum of its total real property interests (U.S. and foreign) and its trade or business assets. To ensure collection, any purchaser of a U.S. real property interest must withhold a tax equal to 10% of the amount realized by the foreign person on the sale.[49]

.02 Foreign Persons Doing Business in the United States

A foreign person that is engaged in a U.S. trade or business is subject to U.S. tax on the income effectively connected with the conduct of that U.S. trade or business.[50] Case law suggests that a foreign person's activities within the United

---

[41] Code Secs. 871(b) and 882.
[42] Code Sec. 871(a) and 881.
[43] Code Secs. 1441 and 1442.
[44] Articles 10, 11 and 12 of the U.S. Model Treaty.
[45] Code Secs. 871(h) and 881(c).

[46] Reg. § 1.1441-2(b)(2).
[47] Code Secs. 1441 and 1442.
[48] Code Sec. 1461.
[49] Code Sec. 1445.
[50] Code Secs. 871(b) and 882.

States must be considerable, continuous, and regular to constitute a U.S. trade or business. If the foreign person is a resident of a country that has entered into an income tax treaty with the United States, then the foreign person's business profits are exempt from U.S. taxation unless those profits are attributable to a "permanent establishment" (i.e., a fixed place of business) located within the United States.[51]

Effectively connected income includes all of the foreign person's U.S.-source income, except for U.S. source investment-type income that is subject to U.S. withholding tax.[52] In computing its effectively connected income, a foreign person may deduct expenses which are directly or indirectly related to the effectively connected gross income.

The progressive rate schedules applicable to domestic corporations and U.S. citizens also apply to the effectively connected income of foreign corporations and nonresident aliens, which means the tax rates range from 10% to 35% in the case of nonresident aliens and 15% to 35% in the case of foreign corporations. Effectively connected income is also subject to the alternative minimum tax.[53]

A foreign corporation engaged a U.S. trade or business is also subject to the Code Sec. 884 branch profits tax, the purpose of which is to better equate the tax treatment of branch and subsidiary operations. The branch profits tax equals 30% (subject to treaty reductions) of a foreign corporation's dividend equivalent amount, which is an estimate of the amount of effectively connected earnings and profits that a U.S. branch remits to its foreign home office during the year. A foreign corporation's U.S. branch operation may also be subject to the tax on excess interest.

Congress enacted the Code Sec. 163(j) anti-earnings stripping provisions to prevent foreign corporations from avoiding U.S. tax by "stripping" out the earnings of a U.S. subsidiary through intercompany interest payments, rather than repatriating the U.S. subsidiary's earnings through nondeductible dividend distributions. If certain requirements are met, Code Sec. 163(j) denies a domestic corporation a deduction for interest that is paid to a related person and is exempt from U.S. tax, as well as any interest paid to an unrelated person on a loan that is guaranteed by a related foreign person and the interest income is not subject to U.S. withholding tax. Interest deductions are disallowed only if the domestic corporation's debt-to-equity ratio exceeds 1.5 to 1 and it has excess interest expense. The amount of disallowed interest deductions may not exceed the corporation's excess interest expense, and any disallowed deductions may be carried forward.

¶ 104 ISSUES COMMON TO OUTBOUND AND INBOUND ACTIVITIES

.01 Transfer Pricing

The operating units of a multinational corporation usually engage in a variety of intercompany transactions. For example, a U.S. manufacturer may market its products abroad through foreign marketing subsidiaries. A domestic parent corpo-

---

[51] Articles 5 and 7 of the U.S. Model Treaty.
[52] Code Sec. 864.

[53] Code Secs. 871(b) and 882.

ration also may provide managerial, technical, and administrative services for its subsidiaries, and may license its manufacturing and marketing intangibles to its foreign subsidiaries for commercial exploitation abroad. A "transfer price" must be computed for each of these controlled transactions. Although a transfer price does not affect the combined income of commonly controlled corporations, it does affect how that income is allocated among the group members. Therefore, when tax rates vary across countries, transfer pricing can have a significant effect on a multinational corporation's total tax costs.

Congress enacted Code Sec. 482 to ensure that related corporations report and pay tax on their actual share of income arising from controlled transactions. The Regulations under Code Sec. 482 adopt an arm's-length standard for evaluating the appropriateness of a transfer price. Under this standard, a taxpayer should recognize the same amount of income from a controlled transaction as an uncontrolled party would have recognized from a similar transaction under similar circumstances.

To arrive at an arm's-length result, the taxpayer must select and apply the method that provides the most reliable estimate of an arm's-length price. The reliability of a pricing method is primarily a function of the degree of comparability between the controlled and uncontrolled transactions. As a practical matter, however, comparable transactions often are not readily available. For example, inventory sales between affiliated companies often involve component parts and semi-finished goods that are unique and are not sold in public markets. As a consequence, the appropriate arm's length price is often ambiguous.

The regulations under Code Sec. 482 provide specific methods for determining an arm's length transfer price for various types of transactions, including transfers of tangible property, transfers of intangible property, loans, and services. For example, the regulations provide five specified methods for estimating an arm's-length charge for transfers of tangible property, including the comparable uncontrolled price method, the resale price method, the cost plus method, the comparable profits method, and the profit split method.

To promote compliance with the arm's-length standard, Congress enacted the Code Sec. 6662(e) transactional and net adjustment penalties. Both penalties equal 20% of the tax underpayment related to an IRS transfer pricing adjustment. The transactional penalty applies if the transfer price used by the taxpayer is 200% or more (or 50% or less) of the amount determined under Code Sec. 482 to be correct. The net adjustment penalty applies if the net increase in taxable income for a year as a result of Code Sec. 482 adjustments exceeds the lesser of $5 million or 10% of the taxpayer's gross receipts. The penalties may be waived if the taxpayer can demonstrate that it had reasonable cause and acted in good faith. In the case of the net adjustment penalty, the reasonable cause and good faith requirements can be met only if the taxpayer also satisfies certain contemporaneous documentation requirements.

¶104.01

.02 Income Tax Treaties

The major purpose of an income tax treaty is to mitigate international double taxation through tax reductions and exemptions for certain types of income derived by residents of one treaty country from sources within the other treaty country. Because tax treaties often substantially modify U.S. and foreign tax consequences, a taxpayer must consider the impact of the applicable treaty on the tax consequences of any outbound or inbound transaction. In addition to treaties governing income taxes, the United States has also entered into bilateral tax treaties governing social security taxes, estate and gift taxes, and international shipping and aviation. The United States currently has income tax treaties with about 60 countries, including most of its major trading partners.

The income tax treaties to which the United States is a party are generally similar to the United States Model Income Tax Convention of November 15, 2006 (hereinafter, the "U.S. Model Treaty"), which reflects the baseline negotiating position of the United States in establishing income tax treaties with other countries.

Treaty tax reductions and exemptions are generally available only to a resident of one of the treaty countries. Under the U.S. Model Treaty, a resident is any person who, under a country's internal laws, is subject to taxation by reason of domicile, residence, citizenship, place of management, place of incorporation, or other criterion of a similar nature.[54]

Most income tax treaties contain a permanent establishment provision, under which the business profits of a resident of one treaty country are exempt from taxation by the other treaty country, unless those business profits are attributable to a "permanent establishment" (i.e., a fixed place of business) located within the host country.[55]

Income tax treaties also usually limit the withholding tax rates imposed on dividend, interest, and royalty income derived from sources within the treaty country to 15% or less.[56] In many cases, treaties exempt such income from host country taxation. Treaties also generally exempt from host country taxation any gains from the disposition of property, such as capital gains on the sale of stocks or bonds. This exemption does not apply to gains from dispositions of real property, or gains from dispositions of personal property that are attributable to a permanent establishment.[57]

Because income tax treaties provide lower withholding tax rates on dividend, interest, and royalty income, a multinational corporation may be able to reduce its foreign withholding taxes by owning its operating subsidiaries through strategically located holding companies, a practice known as "treaty shopping." To restrict the ability of taxpayers to engage in treaty shopping, many treaties contain anti-treaty shopping rules, which are formally known as limitation on benefits provisions. The basic thrust of these provisions is to deny treaty benefits to a corporation that is organized in a treaty country by a resident of a non-treaty country merely to obtain the benefits of that country's income tax treaty.[58]

---

[54] Article 4 of the U.S. Model Treaty.

[55] Articles 5 and 7 of the U.S. Model Treaty.

[56] Articles 10, 11 and 12 of the U.S. Model Treaty.

[57] Article 13 of the U.S. Model Treaty.

[58] Article 22 of the U.S. Model Treaty.

Chapter 2

Tax Jurisdiction

¶ 201 JURISDICTIONAL ISSUES

.01 *Bases for Asserting Jurisdiction*

A government must answer two basic questions in determining how to tax international transactions: Which "persons" should be taxed? and What "income" is subject to tax? One basis upon which countries assert tax jurisdiction is a personal relationship between the taxpayer and the country. For example, a country may wish to tax any individual who is either a citizen or a resident of the country. The concept of a personal relationship also applies to corporations and other types of entities. A corporation may be considered a citizen of the country in which it is organized. Similarly, a corporation can be considered a resident of the country in which its seat of management or principal place of business is located.

A second basis upon which countries assert tax jurisdiction is an economic relationship between the taxpayer and the country. An economic relationship exists whenever a person derives income from property or activities that are located within a country's borders. The set of persons deriving income from sources within a country includes not only citizens and residents (those persons who already have a personal relationship with the country), but also foreign persons who are neither citizens nor residents of the taxing country.

Under the current U.S. system, personal relationships are the basis for taxing U.S. citizens, resident aliens, and domestic corporations, whereas the source of income is the basis for taxing nonresident aliens and foreign corporations.

.02 *Territorial versus Credit Systems*

A double taxation problem usually arises when a taxpayer who has a personal relationship with one country (the home country) derives income from sources within another country (the host country). The host country usually will assert jurisdiction on the basis of its economic relationship with the taxpayer. The home country also may assert jurisdiction over the income on the basis of its personal relationship with the taxpayer. In these situations, the countries involved must decide whether and how to adjust their tax systems so as to avoid international double taxation. Traditionally, it has been up to the home country to solve the double taxation problems of its citizens and residents. The home country can accomplish this only by forfeiting part or all of its jurisdictional claim over the foreign-source income of its citizens and residents, either through a territorial system or a credit system.

Under a territorial system, the home country taxes citizens and residents on income derived from sources within the home country, but allows them to exclude from taxation all income derived from foreign sources. For example, the home country would tax a citizen's wages that were earned domestically, but would exempt from tax any wages earned abroad. This leaves only the host country to tax the citizen's foreign-source income. Therefore, under a territorial system, the foreign income of a citizen or resident is taxed only one time at the host country's rate.

Under a credit system, the home country taxes the foreign income of its citizens and residents, but allows a credit for any taxes paid on that foreign income to the host country. In effect, the home country asserts secondary jurisdiction over the foreign income of its citizens and residents. The claim is secondary in the sense that taxpayers are allowed to claim a foreign tax credit to the extent their foreign income is taxed by the host country. The net result is that foreign income is taxed only one time at the higher of the host country's rate or the home country's rate.

> **Example 2.1:** ABC Corporation has taxable income of $100, all of which is derived from foreign sources. Assume the home country tax rate is 30% and the host country tax rate is 20%.

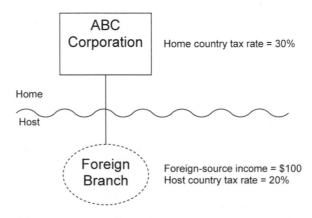

Case 1—No mechanism for mitigating double taxation: If the home country provides no mechanism for mitigating international double taxation, the total

tax on ABC's $100 of foreign-source income is $50 [$30 home country tax + $20 host country tax], computed as follows:

Home country tax return	
Taxable income	$100
Tax rate	× .30
Tax	$ 30

Host country tax return	
Taxable income	$100
Tax rate	× .20
Tax	$ 20

Case 2—Territorial system: Under a territorial system, the total tax on ABC's foreign-source income is $20 [$0 home country tax + $20 host country tax], computed as follows:

Home country tax return	
Taxable income	$0
Tax rate	× .30
Tax	$ 0

Host country tax return	
Taxable income	$100
Tax rate	× .20
Tax	$ 20

Case 3—Credit system: Under a credit system, the total tax on ABC's foreign-source income is $30 [$10 home country tax + $20 host country tax], computed as follows:

Home country tax return	
Taxable income	$100
Tax rate	× .30
Pre-credit tax	$30
Foreign tax credit	– 20
Tax	$10

Host country tax return	
Taxable income	$100
Tax rate	× .20
Tax	$ 20

A credit system and a territorial system both solve ABC's double taxation problem, but they do so in fundamentally different ways. A territorial system eliminates the $30 home country tax on ABC's foreign-source income, resulting in taxation once at the lower foreign rate. In contrast, from ABC's perspective a credit system effectively eliminates the $20 host country tax on ABC's foreign-source income, resulting in taxation once at the higher home country rate.

As Example 2.1 illustrates, territorial and credit systems produce different results when the host country tax rate is lower than the home country rate. Under a territorial system, the taxpayer pays only the lower host country tax. Under a credit

¶201.02

system, the taxpayer pays not only the host country tax, but also any home country tax in excess of the lower host country tax.

In contrast, when the host country tax rate is higher than the home country rate, territorial and credit systems produce equivalent results. Under a territorial system, foreign-source income is taxed once at the higher foreign rate. A credit system also results in taxation once at the higher host country rate, since the foreign tax credit completely offsets the pre-credit home country tax on the foreign-source income. Therefore, no home country tax is collected on the high-tax foreign-source income under either system.

Example 2.2: The facts are the same as in Example 2.1, except now assume that the host country tax rate is 40%, rather than 20%.

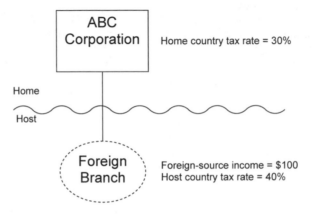

Case 1—Territorial system: Under a territorial system, the total tax on ABC's foreign-source income is $40 [$0 home country tax + $40 host country tax], computed as follows:

Home country tax return		Host country tax return	
Taxable income	$0	Taxable income	$100
Tax rate	× .30	Tax rate	× .40
Tax	$ 0	Tax.	$ 40

Case 2—Credit system: Under a credit system, the total tax on ABC's foreign-source income also is $40 [$0 home country tax + $40 host country tax], computed as follows:

Home country tax return	
Taxable income	$100
Tax rate	× .30
Pre-credit tax	$ 30
Foreign tax credit	– 30
Tax	$ 0

Host country tax return	
Taxable income	$100
Tax rate	× .40
Tax	$ 40

.03 Tax Treaties

Territorial and credit systems represent unilateral solutions to the international double taxation problem in the sense that they are created by individual countries. Tax treaties, on the other hand, represent bilateral solutions to the international double taxation problem since they are created by and apply to both of the countries that are parties to the agreement. In general, tax treaties mitigate double taxation through reciprocal tax exemptions and lower tax rates for income derived by residents of one treaty country from sources within the other treaty country. For example, under the income tax treaty between the United States and the United Kingdom, the United Kingdom agrees not to tax U.S. residents on any interest derived from sources within the United Kingdom. In exchange, the United States agrees not to tax U.K. residents on any interest derived from sources within the United States.[1] Thus, tax treaties shift the claim of primary tax jurisdiction from the host country to the home country, thereby saving a larger share of the tax on international transactions for the home country. The increase in the home country's tax revenues comes at the host country's expense, however, which explains why tax treaty provisions are always reciprocal in nature. Tax treaties are discussed in more detail in Chapter 13 (¶ 1301).

¶ 202 OVERVIEW OF U.S. JURISDICTIONAL SYSTEM

.01 Foreign Activities of U.S. Persons

The United States taxes U.S. persons on their worldwide income.[2] U.S. persons include the following:[3]

(i) *U.S. citizens*

(ii) *Resident alien individuals*—Citizens of foreign countries who meet either the green card test or the substantial presence test.[4]

(iii) *Domestic corporations*—Corporations created or organized under the laws of one of the 50 states or the District of Columbia.[5] The location of a corporation's headquarters office or seat of management is irrelevant for

---

[1] Article 11 of the U.S.-U.K. Income Tax Treaty.

[2] Code Sec. 61(a).

[3] Code Sec. 7701(a)(30).

[4] Code Sec. 7701(b)(1)(A).

[5] Code Sec. 7701(a)(4) and (a)(9). A corporation organized or created under the laws of a U.S. possession is considered a foreign corporation.

purposes of determining whether a corporation is domestic or foreign under U.S. tax principles.

(iv) *Domestic partnerships*—Partnerships created or organized under the laws of one of the 50 states or the District of Columbia, unless the Secretary provides otherwise by regulations.[6]

(v) Any *estate* other than a foreign estate. An estate is foreign if its foreign-source income, other than any income effectively connected with a U.S. trade or business, is not subject to U.S. taxation.[7]

(vi) Any *trust* if a U.S. court is able to exercise primary supervision over the administration of the trust and one or more U.S. persons have the authority to control all substantial decisions of the trust.[8]

The United States uses a credit system to mitigate international double taxation. Therefore, a U.S. person can claim a credit for the foreign income taxes imposed on foreign-source income.[9] Under this credit system, foreign-source income is taxed one time at the higher of the U.S. tax rate or the foreign rate. In other words, the United States collects any residual U.S. tax due on foreign-source income that the host country taxes at a rate lower than the U.S. rate. On the other hand, if the foreign tax rate exceeds the U.S. rate, no U.S. tax is collected on that foreign-source income because the available foreign tax credits are sufficient to offset the pre-credit U.S. tax on that income.

A key feature of the U.S. credit system is the foreign tax credit limitation, which restricts the credit to the portion of the pre-credit U.S. tax that is attributable to foreign-source income.[10] The purpose of the limitation is to confine the effects of the credit to mitigating double taxation of foreign-source income. The limitation accomplishes this by preventing U.S. persons operating in high-tax foreign countries from offsetting those higher foreign taxes against the U.S. taxes on U.S.-source income.

Example 2.3: USAco, a domestic corporation, has $200 of U.S.-source taxable income and $100 of foreign-source taxable income. Assume that the foreign tax rate is 45% and the U.S. rate is 35%.

---

[6] Code Sec. 7701(a)(4) and (a)(9).
[7] Code Sec. 7701(a)(30)(D) and (a)(31)(A).
[8] Code Sec. 7701(a)(30)(E).

[9] Code Sec. 901(a).
[10] Code Sec. 904(a).

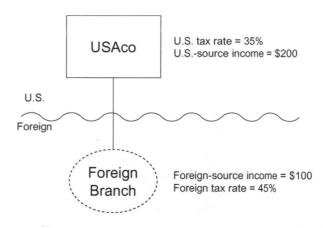

Case 1—Credit is limited: If the foreign tax credit is limited to the U.S. tax on foreign-source income (i.e., 35% × $100 = $35), the total tax on USAco's $300 of worldwide income is $115 [$70 U.S. tax + $45 foreign tax], computed as follows:

U.S. tax return	
Taxable income	$300
U.S. tax rate	× .35
Pre-credit tax	$105
Foreign tax credit	– 35
U.S. tax	$ 70

Foreign tax return	
Taxable income	$100
Foreign tax rate	× .45
Foreign tax	$ 45

Case 2—No limitation: If there were no limitation on the foreign tax credit, the total tax on USAco's $300 of worldwide income would drop from $115 to $105 [$60 U.S. tax + $45 foreign tax], computed as follows:

U.S. tax return	
Taxable income	$300
U.S. tax rate	× .35
Pre-credit tax	$105
Foreign tax credit	– 45
U.S. tax	$ 60

Foreign tax return	
Taxable income	$100
Foreign tax rate	× .45
Foreign tax	$ 45

Without the limitation, the net U.S. tax on the $100 of foreign-source income is negative $10 [$35 pre-credit U.S. tax – $45 credit], which reduces the effective U.S. tax rate on USAco's U.S.-source income to only 30% ($60/$200). Thus,

¶202.01

without the limitation, the U.S. Treasury does not collect the full 35% U.S. tax on U.S.-source income.

One major exception to the U.S. credit system is the deferral privilege, whereby the United States does not tax foreign-source income earned by a U.S. person through a foreign corporation until those profits are repatriated by the domestic shareholder through a dividend distribution. The deferral privilege is the result of several features of U.S. tax law. First, U.S. consolidated reporting rules take a "domestic" consolidation approach, whereby affiliates organized in foreign countries are not allowed to join their U.S. counterparts in filing a federal consolidated income tax return.[11] Second, the earnings of a regular corporation are not taxed to its shareholders until distributed as a dividend. Finally, the United States does not tax the foreign-source income of foreign corporations. Therefore, as long as a foreign subsidiary derives only foreign-source income, those earnings will not enter the U.S. tax base until they are distributed to the U.S. parent corporation as a dividend.

> *Example 2.4:* USAco, a domestic corporation, owns 100% of FORco, a foreign corporation. FORco operates a factory in a country that has granted FORco a 10-year tax holiday. In its first year of operations, FORco has $10 million of foreign-source income and repatriates $4 million of those earnings to USAco through a dividend distribution. Because FORco is a foreign corporation, the United States does not tax FORco on its $10 million of foreign-source income. However, the United States does tax USAco on the $4 million dividend that it receives from FORco. The dividend is included in USAco's gross income, and there is no offsetting dividends-received deduction.

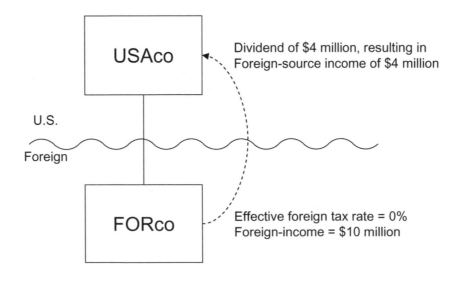

USAco

Dividend of $4 million, resulting in Foreign-source income of $4 million

U.S.

Foreign

FORco

Effective foreign tax rate = 0%
Foreign-income = $10 million

---

[11] Code Sec. 1504. In contrast, U.S. accounting principles require a "worldwide" consolidation, whereby all majority-owned subsidiaries, domestic and foreign alike, must be consolidated with the U.S. parent corporation for financial reporting purposes. ASC-810.

The policy rationale for deferral is that it allows U.S. companies to compete in foreign markets on a tax parity with their foreign competitors. However, deferral also opens the door to tax avoidance, particularly with respect to passive investment income, the source of which can easily be shifted to a foreign country. Congress enacted the Subpart F and passive foreign investment company regimes to prevent taxpayers from using deferral as a device to avoid U.S. tax. Under these two anti-deferral regimes (which are discussed in Chapter 5 (¶ 501)), certain types of unrepatriated earnings of a foreign corporation, such as passive investment income, are subject to immediate U.S. taxation.

A second major exception to the U.S. credit system is the foreign earned income exclusion. Under the general rules, the United States taxes U.S. citizens and resident aliens on their worldwide income, even when they live and work abroad for extended periods of time. To provide some relief, a U.S. expatriate who meets certain requirements can exclude from U.S. taxation a limited amount of foreign earned income plus a housing cost amount.[12] The foreign earned income exclusion is discussed later in this chapter.

Before discussing how the United States taxes the U.S. activities of foreign persons, it is worth noting how the jurisdictional scheme for domestic corporations impacts tax planning for foreign operations. Because the foreign earnings of U.S. companies are subject to both U.S. and foreign income taxes, a commonly used metric for evaluating these tax costs is the total effective tax rate on foreign earnings. When evaluating a U.S. corporation's effective tax rate, the de facto benchmark is the top U.S. statutory rate of 35 percent.[13] However, it is quite common for the total tax rate on foreign earnings to be greater than or less than 35 percent. The total tax rate can exceed 35 percent when the foreign jurisdiction taxes corporate income at a rate in excess of 35 percent (as, for example, in Japan), and the foreign tax credit limitation prevents U.S. companies from claiming a credit for those "excess" foreign taxes. In contrast, the total tax rate on foreign earnings can fall below 35 percent when the foreign jurisdiction taxes corporate income at a rate less than 35 percent (as, for example, in Hong Kong, Ireland, or Switzerland), and the U.S. company takes advantage of its ability to defer the residual U.S. tax on low-tax foreign earnings until those foreign profits are repatriated by the U.S. parent corporation through a dividend distribution. Tax planning for foreign operations is discussed in detail in Chapter 8 (¶ 801).

.02 U.S. Activities of Foreign Persons

U.S. tax law contains a two-pronged territorial system for taxing the U.S.-source income of foreign persons. Foreign persons include the following:

(i) *Nonresident alien individuals*—Individuals who are neither citizens nor residents of the United States.[14]

(ii) *Foreign corporations*—Corporations created or organized under the laws of a foreign country or U.S. possession.[15]

---

[12] Code Sec. 911.
[13] Code Sec. 11.

[14] Code Sec. 7701(b)(1)(B).
[15] Code Sec. 7701(a)(5).

(iii) *Foreign partnerships*—Partnerships created or organized under the laws of a foreign country or U.S. possession.[16]

(iv) *Foreign estate*—Any estate that is not subject to U.S. taxation on its foreign-source income which is not effectively connected with a U.S. trade or business.[17]

(v) *Foreign trust*—A trust is foreign if no U.S. court is able to exercise primary supervision over the administration of the trust or no U.S. persons have the authority to control all substantial decisions of the trust.[18]

The United States taxes foreign persons at graduated rates on the net amount of income effectively connected with the conduct of a trade or business within the United States.[19] On the other hand, the United States taxes the gross amount of a foreign person's U.S.-source investment-type income at a flat rate of 30%.[20] The U.S. person controlling the payment of U.S.-source investment income to a foreign person must deduct and withhold the 30% U.S. tax.[21] Withholding is required because it is the only sure way to collect taxes from passive offshore investors. In order to withhold, the withholding agent must be able to readily ascertain both the tax base and the applicable rate. This explains both the gross basis taxation and the use of a flat tax rate because the U.S. withholding agent may not have any way of determining a foreign person's allocable expenses and appropriate tax bracket.

There are several major exceptions to the general rules for taxing foreign persons. For example, income tax treaties usually reduce the withholding tax rate on interest, dividend, and royalty income from the statutory rate of 30% to 15% or less. In addition, portfolio interest income is exempt from U.S. tax.[22] Capital gains are also exempt from U.S. tax,[23] except for gains from the sale of U.S. real property, which are taxed in the same manner as income effectively connected with the conduct of a U.S. trade or business.[24] Table 2.1 summarizes the general rules regarding U.S. taxation of international transactions.

TABLE 2.1. U.S. TAXATION OF INTERNATIONAL TRANSACTIONS—GENERAL RULES

Type of person	*Type of income*	*U.S. taxation*
U.S. person	Foreign-source income	U.S. collects the excess of the pre-credit U.S. tax over the related foreign tax credit
Foreign person	Income effectively connected with a U.S. trade or business	U.S. taxes the net amount of income at graduated rates
	U.S.-source investment-type income	U.S. taxes the gross amount of income at 30%

---

[16] Code Sec. 7701(a)(5).
[17] Code Sec. 7701(a)(31)(A).
[18] Code Sec. 7701(a)(31)(B) and (a)(30)(E).
[19] Code Secs. 871(b) and 882(a).
[20] Code Secs. 871(a) and 881(a).

[21] Code Secs. 1441 and 1442.
[22] Code Secs. 871(h) and 881(c).
[23] Reg. § 1.1441-2(b)(2).
[24] Code Sec. 897(a)(1).

¶ 203 DEFINITION OF RESIDENT ALIEN

The United States taxes resident aliens on their worldwide income, whereas nonresident aliens are taxed only on their U.S.-source income. As a consequence, the taxation of foreign nationals depends critically on whether the alien is considered a U.S. resident. An alien is considered a U.S. resident in any calendar year that he or she meets either the green card test or the substantial presence test.[25]

.01 Green Card Test

Under the so-called green card test, an alien individual is treated as a U.S. resident for a calendar year if, at any time during that calendar year, the alien is a lawful permanent resident of the United States.[26] An alien qualifies as a lawful permanent resident of the United States if he or she has been lawfully accorded, and has not revoked or abandoned, the privilege of residing permanently in the United States as an immigrant.[27] Such "green card" holders are treated as U.S. residents for tax purposes, regardless of whether they are actually physically present in the United States during the year.

This rule forces aliens who have obtained a green card but have not yet moved to the United States on a permanent basis to pay U.S. taxes on their worldwide income. These individuals are expected to pay taxes on the same basis as U.S. citizens because, like U.S. citizens, they have the right to exit and reenter the United States at will.

.02 Substantial Presence Test

An alien who does not hold a green card is considered a U.S. resident for a calendar year if he or she is physically present in the United States for 183 or more days during that year.[28] This substantial presence test is based on the premise that spending more than half of a year in the United States establishes a stronger connection with the United States than with any other country for that year.

> **Example 2.5:** T is not a U.S. citizen and does not hold a green card. However, T is physically present in the United States from January 1 through September 30 of the current year. T is a U.S. resident for that year because she is physically present in the United States for 183 or more days.

---

[25] Code Sec. 7701(b)(1)(A).
[26] Code Sec. 7701(b)(1)(A)(i).

[27] Code Sec. 7701(b)(6).
[28] Code Sec. 7701(b)(3)(A).

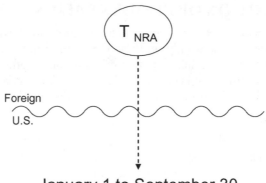

January 1 to September 30

A day is counted as a day of U.S. presence if the alien is physically present in the United States at any time during that day.[29] Therefore, presence for part of a day, such as the day of arrival or departure from the United States, counts as a full day. However, certain types of U.S. presence are disregarded, including commuters from Mexico or Canada,[30] travelers between two foreign points,[31] individuals with medical conditions,[32] and certain exempt individuals.[33] Exempt individuals primarily include qualifying students, teachers, trainees, and foreign-government-related individuals.[34]

A variant of the substantial presence test, called the carryover days test, extends U.S. residence to aliens whose stay in the United States is prolonged, but is less than 183 days in any given calendar year. For example, under the general rule, an alien could be physically present in the United States for the last 182 days of one year and the first 182 days of the succeeding year (for a total of 364 consecutive days in the United States) without establishing U.S. residency. The carryover days test addresses these situations by taking into account days spent in the United States during the two preceding calendar years. Under this test, the 183-day standard is applied by counting a day of presence during the current year as a full day, a day of presence during the first preceding year as one-third of a day, and a day of presence during the second preceding year as one-sixth of a day.[35] In all cases, an individual must be present in the United States at least 31 days during the current calendar year to be considered a resident for that year.[36]

> *Example* **2.6:** T is not a U.S. citizen and does not hold a green card. However, T is physically present in the United States for 90 days during year 1, 150 days during year 2, and 120 days during year 3. The primary 183-day test is not met in any year of the three years. However, the carryover days test is met for the first time in year 3 [120 days + (1/3 of 150 days) + (1/6 of 90 days) = 185 days].

---

[29] Code Sec. 7701(b)(7)(A).

[30] Code Sec. 7701(b)(7)(B).

[31] Code Sec. 7701(b)(7)(C).

[32] Code Sec. 7701(b)(3)(D)(ii).

[33] Code Sec. 7701(b)(3)(D)(i).

[34] Code Sec. 7701(b)(5).

[35] Code Sec. 7701(b)(3)(A)(ii).

[36] Code Sec. 7701(b)(3)(A)(i).

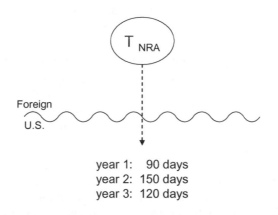

year 1: 90 days
year 2: 150 days
year 3: 120 days

Under the carryover days test, an individual who consistently spends just one-third of the year in the United States (122 days to be exact) is treated as a U.S. resident.[37] This potentially unfair result is mitigated by an exception to the carry-over days test for an alien who satisfies the following requirements:

(i) the alien is present in the United States for less than 183 days during the current year,

(ii) the alien's tax home (i.e., principal or regular place of business) for the current year is in a foreign country, and

(iii) the alien has a closer connection to that foreign country than to the United States.[38]

This exception does not apply, however, if the alien has applied for a green card.[39] Determining whether a taxpayer has a closer connection with a foreign country than with the United States requires a consideration of all the facts and circumstances, such as the location of the individual's family, permanent residence, and personal belongings, as well as the location of the individual's social, political, cultural, and religious relationships.[40]

.03 First Year of Residency

If an alien establishes U.S. residency after January 1, that individual is gener-ally treated as a nonresident alien for the portion of the calendar year preceding the residency starting date and as a resident alien for the remainder of the year.[41] An alien's U.S. residency starting date depends on whether residency is established under the green card test or the substantial presence test. If residency is estab-lished under the substantial presence test, the residency starting date is the first day the taxpayer is physically present in the United States.[42] For this purpose, visits to the United States of 10 days or less, such as a house-hunting trip, are ignored if at the time of the visit the individual had a closer connection to a foreign country

---

[37] 122 days + (1/3 of 122 days) + (1/6 of 122 days) = 183 days.

[38] Code Sec. 7701(b)(3)(B).

[39] Code Sec. 7701(b)(3)(C).

[40] Reg. § 301.7701(b)-2(d).

[41] Code Sec. 7701(b)(2)(A)(i).

[42] Code Sec. 7701(b)(2)(A)(iii).

than to the United States.[43] If residency is established under the green card test, the residency starting date is the first day the taxpayer is physically present in the United States with a green card.[44] If the requirements of both residency tests are satisfied in the first year of residency, the residency starting date is the earlier of the two starting dates.[45] Finally, to prevent a gap in residency when an alien is a resident in two consecutive calendar years, the residency starting date for a taxpayer who was a U.S. resident in the preceding year is January 1, regardless of when the green card test or the substantial presence test was first met for the succeeding year.[46]

    ***Example* 2.7:** T is not a U.S. citizen and does not hold a green card. However, T is physically present in the United States from June 1 through December 31 of the current year. T is a U.S. resident for the year because she is physically present in the United States for 183 or more days, with the date of residency beginning on June 1. Therefore, T's tax year is split and T is a nonresident alien from January 1 through May 31 and a resident alien from June 1 through December 31.

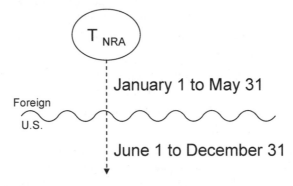

A special first-year residency election is available to certain qualifying aliens. Under this provision, in the first year that an alien satisfies either the green card test or the substantial presence test, he or she can elect to be taxed as a U.S. resident for a portion of the preceding year, if any, in which he or she was present in the United States.[47] This election allows the alien to itemize his or her deductions and claim a foreign tax credit, beginning with the entry date into the United States. However, it also exposes all of the alien's income to U.S. taxation, including his or her foreign-source income.

.04 Last Year of Residency

    An alien's U.S. residency termination date is the last day of the year on which the individual was physically present in the United States under the substantial presence test or the last day he or she had a green card, provided the taxpayer establishes that for the remainder of the year he or she had a closer connection to,

---

[43] Code Sec. 7701(b)(2)(C).
[44] Code Sec. 7701(b)(2)(A)(ii).
[45] Reg. §301.7701(b)-4(a).

[46] Reg. §301.7701(b)-4(e)(1).
[47] Code Sec. 7701(b)(4).

and a tax home in, a foreign country.[48] If this exception applies, the alien is taxed as a U.S. resident from January 1 to the residency termination date and as a nonresident for the remainder of the year.

> *Example 2.8:* T is not a U.S. citizen, but has been a resident of the United States for several years pursuant to the substantial presence test. On July 31, T leaves the United States and returns to her country of citizenship where she has taken a job and purchases a home. Because T has established a closer connection to her country of citizenship and has a tax home there, T's residency in the United States ends on July 31. T is a nonresident alien from August 1 through December 31.

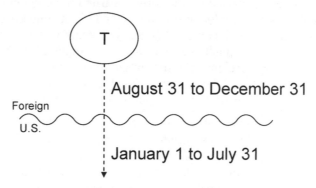

If an alien qualifies as a resident during the current year under both the green card and the substantial presence tests, the residency termination date is the later of the termination dates under either of the two residency tests.[49]

To prevent a gap in residency when an alien is a resident in two consecutive calendar years, the normal residency termination date rules do not apply if the alien is a U.S. resident in the succeeding year. In such cases, the alien is a resident through December 31, regardless of when the green card test or the substantial presence test was last met for the year.[50]

.05 Filing a Joint Return

A married couple generally is not eligible to file a joint return for a given taxable year if, at any time during that year, one or both spouses was a nonresident alien.[51] However, if a nonresident spouse becomes a U.S. resident during the year, the couple may elect to treat that spouse as a U.S. resident for the entire taxable year.[52] A similar election is also available when the spouse is a nonresident alien for the entire year.[53]

¶ 204 EXCLUSION FOR FOREIGN EARNED INCOME

The United States ordinarily taxes U.S. citizens and resident aliens on their worldwide income, even when they live and work abroad for an extended period of

---

[48] Code Sec.7701(b)(2)(B).

[49] Reg. §301.7701(b)-4(b)(2).

[50] Reg. §301.7701(b)-4(e)(2).

[51] Code Sec. 6013(a)(1).

[52] Code Sec. 6013(h) and Reg. §1.6013-7.

[53] Code Sec. 6013(g) and Reg. §1.6013-6.

time. To provide some relief, a U.S. citizen or resident who meets certain requirements can elect to exclude from U.S. taxation a limited amount of foreign earned
income plus a housing cost amount.[54] A double tax benefit is not allowed, however,
and a taxpayer cannot claim a credit for foreign income taxes related to excluded
foreign earned income.[55]

.01 Exclusion versus Credit

Because the foreign earned income exclusion is elective, an expatriate must
decide whether to elect the exclusion or to rely on the foreign tax credit.[56] A key
factor in deciding which option is more advantageous is the relative amounts of
U.S. and foreign taxes imposed on the foreign earned income before the exclusion
or credit. The exclusion completely eliminates the U.S. income tax on the qualifying
amount of foreign earned income. This allows expatriates who work in low-tax
foreign countries or who qualify for special tax exemptions in those countries to
benefit from the lower foreign tax rates. In contrast, under the foreign tax credit
option, the United States collects any residual U.S. tax on lightly-taxed foreign-
source income and the expatriate derives no benefit from the lower foreign rates.

The exclusion also eliminates the U.S. tax on the qualifying amount of foreign
earned income derived by an expatriate working in a high-tax foreign jurisdiction.
The credit option also achieves this result, since the higher foreign taxes are
sufficient to fully offset the U.S. tax on the foreign earned income. In addition,
under the credit option, the expatriate receives a potential added benefit in the form
of a foreign tax credit carryover. Foreign taxes in excess of the foreign tax credit
limitation can be carried back one year and forward up to ten years.[57] Therefore, an
expatriate can use these excess credits in a carryover year in which he or she has
foreign-source income that attracts little or no foreign tax.[58] For example, expatriates who return to the United States may be able to use their foreign tax credit
carryforwards to the extent their future compensation is attributable to foreign
business trips.[59]

.02 Qualified Individuals

The foreign earned income exclusion is available only to U.S. citizens or
resident aliens who meet the following two requirements:

(i) the individual is physically present in a foreign country (or foreign
countries) for at least 330 full days[60] during a 12-month period or (in the

---

[54] Code Sec. 911.

[55] Code Sec. 911(d)(6) and Reg. §1.911-6(c). The foreign earned income exclusion does not apply to FICA
taxes. A U.S. citizen or resident alien employed abroad by
an "American employer" (as defined in Code Sec.
3121(h)) is subject to FICA taxes on his or her wages,
unless there is a social security totalization agreement (a
type of tax treaty) between the United States and the host
foreign country. Code Sec. 3121(b). Expatriates who do
not work for an American employer normally are exempt
from FICA taxes.

[56] It also is possible to deduct foreign income taxes.
Code Sec. 164(a). Typically, however, a credit or exclusion is more advantageous.

[57] Code Sec. 904(c).

[58] Under the separate-category-of-income foreign tax
credit limitations, excess foreign tax credits related to
foreign earned income ordinarily are assigned to the
general limitation basket and can only offset an excess
limitation from that basket. Code Sec. 904(d).

[59] Compensation is treated as foreign-source income to
the extent the related services are performed abroad.
Code Sec. 862(a)(3).

[60] Partial days do not count.

case of a U.S. citizen) is a bona fide resident of a foreign country for an uninterrupted period that includes an entire taxable year, and

(ii) the individual's tax home is in a foreign country.[61]

In applying the 330-day physical presence test, every full day in a foreign country is counted.[62] Therefore, a series of foreign stays, including foreign vacations, can be pieced together to meet the 330-day test. For this purpose, U.S. possessions are not considered foreign countries.[63] U.S. citizens who are unable to meet the objective 330-day physical presence test must satisfy the subjective bona fide foreign resident test. Whether an individual is a bona fide foreign resident is determined by his or her intentions with regard to the length and nature of the stay.[64] Factors which suggest that an expatriate is a bona fide foreign resident include the presence of family, the acquisition of a foreign home or long-term lease, and involvement in the social life of the foreign country.[65]

The second requirement is that the individual has a foreign tax home.[66] An individual's tax home is his or her principal or regular place of business, provided that an individual is not treated as having a tax home in a foreign country during any period in which the taxpayer's abode is in the United States.[67] An individual's abode is in the United States if that is where his or her economic, social, and personal ties are closest.[68]

When both spouses are working abroad, qualification for the foreign earned income exclusion is determined separately for each spouse and each spouse individually makes an election to claim the exclusion.[69] Therefore, it is possible for one qualifying spouse to elect the exclusion, while the other qualifying spouse chooses not to exclude any foreign earned income.

.03 Computing the Exclusion

The maximum amount of foreign earned income that is eligible for the exclusion is adjusted annually for inflation, and is prorated for the number of qualifying days in a taxable year.[70] The maximum exclusion amount is $91,500 for 2010,[71] and $92,900 for 2011.[72] A qualifying day is any day within the period during which the individual meets the foreign tax requirement and either the bona fide resident requirement or the 330-day physical presence requirement.[73]

Example 2.9: During 2010, T satisfied the requirement for claiming a foreign earned income exclusion and had 292 qualifying days for the year.

---

[61] Code Sec. 911(d)(1).

[62] Reg. § 1.911-2(d)(2).

[63] Reg. § 1.911-2(g).

[64] Reg. §§ 1.911-2(c) and 1.871-2(b). An individual with earned income from sources within a foreign country is not a bona fide resident of that country if the individual claims to be a nonresident of that country for local tax purposes. Reg. § 1.911-2(c).

[65] For example, *see G.H. Jones,* CA-5, 91-1 USTC ¶ 50,174, 927 F2d 849. Rev'g and rem'g 58 TCM 689, Dec. 46,157 (M), TC Memo. 1989-616.

[66] Code Sec. 911(d)(1).

[67] Code Sec. 911(d)(3) and Reg. § 1.911-2(b).

[68] For example, *see J.T. Lemay,* CA-5, 88-1 USTC ¶ 9182, 837 F2d 681 (5th Cir. 1988). Aff'g 53 TCM 862, Dec. 43,931(M), TC Memo. 1987-256; *and D.P. Lansdown,* 68 TCM 680, Dec. 50,114(M), TC Memo. 1994-452. Aff'd, 73 F3d 373 (10th Cir. 1995).

[69] Reg. § 1.911-5.

[70] Code Sec. 911(b)(2)(D)(i).

[71] Rev. Proc. 2009-50, IRB 2009-45.

[72] Rev. Proc. 2010-40, IRB 2010-46.

[73] Reg. § 1.911-3(d)(3).

Therefore, T's maximum earned income exclusion is $73,200 [$91,500 × (292 days ÷ 365 days)].

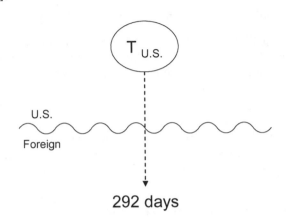

292 days

The exclusion is available only for foreign-source income that was earned during the period in which the taxpayer meets the foreign tax home requirement, and either the bona fide foreign resident or 330-day physical presence test.[74] Therefore, when identifying compensation that qualifies for the exclusion, the determinative factor is whether a paycheck or taxable reimbursement is attributable to services performed during the qualifying period, not whether the expatriate actually received the compensation during that period.[75] A deferred payment, such as a bonus, qualifies for the exclusion only if it is received before the close of the taxable year following the year in which it was earned.[76] Pension income does not qualify for the exclusion.[77]

Employment-related allowances, such as foreign housing and automobile allowances, also qualify for the exclusion if the allowance represents compensation for services performed abroad during the qualifying period. In this regard, any taxable reimbursements received for expenses incurred in moving from the United States to a foreign country ordinarily are treated as compensation for services performed abroad. On the other hand, any taxable reimbursements received for expenses incurred in moving back to the United States ordinarily are treated as U.S.-source income.[78]

Any deductions allocable to excluded foreign earned income, such as unreimbursed employee business expenses, are disallowed.[79] Certain deductions are considered unrelated to any specific item of gross income and are always deducted in full. These include medical expenses, charitable contributions, alimony pay-

---

[74] Code Sec. 911(b)(1)(A). For this purpose, U.S. possessions are considered part of the United States. Reg. § 1.911-2(g).

[75] Reg. § 1.911-3(e)(1).

[76] Code Sec. 911(b)(1)(B)(iv).

[77] Code Sec. 911(b)(1)(B)(i).

[78] Reg. § 1.911-3(e)(5)(i). An exception applies if, prior to moving abroad, there was a written agreement that the expatriate would be reimbursed for the expense of moving back to the United States, even if he or she were to leave the employer upon returning to the United States. In such cases, the reimbursement is treated as foreign-source income.

[79] Code Sec. 911(d)(6).

ments, IRA contributions, real estate taxes and mortgage interest on a personal residence, and personal exemptions.[80]

.04 Housing Cost Amount

An expatriate that qualifies for the foreign earned income exclusion also can claim an exclusion for the housing cost amount.[81] The housing cost amount equals the excess of eligible expenses incurred for the expatriate's foreign housing over a stipulated base amount ($14,640 in 2010), which is prorated for the number of qualifying days in the year.[82]

Eligible housing expenses normally include rent, utilities (other than telephone charges), real and personal property insurance, certain occupancy taxes, nonrefundable security deposits, rental of furniture and accessories, household repairs, and residential parking. Housing expenses do not include the costs of purchasing or making improvements to a house, mortgage interest and real estate taxes related to a house that the taxpayer owns, purchased furniture, pay television subscriptions, or domestic help.[83]

> **Example 2.10:** During 2010, T satisfies the requirements for claiming a foreign earned income exclusion and has 300 qualifying days for the year. Therefore, T's base amount for 2010 is $12,033 [$14,640 base amount for 2010 × (300 days ÷ 365 days)]. T's eligible housing expenses include $15,000 of apartment rentals, $2,000 of utility expenses (not including telephone charges), $5,000 of rental expenses for furniture and accessories, and $1,500 of residential parking expenses. Therefore, T's housing cost amount for 2010 is $11,467 [($15,000 + $2,000 + $5,000 + $1,500) − $12,033].

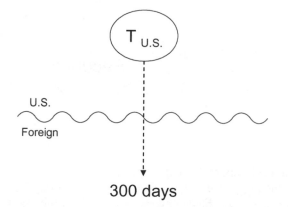

.05 Electing the Exclusion

The election to claim the foreign earned income exclusion and housing cost amount is made by filing Form 2555, Foreign Earned Income Exclusion, and

---

[80] Reg. § 1.911-6(a).

[81] Code Sec. 911(a)(2).

[82] Code Sec. 911(c)(1) and IRS Pub. No. 54 (Nov. 23, 2010).

[83] Reg. § 1.911-4(b). Special rules apply to the computation of a married couple's housing cost amount. Reg. § 1.911-5(a)(3).

remains in effect until revoked by the taxpayer.[84] A taxpayer can revoke an exclusion election, but must then wait five years to reinstate the exclusion.[85] If significant uncertainties exist regarding whether to elect the exclusion, a taxpayer can file an original return without making the election, and then file an amended return at a later date electing the exclusion.[86] (Form 2555 is reproduced in the appendix to this chapter.)

¶ 205 MARK-TO-MARKET FOR EXPATRIATES

As discussed above, U.S. persons (i.e., U.S. corporations, U.S. citizens, and U.S. resident aliens) are subject to U.S. tax on their worldwide income, whereas foreign persons (i.e., foreign corporations and nonresident aliens) are subject to U.S. tax only on certain types of U.S. source income. As one might imagine, this difference in treatment could lead U.S. persons to strategically forfeit their U.S. citizenship.

> *Example 2.11:* Benedict Arnold, a U.S. citizen, is a man of leisure who enjoys clipping coupons. Benedict owns securities with an adjusted basis of $10 million and a fair market value of $30 million. During the last 5 years, his annual net income tax obligation to the United States has averaged $400,000. Aware that foreign persons would not be subject to tax on gain on the sale of securities, Benedict forfeits his citizenship and takes residence in a tropical tax haven.

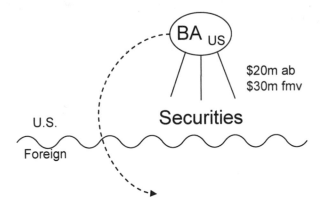

To combat such tax-motivated expatriations, Congress deems a citizen as having sold all his assets for fair market value on the day before the expatriation occurs; if the expatriate (a) has an average annual net income tax obligation to the United States for the 5 years preceding the expatriation that exceeds an inflation-adjusted base amount of tax ($147,000 in 2011), (b) has a net worth greater than or equal to $2 million as of the date of the expatriation or (c) fails to certify to the IRS that he or she complied with U.S. federal tax obligations for the 5 years preceding the expatriation (or to provide the IRS with evidence of such compliance).[87] Finally,

---

[84] Reg. § 1.911-7(a)(1).
[85] Reg. § 1.911-7(b).

[86] Reg. § 1.911-7(a)(2)(i)(B).
[87] Code Sec. 877(a), and Rev. Proc. 2010-40, IRB 2010-46.

a taxpayer may exclude an inflation-adjusted base amount of mark-to-market gain ($636,000 in 2011).[88]

> ***Example 2.12:*** Assume the same factors as in Example 2.11. Despite his expatriation, the $20 million of gain ($30 million fair market value of the securities less the $10 million basis), less the $636,000 exclusion, will result in $19,364,000 of gain subject to U.S. income tax.

This regime similarly applies to long term residents, which are defined as aliens who are residents due to the lawful permanent residence (Green Card) test in 8 of the prior 15 taxable years.

> ***Example 2.13:*** Kato, a foreign national, has been a U.S. resident since acquiring his Green Card in 1967. Kato owns shares in Black Beauty, Inc. with an adjusted basis of $10 million and a fair market value of $30 million. During the last 5 years, his annual net income tax obligation to the United States has averaged $400,000. Aware that foreign persons would not be subject to tax on gain on the sale of securities, Kato forfeits his Green Card and takes up residence in a tropical tax haven.

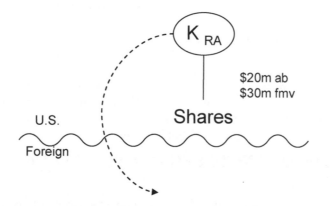

Because Kato has been a long term resident, the $20 million of gain ($30 million fair market value of the shares less the $10 million basis), less the $636,000 exclusion, will result in $19,364,000 of gain subject to U.S. income tax.

¶ 206 REPORTING OF FOREIGN FINANCIAL ASSETS

Since the enactment of the Bank Secrecy Act of 1970, U.S. persons with foreign financial accounts have had to file a Form TD F 90-22.1, Report of Foreign Bank and Financial Accounts (or FBAR). A U.S. person must file a FBAR if it has a financial interest in or signature authority over any financial account in a foreign country, and the aggregate value of these accounts exceeds $10,000 at any time during the calendar year. The FBAR is an annual report which is due by June 30 of the subsequent year. The FBAR is not attached to the U.S. person's annual income tax return, but instead is filed separately with the Treasury Department (¶ 1609.01).

---

[88] Rev. Proc. 2010-40, IRB 2010-46.

Despite the FBAR reporting requirement, Congress believed that many wealthy U.S. citizens continued to evade U.S. tax through the use of unreported foreign financial assets, and that this tax evasion resulted in a significant loss of tax revenues. As a consequence, as part of the Hiring Incentives to Restore Employment (or HIRE) Act of 2010 (P.L. 111-147), Congress enacted new reporting requirements with respect to foreign financial assets held by individuals, as well as new reporting and withholding requirements with respect to foreign financial institutions that potentially hold assets of U.S. persons.

Under new Code Sec. 6038D, individuals who hold an interest in specified foreign financial assets during the tax year must attach to their annual income tax returns certain information with respect to each asset if the aggregate value of all the assets exceeds $50,000. Specified foreign financial assets generally include foreign financial accounts, stock, securities, instruments and other interests in foreign entities. A taxpayer must disclose the maximum value of the foreign financial assets during the tax year and other information specific to each type of asset. The new reporting requirements are effective for tax years beginning after March 18, 2010.

Under new Code Secs. 1471 to 1474, new information reporting and withholding requirements are imposed on foreign financial institutions that potentially hold assets of U.S. persons. Generally, a withholding agent must deduct and withhold a 30% tax on any U.S. source fixed or determinable annual or periodical income paid to a foreign financial institution. Withholding is not required, however, if the foreign financial institution satisfies certain reporting requirements. Similar rules also apply to non-financial foreign entities. These provisions are generally effective for payments made after December 31, 2012. The IRS has provided preliminary guidance for implementing the withholding rules.[89]

¶ 207 A POLICY NOTE REGARDING THE CURRENT U.S. SYSTEM

The current U.S. jurisdictional system reflects a variety of tax policy objectives, including fairness, the need to collect tax revenues, economic neutrality, and enforcement constraints. The concept of fairness encompasses both horizontal equity and vertical equity. Horizontal equity requires similar treatment of taxpayers in similar economic situations, whereas vertical equity requires more taxes paid by higher-income taxpayers. The U.S. government's use of a credit system to mitigate international double taxation generally enhances vertical equity. Under a territorial system, U.S. persons could split their total income between domestic and foreign sources. Under a credit system, however, U.S. persons must aggregate their worldwide income and the United States taxes the total amount at graduated rates.

Whether the taxation of a U.S. person's worldwide income enhances or diminishes horizontal equity depends on how one interprets the concept of similarly situated. For example, one could argue that U.S. citizens residing abroad should benefit less from U.S. government expenditures and, therefore, should pay less

---

[89] Notice 2010-60, IRB 2010-37.

U.S. tax than citizens residing at home. The Supreme Court addressed this issue in 1924 in the case of *G.W. Cook v. G.L. Tait*.[90] The Court ruled that the U.S. government could tax the Mexican-source income of a U.S. citizen who was a permanent resident of Mexico on the grounds that government expenditures benefit U.S. citizens regardless of their residence or the source of their income. In other words, the basic rights and protections accorded all U.S. citizens, including the right to exit and reenter the United States at will (and thereby control the enjoyment of these benefits), are the primary determinants of whether individuals are similarly situated.

A second major tax policy objective is the collection of tax revenues to fund public services. The United States mitigates international double taxation by allowing U.S. persons to claim a credit for foreign income taxes imposed on their foreign-source income. The appeal of the credit system, as compared to a territorial system, is that it allows the United States to mitigate international double taxation without completely forgoing jurisdiction over the foreign-source income of U.S. persons. Double taxation is avoided by allowing the host country to claim primary jurisdiction over a U.S. person's foreign-source income. However, the United States does assert secondary jurisdiction and therefore collects any residual U.S. tax on lightly-taxed foreign-source income. Asserting secondary jurisdiction over foreign-source income increases U.S. tax collections and promotes fairness. Under a territorial system, U.S. persons could avoid U.S. taxes simply by shifting their income-producing assets to tax-haven countries that impose little or no income taxes.

A third basic tax policy objective is economic neutrality, or the effect of taxation on business and investment decisions. In terms of international trade, neutrality is an issue with respect to the location of production facilities and investment assets (capital export neutrality) as well as competition between domestic and foreign companies within the same country or market (capital import neutrality). Capital export neutrality exists if the decision to invest capital at home or abroad is unaffected by taxes. Therefore, capital export neutrality does not exist if, for example, tax rates are lower abroad, in which case there is a tax incentive to export capital. U.S. labor groups, in particular, are concerned that the tax laws do not give U.S. companies an incentive to move their manufacturing plants and other facilities overseas. Capital import neutrality exists if domestic and foreign companies competing within the same country or market all face the same total tax rate. Capital import neutrality is a major concern for U.S. companies attempting to compete in foreign markets.

The U.S. system exhibits elements of both capital export and capital import neutrality. For example, subjecting a U.S. company's worldwide income to taxation enhances capital export neutrality. On the other hand, U.S. companies that operate abroad through lightly-taxed foreign subsidiaries can defer payment of most residual U.S. taxes, which enhances capital import neutrality. During the 1950s and 1960s, capital export neutrality was the major U.S. tax policy goal, as U.S. multina-

---

[90] SCt, 1 USTC ¶ 92, 265 US 47, 44 SCt 444.

tional corporations dominated foreign competitors at home and abroad. However, as global competition has intensified during the past few decades, so have concerns about capital import neutrality.

The tensions created by the trade-offs between these two types of tax neutrality have created an on-going political debate. On one side are those U.S. lawmakers and constituency groups (e.g., organized labor organizations) that wish to emphasize capital export neutrality. These groups are concerned that too many high-paying U.S. manufacturing jobs are migrating offshore due, in part, to the tax savings offered by a number of low-tax foreign jurisdictions. These interests have resulted in recurring proposals to eliminate deferral. On the other side are those U.S. lawmakers and constituency groups (e.g., trade associations representing U.S. multinational corporations) that wish to emphasize capital import neutrality. These groups are concerned that U.S. businesses are at a competitive disadvantage in foreign markets, due to what they perceive to be the unusually harsh approach that U.S. lawmakers take in taxing foreign earnings.

Another major policy issue in the international context is enforcement constraints. The United States can enforce a tax on a foreign person only if it can verify the correctness of the resulting tax liability and collect the tax if the taxpayer does not voluntarily pay it. As a practical matter, this is possible only when either the taxpayer or the taxable income is located within U.S. borders. The U.S. system for taxing foreign persons reflects these constraints. For example, because withholding is the only sure way to collect taxes from passive offshore investors, the United States taxes the gross amount of a foreign person's U.S.-source investment income through flat rate withholding.

In sum, the current system for taxing international transactions, like the U.S. tax system generally, represents a compromise between the competing policy objectives of fairness, tax collections, economic neutrality, and enforcement constraints.

¶ 208 APPENDIX

Mr. Brewster, a U.S. citizen, is employed by the OK Oil Company and he accepts a foreign assignment with the OK Oil Company Foreign Affiliate in foreign country F beginning in 2009. During 2010, Mr. Brewster earned $100,000 in foreign country F, which does not impose an income tax, and incurred $20,000 of qualifying housing cost expenses. Mr. Brewster takes both the foreign earned income exclusion and the foreign housing exclusion. Although Mr. Brewster qualifies for the foreign earned income exclusion under either the bona fide residence test or the physical presence test, he completed the attached Form 2555 using the physical presence test.

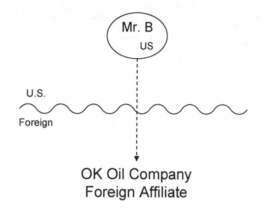

Form **2555**	**Foreign Earned Income**	OMB No. 1545-0074
Department of the Treasury Internal Revenue Service	▶ See separate instructions. ▶ Attach to Form 1040.	**20**10 Attachment Sequence No. **34**

For Use by U.S. Citizens and Resident Aliens Only

Name shown on Form 1040	Your social security number
Mr. Brewster	345-67-8912

Part I   General Information

1 Your foreign address (including country)
1234 Simon Way, Foreign Country F

2 Your occupation
Petroleum Man

3 Employer's name ▶   OK Oil Company Foreign Affiliate

4a Employer's U.S. address ▶

b Employer's foreign address ▶ 5678 RED Road, Foreign Country F

5 Employer is (check any that apply): ▶   **a** ☐ A foreign entity   **b** ☐ A U.S. company   **c** ☐ Self
d ☑ A foreign affiliate of a U.S. company   **e** ☐ Other (specify) ▶

6a If, after 1981, you filed Form 2555 or Form 2555-EZ, enter the last year you filed the form. ▶ **2009**

b If you did not file Form 2555 or 2555-EZ after 1981 to claim either of the exclusions, check here ▶ ☐ and go to line 7.

c Have you ever revoked either of the exclusions? . . . . ☐ Yes ☑ No

d If you answered "Yes," enter the type of exclusion and the tax year for which the revocation was effective. ▶

7 Of what country are you a citizen/national? ▶ United States of America

8a Did you maintain a separate foreign residence for your family because of adverse living conditions at your tax home? See **Second foreign household** on page 3 of the instructions . . . . ☐ Yes ☑ No

b If "Yes," enter city and country of the separate foreign residence. Also, enter the number of days during your tax year that you maintained a second household at that address. ▶

9 List your tax home(s) during your tax year and date(s) established. ▶ Foreign Country F, established January 1

Next, complete either Part II or Part III. If an item does not apply, enter "NA." If you do not give the information asked for, any exclusion or deduction you claim may be disallowed.

Part II   Taxpayers Qualifying Under Bona Fide Residence Test (see page 2 of the instructions)

10 Date bona fide residence began ▶ , and ended ▶

11 Kind of living quarters in foreign country ▶   **a** ☐ Purchased house   **b** ☐ Rented house or apartment   **c** ☐ Rented room
d ☐ Quarters furnished by employer

12a Did any of your family live with you abroad during any part of the tax year? . . . . ☐ Yes ☐ No

b If "Yes," who and for what period? ▶

13a Have you submitted a statement to the authorities of the foreign country where you claim bona fide residence that you are not a resident of that country? See instructions . . . . ☐ Yes ☐ No

b Are you required to pay income tax to the country where you claim bona fide residence? See instructions . ☐ Yes ☐ No

If you answered "Yes" to 13a and "No" to 13b, you do not qualify as a bona fide resident. Do not complete the rest of this part.

14 If you were present in the United States or its possessions during the tax year, complete columns **(a)–(d)** below. **Do not** include the income from column **(d)** in Part IV, but report it on Form 1040.

(a) Date arrived in U.S.	(b) Date left U.S.	(c) Number of days in U.S. on business	(d) Income earned in U.S. on business (attach computation)	(a) Date arrived in U.S.	(b) Date left U.S.	(c) Number of days in U.S. on business	(d) Income earned in U.S. on business (attach computation)

15a List any contractual terms or other conditions relating to the length of your employment abroad. ▶

b Enter the type of visa under which you entered the foreign country. ▶

c Did your visa limit the length of your stay or employment in a foreign country? If "Yes," attach explanation . ☐ Yes ☐ No

d Did you maintain a home in the United States while living abroad? . . . . ☐ Yes ☐ No

e If "Yes," enter address of your home, whether it was rented, the names of the occupants, and their relationship to you. ▶

For Paperwork Reduction Act Notice, see the Form 1040 instructions.   Cat. No. 11900P   Form **2555** (2010)

¶208

Form 2555 (2010)   Page **2**

| **Part III** | Taxpayers Qualifying Under Physical Presence Test (see page 2 of the instructions) |

16 The physical presence test is based on the 12-month period from ▶   January 1   through ▶   December 31

17 Enter your principal country of employment during your tax year. ▶   Foreign Country F

18 If you traveled abroad during the 12-month period entered on line 16, complete columns **(a)–(f)** below. Exclude travel between foreign countries that did not involve travel on or over international waters, or in or over the United States, for 24 hours or more. If you have no travel to report during the period, enter "Physically present in a foreign country or countries for the entire 12-month period." **Do not** include the income from column **(f)** below in Part IV, but report it on Form 1040.

(a) Name of country (including U.S.)	**(b)** Date arrived	**(c)** Date left	**(d)** Full days present in country	**(e)** Number of days in U.S. on business	**(f)** Income earned in U.S. on business (attach computation)
Physically present in foreign country F the entire taxable year.			365		

| **Part IV** | All Taxpayers |

Note: *Enter on lines 19 through 23 all income, including noncash income, you earned and actually or constructively received during your 2010 tax year for services you performed in a foreign country. If any of the foreign earned income received this tax year was earned in a prior tax year, or will be earned in a later tax year (such as a bonus), see the instructions.* **Do not** *include income from line 14, column* **(d)**, *or line 18, column* **(f)**. *Report amounts in U.S. dollars, using the exchange rates in effect when you actually or constructively received the income.*

> **If you are a cash basis taxpayer, report on Form 1040 all income you received in 2010, no matter when you performed the service.**

2010 Foreign Earned Income		**Amount** (in U.S. dollars)	
19 Total wages, salaries, bonuses, commissions, etc.	**19**	100,000	00
20 Allowable share of income for personal services performed (see instructions):			
a In a business (including farming) or profession	**20a**		
b In a partnership. List partnership's name and address and type of income. ▶ _____			
	20b		
21 Noncash income (market value of property or facilities furnished by employer—attach statement showing how it was determined):			
a Home (lodging)	**21a**		
b Meals	**21b**		
c Car	**21c**		
d Other property or facilities. List type and amount. ▶ _____	**21d**		
22 Allowances, reimbursements, or expenses paid on your behalf for services you performed:			
a Cost of living and overseas differential **22a**			
b Family **22b**			
c Education **22c**			
d Home leave **22d**			
e Quarters **22e**			
f For any other purpose. List type and amount. ▶ _____ **22f**			
g Add lines 22a through 22f	**22g**		
23 Other foreign earned income. List type and amount. ▶ _____	**23**		
24 Add lines 19 through 21d, line 22g, and line 23	**24**	100,000	00
25 Total amount of meals and lodging included on line 24 that is excludable (see instructions)	**25**		
26 Subtract line 25 from line 24. Enter the result here and on line 27 on page 3. This is your **2010 foreign earned income** . . . . ▶	**26**	100,000	00

Form **2555** (2010)

¶**208**

Form 2555 (2010)   Page **3**

Part V	All Taxpayers

27	Enter the amount from line 26	27	100,000	00

Are you claiming the housing exclusion or housing deduction?

☑ **Yes.** Complete Part VI.
☐ **No.** Go to Part VII.

Part VI	Taxpayers Claiming the Housing Exclusion and/or Deduction

28	Qualified housing expenses for the tax year (see instructions)	28	20,000	00
29a	Enter location where housing expenses incurred (see instructions) ▶ Foreign Country F			
b	Enter limit on housing expenses (see instructions)	29b	26,280	00
30	Enter the **smaller** of line 28 or line 29b	30	20,000	00
31	Number of days in your qualifying period that fall within your 2010 tax year (see instructions) . . . . [31	365	days]			
32	Multiply $40.11 by the number of days on line 31. If 365 is entered on line 31, enter $14,640.00 here	32	14,640	00
33	Subtract line 32 from line 30. If the result is zero or less, do not complete the rest of this part or any of Part IX	33	5,360	00
34	Enter employer-provided amounts (see instructions) . . . . . . [34	100,000	00]			
35	Divide line 34 by line 27. Enter the result as a decimal (rounded to at least three places), but do not enter more than "1.000"	35	× 1 .	00
36	**Housing exclusion.** Multiply line 33 by line 35. Enter the result but do not enter more than the amount on line 34. Also, complete Part VIII . . . . ▶	36	5,360	00

Note: *The housing deduction is figured in Part IX. If you choose to claim the foreign earned income exclusion, complete Parts VII and VIII before Part IX.*

Part VII	Taxpayers Claiming the Foreign Earned Income Exclusion

37	Maximum foreign earned income exclusion	37	$91,500	00
38	• If you completed Part VI, enter the number from line 31. • All others, enter the number of days in your qualifying period that fall within your 2010 tax year (see the instructions for line 31). [38	365 days]			
39	• If line 38 and the number of days in your 2010 tax year (usually 365) are the same, enter "1.000." • Otherwise, divide line 38 by the number of days in your 2010 tax year and enter the result as a decimal (rounded to at least three places).	39	× 1 .	00
40	Multiply line 37 by line 39	40	91,500	00
41	Subtract line 36 from line 27	41	94,640	00
42	**Foreign earned income exclusion.** Enter the **smaller** of line 40 or line 41. Also, complete Part VIII ▶	42	91,500	00

Part VIII	Taxpayers Claiming the Housing Exclusion, Foreign Earned Income Exclusion, or Both

43	Add lines 36 and 42	43	96,860	00
44	Deductions allowed in figuring your adjusted gross income (Form 1040, line 37) that are allocable to the excluded income. See instructions and attach computation	44		
45	Subtract line 44 from line 43. Enter the result here and in parentheses on **Form 1040, line 21.** Next to the amount enter "Form 2555." On Form 1040, subtract this amount from your income to arrive at total income on Form 1040, line 22	45	96,860	00

Part IX	Taxpayers Claiming the Housing Deduction— Complete this part only if **(a)** line 33 is more than line 36 and **(b)** line 27 is more than line 43.

46	Subtract line 36 from line 33	46		
47	Subtract line 43 from line 27	47		
48	Enter the **smaller** of line 46 or line 47	48		

Note: *If line 47 is **more than** line 48 and you could not deduct all of your 2009 housing deduction because of the 2009 limit, use the worksheet on page 4 of the instructions to figure the amount to enter on line 49. Otherwise, go to line 50.*

49	Housing deduction carryover from 2009 (from worksheet on page 4 of the instructions) . . .	49		
50	**Housing deduction.** Add lines 48 and 49. Enter the total here and on Form 1040 to the left of line 36. Next to the amount on Form 1040, enter "Form 2555." Add it to the total adjustments reported on that line . . . . ▶	50		

Form **2555** (2010)

Chapter 3

Source-of-Income Rules

¶ 301 IMPORTANCE OF SOURCE RULES

.01 U.S. Persons

The United States taxes U.S. persons on all of their income, from whatever source derived.[1] Therefore, the source of income generally has no effect on the computation of a U.S. person's taxable income. Sourcing can have a significant effect, however, on the computation of a U.S. person's foreign tax credit limitation, which equals the portion of the pre-credit U.S. tax that is attributable to foreign-source income (see Figure 3.1).[2] The limitation establishes a ceiling on the amount of foreign taxes that can offset U.S. taxes and is designed to prevent U.S. persons operating in high-tax foreign countries from offsetting those higher foreign taxes against the U.S. tax on domestic income.

Figure 3.1 Foreign Tax Credit Limitation

$$\text{Foreign tax credit limitation} = \text{Pre-credit U.S. tax} \times \frac{\text{Foreign-source taxable income}}{\text{Worldwide taxable income}}$$

The limitation is important to the extent it prevents taxpayers from crediting all of their foreign income taxes. When a U.S. person's creditable foreign taxes are less than the limitation, the cost of paying foreign income taxes is entirely offset by the U.S. tax savings associated with the credit and, therefore, foreign taxes do not represent an out-of-pocket tax cost for the U.S. person. In contrast, when a U.S. person's creditable foreign taxes exceed the limitation, the noncreditable foreign income taxes increase the U.S. person's total tax burden beyond what it would have been if only the United States had taxed the foreign-source income.[3] Therefore, the computation of the foreign tax credit limitation determines whether foreign taxes have an incremental effect on a U.S. person's worldwide tax costs.

---

[1] Code Sec. 61(a).

[2] Code Sec. 904(a).

[3] Although creditable foreign taxes in excess of the limitation cannot be taken in the current year, they can be carried back one year and carried forward up to ten years, and taken as a credit in a year in which the limitation exceeds the amount of creditable foreign taxes. Code Sec. 904(c).

Example 3.1: USAco, a domestic corporation, has taxable income of $100, all of which is attributable to a foreign branch operation. Assume the U.S. tax rate is 35%.

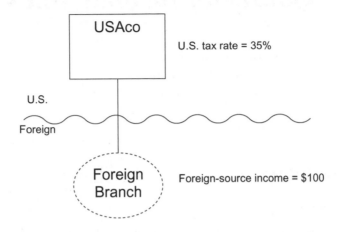

Case 1—Operating in a low-tax foreign country: If USAco's foreign branch is subject to foreign taxation at a 30% rate, USAco can claim a credit for the entire $30 of foreign taxes paid, as follows.

Foreign tax return	
Taxable income	$100
Tax rate	×.30
Foreign tax	$30

U.S. tax return	
Taxable income	$100
Tax rate	×.35
Pre-credit tax	$ 35
Foreign tax credit	– 30
U.S. tax	$ 5

The total tax burden on USAco's foreign profits is $35 [$5 U.S. tax + $30 foreign tax]. Foreign taxes do not represent an incremental tax cost in this case. For example, if USAco were able to reduce its foreign tax from $30 to $29, the foreign tax savings would be completely offset by an increase in U.S. taxes from $5 to $6.

Case 2—Operating in a high-tax foreign country: If USAco's branch is subject to foreign taxation at a 40% rate, the foreign tax credit limitation (which equals the U.S. tax of $35 on USAco's foreign-source income) will prevent USAco from claiming a credit for $5 of the $40 of foreign taxes paid, as follows.

Foreign tax return	
Taxable income	$100
Tax rate	×.40
Foreign tax	$40

U.S. tax return	
Taxable income	$100
Tax rate	×.35
Pre-credit tax	$ 35
Foreign tax credit	– 35
U.S. tax	$ 0

Foreign taxation now increases the total tax burden on USAco's foreign profits from $35 to $40, resulting in a $5 out-of-pocket tax cost.

¶301.01

Foreign taxes in excess of the foreign tax credit limitation are referred to as "excess credits." One strategy for eliminating excess credits is to increase the percentage of total taxable income that is classified as foreign-source for U.S. tax purposes. As a consequence, the rules for sourcing gross income and deductions play an important role in eliminating excess credits. For example, the title passage rule for sourcing income from inventory sales provides U.S. exporters with a significant opportunity for increasing their foreign-source income.[4] By arranging for the passage of title in the importing country, rather than in the United States, export sales will generate foreign-source income and thereby increase the taxpayer's foreign tax credit limitation. Recharacterizing deductions is also an effective strategy for eliminating excess credits. A deduction reduces a taxpayer's pre-credit U.S. tax, regardless of how it is sourced. However, deductions allocated to foreign-source income also reduce the foreign tax credit limitation. In contrast, deductions allocated to U.S.-source income do not affect the foreign tax credit limitation and, therefore, provide a full U.S. tax benefit.

.02 Foreign Persons

The source rules play a more prominent role in the taxation of foreign persons, since they effectively define the boundaries of U.S. taxation. The United States taxes the gross amount of a foreign person's U.S.-source investment-type income at a flat rate of 30%.[5] The United States also taxes foreign persons at graduated rates on the net amount of income effectively connected with the conduct of a U.S. trade or business.[6] As a result, the United States generally taxes the U.S.-source income of foreign persons and exempts their foreign-source income. The source of a foreign person's income also is an important issue for potential U.S. withholding agents since they are liable for any withholding taxes that they fail to withhold from a foreign person's U.S.-source investment-type income. U.S. withholding taxes are discussed in Chapter 9 (¶ 901).

> **Example 3.2:** Norman Ray Allen (NRA), a nonresident alien, owns 100 shares of a U.S. company, 3W. If 3W pays a dividend of $100 to NRA, all $100 is U.S.-source income, which may be subject to withholding.

---

[4] Reg. § 1.861-7(c).
[5] Code Secs. 871(a) and 881(a).

[6] Code Secs. 871(b) and 882(a).

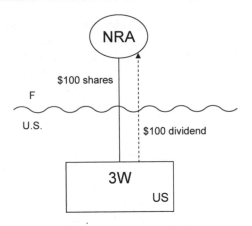

***Example* 3.3:** Norman Ray Allen (NRA), a nonresident alien, collects and trades widgets. NRA comes to the United States for three months where he buys and sells widgets from his hotel room in Peoria, Illinois. If NRA is conducting a U.S. trade or business, his income is U.S.-source income that is subject to tax at graduated rates on the net amount.

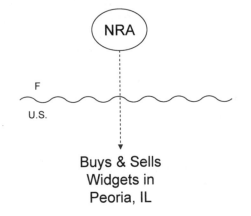

¶ 302 SOURCE RULES FOR GROSS INCOME

.01 *Introduction*

The source rules for gross income are organized by categories of income, such as interest, dividends, personal services income, rentals, royalties, and gains from the disposition of property.[7] Therefore, the first step in the sourcing process is to determine the applicable statutory category. This determination is sometimes ambiguous. For example, the same transaction may exhibit characteristics of both an installment sale and a lease. This distinction is important because a lease generates rental income, which is sourced on the basis of where the property is located, whereas an installment sale results in a gain on the sale as well as interest income, both of which are sourced under different rules. Therefore, the same item

---

[7] Code Secs. 861 and 862.

of income may be allocated between U.S. and foreign sources differently, depending on how it is categorized.

> *Example 3.4:* T is an orchestra conductor. A U.S. record company hired T to conduct various songs at a recording session that took place in the United States. T was compensated based on a percentage of the sales of the recording, which is owned by the record company. Most of the CD sales took place outside the United States. Under U.S. tax principles, personal services income is sourced on the basis of where the services are performed, whereas royalty income is sourced on the basis of where the intangible is used. Therefore, T's income is entirely U.S.-source income if it is classified as personal services income, but is mainly foreign-source income if it is classified as royalty income.[8]

Recording session
Few CD sales

U.S.

〜〜〜〜〜〜〜〜

Foreign

Most CD sales

In sum, an item of gross income cannot be sourced without first assigning the item to a statutory category and the appropriate category may be ambiguous.

An example of the importance of determining the applicable category of income is a transaction involving computer programs, which must be classified as one of the following:

(i) a transfer of a copyright right in the computer program,

(ii) a transfer of a copyrighted article (a copy of the computer program),

(iii) the provision of services for the development or modification of the computer program, or

(iv) the provision of know-how relating to computer programming techniques.[9]

For example, transactions involving mass-market software generally are classified as transfers of copyrighted articles.[10] Therefore, the source of income derived from the transfer of a copyrighted article is determined under the rules applicable to a sale of inventory if the underlying transfer provides all substantial rights. However, the copyrighted article is a lease of tangible personal property if the rights to use the copyrighted article are limited.[11] Sales are sourced under the title passage rule or the 50-50 method,[12] whereas leases are sourced under a place of use rule.[13]

---

[8] For example, *see P. Boulez,* 83 TC 584, Dec. 41,557; FSA 199970.

[9] Reg. § 1.861-18(b)(1).

[10] Reg. § 1.861-18(f)(2).

[11] Reg. § 1.861-18(h), Examples 1 and 2.

[12] Reg. § 1.861-7(c) and § 1.863-3.

[13] Code Secs. 861(a)(4) and 862(a)(4).

Once a taxpayer has determined the appropriate category of income, the next step is to apply the applicable source rule to classify the item of income as either U.S.- or foreign-source. In general, these rules for sourcing income are based on the location of the underlying income-producing property or activity. The general rules for sourcing gross income, which are described in detail in the following pages, are summarized in Table 3.1.

TABLE 3.1. GENERAL RULES FOR SOURCING GROSS INCOME

Type of income	U.S.-source income if:	Foreign-source income if:
Interest income	Debtor is a U.S. resident or a domestic corporation	Debtor is a foreign resident or a foreign corporation
Dividends	Payer is a domestic corporation	Payer is a foreign corporation
Personal services income	Services are performed in U.S.	Services are performed abroad
Rentals and royalties	Property is used in U.S.	Property is used abroad
Gain on sale of real property	Property is located in U.S.	Property is located abroad
Gain on sale of personal property	Seller is a U.S. resident	Seller is a foreign resident
Gain on sale of inventory purchased for resale	Title passes in U.S.	Title passes abroad
Gain on sale of inventory manufactured by taxpayer	Allocated between U.S. and foreign source income using the 50-50 method	
Gain on sale of depreciable property	Title passes in U.S.[a]	Title passes abroad[a]
Gain on sale of patents and other intangibles	Seller is a U.S. resident[b]	Seller is a foreign resident[b]

[a]Different rules apply to the portion of the gain attributable to prior-year depreciation deductions.

[b]Different rules apply if the intangible is sold for a contingent price, or if a portion of the gain is attributable to prior-year amortization deductions.

For purposes of sourcing income, the United States includes the 50 states and the District of Columbia, but not other U.S. possessions (i.e., Puerto Rico, the Virgin Islands, Guam, the Northern Mariana Islands, and American Samoa).[14] However, for purposes of sourcing personal services income from mines, oil and

---

[14] Code Sec. 7701(a)(9).

¶302.01

gas wells, and other natural deposits, the United States also includes continental shelf areas.[15]

.02 Interest Income

Interest income is U.S.-source income if the payer is a domestic corporation or U.S. resident and foreign-source income if the payer is a foreign corporation or a nonresident.[16] U.S.-source interest also includes interest paid by the United States government or any agency or instrumentality thereof (not including U.S. possessions), one of the 50 states or any political subdivisions thereof, or the District of Columbia.[17] For this purpose, the following taxpayers are considered to be U.S. residents:

(i) individuals who, at the time the interest is paid, are residents of the United States;

(ii) domestic corporations;

(iii) domestic partnerships which at any time during the taxable year were engaged in a U.S. trade or business; and

(iv) foreign corporations or foreign partnerships which at any time during the taxable year were engaged in a U.S. trade or business.[18]

Factors other than the residence (or the place of incorporation) of the debtor, such as where the debt was incurred or where the interest is paid are irrelevant. Although this approach is relatively objective, it can produce dubious results.

> **Example 3.5:** USAco, a domestic corporation, is a retailer of women's apparel. Five years ago, USAco opened a retail store in London, which was structured as an unincorporated branch. USAco financed the store through a $10 million loan from a U.K. bank. The loan is being repaid out of the profits of the U.K. branch. Therefore, the acquisition, use, and repayment of funds all occurred abroad. Nevertheless, under the residence-of-debtor source rule, the interest that USAco pays to the U.K. bank is U.S.-source income because USAco is a domestic corporation.

---

[15] Code Sec. 638.

[16] Code Secs. 861(a)(1) and 862(a)(1). For this purpose, interest income includes original issue discount, as well as any imputed interest. Reg. § 1.861-2(a)(4).

[17] Reg. § 1.861-2(a)(1). Determining the residency of trusts and estates is more complex. Generally, a trust that is a U.S. trust under Code Sec. 7701(a)(30)(E) will also be a U.S. trust for interest sourcing purposes. Additionally, the estate of a U.S. citizen or resident will also be treated as a U.S. resident. *See* Rev. Rul. 81-112, 1981-1 CB 598; Rev. Rul. 62-154, 1962-2 CB 148.

[18] Reg. § 1.861-2(a)(2). Note that interest paid by a U.S. citizen residing abroad is treated as foreign-source income.

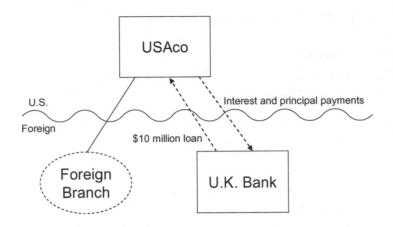

Congress has repealed an exception that would look beyond the debtor's residence to the location of the debtor's operations.[19]

Other major exceptions to the general rules for sourcing interest income include the following:

(i) Interest received from deposits made with a foreign branch of a domestic corporation or partnership engaged in the commercial banking business is treated as foreign-source income.[20]

(ii) Interest paid by a foreign corporation that is at least 50% owned by U.S. persons is U.S.-source income to the extent the interest payment is attributable to income that the foreign corporation derived from U.S. sources.[21] This exception applies only for purposes of computing the foreign tax credit limitation of a U.S. shareholder or other related person of the U.S.-owned foreign corporation and is designed to prevent U.S. persons from artificially increasing their foreign tax credit limitation by routing U.S.-source income through a U.S.-owned foreign corporation.

(iii) Interest paid by a U.S. branch of a foreign corporation is treated as if it were paid by a domestic corporation,[22] which generally makes the interest U.S.-source income. This exception is part of the branch profits tax regime, which is a withholding-type tax imposed on a U.S. branch's dividend equivalent amount. The branch profits tax is discussed in Chapter 10 (¶ 1002).

.03 Dividend Income

Dividends are U.S.-source income if the payer is a domestic corporation and foreign-source income if the payer is a foreign corporation.[23] Unlike interest income, there is no look-through rule for determining whether a domestic corpora-

---

[19] Former Code Secs. 861(a)(1)(A) and (c)(1), as repealed by P.L. 111-26 for tax years beginning after December 31, 2010.

[20] Code Sec. 861(a)(1)(B)(i).

[21] Code Sec. 904(h)(3). This exception does not apply if less than 10% of the U.S.-owned foreign corporation's

earnings are attributable to U.S.-source income. Code Sec. 904(h)(5).

[22] Code Sec. 884(f)(1)(A).

[23] Code Secs. 861(a)(2) and 862(a)(2).

tion is distributing earnings that were derived predominantly from foreign sources.[24] However, there is a look-through rule that applies to a foreign corporation if, during the preceding three taxable years, 25% or more of its gross income was effectively connected with the conduct of a U.S. trade or business. If a foreign corporation meets the 25% test, the U.S. source-portion equals the amount of the dividend times the ratio of gross income that was effectively connected with a U.S. trade or business during the three-year test period to the foreign corporation's total gross income for that period.[25]

> **Example 3.6:** FORco, a foreign corporation, derived 40% of its gross income for the three preceding taxable years from a U.S. branch operation. Under the 25% look-through rule, 40% of any dividends that FORco pays are U.S.-source income. The remaining 60% is foreign-source income by reason of FORco's foreign corporation status.

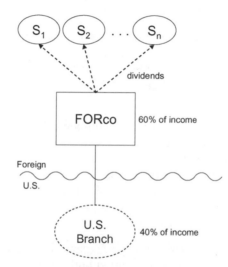

There is a major exception to the general rule for sourcing dividend income. More specifically, dividends paid by a foreign corporation that is at least 50% owned by U.S. persons are U.S.-source income to the extent the dividend is attributable to income that the foreign corporation derived from U.S. sources.[26] This exception applies only for purposes of computing the foreign tax credit limitation and is designed to prevent U.S. persons from artificially increasing their foreign tax credit limitation by routing U.S.-source income through a U.S.-owned foreign corporation.

.04 Personal Services Income

Compensation for personal services performed in the United States is U.S.-source income and compensation for personal services performed abroad is for-

---

[24] Nevertheless, a portion of the dividends that a foreign person receives from a domestic corporation is exempt from U.S. withholding tax if the payer meets an 80%-active-foreign-business test. Code Secs. 871(i)(2)(B) and 881(d).

[25] Code Sec. 861(a)(2)(B).

[26] Code Sec. 904(h)(4). This exception does not apply if less than 10% of the U.S.-owned foreign corporation's earnings are attributable to U.S.-source income. Code Sec. 904(h)(5).

¶302.04

eign-source income.[27] Personal services income includes salaries, wages, fees, and commissions, including any payments that an employer receives as compensation for services performed by employees or other agents.

Under a *de minimis* rule, income of a nonresident alien that is attributable to U.S. services is recharacterized as foreign-source income if the following requirements are met:

(i) the nonresident alien is present in the United States for 90 days or less during the taxable year,

(ii) the nonresident alien receives no more than $3,000 for his or her U.S. services, and

(iii) the nonresident alien works as an employee or under contract for either a foreign person who is not engaged in a U.S. trade or business or the foreign office of a U.S. person.[28]

This exception allows nonresident aliens to make short business trips to the United States free of U.S. taxes. Income tax treaties often contain more generous exemptions which allow for longer stays and, more importantly, increase or eliminate the limitation on earnings for business travelers from treaty countries (see Chapter 13 (¶ 1301)).

Another exception applies to the compensation of nonresident aliens engaged in international transportation services. Under this exception, compensation for services performed by a nonresident alien in connection with the individual's temporary presence in the United States as a regular member of a foreign vessel engaged in transportation between the United States and a foreign country or U.S. possession is generally treated as foreign-source income that is exempt from U.S. tax.[29]

An allocation issue arises when a taxpayer is paid a lump-sum amount, such as an annual salary, for services performed both within and without the United States. In these situations, the lump-sum amount is apportioned between U.S.- and foreign-source income, typically on the basis of the relative number of days worked in the United States and abroad.[30]

> *Example 3.7:* T lived and worked in the United States throughout the current year, except for a five-week foreign business trip. T received an annual salary of $60,000 for a total of 250 working days, including the 25 days spent working abroad. The foreign-source component of T's $60,000 salary is $6,000 [$60,000 × (25 days ÷ 250 days)], and the remaining $54,000 is U.S.-source income.

---

[27] Code Secs. 861(a)(3) and 862(a)(3).

[28] Code Sec. 861(a)(3). A nonresident alien who meets these requirements also is considered not to be engaged in a U.S. trade or business. Code Sec. 864(b)(1).

[29] Code Sec. 861(a)(3). This exception does not apply for purposes of Code Sec. 79 (group-term life insurance),

Code Sec. 105 (amounts received under accident and health plans), and Subchapter D (pertaining to deferred compensation, retirement plans, and other employee benefits).

[30] Reg. § 1.861-4(b).

¶302.04

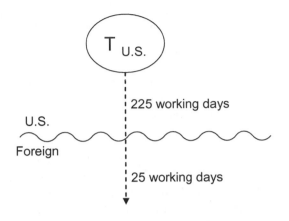

The need to allocate compensation between U.S. and foreign sources also can arise with respect to payments from a defined benefit plan. Pension income has two basic components: employer contributions for services performed and interest on those contributions. The compensation component is sourced under the general rules for sourcing personal services income. As a result, the compensation component of pension income received by an individual for services performed both within and without the United States must be allocated between U.S.- and foreign-source income based on the ratio of employer contributions made while the retiree was working abroad to the total of all employer contributions made for that retiree.[31]

> *Example* **3.8:** T receives an annual pension of $15,000 from a domestic trust, $5,000 of which is attributable to the earnings of the pension plan, and the remaining $10,000 to employer contributions. T's former employer contributed a total of $100,000 to the pension plan on T's behalf, $20,000 of which (30%) was contributed while T was on foreign assignments. Assuming the $5,000 of interest income is U.S. source, the foreign-source portion of T's annual pension is $2,000 [$10,000 × ($20,000 ÷ $100,000)].

The exercise of nonqualified stock options also gives rise to personal services income. If the taxpayer performed services both within and without the United States during the period beginning on the grant date and ending on the exercise date, the resulting compensation must be allocated between U.S.- and foreign-source income based on the relative number of months worked in the United States and abroad from the grant date to the exercise date.[32]

> *Example* **3.9:** T is granted a stock option on January 1 of year 1. T exercises the option on June 30 of year 2, and recognizes $30,000 of compensation income. T worked in the United States throughout year 1, but was on a

---

[31] Rev. Rul. 79-388, 1979-2 CB 270, and Rev. Rul. 79-389, 1979-2 CB 281. The interest component of pension income is sourced based on the residence of the payer. Code Secs. 861(a)(1) and 862(a)(2). *See* Rev. Proc. 2004-37, IRB 2004-26, for a method of determining the source of income for defined-benefit pension plan payments made to nonresident aliens where the trust is organized in the United States.

[32] Reg. § 1.911-3(e)(4).

foreign assignment throughout year 2. The foreign-source portion of T's option income is $10,000 [$30,000 × (6 months ÷ 18 months)].

.05 Rental and Royalty Income

Rentals and royalties are U.S.-source income if the property is located or used in the United States and foreign-source income if the property is located or used abroad.[33] All other factors, such as where the property was produced or the place of contract, are ignored.

Example **3.10:** A California production company produces a motion picture at its Hollywood studio. The movie is licensed for use in, among other places, London, England. Royalties received for the presentation of the movie in London theaters are foreign-source income, even though the movie was produced entirely in the United States.

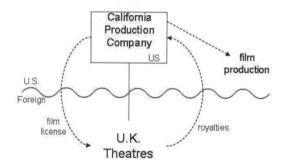

The characterization of income as a royalty, rather than gains from a sale, depends not only on where the intangible is actually used, but also on whether the licensee is legally entitled to use, and legally protected in using, the intangible in that country.[34] For this purpose, an intangible includes any patent, copyright, secret process or formula, goodwill, trademark, trade brand, franchise, or other like property.[35]

The place of use of personal property may be both within and without the United States, in which case the taxpayer must apportion the rental income between U.S. and foreign sources. This apportionment may be done on the basis of time, mileage, or some other appropriate base.

Example **3.11:** The taxpayer leases testing equipment to a manufacturer for a flat fee. The lessee uses the equipment at manufacturing plants located both in the United States and abroad. Therefore, the lessor must apportion its rental income between U.S. and foreign sources, probably on the basis of the relative amount of time the lessee uses the equipment at its U.S. and foreign plants.

---

[33] Code Secs. 861(a)(4) and 862(a)(4).

[34] For example, *see* Rev. Rul. 84-78, 1984-1 CB 173.

[35] Code Sec. 861(a)(4).

¶302.05

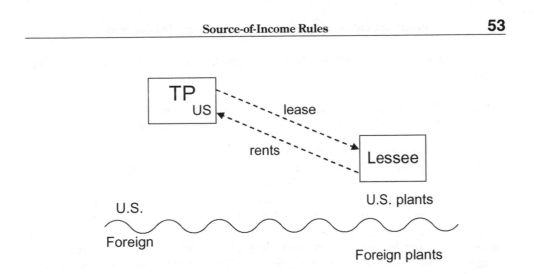

.06 Income from the Disposition of Property

Real property. A gain on the sale or exchange of a U.S. real property interest is U.S.-source income, whereas a gain on the sale or exchange of real property located abroad is foreign-source income.[36] All other factors, including where the selling activities took place, are ignored. For example, a gain on the sale of a U.S. office building to foreign investors is U.S.-source income, even if all of the related sale activities take place abroad.

Example **3.12:** Norman Ray Allen (NRA) is a nonresident alien who owns Blackacre, which is located in Music City, USA. Several years later, NRA sells Blackacre for a gain. Because Blackacre is located in the United States, the gain on NRA's sale is U.S.-source income.

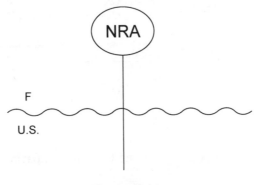

A U.S. real property interest includes the following types of interests located within the United States or the U.S. Virgin Islands: land, buildings, other inherently permanent structures, mines, wells, and other natural deposits, growing crops (but not harvested) and timber, and personal property associated with the use of real property (such as mining and farming equipment). U.S. real property interests also

---

[36] Code Secs. 861(a)(5) and 862(a)(5).

include shares of a corporation that is, or was, a U.S. real property holding corporation at any time during the five-year period preceding the disposition. A U.S. real property holding corporation is any corporation that holds U.S. real property with a market value equal to 50% or more of the market value of all the corporation's real property (U.S. and foreign) plus any property used in a trade or business.[37]

Personal property—general rule. Personal property includes a wide variety of assets, including stocks and securities, inventories, machinery and equipment, and intangibles such as patents, trademarks, and copyrights. As a general rule, a gain on the sale of personal property is U.S.-source income if the taxpayer is a U.S. resident and foreign-source income if the taxpayer is a nonresident.[38] However, there are numerous exceptions to this residence-of-seller rule, including special source rules for depreciable property, intangibles, inventories, and stock of a foreign affiliate. As a consequence, the residence-of-seller source rule applies primarily to security sales.

Example **3.13:** T, a citizen and resident of Ireland, sells at a gain 100 shares of USAco, a U.S. utility company whose shares are traded on the New York Stock Exchange. Even though USAco is a domestic corporation that conducts business operations only within the United States, T's gain is nevertheless treated as foreign-source income because T is a nonresident.

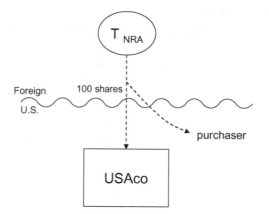

For purposes of this source rule, the following taxpayers are considered to be U.S. residents:

    (i) a domestic corporation,

    (ii) a U.S. citizen or resident alien who does not have a tax home in a foreign country,

    (iii) a nonresident alien who has a tax home in the United States, and

---

[37] Code Sec. 897(c). The definition of U.S. property interests is discussed in more detail in Chapter 9 (¶ 901).

[38] Code Sec. 865(a). For this purpose, the term "sale" includes an exchange or any other disposition. Code Sec. 865(i)(2).

¶302.06

(iv) a trust or estate whose situs is in the United States.[39]

A nonresident is any person other than a U.S. resident.[40] An individual's tax home is his or her principal or regular place of business, provided that the individual is not treated as having a tax home in a foreign country during any period in which his or her abode is in the United States.[41]

One implication of these residency rules is that a gain realized by a U.S. citizen or resident alien who has a foreign tax home is treated as foreign-source income, which has the beneficial side effect of increasing the taxpayer's foreign tax credit limitation. However, if the taxpayer's gain is not subject to foreign tax at a rate of 10% or more, the gain is treated as U.S.-source income, despite the taxpayer's foreign tax home.[42] Another special rule applies to U.S. residents who maintain an office or other fixed base in a foreign country. If a sale is attributable to that foreign office and the gain on the sale is subject to foreign tax at a rate of 10% or more, then the gain is treated as foreign-source income, despite the taxpayer's U.S. residency. This exception does not apply to sales of intangibles for a contingent price, inventory, depreciable personal property, goodwill, or stock of certain foreign affiliates.[43] For purposes of this exception, income is attributable to a foreign office if the office is a material factor in making the sale and the office regularly engages in these types of sales activities.[44]

> *Example* **3.14:** Uncle Sam, a U.S. citizen, operates an office in a European country where he buys and sells shares of stock. Assume that Uncle Sam earns a gain of $100,000 from the sale of shares. If that gain incurs tax of $10,000 or more (a 10% or greater tax rate), the gain from that sale is foreign-source. However, if the tax is less than $10,000 (a less than 10% rate), the gain from the sale of shares is U.S.-source income.

---

[39] Code Sec. 865(g)(1)(A). In the case of a sale of property by a partnership, the determination of residency generally is made at the partner level. Code Sec. 865(i)(5).

[40] Code Sec. 865(g)(1)(B).

[41] Code Sec. 911(d)(3) and Reg. § 1.911-2(b). An individual's abode is in the United States if that is where his or her economic, social, and personal ties are closest. For

example, *see J.T. Lemay,* CA-5, 88-1 USTC ¶ 9182, 837 F2d 681 (5th Cir. 1988). Aff'g 53 TCM 862, Dec. 43,931(M), TC Memo. 1987-256; *and D.P. Lansdown,* 68 TCM 680, Dec. 50,114(M), TC Memo. 1994-452. Aff'd, 73 F3d 373 (10th Cir. 1995).

[42] Code Sec. 865(g)(2).

[43] Code Sec. 865(e)(1).

[44] Code Secs. 865(e)(3) and 864(c)(5)(b).

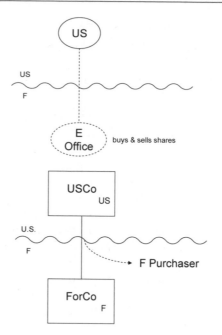

For purposes of the source-of-income rules, inventory includes personal property (and not real property) that is held by the taxpayer primarily for sale to customers in the ordinary course of business.[45] Developing an accurate, yet simple, source rule for income from the sale of inventories is a difficult task, given the complex nature of the underlying income-producing activities. For example, income from the sale of inventory by a wholesaler or retailer may be attributable to a number of geographically dispersed economic activities, such as purchasing, marketing, and distribution. The problem of tracing inventory profits to the underlying income-producing activities is more severe for manufacturers. In addition to the functions outlined above for retailers and wholesalers, manufacturers also engage in research and development, production, and post-sale warranty activities. One way in which U.S. lawmakers have sought to address these complexities is to promulgate separate source rules for inventory purchased for resale, as opposed to inventory manufactured by the taxpayer.

Inventory purchased for resale. Gross income from the sale of inventory that the taxpayer purchased for resale is sourced on the basis of where the sale occurs.[46] Therefore, such income is U.S.-source income if the sale occurs within the United States and foreign-source income if the sale occurs abroad. Other functions performed by a wholesaler or retailer, such as purchasing and distribution, are ignored. The place of sale is generally determined by where title to the goods passes from the seller to the buyer.[47]

Example **3.15:** USAco, a domestic corporation, is an independent broker that purchases used commercial aircraft from U.S. airlines for resale abroad.

---

[45] Code Secs. 865(i)(1) and 1221(1).
[46] Code Secs. 861(a)(6) and 862(a)(6).

[47] Reg. § 1.861-7(c).

¶302.06

During the current year, USAco purchased 20 planes from a regional airline based in Texas and then resold the planes to a Spanish airline. The Spanish airline first learned about USAco's services at a trade show held in Las Vegas, Nevada. The sales agreement between USAco and the Spanish airline was negotiated and signed in Florida. Title to the airplanes passed in Spain upon delivery at the Madrid airport. Even though all of the selling activities, including solicitation, negotiation, and closing, took place within the United States, the entire profit from the sale of the airplanes is foreign-source income because title passed abroad.

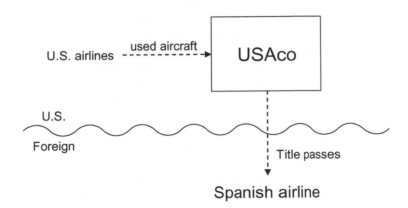

Passing title at the destination point rather than at the shipping point generally is not of great economic consequence to a U.S. exporter, since it is a common business practice to insure shipments and obtain letters of credit from offshore customers. Therefore, the title passage rule provides U.S. exporters with a significant opportunity for increasing their foreign tax credit limitation. Foreign title passage has some potential disadvantages, however, such as the burden of satisfying local customs requirements and the possibility of creating nexus in certain developing countries.

An exception to the title passage rule prevents nonresidents from avoiding U.S. tax by passing title abroad on sales to U.S. customers. This exception applies if a foreign resident maintains an office or other fixed base in the United States and the U.S. office is a material factor in making the sale and regularly engages in these types of sales activities. Income from such sales is treated as U.S.-source income, unless the inventory is sold for use, disposition, or consumption outside the United States and a foreign office of the taxpayer materially participates in the sale.[48]

Inventory manufactured by taxpayer. In contrast to the all-or-nothing approach of the title passage rule used to source gross income from the sale of inventory purchased for resale, income from the sale of inventory that the taxpayer

---

[48] Code Sec. 865(e)(2) and (3). Another exception applies to income from the sale of unprocessed timber which is softwood and which was cut from an area within the United States. Such income is treated as U.S.-source income, regardless of where title passes. Code Sec. 865(b).

produces in the United States and sells abroad is apportioned between U.S. and foreign-source income using one of three methods: the 50-50 method, the independent factory price method, or the taxpayer's own books and records.[49] Taxpayers are generally required to use the 50-50 method.[50]

The 50-50 method is analogous to the apportionment formulas used to source a corporation's income for state income tax purposes. Under the 50-50 method, a U.S. manufacturer apportions 50% of the gross income from export sales based on a sales activity factor and the other 50% based on a production activity factor.[51] The sales activity factor equals the ratio of the gross amount of export sales that are classified as foreign (using the title passage rule) to the gross amount of all export sales.[52] The production activity factor equals the ratio of the average adjusted basis of the taxpayer's production assets located abroad to the average adjusted basis of the taxpayer's production assets everywhere. The average adjusted basis is computed by averaging the adjusted basis of production assets at the beginning and end of the taxable year. Production assets include tangible and intangible assets owned by the taxpayer and directly used to produce inventory sold abroad (e.g., a factory building, machinery and equipment, and patents). Production assets do not include accounts receivables, intangibles not related to the production of inventory (e.g., marketing intangibles, including trademarks and customer lists), transportation assets, warehouses, the inventory itself, raw materials, or work-in-process. In addition, production assets do not include cash or other liquid assets (including working capital), investment assets, prepaid expenses, or stock of a subsidiary.[53]

If a U.S. manufacturer's foreign production assets are insignificant or nonexistent and the taxpayer passes title abroad on all foreign sales, the 50-50 method will allocate roughly 50% of the taxpayer's gross income from export sales to foreign-source income.[54]

> *Example* **3.16:** USAco, a domestic corporation, manufactures computers at its U.S. plant at a cost of $1,200 per unit. USAco markets its computers in Mexico through a branch sales office located in Mexico City with title passing in Mexico on these Mexican sales. During the year, USAco sold 1,000 computers through its Mexican branch at a price of $2,000 per unit. Therefore, USAco realized gross income of $800,000 [1,000 units × ($2,000 sales price – $1,200 cost of goods sold)] from its Mexican sales. USAco has no production assets located abroad, whereas the average value of its U.S. production assets is $5 million. As a result, the sales activity factor apportions $400,000 of income

---

[49] Code Sec. 863(b). Production means an activity that creates, fabricates, manufactures, extracts, processes, cures, or ages inventory. Reg. § 1.863-3(c)(1)(i)(A). Reg. § 1.863-3(a)(1) and (b). Special rules apply to the sale of goods manufactured in the United States and sold in a U.S. possession (or vice versa). Reg. §§ 1.863-3(f) and 1.863-3A(c).

[50] Reg. § 1.863-3(b)(1).

[51] Reg. § 1.863-3(b)(1) and (c).

[52] Reg. § 1.863-3(c)(2).

[53] Reg. § 1.863-3(c)(1). Production assets used to produce inventory sold both domestically and abroad are included in the formula based on the ratio of export sales of the related inventory to sales everywhere of that inventory.

[54] The regulations are generally less favorable for exporters of natural resources, which must apply a special export terminal rule. Reg. § 1.863-1(b). This rule applies to sales outside the United States of products derived from the ownership or operation of any farm, mine, oil or gas well, other natural deposit, or timber within the United States. Reg. § 1.863-1(b)(1). However, any income from the sale of unprocessed timber which is softwood and was cut from an area within the United States is always treated as U.S. source income. Code Sec. 865(b).

to foreign sources [50% × $800,000 × ($2 million of foreign export sales ÷ $2 million of total export sales)], and the production activity factor apportions no income to foreign sources [50% × $800,000 × ($0 of foreign production assets ÷ $5 million of production assets worldwide)]. In sum, the foreign-source portion of USAco's export gross income is $400,000 and the remaining $400,000 is U.S. source income.

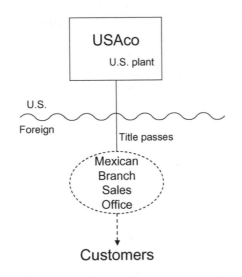

After a taxpayer has apportioned the gross income from export sales based on the sales activity and production activity factors, the taxpayer then apportions any related deductions between U.S. and foreign source income on a pro rata basis.[55]

If the taxpayer regularly sells part of its output to independent distributors such that an independent factory price can be fairly established, the taxpayer may elect to use the independent factory price method.[56] Under the independent factory price method, any gross profit on export sales beyond that earned on sales to independent distributors is foreign-source income. The 50-50 method generally will classify more of a U.S. manufacturer's export profits as foreign-source income than will the independent factory price method. Therefore, it will typically not be advantageous for purposes of the U.S. foreign tax credit to elect the independent factory price method. A taxpayer may also elect to use the books and records method, but only if the taxpayer receives advance permission from the IRS.[57]

An overriding rule applies to nonresidents who maintain an office or other fixed base in the United States. If a sale is attributable to that U.S. office, the gain is treated as U.S.-source income, despite the taxpayer's foreign residency. This exception applies to all types of personal property, including inventory, that a taxpayer sells for use, disposition, or consumption outside the United States, where the

---

[55] Reg. § 1.863-3(d). An exception applies to research and experimental expenditures.

[56] Reg. § 1.863-3(b)(2).
[57] Reg. § 1.863-3(b)(3).

taxpayer has a foreign office which materially participates in the sale and overrides all other sourcing rules.[58]

Example **3.17**: ForCo, a foreign corporation that manufactures and sells widgets, has a U.S. branch that is comprised of sales and warehousing functions. A Canadian customer purchases a widget that the U.S. branch office ships from its warehouse. If ForCo materially participates in the sale, the sale is foreign-source income. If ForCo does not materially participate in the sale (e.g., the sales personnel in the U.S. branch materially participated), the income is U.S.-source income.

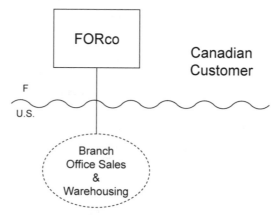

Depreciable personal property. Depreciation deductions reduce a taxpayer's basis in the depreciable property and thereby increase the gain computed on the disposition of that property. The portion of the gain on the disposition of depreciable personal property that is attributable to prior depreciation deductions is treated as having the same source as the related deductions.[59] For example, if the prior depreciation deductions offset both U.S.- and foreign-source income in prior years, the depreciation recapture portion of the gain is generally allocated between U.S.- and foreign-source income in the same proportion as the prior deductions. When the total gain exceeds the prior depreciation deductions (i.e., the property has appreciated in value since its acquisition), that appreciation is sourced using the rules applicable to inventories.[60] This generally means the gain is sourced based upon where title to the property passes from seller to buyer.[61]

Example **3.18**: During the current year, USAco (a domestic corporation) sold a machine to a Canadian company for $230,000, with title passing to the buyer upon delivery in Canada. USAco purchased the machine several years

---

[58] Code Sec. 865(e)(2).

[59] Code Sec. 865(c)(1). In determining whether prior depreciation deductions were allocated to U.S.-or foreign-source income, a special rule applies to property used predominantly inside or outside the United States. All of the depreciation related to such property is deemed to have been allocated to either U.S.- or foreign-source income, depending on the location of the property's predominant use. Code Sec. 865(c)(3)(B). For an example, *see* Temp. Reg. § 1.865-1T(e), Example 1. This exception

does not apply to property described in Code Sec. 168(g)(4).

[60] Code Sec. 865(c)(2).

[61] Code Sec. 865(b) and Reg. § 1.861-7(c). An exception applies if a foreign resident maintains an office or other fixed base in the United States, and the U.S. office is a material factor in making the sale and regularly engages in these types of sales activities. In such cases, the gain on the sale of depreciable property is treated as U.S.-source income. Code Sec. 865(e)(2) and (3).

¶302.06

ago for $200,000 and took $120,000 of depreciation deductions on the machine, all of which was apportioned to U.S.-source income. Therefore, USAco's adjusted basis in the machine is $80,000 [$200,000 original cost − $120,000 of accumulated depreciation] and the total gain on the sale of the machine is $150,000 [$230,000 sales price − $80,000 adjusted basis]. The $120,000 depreciation recapture portion of the gain is U.S.-source income, whereas the $30,000 of appreciation is foreign-source income.

Intangibles. For purposes of the source-of-income rules, an intangible is any patent, copyright, secret process or formula, goodwill, trademark, trade brand, franchise, or other like property.[62] As with depreciable personal property, a gain on the disposition of an intangible may be attributable in whole or in part to prior amortization deductions. The portion of the gain which is attributable to prior amortization deductions is treated as having the same source as the related deductions, determined using the same tracing rule applicable to depreciation on tangible personal property.[63] Unlike tangible personal property, however, the inventory source rules do not apply to any gain in excess of the depreciation recapture income.[64] Instead, any gain attributable to appreciation in the value of the intangible is sourced using the residence-of-seller rule, assuming the intangible is sold for a price that is not contingent on its productivity, use, or disposition.[65] If the intangible is sold for a price that is contingent on its productivity, use, or disposition, then the appreciation portion of the gain is sourced as if it were a royalty payment.[66] As discussed above, royalties are sourced based on the location of the actual use of, or the right to use, the underlying intangible.[67] A special rule also applies to a gain on the disposition of goodwill, which is treated as arising from sources within the country in which the goodwill was generated.[68]

Sale of stock of a foreign affiliate. Under the general rule, a U.S. resident treats a gain on the sale of stock as U.S.-source income.[69] However, if certain requirements are met, a U.S. resident can treat a gain on the sale of the stock of a foreign affiliate as foreign-source income, which has the beneficial side effect of increasing the taxpayer's foreign tax credit limitation (albeit in the passive basket). This exception applies if the following requirements are met:

    (i) the U.S. resident sells stock in an affiliate that is a foreign corporation,

   (ii) the sale occurs in a foreign country in which the affiliate is engaged in the active conduct of a trade or business, and

  (iii) the affiliate derived more than 50% of its gross income during the preceding three taxable years from the active conduct of a trade or business in such foreign country.[70]

---

[62] Code Sec. 865(d)(2).

[63] Code Sec. 865(d)(4)(A).

[64] Code Sec. 865(d)(4)(B).

[65] Code Sec. 865(d)(1)(A).

[66] Code Sec. 865(d)(1)(B).

[67] Code Secs. 861(a)(4) and 862(a)(4). Another special rule applies if a foreign resident maintains an office or other fixed base in the United States, and the U.S. office is a material factor in making the sale and regularly engages in these types of sales activities. In such cases, the gain on the sale of the intangible is treated as U.S.-source income. Code Sec. 865(e)(2) and (3).

[68] Code Sec. 865(d)(3).

[69] Code Sec. 865(a).

[70] Code Sec. 865(f). For this purpose, an affiliate is a member of the same affiliated group as defined in Code Sec. 1504(a), but without regard to the domestic corporation requirement of Code Sec. 1504(b). Code Sec.

¶302.06

Example **3.19**: A U.S. company, USCo, owns all the shares of a foreign company, ForCo. Over the last three years, ForCo has earned approximately 60% of its gross income from the active conduct of a trade or business in foreign country F. USCo personnel travel to foreign country F where they offer to sell all the USCo-owned shares of ForCo to a foreign purchaser. The deal is negotiated and closed in foreign country F. As a result, the gain on the sale of the ForCo shares is foreign-source income.

.07 Other Types of Income

Currency exchange gains and losses. Special source-of-income rules apply to a defined group of transactions referred to as "Section 988 transactions." Section 988 transactions include the following:

> (i) dispositions of a nonfunctional currency, and
>
> (ii) debt instruments, receivables and payables, and currency forward, futures, and option contracts, where the amount the taxpayer is entitled to receive, or required to pay, is denominated in (or determined by reference to) a nonfunctional currency.[71]

An example of a Section 988 transaction is a U.S. company that makes a sale on account to a foreign customer where the sales price is denominated in the customer's local currency instead of the U.S. dollar.

Exchange gains and losses attributable to a Section 988 transaction are sourced by reference to the residence of the taxpayer or the qualified business unit of the taxpayer (e.g., a foreign branch or subsidiary) on whose books the underlying asset, liability, or item of income or expense is properly reflected.[72] For purposes of this source rule, a U.S. resident is any corporation, partnership, trust, or estate that is a U.S. person, as well as any individual who has a tax home in the United States.[73] An individual's tax home is his or her principal or regular place of business, provided that an individual is not treated as having a tax home in a foreign country during any period in which the taxpayer's abode is in the United States.[74] A foreign resident is any corporation, partnership, trust, or estate that is a foreign person, as well as any individual who has a tax home in a foreign country.[75] The residence of a qualified business unit of the taxpayer is the country in which the qualified business unit's principal place of business is located.[76]

(Footnote Continued)

865(i)(4). In addition, for purposes of satisfying requirements (ii) and (iii), the U.S. resident can elect to treat the affiliate and all the corporations which are wholly owned, directly or indirectly, by the affiliate as one corporation.

[71] Code Sec. 988(c)(1).

[72] Code Sec. 988(a)(3)(A). However, any exchange gain or loss realized by a foreign person from the conduct of a U.S. trade or business is treated as U.S.-source income. Reg. § 1.988-4(c).

[73] Code Sec. 988(a)(3)(B)(i)(I) and (II).

[74] Code Sec. 911(d)(3) and Reg. § 1.911-2(b). An individual's abode is in the United States if that is where his

or her economic, social, and personal ties are closest (for example, *see J.T. Lemay*, CA-5, 88-1 USTC ¶ 9182, 837 F2d 681 (5th Cir. 1988). Aff'g 53 TCM 862, Dec. 43,931(M), TC Memo. 1987-256; *and D.P. Lansdown*, 68 TCM 680, Dec. 50,114(M), TC Memo. 1994-452. Aff'd, 73 F3d 373 (10th Cir. 1995)). An individual who does not have a tax home is treated as a U.S. resident if the individual is a U.S. citizen or resident alien, and a foreign resident if the individual is not a U.S. citizen or resident alien. Code Sec. 988(a)(3)(B)(i).

[75] Code Sec. 988(a)(3)(B)(i)(I) and (III).

[76] Code Sec. 988(a)(3)(B)(ii).

A different source rule applies if the currency exchange gain or loss arises as a result of a branch remittance. If a foreign branch that has a functional currency other than the U.S. dollar remits its earnings to the U.S. home office, then the taxpayer must recognize a currency exchange gain or loss equal to the difference between the dollar value of the remittance and the taxpayer's basis in the distributed earnings.[77] In such cases, the resulting gain or loss has the same source as the income giving rise to the branch's distributed earnings.[78] In a similar vein, if a U.S. shareholder receives a distribution from a foreign corporation of earnings previously taxed as either a Subpart F inclusion or a qualified electing fund inclusion, the U.S. shareholder must recognize a currency exchange gain or loss equal to the difference between the dollar value of the distribution and the U.S. shareholder's basis in the distributed earnings.[79] Such gains have the same source as the associated Subpart F or qualified electing fund inclusion.[80]

See Chapter 6 (¶ 601) for a more detailed discussion of currency exchange gains and losses.

Insurance underwriting income. Insurance income generally is sourced on the basis of where the insured risk is located. Therefore, premiums from issuing or reinsuring any insurance or annuity contract in connection with property located in the United States, a liability arising out of an activity located in the United States or in connection with the lives or health of residents of the United States, is treated as U.S.-source income.[81] Under an exception to prevent abuse, U.S.-source insurance income also includes income from insuring risks located outside the United States if, as a result of an arrangement, another corporation receives a substantially equal amount of premiums for insuring risks located within the United States.[82] Any other type of underwriting income is treated as foreign-source income.[83]

International communications income. International communications income includes income derived from the transmission of communications or data from the United States to a foreign country or from a foreign country to the United States.[84] Examples include transmitting telephone calls or other data, images, or sounds by satellite or underwater cable. The source rule for international communications income varies depending on whether the taxpayer is a U.S. person or a foreign person. In the case of a U.S. person, 50% of international communications income is treated as U.S.-source income and the other 50% is treated as foreign-source income.[85] In contrast, a foreign person generally treats all international communications income as foreign-source income, unless that person maintains an office or other fixed place of business within the United States, in which case any income attributable to that fixed place of business is treated as U.S.-source income.[86]

Scholarships and fellowships. Scholarships and fellowships received by someone who is not required to perform services for the payer are sourced based

---

[77] Prop. Reg. § 1.987-2.
[78] Code Sec. 987(3)(B).
[79] Code Sec. 986(c)(1).
[80] Code Sec. 986(c)(1).
[81] Code Sec. 861(a)(7)(A).
[82] Code Sec. 861(a)(7)(B).
[83] Code Sec. 862(a)(7).
[84] Code Sec. 863(e)(2).
[85] Code Sec. 863(e)(1)(A).
[86] Code Sec. 863(e)(1)(B).

on the residence of the payer. Therefore, an award is treated as U.S.- source income if it is made by a U.S. citizen or resident, a domestic corporation, the United States (or any instrumentality or agency thereof), one of the 50 states (or any political subdivision thereof), or the District of Columbia. On the other hand, awards made by a nonresident alien, a foreign corporation, a foreign government (or any instrumentality, agency, or political subdivision thereof), or an international agency, are treated as foreign-source income.[87]

Social security benefits. U.S. social security benefits are considered U.S.-source income,[88] regardless of whether the recipient spent his or her employment years working in the United States or abroad.

Space and ocean activities. Space and ocean activities include any activity conducted in space, any activity conducted on or under water not within the jurisdiction of a foreign country or the United States and any activity conducted in Antarctica.[89] Examples include fishing and mining activities undertaken on the high seas. Space and ocean activities are unique in the sense that they do not take place within the territory of any country. As a result, income from space and ocean activities is treated as U.S.-source income if derived by a U.S. person and as foreign-source income if derived by a foreign person.[90] Space and ocean activities do not include any activity that gives rise to transportation income or international communications income, or any activity connected with a mine, oil and gas well, or other natural deposit in a continental shelf area.[91]

Transportation income. Transportation income includes income derived from the use or lease of a vessel or aircraft (including any container used in connection with a vessel or aircraft) or from the performance of services directly related to the use of a vessel or aircraft.[92] Income from transportation that both begins and ends within the United States is treated as U.S.-source income.[93] If the transportation begins in the United States and ends abroad or begins abroad and ends in the United States, then 50% of the resulting income is treated as U.S.-source income and the other 50% is treated as foreign-source income.[94] This rule generally does not apply to transportation income derived from personal services performed by the taxpayer.[95] Therefore, flight and ship personnel source their compensation using the source rule for personal services income.

---

[87] Reg. § 1.863-1(d). An exception applies if a nonresident alien receives an award for study or research activities to be conducted outside the United States. Such grants are treated as foreign-source income, irrespective of the residence of the payer.

[88] Code Sec. 861(a)(8).

[89] Code Sec. 863(d)(2)(A).

[90] Code Sec. 863(d)(1).

[91] Code Sec. 863(d)(2)(B).

[92] Code Sec. 863(c)(3). Transportation income does not include income derived from transporting passengers or property between the United States and a foreign country by truck, rail, or bus, which is sourced under different rules (see Reg. § 1.863-4).

[93] Code Sec. 863(c)(1). Round trip travel from the United States to a foreign country is not transportation that begins and ends in the United States.

[94] Code Sec. 863(c)(2)(A). The source of transportation income may be of little or no consequence to a foreign person since both the Code and numerous tax treaties provide exemptions for income from the international operation of a vessel or aircraft. For example, see Code Secs. 872(b) and 883(a).

[95] Code Sec. 863(c)(2)(B).

¶302.07

.08 Distributive Share of Income from a Pass-Through Entity

In the case of partnerships and S corporations, the source of income usually is determined at the entity level and that source characterization carries over to the partners or shareholders in their distributive shares of income.[96] For example, a partner's distributive share of a partnership's foreign-source dividend income is foreign-source income to the partner. The same principle applies to trusts. As a result, distributions from a trust have the same character in the hands of the beneficiary as in the hands of the trust.[97] An exception applies to the sale of personal property by a partnership, in which case the applicable source rule is applied at the partner level rather than the partnership level.[98]

> **Example 3.20:** SCorp is a U.S. company owned by Larry (25%), Curly (25%) and Moe (50%). SCorp earns $100,000 of income, $20,000 of which is U.S.-source and $80,000 of which is foreign-source. As 25% shareholders, Larry and Curly each have $5,000 of U.S.-source income and $20,000 of foreign-source income. As 50% shareholder, Moe has $10,000 of U.S.-source income and $40,000 of foreign-source income.

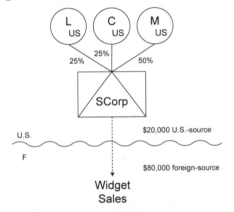

¶ 303 SOURCE RULES FOR DEDUCTIONS

.01 Introduction

Sourcing a taxpayer's gross income will be sufficient in some situations. For example, there is no need to source the deductions of a foreign person whose only connection to the United States is as a passive investor deriving U.S.-source nonbusiness income, since such income is taxed on a gross basis through a flat rate withholding tax.[99] In other cases, however, the operative tax attribute is net taxable income, which necessitates the sourcing of items of both gross income and deduction. For example, a foreign corporation with a branch office in the United States is taxed on the net amount of income effectively connected with the conduct of that U.S. trade or business.[100] Similarly, a U.S. person's foreign tax credit

---

[96] Code Secs. 702(b) and 1366(b).
[97] Code Secs. 652(b) and 662(b).
[98] Code Sec. 865(i)(5).

[99] Code Secs. 871(a) and 881(a).
[100] Code Sec. 882(a).

limitation is based on the ratio of net taxable income from foreign sources to net taxable income from all sources.[101]

In computing taxable income from sources within (or without) the United States, the taxpayer is allowed deductions for expenses and losses directly related to either U.S.- or foreign-source gross income, as well as a ratable portion of expenses and losses that are not definitely related to any specific item of gross income.[102] The taxpayer makes these determinations through a two-step process referred to as "allocation and apportionment."

.02 Allocation

The first step in sourcing a deduction is to allocate it to a related income-producing activity or class of gross income.[103] Examples of potential classes of gross income include compensation for services (including fees and commissions), gross income derived from business, gains derived from dealings in property, interest, rents, royalties, and dividends (see Figure 3.2).[104] A deduction is related, and therefore allocable, to a class of gross income if it is incurred as a result of, or incident to, the activity or property from which the gross income is derived. Therefore, the allocation rules emphasize the factual relationship between a deduction and a class of gross income. The classes of gross income are not predetermined, but instead, are determined on the basis of the deductions to be allocated. Although most deductions are definitely related to a specific class of gross income, some deductions are related to all gross income.[105] Examples include overhead, general and administrative, and supervisory expenses. These deductions ordinarily are allocated to a class consisting of all of the taxpayer's gross income.[106]

> **Example 3.21:** USCo, a U.S. corporation, conducts research and development activities (R&D). USCo earns $1 million as compensation for performing contract R&D services and $500,000 from sales of dental floss. The only expenses incurred by USCo include $500,000 of salaries paid to the lab technicians that wear white coats, $200,000 of commissions to sales people that wear plaid coats (and pearly-white smiles) and $100,000 of rent on the USCo worldwide headquarters. Based on gross receipts, two-thirds of the overhead expense of $100,000 of rent ($67,000) should be allocated to R&D services and one-third of the $100,000 of overhead expenses ($33,000) should be allocated to sales. Consequently, net income for services should be $433,000 ($1 million less $500,000 less $67,000). Income for sales should be $267,000 ($500,000 less $200,000 less $33,000).

---

[101] Code Sec. 904(a).

[102] Code Secs. 861(b) and 862(b).

[103] Reg. § 1.861-8(a)(2).

[104] Reg. § 1.861-8(a)(3).

[105] Reg. § 1.861-8(b)(1) and (b)(2).

[106] Temp. Reg. § 1.861-8T(b)(3). If the taxpayer incurring the expenses is a corporation that is a member of an affiliated group, the expense is allocated and apportioned as if all members of the group were a single corporation. Code Sec. 864(e)(6) and Temp. Reg. § 1.861-14T.

¶303.02

$1 million contract R&D $500,000 dental floss sales	**USCo**	$500,000 salaries $200,000 commission $100,000 rent

Figure 3.2 Allocation and apportionment of deductions

Step 1: Allocate deductions to a class of gross income

- Compensation for services
- Gross income from business
- Gains from dealings in property
- Interest
- Rents
- Royalties
- Dividends

Step 2: Apportion deductions between U.S. and foreign sources

- Gross income
- Gross sales
- Units sold
- Cost of goods sold
- Profit contributions
- Expenses incurred
- Assets used
- Salaries paid
- Space utilized
- Time spent

.03 Apportionment

The second step in sourcing a deduction is to apportion the deduction between U.S.- and foreign-source gross income.[107] This is accomplished by using an apportionment base that reflects, to a reasonably close extent, the factual relationship between the deduction and the gross income. Examples of potential apportionment bases include gross income, gross receipts or sales, units sold, cost of goods sold, profit contributions, expenses incurred, assets used, salaries paid, space utilized, and time spent (see Figure 3.2). The effect of the resulting apportionment on the tax liability and the related record-keeping burden are both considered when determining whether or not the apportionment is sufficiently precise.[108]

Unfortunately, the relationship between deductions and U.S. and foreign operations often is ambiguous. For example, in concept, a U.S. exporter should apportion its marketing expenses between U.S. and foreign sources based upon the relative amounts of marketing resources expended to generate U.S., as opposed to foreign, sales. However, often it is unclear which, if any, of the conventional apportionment bases, such as unit sales, gross sales, or gross margin, accurately reflects this relation. Moreover, if the mix of products sold in the United States differs from the mix of products sold abroad, the use of different apportionment bases will lead to different results.

---

[107] Reg. § 1.861-8(a)(2).   [108] Temp. Reg. § 1.861-8T(c)(1).

Example 3.22: USAco is a domestic corporation that sells its products both in the United States and abroad. During the current year, USAco had $10 million of sales and a gross profit of $5 million, and incurred $1 million of selling, general, and administrative (SG&A) expenses. USAco's $10 million of sales included $6 million of foreign sales and $4 million of domestic sales. On the other hand, because USAco's domestic sales generally involved higher-margin products than its foreign sales, USAco's gross profit of $5 million was split 50-50 between U.S. and foreign sources. So, if USAco uses gross profit as an apportionment base, it would apportion $500,000 of SG&A expenses to foreign-source income [50% × $1 million of SG&A expenses], as opposed to $600,000 if gross sales is used as an apportionment base [($6 million of foreign sales ÷ $10 million of total sales) × $1 million of SG&A expenses].

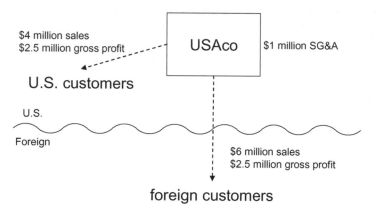

The selection of an apportionment base also is impacted by the type of records that the taxpayer maintains.

Example 3.23: The facts are the same as in Example 3.15, except now assume that USAco's SG&A expenses of $1 million consist of the president's salary of $250,000, the sales manager's salary of $100,000, and other SG&A expenses of $650,000. Also assume that USAco's president and sales manager maintain time records which indicate that the president devoted 30% of her time to foreign operations and 70% to domestic operations, while the sales manager devoted 40% of her time to foreign operations and 60% to domestic operations. USAco should now apportion the salaries of the president and sales manager on the basis of time spent and apportion the other SG&A expenses on the basis of gross profit. Therefore, USAco apportions to foreign-source income $75,000 of the president's salary [30% × $250,000], $40,000 of the sales manager's salary [40% × $100,000], and $325,000 of the remaining SG&A expenses [50% × $650,000], for a total of $440,000 of SG&A expenses apportioned to foreign-source income.[109]

---

[109] Compare Reg. § 1.861-8(g), Examples (19) and (20).

¶303.03

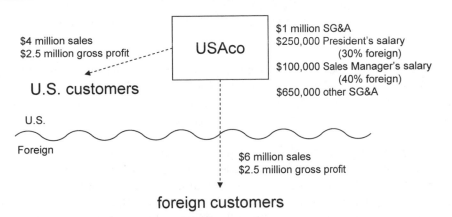

$4 million sales
$2.5 million gross profit

USAco

$1 million SG&A
$250,000 President's salary
(30% foreign)
$100,000 Sales Manager's salary
(40% foreign)
$650,000 other SG&A

U.S. customers

U.S.

Foreign

$6 million sales
$2.5 million gross profit

foreign customers

.04 Specialized Apportionment Rules

Interest expense. All income-producing activities require some degree of funding and a taxpayer often has considerable flexibility as to the source and use of funds. For example, a multinational corporation could use the proceeds from a second mortgage on a U.S. factory to acquire an office building located abroad. Moreover, when money is borrowed for a specific purpose, such borrowing generally will free other funds for other purposes. Because money is fungible, interest expense is assumed to be related to all of the taxpayer's activities and property, regardless of the specific purpose of the borrowing. Therefore, interest expense is allocated to all of the taxpayer's gross income.[110] If the taxpayer is a corporation that is a member of an affiliated group, interest expense is allocated and apportioned as if all members of the group were a single corporation.[111]

Interest expense is apportioned between U.S.- and foreign-source income using the relative basis of U.S. and foreign assets as an apportionment base.[112] For example, if 20% of a taxpayer's assets are foreign in nature, then that taxpayer must apportion 20% of its interest expense to foreign-source income. For this purpose, an asset is characterized as U.S. or foreign based upon whether the asset produces U.S.-or foreign-source income.[113] For example, inventory is characterized as a foreign asset to the extent that inventory sales give rise to foreign-source income.[114] The physical location of the asset is not relevant. Normally, the asset figures for a taxable year are the averages of the adjusted basis amounts at the beginning and the end of the year.[115] In lieu of using adjusted basis amounts, a taxpayer may elect to apportion interest expense on the basis of the fair market value of its assets, which may be advantageous if the adjusted basis of the taxpayer's U.S. assets is lower than their market value or if the adjusted basis of the taxpayer's foreign assets is higher than their market value.[116]

For example, tax-exempt assets are not taken into account when computing a taxpayer's U.S. versus foreign assets.[117] In addition, for purposes of computing asset

---

[110] Temp. Reg. § 1.861-9T(a).
[111] Code Sec. 864(e)(1).
[112] Code Sec. 864(e)(2).
[113] Temp. Reg. § 1.861-9T(g)(3).

[114] Temp. Reg. § 1.861-12T(b).
[115] Temp. Reg. § 1.861-9T(g).
[116] Reg. § 1.861-9T(g)(1)(ii).
[117] Code Sec. 864(e)(3).

amounts, a taxpayer's basis in any nonaffiliated, 10%-or-more-owned corporation is adjusted for changes in that company's earnings and profits over time.[118]

Interest expense. Under current law, the interest expense of U.S. affiliates is apportioned between U.S.-source and foreign-source income; on the other hand, contrary to the fungibility assumption, the interest expense of foreign affiliates is effectively allocated 100% to foreign-source income.

Example **3.24:** USP, a domestic corporation, owns all the stock of FSub, a foreign corporation. USP has a basis of $1,000 in its U.S. operating assets and a basis of $500 in its shares of FSub. FSub has foreign operating assets with a basis of $600 as well as $200 of debt, on which FSub pays $20 of interest expense. Under current law, the full amount of FSub's $20 of interest expense is effectively allocated against USP's foreign-source income because it reduces FSub's earnings and profits and ultimately any dividends it pays to USP by $20.

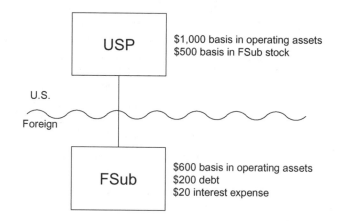

Example **3.25:** The facts are the same as in Example 3.24, except that USP now has $300 of debt, on which it pays $30 of interest expense. Under current law, USP apportions $20 of interest expense to U.S.-source income ([$1,000 U.S. operating assets / $1,500 total assets] × $30 interest expense), and $10 of interest expense to foreign-source income ([$500 basis in FSub shares / $1,500 total assets] × $30 interest expense). Thus, any foreign-source dividend income derived by USP from FSub is reduced by the full amount of FSub's $20 in interest expense, as well as $10 (or one-third) of USP's interest expense. In sum, USP's foreign-source taxable income is arguably understated due to the asymmetric treatment of the interest expense incurred by USP and FSub.

---

[118] Code Sec. 864(e)(4). *See also* Temp. Reg. §§1.861-9T and 1.861-11T through 1.861-13T for addi- tional guidance regarding the allocation and apportion- ment of interest expense.

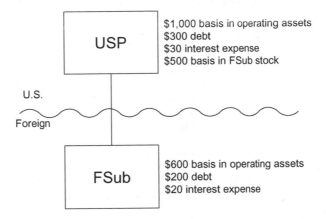

To address this issue, Code Sec. 864(f) permits a domestic corporation to elect to apportion interest expense on the basis of the taxpayer's worldwide affiliated group, which includes all 80% or more owned U.S. and foreign affiliates (other than certain financial institutions). However, in an attempt to balance the budget, Congress has delayed the effective date (as a revenue raiser) several times such that Code Sec. 864(f) will not be effective until taxable years beginning after December 31, 2020.[119]

Congress was concerned that domestic corporations would borrow money and re-loan those funds to its foreign subsidiaries (whereby only some of the interest expense would be allocable to reduce foreign-source income) in lieu of the foreign subsidiaries directly borrowing funds (whereby all of the interest expense would reduce foreign-source income). To avoid this potential abuse, the controlled foreign corporation netting rule specifically allocates certain interest expense deductions against foreign-source interest income derived from a controlled foreign corporation in computing its foreign tax credit limitation.[120] This rule applies when a domestic corporation has excess related-person indebtedness (the domestic corporation's indebtedness is much greater than the controlled foreign corporation's indebtedness).

Research and development expenditures. Any research and development (R&D) expenditures incurred solely to meet legal requirements imposed by a jurisdiction (the United States or a foreign country) are apportioned to that jurisdiction. Further R&D expenses attributable to activities conducted in the United States will result in a 50% apportionment to U.S.-source income; further R&D expenses attributable to activities conducted outside the United States will result in a 50% apportionment to foreign-source income. Any remaining R&D expenses are apportioned between U.S. and foreign sources according to either sales or gross income.[121]

---

[119] Hiring Incentives to Restore Employment Act of 2010.

[120] Reg. § 1.861-10.

[121] Code Sec. 864(g); Reg. § 1.861-17. To the extent R&D expenses are apportioned on the basis of gross income, the amount apportioned to foreign-source income must be at least 30% of the amount apportioned to

Figure 3.3 Apportionment priority of research and development expenditures

	Apportionment Priority
Step 1	R&D expenditures incurred solely to meet legal requirements imposed by a jurisdiction (U.S. or foreign) are allocated to that jurisdiction
Step 2	Apportion half of the remaining R&D expenses to U.S. or foreign-source income if R&D activities are conducted either in the United States or abroad.
Step 3	Other 50% of R&D expenditures is apportioned between U.S. and foreign sources using sales or gross income as an apportionment base

Losses from disposition of stock and other personal property. Losses from the sale or other disposition of stock and other personal property are generally sourced under the same rules that apply to gains from such property, that is, based on the residence of the seller.[122] For example, a loss from the sale of stocks and bonds issued by U.S. corporations are classified as foreign source income if the seller resides outside the United States. However, as with the source rules governing gains from personal property, there is a wide range of exceptions to the general rule. Exceptions governing stock sales include a recapture rule with respect to dividends received within 24 months of the stock sale,[123] stock attributable to a foreign office,[124] stock of an S corporation[125] and stock of a real property holding company.[126] Exceptions governing sales of personal property other than stock include inventory sales,[127] depreciable property,[128] foreign currency and certain financial instruments,[129] losses attributable to a foreign office[130] and trade receivables and certain interest equivalents.[131]

Other specialized rules. Additional guidance also is provided regarding the following types of deductions:

> (i) *Legal and accounting expenses*—Legal and accounting expenses incurred with respect to a specific property or activity (for example, to obtain a

---

(Footnote Continued)

foreign-source income using sales. See Figure 3.3 for a summary.

[122] Reg. § 1.865-2 (stock) and Reg. § 1.865-1 (personal property).

[123] A de minimis exception applies when the dividend is less than 10% of the recognized loss. Reg. § 1.865-2(b)(1).

[124] Reg. § 1.865-2(a)(2).

[125] Reg. § 1.865-2(b)(3).

[126] Reg. § 1.865-2(a)(4).

[127] Reg. § 1.865-1(c)(2).

[128] Reg. § 1.865-1(b)(1).

[129] Reg. § 1.865-1(c)(1).

[130] Reg. § 1.865-1(a)(2).

[131] Reg. § 1.865-1(c)(3).

patent) are allocated to the gross income produced by that property or activity (for example, royalties from the patent). On the other hand, the cost of general legal and accounting functions is allocated to all gross income and apportioned on the basis of gross income.[132]

(ii) *State income taxes*—State income taxes are allocated to the gross income on which the taxes were imposed and apportioned on the basis of gross income.[133]

(iii) *Net operating losses*—A net operating loss deduction allowed under Code Sec. 172 shall be allocated and apportioned in the same manner as the deductions giving rise to the net operating loss deduction.[134]

(iv) *Stewardship expenses*—Expenses associated with stewardship activities (e.g., activities undertaken by a parent corporation as an investor in a subsidiary) are allocated to the class of gross income that includes the dividends received from the subsidiary.[135]

(v) *Standard deduction*—The standard deduction is allocated to all of the individual taxpayer's gross income and apportioned on the basis of gross income.[136]

(vi) *Certain personal expenses*—An individual taxpayer's deductions for real estate taxes on a personal residence, medical expenses, and alimony payments are allocated to all of the taxpayer's gross income and apportioned on the basis of gross income.[137]

(vii) *Personal exemption*—Personal exemption deductions are not taken into account for purposes of allocating and apportioning deductions.[138]

(viii) *Charitable contributions*—Charitable contributions are allocated to all of the taxpayer's gross income and apportioned on the basis of gross income.[139]

---

[132] Reg. § 1.861-8(e)(5).
[133] Reg. § 1.861-8(e)(6).
[134] Reg. § 1.861-8(e)(8).
[135] Reg. § 1.861-8(e)(4).

[136] Code Secs. 861(b) and 862(b).
[137] Reg. § 1.861-8(e)(9).
[138] Reg. § 1.861-8(e)(11).
[139] Temp. Reg. § 1.861-8(e)(12).

Chapter 4
Foreign Tax Credit

¶ 401 INTRODUCTION

The United States mitigates international double taxation by allowing U.S. persons a credit for any foreign income taxes paid on their foreign-source income. Chapter 4 explains how to compute the foreign tax credit, describes the role that the foreign tax credit limitation plays in this process, and introduces some basic planning strategies for maximizing the credit. Chapter 4 also discusses the deemed paid foreign tax credit, which is the mechanism by which a domestic corporation can claim a credit for the foreign income taxes paid by a 10%-or-more-owned foreign corporation.

> ***Example 4.1:*** USAco operates an Asian branch that produces $10 million of foreign-source income and pays $2 million of foreign income taxes. USAco may take a direct foreign tax credit of $2 million against it pre-credit U.S. tax of $3.5 million (35% of $10 million of foreign-source taxable income) and pay only $1.5 million to the United States.

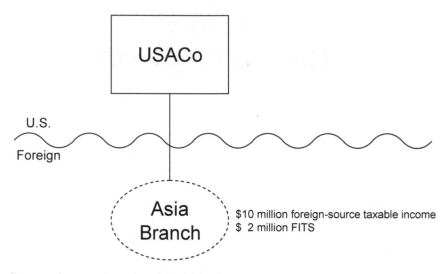

.01 Computing the Foreign Tax Credit

The United States taxes U.S. persons on all of their income, regardless of its source.[1] This creates a double taxation problem with respect to a U.S. person's foreign-source income, since foreign countries usually tax all the income earned within their borders, including that derived by U.S. persons. If the United States did nothing to mitigate international double taxation, U.S. companies would be at a competitive disadvantage in overseas markets, since their total tax rate would exceed that of their foreign competitors by the amount of the U.S. tax burden on foreign-source income. The centerpiece of the U.S. system for mitigating international double taxation is the foreign tax credit.[2]

The computation of the foreign tax credit is a three-step process, as follows:

Step 1—Compute creditable foreign income taxes. To be creditable, a foreign levy must be a tax, the predominant character of which is an income tax in the U.S. sense.[3]

Step 2—Compute the foreign tax credit limitation. A key feature of the U.S. credit system is the foreign tax credit limitation, which restricts the credit to the portion of the pre-credit U.S. tax that is attributable to foreign-source income.[4] The purpose of the limitation is to confine the effects of the credit to mitigating double taxation of foreign-source income. The limitation accomplishes this by preventing U.S. persons operating in high-tax foreign countries from offsetting those higher foreign taxes against the U.S. taxes on U.S.-source income.

Step 3—Determine the lesser of creditable foreign income taxes (step 1) or the foreign tax credit limitation (step 2). Creditable foreign taxes in excess of the limitation cannot be claimed as a credit in the current year. However, these excess credits can be carried back one year and carried forward up to ten

---

[1] Code Sec. 61(a).
[2] Code Sec. 901(a).

[3] Reg. § 1.901-2(a)(1).
[4] Code Sec. 904(a).

¶401.01

years and taken as a credit in a year that the limitation exceeds foreign income taxes.[5]

Example 4.2: USAco, a domestic corporation, has $10 million of taxable income, including $3 million of foreign-source taxable income, on which USAco paid $1.5 million in foreign income taxes. Assume that the U.S. tax rate is 35%.

Step 1: Compute the foreign income taxes	$1.5 million
Step 2: Compute the foreign tax credit limitation	
(A) Worldwide taxable income	$10 million
(B) Pre-credit U.S. tax [35% × $10 million] . .	$3.5 million
(C) Foreign-source taxable income	$3 million
Limitation = [line B × (C ÷ A)]	
= [$3.5 million × ($3 million ÷ $10 million)] .	$1,050,000
Step 3: Credit equals the lesser of creditable taxes ($1.5 million) or the limitation ($1,050,000)	$1,050,000

USAco can carry its excess credits of $450,000 [$1,500,000 – $1,050,000] back one year and forward ten years.

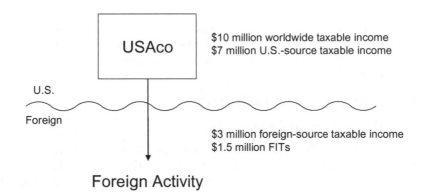

USAco

$10 million worldwide taxable income
$7 million U.S.-source taxable income

U.S.

Foreign

$3 million foreign-source taxable income
$1.5 million FITs

Foreign Activity

.02 Credit versus Deduction

Taxpayers have the option of deducting foreign income taxes in lieu of taking a credit.[6] A double tax benefit is not allowed, however, and a taxpayer cannot both deduct and claim a credit for the same foreign income taxes.[7] Generally, a credit is more advantageous than a deduction because a credit reduces a person's tax dollar for dollar as opposed to a reduction in taxable income. For example, if a domestic corporation is subject to U.S. tax at a 35% rate, deducting $1 of foreign income taxes saves only $0.35 in taxes, compared to $1 in tax savings from a credit.

---

[5] Code Sec. 904(c).
[6] Code Sec. 164(a).

[7] Code Sec. 275(a)(4)(A).

The choice between a deduction and a credit applies to all foreign income taxes paid or accrued during the year.[8] In other words, a taxpayer cannot claim a credit for a portion of the foreign income taxes incurred in a taxable year and claim a deduction for the remaining foreign income taxes. However, taxpayers can change their election from year to year. In addition, taxpayers can change their election any time before the expiration of the statute of limitations, which is 10 years in the case of a refund claim based on the foreign tax credit.[9] A taxpayer makes the annual election to claim a credit by including with its tax return Form 1118 (for domestic corporations) or Form 1116 (for individuals).[10] In the case of a partnership or S corporation, the election to claim a credit in lieu of a deduction for the foreign income taxes paid or accrued by the partnership or S corporation is made at the partner or shareholder level.[11]

.03 Who Can Claim a Credit

Taxpayers entitled to claim a foreign tax credit primarily include U.S. citizens, resident aliens, and domestic corporations.[12] An affiliated group of U.S. corporations that files a consolidated return computes its foreign tax credit on a consolidated basis.[13] A U.S. citizen, resident alien or domestic corporation that is a partner in a partnership or a beneficiary of an estate or trust may also claim a credit for a proportionate share of the creditable foreign taxes incurred by the partnership, estate, or trust.[14] The rules applicable to partners in a partnership also apply to shareholders in an S corporation.[15]

In certain limited situations, nonresident alien individuals and foreign corporations can claim a foreign tax credit against the U.S. tax on their income effectively connected to the conduct of a U.S. trade or business.[16] See the discussion in Chapter 10 (¶ 1001).

¶ 402 CREDITABLE FOREIGN INCOME TAXES

.01 Qualifying Foreign Levies

The foreign tax credit is intended to mitigate international double taxation of a U.S. person's foreign-source income. Therefore, the United States restricts the credit to foreign income taxes that replicate the U.S. income tax against which the credit is taken. Specifically, to be creditable, a levy must satisfy the following two requirements:

(i) the levy must be a compulsory payment to a foreign country, a political subdivision of a foreign country, or a U.S. possession (i.e., Puerto Rico, the Virgin Islands, Guam, the Northern Mariana Islands, and American Samoa), and

(ii) the predominant character of the tax must be that of an income tax in the U.S. sense.[17]

---

[8] Reg. § 1.901-1(c).
[9] Reg. § 1.901-1(d) and Code Sec. 6511(d)(3)(A).
[10] Reg. § 1.905-2(a).
[11] Code Secs. 703(b)(3) and 1363(c)(2)(B).
[12] Code Sec. 901(b)(1)–(3).

[13] Reg. § 1.1502-4(c).
[14] Code Sec. 901(b)(5).
[15] Code Sec. 1373(a).
[16] Code Secs. 901(b)(4) and 906.
[17] Code Sec. 901(b) and Reg. § 1.901-2(a)(1).

If a foreign levy satisfies the first requirement but not the second, the levy may still be creditable if the tax is imposed "in lieu of" an income tax.[18] Foreign taxes other than income taxes, such as sales and property taxes, are not creditable but generally are deductible.[19]

Payment of the foreign levy is not considered compulsory to the extent the amount paid exceeds the amount of the liability under foreign laws. More specifically, the taxpayer is obligated to reduce its foreign tax liability to the lowest amount possible by reasonably interpreting and applying the substantive and procedural provisions of foreign law while exhausting all effective and practical administrative remedies. The policy behind these requirements is that the United States does not want to cede primary taxing jurisdiction with respect to credits for foreign taxes that did not have to be paid. As a practical matter, the taxpayer should obtain an opinion from foreign counsel stating that only the proper amount of foreign taxes have been paid and that it would be unreasonable, ineffective and unpractical to try to lower the amount of foreign taxes through further administrative procedures.[20]

> **Example 4.3:** USCo owns UKCo, a United Kingdom company, which owns DutchCo, a Dutch company that is a disregarded entity for U.S. tax purposes due to a time-filed check-the-box election. Due to a transfer pricing dispute on the purchase by DutchCo of products from UKCo, DutchCo pays an assessment for additional Dutch taxes. DutchCo procures Dutch counsel, which opines that it would be impossible to reduce the Dutch tax further through further appeal of the assessment, which would include pursuing competent authority procedures. As a result, if DutchCo paid the additional assessment, DutchCo would have additional creditable foreign income taxes.

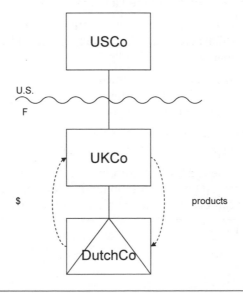

---

18 Code Sec. 903.
19 Code Sec. 164(a).

20 *Procter & Gamble v. Comm'r*, 2010-2 USTC ¶ 50,593 (S.D. Oh).

Tax requirement. A tax is a compulsory payment that a country imposes in order to raise funds for public purposes. Penalties, fines, interest and custom duties do not qualify. A foreign levy also does not qualify as a tax if the payer receives a specific economic benefit in exchange for the levy.[21] Historically, the problem of distinguishing taxes from payments for specific economic benefits has been most difficult in the petroleum industry. In countries where the government owns the oil resources, the treasury is in a position to both collect taxes on an oil company's profits and receive royalties from those same companies. Therefore, the foreign government might designate as a tax what is actually a royalty, without affecting its total revenues. If the characterization of the payment as a tax is accepted for U.S. tax purposes, a U.S. oil company could be able to claim a credit for what should be only a deductible royalty expense.

To prevent this result, a foreign levy is not considered a tax to the extent the taxpayer receives a specific economic benefit in exchange for the levy. A person who is both a taxpayer and the recipient of a specific economic benefit is referred to as a dual-capacity taxpayer. Dual-capacity taxpayers have the burden of establishing what portion of a levy is a tax[22] and can use either a facts and circumstances approach or an elective safe-harbor method to satisfy their burden of proof.[23]

Income tax requirement. It generally is obvious whether a particular levy is a tax on income, as opposed to a tax on some other base. However, governments occasionally impose hybrid taxes that are difficult to classify, such as a tax on the gross value of minerals extracted from mining or a tax on the gross receipts from banking.[24] Such taxes are creditable only if their predominant character is that of an income tax in the U.S. sense.[25] In this regard, three aspects of U.S. income taxation are considered fundamental and the foreign levy must exhibit each of these characteristics in order to be considered an income tax.[26]

   (i) *Realization test*—The tax must be imposed on income resulting from an exchange transaction or other event that would trigger a realization of income under U.S. principles.[27]

   (ii) *Gross receipts test*—The tax must be imposed either upon actual gross receipts or according to a formulary method that is not likely to produce an amount that is greater than fair market value.[28]

   (iii) *Net income test*—The tax base must permit the recovery of significant costs and expenses attributable to the taxpayer's gross income.[29]

Even if a tax satisfies all three requirements, the tax will still be denied income tax status if it is a soak-up tax.[30] A soak-up tax is a levy that a host country imposes only if the taxpayer can claim the tax as a credit on its home country tax return.[31]

---

[21] Reg. § 1.901-2(a)(2)(i).

[22] Reg. § 1.901-2(a)(2)(i).

[23] Reg. § 1.901-2A(c) and (d).

[24] For an example, *see Texasgulf, Inc.*, FedCl, 99-2 USTC ¶ 50,915.

[25] Reg. § 1.901-2(a)(1).

[26] Reg. § 1.901-2(a)(3)(i) and (b)(1).

[27] Reg. § 1.901-2(b)(2).

[28] Reg. § 1.901-2(b)(3).

[29] Reg. § 1.901-2(b)(4). Moreover, Code Sec. 901(m) essentially permits a creditable tax under U.S. tax accounting standards whenever the foreign taxes are a result of a covered asset acquisition.

[30] Reg. § 1.901-2(a)(3)(ii).

[31] Reg. § 1.901-2(c)(1).

¶402.01

Soak-up taxes allow a country to collect taxes on inbound investments with the cost borne solely by the foreign investors' home country. Income tax status also is denied to any foreign levy that a foreign country uses to provide some type of subsidy to the taxpayer, a related person, or any party to a transaction to which the taxpayer is a party.[32]

Foreign withholding taxes. Creditable taxes also include any foreign taxes imposed "in lieu of" an income tax.[33] The most common type of in-lieu-of tax is the flat rate withholding tax that countries routinely impose on the gross amount of interest, dividends, rents, and royalties derived by passive offshore investors. Withholding is required because it is the only sure way to collect taxes from passive offshore investors. In order to withhold, the withholding agent must be able to readily ascertain both the tax base and the applicable rate. This explains both the gross basis taxation and the use of a flat tax rate since it would be difficult for the withholding agent to determine the offshore investor's allocable expenses and appropriate tax bracket based on worldwide income. A withholding tax generally does not qualify as an income tax because no deductions are allowed in computing the tax base, which results in failing the net income test (test iii, above).[34] A withholding tax is creditable, however, if it is imposed in lieu of the foreign country's general income tax, which is generally the case.[35]

A taxpayer can not claim a tax credit for foreign withholding taxes paid unless a holding period requirement is satisfied. For example, with respect to a dividend, a 16-day holding period for the dividend-paying stock (or a 46-day holding period for certain dividends on preferred stock) must be satisfied. The 16-day holding period requirement must be met within the 30-day period beginning 15 days before the ex-dividend date. If the stock is held for 15 days or less during the 30-day period, the foreign tax credit for the withholding tax is disallowed. The holding period generally does not include any period during which the taxpayer is protected from risk of loss (e.g., by use of an option). However, taxpayers that fail to meet the holding period requirement can still take a deduction equal to the foreign tax credits disallowed. In addition, an exception to the holding period requirement is available to security dealers.[36] Congress enacted these provisions to curtail transactions designed to transfer foreign tax credits from persons unable to benefit from them to persons that can use the credits.[37] Moreover, these minimum holding period requirements apply to credits for foreign withholding taxes imposed on income other than dividends, such as interest, rent and royalty income.[38]

Denial of credit for certain taxes. In an attempt to further U.S. foreign policy objectives, a credit is denied to any foreign income taxes paid to a country whose government the United States does not recognize, does not conduct diplomatic relations with, or has designated as a government that repeatedly supports acts of

---

[32] Code Sec. 901(i) and Reg. § 1.901-2(e)(3).

[33] Code Sec. 903.

[34] Reg. § 1.901-2(b)(4).

[35] Reg. § 1.903-1(b)(3), Example 2.

[36] Code Sec. 901(k).

[37] *See* Notice 98-5, 1998-1 CB 334, and Notice 2004-19, IRB 2004-11.

[38] Code Sec. 901(l).

international terrorism.[39] Countries to which this provision has applied in the past or present include Cuba, Iran, North Korea, Sudan, and Syria.[40]

In addition, any taxpayer who participates in or cooperates with an international boycott must reduce its creditable foreign taxes by an international boycott factor.[41] Countries that may require participation in or cooperation with an international boycott include Kuwait, Lebanon, Libya, Qatar, Saudi Arabia, Syria, United Arab Emirates, and the Republic of Yemen.[42]

.02 Accounting Method

Accrual-basis taxpayers compute the foreign tax credit on an accrual basis.[43] Under the accrual method, creditable foreign income taxes equal the taxpayer's foreign tax liability for the current year, regardless of when those taxes are actually paid. Normal accrual-basis accounting principles apply when determining the liability for the year. Therefore, a foreign tax liability cannot be accrued unless all the events have occurred that determine the fact of the liability and the amount of the liability can be determined with reasonable accuracy.[44]

Cash-basis taxpayers generally compute the credit on a cash basis.[45] Under the cash method, creditable foreign taxes equal the amount of foreign income taxes paid during the year, regardless of whether the payment relates to the current year or some other year. A tax payment is not creditable, however, to the extent that it is reasonably certain that the amount will be refunded in the future.[46]

Cash-basis taxpayers can elect to compute the credit on an accrual basis. Once made, this election applies for all subsequent years.[47] Allowing cash-basis taxpayers to account for foreign income taxes on an accrual basis may provide a better matching of foreign income taxes to the associated foreign-source income. Matching is important because the foreign tax credit limitation for a given year is based on the amount of foreign-source income recognized in that year.

.03 Currency Translation

Because foreign income taxes are paid in the local currency, taxpayers must translate foreign taxes into their U.S. dollar equivalents in order to determine the credit. Taxpayers that account for foreign income taxes on an accrual basis generally translate foreign income taxes accrued into U.S. dollars using the average exchange rate for the tax year to which the taxes relate.[48] On the other hand, taxpayers that account for foreign taxes on a cash basis generally translate foreign income taxes accrued into U.S. dollars using the spot rate for the date that the taxes were paid.[49] An accrual basis taxpayer may elect to translate foreign taxes into U.S. dollars using the spot rate.[50] See Chapter 6 (¶ 602) for more details.

---

[39] Code Sec. 901(j).

[40] Rev. Rul. 2005-3, IRB 2005-3.

[41] Code Sec. 908.

[42] Iraq is under review. 76 F.R. 27377.

[43] Reg. § 1.905-1(a).

[44] Reg. § 1.446-1(c)(1)(ii). The economic performance requirement does not apply to an accrual for foreign taxes. Reg. § 1.461-4(g)(6)(iii)(B).

[45] Reg. § 1.905-1(a).

[46] Reg. § 1.901-2(e)(2)(i).

[47] Code Sec. 905(a).

[48] Code Sec. 986(a)(1).

[49] Code Sec. 986(a)(2).

[50] Code Sec. 986(a)(1)(D).

¶ 403 EXCESS CREDIT VERSUS EXCESS LIMITATION POSITIONS

.01 Purpose of Limitation

After a taxpayer has computed the amount of creditable foreign income taxes, the next step is to compute the foreign tax credit limitation. The limitation equals the portion of the pre-credit U.S. tax that is attributable to foreign-source income.[51] The purpose of the limitation is to confine the effects of the credit to mitigating double taxation of foreign-source taxable income. The limitation accomplishes this by preventing U.S. persons operating in high-tax foreign countries from offsetting those higher foreign taxes against the U.S. tax on U.S.-source taxable income.

Example 4.4: USAco is a domestic corporation. During the current year, USAco has $200 of U.S.-source taxable income and $100 of foreign-source taxable income that is subject to foreign income taxation. Assume that the foreign tax rate is 45% and the U.S. tax rate is 35%.

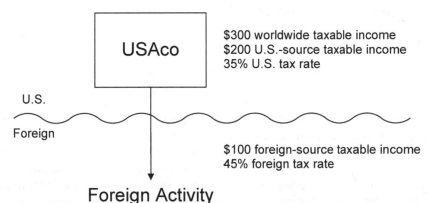

Case 1—Credit is limited: If the foreign tax credit is limited to the U.S. tax on foreign-source income (i.e., 35% × $100 = $35), the total tax on USAco's $300 of worldwide income is $115, computed as follows:

Foreign tax return		U.S. tax return	
Taxable income	$100	Taxable income	$300
Foreign tax rate	× .45	U.S. tax rate	× .35
Foreign tax	$ 45	Pre-credit tax	$105
		Foreign tax credit	− 35
		U.S. tax	$ 70

---

[51] Code Sec. 904(a).

Case 2—No limitation: If there were no limitation on the foreign tax credit, the total tax on USAco's worldwide income would drop from $115 to $105, computed as follows:

Foreign tax return		*U.S. tax return*	
Taxable income	$100	Taxable income	$300
Foreign tax rate	× .45	U.S. tax rate	× .35
Foreign tax	$ 45	Pre-credit tax	$105
		Foreign tax credit	− 45
		U.S. tax	$ 60

Without the limitation, the net U.S. tax on the $100 of foreign-source taxable income is negative $10 [$35 pre-credit U.S. tax – $45 credit], which reduces the U.S. tax on USAco's domestic profits from $70 to $60.

Taxpayers compute their foreign tax credit limitation using the following formula.[52]

$$\text{Pre-credit U.S. tax on Worldwide Taxable Income} \times \frac{\text{Foreign-source taxable income}}{\text{Worldwide taxable income}}$$

With a single foreign tax credit limitation, all foreign-source income, regardless of its character (e.g., active business versus passive investment) or country of origin (e.g., low-tax country versus high-tax country), is commingled to arrive at a single limitation. It also is possible to make more precise comparisons of the U.S. and foreign tax burdens on foreign-source income, including separate income limitations and separate country limitations. As discussed later in this chapter, taxpayers currently must compute separate limitations for two different categories of income.[53]

.02 Exemption for Individuals with *De Minimis* Foreign Tax Credits

An individual with $300 or less of creditable foreign income taxes is exempt from the foreign tax credit limitation, provided he or she has no foreign-source income other than passive investment income. The $300 amount is increased to $600 in the case of married persons filing a joint return. To qualify, an individual must elect to take the exemption for the tax year. Congress enacted this rule to relieve the tax reporting burden (specifically, the need to complete Form 1116) in situations where the amount of foreign taxes paid and the corresponding credit was small. However, certain restrictions apply. An individual electing exemption from the foreign tax credit limitation may not carry over any excess foreign income taxes paid or accrued to or from a tax year in which the election applies. Also, for purposes of the election, creditable foreign income taxes are limited to those shown

---

[52] Code Sec. 904(a).   [53] Code Sec. 904(d).

¶403.02

on a payee statement furnished to the taxpayer. Finally, the election is not available to estates or trusts.[54]

.03 Importance of Relative Tax Rates

The relation of U.S. and foreign tax rates is a major determinant of whether a taxpayer is in an excess limitation or an excess credit position. Taxpayers will be in an excess limitation position when the foreign tax rate is lower than the U.S. rate and in an excess credit position when the foreign tax rate is higher than the U.S. rate. Any other factors that impact the effective foreign tax rate, such as the use of different accounting methods or local country tax incentives, will also affect whether a taxpayer is in an excess limitation or an excess credit position.

Example **4.5***:* USAco, a domestic corporation, has foreign-source taxable income of $100 and no U.S.-source taxable income. Assume the U.S. tax rate is 35%.

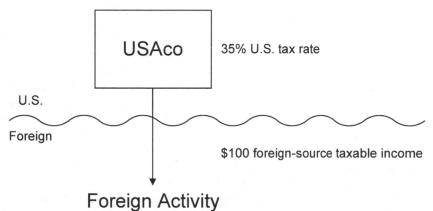

Case 1—*Foreign tax rate is 30%:* If all the foreign-source taxable income is subject to foreign income tax at a rate of 30%, USAco can claim a credit for the entire $30 of foreign income taxes paid, as follows:

U.S. tax return		*Foreign tax return*	
Taxable income	$100	Taxable income	$100
U.S. tax rate	× .35	Foreign income tax rate . . .	× .30
Pre-credit tax	$ 35	Foreign income tax	$ 30
Foreign tax credit	– 30		
U.S. tax	$ 5		

Case 2—*Foreign tax rate is 40%:* If a foreign income tax rate of 40% applies to all the foreign-source taxable income, the foreign tax credit limitation (which

---

[54] Code Sec. 904(k).

equals the U.S. tax of $35 on USAco's $100 of foreign-source income) will prevent USAco from claiming a credit for $5 of the $40 of foreign income taxes paid, as follows:

U.S. tax return	
Taxable income	$100
U.S. tax rate	× .35
Pre-credit tax	$ 35
Foreign tax credit	– 35
U.S. tax	$ 0

Foreign tax return	
Taxable income	$100
Foreign income tax rate . . .	× .40
Foreign income tax	$ 40

.04 Planning Implications

The foreign tax credit limitation determines whether foreign taxes have an incremental effect on a U.S. person's total tax costs. When a taxpayer is in an excess limitation position (i.e., the taxpayer's creditable foreign taxes are less than the limitation), foreign taxes do not represent an out-of-pocket tax cost since the cost of paying those taxes is entirely offset by the U.S. tax savings associated with the credit. Therefore, tax planning focuses on reducing the residual U.S. tax due on foreign-source income. In contrast, when a taxpayer is in an excess credit position (i.e., creditable foreign taxes exceed the limitation), no U.S. tax is collected on foreign-source income because the credit fully offsets the pre-credit U.S. tax on that income. In addition, the noncreditable foreign income taxes increase the total tax burden on foreign-source income beyond what it would have been if only the United States had taxed that income.[55] Therefore, planning focuses on reducing those excess credits.

¶ 404 STRATEGIES FOR ELIMINATING EXCESS CREDITS

Strategies for eliminating excess credits include foreign tax reduction planning, increasing the limitation, and cross-crediting.

.01 Foreign Tax Reduction Planning

When a taxpayer is in an excess limitation position, any decrease in foreign tax costs is accompanied by an offsetting increase in the residual U.S. tax on foreign income. As a result, foreign tax reduction planning has no effect on the taxpayer's total tax costs.[56] The circumstances are quite different, however, for U.S. persons in excess credit positions. Foreign taxes increase the total tax costs of such taxpayers by the amount of the excess credits. As a consequence, every dollar of foreign

---

[55] Although creditable foreign taxes in excess of the limitation cannot be taken in the current year, they can be carried back one year and carried forward up to ten years and taken as a credit in a year in which the limitation exceeds the amount of creditable foreign taxes. Code Sec. 904(c).

[56] However, foreign tax reduction planning does affect the allocation of tax revenues between the United States and other countries. Reducing foreign taxes reduces the foreign tax credit and, in turn, increases U.S. tax revenues.

income taxes saved reduces the taxpayer's total tax costs by a dollar, up to the amount of excess credits.

The techniques that a U.S. person can use to reduce foreign income taxes often are the same as those used to reduce income taxes in a purely domestic context. Examples include taking advantage of any special exemptions, deductions, or credits provided by local law, realizing income in a form that is taxed at a lower rate (such as a preferential rate for capital gains), deferring the recognition of gross income, and accelerating the recognition of deductions. Other foreign tax reduction planning strategies, including the use of debt financing, transfer pricing, and tax treaties, are discussed in Chapter 8 (¶ 801).

> ***Example* 4.6:** USCo contemplates expanding to a foreign country by building a new plant. USCo likes the opportunities in foreign country F but does not like the 40% income tax rate (5 percentage points above the U.S. corporate tax rate of 35%) because USCo already has excess foreign tax credits. Taking advantage of foreign country F's vulnerability due to F's chronically-high unemployment rate, USCo negotiates tax holiday with foreign country F whereby USCo will pay tax at only a 25% rate in foreign country F for ten years, which may create additional limitation to sop up the excess foreign tax credits without creating additional excess foreign tax credits.

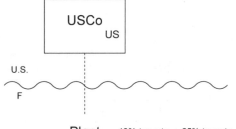

Plant   40% tax rate → 25% tax rate

.02 Increasing the Limitation

A second basic strategy for reducing excess credits is to increase the foreign tax credit limitation by increasing the proportion of worldwide income that is classified as foreign-source income for U.S. tax purposes. As a consequence, the U.S. rules for sourcing gross income and deductions can play a decisive role in eliminating excess credits. For example, the title-passage rule for sourcing the income from inventory sales provides U.S. companies with a significant opportunity to increase foreign-source income. By arranging for the passage of title in the foreign country rather than the United States, export sales will generate foreign-source income.

Recharacterizing deductions also is an effective strategy for eliminating excess credits. Deductions reduce a taxpayer's pre-credit U.S. tax, regardless of how they are sourced. However, if the deduction is allocated to foreign-source income, the deduction also reduces the foreign tax credit limitation. As a result, a taxpayer in an excess credit position derives no net U.S. tax benefit from deductions allocated to foreign-source income. In contrast, deductions allocated to U.S.-source income do not affect the foreign tax credit limitation and, therefore, provide a full U.S. tax benefit. An example of how a taxpayer can recharacterize deductions is the use of alternative apportionment bases for sourcing selling, general, and administrative expenses that reduce the amount of these deductions allocated to foreign-source income (see ¶ 303).

As with any international tax planning strategy, reducing excess credits by resourcing gross income and deductions requires a careful analysis of both U.S. and foreign tax consequences. In particular, if a taxpayer takes an action that increases foreign-source income for both U.S. and foreign tax purposes, the resourced income may increase the taxpayer's foreign tax costs more than it increases the taxpayer's foreign tax credit limitation. If this happens, the net effect of the action may be an increase, rather than the desired decrease, in the taxpayer's excess credits. Therefore, the effectiveness of resourcing income as a strategy for eliminating excess credits depends on the existence of differences between the source-of-income rules used by the United States and other countries.

>*Example* **4.7:** USAco, a domestic corporation, has $2 million of U.S.-source taxable income and $4 million of foreign-source taxable income that is subject to foreign income tax. Further assume that the foreign income tax rate is 50% and the U.S. rate is 35%.

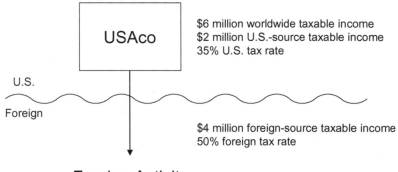

Foreign Activity

USAco has $600,000 of excess credits, computed as follows:

Foreign income taxes [$4 million × 50%]	$2 million
Foreign tax credit limitation:	
(A) Worldwide taxable income	$ 6 million
(B) Pre-credit U.S. tax [$6 million × 35%] . . .	$2.1 million
(C) Foreign-source taxable income	$ 4 million
Limitation = [line B × (C ÷ A)]	
= [$2.1 million × ($4 million ÷ $6 million)] . .	− $1.4 million
Excess foreign tax credits	$600,000

Now assume that USAco can recharacterize $1 million of its U.S.-source income as foreign-source income, but only for U.S. tax purposes so that there is now $5 million of foreign-source taxable income (under the U.S. rules) even though only $4 million is subject to income tax in the foreign country. Every dollar of resourced income increases USAco's limitation and has no effect on USAco's foreign taxes. The net effect is a reduction in USAco's excess credits from $600,000 to $250,000, computed as follows:

Foreign income taxes [$4 million × 50%] . . . . $2 million
Foreign tax credit limitation:
               (A) Worldwide taxable income . . . . $ 6 million
               (B) Pre-credit U.S. tax [$6 million × 35%] . . . $2.1 million
               (C) Foreign-source taxable income . . . . $ 5 million
    Limitation   = [line B × (C ÷ A)]
                = [$2.1 million × ($5 million ÷ $6 million)] . .   – $1.75 million

Excess foreign tax credits $250,000

On the other hand, if the resourcing of USAco's income for U.S. tax purposes somehow increases USAco's taxable income for foreign tax purposes (an extremely rare occurrence), the $1 million of resourced income will increase USAco's foreign income taxes at a faster rate than it will increase its limitation. The net effect will be an increase in USAco's excess credits from $600,000 to $750,000, computed as follows.

Foreign income taxes [$5 million × 50%] . . . . $2.5 million
Foreign tax credit limitation:
               (A) Worldwide taxable income . . . . $ 6 million
               (B) Pre-credit U.S. tax [$6 million × 35%] . . . $2.1 million
               (C) Foreign-source taxable income . . . . $ 5 million
    Limitation   = [line B × (C ÷ A)]
                = [$2.1 million × ($5 million ÷ $6 million)] . .   – $1.75 million

Excess foreign tax credits $750,000

.03 Cross-Crediting

A third basic strategy for eliminating excess credits is cross-crediting. This strategy is based on the fact that different items of foreign-source income have distinctly different effects on a taxpayer's excess credits. Foreign income that bears foreign income taxes at a rate higher than the U.S. tax rate increases a taxpayer's excess credits, whereas foreign income that bears a low rate of foreign income tax results in an excess limitation. If there were a single foreign tax credit limitation, the excess credits on heavily-taxed foreign income would be credited against the excess limitation on lightly-taxed foreign income. Through this process, known as "cross-crediting," the effects of individual items of heavily and lightly taxed foreign-source income are averaged. This averaging process produces an excess credit only when the average foreign tax rate on all of the items of income within a single limitation is higher than the U.S. rate.

Example **4.8:** USAco, a domestic corporation, has $1 million of country X source income and no U.S.-source income. Assume the U.S. tax rate is 35% and the country X rate of 40% applies to the $1 million of X income.

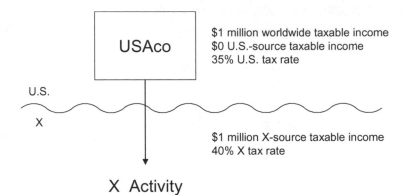

USAco

$1 million worldwide taxable income
$0 U.S.-source taxable income
35% U.S. tax rate

U.S.

X

$1 million X-source taxable income
40% X tax rate

X Activity

USAco has $50,000 of excess credits, computed as follows:

Foreign income taxes [$1 million × 40%]	$400,000
Foreign tax credit limitation:	
(A) Worldwide taxable income	$ 1 million
(B) Pre-credit U.S. tax [$1 million × 35%]	$350,000
(C) Foreign-source taxable income	$ 1 million
Limitation = [line B × (C ÷ A)]	
= [$350,000 × ($1 million ÷ $1 million)]	$350,000
Excess foreign tax credits	$50,000

Now assume that in addition to the $1 million of country X income, USAco also has $1 million of country Y income, which is subject to foreign tax at a 30% rate. Further assume that the Country Y income is assigned to the same limitation category as the Country X income.

¶404.03

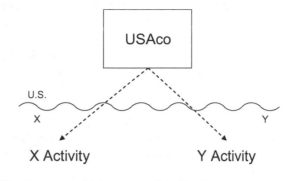

$1 million X-source taxable income
40% X tax rate

$1 million Y-source taxable income
30% Y tax rate

Cross-crediting will eliminate the $50,000 of excess credits as follows:

Foreign income taxes [($1 million × 40%) + ($1 million × 30%)] . . . $700,000

Foreign tax credit limitation:

   (A) Worldwide taxable income
    [$1 million + $1 million] . . . . $ 2 million

   (B) Pre-credit U.S. tax [$2 million × 35%] $700,000

   (C) Foreign-source taxable income . . . . $ 2 million

 Limitation = [line B × (C ÷ A)]

    = [$700,000 × ($2 million ÷ $2 million)] $700,000

Excess foreign tax credits . . . .   None

USAco no longer has any excess credits because the average rate of foreign income tax is now 35% (foreign taxes of $700,000 ÷ $2 million of foreign income), which is the same as the U.S. rate.

The third strategy for eliminating excess credits exploits the cross-crediting phenomenon. If a taxpayer can blend low-tax and high-tax foreign-source income within a single limitation, then the excess limitation on the low-tax income will soak up the excess credits on the high-tax income.

¶ 405 RESTRICTIONS ON CROSS-CREDITING

.01 History

Cross-crediting is possible only to the extent the operative foreign tax credit limitation encompasses both lightly-taxed and highly-taxed foreign-source income. Foreign income tax rates vary not only across countries, but also across different types of income within the same country. For example, countries often tax the local business profits of foreign taxpayers at a higher rate than on their passive investment income. Therefore, restrictions on cross-crediting can be implemented by imposing either separate country or separate income limitations on the foreign tax credit.

If there were a separate country limitation system, a separate limitation would be computed for each foreign country. Separate country limitations prevent cross-crediting on income derived from different countries, but still allow cross-crediting on lightly-taxed and highly-taxed income derived from the same foreign country. Under a separate income limitation approach, a separate limitation is applied to each category of income designated by lawmakers. Cross-crediting is allowed between countries but not between different categories of income. For example, a separate limitation may be required for interest income. Interest income is a prime target for lawmakers wishing to restrict cross-crediting because interest income often bears little or no foreign taxes and because interest-producing assets are easily moved overseas.

Over the years, U.S. lawmakers have employed both separate country and separate income systems (see Table 4.1).

TABLE 4.1. U.S. RESTRICTIONS ON CROSS-CREDITING

Time period	Type of foreign tax credit limitation	Prohibited form of cross-crediting
1918 to 1921	No limitation	n.a.
1922 to 1931	Overall limitation	None
1932 to 1975	Various types of separate country limitations	Between countries
1976 to 1986	Limited number of separate income limitations	Between categories of income
1987 to 2002	Nine separate income limitation categories	Between categories of income
2003 to 2006	Eight separate income limitation categories	Between categories of income
Post-2006	Two separate income limitation categories	Between categories of income

.02 Separate Income Limitations

The primary purpose of the current separate income limitation system is to prevent cross-crediting between lightly-taxed passive foreign investment income and more heavily-taxed active foreign business profits. Cross-crediting is still allowed, however, with respect to business profits derived from different foreign countries or investment income derived from different foreign countries. Congress enacted the current system because it believed that little residual U.S. tax was being collected on foreign-source investment income, even though this income often bears little or no foreign tax. Congress attributed these negligible tax collections to the ability of U.S. multinational corporations to credit the excess foreign taxes on their foreign business profits against the residual U.S. tax on foreign-source investment income. Congress also believed that cross-crediting provided an undesirable tax incentive to shift investment capital overseas.[57]

The formula for computing the separate income limitations is the same as that for computing the overall limitation, except that the numerator of the fraction is now separate category foreign taxable income, as follows:

$$\text{Pre-credit U.S. tax} \times \frac{\text{Separate category foreign-source taxable income}}{\text{Worldwide taxable income}}$$

The credit allowed with respect to each category of income is the lesser of that category's limitation or the foreign income taxes related to that category. A taxpayer's total credit for the year is the sum of the credits for each of the individual limitation categories.

For taxable years beginning in 2007, taxpayers must compute a separate limitation for only the following two categories of income:[58]

  (i) passive category income, and

  (ii) general category income (the residual category for income not assigned to the passive income category).

Example 4.9: USAco, a domestic corporation, has $12 million of U.S.-source taxable income, $8 million of foreign-source general limitation taxable income (on which USAco paid $3 million in foreign income taxes), and $2 million of foreign-source passive taxable income (on which USAco paid $400,000 in foreign income taxes). Assume that the U.S. tax rate is 35%.

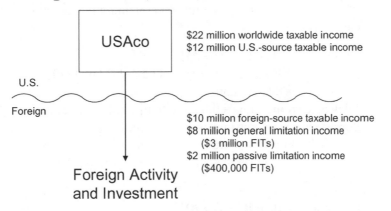

Under a single overall limitation, all of USAco's foreign taxes are creditable, as follows:

---

[57] S. Rep. No. 445 (100th Cong., 2d Sess. 217 (1988)).

[58] Code Sec. 904(d)(1). For taxable years beginning before 2007, taxpayers had to compute a separate limitation for each of the following eight categories of income: passive income, high withholding tax interest, financial services income, shipping income, certain dividends from a domestic international sales corporation, a foreign sales corporation's taxable income attributable to foreign trade income, certain distributions from a foreign sales corporation, and general limitation income.

¶405.02

Foreign income taxes [$3 million + $400,000]	$3.4 million
Foreign tax credit limitation:	
(A) Worldwide taxable income	
[$12 million + $8 million + $2 million]	$ 22 million
(B) Pre-credit U.S. tax [$22 million × 35%] . .	$7.7 million
(C) Foreign-source taxable income	
[$8 million + $2 million]	$ 10 million

Overall
limitation   = [line B × (C ÷ A)]

           = [$7.7 million × ($10 million ÷ $22 million)]

. . . .	$3.5 million
Foreign tax credit (equals creditable foreign taxes)	$3.4 million

In contrast, under the separate income limitations, USAco has $200,000 of excess credits within the general limitation category and $300,000 of excess limitation in the passive limitation category, computed as follows:

Pre-credit U.S. tax:

(A) Worldwide taxable income	$ 22 million
(B) Pre-credit U.S. tax [$22 million × 35%] . .	$7.7 million

Foreign tax credit:

Foreign income taxes on general income	$ 3 million
General income limitation:	
(C) Foreign-source general limitation income	$ 8 million

General
Income
Limitation   = [line B × (C ÷ A)]

           = [$7.7 million × ($8 million ÷ $22 million)]

           = $2.8 million

Allowable credit [equals the limitation]	$2.8 million
Foreign income taxes on passive income	$ 400,000
Passive income limitation:	
(D) Foreign-source passive income	$ 2 million

Passive
Income
Limitation   = [line B × (D ÷ A)]

           = [$7.7 million × ($2 million ÷ $22 million)]

           = $700,000

Allowable credit [equals foreign income taxes]	$ 400,000
Total foreign tax credit	$3.2 million

Although the Internal Revenue Code contains both an overall income limitation and the separate income limitation categories, as a practical matter, the IRS has only implemented the separate income limitation categories.[59]

---

[59] See Forms 1116 and 1118 in the Appendix.

¶405.02

General income limitation category. The general income limitation category includes all income not described by one of the other categories of income. Because it is the residual category, there is no specific definition of the types of income that are allocated to this category. However, most of the income from active foreign business operations, including manufacturing, marketing, and services, falls into this category.

Passive income limitation category. Passive income primarily includes the following items of gross income:

(i) dividends, interest, royalties, rents, and annuities,

(ii) net gains from the disposition of property that produces dividend, interest, rent, and royalty income (except for net gains from certain dealer sales and inventory sales),

(iii) net gains from commodity and foreign currency transactions (except for certain net gains from active business or hedging transactions),[60]

(iv) certain income received from domestic international sales corporations and foreign sales corporations,[61] and

(v) income of a passive foreign investment company that has made a qualified electing fund election.[62]

However, there are numerous exceptions to the rules for passive income, including the following, which belong to the general limitation income category:

(i) *Highly-taxed income*—Passive income does not include any income that qualifies as highly-taxed income.[63] For example, a corporate taxpayer's, income is highly-taxed if, after allocating the corporation's expenses to the income, the creditable foreign taxes related to the income exceed the product of the amount of that income multiplied by 35% (the maximum U.S. corporate tax rate).[64] This exception removes from the passive income category any investment income that gives rise to excess credits and thereby prevents cross-crediting of low-tax and high-tax passive income.

(ii) *Controlled foreign corporation and 10/50 company look-through rules*—A U.S. shareholder allocates payments received from a controlled foreign corporation, including dividends, interest, rents, and royalties, to the separate categories of income based on the character of the controlled foreign corporation's earnings.[65] A look-through rule also applies to dividends received from a noncontrolled Code Sec. 902 corporation (10/50 company).[66] These look-through rules are discussed in detail later in this chapter.

(iii) *Active rents and royalties*—Passive income does not include rents and royalties that are derived in the active conduct of a trade or business.[67]

---

[60] Code Secs. 904(d)(2)(B)(i) and 954(c)(1).
[61] Code Sec. 904(d)(2)(B)(v).
[62] Code Sec. 904(d)(2)(B)(ii).
[63] Code Sec. 904(d)(2)(B)(iii)(II).

[64] Code Sec. 904(d)(2)(F) and Reg. § 1.904-4(c)(1).
[65] Reg. § 1.904-4(b)(1)(i) and Code Sec. 904(d)(3).
[66] Code Sec. 904(d)(4).
[67] Reg. § 1.904-4(b)(2).

(iv) *Export financing interest*—Passive income does not include export financing interest.[68] Export financing interest is any interest (other than related-person factoring income) that is derived from financing the sale or other disposition of property for use or consumption outside the United States if the property is manufactured, produced, grown, or extracted in the United States by the taxpayer or a related person and if not more than 50% of the fair market value of the property is attributable to products imported into the United States.[69]

(v) *Financial services income.* Financial services income includes income derived in the active conduct of a banking, insurance, financing or similar business by a person predominantly engaged in the active conduct of such a business.[70] This allows financial services companies to engage in cross-crediting in the general limitation income category with respect to all of their financial services income, including both investment-type income and income from services, such as investment advisory, brokerage, fiduciary, investment banking, and trust services.[71]

Foreign income taxes paid or accrued in a year prior to 2007 and carried to any subsequent tax year are put into either the passive income or general limitation categories as if only these two limitation categories existed during the year the foreign income taxes were paid or accrued.[72]

.03 Look-Through Rules

There are two look-through rules. One look-through rule is for a number of items of income received from a controlled foreign corporation. The second look-through rule is for dividends received from 10/50 companies.

Controlled foreign corporations. Under the general rules, the separate income limitations would yield significantly different results for domestic corporations operating abroad through foreign subsidiaries as opposed to foreign branches. For example, if a domestic corporation structures a foreign manufacturing operation as a branch, the related income and foreign income taxes are assigned to the general income limitation category. In contrast, if the domestic corporation were to structure the same manufacturing operation as a subsidiary, the dividend distributions from that manufacturing subsidiary would be assigned to the passive income limitation category. To better equate the treatment of branches and subsidiaries, a U.S. shareholder allocates income derived from a controlled foreign corporation (or CFC), including dividends, interest, rents, and royalties, to the separate income categories based on the character of the controlled foreign corporation's earnings, the so called "look-through" rules.

A foreign corporation is a controlled foreign corporation if, on any day during the foreign corporation's taxable year, U.S. shareholders own more than 50% of the

---

[68] Code Sec. 904(d)(2)(B)(iii)(I).

[69] Code Sec. 904(d)(2)(G).

[70] Code Sec. 904(d)(2)(C). Excluded from the definition of financial services income are export financing interest that is subject to withholding tax at a rate of less than 5%, and high withholding tax interest (unless it is also export financing interest). Code Sec. 904(d)(2)(C)(iii) and Reg. § 1.904-4(e)(5).

[71] Code Sec. 904(d)(1)(C).

[72] Code Sec. 904(d)(2)(K) and Temp. Reg. § 1.904-2T.

combined voting power of all classes of stock or 50% of the total value, of the foreign corporation.[73] A U.S. shareholder is any U.S. person owning at least 10% of the total combined voting power of all classes of voting stock of the foreign corporation.[74]

The specific look-through rule varies with the type of income derived from the CFC, as follows:

(i) *Dividends*—Dividends paid by a CFC to a taxpayer who is a U.S. shareholder of that CFC are prorated among the separate categories of income based on the ratio of the CFC's earnings and profits within each separate income category to the CFC's total earnings and profits.[75] For example, if a CFC has $1 million of earnings and profits, $900,000 of which is attributable to general income limitation income and the other $100,000 to passive income, then 90% of a dividend distribution from the CFC is assigned to the general income limitation category and the other 10% is assigned to the passive income limitation category.

(ii) *Rents and royalties*—Rent and royalty income derived from a CFC by a U.S. shareholder of that CFC is allocated among the separate categories of income based on the extent to which the related deduction (at the CFC level) is properly allocable to the CFC's income in that category.[76] For example, if the entire amount of a CFC's current-year taxable income is general income limitation category, then any royalty paid to a U.S. shareholder is assigned to the general income limitation category.

(iii) *Interest*—Interest income derived from a CFC by a U.S. shareholder of that CFC is assigned to the passive income category to the extent of the CFC's foreign personal holding company income.[77] Any interest income in excess of the CFC's foreign personal holding company income is apportioned among the separate income categories other than passive income.[78] This rule prevents a U.S. shareholder from artificially increasing income in the general income limitation category by loaning money to a CFC that could be recharacterized under the look-through rules.

(iv) *Subpart F inclusion*—A Subpart F inclusion for an increase in a CFC's earnings invested in U.S. property is allocated among the separate categories of income using the same rule that applies to actual dividend distributions (see discussion above).[79] In contrast, a Subpart F inclusion for Subpart F income is allocated among the separate categories of income based on the nature of the CFC's taxable income which gave rise to the Subpart F inclusion.[80] For example, if a CFC has $1 million of Subpart F income, including $850,000 of foreign base company sales income and $150,000 of foreign personal holding company income,

---

[73] Code Sec. 957(a).

[74] Code Sec. 951(b). All forms of ownership, including direct, indirect (i.e., beneficial ownership through intervening entities), and constructive (i.e., attribution of ownership by one related party to another), are considered in applying both the 10% shareholder and the 50% aggregate ownership tests. Code Sec. 958.

[75] Code Sec. 904(d)(3)(D) and Reg. § 1.904-5(c)(4)(i).

[76] Code Sec. 904(d)(3)(C) and Reg. § 1.904-5(c)(3).

[77] Code Sec. 954(b)(5). *See* Chapter 5 (¶ 501) for a definition of foreign personal holding company income.

[78] Code Sec. 904(d)(3)(C). *See* Reg. § 1.904-5(c)(2)(ii) regarding the applicable apportionment method.

[79] Code Sec. 904(d)(3)(G) and Reg. § 1.904-5(c)(4)(i).

[80] Code Sec. 904(d)(3)(B) and Reg. § 1.904-5(c)(1)(i).

$850,000 of the Subpart F inclusion is assigned to the general limitation category and the other $150,000 is assigned to the passive income category.[81]

(v) *Passive foreign investment company inclusion*—If the taxpayer is a U.S. shareholder of a CFC that also is a passive foreign investment company that has made a qualified electing fund (or QEF) election, then the look-through rule that applies to Subpart F inclusions also applies to a QEF inclusion from that CFC.[82] If the QEF is neither a CFC nor a 10/50 company, the QEF inclusion is assigned to the passive income category.[83]

Example **4.10:** USAco has always owned 100% of FORco, a CFC. FORco has accumulated earnings and profits of $1 million, $900,000 of which constitutes general limitation income and $100,000 of which constitutes passive income. FORco distributes a $100,000 dividend to USAco.

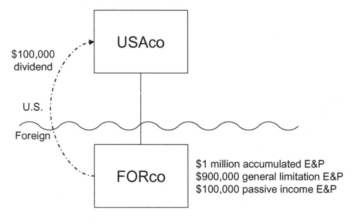

Pursuant to the look-through rule, the $100,000 dividend is allocated to various limitation categories based on the nature of FORco's accumulated earnings and profits. Because 90% of FORco's accumulated earnings and profits were earned in the general limitation income category 90% of the dividend, $90,000, constitutes general limitation income to USAco. Because 10% of FORco's accumulated earnings and profits were earned in the passive limitation income category, 10% of the dividend, $10,000, is allocated to USAco's passive limitation income.

10/50 companies. A look-through rule also applies only to dividends received by a domestic corporation from a noncontrolled Code Sec. 902 corporation (10/50 company).[84] A foreign corporation is a 10/50 company if a domestic corporation owns between 10% and 50% of the foreign corporation, in which case the U.S. corporate shareholder satisfies the 10% or more ownership requirement for claiming a deemed paid credit with respect to a dividend from the foreign corporation,

---

[81] Reg. § 1.904-5(c)(1)(ii), Example (1).

[82] Code Sec. 904(d)(3)(I) and Reg. § 1.904-5(j).

[83] Code Sec. 904(d)(2)(A)(ii).

[84] Code Sec. 904(d)(4).

but the foreign corporation does not meet the more than 50% U.S. ownership requirement for CFC status (¶ 501.03).

Under the 10/50 company look-through rule, a dividend is assigned to a separate category of income limitation in proportion to the ratio of the 10/50 company's earnings and profits attributable to income in that category to the 10/50 company's total earnings and profits, which is the same as the rule for dividends from CFCs. In contrast to a CFC, however, look-through treatment does not apply to interest, rents, and royalties received from a 10/50 company.

.04 Partnerships

A partner's distributive share of partnership income is assigned to the partner's separate income limitations based on the character of the income at the partnership level.[85] For example, if a partnership has $800,000 of general limitation income and $200,000 of passive income, 80% of the partner's distributive share of the partnership's income is general limitation income and the other 20% is passive income. A look-through rule also applies, in certain circumstances, to payments of interest, rents, and royalties by a partnership to a partner.[86] These look-through rules do not apply to a limited partner or corporate general partner that owns less than 10% of the value of the partnership. In such cases, the partner's distributive share of partnership income generally is treated as passive income, unless the partnership interest is held in the ordinary course of the partner's trade or business, in which case the general look-through rule applies.[87] The rules applicable to partners in a partnership also apply to shareholders in an S corporation.[88]

.05 Allocating Foreign Income Taxes

In order to apply the separate category of income limitations, foreign income taxes also must be allocated among the two income categories. Foreign income taxes are allocated to the category of income that includes the income on which the foreign taxes were imposed.[89] For example, foreign withholding taxes imposed on interest income included in the passive income category are assigned to the passive category, whereas withholding taxes imposed on royalty income included in the general limitation category are assigned to the general limitation category.

If the base upon which a foreign income tax is imposed includes income from more than one category, the taxpayer prorates the foreign taxes among the separate limitation categories of income using the following formula:[90]

$$\begin{array}{c} \text{Foreign income taxes} \\ \text{related to more than} \\ \text{one income category} \end{array} \times \dfrac{\text{Net income subject to the foreign tax}}{\text{included in the separate limitation category}}{\text{Total net income subject to the foreign tax}}$$

Net income for this purpose is determined under the tax accounting rules of the foreign country to which the tax was paid or accrued, rather than under U.S. law.

---

[85] Reg. § 1.904-5(h)(1).

[86] Reg. § 1.904-5(h)(1).

[87] Reg. § 1.904-5(h)(2). A gain on the sale of a partnership interest also is treated as passive income. Reg. § 1.904-5(h)(3).

[88] Code Sec. 1373(a).

[89] Reg. § 1.904-6(a)(1)(i).

[90] Reg. § 1.904-6(a)(1)(ii).

Example **4.11**: USAco, a domestic corporation, paid $300,000 of foreign income taxes on $1 million of foreign-source taxable income. The $1 million of foreign-source taxable income consists of $800,000 of general limitation income and $200,000 of passive income.

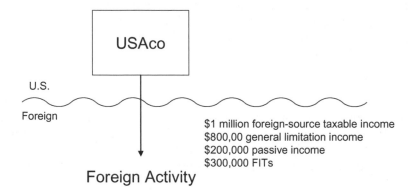

USAco

U.S.

Foreign

$1 million foreign-source taxable income
$800,00 general limitation income
$200,000 passive income
$300,000 FITs

Foreign Activity

For purposes of applying the separate income limitations, USAco allocates $240,000 of foreign taxes [$300,000 × ($800,000 ÷ $1,000,000)] to the general limitation category and the remaining $60,000 of foreign taxes [$300,000 × ($200,000 ÷ $1,000,000)] to the passive income limitation category.

A problem arises when the foreign income tax base includes an item of income that is nontaxable for U.S. purposes. Under the general allocation rules, the income in question is not reflected in the numerators of any separate income limitation category and, therefore, the related foreign income tax will not be allocated to any of the separate income limitation categories. To prevent this result, a taxpayer may elect to treat such taxes as imposed on general limitation income.[91] A similar problem arises when an item of income is subject to taxation in different years for U.S. and foreign tax purposes. For purposes of allocating the related foreign income taxes, such income is deemed to be recognized for U.S. tax purposes in the same year that it is recognized for foreign tax purposes.[92]

¶ 406 OTHER COMPLEXITIES OF THE LIMITATION

.01 Capital Gains and Losses

Under general U.S. tax principles, capital gains and losses receive special treatment in the form of the netting of individual capital gains and losses, a maximum tax rate on a noncorporate taxpayer's net long-term capital gain,[93] and limited deductibility of a net capital loss.[94] This special treatment can distort the accuracy of the foreign tax credit limitation as an estimate of the U.S. tax burden on foreign-source income. To prevent these distortions, taxpayers with capital gains and losses must make various special adjustments to the limitation.

---

[91] Code Sec. 904(d)(2)(H) and Reg. § 1.904-6(a)(1)(iv).
[92] Reg. § 1.904-6(a)(1)(iv).
[93] Code Sec. 1(h).
[94] Code Sec. 1211.

One potential distortion arises when a taxpayer nets a foreign-source capital gain against a U.S.-source capital loss in computing the net capital gain or loss for the year. Because capital losses are generally deductible only against capital gains, one U.S. tax benefit derived from the foreign-source capital gain is to soak up the U.S.-source capital loss. If the taxpayer also includes the foreign-source capital gain in the numerator of the foreign tax credit limitation, a second U.S. tax benefit may be realized in the form of additional foreign tax credits. To prevent this double tax benefit, a foreign-source capital gain is excluded from the numerator of the foreign tax credit limitation to the extent it offsets a U.S.-source capital loss.[95]

A second potential distortion arises when the tax rate applied to a taxpayer's net long-term capital gain is lower than the tax rate applied to the taxpayer's ordinary income. Under current tax law, there is no capital gain rate differential for corporations, but there is a significant rate differential for individuals. When a capital gain rate differential exists, the attribution of the pre-credit U.S. tax to foreign-source taxable income for purposes of computing the foreign tax credit limitation will be based on the "average" rate of U.S. tax on both ordinary income and the net long-term capital gain. This is advantageous when the long-term capital gain is from foreign sources, since the average U.S. rate is greater than the actual U.S. tax burden on the foreign-source capital gain. This result is disadvantageous, however, when the long-term capital gain is from U.S. sources, since the average U.S. rate underestimates the actual U.S. tax burden on foreign-source income, which is all ordinary in nature.

To prevent these distortions, a taxpayer that has a capital gain rate differential must reduce the numerator of the foreign tax credit limitation fraction by a portion of any foreign-source capital gain net income.[96] The taxpayer also must reduce the denominator of the limitation by a portion of the overall capital gain net income.[97] The amount of these reductions is determined by the magnitude of the capital gain rate differential enjoyed by the taxpayer and is computed so as to remove the precise amount of bias in the unadjusted foreign tax credit limitation.

This adjustment, due to the capital gain rate differential, should only impact the foreign tax credit limitation for U.S. individuals receiving foreign-source dividends in unique situations. More specifically, if the only item of foreign-source income is a dividend received from a foreign corporation incorporated in a treaty country, which would typically not incur a withholding tax at a rate greater than 15%, the qualified dividend would incur pre-U.S. credit U.S. tax at the 15% capital gain rate.[98] These facts would render all of the withholding taxes creditable. However, if there is an effective rate of foreign tax on the dividend that is greater than 15%, due to either an allocation and apportionment of expenses to the foreign-source dividend or a high treaty withholding rate, the capital gain rate differential adjustment may result in some uncreditable foreign withholding taxes.

A capital gain rate differential also can similarly create a distortion when a taxpayer in a net long-term capital gain position nets a foreign-source capital loss

---

[95] Code Sec. 904(b)(2)(A).
[96] Code Sec. 904(b)(2)(B)(i).

[97] Code Sec. 904(b)(2)(B)(ii).
[98] Code Sec. 1(h)(11)(C).

against a U.S.-source long-term capital gain. Under the general rules, the effect of the foreign-source capital loss on the foreign tax credit limitation is based on the average rate of U.S. tax on both ordinary income and the net long-term capital gain. This average rate overstates the U.S. tax benefit of the foreign-source capital loss and, therefore, understates the U.S. tax burden on foreign-source taxable income. To prevent this result, a taxpayer that has a capital gain rate differential can increase the numerator of the foreign tax credit limitation fraction by a portion of the foreign-source capital loss.[99]

.02 Impact of Losses

Under basic U.S. tax principles, a loss from one business activity ordinarily is deductible against income from any other business activity. This principle ignores two important distinctions that must be made when computing the foreign tax credit limitation: the distinction between U.S.- and foreign-source income and the assignment of income to one of the two separate categories of income limitations. As a consequence, for purposes of computing the taxpayer's foreign tax credit limitation, numerous special rules apply when a taxpayer's business activities give rise to a net loss.

Overall foreign losses. An overall foreign loss occurs when the taxpayer's foreign-source deductions exceed foreign-source gross income.[100] A taxpayer can receive a current year tax benefit from an overall foreign loss ("OFL") by using that loss to offset U.S.-source income. If this occurs, the U.S. tax burden on foreign-source income is, in effect, negative in the year of the overall foreign loss. Moreover, there is no guarantee that future U.S. tax collections on foreign-source income will compensate for this initial tax benefit. More specifically, the United States collects only the residual U.S. tax on foreign-source income, and there is no residual U.S. tax on foreign-source income that is taxed at a rate higher than the U.S. rate. Therefore, an OFL presents the possibility of the best of both worlds: the immediate utilization of foreign losses to shelter U.S.-source income and the potential availability of foreign tax credits in profitable years to shield foreign-source income from U.S. tax.

To prevent this result, a taxpayer that sustains an OFL must, in each succeeding year, recapture as U.S.-source income the lesser of the following two amounts:

  (i) 50% (or a larger percentage if the taxpayer so elects) of its foreign-source taxable income for that succeeding year, or

  (ii) the amount of the OFL that has not been previously recaptured.[101]

This recapture rule prevents a double U.S. tax benefit by denying the taxpayer foreign tax credits on foreign-source income earned in the succeeding tax years.

Example 4.12: USAco has operations in both the United States and foreign country F. In year 1, the foreign country F operations produced an OFL

---

[99] Code Sec. 904 (b) (2) (B) (iii).
[100] Code Sec. 904 (f) (2).

[101] Code Sec. 904 (f) (1). A gain on the disposition of appreciated foreign business property or stock of a CFC also results in the recapture of an overall foreign loss. Code Sec. 904 (f) (3).

of $100,000. In the United States, USAco's operations produced taxable income of $100,000, on which USAco would otherwise pay $35,000 of U.S. tax. However, the OFL reduces USAco's net profit to $0, so USAco does not pay any U.S. income tax. In year 2, USAco again has $100,000 of U.S.-source income. However, the foreign operations turn around and produce a profit of $100,000 for worldwide income of $200,000.

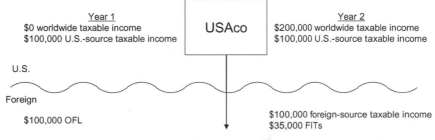

Foreign Activity

In year 2, USAco must recapture as U.S.-source income $50,000, which is the lesser of 50% of foreign-source taxable income in year 2 or the previously unrecaptured OFL of $100,000. As a result, USAco's foreign tax credit limitation for year 2 is computed as follows:

$$\text{Precredit U.S. tax on WWI} \quad \times \quad \frac{\text{Foreign-source taxable income}}{\text{Worldwide taxable income}}$$

$$35\% \times \$200,000 \quad \times \quad \frac{\$50,000}{\$200,000}$$

$$= \quad \$17,500$$

The upshot of the OFL is a reduction of foreign-source taxable income in the numerator of the limitation calculation due to $50,000 of income recaptured as U.S.-source income.

Separate foreign limitation losses. To apply the separate income limitation rules, a taxpayer must make a separate computation of foreign-source taxable income or loss for both of the two separate limitation categories. When a computation results in a net loss in a separate limitation category, that loss is a separate limitation loss.[102] Separate limitation losses are subject to special ordering and recharacterization rules.

The ordering rule is that a separate limitation loss (which, by definition, is a foreign-source loss) must be deducted against income in another separate limitation category (i.e., other foreign-source income) before it can be deducted against any U.S.-source income.[103] Taxpayers would prefer to initially offset their foreign losses against U.S.-source income and only then reduce the numerators of the other separate income limitation categories.

---

[102] Code Sec. 904(f)(5)(E)(iii). [103] Code Sec. 904(f)(5)(A).

To further maintain the integrity of the separate income limitation categories, in succeeding years, income earned in the category from which a separate limitation loss arose is recharacterized as income in the category to which the loss deduction was allocated and deducted.[104] For example, if a loss from the general income limitation category is used to offset income in the passive income limitation category, then any general limitation income earned in succeeding tax years is recharacterized as passive income to the extent of the prior year loss deduction.[105]

Example **4.13:** USAco has operations in both the United States and a foreign country. The foreign country operations produce income in both the general income limitation category and the passive income limitation category. In year 1, USAco has a loss of $50,000 in the general income limitation category, but profits of $100,000 in the passive income limitation category and $100,000 from U.S.-source taxable income. Although USAco would like to allocate the $50,000 loss in the general income limitation category to U.S.-source taxable income, the separate foreign limitation loss rules require the $50,000 general income limitation category loss to be applied against the income in the passive income limitation category. As a result, for year 1, USAco now has $50,000 in the passive income limitation category and $100,000 of U.S.-source taxable income. In year 2, USAco's operations that produce income in the general income limitation category turn around and produce $75,000 of income. Once again, USAco's passive income limitation category produces $100,000 of profits and USAco also earns $100,000 of U.S.-source taxable income. However, because USAco's passive income limitation category income was previously reduced by the $50,000 year 1 loss in the general income limitation category, $50,000 of the $75,000 earned in year 2 in the general income limitation category is recharacterized as passive income limitation category income. As a result, in year 2, when determining its foreign tax credit limitations, USAco has $25,000 in the general income limitation category, $150,000 in the passive income limitation category, and $100,000 of U.S.-source taxable income.

	Foreign-Source Income		
Year	General	Passive	U.S.-Source Income
1	($50,000)	$100,000	$100,000
1 recharacterized	0	$50,000	$100,000
2	$75,000	$100,000	$100,000
2 recharacterized	$25,000	$150,000	$100,000

Overall domestic losses. A taxpayer sustains an overall domestic loss ("ODL") in a taxable year in which the taxpayer's U.S.-source deductions exceed U.S.-source gross income. A U.S.-source loss reduces the denominator of the

---

[104] Code Sec. 904(f)(5)(C).

[105] A gain from the disposition of appreciated foreign business property that is related to a separate limitation loss also is subject to recharacterization. Code Sec. 904(f)(5)(F).

¶406.02

foreign tax credit limitation (i.e., total taxable income) and also offsets foreign-source taxable income so that no U.S. tax is due.[106]

By reducing the taxpayer's foreign-source income, an ODL may deny a taxpayer foreign tax credits. Therefore, a taxpayer may recapture and treat as foreign-source income an amount equal to the lesser of 50% of the taxpayer's U.S.-source taxable income in the succeeding taxable year or the amount of the ODL that was not recaptured in prior taxable years.[107]

Example **4.14:** USAco has operations in both the United States and foreign country F. In year 1, the foreign country F operations produced taxable income of $100,000 on which USAco pays $35,000 of tax to foreign country F. In the United States, USAco has an ODL of $100,000. USAco is in the unenviable position of paying $35,000 of tax (the taxes paid to foreign country F) without any worldwide taxable income.

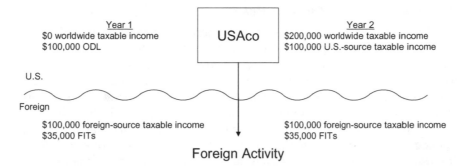

Foreign Activity

In year 2, USAco again has $100,000 of foreign-source taxable income on which it pays $35,000 of foreign income taxes. However, the U.S. operations turn around and produce a profit of $100,000. In year 2, USAco must recapture as foreign-source income $50,000, which is the lesser of 50% of the U.S.-source taxable income in year 2 or the previously unrecaptured ODL of $100,000. As a result, USAco's foreign tax credit limitation for year 2 is computed as follows:

$$\text{Precredit U.S. tax on WWI} \quad \times \quad \frac{\text{Foreign-source taxable income}}{\text{Worldwide taxable income}}$$

$$35\% \times \$200,000 \quad \times \quad \frac{\$150,000}{\$200,000}$$

$$= \quad \$\,52,500$$

As a result, USAco can now carry over $17,500 of the excess credits from year 1 to year 2 and may be able to use them in future years as USAco's U.S.-source income is recaptured as foreign-source income.

.03 Oil and Gas Activities

Special restrictions prevent oil and gas companies from using excess credits on foreign oil and gas income to soak up the residual U.S. tax on other types of

---

[106] Code Sec. 904(f)(5)(D).

[107] Code Sec. 904(g).

income. Congress enacted these restrictions because it believed that high rates of foreign tax on extraction income may have represented disguised royalties for the right to extract oil and gas resources from government-owned land. As discussed earlier in this chapter, one way in which lawmakers attempt to resolve this issue is by denying a credit for a foreign levy if the taxpayer receives a specific economic benefit in exchange for the payment.[108] In addition, a corporate taxpayer's creditable foreign oil and gas related income taxes are limited to an amount equal to the taxpayer's combined foreign oil and gas extraction income (FOGEI) and foreign oil-related income (FORI, which is income from refining, processing, transporting, distributing, or selling oil and gas or primary products derived from oil and gas),[109] multiplied by 35% (the maximum U.S. corporate tax rate).[110] Foreign taxes that are disallowed because of this restriction can be carried back one year or forward up to ten years and taken as a credit in a year in which the taxpayer has an excess limitation on the combined FOGEI and FORI.[111]

.04 Special Source-of-Income Rules

As discussed in Chapter 3 (¶ 301), there are several source-of-income rules which apply solely for purposes of computing the foreign tax credit limitation. For example, certain types of income derived from a foreign corporation that is at least 50% owned by U.S. persons are recharacterized as U.S.-source income to the extent the income is attributable to earnings that the foreign corporation derived from U.S. sources. This rule applies to interest, dividends, Subpart F inclusions, and income derived from a passive foreign investment corporation that has made a qualified electing fund election.[112] Another example is the CFC netting rule, which requires a domestic corporation to specifically allocate certain interest expense deductions against foreign-source interest income derived from a controlled foreign corporation in computing its foreign tax credit limitation (see ¶ 303.04).[113]

¶ 407 EXCESS CREDIT CARRYOVERS

Foreign taxes that exceed the limitation in a given taxable year can be carried back one year and forward up to ten years and taken as a credit in a year that the limitation exceeds the amount of creditable foreign taxes.[114] This carryover process must take place, however, within the confines of the separate income categories. In other words, excess credits from one income limitation category can offset only past or future excess limitations on that same type of income.[115] Excess credits that are carried back or forward to another taxable year must be credited and cannot be deducted in the carryback or carryforward year.[116]

This carryover provision prevents U.S. persons from being denied a foreign tax credit solely because of changes in the effective rate of foreign taxation over time.

---

[108] Reg. § 1.901-2(a)(2)(i).

[109] Code Sec. 907(c)(2). Under a look-through rule, FORI also includes dividends and interest derived from a 10%-or-more-owned foreign corporation to the extent the interest or dividends are attributable to FORI. Code Sec. 907(c)(3).

[110] Code Sec. 907(a). Individual taxpayers are subject to a different limitation.

[111] Code Sec. 907(f).

[112] Code Sec. 904(g)(1). This rule does not apply if less than 10% of the U.S.-owned foreign corporation's earnings are attributable to U.S.-source income. Code Sec. 904(g)(5).

[113] Reg. § 1.861-10.

[114] Code Sec. 904(c).

[115] Code Sec. 904(d)(1).

[116] Code Sec. 904(c).

Such fluctuations arise when a country changes its statutory tax rates, when income or expense is recognized at different times for U.S. and foreign tax purposes, or when a country enacts or eliminates tax preference items.

> *Example* **4.15:** USAco, a domestic corporation, realizes $20 million of foreign-source gross income in both year 1 and year 2 that is subject to tax in a foreign country. Assume that the U.S. and foreign tax rates are both 35%. The only deduction allocable against this income is a $20 million expenditure that is deducted over two years for U.S. tax purposes, but just one year for foreign tax purposes. As a consequence, USAco's foreign taxes are $0 in year 1 and $7 million in year 2 [35% × $20 million of foreign taxable income]. In contrast, USAco's foreign-source taxable income for U.S. tax purposes is $10 million [$20 million of gross income – $10 million of deductions] in both year 1 and year 2. Therefore, USAco's foreign tax credit limitation is $3.5 million in each year [$10 million × 35%]. If there were no excess credit carryover provision, USAco could claim a credit (in year 2) for only $3.5 million of the $7 million in foreign taxes paid. With the carryover provisions, USAco can carry the excess credits from year 2 back to year 1 and credit them against the excess limitation of $3.5 million for that year.

¶ 408 COMPUTING THE ALTERNATIVE MINIMUM TAX FOREIGN TAX CREDIT

U.S. persons can use foreign tax credits to offset not only their regular income tax for the year, but also their alternative minimum tax (or AMT). A U.S. person is subject to the AMT if the taxpayer's tentative minimum tax exceeds the regular tax for the year.[117] A corporate taxpayer's tentative minimum tax equals 20% (in the case of noncorporate taxpayers, a two-tiered rate schedule of 26% and 28% applies) of the taxpayer's alternative minimum taxable income less an exemption amount while being reduced by the alternative minimum foreign tax credit.[118]

A taxpayer computes the AMT foreign tax credit in the same manner as the credit for regular tax purposes, with one major exception. For regular tax purposes, the limitation equals the pre-credit U.S. tax multiplied by the ratio of foreign-source taxable income to worldwide income, with separate income limitation categories computed for both separate categories of income. For AMT purposes, the same basic formula and separate income limitation categories apply, except that the pre-credit U.S. tax amount is now the tentative minimum tax (before any foreign tax credits) and the foreign-source and worldwide income amounts are computed on the basis of alternative minimum taxable income.[119] For example, the AMT limitation for the passive income category equals the pre-credit tentative minimum tax multiplied by the ratio of foreign-source passive alternative minimum taxable income to worldwide alternative minimum taxable income.

Taxpayers may elect to use a simplified AMT foreign tax credit limitation when calculating their AMT foreign tax credit. The simplified limitation is the ratio of the

---

[117] Code Sec. 55(a).
[118] Code Sec. 55(b)(1).

[119] Code Sec. 59(a)(1).

taxpayer's foreign-source regular taxable income to the entire alternative minimum taxable income (AMTI). Because the simplified limitation uses foreign-source regular taxable income, rather than foreign-source AMTI, the taxpayer is not required to reallocate and reapportion deductions for AMTI purposes based on assets and income that reflect AMT adjustments (including depreciation). The AMT foreign tax credit limitation under the simplified method is computed using the following formula:[120]

$$\frac{\text{Foreign-source regular taxable income}}{\text{Worldwide AMTI}} \times \begin{array}{c}([\text{Worldwide AMTI} - \text{AMT exemption}] \\ \times [\text{AMT rate}])\end{array}$$

The election may be made only in the taxpayer's first tax year for which the taxpayer claims an AMT foreign tax credit. The election applies to all subsequent tax years and can be revoked only with the consent of the IRS.[121]

¶ 409 THE FOREIGN TAX CREDIT FOR DIVIDEND REPATRIATIONS—OVERVIEW

.01 Gross Income

A domestic corporation generally cannot claim a dividends-received deduction for a dividend from a foreign corporation, even if that foreign corporation is a wholly-owned subsidiary.[122] Therefore, a domestic corporation generally must include the entire amount of such a dividend in U.S. taxable income. A dividends-received deduction is not allowed because the domestic parent corporation's receipt of a dividend from a foreign corporation is normally the U.S. Treasury's first opportunity to tax the underlying foreign-source earnings. In contrast, a dividends-received deduction is allowed for a dividend received from a domestic corporation, based on the premise that the United States has already taxed the underlying earnings at the subsidiary corporation level and, therefore, those earnings should not be taxed again at the parent corporation level.

An exception applies if a domestic corporation owns 10% or more of a foreign corporation and that foreign corporation distributes a dividend out of post-1986 undistributed earnings that are attributable to either income effectively connected with the conduct of a U.S. trade or business or dividends received from a domestic subsidiary corporation.[123] The domestic corporation can claim a dividends-received deduction in this situation because the dividends represent a distribution of earnings that have already been taxed by the United States.

.02 Direct Foreign Tax Credit

Most foreign countries impose flat rate withholding taxes on the gross amount of dividends paid by a locally organized corporation to a U.S. shareholder. Tax treaties usually reduce the statutory withholding tax rate to 15% or less and the treaty withholding rate often is lower for controlling shareholders (e.g., a share-

---

[120] For purposes of the simplified limitation, foreign-source regular taxable income cannot exceed the taxpayer's entire AMTI.

[121] Code Sec. 59(a)(3).

[122] Code Sec. 243(a).

[123] Code Sec. 245(a). *See also* Code Sec. 245(b).

holder owning 10% or more of the payer's stock) than for noncontrolling shareholders.

A U.S. person can claim a direct foreign tax credit for any foreign withholding taxes it incurs on a dividend from a foreign corporation.[124] However, a credit generally is not allowed for any foreign withholding taxes related to the U.S.-source portion of a dividend from a foreign corporation (the taxpayer would have been entitled to a dividends-received deduction).[125]

.03 Deemed Paid Foreign Tax Credit

In addition to the direct foreign credit for foreign withholding taxes, a domestic corporation also can claim a deemed paid foreign tax credit if it owns 10% or more of the voting stock of the foreign corporation from which it receives a dividend distribution.[126] The term "deemed paid" is a reference to how the foreign income taxes paid by a foreign corporation are made available as a credit to the domestic corporation. Specifically, the domestic corporation is deemed to have paid the foreign corporation's foreign income taxes upon receipt of a dividend from that subsidiary.

> ***Example* 4.16:** USAco, a domestic corporation, owns 100% of FORco, a foreign corporation. During its first year of operations, FORco derives $1 million of foreign-source taxable income, pays $250,000 of foreign income taxes, and distributes its $750,000 of after-tax earnings to USAco as a dividend. The $750,000 dividend is subject to foreign withholding taxes at a 5% rate. USAco can claim a direct foreign tax credit for the foreign withholding taxes of $37,500 [$750,000 dividend × 5% withholding rate]. In addition, because USAco owns 10% or more of FORco and receives a dividend distribution from FORco during the year, USAco also can claim a deemed paid credit for the $250,000 of foreign income taxes related to the earnings distribution. As discussed in the next section, USAco also has $250,000 of Code Sec. 78 gross-up income.

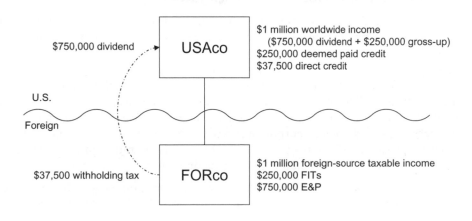

---

[124] Reg. § 1.903-1(b)(3), Example (2).
[125] Code Sec. 245(a)(8).

[126] Code Sec. 902(a).

Congress enacted the deemed paid credit to protect domestic corporations with foreign subsidiaries against double taxation, as well as to better equate the tax treatment of U.S. companies with foreign subsidiaries to those with foreign branches. A domestic corporation operating abroad through a branch can claim a direct foreign tax credit for the foreign taxes it pays directly on its foreign earnings.[127] In contrast, a domestic corporation operating abroad through a foreign subsidiary cannot claim a direct credit because the foreign subsidiary, not the domestic parent, is the entity paying the foreign taxes. Allowing domestic corporations to claim a credit for the foreign taxes paid by their foreign subsidiaries allows domestic corporations to make legal form decisions on the basis of general business considerations rather than U.S. tax consequences. Sometimes the deemed paid foreign tax credit is referred to as the indirect foreign tax credit because, in contrast to the direct foreign tax credit for taxes that are directly paid by the U.S. taxpayer, the indirect foreign tax credit is for taxes that are indirectly paid by the domestic corporation via the foreign subsidiary.

Taxpayers cannot claim a credit for foreign income taxes deemed paid with respect to a dividend unless a 16-day holding period for the dividend-paying stock (or a 46-day holding period for certain dividends on preferred stock) is satisfied with respect to each corporation in the chain of corporations for which the deemed paid credit is claimed. The 16-day holding period requirement must be met within the 30-day period beginning 15 days before the ex-dividend date. If the stock is held for 15 days or less during the 30-day period, the foreign tax credit for the deemed paid tax is disallowed. The holding period generally does not include any period during which the taxpayer is protected from risk of loss (e.g., by use of an option). An exception to the holding period requirement is available to security dealers.[128] Congress enacted these provisions to curtail transactions designed to transfer foreign tax credits from persons unable to benefit from them to persons that can use the credits.

.04 Gross-Up for Deemed Paid Foreign Taxes

Because a dividend represents a distribution from earnings and profits (after-tax earnings), the amount of income that a domestic corporation recognizes upon receiving a dividend from a foreign corporation is net of all the foreign income taxes paid by that foreign corporation. In effect, the domestic corporation is allowed a deduction for the foreign corporation's income taxes when computing the gross income from a dividend. To prevent a double tax benefit in the form of both an implicit deduction and a deemed paid credit with respect to the same foreign income taxes, a domestic corporation must gross up its dividend income by the amount of the deemed paid credit.[129] This gross-up requirement prevents the double tax benefit by eliminating the implicit deduction.

Example **4.17:** USAco, a domestic corporation, owns 100% of ASIAco, a foreign corporation. During its first year of operations, ASIAco derives $10

---

[127] Code Sec. 901(a).
[128] Code Sec. 901(k).

[129] Code Sec. 78. The gross-up requirement does not apply if the taxpayer is denied a credit by virtue of not satisfying the holding period requirement of Code Sec. 901(k).

million of foreign-source taxable income, pays $2 million of foreign income taxes, and distributes its $8 million of after-tax earnings to USAco as a dividend. Assume the dividend is not subject to foreign withholding taxes and that the U.S. tax rate is 35%.

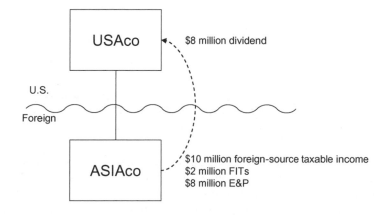

Because USAco owns 10% or more of ASIAco and received a dividend distribution from ASIAco during the year, USAco can claim a deemed paid credit for the $2 million of foreign income taxes related to the $8 million of earnings and profits that were distributed. After the gross-up of $2 million of foreign income taxes, USAco has a pre-credit U.S. tax of $3.5 million [35% × ($8 million dividend + $2 million gross-up)], $2 million of deemed paid credits, and a residual U.S. tax of $1.5 million. Therefore, the total tax on the $10 million of repatriated foreign earnings is $3.5 million [$2 million of foreign taxes + $1.5 million of U.S. taxes], which indicates that ASIAco's earnings are being taxed only once at the higher U.S. rate of 35%. In other words, the deemed paid credit in conjunction with the gross-up achieves its intended effect, which is to prevent both an implicit deduction and a credit for foreign income taxes paid.

The gross-up is also consistent with the policy of equating operating abroad as a foreign subsidiary with operating abroad as a foreign branch by rendering equal results. In branch form, the Asian operations would still have $10 million of foreign-source taxable income and $2 million of foreign income taxes paid. On its U.S. return, USAco would report $10 million of world-wide income (the $10 million of foreign-source taxable income earned by the Asian branch) on which it would have a pre-credit U.S. tax of $3.5 million. USAco would take a $2 million direct foreign tax credit against the $3.5 million pre-credit U.S. tax and pay only a residual U.S. tax of $1.5 million. Again, the total tax on the $10 million of foreign earnings is $3.5 million [$2 million of foreign taxes + $1.5 million of U.S. taxes], which indicates that the Asian earnings are being taxed only once at the higher U.S. rate of 35% (compare with Example 4.1 for a comparable result under the direct foreign tax credit when operating abroad as a branch).

¶409.04

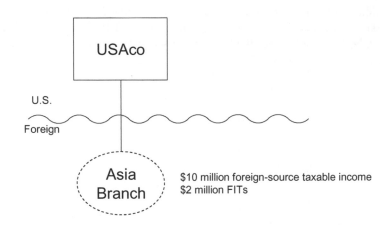

Furthermore, without the gross-up the residual U.S. tax on ASIAco's repatriated earnings would drop from $1.5 million to $800,000 [(35% U.S. rate × $8 million dividend) – $2 million deemed paid credit]. The $700,000 reduction in the residual U.S. tax reflects the U.S. tax benefit of an implicit deduction for ASIAco's $2 million of foreign income taxes that arises because USAco included only ASIAco's after-tax earnings in U.S. taxable income.

¶ 410 WHO CAN CLAIM A DEEMED PAID CREDIT

Only a domestic C corporation is eligible to claim a deemed paid foreign tax credit. A domestic C corporation can claim a deemed paid foreign tax credit only if it owns 10% or more of the voting stock of a foreign corporation and receives a dividend distribution from that foreign corporation.[130] For this purpose, stock of a foreign corporation that is owned by a partnership is considered to be owned proportionately by its corporate partners.[131] As a result, a domestic C corporation which is a partner in a partnership that owns stock of a foreign corporation is eligible to claim a deemed paid credit with respect to the foreign corporation if the domestic C corporation indirectly owns at least 10% of the voting stock of the foreign corporation and the foreign corporation distributes a dividend. In addition, for purposes of the deemed paid credit, the term "dividend" means a distribution of property out of a foreign corporation's earnings and profits, as well as other transactions that are treated as dividends under the Code, such as a Code Sec. 302(d) stock redemption or a Code Sec. 1248 gain on the sale of stock of a CFC.[132]

U.S. persons other than a domestic C corporation, such as a U.S. citizen or resident alien, are not eligible for the deemed paid credit. This includes an S corporation since, for purposes of the deemed paid credit, an S corporation is treated as a partnership.[133] An S corporation's shareholders, who by statute must be individuals, estates, or trusts, also cannot claim a deemed paid credit. Therefore, an

---

[130] Code Sec. 902(a). Members of an affiliated group may not aggregate their ownership interests for purposes of satisfying the 10% ownership requirement. *First Chicago NBD Corp.*, CA-7, 98-1 USTC ¶ 50,169, 135 F3d 457 (7th Cir. 1998). Aff'g 96 TC 421, Dec. 47,218. Rev. Rul. 85-3, 1985-1 CB 222.

[131] Code Sec. 902(c)(7).

[132] Reg. § 1.902-1(a)(11).

[133] Code. Sec. 1373(a), and Reg. § 1.902-1(a)(1).

S corporation may wish to structure its foreign operations as a branch or a partnership rather than a foreign corporation, in which case the S corporation's shareholders can claim a direct credit for the foreign income taxes incurred by the foreign branch or partnership.[134] The remainder of this chapter will assume that all domestic corporations are domestic C corporations.

In the alternative, because the maximum tax on most dividends (those paid by foreign corporations as well as those paid by U.S. corporations) is 15%, U.S. individuals owning foreign corporations in treaty countries either directly or through a pass through entity pay a lower rate of tax (15% instead of 35%) when repatriating the earnings of a foreign corporation.[135]

Foreign income taxes are not creditable until the underlying foreign income is taken into account for U.S. federal income tax purposes.[136] This rule applies to both direct foreign tax credits[137] and deemed paid foreign tax credits.[138] A foreign tax credit splitting event occurs when income (or earnings and profits) giving rise to a tax is taken into account by a "covered person." A "covered person" is anyone directly or indirectly owning or owned by the actual payor of the foreign tax. The rule's policy is to prevent a payor from circumventing the foreign tax credit limitations by entering transactions with related parties that split foreign income taxes from their income.

Example 4.18: USCo wholly owns CFC 1, which wholly owns CFC 2. CFC 2 earns $100 of income. CFC 2 issues a hybrid instrument to CFC 1, which is treated as equity for U.S. tax purposes, but is debt for foreign tax purposes. Because CFC 2 accrues interest to CFC 1 of $100, CFC 2 does not have any income for foreign country purposes while CFC 1 has $100 of income that is subject to foreign country tax at a 30% rate for $30.

For U.S. tax purpose, CFC 2 still has $100 of e&p (the U.S. ignores the accrued interest expense because the hybrid instrument is treated as equity for U.S. tax purposes). Pursuant to the anti-splitter rule, the related income with respect to the $30 of foreign income taxes paid by CFC 1 is the $100 of e&p of CFC 2. As a result, if CFC 1 pays a dividend to USCo, USCo may not take a deemed paid foreign tax credit of any of the $30.

---

[134] Code Sec. 901.
[135] Code Sec. 1(h)(11)(B)(i).
[136] Code Sec. 909.

[137] Code Sec. 901.
[138] Code Sec. 902.

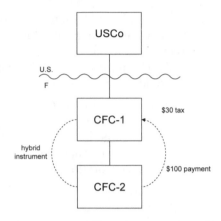

¶ 411 COMPUTING THE DEEMED PAID CREDIT

.01 Tracing Foreign Taxes to Dividend Distributions

Pooling rule. To compute the deemed paid credit, the taxpayer must determine the amount of foreign income taxes that are attributable to a foreign corporation's dividend distribution. In theory, a dividend represents a distribution of corporate earnings from one or more specific taxable years. Associated with each year's earnings are the foreign income taxes for that year. The practical problem is determining the taxable year(s) from which the earnings distribution emanates. If a foreign corporation distributes all of its after-tax earnings each year (an uncommon occurrence), then the tracing problem is relatively easy to solve. The foreign income taxes related to each year's dividend are simply the foreign income taxes paid for that taxable year. However, if a foreign corporation does not distribute all of its earnings and profits each year, a tracing problem arises.

One possible approach to solving this problem is to assume that dividend distributions pull out a foreign corporation's undistributed earnings and profits and the related foreign income taxes in chronological order (a first-in, first-out rule) or in reverse chronological order (a last-in, first-out rule). Another approach is to pool a foreign corporation's undistributed earnings and profits and foreign income taxes, and then assume that a dividend distribution pulls out deemed paid taxes equal to the pool of foreign income taxes multiplied by the ratio of the dividend to the pool of undistributed earnings and profits. If the effective foreign tax rate varies over time, the amount of deemed paid foreign taxes associated with a dividend will vary with the approach taken.

Example 4.19: USAco, a domestic corporation, owns 100% of EURco, a foreign corporation. EURco's earnings and profits, foreign income taxes, and dividend distributions for its first two years of operations are as follows.

Year	Pre-tax earnings	Foreign income taxes	Effective foreign rate	Earnings & Profits	Dividend distributions
Year 1	$10 million	$2 million	20%	$8 million	$0
Year 2	$10 million	$4 million	40%	$6 million	$3 million

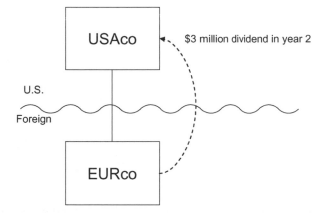

Because the foreign tax rate on EURco's earnings increased from 20% in year 1 to 40% in year 2, the last-in, first-out method would pull out more foreign taxes than the pooling method, as discussed below.

Last-in, first-out method: Under a last-in, first-out tracing rule, the $3 million dividend represents a distribution of 50% of EURco's year 2 earnings and profits of $6 million and, therefore, the dividend pulls out foreign income taxes of $2 million [50% × $4 million of year 2 foreign income taxes].

Pooling method: Prior to the dividend, EURco has undistributed earnings and profits of $14 million [$8 million + $6 million] and foreign income taxes of $6 million [$2 million + $4 million]. Therefore, under a pooling approach, the $3 million dividend pulls out foreign income taxes of roughly $1,285,714 [$6 million of foreign income taxes × ($3 million dividend ÷ $14 million of earnings and profits)].

A pooling approach is required for post-1986 dividends, whereby a domestic corporation that receives a dividend from a 10% or more owned foreign corporation is deemed to have paid the following portion of the foreign corporation's foreign income taxes:[139]

$$\text{Foreign corporation's post-1986 foreign income taxes} \times \frac{\text{Dividend}}{\text{Foreign corporation's post-1986 undistributed E\&P}} \quad [140]$$

Example **4.20:** USAco, a domestic corporation, owns 100% of AFRIco, a foreign corporation. During its first year of operations, AFRIco derives $10 million of foreign-source taxable income, pays $4 million of foreign income taxes, and distributes a $3 million dividend to USAco. The $3 million dividend carries deemed paid taxes of $2 million [$4 million of post-1986 foreign income taxes × ($3 million dividend ÷ $6 million of post-1986 undistributed earnings and profits)].

---

[139] Code Sec. 902(a).

[140] The dividend amount in the numerator does not include the Code Sec. 78 gross-up income.

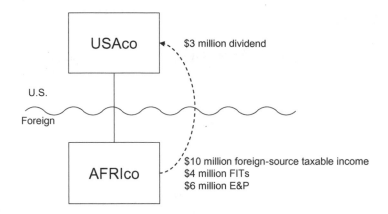

If a dividend exceeds the amount of post-1986 undistributed earnings (i.e., the dividend represents a distribution of pre-1987 earnings), then the tracing rule in effect prior to 1987 is used.[141] Prior to 1987, a last-in, first-out rule was used, whereby pre-1987 annual earnings were layered in chronological order and a dividend pulled out a layer of earnings (and, in turn, a layer of foreign income taxes) in reverse chronological order.[142] The portion of a dividend traced to a pre-1987 year's profits pulls out deemed paid taxes equal to the foreign income taxes for that year multiplied by the ratio of the dividend from that year to the total earnings and profits for that year.

Congress enacted the pooling method in 1986, in part, because it believed that U.S. companies were manipulating the preexisting rule to maximize their deemed paid credits. Under a last-in, first-out rule, there is an advantage to bunching a foreign corporation's taxable income and, in turn, its foreign income taxes into particular years before having the foreign corporation distribute its earnings for those high-tax years. This technique causes deemed paid taxes to flow through to the domestic parent corporation at a higher rate than the long-run average effective rate of foreign taxation. In contrast, under the pooling method, the amount of foreign taxes pulled out by a dividend more accurately reflects the long-run effective rate of foreign taxation.

Post-1986 undistributed earnings and profits. Post-1986 undistributed earnings and profits is computed as of the close of the foreign corporation's taxable year in which it distributes the dividend and equals the cumulative amount of the foreign corporation's undistributed earnings and profits for taxable years beginning after December 31, 1986. Post-1986 undistributed earnings and profits is reduced by actual dividend distributions from prior taxable years, as well as any prior year inclusions of the foreign corporation's earnings and profits in a shareholder's income (e.g., income inclusions under Subpart F). However, post-1986 undistributed earnings and profits are not reduced by the dividend distribution or any other inclusions in a shareholder's income for the current taxable year.[143]

---

[141] Code Sec. 902(c)(6).

[142] Code Sec. 902(c)(1), before amendment in 1986.

[143] Code Sec. 902(c)(1) and Reg. § 1.902-1(a)(9).

Roughly speaking, a foreign corporation's earnings and profits equals its taxable income, plus or minus various adjustments (such as taxes) designed to make earnings and profits a better measure of a corporation's economic income. Examples of the required adjustments include adding back tax-exempt income, adding back the excess of accelerated depreciation over straight-line depreciation, and subtracting foreign income taxes.[144] In all cases, a foreign corporation's earnings and profits are determined according to substantially the same U.S. tax accounting principles that apply to domestic corporations.[145] As a consequence, financial statements prepared under a foreign corporation's local country accounting principles are adjusted to make them consistent with U.S. accounting principles.[146]

Post-1986 foreign income taxes. Post-1986 foreign income taxes equal the cumulative amount of a foreign corporation's foreign income taxes for taxable years beginning after December 31, 1986 (including the foreign income taxes for the year of the dividend), reduced by the amount of foreign income taxes related to prior-year dividend distributions or other inclusions of the foreign corporation's earnings and profits in a shareholder's income (e.g., income inclusions under Subpart F), regardless of whether those other shareholders were eligible to claim a deemed paid credit.[147]

The term "foreign income taxes" has the same meaning for purposes of the deemed paid credit as it does for purposes of the direct foreign tax credit.[148] As a result, to be creditable, a levy paid by a foreign corporation must meet two basic requirements. First, the levy must be a tax (as opposed to a payment in exchange for a specific economic benefit) that is paid to a foreign country or U.S. possession. Second, the predominant character of the tax must be that of an income tax in the U.S. sense.[149] If a foreign levy satisfies the first requirement but not the second, the foreign levy may still be creditable if the tax is imposed in lieu of an income tax.[150] As described below, foreign income taxes also include any taxes that a foreign corporation is deemed to have paid by reason of receiving a dividend from a lower-tier foreign corporation.[151] If two or more commonly controlled foreign corporations file a consolidated foreign income tax return and the corporations are jointly and severally liable for the foreign income tax, then each corporation is treated as having paid a portion of the foreign income tax equal to its proportionate share of the combined income tax base.[152]

Currency translation. Foreign corporations usually conduct a significant part of their activities in an economic environment in which a foreign currency is used and usually keep their books and records in a foreign currency. This creates a currency translation problem for a domestic corporation, which must translate the

---

[144] Code Sec. 312, and Reg. § 1.902-1(a)(9)(iii).

[145] Code Sec. 964(a); *Goodyear Tire & Rubber Co.*, SCt, 89-2 USTC ¶ 9658, 493 US 132, 110 SCt 462.

[146] *See* Reg. § 1.964-1(a) for the applicable computation procedures.

[147] Code Sec. 902(c)(2) and Reg. § 1.902-1(a)(8). However, a domestic corporation generally cannot claim a deemed paid credit for any foreign taxes related to the

U.S.-source portion of a dividend from a foreign corporation for which a domestic corporation claims a dividends-received deduction. Code Sec. 245(a)(8).

[148] Code Sec. 902(c)(4)(A) and Reg. § 1.902-1(a)(7).

[149] Code Sec. 901(b) and Reg. § 1.901-2(a)(1).

[150] Code Sec. 903.

[151] Code Sec. 902(c)(4)(B).

[152] Reg. § 1.901-2(f)(3).

tax attributes of the foreign corporation into U.S. dollars. The currency translation rules for dividend distributions from a foreign corporation, including the computation of the deemed paid credit, are discussed in Chapter 6 (¶ 601).

.02 Credit Derived from Lower-Tier Foreign Corporations

A domestic corporation that operates abroad through multiple tiers of foreign corporations also can obtain deemed paid credits for taxes paid by second- and third-tier foreign corporations (and, under conditions discussed below, fourth-, fifth- and sixth-tier foreign corporations). This is possible because, for purposes of computing the deemed paid credit, a first-tier foreign corporation's foreign income taxes include not only its foreign income taxes actually paid, but also any foreign income taxes it is deemed to have paid by reason of receiving a dividend from a qualifying lower-tier foreign corporation.[153] In general, for deemed paid taxes to pass up from second- and third-tier subsidiaries, (i) each tier must have 10% direct ownership by its immediate parent and (ii) the domestic corporation must indirectly own at least 5% of the lowest tier.

More specifically, foreign income taxes paid by a second-tier foreign corporation pass up a dividend to a first-tier foreign corporation if the following requirements are satisfied:

(i)   the domestic corporation owns 10% or more of the voting stock of the first-tier foreign corporation,

(ii) the first-tier foreign corporation owns 10% or more of the voting stock of the second-tier foreign corporation,

(iii) the domestic corporation indirectly owns at least 5% of the second-tier foreign corporation, determined by multiplying the percentage ownership at the two levels, and

(iv) the first-tier foreign corporation receives a dividend from the second-tier foreign corporation.[154]

Foreign income taxes paid by a third-tier foreign corporation pass up a dividend to a second-tier foreign corporation if the following requirements are satisfied:

(i)   the domestic corporation owns 10% or more of the voting stock of the first-tier foreign corporation,

(ii) the first-tier foreign corporation owns 10% or more of the voting stock of the second-tier foreign corporation,

(iii) the second-tier foreign corporation owns 10% or more of the voting stock of the third-tier foreign corporation,

(iv) the domestic corporation indirectly owns at least 5% of the third-tier foreign corporation, determined by multiplying the percentage ownership at the three levels, and

(v)   the second-tier foreign corporation receives a dividend from the third-tier foreign corporation.[155]

---

[153] Code Sec. 902(c)(4).
[154] Code Sec. 902(b).

[155] Code Sec. 902(b).

Example **4.21**: USAco, a domestic corporation, owns 100% of the shares of FORco1. FORco1 owns 40% of the shares of FORco2 and FORco2 owns 10% of the shares of FORco3.

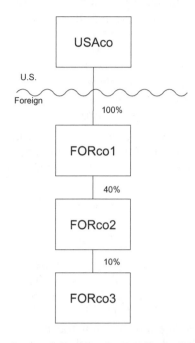

USAco may take a deemed foreign tax credit for foreign income taxes paid by FORco2 because USAco owns more than 10% of FORco1 (100%), FORco1 owns 10% or more of FORco2 (40%) and USAco indirectly owns at least 5% (40%) of FORco2 (100% × 40%). However, even though FORco2 owns at least 10% of FORco3, because the indirect ownership by USAco of FORco3 is less than 5% (only 4%, 100% × 40% × 10%), USAco may not take a deemed foreign tax credit for foreign income taxes paid by FORco3.

The deemed paid credit also extends to taxes paid or accrued by fourth-, fifth-, and sixth-tier foreign corporations on the upstream distribution of a dividend. To qualify, the corporation in question must be a controlled foreign corporation (CFC), the U.S. corporation claiming the credit must be a U.S. shareholder, and the product of the percentage ownership of voting stock at each level from the U.S. corporation down must equal at least five percent. The deemed paid credit is extended to lower tiers only with respect to taxes paid or incurred in years during which the payor is a CFC.[156] A foreign corporation is a CFC if, on any day during the foreign corporation's tax year, U.S. shareholders own more than 50% of the combined voting power of all classes of stock or 50% of the total value of the foreign corporation.[157] A U.S. shareholder is any U.S. person owning at least 10% of the total combined voting power of all classes of voting stock of the foreign corporation.[158]

---

[156] Code Sec. 902(b).
[157] Code Sec. 957(a).

[158] Code Sec. 951(b).

¶**411.02**

The mechanism by which foreign income taxes pass up from a lower-tier foreign corporation to a higher-tier foreign corporation is almost identical to that by which foreign income taxes pass up from a first-tier foreign corporation to a domestic corporation (although there is not a gross-up).[159] For example, when a domestic corporation receives a dividend from a first-tier foreign corporation and, in the same taxable year, the first-tier foreign corporation receives a dividend from a second-tier foreign corporation, then the domestic corporation computes its deemed paid foreign taxes by starting with the lowest-tier corporation and working up.[160] The same types of procedures allow the foreign income taxes paid by a third-tier foreign corporation to pass up to a second-tier foreign corporation, and so on for fourth-, fifth-, and sixth-tier foreign corporations.[161]

Example **4.22:** USAco (a domestic corporation) owns 100% of F1, and F1 owns 100% of F2. F1 and F2 are both foreign corporations. At end of the current year, the undistributed earnings and foreign income taxes of F1 and F2 are as follows:

	Undistributed E&P	*FITs*
F1	$18 million	$4 million
F2	$6 million	$3 million

During the current year, F2 distributes a $2 million dividend to F1 and F1 distributes a $2 million dividend to USAco. The $2 million dividend from F2 pulls out $1 million of deemed paid taxes for F1 [$3 million of post-1986 foreign income taxes × ($2 million dividend ÷ $6 million of post-1986 undistributed earnings)]. After taking into account the $2 million dividend from F2, F1's post-1986 undistributed earnings and profits increase to $20 million [$18 million + $2 million] and (assuming F2's dividend is exempt from local taxation in F1's country) F1's post-1986 foreign income taxes increase to $5 million [$4 million + $1 million]. As a consequence, USAco's receipt of a $2 million dividend from F1 pulls out deemed paid taxes of $500,000 [$5 million of post-1986 foreign income taxes × ($2 million dividend ÷ $20 million of post-1986 undistributed earnings)] and USAco must recognize dividend income of $2.5 million [$2 million dividend + $500,000 gross-up].

---

[159] Code Sec. 902(b)(1). One difference is that the first-tier foreign corporation does not recognize any gross-up income for deemed paid taxes, since the gross-up require-ment applies only to a domestic corporation that claims a credit against its U.S. taxes. Code Sec. 78.

[160] Reg. § 1.902-1(c)(1)(i).

[161] Code Sec. 902(b)(2) and Reg. § 1.902-1(c)(1)(i).

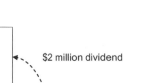

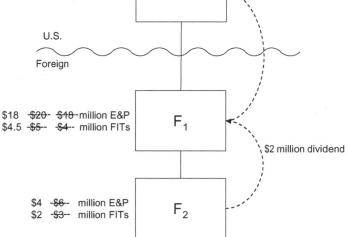

.03 CFC and 10/50 Company Look-through Rules

As discussed in ¶ 405.03 with respect to direct credits, for purposes of computing the separate basket foreign tax credit limitations, look-through rules apply to dividends received from either a CFC or a 10/50 company.[162] The look-through rule also applies to deemed paid credits. If it were not for these look-through rules, the separate category of income limitations would yield significantly different results for domestic corporations operating abroad through foreign subsidiaries as opposed to foreign branches. For example, if a domestic corporation structures a foreign manufacturing operation as a branch, the related income and foreign taxes would be assigned to the general limitation category. In contrast, if a domestic corporation were to structure the same foreign manufacturing operation as a subsidiary, absent a look-through rule, dividend distributions from that foreign manufacturing subsidiary would be assigned to the passive income category.

To better equate the treatment of foreign branch and foreign subsidiary operations, dividends paid by a foreign corporation to a domestic corporation are prorated among the separate categories of income based on the ratio of the foreign corporation's earnings and profits within each separate income category to the foreign corporation's total earnings and profits.[163] For example, if a foreign corporation has $1 million of earnings and profits, $900,000 of which is attributable to general limitation income and the other $100,000 to passive income, then 90% of a dividend distribution from the foreign corporation is assigned to the general limitation category and the other 10% is assigned to the passive income limitation category. The amount of deemed paid foreign taxes related to a dividend attributa-

---

[162] Code Sec. 904(d)(3) and (4).   [163] Code Sec. 904(d)(3)(D) and Reg. § 1.904-5(c)(4)(i).

ble to a specific category of income is then determined using the following formula:[164]

$$\text{Post-1986 foreign income taxes attributable to the separate category of income}^{165} \quad \times \quad \frac{\text{Portion of dividend attributable to the separate income limitation}}{\text{Post-1986 undistributed E\&P attributable to the separate income limitation}}$$

To make these computations, a domestic corporation must maintain separate pools of post-1986 undistributed earnings and profits and post-1986 foreign income taxes for both categories of income with respect to any foreign corporations in which the domestic corporation owns 10% of the outstanding shares.

> *Example* **4.23:** USAco, a domestic corporation, owns 100% of FORco, a foreign corporation. At end of the current year, FORco's pools of post-1986 undistributed earnings and post-1986 foreign income taxes are as follows:

	Post-1986 undistributed earnings and profits	*Post-1986 foreign income taxes*
General limitation income	$8 million	$7 million
Passive income	$4 million	$1 million
Total income	$12 million	$8 million

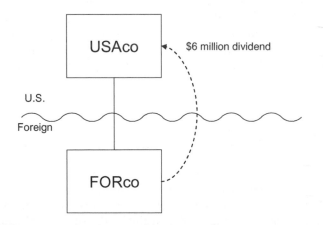

> During the current year, FORco distributed a $6 million dividend to USAco. Under the CFC look-through rule, $4 million of this amount [$6 million × ($8 million ÷ $12 million)] is assigned to the general income limitation category

---

[164] Reg. § 1.902-1(d)(2)(i).

[165] Foreign income taxes are allocated to the category of income that includes the income upon which the foreign taxes were imposed. Reg. § 1.904-6(a)(1)(i). If the base upon which a foreign income tax is imposed includes income from more than one category, the taxpayer prorates the foreign income taxes among the separate categories of income based on the relative amount of foreign taxable income within each category. Reg. § 1.904-6(a)(1)(ii).

and the other $2 million [$6 million × ($4 million ÷ $12 million)] is assigned to the passive income limitation category. Therefore, FORco's $6 million dividend pulls out deemed paid taxes of $3.5 million in the general income limitation category [$7 million of post-1986 foreign income taxes × ($4 million dividend ÷ $8 million of post-1986 undistributed earnings)] and $500,000 in the passive income limitation category [$1 million of post-1986 foreign income taxes × ($2 million dividend ÷ $4 million of post-1986 undistributed earnings)].

.04 Deemed Paid Credits for Subpart F and QEF Inclusions

Subpart F requires a U.S. shareholder of a CFC to recognize a deemed dividend equal to its pro rata share of the CFC's Subpart F income, plus any increase in the CFC's earnings invested in U.S. property.[166] In the case of a domestic corporation that owns 10% or more of the CFC's voting stock, a Subpart F inclusion carries with it a deemed paid foreign tax credit that is conceptually identical to the deemed paid credit that is allowed with respect to actual dividend distributions.[167] Domestic corporations that own 10% or more of the voting stock of a passive foreign investment company that has made a qualified electing fund election can also claim a deemed paid credit with respect to the qualified electing fund income inclusion.[168] The taxation of Subpart F and qualified electing fund inclusions, including the computation of the related deemed paid foreign tax credit, is discussed in Chapter 5.

¶ 412 COMPLIANCE REQUIREMENTS

A corporation claiming a foreign tax credit must attach Form 1118 to its tax return, whereas an individual claiming a foreign tax credit must attach Form 1116 to his or her tax return (both forms are reproduced in the appendix to this chapter).[169] A domestic corporation claiming a deemed paid foreign tax credit generally must satisfy the same filing and documentation requirements that apply to the direct credit.[170] If the taxpayer has foreign income taxes in both the general category and passive category baskets, a separate Form 1118 (or Form 1116) is completed for each separate limitation.

Regardless of whether the foreign tax credits taken are direct credits or deemed paid credits, IRS agents may ask for proof of the foreign income taxes paid or incurred. The primary substantiation for foreign income taxes paid by a cash basis taxpayer is a receipt for payment. The primary substantiation for foreign income taxes paid or incurred by an accrual basis taxpayer is the foreign tax return.[171] If the IRS, in its discretion, is satisfied that a taxpayer cannot furnish primary substantiation, a taxpayer may furnish secondary substantiation.[172] In lieu of a receipt for payment of foreign income taxes, a cash basis taxpayer must be able to provide a photocopy of the check, draft or other medium of payment showing the amount and date, with evidence establishing that the tax was paid. In lieu of a foreign tax return showing the foreign income taxes incurred, an accrual basis

---

[166] Code Sec. 951(a)(1).
[167] Code Sec. 960(a)(1).
[168] Code Sec. 1293(f)(1).
[169] Reg. § 1.905-2(a)(1).

[170] Reg. § 1.902-1(e).
[171] Reg. § 1.905-2(a)(2).
[172] Reg. § 1.905-2(b).

taxpayer must be able to provide a certified statement of the accrued amount, with excerpts from its books showing the computation of the accrued amount.

Foreign withholding taxes represent unique problems, since they are not paid directly by the taxpayer. Indirect evidence, such as a letter from the foreign payer stating that the tax was withheld and paid, may not provide sufficient proof of payment to claim a credit. Instead, the taxpayer may be required to produce evidence that the foreign payer actually remitted the foreign withholding taxes to the foreign government.[173] Whenever possible, taxpayers should obtain a government receipt for any foreign withholding taxes that it paid.

Although these substantiation rules apply to both direct and deemed paid credits, record retention can be a challenge for a corporation claiming the deemed paid credit. Considering that the deemed paid credit is based on pools of foreign taxes and earnings and profits that have accumulated since 1987, domestic corporations should ensure that they are keeping primary substantiation and, if they do not have primary substantiation, putting together the appropriate secondary substantiation.

> **Example 4.24:** USAco is a U.S. based multinational with many subsidiaries, one of which is FORco, a country F corporation. USAco has owned FORco since 1990. On December 31, 2010, FORco distributes its first dividend ever to USAco. When filing its return for the 2010 tax year, USAco claims the deemed paid credit with respect to the dividend received from FORco. In June 2012, the IRS audits USAco and requests substantiation of the foreign income taxes paid by FORco. If USAco cannot substantiate the foreign income taxes paid by FORco going back to 1990, the IRS may deny the deemed paid credit.

If an adjustment by a foreign tax authority (i.e., a "redetermination") results in an increase in the amount of foreign taxes paid, the taxpayer has 10 years from the date the U.S. return was originally filed to claim a refund of U.S. taxes for the increase in creditable foreign taxes.[174] On the other hand, if the foreign tax redetermination results in a refund of foreign taxes, the taxpayer must notify the IRS by filing an amended tax return on which the taxpayer recomputes the U.S. tax liability for the year in which the foreign tax credit was originally claimed.[175] In addition, special IRS notification rules apply to taxpayers under the jurisdiction of the Large Business and International Division.[176] A failure to provide notification to the IRS can result in a penalty of up to 25% of the amount of the deficiency associated with the redetermination.[177] In the case of a redetermination of the foreign taxes of a foreign corporation that are deemed paid by a domestic corporation under Code Sec. 902 or 960, adjustments are made to the foreign corporation's pools of post-1986 foreign income taxes and post-1986 undistributed earnings.[178] Special currency translation rules apply to redeterminations.[179]

---

[173] Reg. § 1.905-2(b)(3), *Continental Illinois Corp.*, CA-7, Dec. 47,178(M), 998 F2d 513 (7th Cir. 1993), aff'g, rev'g, and rem'g 61 TCM 1916, Dec. 47,178(M), TC Memo. 1991-66; and *Norwest Corp.*, 70 TCM 779, Dec. 50,906(M), TC Memo. 1995-453.

[174] Code Sec. 6511(d)(3)(A).

[175] Temp. Reg. § 1.905-4T(b)(2). The amended tax return must be filed within 180 days of the redetermination.

[176] Temp. Reg. § 1.905-4T.

[177] Code Sec. 6689.

[178] Code Sec. 905(c).

[179] Temp. Reg. § 1.905-3T.

¶ 413 PLANNING FOR DIVIDEND REPATRIATIONS

The decision to repatriate earnings from a foreign subsidiary may be influenced by a variety of factors, such as the cash needs of the domestic parent corporation, the preferences of foreign managers, financial reporting considerations, local company laws requiring the maintenance of reserves, as well as U.S. and foreign tax consequences. As discussed below, the precepts of U.S. tax planning for dividend repatriations include cross-crediting, minimizing foreign withholding taxes, and considering alternative methods of repatriating earnings.

.01 Cross-Crediting

The U.S. tax consequences of a dividend repatriation depend on whether the foreign corporation is operating in a low- or high-tax foreign jurisdiction. No U.S. tax is due on a dividend from a foreign corporation operating in a high-tax foreign jurisdiction, because the deemed foreign tax credits more than offset the pre-credit U.S. tax. Therefore, planning focuses on reducing these excess credits. In contrast, a dividend from a foreign corporation operating in a low-tax foreign jurisdiction results in a residual U.S. tax. In such situations, planning focuses on reducing that residual U.S. tax. For example, through cross-crediting, the excess credits on dividends from highly-taxed foreign subsidiaries can be used to soak up the residual U.S. tax due on dividends from lightly-taxed foreign subsidiaries. The look-through rule makes cross-crediting possible with respect to dividends from foreign corporations located in low- and high-tax foreign jurisdictions, as long as the underlying earnings of the foreign corporation are assigned to the same category of income limitation (e.g., the general limitation category).

> **Example 4.25:** USAco is a domestic corporation that owns 100% of both LOWco and HIGHco, two foreign corporations. At end of the current year, LOWco's and HIGHco's pools of undistributed earnings and profits and foreign income taxes are as follows:

	LOWco	HIGHco
Post-1986 undistributed E&P in general income limitation category	$8 million	$6 million
Post-1986 foreign income taxes in general income limitation category	$2 million	$9 million

Assume the U.S. tax rate is 35%, and that any dividends that LOWco or HIGHco distribute to USAco are not subject to foreign withholding taxes.

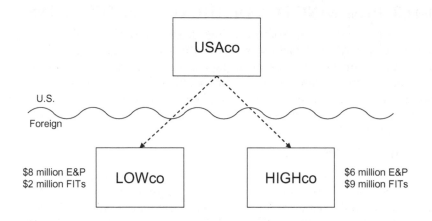

Case 1—Repatriate earnings from low-tax subsidiary: Assume LOWco distributes a $4 million dividend to USAco. The dividend would pull out $1 million of deemed paid taxes [$2 million of post-1986 foreign income taxes × ($4 million dividend ÷ $8 million of post-1986 undistributed earnings and profits)]. With the gross-up of $1 million, USAco would have dividend income of $5 million [$4 million dividend + $1 million gross-up]. Under the look-through rule, the entire amount of this dividend and the related foreign income taxes would be assigned to the general limitation category. Therefore, within USAco's general limitation, there would be a limitation of $1.75 million [35% U.S. rate × $5 million], deemed paid taxes of $1 million, and a residual U.S. tax of $750,000 [$1.75 million – $1 million].

Case 2—Repatriate earnings from both low- and high-tax subsidiaries: Every dollar of dividends from HIGHco increases the deemed paid taxes within USAco's general limitation by $1.50 [$9 million of post-1986 foreign income taxes × ($1 dividend ÷ $6 million of post-1986 undistributed earnings and profits)] and also increases USAco's general limitation by $0.875 [35% U.S. tax rate × ($1.00 dividend + $1.50 gross-up)]. The net effect is an excess credit of $0.625 for every dollar of dividends [$1.50 of additional deemed paid taxes – $0.875 of additional limitation]. Therefore, USAco can completely eliminate the $750,000 residual U.S. tax on LOWco's $4 million dividend by having HIGHco distribute a dividend of $1.2 million [$750,000 ÷ $0.625]. A $1.2 million dividend from HIGHco would pull out $1.8 million of deemed paid taxes [$9 million of post-1986 foreign income taxes × ($1.2 million dividend ÷ $6 million of post-1986 undistributed earnings and profits)] and increase USAco's general limitation by $1,050,000 [35% U.S. tax rate × ($1.2 million dividend + $1.8 million gross-up)], for an additional credit of $750,000 to eliminate the residual U.S. tax.

.02 Minimizing Foreign Withholding Taxes

Most foreign countries impose flat rate withholding taxes on the gross amount of dividends paid by a locally organized corporation to its U.S. shareholders. Foreign withholding taxes can exacerbate the excess credit problem created by dividends from foreign subsidiaries operating in high-tax foreign jurisdictions as the creditable foreign taxes include both the deemed paid taxes and the withholding taxes. However, tax treaties usually reduce the statutory withholding rate on dividends to 15% or less. Moreover, the treaty withholding rate often is lower for controlling shareholders (e.g., entities owning 10% or more of the payer's stock) than for noncontrolling shareholders. Therefore, a domestic corporation may be able to use tax treaties to reduce foreign withholding taxes by, for example, owning foreign operating subsidiaries through a foreign holding company located in a country with a favorable treaty network that contains lenient limitation of benefits articles.

.03 Alternatives to Dividend Repatriations

It may be advantageous for a domestic parent corporation to repatriate the earnings of a foreign subsidiary through interest, rental, and royalty payments and higher transfer prices, rather than dividend distributions. A foreign subsidiary usually can claim a tax deduction for interest, rents, and royalties paid to its domestic parent as well as for higher transfer prices, whereas dividend distributions typically are not deductible. On the other hand, only a dividend distribution can provide the domestic parent with a deemed paid credit. Nevertheless, if the foreign subsidiary is operating in a high-tax foreign jurisdiction, the benefits of a deduction at the foreign subsidiary level may exceed the costs of losing the deemed paid credit at the domestic parent level.

> *Example 4.26:* USAco, a domestic corporation, owns 100% of ASIAco, a foreign corporation. During its first year of operations, ASIAco's taxable income is $10 million and no deductible interest payments are made to USAco. Assume that the foreign income tax rate of 45% applies to the $10 million of income, the U.S. rate is 35%, and no foreign withholding taxes are imposed on any dividend distributions or interest payments that ASIAco makes to USAco.

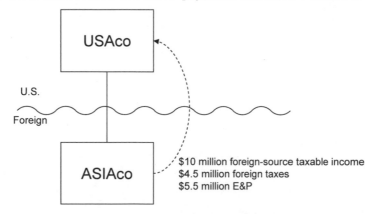

Case 1—Repatriate earnings through dividend: If USAco repatriated all of ASIAco's after-tax earnings through a dividend, the foreign tax on those earnings would be $4.5 million [$10 million of taxable income × 45% foreign tax rate]. USAco would receive a $5.5 million dividend distribution, which would pull out $4.5 million of deemed paid foreign taxes [$4.5 million of post-1986

¶413.03

foreign income taxes × ($5.5 million dividend ÷ $5.5 million of post-1986 earnings and profits)]. With the gross-up, USAco would have dividend income of $10 million [$5.5 million dividend + $4.5 million gross-up] and its pre-credit U.S. tax would be $3.5 million [$10 million × 35% U.S. tax rate]. There would be no residual U.S. tax due on the dividend income since USAco's deemed paid credits would offset the entire pre-credit U.S. tax. In sum, if USAco repatriates ASIAco's earnings through a dividend distribution, the total tax on those earnings would equal the foreign tax of $4.5 million.

Case 2—Repatriate earnings through interest payments: USAco may be able to reduce the total tax burden on ASIAco's earnings by repatriating those earnings through deductible interest payments, as opposed to dividend distributions. As an extreme example, if USAco financed ASIAco in a way that provided ASIAco with $10 million of deductible interest payments, that interest expense would reduce ASIAco's taxable income to $0. On the other hand, USAco would owe a $3.5 million U.S. tax on the interest payments it received from ASIAco [$10 million of interest income × 35% U.S. rate]. Nevertheless, the total tax on ASIAco's repatriated earnings would equal the U.S. tax of $3.5 million, which is $1 million less than the total tax if ASIAco's earnings are repatriated through a dividend distribution.

The tax implications of using debt financing for a foreign subsidiary are discussed in more detail in Chapter 8 (¶ 805).

¶ 414 APPENDIX

An S corporation is owned by Uncle Sam, a U.S. citizen who pays tax at a 35% U.S. rate. The S corporation earns $300,000 of worldwide gross profits, $150,000 of which is attributable to its U.S. sales. A sales branch office in foreign country F earns $150,000 of gross profits. All of the goods sold abroad (with title passing abroad) are manufactured at the S corporation's manufacturing facility in East Palo Alto, California. The foreign sales branch pays $40,000 of foreign taxes on December 31 of the year. The S corporation incurs $100,000 of expenses to be allocated and apportioned, $12,000 of which are itemized. Uncle Sam's pre-credit U.S. tax liability on the worldwide taxable income of $200,000 is $70,000. Under the 50-50 method, $75,000 of the gross profit on foreign sales is gross foreign-source income and, after an allocation and apportionment of expenses, Uncle Sam has only $50,000 of net foreign source income. Therefore, some of the foreign income taxes paid will not be creditable due to the foreign tax credit limitation. On his Form 1116, Uncle Sam will only be able to credit $17,500 of foreign income taxes paid. The remaining $22,500 of foreign income taxes paid constitutes an excess foreign tax credit that may be carried back or carried forward.

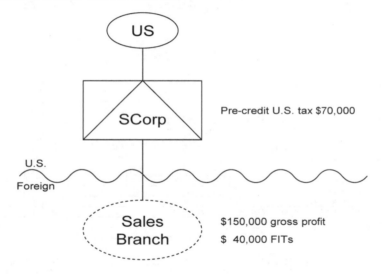

Form **1116**	**Foreign Tax Credit**	OMB No. 1545-0121
Department of the Treasury Internal Revenue Service (99)	**(Individual, Estate, or Trust)** ► Attach to Form 1040, 1040NR, 1041, or 990-T. ► See separate instructions.	**20**10 Attachment Sequence No. **19**

Name Uncle Sam	Identifying number as shown on page 1 of your tax return 123-45-6789

Use a separate Form 1116 for each category of income listed below. See **Categories of Income** in the instructions. Check only one box on each Form 1116. Report all amounts in U.S. dollars except where specified in Part II below.

a ☐ Passive category income   c ☐ Section 901(j) income   e ☐ Lump-sum distributions

b ☑ General category income   d ☐ Certain income re-sourced by treaty

f Resident of (name of country) ►

Note: *If you paid taxes to only one foreign country or U.S. possession, use column A in Part I and line A in Part II. If you paid taxes to* ***more than one*** *foreign country or U.S. possession, use a separate column and line for each country or possession.*

Part I **Taxable Income or Loss From Sources Outside the United States (for Category Checked Above)**

		Foreign Country or U.S. Possession				Total
		A	**B**	**C**		(Add cols. A, B, and C.)
g	Enter the name of the foreign country or U.S. possession . . . . ►	F				
1a	Gross income from sources within country shown above and of the type checked above (see instructions): _____					
	--					
	--	75,000			**1a**	75,000
b	Check if line 1a is compensation for personal services as an employee, your total compensation from all sources is $250,000 or more, and you used an alternative basis to determine its source (see instructions) . . ► ☐					
Deductions and losses (*Caution: See instructions*):						
2	Expenses **definitely related** to the income on line 1a (attach statement)					
3	Pro rata share of other deductions **not definitely related:**					
a	Certain itemized deductions or standard deduction (see instructions)	12,000				
b	Other deductions (attach statement)	88,000				
c	Add lines 3a and 3b	100,000				
d	Gross foreign source income (see instructions) .	75,000				
e	Gross income from all sources (see instructions) .	300,000				
f	Divide line 3d by line 3e (see instructions) . . .	.25				
g	Multiply line 3c by line 3f	25,000				
4	Pro rata share of interest expense (see instructions):					
a	Home mortgage interest (use worksheet on page 14 of the instructions)					
b	Other interest expense					
5	Losses from foreign sources					
6	Add lines 2, 3g, 4a, 4b, and 5	25,000			**6**	25,000
7	Subtract line 6 from line 1a. Enter the result here and on line 14, page 2 . . . . ►				**7**	50,000

Part II **Foreign Taxes Paid or Accrued** (see instructions)

Country	Credit is claimed for taxes (you must check one)		Foreign taxes paid or accrued								
	(h) ☑ Paid		In foreign currency				In U.S. dollars				
	(i) ☐ Accrued		Taxes withheld at source on:			(n) Other foreign taxes paid or accrued	Taxes withheld at source on:			(r) Other foreign taxes paid or accrued	(s) Total foreign taxes paid or accrued (add cols. (o) through (r))
	(j) Date paid or accrued		(k) Dividends	(l) Rents and royalties	(m) Interest		(o) Dividends	(p) Rents and royalties	(q) Interest		
A	12/31/10									40,000	40,000
B											
C											
8	Add lines A through C, column (s). Enter the total here and on line 9, page 2 . . . . ►								**8**		40,000

For Paperwork Reduction Act Notice, see instructions.   Cat. No. 11440U   Form **1116** (2010)

¶414

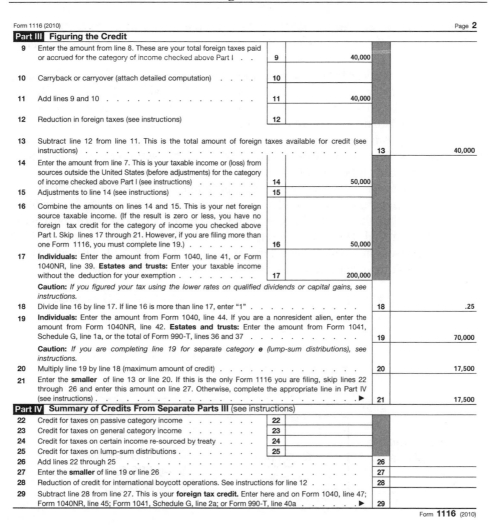

Part III Figuring the Credit

9 Enter the amount from line 8. These are your total foreign taxes paid or accrued for the category of income checked above Part I . . | **9** | 40,000

10 Carryback or carryover (attach detailed computation) . . . . | **10** |

11 Add lines 9 and 10 . . . . | **11** | 40,000

12 Reduction in foreign taxes (see instructions) | **12** |

13 Subtract line 12 from line 11. This is the total amount of foreign taxes available for credit (see instructions) . . . . | **13** | 40,000

14 Enter the amount from line 7. This is your taxable income or (loss) from sources outside the United States (before adjustments) for the category of income checked above Part I (see instructions) . . . . . . | **14** | 50,000

15 Adjustments to line 14 (see instructions) . . . . | **15** |

16 Combine the amounts on lines 14 and 15. This is your net foreign source taxable income. (If the result is zero or less, you have no foreign tax credit for the category of income you checked above Part I. Skip lines 17 through 21. However, if you are filing more than one Form 1116, you must complete line 19.) . . . . | **16** | 50,000

17 **Individuals:** Enter the amount from Form 1040, line 41, or Form 1040NR, line 39. **Estates and trusts:** Enter your taxable income without the deduction for your exemption . . . . | **17** | 200,000

Caution: If you figured your tax using the lower rates on qualified dividends or capital gains, see instructions.

18 Divide line 16 by line 17. If line 16 is more than line 17, enter "1" . . . . | **18** | .25

19 **Individuals:** Enter the amount from Form 1040, line 44. If you are a nonresident alien, enter the amount from Form 1040NR, line 42. **Estates and trusts:** Enter the amount from Form 1041, Schedule G, line 1a, or the total of Form 990-T, lines 36 and 37 . . . . | **19** | 70,000

*Caution: If you are completing line 19 for separate category **e** (lump-sum distributions), see instructions.*

20 Multiply line 19 by line 18 (maximum amount of credit) . . . . | **20** | 17,500

21 Enter the **smaller** of line 13 or line 20. If this is the only Form 1116 you are filing, skip lines 22 through 26 and enter this amount on line 27. Otherwise, complete the appropriate line in Part IV (see instructions) . . . . ▶ | **21** | 17,500

Part IV Summary of Credits From Separate Parts III (see instructions)

22 Credit for taxes on passive category income . . . . | **22** |

23 Credit for taxes on general category income . . . . | **23** |

24 Credit for taxes on certain income re-sourced by treaty . . . . | **24** |

25 Credit for taxes on lump-sum distributions . . . . | **25** |

26 Add lines 22 through 25 . . . . | **26** |

27 Enter the **smaller** of line 19 or line 26 . . . . | **27** |

28 Reduction of credit for international boycott operations. See instructions for line 12 . . . . . | **28** |

29 Subtract line 28 from line 27. This is your **foreign tax credit.** Enter here and on Form 1040, line 47; Form 1040NR, line 45; Form 1041, Schedule G, line 2a; or Form 990-T, line 40a . . . . . . ▶ | **29** |

Form **1116** (2010)

M&M Enterprises, Inc. (M&M), a U.S. C corporation, earns $200,000 of gross profit from U.S.-sources and owns a foreign subsidiary that operates a manufacturing/sales facility. The foreign subsidiary earns $100,000 on which $40,000 of foreign incomes taxes are paid. On December 31, the foreign subsidiary distributes a $30,000 dividend on which Country F imposes a 10% withholding tax of $3,000. M&M incurs $28,000 of expenses, $7,000 of which is apportioned to foreign-source income. The remaining $21,000 of expenses is apportioned to the $150,000 of gross income from operations in the United States. M&M will take two types of foreign tax credits—an "in lieu of" foreign tax credit for the withholding taxes and a "deemed paid" foreign tax credit for the foreign income taxes paid by the foreign subsidiary that come with the dividend repatriation. Only half of the $40,000 of accumulated foreign taxes paid by the foreign subsidiary comes with the dividend because only half of the accumulated earnings and profits of $60,000 are repatriated as a $30,000 dividend. Due to the foreign tax credit limitation, the Form 1118 for M&M Enterprises, Inc. will show a foreign tax credit of $15,229, with an excess foreign tax credit of $7,771 that may be carried back or carried forward.

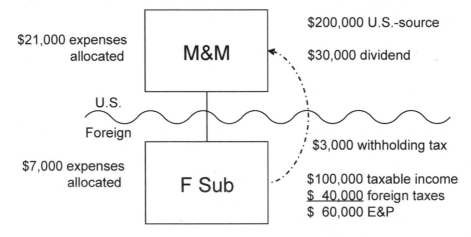

Form **1118**
(Rev. December 2009)
Department of the Treasury
Internal Revenue Service

Foreign Tax Credit—Corporations

▶See separate instructions.
▶ Attach to the corporation's tax return.

OMB No. 1545-0122

For calendar year 20 **10** , or other tax year beginning , 20 , and ending , 20 .

Name of corporation

M&M Enterprises, Inc.

Employer identification number

Use a **separate** Form 1118 for each applicable category of income listed below. See **Categories of Income** in the instructions. Also, see **Specific Instructions.**
Check only one box on each form.

☐ Passive Category Income
☐ General Category Income
☑ General Category Income

☐ Section 901(j) Income: Name of Sanctioned Country ▶
☐ Income Re-sourced by Treaty: Name of Country ▶

Schedule A   Income or (Loss) Before Adjustments *(Report all amounts in U.S. dollars. See **Specific Instructions**.)*

Gross Income or (Loss) From Sources Outside the United States (*INCLUDE* Foreign Branch Gross Income here *and* on Schedule F)

1. Foreign Country or U.S. Possession (Enter two-letter code; see instructions. Use a separate line for each.) *	2. Deemed Dividends (see instructions)		3. Other Dividends		4. Interest	5. Gross Rents, Royalties, and License Fees	6. Gross Income From Performance of Services	7. Other (attach schedule)	8. Total (add columns 2(a) through 7)
	(a) Exclude gross-up	(b) Gross-up (sec. 78)	(a) Exclude gross-up	(b) Gross-up (sec. 78)					
A F			30,000	20,000					50,000
B									
C									
D									
E									
F									
Totals (add lines A through F)									50,000

* For section 863(b) income, NOLs, income from RICs, and high-taxed income, use a single line (see instructions).

Deductions (*INCLUDE* Foreign Branch Deductions here *and* on Schedule F)

	9. Definitely Allocable Deductions					10. Apportioned Share of Deductions Not Definitely Allocable (enter amount from applicable line of Schedule H, Part II, column (d))	11. Net Operating Loss Deduction	12. Total Deductions (add columns 9(e) through 11)	13. Total Income or (Loss) Before Adjustments (subtract column 12 from column 8)
	Rental, Royalty, and Licensing Expenses		(c) Expenses Related to Gross Income From Performance of Services	(d) Other Definitely Allocable Deductions	(e) Total Definitely Allocable Deductions (add columns 9(a) through 9(d))				
	(a) Depreciation, Depletion, and Amortization	(b) Other Expenses							
A				7,000	7,000			7,000	43,000
B									
C									
D									
E									
F									
Totals									43,000

For Paperwork Reduction Act Notice, see separate instructions.

Cat. No. 10900F

Form **1118** (Rev. 12-2009)

¶414

Form 1118 (Rev. 12-2009)   Page **2**

Schedule B   Foreign Tax Credit (Report all foreign tax amounts in U.S. dollars.)

Part I—Foreign Taxes Paid, Accrued, and Deemed Paid (see instructions)

	1. Credit is Claimed for Taxes:		2. Foreign Taxes Paid or Accrued (attach schedule showing amounts in foreign currency and conversion rate(s) used)							3. Tax Deemed Paid (from Schedule C—
	☑ Paid ☐ Accrued		Tax Withheld at Source on:		Other Foreign Taxes Paid or Accrued on:				(h) Total Foreign Taxes Paid or Accrued (add columns 2(a) through 2(g))	Part I, column 10, Part II, column 8(b), and Part III, column 8)
	Date Paid	Date Accrued	(a) Dividends	(b) Interest	(c) Rents, Royalties, and License Fees	(d) Section 863(b) Income	(e) Foreign Branch Income	(f) Services Income	(g) Other	
A	12/31		3,000							3,000	20,000
B											
C											
D											
E											
F											
Totals (add lines A through F)			3,000							3,000	20,000

Part II—Separate Foreign Tax Credit (Complete a separate Part II for each applicable category of income.)

1	Total foreign taxes paid or accrued (total from Part I, column 2(h))	1	3,000
2	Total taxes deemed paid (total from Part I, column 3)	2	20,000
3	Reductions of taxes paid, accrued, or deemed paid (enter total from Schedule G)	3	( )
4	Taxes reclassified under high-tax kickout	4	
5	Enter the sum of any carryover of foreign taxes (from Schedule K, line 3, column (xiv)) plus any carrybacks to the current tax year	5	
6	Total foreign taxes (combine lines 1 through 5)	6	23,000
7	Enter the amount from the applicable column of Schedule J, Part I, line 11 (see instructions). If Schedule J is **not** required to be completed, enter the result from the "Totals" line of column 13 of the applicable Schedule A	7	43,000
8a	Total taxable income from all sources (enter taxable income from the corporation's tax return) .	8a	222,000
b	Adjustments to line 8a (see instructions)	8b	
c	Subtract line 8b from line 8a	8c	222,000
9	Divide line 7 by line 8c. Enter the resulting fraction as a decimal (see instructions). If line 7 is greater than line 8c, enter 1	9	.19
10	Total U.S. income tax against which credit is allowed (regular tax liability (see section 26(b)) minus American Samoa economic development credit) . .	10	80,150
11	Credit limitation (multiply line 9 by line 10) (see instructions)	11	15,229
12	**Separate foreign tax credit** (enter the smaller of line 6 or line 11 here and on the appropriate line of Part III)	12	15,229

Part III—Summary of Separate Credits (Enter amounts from Part II, line 12 for **each** applicable category of income. **Do not** include taxes paid to sanctioned countries.)

1	Credit for taxes on passive category income	1	
2	Credit for taxes on general category income	2	15,229
3	Credit for taxes on income re-sourced by treaty (combine all such credits on this line)	3	
4	Total (add lines 1 through 3)	4	
5	Reduction in credit for international boycott operations (see instructions)	5	
6	**Total foreign tax credit** (subtract line 5 from line 4). Enter here and on the appropriate line of the corporation's tax return	6	15,229

Form **1118** (Rev. 12-2009)

Form 1118 (Rev. 12-2009)   Page **3**

Schedule C   Tax Deemed Paid by Domestic Corporation Filing Return

*Use this schedule to figure the tax deemed paid by the corporation with respect to dividends from a first-tier foreign corporation under section 902(a), and deemed inclusions of earnings from a first- or lower-tier foreign corporation under section 960(a). **Report all amounts in U.S. dollars unless otherwise specified.***

Part I—Dividends and Deemed Inclusions From Post-1986 Undistributed Earnings

1. Name of Foreign Corporation (identify DISCs and former DISCs)	2. Tax Year End (Yr-Mo) (see instructions)	3. Country of Incorporation (enter country code from instructions)	4. Post-1986 Undistributed Earnings (in functional currency—attach schedule)	5. Opening Balance in Post-1986 Foreign Income Taxes	6. Foreign Taxes Paid and Deemed Paid for Tax Year Indicated		7. Post-1986 Foreign Income Taxes (add columns 5, 6(a), and 6(b))	8. Dividends and Deemed Inclusions		9. Divide Column 8(a) by Column 4	10. Tax Deemed Paid (multiply column 7 by column 9)
					(a) Taxes Paid	(b) Taxes Deemed Paid (from Schedule D, Part I—see instructions)		(a) Functional Currency	(b) U.S. Dollars		
Foreign Sub	12/31	F	60,000				40,000	40,000		30,000	.5	20,000
Total (Add amounts in column 10. Enter the result here and include on "Totals" line of Schedule B, Part I, column 3.) ▶											20,000

Part II—Dividends Paid Out of Pre-1987 Accumulated Profits

1. Name of Foreign Corporation (identify DISCs and former DISCs)	2. Tax Year End (Yr-Mo) (see instructions)	3. Country of Incorporation (enter country code from instructions)	4. Accumulated Profits for Tax Year Indicated (in functional currency computed under section 902) (attach schedule)	5. Foreign Taxes Paid and Deemed Paid on Earnings and Profits (E&P) for Tax Year Indicated (in functional currency) (see instructions)	6. Dividends Paid		7. Divide Column 6(a) by Column 4	8. Tax Deemed Paid (see instructions)	
					(a) Functional Currency	(b) U.S. Dollars		(a) Functional Currency	(b) U.S. Dollars
Total (Add amounts in column 8b. Enter the result here and include on "Totals" line of Schedule B, Part I, column 3.) ▶									

Part III—Deemed Inclusions From Pre-1987 Earnings and Profits

1. Name of Foreign Corporation (identify DISCs and former DISCs)	2. Tax Year End (Yr-Mo) (see instructions)	3. Country of Incorporation (enter country code from instructions)	4. E&P for Tax Year Indicated (in functional currency translated from U.S. dollars, computed under section 964) (attach schedule)	5. Foreign Taxes Paid and Deemed Paid for Tax Year Indicated (see instructions)	6. Deemed Inclusions		7. Divide Column 6(a) by Column 4	8. Tax Deemed Paid (multiply column 5 by column 7)
					(a) Functional Currency	(b) U.S. Dollars		
Total (Add amounts in column 8. Enter the result here and include on "Totals" line of Schedule B, Part I, column 3.) ▶								

Form **1118** (Rev. 12-2009)

¶414

Form 1118 (Rev. 12-2009)

Page **4**

| Schedule D | Tax Deemed Paid by First- and Second-Tier Foreign Corporations under Section 902(b) |

Use Part I to compute the tax deemed paid by a first-tier foreign corporation with respect to dividends from a second-tier foreign corporation. Use Part II to compute the tax deemed paid by a second-tier foreign corporation with respect to dividends from a third-tier foreign corporation. **Report all amounts in U.S. dollars unless otherwise specified.**

Part I—Tax Deemed Paid by First-Tier Foreign Corporations

Section A—Dividends Paid Out of Post-1986 Undistributed Earnings (Include the column 10 results in Schedule C, Part I, column 6(b).)

1. Name of Second-Tier Foreign Corporation and Its Related First-Tier Foreign Corporation	2. Tax Year End (Yr-Mo) (see instructions)	3. Country of Incorporation (enter country code from instructions)	4. Post-1986 Undistributed Earnings (in functional currency—attach schedule)	5. Opening Balance in Post-1986 Foreign Income Taxes	6. Foreign Taxes Paid and Deemed Paid for Tax Year Indicated		7. Post-1986 Foreign Income Taxes (add columns 5, 6(a), and 6(b))	8. Dividends Paid (in functional currency)		9. Divide Column 8(a) by Column 4	10. Tax Deemed Paid (multiply column 7 by column 9)
					(a) Taxes Paid	(b) Taxes Deemed Paid (see instructions)		(a) of Second-tier Corporation	(b) of First-tier Corporation		

Section B—Dividends Paid Out of Pre-1987 Accumulated Profits (Include the column 8(b) results in Schedule C, Part I, column 6(b).)

1. Name of Second-Tier Foreign Corporation and Its Related First-Tier Foreign Corporation	2. Tax Year End (Yr-Mo) (see instructions)	3. Country of Incorporation (enter country code from instructions)	4. Accumulated Profits for Tax Year Indicated (in functional currency—attach schedule)	5. Foreign Taxes Paid and Deemed Paid for Tax Year Indicated (in functional currency—see instructions)	6. Dividends Paid (in functional currency)		7. Divide Column 6(a) by Column 4	8. Tax Deemed Paid (see instructions)	
					(a) of Second-tier Corporation	(b) of First-tier Corporation		(a) Functional Currency of Second-tier Corporation	(b) U.S. Dollars

Part II—Tax Deemed Paid by Second-Tier Foreign Corporations

Section A—Dividends Paid Out of Post-1986 Undistributed Earnings (Include the column 10 results in Section A, column 6(b), of Part I above.)

1. Name of Third-Tier Foreign Corporation and Its Related Second-Tier Foreign Corporation	2. Tax Year End (Yr-Mo) (see instructions)	3. Country of Incorporation (enter country code from instructions)	4. Post-1986 Undistributed Earnings (in functional currency—attach schedule)	5. Opening Balance in Post-1986 Foreign Income Taxes	6. Foreign Taxes Paid and Deemed Paid for Tax Year Indicated		7. Post-1986 Foreign Income Taxes (add columns 5, 6(a), and 6(b))	8. Dividends Paid (in functional currency)		9. Divide Column 8(a) by Column 4	10. Tax Deemed Paid (multiply column 7 by column 9)
					(a) Taxes Paid	(b) Taxes Deemed Paid (from Schedule E, Part I, column 10)		(a) of Third-tier Corporation	(b) of Second-tier Corporation		

Section B—Dividends Paid Out of Pre-1987 Accumulated Profits (Include the column 8(b) results in Section A, column 6(b), of Part I above.)

1. Name of Third-Tier Foreign Corporation and Its Related Second-Tier Foreign Corporation	2. Tax Year End (Yr-Mo) (see instructions)	3. Country of Incorporation (enter country code from instructions)	4. Accumulated Profits for Tax Year Indicated (in functional currency—attach schedule)	5. Foreign Taxes Paid and Deemed Paid for Tax Year Indicated (in functional currency—see instructions)	6. Dividends Paid (in functional currency)		7. Divide Column 6(a) by Column 4	8. Tax Deemed Paid (see instructions)	
					(a) of Third-tier Corporation	(b) of Second-tier Corporation		(a) In Functional Currency of Third-tier Corporation	(b) U.S. Dollars

Form **1118** (Rev. 12-2009)

¶414

Form 1118 (Rev. 12-2009)   Page **5**

| Schedule E | Tax Deemed Paid by Certain Third-, Fourth-, and Fifth-Tier Foreign Corporations Under Section 902(b) |

Use this schedule to report taxes deemed paid with respect to dividends paid with respect to dividends from eligible post-1986 undistributed earnings of fourth-, fifth- and sixth-tier controlled foreign corporations. **Report all amounts in U.S. dollars unless otherwise specified.**

Part I—Tax Deemed Paid by Third-Tier Foreign Corporations (Include the column 10 results in Schedule D, Part II, Section A, column 6(b).)

| 1. Name of Fourth-Tier Foreign Corporation and Its Related Third-Tier Foreign Corporation | 2. Tax Year End (Yr-Mo) (see instructions) | 3. Country of Incorporation (enter country code from instructions) | 4. Post-1986 Undistributed Earnings (in functional currency—attach schedule) | 5. Opening Balance in Post-1986 Foreign Income Taxes | 6. Foreign Taxes Paid and Deemed Paid for Tax Year Indicated | | 7. Post-1986 Foreign Income Taxes (add columns 5, 6(a), and 6(b)) | 8. Dividends Paid (in functional currency) | | 9. Divide Column 8(a) by Column 4 | 10. Tax Deemed Paid (multiply column 7 by column 9) |
					(a) Taxes Paid	(b) Taxes Deemed Paid (from Part II, column 10)		(a) Of Fourth-tier CFC	(b) Of Third-tier CFC		

Part II—Tax Deemed Paid by Fourth-Tier Foreign Corporations (Include the column 10 results in column 6(b) of Part I above.)

| 1. Name of Fifth-Tier Foreign Corporation and Its Related Fourth-Tier Foreign Corporation | 2. Tax Year End (Yr-Mo) (see instructions) | 3. Country of Incorporation (enter country code from instructions) | 4. Post-1986 Undistributed Earnings (in functional currency—attach schedule) | 5. Opening Balance in Post-1986 Foreign Income Taxes | 6. Foreign Taxes Paid and Deemed Paid for Tax Year Indicated | | 7. Post-1986 Foreign Income Taxes (add columns 5, 6(a), and 6(b)) | 8. Dividends Paid (in functional currency) | | 9. Divide Column 8(a) by Column 4 | 10. Tax Deemed Paid (multiply column 7 by column 9) |
					(a) Taxes Paid	(b) Taxes Deemed Paid (from Part III, column 10)		(a) Of Fifth-tier CFC	(b) Of Fourth-tier CFC		

Part III—Tax Deemed Paid by Fifth-Tier Foreign Corporations (Include the column 10 results in column 6(b) of Part II above.)

| 1. Name of Sixth-Tier Foreign Corporation and Its Related Fifth-Tier Foreign Corporation | 2. Tax Year End (Yr-Mo) (see instructions) | 3. Country of Incorporation (enter country code from instructions) | 4. Post-1986 Undistributed Earnings (in functional currency—attach schedule) | 5. Opening Balance in Post-1986 Foreign Income Taxes | 6. Foreign Taxes Paid For Tax Year Indicated | 7. Post-1986 Foreign Income Taxes (add columns 5 and 6) | 8. Dividends Paid (in functional currency) | | 9. Divide Column 8(a) by Column 4 | 10. Tax Deemed Paid (multiply column 7 by column 9) |
							(a) Of Sixth-tier CFC	(b) Of Fifth-tier CFC		

Form **1118** (Rev. 12-2009)

¶414

Form 1118 (Rev. 12-2009)

Page **6**

Schedule F — Gross Income and Definitely Allocable Deductions for Foreign Branches

1. Foreign Country or U.S. Possession (Enter two-letter code from Schedule A, column 1. Use a separate line for each.)	2. Gross Income	3. Definitely Allocable Deductions
A		
B		
C		
D		
E		
F		
Totals (add lines A through F)* ▲		

Note: The Schedule F totals are not carried over to any other Form 1118 Schedule. (These totals were already included in Schedule A.) However, the IRS requires the corporation to complete Schedule F under the authority of section 905(b).

Schedule G — Reductions of Taxes Paid, Accrued, or Deemed Paid

A	Reduction of Taxes Under Section 901(e)—Attach separate schedule
B	Reduction of Foreign Oil and Gas Taxes—Enter amount from Schedule I, Part II, line 6
C	Reduction of Taxes Due to International Boycott Provisions— Enter appropriate portion of Schedule C (Form 5713), line 2b. **Important:** Enter only "specifically attributable taxes" here.
D	Reduction of Taxes for Section 6038(c) Penalty— Attach separate schedule
E	Other Reductions of Taxes—Attach schedule(s)
Total (add lines A through E). Enter here and on Schedule B, Part II, line 3 . . . . ▲	

Form **1118** (Rev. 12-2009)

¶414

Form 1118 (Rev. 12-2009)

Page **7**

Schedule H — Apportionment of Deductions Not Definitely Allocable *(complete only once)*

Part I—Research and Development Deductions

	(a) Sales Method					(b) Gross Income Method—Check method used: Option 1 ☐ Option 2 ☐ (See instructions.)		(c) Total R&D Deductions Not Definitely Allocable (enter all amounts from column (a)(v) or all amounts from column (b)(vii))
	Product line #1 (SIC Code:) *		Product line #2 (SIC Code:) *		(v) Total R&D Deductions Under Sales Method (add columns (ii) and (iv))	(vi) Gross Income	(vii) Total R&D Deductions Under Gross Income Method	
	(i) Gross Sales	(ii) R&D Deductions	(iii) Gross Sales	(iv) R&D Deductions				
1 Totals (see instructions)								
2 Total to be apportioned								
3 Apportionment among statutory groupings:								
a General category income								
b Passive category income								
c Section 901(j) income*								
d Income re-sourced by treaty*								
4 Total foreign (add lines 3a through 3d)								

* Important: See *Computer-Generated Schedule H* in instructions.

Form **1118** (Rev. 12-2009)

¶414

Form 1118 (Rev. 12-2009)   Page **8**

Schedule H   **Apportionment of Deductions Not Definitely Allocable** *(continued)*

Part II—Interest Deductions, All Other Deductions, and Total Deductions

(a) Average Value of Assets — Check method used: ☐ Fair market value   ☐ Tax book value   ☐ Alternative tax book value

	(a) (i) Nonfinancial Corporations	(a) (ii) Financial Corporations	(b) Interest Deductions (iii) Nonfinancial Corporations	(b) Interest Deductions (iv) Financial Corporations	(c) All Other Deductions Not Definitely Allocable	(d) Totals (add the corresponding amounts from column (c), Part I; columns (b)(iii) and (b)(iv), Part II; and column (c), Part II). Enter each amount from lines 3a through 3d below in column 10 of the corresponding Schedule A.
1a Totals (see instructions)					28,000	
b Amounts specifically allocable under Temp. Regs. 1.861-10T(e)						
c Other specific allocations under Temp. Regs. 1.861-10T						
d Assets excluded from apportionment formula						
2 Total to be apportioned (subtract the sum of lines 1b, 1c, and 1d from line 1a)						
3 Apportionment among statutory groupings:						
a General category income					7,000	7,000
b Passive category income						
c Section 901(j) income*						
d Income re-sourced by treaty*						
4 Total foreign (add lines 3a through 3d)					7,000	7,000

*Important: See **Computer-Generated Schedule H** in instructions.

Form **1118** (Rev. 12-2009)

Chapter 5
Anti-Deferral Provisions

¶ 501 SUBPART F

.01 Background

The United States generally does not tax foreign business profits earned through a foreign subsidiary until the subsidiary repatriates those earnings through a dividend. This policy, known as "deferral," allows U.S. companies to compete in foreign markets on a tax parity with their foreign competitors. In addition to promoting the competitiveness of U.S. companies abroad, however, deferral also creates an opportunity for avoiding U.S. taxes on passive investment income, inventory trading profits and other income that can be easily shifted to a foreign base company. Various foreign countries, such as the Cayman Islands, Hong Kong, Ireland, and Singapore, offer tax holidays or low tax rates to attract foreign investment. A U.S. multinational can shift income to a base company organized in these tax-haven countries by, for example, selling goods to the base company at an artificially low price. The base company can then resell the goods at a higher price to a sales subsidiary located in the same country as the ultimate foreign customers. The spread between the two transfer prices shifts the profit on the export sale from the countries in which manufacturing and marketing actually take place to a tax-haven country.

> ***Example 5.1:*** USAco is a domestic corporation that manufactures electric generators for sale both in the United States and Germany. German sales are made through GERco, a wholly owned German sales subsidiary. USAco's generators cost $600 to manufacture and $100 to market, and they sell for $1,000 in Germany. Therefore, the combined income from a German sale is $300 per generator [$1,000 final sales price − $600 manufacturing cost − $100 selling expense]. USAco also has a wholly owned Cayman Island subsidiary, CAYco, which performs no significant functions with respect to the manufacture or sale of USAco's generators. Assume that the U.S. tax rate is 35%, that the German rate is 30%, and that the Cayman Islands does not have a corporate income tax.

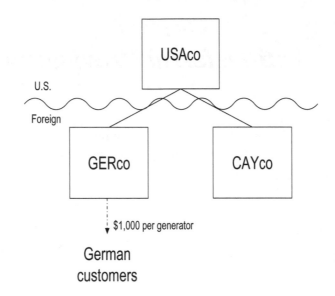

German
customers

Case 1—Do not route sale through base company: If a German sale is not routed through CAYco and the transfer price used for USAco's sale to GERco is, for example, $800, the $300 of profits will be allocated as follows:

Transaction	Effect on USAco	Effect on CAYco	Effect on GERco
Manufacture good	Cost of sales = $600		
Intercompany sale	Sales = $800		Cost of sales = $800
Selling activities			Expense = $100
Final sale			Sales = $1,000
	Net profit = $200	Net profit = $0	Net profit = $100

The total tax on the $300 profit equals $100 [($200 × 35% U.S. tax rate) + ($100 × 30% German tax rate)], which results in an overall effective tax rate of 33.3% ($100/$300).

Case 2—Route sale through base company: Now assume that the German sale is routed through CAYco, a $700 transfer price is used for USAco's sale to CAYco, and an $800 transfer price is used for CAYco's sale to GERco. The $300 of profits is now allocated as follows:

Transaction	Effect on USAco	Effect on CAYco	Effect on GERco
Manufacture good	Cost of sales = $600		
Intercompany sale	Sales = $700	Cost of sales = $700	
Intercompany sale		Sales = $800	Cost of sales = $800
Selling activities			Expense = $100
Final sale			Sales = $1,000
	Net profit = $100	Net profit = $100	Net profit = $100

The total tax on the $300 profit now equals $65 [($100 × 35% U.S. tax rate) + ($100 × 0% Cayman Island tax rate) + ($100 × 30% German tax rate)], which results in an overall effective tax rate of 21.7% ($65/$300). Therefore, ignoring Code Sec. 482 and Subpart F, USAco can reduce the total tax burden on its German sales by routing those sales through a Cayman Island base company.

One tool that the IRS can use against this planning is Code Sec. 482, which gives the IRS the authority to allocate income among domestic and foreign affiliates whenever an allocation is necessary to clearly reflect the income of each party. Historically, the arm's-length standard of Code Sec. 482 has proven difficult to administer, however, due to a lack of information regarding comparable uncontrolled transactions. As a result, in 1962 Congress enacted Subpart F, which automatically denies deferral to certain types of tainted income earned through a foreign corporation.[1]

.02 Subpart F Overview

If a foreign corporation is a controlled foreign corporation (or CFC) for an uninterrupted period of 30 days or more during the taxable year, every person who was a U.S. shareholder of the CFC at any time during the taxable year and who owns stock in such corporation on the last day of the CFC's taxable year must include in gross income its pro rata share of:

    (i) Subpart F income, and

    (ii) Investment of earnings in U.S. property.[2]

A U.S. shareholder's pro rata share is the amount that the shareholder would have received if, on the last day of its taxable year, the CFC had actually distributed

---

[1] The term "Subpart F" refers to the part of the Internal Revenue Code where the applicable statutes, i.e., Code Secs. 951–965, are found.

[2] Code Sec. 951(a)(1). Two other less common types of Subpart F inclusions are (i) previously excluded Subpart F income withdrawn from investments in less developed countries (see Code Sec. 955 as in effect prior to the enactment of the Tax Reduction Act of 1975 (P.L. 94-12)) and (ii) previously excluded Subpart F income withdrawn from foreign base company shipping operations (see Code Sec. 955).

pro rata to all of its shareholders a dividend equal to the Subpart F inclusion.[3] For this purpose, both direct ownership of the CFC's stock and indirect ownership through foreign entities (but not constructive ownership) are considered.[4]

   Example 5.2: USAco, a domestic corporation, owns 100% of the stock of FORco, a foreign corporation. During the current year, FORco derives $10 million of Subpart F income in the form of passive interest income, pays $1 million in foreign income taxes (for an effective foreign rate of 10%), and distributes no dividends. USAco is not allowed to defer the residual U.S. tax due on FORco's earnings. Instead, USAco must recognize a Subpart F inclusion income equal to FORco's $9 million of net Subpart F income.

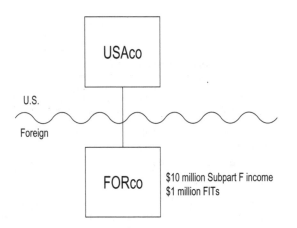

   Consistent with the notion that a Subpart F inclusion is a deemed dividend, a domestic corporation reports a Subpart F inclusion as "Dividends" on Line 4 of Form 1120 (see Schedule C, Line 14). In the case of U.S. shareholders who are U.S. citizens or resident aliens, Subpart F inclusions do not qualify for the reduced rate of tax on qualified dividend income under Code Sec. 1(h).[5]

.03 Definition of a Controlled Foreign Corporation

   Subpart F applies only to a foreign corporation that qualifies as a controlled foreign corporation, or CFC. The determination of whether a business entity is considered a "corporation" is determined under the U.S. check-the-box regulations.[6] A corporation is a "foreign corporation" if it is created or organized outside the United States.[7]

   A foreign corporation is a CFC if, on any day during the foreign corporation's taxable year, U.S. shareholders own more than 50% of the combined voting power of all classes of stock, or more than 50% of the total value, of the foreign corporation.[8] Only U.S. shareholders are considered in applying the 50% test. A U.S.

---

[3] Code Sec. 951(a)(2). The shareholder's pro rata amount may be reduced if the foreign corporation was a CFC for only part of the year or if the U.S. shareholder acquired the CFC's stock during the year.

[4] Code Sec. 958(a).

[5] Notice 2004-70, IRB 2004-44.

[6] Reg. §§ 301.7701-1 to 3.

[7] Code Secs. 7701(a)(4) and (a)(5).

[8] Code Sec. 957(a). The taxable year of a CFC generally must conform to that of its majority U.S. shareholder. Code Sec. 898.

shareholder is defined under Subpart F as any U.S. person owning at least 10% of the total combined voting power of all classes of voting stock of the foreign corporation.[9] All forms of ownership, including direct ownership, indirect or beneficial ownership through intervening foreign entities, and constructive ownership (i.e., attribution of ownership from one related party to another), are taken into account in applying both the 10% ownership test for U.S. shareholder status and the more than 50% ownership test for CFC status.[10] Obviously, a foreign subsidiary that is 100%-owned by a U.S. parent is a CFC. However, determining a foreign corporation's CFC status can be complex and the results may be unexpected.

    ***Example* 5.3:** USAco, a domestic corporation, owns 50% of the stock of F1, a foreign corporation. Unrelated foreign persons own the remaining 50% of F1. USAco also owns 10% of the stock of F2, a foreign corporation. F1 owns 51% of F2, and unrelated foreign persons own the remaining 39%. F1 is not a CFC because USAco, F1's only U.S. shareholder, does not own more than 50% of the stock. USAco also is a U.S. shareholder of F2 because it owns 10% of F2 directly. Under the constructive ownership rules, F1 is treated as constructively owning 100% of F2 because F1 owns more than 50% of F2.[11] Therefore, USAco is treated as owning 60% of F2, 10% directly and 50% through F1 [50% of 100%]. As a consequence, F2 is a CFC.

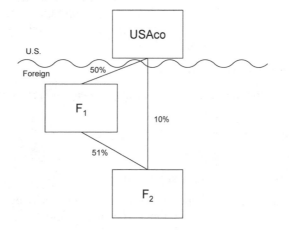

    ***Example* 5.4:** One hundred unrelated U.S. citizens each own 1% of FORco, a foreign corporation. Although FORco is 100%-owned by U.S. persons, none of them satisfies the 10% ownership test for U.S. shareholder status. Thus, FORco is not a CFC.

---

[9] Code Sec. 951(b).
[10] Code Sec. 958.

[11] Code Secs. 318 and 958(b)(2).

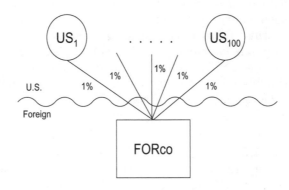

In theory, it is possible to avoid CFC status by spreading ownership of a foreign corporation among 11 U.S. persons, each owning only 9.09% of the company. However, because direct, indirect, and constructive ownership are considered in applying the 10% shareholder test,[12] the 11 U.S. persons would have to be unrelated to one another, by both family and business connections, in order to avoid U.S. shareholder status. In addition, even if the ownership of a foreign corporation can be structured so as to avoid CFC status, the foreign corporation may still qualify as a passive foreign investment company (see ¶ 502). Therefore, planning designed to take advantage of the deferral privilege requires a careful analysis of all of the anti-deferral provisions.

.04 Subpart F Income—Overview

Subpart F income includes the following five categories of income derived by a CFC:[13]

(i) Insurance income,

(ii) Foreign base company income,

(iii) A portion of international boycott income,[14]

(iv) The sum of any illegal bribes or kickbacks paid by or on behalf of the CFC to a government employee or official, and

(v) Income derived from certain disfavored foreign countries.[15]

The amount of a CFC's Subpart F income for any taxable year cannot exceed the CFC's current-year earnings and profits before any reductions for current-year dividend distributions.[16] Insurance income and foreign base company income,

---

[12] Code Sec. 958.

[13] Code Sec. 952(a).

[14] International boycott income is determined under Code Sec. 999. Countries which may require participation in or cooperation with an international boycott include Kuwait, Lebanon, Libya, Qatar, Saudi Arabia, Syria, United Arab Emirates, and the Republic of Yemen. Boycott Notice, (April 2, 2007).

[15] These include foreign countries whose governments the United States does not recognize, does not conduct

diplomatic relations with, or has designated as a government which repeatedly supports acts of international terrorism. Code Sec. 901(j). Countries to which this provision has applied in the past or present include Cuba, Iran, North Korea, Sudan, and Syria. Rev. Rul. 2005-3, IRB 2005-3.

[16] Code Sec. 952(c)(1)(A) and Reg. §1.952-1(c)(1). Under certain conditions, prior-year deficits also can be used to reduce the amount of Subpart F income. Code Sec. 952(c)(1)(B) and (C).

¶501.04

which are the two most prevalent types of Subpart F income, are discussed in detail below.

.05 Insurance Income

Premiums and other income from insurance activities represent the type of portable income that can be readily shifted to a foreign corporation in order to avoid U.S. taxation. Prior to the enactment of Subpart F, a domestic corporation could exploit the portability of insurance income by establishing an offshore insurance company. For example, a U.S. insurance company that had issued policies insuring U.S. risks (e.g., a casualty policy on a U.S. office building) might form a subsidiary in a low-tax jurisdiction and reinsure that U.S. risk with that foreign subsidiary. Assuming there was a bona fide shifting and distribution of risks, the U.S. parent could deduct the premiums paid to the subsidiary against its U.S. taxable income. In addition, assuming the foreign subsidiary had no office or other taxable presence in the United States, the premium income was not subject to U.S. taxation. The net effect was the avoidance of U.S. taxes on the premium income routed through the foreign subsidiary.

To negate the tax benefits of such arrangements, Subpart F income includes any income attributable to issuing or reinsuring any insurance or annuity contract in connection with a risk located outside the CFC's country of incorporation. The location of a risk is determined by where the insured property or activity is located or by where the insured individual resides.[17] Income from insuring risks located within the CFC's country of incorporation also qualifies as Subpart F income if, as a result of an arrangement, another corporation receives a substantially equal amount of premiums for insuring risks located outside the CFC's country of incorporation.[18] The taxable amount of insurance income equals the gross amount of such income, less any deductions properly allocable to such income.[19]

More stringent rules apply to related-person insurance income. Related-person insurance income includes any income attributable to issuing or reinsuring any insurance or annuity contract that directly or indirectly covers a U.S. shareholder or a person related to a U.S. shareholder.[20] For insurance income purposes only, a U.S. shareholder is defined as any U.S. person who owns any stock of the foreign corporation and a CFC is defined as any foreign corporation that is 25% or more owned by such U.S. shareholders.[21] Under this rule, any U.S. person who owns stock of such a CFC is taxed on his or her pro rata share of related-person insurance income.[22]

.06 Foreign Base Company Income

Subpart F income also includes foreign base company income, which consists of the following four categories of income derived by a CFC:

  (i) Foreign personal holding company income,

---

[17] Code Sec. 953(a)(1)(A).
[18] Code Sec. 953(a)(1)(B).
[19] Code Sec. 953(b)(3).
[20] Code Sec. 953(c)(2).

[21] Code Sec. 953(c)(1).
[22] Code Sec. 953(c)(1)(C). Code Sec. 953(c)(3) provides several exceptions to the related-person insurance rules.

    (ii) Foreign base company sales income,

    (iii) Foreign base company services income, and

    (iv) Foreign base company oil-related income.[23]

The taxable amount of foreign base company income equals the gross amount of such income, less any deductions (including foreign income taxes) properly allocable to such income.[24]

    Foreign personal holding company income. Under the general rules, foreign personal holding company income primarily includes:

    (i) Dividends, interest, royalties, rents, and annuities,

    (ii) Net gains from the disposition of property that produces dividend, interest, rent, and royalty income (except for net gains from certain dealer sales and inventory sales), and

    (iii) Net gains from commodity and foreign currency transactions (excluding net gains from active business and hedging transactions).[25]

Numerous special rules exclude selected types of dividend, interest, rent and royalty income from foreign personal holding company income, including:

    (i) Rents and royalties derived from the active conduct of a trade or business and received from an unrelated person.[26]

    (ii) Export financing interest derived in the active conduct of a banking business.[27]

    (iii) Dividends and interest received from related parties incorporated in the same country as the CFC.[28]

    (iv) Rents and royalties received from related parties for the use of property in the CFC's country of incorporation.[29]

    (v) Income derived from the active conduct of a banking, financing, insurance or similar business (temporary exception for tax years of a CFC beginning after 1998 and before 2012).[30]

    (vi) Dividends, interest, rents, and royalties received from a related CFC, provided the payments are attributable to income of the related CFC which is neither Subpart F income nor income that is effectively connected with a U.S. trade or business (temporary exception for tax years of a CFC beginning after 2005 and before 2012). Under this exception, cross-border payments between related CFCs do not constitute Subpart F income as long as the payments are attributable to active foreign business income.[31]

---

[23] Code Sec. 954(a).

[24] Code Sec. 954(b)(5).

[25] Code Sec. 954(c)(1). *See* Reg. § 1.954-2(g)(2) regarding the excludable commodity and foreign currency transactions.

[26] Code Sec. 954(c)(2)(A).

[27] Code Sec. 954(c)(2)(B).

[28] Code Sec. 954(c)(3)(A)(i).

[29] Code Sec. 954(c)(3)(A)(ii).

[30] Code Sec. 954(h) and (i).

[31] Code Sec. 954(c)(6).

Foreign base company sales income. Foreign base company sales income includes any gross profit, commissions, fees, or other income derived from the sale of personal property which meets the following requirements:

(i) The CFC purchases the property from or sells the property to a related person;

(ii) The property is manufactured, produced, grown, or extracted outside the CFC's country of incorporation;

(iii) The property is not manufactured, produced, or constructed by the CFC; and

(iv) The property is sold for use, consumption, or disposition outside the CFC's country of incorporation.[32]

The definition of foreign base company sales income is based on the premise that if a good is neither manufactured nor sold for use in the CFC's country of incorporation, then the CFC may not be a bona-fide manufacturing or sales subsidiary, but rather a base company organized primarily to avoid tax.

Example 5.5: USAco, a domestic corporation, manufactures consumer goods for sale both in the United States and Norway. Norwegian sales are made through NORco, a wholly owned Norwegian marketing subsidiary. USAco also has a wholly owned Belgian subsidiary, BELco, which performs no real functions with respect to the manufacture or sale of USAco's products. The gross profit realized by NORco on the resale of goods to Norwegian customers is not foreign base company sales income because the goods are sold for use in NORco's country of incorporation. In contrast, if a sale to a Norwegian customer is made by BELco, the gross profit realized by BELco is foreign base company sales income because the good was neither manufactured nor sold for use in Belgium.

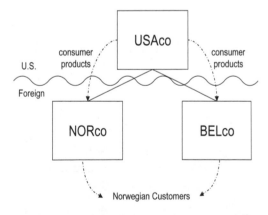

The regulations effectively provide four independent tests for determining whether a CFC manufactured or produced a good, including: (i) a substantial transformation test, (ii) generally considered manufacturing test, (iii) a safe-harbor

---

[32] Code Sec. 954(d)(1); Reg. § 1.954-3(a)(4)(i).

test, and (iv) a substantial contribution test. A CFC needs to satisfy only one of these tests to avoid the foreign base company sales income taint.

A CFC is considered to have manufactured a good if it substantially transforms the goods. Examples of substantial transformation include converting wood pulp to paper, steel rods to screws and bolts, and fresh fish to canned fish. Whether or not the substantial transformation test is met depends on the facts and circumstances of each case.[33]

Manufacturing also occurs if a CFC purchases component parts and its activities in the assembly or conversion of the component parts into the final product are substantial in nature and generally considered to constitute manufacturing, based on the facts and circumstances.[34]

Under the safe-harbor test, manufacturing is deemed to occur if the CFC's conversion costs (i.e., direct labor and factory burden) account for 20% or more of the total cost of the goods sold. In no case, however, is mere packaging, repackaging, labeling, or minor assembly considered manufacturing.[35]

> ***Example 5.6:*** USAco, a domestic corporation, owns 100% of the stock of CANco, a Canadian corporation. CANco sells industrial engines for use outside of its country of incorporation. CANco performs some machining and assembly operations with respect to the engines it sells, but purchases the component parts for these engines from related and unrelated suppliers. On a per-engine basis, CANco's direct material costs are $30,000 and its conversion costs (direct labor and factory burden) are $10,000. Although it is unclear whether CANco meets either the substantial transformation test or the generally considered manufacturing test, it does meet the safe-harbor test because conversion costs are 25% of the total costs of goods sold [$10,000 ÷ ($10,000 + $30,000)]. As a result, CANco's gross profit from the sale of engines is not foreign base company sales income.[36]

---

[33] Reg. § 1.954-3(a)(4)(ii).
[34] Reg. § 1.954-3(a)(4)(iii).
[35] Reg. § 1.954-3(a)(4)(iii).
[36] Compare Reg. § 1.954-3(a)(4)(iii), Example (1).

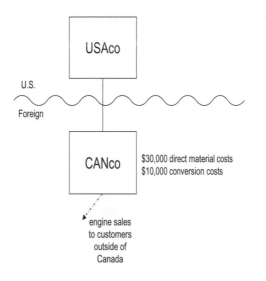

Finally, the substantial contribution test treats a CFC as a manufacturer of goods if, based on the facts and circumstances, the CFC substantially contributed to the manufacturing process, even if the CFC did not physically manufacture the goods. The following non-exclusive list provides various activities to consider when determining whether the CFC has substantially contributed to the manufacturing process:[37]

- oversight and direction of manufacturing activities;
- material and vendor selection; control of raw materials;
- management of manufacturing costs or capacities;
- control of manufacturing-related logistics;
- quality control; and
- development of intellectual property.

Branch rule. A potential loophole arises if a CFC's country of incorporation does not tax income derived from sources outside its borders (i.e., employs a territorial system). In such countries, the foreign base company sales income taint could be avoided by having a CFC sell goods through a sales branch located in a low-tax country, because there would be no related-party sale between the CFC and its sales branch. A similar tax result could be obtained if a CFC manufactures its goods in another foreign country through a branch rather than a subsidiary.

The so-called branch rule closes this potential loophole by treating a branch as if it were a subsidiary of the CFC if the activities of the branch have substantially the same effect as a subsidiary.[38] This requirement is met if there is a substantial tax rate disparity between the country in which the branch is located and the CFC's country of incorporation.[39] In the case of a sales branch, this is defined as an

---

[37] Reg. § 1.954-3(a)(iv)(b).
[38] Code Sec. 954(d)(2).

[39] Reg. § 1.954-3(b). The determination of what constitutes a foreign branch is an unsettled issue. In *Ashland Oil, Inc.*, 95 TC 348 (1990), the Tax Court ruled that an

¶501.06

effective tax rate that is less than 90% of, and at least 5 percentage points less than, the effective rate of tax in the CFC's country of incorporation.[40] For example, assume the tax rate in the CFC's country of incorporation is 30%, and the CFC establishes a sales branch in a country that has a 10% tax rate. The tax rate disparity test is met because 10% is less than 90% of 30%, and 10% is also at least 5 percentage points less than 30%. Therefore, the sales branch is treated as a subsidiary of the CFC, and the income from sales made through the branch may qualify as foreign base company sales income.

Foreign base company services income. Foreign base company services income includes any compensation, commissions, fees, or other income derived from the performance of technical, managerial, engineering, architectural, scientific, skilled, industrial, commercial, and like services, where the CFC performs the services for or on behalf of a related person and the services are performed outside the CFC's country of incorporation.[41] This provision denies deferral to a foreign service subsidiary that is separated from its manufacturing and sales affiliates and that is organized in another country.

Example **5.7:** USAco, a domestic corporation, owns 100% of GERco, a German corporation. USAco is in the business of manufacturing drill presses for industrial use. During the year, USAco sells drill presses to both French and German customers. A condition of these sales is that USAco will install and provide maintenance services with respect to the drill presses. GERco performs these services on USAco's behalf in both France and Germany. The fees that GERco receives for services performed in Germany are not foreign base company services income. In contrast, the fees that GERco receives for services performed in France are foreign base company services income.

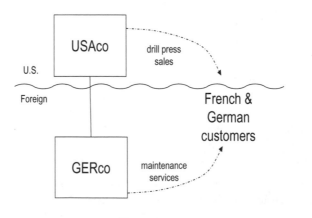

(Footnote Continued)

unrelated contract manufacturer of a CFC was not a branch.

[40] Reg. § 1.954-3(b)(1)(ii)(B).

[41] Code Sec. 954(e)(1). An exception applies to services which are directly related to the sale of property which was manufactured, produced, grown, or extracted by the CFC, and the services are performed before the time of the sale. Code Sec. 954(e)(2).

Foreign base company oil-related income. Foreign base company oil-related income includes foreign-source income derived from refining, processing, transporting, distributing, or selling oil and gas or primary products derived from oil and gas. However, it does not include oil-related income derived from sources within a foreign country in which such oil or gas is either extracted or used. Under a look-through rule, foreign base company oil-related income also includes dividends and interest derived from a 10%-or-more-owned foreign corporation to the extent such dividends or interest are attributable to foreign base company oil-related income.[42]

.07 Special Exclusions and Inclusions

There are several exceptions to the general rules for computing Subpart F income. First, if any part of a CFC's Subpart F income is U.S.-source income that is effectively connected to the conduct of a U.S. trade or business, such income is excluded from Subpart F income. There is no reason to tax effectively connected income to the U.S. shareholder because, under Code Sec. 882(a), it is already subject to U.S. taxation at the regular graduated rates at the CFC level. This exception does not apply, however, to any effectively connected income that is exempt from U.S. taxation or that is subject to a reduced rate of tax by reason of a tax treaty.[43]

The second exception is a *de minimis* rule, under which no part of a CFC's income is treated as insurance or foreign base company income if the sum of the CFC's gross insurance and gross foreign base company income for the taxable year (before taking into account any deductions) is less than both $1 million and 5% of the CFC's total gross income for the year.[44]

> **Example 5.8:** During the current year, ASIAco (a CFC) has gross income of $30 million, including $800,000 of interest income and $29.2 million of gross income from the sale of inventory that ASIAco manufactured at a factory located within its country of incorporation. Under the general rules, the $800,000 of interest income would be treated as foreign base company income because the interest is foreign personal holding company income. Under the *de minimis* rule, however, none of ASIAco's income is foreign base company income because $800,000 is less than both $1 million and 5% of ASIAco's gross income or $1.5 million (5% × $30 million).

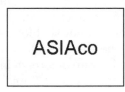

$800,000 of interest income

$29.2 million of gross income
from sales of inventory

---

[42] Code Secs. 954(g)(1) and 907(c)(2) and (3). An exception applies to foreign corporations which are not "large oil producers," as defined in Code Sec. 954(g)(2).

[43] Code Sec. 952(b) and Reg. § 1.952-1(b)(2).

[44] Code Sec. 954(b)(3)(A). This exception also does not apply to any U.S.-source portfolio interest derived by a CFC from an unrelated U.S. person. Code Sec. 881(c)(5)(A)(i).

The third exception is a full inclusion rule, under which all of a CFC's gross income is treated as Subpart F income if the sum of the CFC's gross insurance income and gross foreign base company income for the taxable year (before taking into account any deductions) exceeds 70% of the CFC's total gross income for the year.[45]

Example **5.9:** During the current year, AFRIco (a CFC) has gross income of $20 million, including $16 million of interest income and $4 million of gross income from the sale of inventory that AFRIco manufactured at a factory located within its country of incorporation. Foreign base company income ordinarily would include only the $16 million of interest income. Under the full-inclusion rule, however, AFRIco's entire $20 million of gross income is Subpart F income since the $16 million of gross foreign base company income exceeds 70% of AFRIco's total gross income.

AFRIco

$16 million of interest income

$4 million of gross income from sales of inventory

The final exception is an elective high-tax rule, under which a U.S. shareholder can elect to exclude from Subpart F income any insurance or foreign base company income that is subject to foreign income tax at an effective rate exceeding 90% of the maximum U.S. corporate rate.[46] The effective rate of foreign tax on an item of foreign income equals the amount of foreign income taxes paid or accrued with respect to that income divided by the net amount of that income, as determined under U.S. tax principles.[47] The high-tax exception reflects the reality that there is little or no residual U.S. tax for the U.S. Treasury to collect when the foreign tax rate exceeds 90% of the U.S. rate. At present, this exception is available whenever the effective foreign rate exceeds 31.5% (90% × 35%).

Example **5.10:** USAco, a domestic corporation, owns 100% of the stock of SWISSco, a Swiss corporation. SWISSco purchases goods that USAco manufactures in the United States, and then resells them to foreign customers located outside of Switzerland. SWISSco's taxable income from inventory sales is $9 million, on which SWISSco pays $3 million in foreign income taxes. The entire $9 million of taxable income is foreign base company sales income because the goods were neither manufactured nor sold for use within Switzerland. However, USAco can elect to exclude the $9 million of taxable income from Subpart F income because the effective rate of foreign income tax on that income of 33% [$3 million of foreign income taxes ÷ $9 million of net foreign base company sales income] exceeds 90% of the maximum U.S. corporate rate of 35%.

---

[45] Code Sec. 954(b)(3)(B).
[46] Code Sec. 954(b)(4). The high-tax exception does not apply to foreign base company oil-related income.

[47] Reg. § 1.954-1(d)(2).

¶501.07

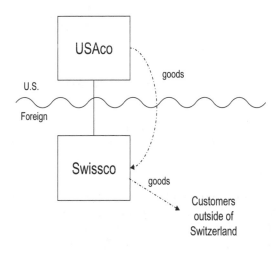

.08 Investment of Earnings in U.S. Property

A CFC's investment of earnings in U.S. property can be substantially equivalent to distributing a dividend to its U.S. shareholders. For example, a loan made by a CFC to its U.S. parent makes funds available for the U.S. parent's use in the same manner as a dividend distribution. The advantage of disguising a dividend as a loan used to be that, under the general rules, a loan did not trigger a shareholder-level tax on the CFC's earnings. Congress closed this loophole in 1962 by enacting provisions which automatically recharacterize investments made by a CFC in U.S. property as an income inclusion. Under this provision, a U.S. shareholder must include in gross income the excess of the shareholder's pro rata share of the CFC's current-year investment in U.S. property over investments in U.S. property taxed to the U.S. shareholder in prior tax years, but only to the extent the CFC has undistributed earnings which have not yet been taxed to U.S. shareholders.[48]

The amount of a CFC's investment in U.S. property is the quarterly average of the adjusted basis of U.S. property held (directly or indirectly) by the CFC, reduced by any liabilities to which the property is subject.[49] To determine the quarterly average, the taxpayer determines the amount of a CFC's investment in U.S. property at the end of each quarter, totals the quarterly amounts, and divides by four.

> **Example 5.11:** During the current year, FORco (a CFC) has no investments in U.S. property at the end of either the first or the second quarter, $5 million invested in U.S. property at the end of the third quarter and $11 million invested in U.S. property at the end of the fourth quarter. FORco's average quarterly investment in U.S. property for the year is $4 million [($0 + $0 + $5 million + $11 million) ÷ 4].

---

[48] Code Secs. 951(a)(1)(B) and 956(a).   [49] Code Sec. 956(a).

The definition of "U.S. property" attempts to distinguish U.S. investments that are equivalent to a dividend distribution from U.S. investments that are part of the CFC's normal business operations. The principal types of U.S. property are as follows:

(i) *Debt obligations*—U.S. property includes an obligation of a U.S. person, such as a loan to a U.S. shareholder,[50] including any pledge or guarantee by a CFC of a U.S. person's obligation.[51] There are exceptions for obligations of unrelated domestic corporations,[52] obligations of the United States and deposits with a U.S. bank,[53] obligations that arise from regular business transactions to the extent such amounts are ordinary and necessary,[54] certain deposits of cash or securities made or received by a securities or commodities dealer,[55] and obligations to U.S. persons who are neither U.S. shareholders of the CFC nor entities related to the CFC.[56]

(ii) *Certain receivables*—U.S. property includes trade or service receivables acquired, directly or indirectly, from a related U.S. person where the obligor is a U.S. person.[57]

(iii) *Stock*—U.S. property includes stock of a U.S. shareholder or other related domestic corporation, but not stock of unrelated domestic corporations.[58]

(iv) *Tangible property*—U.S. property includes any tangible property located in the United States, such as a U.S. manufacturing facility.[59] There are exceptions for property that is purchased in the United States for export to or use in foreign countries,[60] as well as aircraft, railroad rolling stock, vessels, motor vehicles, and transport containers used predominantly outside the United States.[61]

(v) *Intangibles*—U.S. property includes any right to use in the United States a patent, copyright, invention, model, design, secret formula or process, or any similar property right.[62]

***Example* 5.12:** CANco is a wholly owned Canadian subsidiary of USAco, a domestic corporation. During the year, USAco obtains a $2 million loan from

---

[50] Code Sec. 956(c)(1)(C).
[51] Code Sec. 956(d).
[52] Code Sec. 956(c)(2)(F).
[53] Code Sec. 956(c)(2)(A).
[54] Code Sec. 956(c)(2)(C).
[55] Code Sec. 956(c)(2)(J).
[56] Code Sec. 956(c)(2)(M).

[57] Code Sec. 956(c)(3).
[58] Code Sec. 956(c)(1)(B) and (2)(F).
[59] Code Sec. 956(c)(1)(A).
[60] Code Sec. 956(c)(2)(B).
[61] Code Sec. 956(c)(2)(D).
[62] Code Sec. 956(c)(1)(D).

¶501.08

a U.S. bank. At the bank's request, the loan agreement contains a provision whereby the loan is guaranteed by all of USAco's affiliates, including CANco. CANco's guarantee of USAco's loan from the U.S. bank may inadvertently trigger an investment in U.S. property.

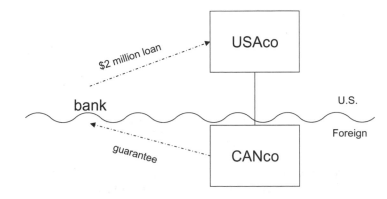

.09 Deemed Paid Foreign Tax Credit

Consistent with the notion that a Subpart F inclusion represents a deemed dividend, a domestic corporation which directly owns 10% or more of a CFC's voting stock can claim a deemed paid foreign tax credit for the CFC's foreign income taxes in the same year that the shareholder is taxed on the CFC's earnings.[63] The deemed paid credit that is allowed with respect to a Subpart F inclusion generally is identical to the deemed paid credit that is allowed with respect to actual dividend distributions.[64]

> *Example* 5.13: USAco, a domestic corporation, owns 100% of the stock of ASIAco, a foreign corporation. During its first year of existence, ASIAco had $20 million of Subpart F income, paid $2 million in foreign income taxes, and distributed no dividends. Because ASIAco is a CFC, USAco must include in income its share of ASIAco's net Subpart F income, which is $18 million [$20 million of Subpart F income – $2 million of foreign income taxes]. The inclusion of Subpart F income carries with it a deemed paid foreign tax credit of $2 million [ASIAco's post-1986 foreign income taxes of $2 million × ($18 million Subpart F inclusion ÷ $18 million of post-1986 undistributed earnings)]. With the $2 million gross-up, USAco has $20 million of taxable income and $2 million of deemed paid foreign tax credits.

---

[63] Code Sec. 960(a)(1). A U.S. shareholder who is an individual can elect to have a Subpart F inclusion taxed as if the taxpayer were a domestic corporation, in which case the individual can claim a deemed paid credit. Code Sec. 962.

[64] Reg. §§ 1.960-1–1.960-7.

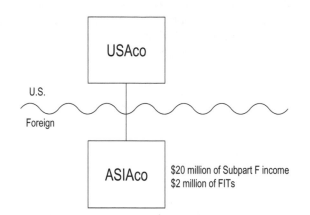

For foreign tax credit limitation purposes, a Subpart F inclusion is allocated among the separate categories of income under one of two CFC look-through rules. A Subpart F inclusion for an increase in a CFC's investment in U.S. property is allocated between general category income and passive category income based on the ratio of the CFC's post-1986 undistributed earnings within each separate category of income to the CFC's total post-1986 undistributed earnings.[65]

Example **5.14:** USAco, a domestic corporation, owns 100% of the stock of MEXco, a Mexican corporation. As of the end of the current year, MEXco has $100 million of post-1986 undistributed earnings, including $90 million of earnings attributable to general category income and $10 million attributable to passive category income. During the current year, MEXco made a $1 million loan to USAco, which resulted in a $1 million Subpart F inclusion for an investment in U.S. property. Under the CFC look-through rule, $900,000 of this amount [$1 million × ($90 million ÷ $100 million)] is general category income, and the other $100,000 [$1 million × ($10 million ÷ $100 million)] is passive category income.

---

[65] Code Sec. 904(d)(3)(G).

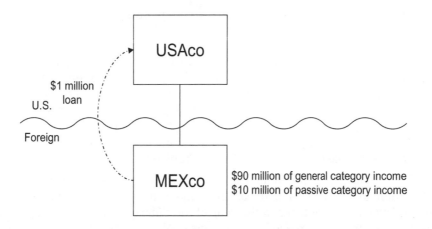

A Subpart F inclusion for Subpart F income is allocated between the general and passive categories of income based on the nature of the CFC's current year taxable income which gave rise to the Subpart F inclusion.[66]

    Example **5.15:** USAco, a domestic corporation, owns 100% of the stock of EURco, a foreign corporation. During the current year, EURco has $1 million of Subpart F income that is taxed to USAco, including $850,000 of foreign base company sales income and $150,000 of foreign personal holding company income. Under the CFC look-through rule, $850,000 of this amount is general category income and the other $150,000 is passive category income.[67]

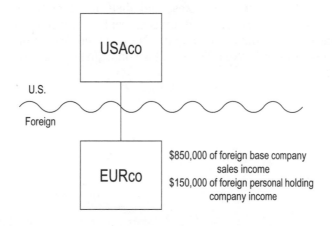

.10 Mechanisms to Prevent Double Taxation

    To avoid taxing the same earnings twice, the current taxation of a CFC's undistributed earnings to its U.S. shareholders must be coordinated with the taxation of actual dividend distributions made by the CFC, as well as the taxation of dispositions of the CFC's stock.

---

[66] Code Sec. 904(d)(3)(B).

[67] Compare Reg. § 1.904-5(c)(1)(ii), Example (1).

Distributions of previously-taxed earnings and profits. A U.S. shareholder can exclude from income distributions of a CFC's earnings and profits that were previously-taxed to U.S. shareholders by reason of a Subpart F inclusion.[68] For this purpose, distributions made by a CFC are traced first to previously-taxed earnings and profits attributable to a Subpart F inclusion for an investment in U.S. property, and then to previously-taxed earnings and profits attributable to a Subpart F inclusion for Subpart F income. The remaining portion of the distribution, if any, is traced to the CFC's other earnings and profits.[69] Only the portion of a distribution traced to other earnings and profits (i.e., non-Subpart F earnings and profits) represents a taxable dividend to the U.S. shareholder.

A U.S. shareholder cannot claim a deemed paid credit with respect to a distribution of previously-taxed earnings and profits to the extent a credit was already taken for those taxes in the year of the Subpart F inclusion.[70] However, the U.S. shareholder can increase its foreign tax credit limitation by the lesser of (i) the amount of excess limitation, if any, created in the prior year by the Subpart F inclusion or (ii) the amount of foreign withholding taxes imposed on the distribution of previously-taxed earnings and profits.[71] This adjustment is designed to prevent a U.S. shareholder from being unfairly denied a Code Sec. 903 "in lieu of" credit for any foreign withholding taxes imposed on an actual dividend distribution simply because, for U.S. tax purposes, the dividend income was recognized in a prior year.

> *Example 5.16:* USAco, a domestic corporation, owns 100% of the stock of AFRIco, a foreign corporation which was organized in year 1. During year 1, AFRIco had $10 million of foreign personal holding company income, paid $2 million in foreign income taxes, and distributed no dividends. In year 2, AFRIco had no earnings and profits, paid no foreign income taxes, and distributed an $8 million dividend. The dividend was subject to $800,000 of foreign withholding taxes. The U.S. tax consequences of AFRIco's activities are as follows.

---

[68] Code Sec. 959(a). In addition, a distribution of previously taxed income by a lower-tier CFC is not included in the income of a higher-tier CFC. Code Sec. 959(b).

[69] Code Sec. 959(c).

[70] Code Sec. 960(a)(2).

[71] Code Sec. 960(b)(1). A U.S. shareholder keeps track of these excess limitation amounts by establishing an excess limitation account in the year of the Subpart F inclusion. Code Sec. 960(b)(2).

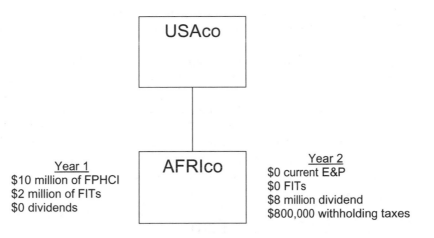

Year 1
$10 million of FPHCI
$2 million of FITs
$0 dividends

USAco

AFRIco

Year 2
$0 current E&P
$0 FITs
$8 million dividend
$800,000 withholding taxes

Year 1. Because AFRIco is a CFC, USAco must include in gross income its share of AFRIco's net Subpart F income, which is $8 million [$10 million of Subpart F income − $2 million of foreign income taxes]. The inclusion of Subpart F income carries with it a deemed paid credit of $2 million [AFRIco's post-1986 foreign income taxes of $2 million × ($8 million Subpart F inclusion ÷ $8 million of post-1986 undistributed earnings)]. With the gross-up, USAco has $10 million of foreign-source passive category income and a pre-credit U.S. tax of $3.5 million (assuming a 35% U.S. rate). Therefore, USAco's residual U.S. tax on the Subpart F income is $1.5 million [$3.5 million pre-credit U.S. tax − $2 million foreign tax credit].

Year 2. USAco can exclude the $8 million dividend from U.S. taxation because it represents a distribution of previously-taxed earnings and profits. In addition, USAco cannot claim a deemed paid credit because it claimed a credit for AFRIco's income taxes in year 1. However, USAco can claim an "in lieu of" credit for the $800,000 of foreign withholding taxes. USAco's foreign tax credit limitation equals the lesser of the excess limitation from year 1 of $1.5 million or the $800,000 of withholding taxes imposed on the distribution of previously-taxed earnings and profits and, therefore, USAco can claim a credit for the full amount of withholding taxes.

CFC stock basis adjustments. A U.S. shareholder increases its basis in the stock of a CFC by the amount of a Subpart F inclusion.[72] This adjustment prevents double taxation of any proceeds from the sale or exchange of a CFC's stock that are attributable to earnings and profits that were already taxed to the U.S. shareholder as a Subpart F inclusion. When the CFC distributes the previously-taxed earnings and profits, the U.S. shareholder treats the distribution as a nontaxable return-of-capital which reduces its basis in the stock of a CFC.[73]

> **Example 5.17:** In January of year 1, Tom (a U.S. citizen) organizes FORco, a wholly owned foreign corporation, and contributes $10 million of

---

[72] Code Sec. 961(a).

[73] Code Sec. 961(b).

cash to FORco in exchange for 100% of its stock. During year 1, FORco derives $2 million of Subpart F income (net of foreign income taxes and other allocable deductions), which is taxed to Tom in year 1 as a Subpart F inclusion. In January of year 2, Tom completely liquidates FORco and receives a $12 million liquidating distribution. If no adjustments are made to Tom's basis in FORco's stock, Tom would recognize a $2 million capital gain on the receipt of the liquidating distribution [$12 million amount realized – $10 million original basis].[74] In effect, FORco's year 1 Subpart F income of $2 million would be subject to U.S. taxation for a second time. However, because Tom is allowed to increase his basis in the FORco stock by the $2 million Subpart F inclusion, he recognizes no gain on the receipt of the liquidating distribution.

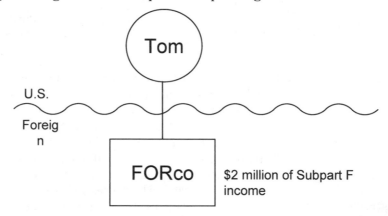

.11 Currency Translation

CFCs usually conduct business and keep their books and records in a foreign currency. This creates currency translation issues for U.S. shareholders, who must report Subpart F inclusions in U.S. dollars. The currency translation rules for Subpart F inclusions are discussed in detail in Chapter 6 (¶ 602). Briefly, to determine the amount of a Subpart F inclusion, Subpart F income is translated into U.S. dollars using the average exchange rate for the tax year, and an investment in U.S. property is translated into U.S. dollars using the spot rate on the last day of the tax year.[75] If the exchange rate fluctuates between the time of the Subpart F inclusion and the time the previously-taxed earnings and profits are distributed, the U.S. shareholder recognizes a foreign currency gain or loss.[76]

.12 Earnings and Profits

A CFC's earnings and profits play an important role in determining a U.S. shareholder's Subpart F inclusions. For example, the amount of a U.S. share-holder's Subpart F inclusion for Subpart F income is limited to the CFC's current earnings and profits.[77] Likewise, the amount of a U.S. shareholder's Subpart F inclusion for an investment in U.S. property is limited to the sum of the CFC's

---

[74] Code Sec. 331.
[75] Code Secs. 986(b) and 989(b).

[76] Code Sec. 986(c). The procedure for computing the gain is described in Notice 1988-71, 1988-2 CB 374.
[77] Code Sec. 952(c)(1)(A).

¶501.11

current and accumulated earnings and profits.[78] The earnings and profits of a CFC are computed substantially as if the CFC were a domestic corporation, by starting with the CFC's profit and loss statement, and then making any adjustments necessary to conform the profit and loss statement to U.S. GAAP and tax accounting standards.[79]

.13 Information Reporting for CFCs

In order to provide the IRS with the information necessary to ensure compliance with Subpart F, each year a U.S. person who owns more than 50% of the stock, by vote or value, of a foreign corporation must file a Form 5471, Information Return of U.S. Persons With Respect to Certain Foreign Corporations.[80] Other persons who must file a Form 5471 include (i) U.S. persons who acquire a 10% ownership interest, acquire an additional 10% ownership interest, or dispose of stock holdings to reduce their ownership in the foreign corporation to less than 10%[81] and (ii) U.S. citizens and residents who are officers or directors of a foreign corporation in which a U.S. person acquires a 10% ownership interest or an additional 10% interest.[82]

In Form 5471, the reporting agent must provide the following information regarding the CFC:[83]

   (i) Stock ownership, including current year acquisitions and dispositions,

   (ii) U.S. shareholders,

   (iii) GAAP income statement and balance sheet,

   (iv) Foreign income taxes,

   (v) Current and accumulated earnings and profits, including any actual dividend distributions during the year,

   (vi) The U.S. shareholder's pro rata share of Subpart F income and any increase in earnings invested in U.S. property, and

   (vii) Transactions between the CFC and shareholders or other related persons.

A Form 5471 ordinarily is filed by attaching it to the U.S. person's regular federal income tax return.[84] Any U.S. person who fails to furnish the required information may be subject to an annual penalty of $10,000, as well as a reduction in the taxpayer's foreign tax credit.[85] A completed Form 5471 is included in the appendix to this chapter.

Reporting requirements also apply to controlled foreign partnerships and foreign disregarded entities. Any U.S. person that is a more-than-50% partner must annually file Form 8865, Return of U.S. Persons With Respect to Certain Foreign Partnerships,[86] and any U.S. person that is a tax owner of a foreign disregarded entity must annually file Form 8858, Information Return of U.S. Persons with Respect to Foreign Disregarded Entities (see ¶ 809). U.S. persons that are required

---

[78] Code Sec. 956(a)(2).
[79] Reg. § 1.964-1(a)(1).
[80] Reg. § 1.6038-2(a) and (b).
[81] Reg. § 1.6046-1(c)(1).
[82] Reg. § 1.6046-1(a)(2)(i) and Code Sec. 6046(a).

[83] Reg. § 1.6038-2(f) and (g).
[84] Reg. § 1.6038-2(i).
[85] Code Sec. 6038(b) and (c).
[86] Reg. § 1.6038-3(a)(1).

to file Form 5471 with respect to a CFC that is a tax owner of a foreign disregarded entity also must file Form 8858.

¶ 502 PASSIVE FOREIGN INVESTMENT COMPANIES

.01 Background

U.S. investors in a domestic mutual fund (i.e., a regulated investment company) are taxed currently on the fund's investment income because a domestic fund must distribute at least 90% of its income each year in order to avoid U.S. taxation at the corporate level.[87] In contrast, prior to 1987, investors in foreign mutual funds were able to avoid current U.S. taxation. The fund itself avoided U.S. tax because it was a foreign corporation that derived only foreign-source income. The U.S. investors avoided U.S. tax because the fund paid no dividends. These funds are able to avoid the CFC taint because the ownership of the fund was dispersed among a large number of U.S. and foreign investors, each owning a relatively small percentage of the fund. Another significant tax benefit of foreign mutual funds was that when U.S. investors eventually did realize the fund's earnings through the sale of the fund's stock, they were able to effectively convert the fund's ordinary income (dividends and interest) into capital gains.

The enactment in 1986 of the passive foreign investment company (or PFIC) regime significantly expanded the reach of U.S. taxing authorities with respect to passive investment income earned by U.S. persons through foreign corporations.[88] Congress enacted the PFIC provisions to deal with perceived abuses by U.S. investors in foreign mutual funds. However, the PFIC rules apply to any foreign corporation that meets either the PFIC income test or assets test, regardless of whether U.S. shareholders individually or in the aggregate have a significant ownership stake in the company. The lack of a U.S. control requirement represents a major policy shift from Subpart F, which applies only to foreign corporations with controlling U.S. shareholders.

Under an overlap rule, a foreign corporation that qualifies as both a CFC and a PFIC is not treated as a PFIC by a U.S. shareholder (i.e., a U.S. person who owns 10% or more of the stock). Thus, a shareholder that is subject to the current inclusion rules of Subpart F is not also subject to the PFIC rules with respect to the same stock.[89] On the other hand, the PFIC provisions do apply to any U.S. persons who are less than 10% shareholders of the foreign corporation.

.02 Definition of a PFIC

A foreign corporation is a PFIC if it meets either an income test or an asset test.[90]

Income test. Under the income test, a foreign corporation is a PFIC if 75% or more of the corporation's gross income for the taxable year is passive income.[91]

---

[87] Code Secs. 851 and 852.

[88] Code Secs. 1291–1298.

[89] Code Sec. 1297(d).

[90] Code Sec. 1297(a). Exceptions to the income test and asset test apply to a foreign corporation's first taxable

year and to a year in which a foreign corporation experiences a change in business. Code Sec. 1298(b)(2) and (3).

[91] Code Sec. 1297(a)(1).

Passive income is foreign personal holding company income (as defined for purposes of Subpart F),[92] with certain adjustments. The adjustments include exclusions for income derived from the active conduct of a banking, insurance, or securities business, as well as any interest, dividends, rents, and royalties received from a related person to the extent such income is properly allocable to nonpassive income of the related person.[93] In addition, to prevent foreign holding companies of operating subsidiaries from being treated as PFICs, a foreign corporation that owns directly or indirectly at least 25% (by value) of the stock of another corporation is treated as if it earned a proportionate share of that corporation's income.[94]

Assets test. Under the assets test, a foreign corporation is a PFIC if the average market value of the corporation's passive assets during the taxable year is 50% or more of the corporation's total assets. In the case of a CFC, the assets test is based on adjusted basis, rather than market values. Non-publicly traded foreign corporations also may elect to use adjusted basis to apply the assets test.[95] Passive assets are assets that produce passive income (as defined for purposes of the PFIC income test), with certain adjustments. For example, a CFC can increase its total assets by the amount of research or experimental expenditures incurred by the CFC during the current and preceding two taxable years, and by an amount equal to 300% of the payments made by the CFC for certain licensed intangibles used by the CFC in the active conduct of a trade or business.[96] In addition, a foreign corporation is treated as the owner of any tangible personal property with respect to which it is a lessee under a lease with a term of 12 or more months.[97] Finally, as with the income test, a foreign corporation that owns directly or indirectly at least 25% (by value) of the stock of another corporation is treated as if it owned directly a proportionate share of that corporation's assets.[98]

The assets of a publicly traded PFIC are measured using a special fair market value computation. Therefore, a publicly traded foreign corporation is a PFIC if the fair market value of its passive income-producing assets equals or exceeds 50% of the sum of the market value of its outstanding stock plus its liabilities.[99]

.03 Taxation of a PFIC

A PFIC's undistributed earnings are subject to U.S. taxation under one of three methods, each of which is designed to eliminate the benefits of deferral. These include the qualified electing fund method, excess distribution method, and mark-to-market method.

Under the qualified electing fund (or QEF) method, shareholders who can obtain the necessary information can elect to be taxed currently on their pro rata share of the PFIC's earnings and profits. The income inclusion is treated as ordinary income to the extent of the taxpayer's pro rata share of the QEF's ordinary income and capital gains to the extent of the taxpayer's pro rata share of the QEF's

---

[92] Code Sec. 1297(b)(1) by reference to Code Sec. 954(c).

[93] Code Sec. 1297(b)(2).

[94] Code Sec. 1297(c)(2).

[95] Code Sec. 1297(e)(2).

[96] Code Sec. 1298(e). This provision does not apply if the licenser is a related foreign person.

[97] Code Sec. 1298(d). This provision does not apply if the lessor is a related person.

[98] Code Sec. 1297(c)(1).

[99] Code Sec. 1297(e) [sic (f)].

net capital gain.[100] A taxpayer's pro rata share is the amount that the taxpayer would have received if, on each day of the QEF's taxable year, the QEF had actually distributed to each of its shareholders a pro rata share of that day's ratable share of the QEF's ordinary earnings and net capital gains for the year.[101] To prevent double taxation of the QEF's earnings, any actual distributions made by a QEF out of its previously taxed income are tax-free to the U.S. investor.[102] In addition, a U.S. investor increases its basis in the QEF's stock for any income inclusions and reduces its basis in the stock when it receives a distribution of previously taxed income.[103]

Under the excess distribution method, the taxpayer is allowed to defer taxation of the PFIC's undistributed income until the PFIC makes an excess distribution. An excess distribution includes the following:

(i) A gain realized on the sale of PFIC stock,[104] and

(ii) Any actual distribution made by the PFIC, but only to the extent the total actual distributions received by the taxpayer for the year exceeds 125% of the average actual distribution received by the taxpayer in the preceding three taxable years (or, if shorter, the taxpayer's holding period before the current taxable year).[105]

The amount of an excess distribution is treated as if it had been realized pro rata over the holding period for the PFIC's stock and the tax due on an excess distribution is the sum of the deferred yearly tax amounts (computed using the highest tax rate in effect in the years the income was accumulated), plus interest.[106] Therefore, the excess distribution method eliminates the benefits of deferral by assessing an interest charge on the deferred yearly tax amounts. Any actual distributions that fall below the 125% threshold are treated as dividends (assuming they represent a distribution of earnings and profits), which are taxable in the year of receipt and are not subject to the special interest charge.[107] Taxpayers can claim a Code Sec. 903 "in lieu of" foreign tax credit with respect to any withholding taxes imposed on a distribution by a PFIC, and a domestic corporation owning 10% or more of the PFIC's voting stock also can claim a deemed paid foreign tax credit.[108]

> ***Example* 5.18:** On January 1, 20Y1, Ann (a U.S. citizen) purchases 1% of the stock of Fm, a foreign mutual fund that qualifies as a PFIC. Ann does not make a QEF or mark-to-market election. Fm is highly profitable, but it does not make a distribution until December 31, 20Y3, when it pays Ann a dividend of

---

[100] Code Secs. 1293(a) and 1295(a). When the QEF method and Subpart F apply to the same income, the item is included in the U.S. shareholder's gross income under Subpart F. Code Sec. 951(f).

[101] Code Sec. 1293(b).

[102] Code Sec. 1293(c).

[103] Code Sec. 1293(d). Domestic corporations owning 10% or more of the QEF's voting stock can claim a deemed paid foreign tax credit with respect to a QEF income inclusion. Code Sec. 1293(f)(1). However, U.S. individuals must pay tax at ordinary rates and are not entitled to the preferential rate of tax on qualified dividends. Code Sec. 1(h)(11)(C)(iii).

[104] Code Sec. 1291(a)(2).

[105] Code Sec. 1291(b)(1) and (2)(A). Any amounts currently or previously included in the U.S. investor's gross income by reason of Subpart F are not treated as excess distributions. Prop. Reg. § 1.1291-2(b)(2). In addition, it is not possible to have an excess distribution in the year that the taxpayer first acquires shares in the PFIC. Code Sec. 1291(b)(2)(B).

[106] Code Sec. 1291(a)(1) and (c). The interest is the underpayment rate, which is the AFR short term rate plus 3%. Code Secs. 1291(c)(3) and 6621.

[107] Prop. Reg. § 1.1291-2(e)(1).

[108] Code Sec. 1291(g) and Prop. Reg. § 1.1291-5.

¶502.03

$300,000. Under the excess distribution method, the dividend is treated as if it were received ratably ($100,000 per year) over 20Y1, 20Y2 and 20Y3, taxed at the highest rate in effect each year, and subject to an interest charge.

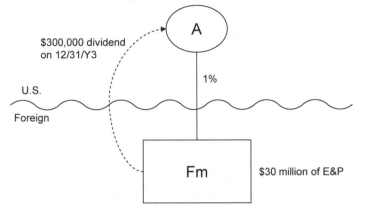

If the stock of a PFIC is marketable, the taxpayer may elect to use the mark-to-market. Under this election, any excess of the fair market value of the PFIC stock at the close of the tax year over the shareholder's adjusted basis in the stock is included in the shareholder's income. The shareholder may deduct any excess of the adjusted basis of the PFIC stock over its fair market value at the close of the tax year. However, deductions are limited to the net mark-to-market gains on the stock that the shareholder included in income in prior years, or so-called "unreversed inclusions." Any income or loss recognized under the mark-to-market election is treated as ordinary in nature. In addition, a shareholder's adjusted basis of PFIC stock is increased by the income recognized under the mark-to-market election and decreased by the deductions allowed under the election.[109] The mark-to-market election was enacted to extend a current income inclusion method to PFIC shareholders who could not obtain the information from the PFIC necessary to making a QEF election and, therefore, were forced to use the complex and burdensome interest-charge method.

  Example **5.19:** On January 1, 20Y1, Ann (a U.S. citizen) pays $1 million for 1% of the stock of Fm, a foreign mutual fund that qualifies as a PFIC. The stock of Fm is marketable and Ann makes a mark-to-market election. On December 31, 20Y1, the stock is worth $1.2 million, and Ann recognizes $200,000 of income.

---

[109] Code Sec. 1296.

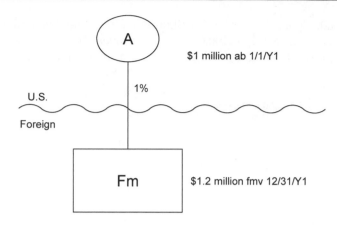

.04 Information reporting for PFICs

Effective March 18, 2010, new Code Sec. 1298(f) requires each U.S. person who is a shareholder of a PFIC to file an annual report. In Notice 2010-34, the IRS announced that it is developing further guidance regarding the reporting obligations under Code Sec. 1298(f).[110] In the meantime, persons who were required to file Form 8621, Return by a Shareholder of a Passive Foreign Investment Company or a Qualified Electing Fund, prior to March 18, 2010, must continue to file Form 8621, as provided in the instructions (e.g., upon the disposition of stock, or with respect to a QEF election). A completed Form 8621 is included in the appendix to this chapter.

¶ 503 GAIN FROM THE SALE OR EXCHANGE OF A CFC'S STOCK

A gain on the sale or exchange of stock of a foreign corporation normally is capital in nature.[111] However, an exception applies if, at any time during the five-year period ending on the date of the sale or exchange, the taxpayer was a U.S. shareholder of the foreign corporation when the foreign corporation qualified as a CFC. In such cases, the U.S. person must treat the gain on the sale or exchange of the foreign corporation's stock as a dividend to the extent of the shareholder's pro rata share of the corporation's post-1962 earnings and profits that were accumulated while the shareholder owned the stock and the corporation was a CFC.[112] Any gain in excess of the deemed dividend is still accorded capital gain treatment. For purposes of this provision, earnings and profits does not include certain amounts already subjected to U.S. tax, including prior-year Subpart F inclusions, income effectively connected with the conduct of a U.S. trade or business, and an inclusion from a PFIC that has made a QEF election.[113]

Congress enacted this provision in 1962 to ensure that the U.S. Treasury collects the "full U.S. tax" when a U.S. shareholder repatriates a CFC's foreign

---

[110] IRB 2010-17, Apr. 6, 2010.

[111] Code Sec. 1221.

[112] Code Sec. 1248(a). In the case of U.S. shareholders who are individuals, the tax attributable to the deemed dividend inclusion cannot exceed the tax that would have been due if the foreign corporation had been a domestic corporation. Code Sec. 1248(b).

[113] Code Sec. 1248(d).

earnings. Before 1963, a U.S. shareholder that operated abroad through a CFC could defer U.S. taxes on the CFC's earnings, and then repatriate those earnings through the sale of the CFC's stock (rather than a dividend distribution), in which case the CFC's earnings were subject to U.S. tax at a lower capital gains rate. The requirement that U.S. shareholders treat part or all of the gain on the sale of a CFC's stock as a dividend ensures that the United States is allowed to tax the CFC's accumulated earnings at ordinary income rates.

At present, there is a capital gains rate differential for noncorporate taxpayers, but not for corporate taxpayers. Nevertheless, because a dividend carries with it deemed paid foreign tax credits, the re-characterization of a gain as a dividend remains an important feature of the law for domestic corporations that are U.S. shareholders of a CFC.[114] Therefore, this anti-abuse provision can work to a domestic corporation's advantage by allowing it to claim deemed paid foreign tax credits that can be used to offset the tax on the disposition of a CFC's stock.

Example **5.20:** ASIAco is a wholly-owned manufacturing subsidiary of USAco, a domestic corporation. USAco has been ASIAco's sole shareholder since ASIAco was organized several years ago. At the end of the current year, USAco sells all of ASIAco's stock to an unrelated foreign buyer for $15 million. At that time, ASIAco had $3 million of post-1986 undistributed earnings and profits and $1 million of post-1986 foreign income taxes. USAco's basis in ASIAco's stock was $10 million immediately prior to the sale. Assume USAco's capital gain on the sale of ASIAco's stock is not subject to foreign taxation and that the U.S. corporate tax rate is 35%.

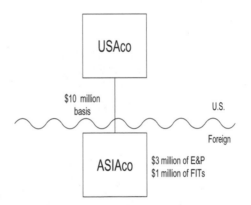

USAco realizes a gain on the sale of ASIAco's stock of $5 million [$15 million amount realized – $10 million basis in ASIAco's stock]. The dividend portion of the gain equals ASIAco's undistributed earnings of $3 million, and the remaining $2 million is treated as a capital gain. The $3 million dividend carries with it $1 million of deemed paid foreign taxes. As a result, with the gross-up, ASIAco has $4 million of foreign-source dividend income. The $2 million capital gain also is foreign-source income.[115] Therefore, the pre-credit U.S. tax on the stock

---

[114] Reg. § 1.1248-1(d).   [115] Code Sec. 865(f).

sale is $2.1 million [35% U.S. tax rate × ($4 million dividend + $2 million capital gain)], the credit is $1 million, and USAco has a residual U.S. tax of $1.1 million. In contrast, if the entire $5 million gain had been treated as a capital gain, the residual U.S. tax would have been $1.75 million [35% U.S. tax rate × $5 million capital gain].

¶ 504 APPENDIX

Mark Twain, a resident of Hannibal, Missouri, owns 51 of the 100 outstanding common shares of BritCo, a United Kingdom corporation headquartered in Cambridge, England. The remaining 49 outstanding common shares are owned by diverse foreign interests. BritCo purchases bowling balls from Mark Twain for resale throughout Europe. Although all of BritCo's purchases and sales are in British pounds, approximately 25% of BritCo's sales are to customers in Finland.

Mark Twain, as President, is the only officer and director of BritCo. The small business tax rate in the United Kingdom is 20%. Both Mark Twain and BritCo are on the calendar year. BritCo does not pay any dividends and neither Mark Twain nor BritCo own an interest in any other foreign entities. Furthermore, none of the shares are considered securities or debt for U.S. tax purposes. During 2010, the average exchange rate for the pound was $1.50, which was also the spot rate on December 31, 2010. BritCo keeps all its cash in a non-interest bearing account.

Mark Twain acquired his shares of BritCo, as did all the other foreign shareholders, on January 1, 2010, based on his capital contribution of £5,100,000 for common shares. Mark Twain files his return with the Kansas City Service Center on April 15 of each year, without ever pursuing an extension.

The chartered accountant in Cambridge provides you with the following account information for the year ended December 31, 2010:

Sales:	£ 25,000,000
Cost of Good Sold:	£ 15,000,000
Compensation to U.K. employees:	£ 2,000,000
Taxes:	£ 1,600,000
Cash:	£ 16,400,000
Inventory:	£ 15,000,000
Accounts Payable:	£ 15,000,000
Common Stock:	£ 10,000,000
Retained Earnings:	£ 6,400,000

When filing Form 5471, Mark Twain is a Category 2 filer because he is a U.S. citizen who is an officer or director of BritCo and he has acquired at least 10% of his shares during 2010. He is a Category 3 filer because he is a U.S. shareholder (at least 10% share holdings). He controls a foreign corporation, BritCo, for an uninterrupted period of at least 30 days during 2010 and, accordingly, is a Category 4 filer. He is a Category 5 filer because he is a U.S. shareholder of BritCo, which was a CFC, on the last day of the 2010 taxable year.

Mark Twain will report $1,530,000 of Subpart F income, which constitutes foreign-based company sales income from BritCo's purchase of bowling balls from Mark and BritCo's resale to customers in Finland. Twenty-five percent of net income from Finnish sales is £2 million, of which Mark's 51% share was £1,020,000. At the exchange rate of $1.50 per pound, the Subpart F income inclusion is $1,530,000.

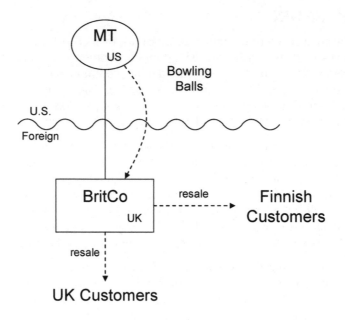

Form **5471**	**Information Return of U.S. Persons With Respect To Certain Foreign Corporations**	OMB No. 1545-0704
(Rev. December 2007)	▶ See separate instructions.	
Department of the Treasury Internal Revenue Service	Information furnished for the foreign corporation's annual accounting period (tax year required by section 898) (see instructions) beginning **Jan 1** , 20 **10** , and ending **Dec 31** , 20 **10**	Attachment Sequence No. **121**

Name of person filing this return **Mark Twain**	**A** Identifying number **123-45-6789**

Number, street, and room or suite no. (or P.O. box number if mail is not delivered to street address) **1234 Main Street**	**B** Category of filer (See instructions. Check applicable box(es)): 1 (repealed) 2 ☑ 3 ☑ 4 ☑ 5 ☑

City or town, state, and ZIP code **Hannibal, MO 63401**	**C** Enter the total percentage of the foreign corporation's voting stock you owned at the end of its annual accounting period . . . . %

Filer's tax year beginning **January 1** , 20 **10** , and ending **December 31** , 20 **10**

D Person(s) on whose behalf this information return is filed:

(1) Name	(2) Address	(3) Identifying number	(4) Check applicable box(es)		
			Shareholder	Officer	Director

Important: *Fill in all applicable lines and schedules. All information **must** be in English. All amounts **must** be stated in U.S. dollars unless otherwise indicated.*

1a Name and address of foreign corporation	**b** Employer identification number, if any
BritCo **Cambridge, England**	**c** Country under whose laws incorporated **United Kingdom**

d Date of incorporation	e Principal place of business	f Principal business activity code number	g Principal business activity	h Functional currency
1/1/2010	**United Kingdom**	**423910**	**Sporting & Recreational Goods & Supplies**	**British Pound**

2 Provide the following information for the foreign corporation's accounting period stated above.

a Name, address, and identifying number of branch office or agent (if any) in the United States	b If a U.S. income tax return was filed, enter:	
	(i) Taxable income or (loss)	*(ii)* U.S. income tax paid (after all credits)

c Name and address of foreign corporation's statutory or resident agent in country of incorporation	d Name and address (including corporate department, if applicable) of person (or persons) with custody of the books and records of the foreign corporation, and the location of such books and records, if different **Controller** **Cambridge, United Kingdom**

Schedule A Stock of the Foreign Corporation

(a) Description of each class of stock	(b) Number of shares issued and outstanding	
	(i) Beginning of annual accounting period	*(ii)* End of annual accounting period
Common Stock	**0**	**100**

For Paperwork Reduction Act Notice, see instructions.   Cat. No. 49958V   Form **5471** (Rev. 12-2007)

Form 5471 (Rev. 12-2007)   Page **2**

Schedule B   **U.S. Shareholders of Foreign Corporation** (see instructions)

(a) Name, address, and identifying number of shareholder	(b) Description of each class of stock held by shareholder. **Note:** This description should match the corresponding description entered in Schedule A, column (a).	(c) Number of shares held at beginning of annual accounting period	(d) Number of shares held at end of annual accounting period	(e) Pro rata share of subpart F income (enter as a percentage)
Mark Twain 1234 Main Street Hannibal, MO 63401	Common Stock	None	51	51%

Schedule C   **Income Statement** (see instructions)

Important: *Report all information in functional currency in accordance with U.S. GAAP. Also, report each amount in U.S. dollars translated from functional currency (using GAAP translation rules). However, if the functional currency is the U.S. dollar, complete only the U.S. Dollars column. See instructions for special rules for DASTM corporations.*

			Functional Currency	U.S. Dollars
Income	**1a** Gross receipts or sales	1a	25,000,000	37,500,000
	b Returns and allowances	1b		
	c Subtract line 1b from line 1a	1c	25,000,000	37,500,000
	2 Cost of goods sold	2	15,000,000	22,500,000
	3 Gross profit (subtract line 2 from line 1c)	3	10,000,000	15,000,000
	4 Dividends	4		
	5 Interest	5		
	6a Gross rents	6a		
	b Gross royalties and license fees	6b		
	7 Net gain or (loss) on sale of capital assets	7		
	8 Other income (attach schedule)	8		
	9 Total income (add lines 3 through 8)	9	10,000,000	15,000,000
Deductions	**10** Compensation not deducted elsewhere	10	2,000,000	3,000,000
	11a Rents	11a		
	b Royalties and license fees	11b		
	12 Interest	12		
	13 Depreciation not deducted elsewhere	13		
	14 Depletion	14		
	15 Taxes (exclude provision for income, war profits, and excess profits taxes)	15		
	16 Other deductions (attach schedule—exclude provision for income, war profits, and excess profits taxes)	16		
	17 Total deductions (add lines 10 through 16)	17	2,000,000	3,000,000
Net Income	**18** Net income or (loss) before extraordinary items, prior period adjustments, and the provision for income, war profits, and excess profits taxes (subtract line 17 from line 9)	18	8,000,000	12,000,000
	19 Extraordinary items and prior period adjustments (see instructions)	19		
	20 Provision for income, war profits, and excess profits taxes (see instructions)	20	1,600,000	2,400,000
	21 Current year net income or (loss) per books (combine lines 18 through 20)	21	6,400,000	9,600,000

Form **5471** (Rev. 12-2007)

¶504

Form 5471 (Rev. 12-2007) Page **3**

Schedule E	Income, War Profits, and Excess Profits Taxes Paid or Accrued (see instructions)			
		Amount of tax		
	(a) Name of country or U.S. possession	(b) In foreign currency	(c) Conversion rate	(d) In U.S. dollars
1	U.S.			
2	United Kingdom	1,600,000	0.66667	2,400,000
3				
4				
5				
6				
7				
8	Total . . . . ▶			2,400,000

Schedule F	Balance Sheet

Important: *Report all amounts in U.S. dollars prepared and translated in accordance with U.S. GAAP. See instructions for an exception for DASTM corporations.*

	Assets		(a) Beginning of annual accounting period	(b) End of annual accounting period
1	Cash	1	--	24,600,000
2a	Trade notes and accounts receivable	2a		
b	Less allowance for bad debts	2b	( )	( )
3	Inventories	3	--	22,500,000
4	Other current assets (attach schedule)	4		
5	Loans to shareholders and other related persons	5		
6	Investment in subsidiaries (attach schedule)	6		
7	Other investments (attach schedule)	7		
8a	Buildings and other depreciable assets	8a		
b	Less accumulated depreciation	8b	( )	( )
9a	Depletable assets	9a		
b	Less accumulated depletion	9b	( )	( )
10	Land (net of any amortization)	10		
11	Intangible assets:			
a	Goodwill.	11a		
b	Organization costs	11b		
c	Patents, trademarks, and other intangible assets	11c		
d	Less accumulated amortization for lines 11a, b, and c	11d	( )	( )
12	Other assets (attach schedule)	12		
13	Total assets	13	--	47,100,000
	Liabilities and Shareholders' Equity			
14	Accounts payable.	14	--	22,500,000
15	Other current liabilities (attach schedule)	15		
16	Loans from shareholders and other related persons	16		
17	Other liabilities (attach schedule)	17		
18	Capital stock:			
a	Preferred stock	18a		
b	Common stock	18b	--	15,000,000
19	Paid-in or capital surplus (attach reconciliation)	19		
20	Retained earnings	20	--	9,600,000
21	Less cost of treasury stock	21	( )	( )
22	Total liabilities and shareholders' equity	22	--	47,100,000

Form **5471** (Rev. 12-2007)

Form 5471 (Rev. 12-2007)   Page **4**

Schedule G   Other Information

		Yes	No
1	During the tax year, did the foreign corporation own at least a 10% interest, directly or indirectly, in any foreign partnership?	☐	☑
	If "Yes," see the instructions for required attachment.		
2	During the tax year, did the foreign corporation own an interest in any trust?	☐	☑
3	During the tax year, did the foreign corporation own any foreign entities that were disregarded as entities separate from their owners under Regulations sections 301.7701-2 and 301.7701-3 (see instructions)?	☐	☑
	If "Yes," you are generally required to attach Form 8858 for each entity (see instructions).		
4	During the tax year, was the foreign corporation a participant in any cost sharing arrangement?	☐	☑
5	During the course of the tax year, did the foreign corporation become a participant in any cost sharing arrangement?	☐	☑

Schedule H   Current Earnings and Profits (see instructions)

Important: *Enter the amounts on lines 1 through 5c in **functional** currency.*

1	Current year net income or (loss) per foreign books of account	**1**	8,000,000

2	Net adjustments made to line 1 to determine current earnings and profits according to U.S. financial and tax accounting standards (see instructions):	Net Additions	Net Subtractions
a	Capital gains or losses		
b	Depreciation and amortization		
c	Depletion		
d	Investment or incentive allowance		
e	Charges to statutory reserves.		
f	Inventory adjustments		
g	Taxes.		1,600,000
h	Other (attach schedule)		
3	Total net additions		
4	Total net subtractions		

5a	Current earnings and profits (line 1 plus line 3 minus line 4)	**5a**	6,400,000
b	DASTM gain or (loss) for foreign corporations that use DASTM (see instructions)	**5b**	--
c	Combine lines 5a and 5b	**5c**	6,400,000
d	Current earnings and profits in U.S. dollars (line 5c translated at the appropriate exchange rate as defined in section 989(b) and the related regulations (see instructions))	**5d**	9,600,000

Enter exchange rate used for line 5d ▶ **1.50**

Schedule I   Summary of Shareholder's Income From Foreign Corporation (see instructions)

1	Subpart F income (line 38b, Worksheet A in the instructions)	**1**	1,530,000
2	Earnings invested in U.S. property (line 17, Worksheet B in the instructions)	**2**	
3	Previously excluded subpart F income withdrawn from qualified investments (line 6b, Worksheet C in the instructions)	**3**	
4	Previously excluded export trade income withdrawn from investment in export trade assets (line 7b, Worksheet D in the instructions).	**4**	
5	Factoring income	**5**	
6	Total of lines 1 through 5. Enter here and on your income tax return. See instructions.	**6**	1,530,000
7	Dividends received (translated at spot rate on payment date under section 989(b)(1))	**7**	
8	Exchange gain or (loss) on a distribution of previously taxed income	**8**	

	Yes	No
● Was any income of the foreign corporation blocked?.	☐	☑
● Did any such income become unblocked during the tax year (see section 964(b))?.	☐	☑

If the answer to either question is "Yes," attach an explanation.

Form **5471** (Rev. 12-2007)

SCHEDULE J
(Form 5471)
(Rev. December 2005)
Department of the Treasury
Internal Revenue Service

Accumulated Earnings and Profits (E&P)
of Controlled Foreign Corporation
▶ Attach to Form 5471. See Instructions for Form 5471.

OMB No. 1545-0704

Name of person filing Form 5471
Mark Twain

Identifying number
123-45-6789

Name of foreign corporation
BritCo

Important: Enter amounts in functional currency.	**(a)** Post-1986 Undistributed Earnings (post-86 section 959(c)(3) balance)	**(b)** Pre-1987 E&P Not Previously Taxed (pre-87 section 959(c)(3) balance)	**(c)** Previously Taxed E&P (see instructions) (sections 959(c)(1) and (2) balances)			**(d)** Total Section 964(a) E&P (combine columns (a), (b), and (c))
			(i) Earnings Invested in U.S. Property	*(ii)* Earnings Invested in Excess Passive Assets	*(iii)* Subpart F Income	
1 Balance at beginning of year	–					
2a Current year E&P	6,400,000					
b Current year deficit in E&P						
3 Total current and accumulated E&P not previously taxed (line 1 plus line 2a **or** line 1 minus line 2b)	6,400,000					
4 Amounts included under section 951(a) or reclassified under section 959(c) in current year	(1,020,000)				1,020,000	
5a Actual distributions or reclassifications of previously taxed E&P						
b Actual distributions of nonpreviously taxed E&P						
6a Balance of previously taxed E&P at end of year (line 1 plus line 4, minus line 5a)					1,020,000	
b Balance of E&P not previously taxed at end of year (line 3 minus line 4, minus line 5b)	5,380,000					
7 Balance at end of year. (Enter amount from line 6a or line 6b, whichever is applicable.)	5,380,000				1,020,000	6,400,000

For Paperwork Reduction Act Notice, see the Instructions for Form 5471.   Cat. No. 21111K   Schedule J (Form 5471) (Rev. 12-2005)

¶504

SCHEDULE M (Form 5471)	Transactions Between Controlled Foreign Corporation and Shareholders or Other Related Persons	
(Rev. December 2010) Department of the Treasury Internal Revenue Service	► Attach to Form 5471. See Instructions for Form 5471.	OMB No. 1545-0704

Name of person filing Form 5471	Identifying number
Mark Twain	123-45-6789

Name of foreign corporation

BritCo

Important: Complete a **separate** Schedule M for each controlled foreign corporation. Enter the totals for each type of transaction that occurred during the annual accounting period between the foreign corporation and the persons listed in columns (b) through (f). All amounts must be stated in U.S. dollars translated from functional currency at the average exchange rate for the foreign corporation's tax year. See instructions.

Enter the relevant functional currency and the exchange rate used throughout this schedule ▶   **British pound at $1.50**

(a) Transactions of foreign corporation	(b) U.S. person filing this return	(c) Any domestic corporation or partnership controlled by U.S. person filing this return	(d) Any other foreign corporation or partnership controlled by U.S. person filing this return	(e) 10% or more U.S. shareholder of controlled foreign corporation (other than the U.S. person filing this return)	(f) 10% or more U.S. shareholder of any corporation controlling the foreign corporation
1 Sales of stock in trade (inventory) . . .					
2 Sales of tangible property other than stock in trade					
3 Sales of property rights (patents, trademarks, etc.)					
4 Platform contribution transaction payments received					
5 Cost sharing transaction payments received					
6 Compensation received for technical, managerial, engineering, construction, or like services					
7 Commissions received					
8 Rents, royalties, and license fees received					
9 Dividends received (exclude deemed distributions under subpart F and distributions of previously taxed income)					
10 Interest received					
11 Premiums received for insurance or reinsurance					
12 Add lines 1 through 11					
13 Purchases of stock in trade (inventory) .	22,500,000				
14 Purchases of tangible property other than stock in trade					
15 Purchases of property rights (patents, trademarks, etc.)					
16 Platform contribution transaction payments paid					
17 Cost sharing transaction payments paid .					
18 Compensation paid for technical, managerial, engineering, construction, or like services					
19 Commissions paid					
20 Rents, royalties, and license fees paid .					
21 Dividends paid					
22 Interest paid					
23 Premiums paid for insurance or reinsurance					
24 Add lines 13 through 23	22,500,000				
25 Amounts borrowed (enter the maximum loan balance during the year) — see instructions					
26 Amounts loaned (enter the maximum loan balance during the year) — see instructions					

For Paperwork Reduction Act Notice, see the Instructions for Form 5471.   Cat. No. 49963O   Schedule M (Form 5471) (Rev. 12-2010)

¶504

SCHEDULE O (Form 5471) (Rev. December 2005) Department of the Treasury Internal Revenue Service	**Organization or Reorganization of Foreign Corporation, and Acquisitions and Dispositions of its Stock** ▶ Attach to Form 5471. See Instructions for Form 5471.	OMB No. 1545-0704

Name of person filing Form 5471	Identifying number
Mark Twain	**123-45-6789**

Name of foreign corporation

BritCo

Important: *Complete a **separate** Schedule O for each foreign corporation for which information must be reported.*

Part I   To Be Completed by U.S. Officers and Directors

(a) Name of shareholder for whom acquisition information is reported	(b) Address of shareholder	(c) Identifying number of shareholder	(d) Date of original 10% acquisition	(e) Date of additional 10% acquisition
Mark Twain	**1234 Main Street Hannibal, MO 63401**	**123-45-6789**	**1/1/2010**	

Part II   To Be Completed by U.S. Shareholders

Note: *If this return is required because one or more shareholders became U.S. persons, attach a list showing the names of such persons and the date each became a U.S. person.*

Section A—General Shareholder Information

(a) Name, address, and identifying number of shareholder(s) filing this schedule	(b) For shareholder's latest U.S. income tax return filed, indicate:			(c) Date (if any) shareholder last filed information return under section 6046 for the foreign corporation
	(1) Type of return (enter form number)	(2) Date return filed	(3) Internal Revenue Service Center where filed	
Mark Twain 1234 Main Street Hannibal, MO 63401	**1040**	**4/15/2010**	**Kansas City, MO**	

Section B—U.S. Persons Who Are Officers or Directors of the Foreign Corporation

(a) Name of U.S. officer or director	(b) Address	(c) Social security number	(d) Check appropriate box(es)	
			Officer	Director
Mark Twain	**1234 Main Street Hannibal, MO 63401**	**123-45-6789**	✓	✓

Section C—Acquisition of Stock

(a) Name of shareholder(s) filing this schedule	(b) Class of stock acquired	(c) Date of acquisition	(d) Method of acquisition	(e) Number of shares acquired		
				(1) Directly	(2) Indirectly	(3) Constructively
Mark Twain	**Common**	**1/1/2010**	**Contribution**	**51**		

For Paperwork Reduction Act Notice, see the Instructions for Form 5471.   Cat. No. 61200O   **Schedule O (Form 5471)** (Rev. 12-2005)

¶504

(f) Amount paid or value given	(g) Name and address of person from whom shares were acquired

Section D—Disposition of Stock

(a) Name of shareholder disposing of stock	(b) Class of stock	(c) Date of disposition	(d) Method of disposition	(e) Number of shares disposed of		
				(1) Directly	(2) Indirectly	(3) Constructively

(f) Amount received	(g) Name and address of person to whom disposition of stock was made

Section E—Organization or Reorganization of Foreign Corporation

(a) Name and address of transferor	(b) Identifying number (if any)	(c) Date of transfer

(d) Assets transferred to foreign corporation			(e) Description of assets transferred by, or notes or securities issued by, foreign corporation
(1) Description of assets	(2) Fair market value	(3) Adjusted basis (if transferor was U.S. person)	

Section F—Additional Information

(a) If the foreign corporation or a predecessor U.S. corporation filed (or joined with a consolidated group in filing) a U.S. income tax return for any of the last 3 years, attach a statement indicating the year for which a return was filed (and, if applicable, the name of the corporation filing the consolidated return), the taxable income or loss, and the U.S. income tax paid (after all credits).

(b) List the date of any reorganization of the foreign corporation that occurred during the last 4 years while any U.S. person held 10% or more in value or vote (directly or indirectly) of the corporation's stock ▶

(c) If the foreign corporation is a member of a group constituting a chain of ownership, attach a chart, for each unit of which a shareholder owns 10% or more in value or voting power of the outstanding stock. The chart must indicate the corporation's position in the chain of ownership and the percentages of stock ownership (see instructions for an example).

Schedule O **(Form 5471)** (Rev. 12-2005)

On January 1, 2008, Aunt Harriet pays $500 for one of the 100 outstanding shares in Hong Kong Equities (HKE), a Hong Kong corporation that invests in Asian entities not incorporated in Hong Kong. In the 35% bracket, Aunt Harriet fails to make a qualified electing fund election when filing her U.S. income tax return for 2008. HKE earns ordinary income of $100,000 in 2008, $100,000 in 2009, and $100,000 in 2010. On December 31, 2010, HKE distributes a $3,000 dividend to Aunt Harriet. Aunt Harriet must prepare a Form 8621 reporting the excess distribution in 2010. Two thousand dollars of the $3,000 dividend is attributable to 2008 and 2009. Although the excess distribution regime will not result in any additional tax beyond the $1,050 because Aunt Harriet will remain in the 35% tax bracket, Aunt Harriet will have to pay interest on the deferred tax from 2008 and 2009 on the $350 of tax due each year. At the Code section 6621 underpayment rate of 4%[116], that amount will total $43.

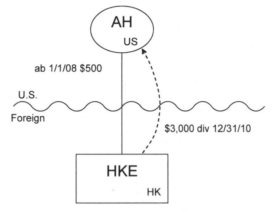

[116] Rev. Rul. 2011-12, 2011-26 IRB 917.

Form **8621** (Rev. December 2004) Department of the Treasury Internal Revenue Service	**Return by a Shareholder of a Passive Foreign Investment Company or Qualified Electing Fund** ▶ **See separate instructions.**	OMB No. 1545-1002
		Attachment Sequence No. **69**

Name of shareholder **Aunt Harriet**	Identifying number (see page 2 of instructions) **987-65-4321**

Number, street, and room or suite no. (If a P.O. box, see page 2 of instructions.)	Shareholder tax year: calendar year 20 .**10** or other tax year beginning .... , 20 ...... and ending.................. 20......

City or town, state, and ZIP code or country
Gotham City

Check type of shareholder filing the return: ☑ Individual ☐ Corporation ☐ Partnership ☐ S Corporation ☐ Nongrantor Trust ☐ Estate

Name of passive foreign investment company (PFIC) or qualified electing fund (QEF) **Hong Kong Equities**	Employer identification number (if any)

Address (Enter number, street, city or town, and country.) **Hong Kong**	Tax year of company or fund: calendar year 20 .**10**. or other tax year beginning .... , 20 ...... and ending..................... , 20 ....

Part I **Elections** (See instructions.)

A ☐ **Election To Treat the PFIC as a QEF.** I, a shareholder of a PFIC, elect to treat the PFIC as a QEF. *Complete lines 1a through 2c of Part II.*

B ☐ **Deemed Sale Election.** I, a shareholder on the first day of a PFIC's first tax year as a QEF, elect to recognize gain on the deemed sale of my interest in the PFIC. *Enter gain or loss on line 10f of Part IV.*

C ☐ **Deemed Dividend Election.** I, a shareholder on the first day of a PFIC's first tax year as a QEF that is a controlled foreign corporation (CFC), elect to treat an amount equal to my share of the post-1986 earnings and profits of the CFC as an excess distribution. *Enter this amount on line 10e of Part IV.*

D ☐ **Election To Extend Time For Payment of Tax.** I, a shareholder of a QEF, elect to extend the time for payment of tax on the undistributed earnings and profits of the QEF until this election is terminated. *Complete lines 3a through 4c of Part II to calculate the tax that may be deferred.*
Note: *If any portion of line 1a or line 2a of Part II is includible under section 551 or 951, you may **not** make this election. Also, see sections 1294(c) and 1294(f) and the related regulations for events that terminate this election.*

E ☐ **Election To Recognize Gain on Deemed Sale of PFIC.** I, a shareholder of a former PFIC or a PFIC to which section 1297(e) applies, elect to treat as an excess distribution the gain recognized on the deemed sale of my interest in the PFIC, or, if I qualify, my share of the PFIC's post-1986 earnings and profits deemed distributed, on the last day of its last tax year as a PFIC under section 1297(a). *Enter gain on line 10f of Part IV.*

F ☐ **Election To Mark-to-Market PFIC Stock.** I, a shareholder of a PFIC, elect to mark-to-market the PFIC stock that is marketable within the meaning of section 1296(e). *Complete Part III.*

Part II **Income From a Qualified Electing Fund (QEF).** All QEF shareholders complete lines 1a through 2c. If you are making Election D, also complete lines 3a through 4c. (See page 5 of instructions.)

1a Enter your pro rata share of the ordinary earnings of the QEF .	**1a**	
b Enter the portion of line 1a that is included in income under section 551 or 951 or that may be excluded under section 1293(g)	**1b**	
c Subtract line 1b from line 1a. Enter this amount on your tax return as dividend income . .		**1c**
2a Enter your pro rata share of the total net capital gain of the QEF	**2a**	
b Enter the portion of line 2a that is included in income under section 551 or 951 or that may be excluded under section 1293(g)	**2b**	
c Subtract line 2b from line 2a. This amount is a net long-term capital gain. Enter this amount in Part II of the Schedule D used for your income tax return. (See instructions.)		**2c**
3a Add lines 1c and 2c		**3a**
b Enter the total amount of cash and the fair market value of other property distributed or deemed distributed to you during the tax year of the QEF. (See instructions.)	**3b**	
c Enter the portion of line 3a not already included in line 3b that is attributable to shares in the QEF that you disposed of, pledged, or otherwise transferred during the tax year	**3c**	
d Add lines 3b and 3c		**3d**
e Subtract line 3d from line 3a, and enter the difference (if zero or less, enter amount in brackets)		**3e**
Important: *If line 3e is greater than zero, and no portion of line 1a or 2a is includible in income under section 551 or 951, you may make Election D with respect to the amount on line 3e.*		
4a Enter the total tax for the tax year (See instructions.)	**4a**	
b Enter the total tax for the tax year determined without regard to the amount entered on line 3e.	**4b**	
c Subtract line 4b from line 4a. **This is the deferred tax, the time for payment of which is extended by making Election D. See instructions**		**4c**

For Paperwork Reduction Act Notice, see page 7 of separate instructions.   Cat. No. 64174H   Form **8621** (Rev. 12-2004)

Part III	Gain or (Loss) From Mark-to-Market Election (See page 5 of instructions.)		

5	Enter the fair market value of your PFIC stock at the end of the tax year	**5**	
6	Enter your adjusted basis in the stock at the end of the tax year	**6**	
7	**Excess.** Subtract line 6 from line 5. If a gain, **stop here.** Include this amount as ordinary income on your tax return. If a loss, go to line 8	**7**	
8	Enter any unreversed inclusions (as defined in section 1296(d)). See instructions.	**8**	
9	Enter the smaller of line 7 or line 8. Include this amount as an ordinary loss on your tax return	**9**	

Part IV	Distributions From and Dispositions of Stock of a Section 1291 Fund (See page 6 of instructions.)
	Complete a **separate** Part IV for each excess distribution (see instructions).

10a	Enter your total distributions from the section 1291 fund during the current tax year with respect to the applicable stock. If the holding period of the stock began in the current tax year, see instructions . .	**10a**	3,000
b	Enter the total distributions (reduced by the portions of such distributions that were excess distributions but not included in income under section 1291(a)(1)(B)) made by the fund with respect to the applicable stock for each of the 3 years preceding the current tax year (or if shorter, the portion of the shareholder's holding period before the current tax year). . . .	**10b**	0
c	Divide line 10b by 3. (See instructions if the number of preceding tax years is less than 3.) .	**10c**	0
d	Multiply line 10c by 125% (1.25)	**10d**	0
e	Subtract line 10d from line 10a. This amount, if more than zero, is the excess distribution with respect to the applicable stock. If zero or less and you did not dispose of stock during the tax year, **do not** complete the rest of Part IV. See instructions if you received more than one distribution during the current tax year. Also, see instructions for rules for reporting a nonexcess distribution on your income tax return . . .	**10e**	3,000
f	Enter gain or loss from the disposition of stock of a section 1291 fund or former section 1291 fund. If a gain, complete line 11. If a loss, show it in brackets and **do not** complete line 11 .	**10f**	0
11a	Attach a statement for each distribution and disposition. Show your holding period for each share of stock or block of shares held. Allocate the excess distribution to each day in your holding period. Add all amounts that are allocated to days in each tax year.		
b	Enter the total of the amounts determined in line 11a that are allocable to the current tax year and tax years before the foreign corporation became a PFIC (pre-PFIC tax years). Enter these amounts on your income tax return as other income	**11b**	1,000
c	Enter the aggregate increases in tax (before credits) for each tax year in your holding period (other than the current tax year and pre-PFIC years). (See instructions.)	**11c**	700
d	Foreign tax credit. (See instructions.)	**11d**	0
e	Subtract line 11d from line 11c. Enter this amount on your income tax return as "additional tax." (See instructions.)	**11e**	700
f	Determine interest on each net increase in tax determined on line 11e using the rates and methods of section 6621. Enter the aggregate amount of interest here. (See instructions.) .	**11f**	43

Part V	Status of Prior Year Section 1294 Elections and Termination of Section 1294 Elections
	Complete a separate column for each outstanding election. Complete lines 9 and 10 only if there is a partial termination of the section 1294 election.

		(i)	(ii)	(iii)	(iv)	(v)	(vi)
1	Tax year of outstanding election						
2	Undistributed earnings to which the election relates						
3	Deferred tax						
4	Interest accrued on deferred tax (line 3) as of the filing date						
5	Event terminating election						
6	Earnings distributed or deemed distributed during the tax year.						
7	Deferred tax due with this return.						
8	Accrued interest due with this return						
9	Deferred tax outstanding after partial termination of election						
10	Interest accrued after partial termination of election . .						

Form **8621** (Rev. 12-2004)

Statement for Part IV, Line 11a

	Dates of Holding	Allocation of Distribution
2008	January 1 to December 31	$1,000
2009	January 1 to December 31	$1,000

Chapter 6
Foreign Currency Translation and Transactions

¶ 601   Introduction
¶ 602   Foreign Currency Translation
¶ 603   Foreign Currency Transactions

¶ 601 INTRODUCTION

The foreign branches and subsidiaries of U.S. companies often conduct business and maintain their books and records in the currency of the host country. This creates a currency translation problem for the domestic parent corporation, which must restate into U.S. dollars the results from its foreign operations. Tax attributes that require translation include the taxable income or loss of a foreign branch, earnings remittances from a foreign branch, actual and deemed distributions from a foreign corporation, and foreign income taxes. Foreign currency translation would be the only issue if currency exchange rates did not fluctuate. However, the U.S. dollar floats freely against other currencies and this results in currency exchange gains and losses on assets and liabilities denominated in other currencies.

Translational exchange gains and losses arise when a foreign branch or subsidiary that has a functional currency other than the U.S. dollar repatriates earnings that were previously taxed to the U.S. parent and the exchange rate has changed since the parent included those earnings in U.S. taxable income. Foreign currency translation, including the tax treatment of translational exchange gains and losses, is discussed in the section entitled "Foreign Currency Translation."

Transactional exchange gains and losses arise when, for example, a U.S. company enters into a transaction denominated in a foreign currency and the exchange rate fluctuates between the time the transaction is entered into and the time the transaction closes. Transactional exchange gains and losses are discussed in the section entitled "Foreign Currency Transactions."

¶ 602 FOREIGN CURRENCY TRANSLATION

.01 Qualified Business Unit

A qualified business unit (QBU) generally must make all of its U.S. tax determinations in its functional currency.[1] A corporation is always considered to be a QBU.[2] In addition, a branch of a corporation can qualify as a QBU if the branch is

---

[1] Code Sec. 985(a).   [2] Reg. § 1.989(a)-1(b)(2)(i).

a separate and clearly identified unit of a trade or business of the corporation for which separate books and records are maintained.[3]

Whether a branch operation constitutes a separate trade or business of the corporation is a question of fact. For this purpose, a trade or business is a specific unified group of activities that constitutes an independent economic activity carried on for profit. This group of activities ordinarily includes every operation which is part of the process by which an enterprise earns a profit, including the collection of income and the payment of expenses. It is not necessary that the trade or business carried out by the branch be of a different type than that carried out by other QBUs of the taxpayer. For example, a sales branch that is located in a different geographic market than the home office sales operation can constitute a separate trade or business. However, activities that are merely ancillary to a trade or business of the corporation do not constitute a separate trade or business.[4]

> **Example 6.1:** [5] USAco, a domestic corporation, manufactures goods for sale both in the United States and abroad. USAco sells goods in the United Kingdom through a branch office located in London. The London office has its own employees who solicit and process orders. USAco maintains separate books and records for all of the transactions entered into by the London office. USAco qualifies as a QBU because of its corporate status. The branch sales office in London also qualifies as a separate QBU because its sales operation constitutes a separate trade or business for which USAco maintains separate books and records.

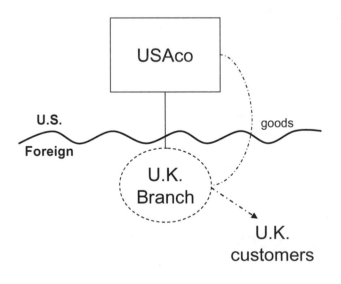

---

[3] Code Sec. 989(a) and Reg. §1.989(a)-1(b)(2)(ii). A separate set of books and records generally includes books of original entry and ledger accounts, both general and subsidiary. Reg. §1.989(a)-1(d).

[4] Reg. §1.989(a)-1(c). An activity of a foreign person which produces income effectively connected with the conduct of a U.S. trade or business is always treated as a separate QBU. Reg. §1.989(a)-1(b)(3).

[5] Compare Reg. §1.989(a)-1(e), Example 1.

¶602.01

Example 6.2: [6] USAco, a domestic corporation, incorporates a wholly-owned subsidiary in Switzerland to market its products in Europe. In addition to its sales operation located in Switzerland, the Swiss subsidiary has branch sales offices in France and Germany that are responsible for all marketing operations in those countries. Each branch has its own employees, solicits and processes orders, and maintains a separate set of books and records. USAco and the Swiss subsidiary are both QBUs because of their corporate status. The French and German branches also are QBUs of the Swiss subsidiary because each sales operation constitutes a separate trade or business for which separate books and records are maintained.

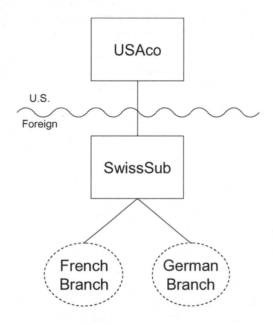

Unlike a corporation, an individual is not a QBU.[7] Moreover, activities of an individual conducted as an employee do not constitute a QBU.[8] However, activities of an individual conducted as a sole proprietor do constitute a QBU if they satisfy the separate trade or business and separate books and records requirements discussed above.[9] As with a corporation, a partnership, trust, or estate is always considered to be a QBU of the partner or beneficiary, regardless of the scope of the entity's activities or whether the entity keeps separate books and records.[10] In addition, each different activity of a partnership, trust, or estate also can qualify as a separate QBU if it satisfies the separate trade or business and separate books and records requirements.[11]

---

[6] Compare Reg. § 1.989(a)-1(e), Example 2.

[7] Reg. § 1.989(a)-1(b)(2)(i).

[8] Reg. § 1.989(a)-1(c).

[9] Reg. § 1.989(a)-1(b)(2)(ii).

[10] Reg. § 1.989(a)-1(b)(2)(i).

[11] Reg. § 1.989(a)-1(b)(2)(ii).

.02 Functional Currency

A QBU's functional currency is the U.S. dollar, unless the QBU conducts a significant part of its activities in an economic environment in which a foreign currency is used and maintains its books and records in that foreign currency.[12] For this purpose, a QBU is presumed to keep its books and records in the currency of the economic environment in which a significant part of its activities are conducted.[13] The taxpayer must consider all of the facts and circumstances in identifying the relevant economic environment, including the currency of the country in which the QBU is a resident, as well as the currencies in which the QBU realizes its cash flows, generates its revenues, incurs its expenses, borrows and lends, sells its products, and makes its pricing and other financial decisions.[14] If a QBU has more than one currency that satisfies these requirements, then the QBU may choose any of those currencies as its functional currency.[15]

The adoption of a functional currency is treated as a method of accounting. As a consequence, the functional currency used in the year of adoption must be used for all subsequent taxable years unless permission to change is granted by the IRS.[16] Permission to change functional currencies generally is not granted unless significant changes in the facts and circumstances of the QBU's economic environment occur. The QBU's functional currency for U.S. financial reporting purposes is a relevant factor in this regard.[17]

.03 Foreign Branches

Code Section 987 addresses foreign currency translation in the context of foreign branch operations. The proposed regulations issued in 2006 provide some guidance as to the IRS's position.[18]

If a foreign branch is a QBU that has a functional currency other than the U.S. dollar, the taxpayer computes the branch's income, gain, deduction and loss for the year in the branch's functional currency and then translates such items into the taxpayer's functional currency, using the yearly average exchange rate, unless the spot rate is either elected or required.[19] The average exchange rate means the simple average of the daily exchange rates, excluding weekends, holidays, and any other nonbusiness days for the taxable year.[20]

> **Example 6.3:** [21] USAco is a U.S. corporation with the dollar as its functional currency. On November 1, 2010, USAco establishes a foreign sales branch in France, which qualifies as a QBU with the euro as its functional

---

[12] Code Sec. 985(b)(1) and Reg. § 1.985-1(c)(1). Activities of a foreign person which produce income effectively connected with the conduct of a U.S. trade or business are always treated as a separate QBU, with the U.S. dollar as its functional currency. Reg. § 1.985-1(b)(1)(v). Special rules also apply to a foreign corporation with two or more QBUs that do not have the same functional currency. Reg. § 1.985-1(d).

[13] Reg. § 1.985-1(c)(3).

[14] Reg. § 1.985-1(c)(2)(i). Other relevant factors include the duration of the qualified business unit's business operations and the significance or volume of the qualified business unit's independent activities.

[15] Reg. § 1.985-1(c)(4).

[16] Reg. § 1.985-4(a).

[17] Reg. § 1.985-4(b). If a QBU is granted permission to change its functional currency, adjustments may be required. Reg. § 1.985-5.

[18] Reg. § 1.987-5. The 2006 proposed regulations withdrew the 1991 proposed regulations.

[19] Code Sec. 987 and Prop. Reg. §§ 1.987-3(b) and 1.987-1(c).

[20] Reg. § 1.989(b)-1.

[21] Based on Prop. Reg. § 1.987-3(f), Ex. 1.

currency. USAco uses the yearly average exchange rate to translate its gross sales income. However, USAco is required to use the spot rate to translate the basis of its inventory.[22]

Assume that the branch purchased 300 units of inventory on November 1 for €1.50 per unit, when the spot rate is €1 = $1.08. As such, the branch's basis in these units is $486 [(300 × €1.50) × $1.08]. Assume also that the yearly average exchange rate for 2009 is €1 = $1.05. Finally, assume the branch sold all 300 units by the end of the year at a price of €3 per unit.

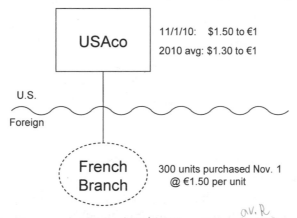

11/1/10: $1.50 to €1
2010 avg: $1.30 to €1

USAco

U.S.
Foreign

French Branch

300 units purchased Nov. 1
@ €1.50 per unit

The gross sales income would be $945 [(300 × €3) × $1.05]. Accordingly, the branch's gross income for 2009 is $459 [$945 – $486].

Currency exchange gains and losses arising from changes in the exchange rate between the date income is earned by the branch and the date such income is remitted to the home office ("987 gain or loss") are also recognized.[23] The rationale behind these rules is that foreign currency is property that has a basis, just as other property has a basis, and that the taxpayer should recognize gain or loss on repatriation when its value on repatriation differs from its basis. This gain and loss essentially equals the product of:

(i) the owner's net unrecognized 987 gain or loss in the owner's functional currency,[24] multiplied by

(ii) the remittance proportion, which is the amount remitted divided by the sum amount remitted plus the QBU's basis in all its assets.[25]

Example 6.4: [26] USAco is a domestic corporation with the dollar as its functional currency. USAco establishes a foreign sales branch in the United Kingdom, which is a QBU with the pound as its functional currency. In the previous year, the branch recognized income of $420, none of which was repatriated, that, under the current exchange rate, now has a value of $500,

---

[22] Prop. Reg. § 1.987-3(b)(2)(ii)(B). Here, the required use of the spot rate is referred to as the historic exchange rate.

[23] Code Sec. 987(3) and Prop. Reg. § 1.987-5. The incorporation or other termination of a branch also triggers

recognition of a currency exchange gain or loss. Prop. Reg. § 1.987-8(d).

[24] Prop. Reg. § 1.987-4.

[25] Prop. Reg. § 1.987-5.

[26] Based on Prop. Reg. § 1.987-5(g), Ex. 1.

resulting in a net unrecognized 987 gain of $80.[27] During the current year, the branch remits $500 worth of pounds to USAco when the UK branch has a basis in its assets of $5,350.

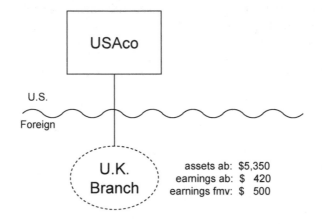

assets ab: $5,350
earnings ab: $ 420
earnings fmv: $ 500

The percent remitted is 0.085 [$500 ÷ ($5,350 + $500)] and the 987 gain is $6.80 [0.085 × $80].

For purposes of determining the taxpayer's basis in a remittance, the remittance is treated as being paid pro rata out of the branch's accumulated earnings. The resulting gain or loss is treated as ordinary income that is sourced by reference to the source of income giving rise to the branch's accumulated earnings.[28]

.04 Foreign Corporations

Dividend distributions. The translation rules for computing the U.S. tax attributes of a dividend distribution from a foreign corporation are as follows:

(i) *Dividend*—If a foreign corporation pays a dividend in a foreign currency, the U.S. taxpayer translates the dividend income into dollars using the spot rate for the date on which the dividend was included in the taxpayer's income.[29]

(ii) *Foreign withholding taxes*—Any foreign withholding taxes imposed on a dividend from a foreign corporation are translated into dollars using the spot rate or the average exchange rate, whichever is applicable (see Foreign Income Taxes, below).[30]

(iii) *Deemed paid foreign tax credit*—For purposes of computing the deemed paid credit, the foreign corporation's dividend distribution and post-1986 undistributed earnings are not translated into U.S. dollars, but are instead maintained in the foreign corporation's functional currency.[31] On the other hand, foreign taxes included in the pool of post-1986 foreign

---

[27] Prop. Reg. § 1.987-4(d)(2)(ii)(A).

[28] Code Sec. 987(3)(A) and (B); *see also* Prop. Reg. § 1.987-6.

[29] Code Secs. 986(b)(2) and 989(b)(1).

[30] Code Sec. 986(a); *see also* Code Sec. 903; Reg. § 1.903-1(b)(3)(Ex. 2).

[31] Code Sec. 986(b)(1).

income taxes are translated into dollars using the spot rate or the average exchange rate, whichever is applicable (see Foreign Income Taxes, below).[32]

Example 6.5: USAco, a domestic corporation, owns 100% of the stock of EURco. EURco is a calendar year, foreign corporation with the Swiss franc (F) as its functional currency. During its first year of operations, EURco derives F10 million of taxable income, pays F2 million in foreign income taxes, and distributes a F4 million dividend to USAco on December 31. The franc was worth $0.15 on December 31 and had an average daily value during the year of $0.14. Therefore, the F4 million dividend translates into $600,000 [F4 million × $0.15], and EURco's foreign income taxes are $280,000 [F2 million × $0.14]. EURco's undistributed earnings and profits are F8 million [F10 million of taxable income – F2 million of foreign income taxes]. As a result, EURco's dividend pulls out deemed paid taxes of $140,000 [$280,000 of foreign income taxes × (F4 million dividend ÷ F8 million of undistributed earnings and profits)], and USAco must recognize dividend income of $740,000 [$600,000 dividend + $140,000 gross-up].

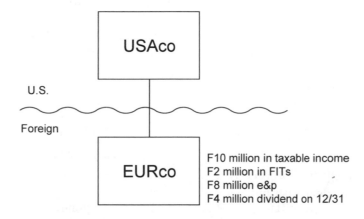

F10 million in taxable income
F2 million in FITs
F8 million e&p
F4 million dividend on 12/31

Subpart F inclusions. The translation rules for computing the tax attributes of a U.S. shareholder's Subpart F inclusion from a controlled foreign corporation (or CFC) are as follows:

(i) *Subpart F inclusion*—The appropriate exchange rate for computing an income inclusion under Subpart F varies with the type of inclusion. An inclusion of Subpart F income is translated into dollars using the average exchange rate for the CFC's taxable year. Inclusions for investments in U.S. property are computed using the spot rate for the last day of the CFC's taxable year.[33]

(ii) *Deemed paid foreign tax credit*—For purposes of computing the deemed paid credit, the CFC's Subpart F inclusion and post-1986 undistributed earnings and profits are not translated into U.S. dollars, but are instead

---

[32] Code Sec. 986(a).

[33] Code Secs. 986(b)(2) and 989(b).

maintained in the CFC's functional currency.[34] On other hand, foreign taxes included in the pool of post-1986 foreign income taxes are translated into dollars using the spot rate or the average exchange rate, whichever is applicable (see Foreign Income Taxes, below).[35]

(iii) *Distributions of previously taxed income*—For purposes of tracing actual dividend distributions to previously taxed income, the taxpayer measures the CFC's earnings in its functional currency.[36] Later, when receiving a distribution of previously taxed income, the U.S. shareholder must recognize a currency exchange gain or loss equal to the difference between:

    (a) The dollar value of the distribution as determined using the spot rate for the date of the distribution and

    (b) The U.S. shareholder's basis in the distribution as determined by the dollar amount at which the taxpayer previously included the earnings in U.S. taxable income.[37]

    Such gains are treated as ordinary income.[38]

Example 6.6: USAco, a domestic corporation, owns 100% of the stock of FORco, which was organized in year 1. FORco is a calendar year, foreign corporation with the euro (€) as its functional currency. FORco's tax attributes for its first two years of operations are as follows:

	Year 1	Year 2
Taxable income	€ 50 million	None
Foreign income taxes	€ 10 million	None
Undistributed E&P	€ 40 million	€ 40 million
Net Subpart F income	€ 20 million	None
Investments in U.S. property	€ 5 million	None
Actual dividend distributions (paid December 31)	None	€ 4 million

[34] Code Sec. 986(b)(1).
[35] Code Sec. 986(a).
[36] Code Sec. 986(b)(1).

[37] Code Sec. 986(c)(1).
[38] Code Sec. 986(c)(1).

¶602.04

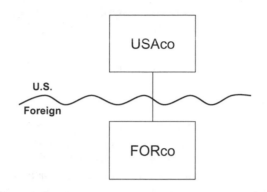

The euro had an average value of $1.10 during year 1, and was worth $1.20 on December 31 of year 1, and $1.40 on December 31 of year 2. USAco's Subpart F income inclusion for year 1 is $28 million [(€ 20 million of Subpart F income × $1.10) + (€ 5 million investment in U.S. property × $1.20)]. With respect to the deemed paid credit, FORco has foreign income taxes of $11 million [€ 10 million × $1.10] and undistributed earnings and profits of € 40 million [€ 50 million of taxable income – € 10 million of foreign income taxes]. Therefore, USAco's deemed paid taxes are $6,875,000 [$11 million of foreign income taxes × (€ 25 million Subpart F inclusion ÷ € 40 million of undistributed earnings)].

USAco can exclude from income the € 4 million dividend received in year 2 because it is traced to FORco's previously taxed income from year 1. For this purpose, USAco measures FORco's earnings in euros and traces the distribution to FORco's € 5 million investment of earnings in U.S. property from year 1.[39] However, the dividend does trigger the recognition of a currency exchange gain produced as a result of the euro strengthening against the dollar. The gain equals $800,000, which represents the excess of the distribution's value of $5.6 million [€ 4 million dividend × $1.40] over USAco's basis in the previously taxed earnings of $4.8 million [€ 4 million × $1.20].

Passive foreign investment company inclusions. A U.S. person translates his or her pro rata share of the undistributed earnings and profits of a qualified electing fund (or QEF) into dollars using the average exchange rate for the QEF's taxable year (the same average exchange rate as for Subpart F income).[40] For purposes of tracing subsequent actual dividend distributions to the QEF's previously taxed income, the taxpayer measures the QEF's earnings in its functional currency.[41] In addition, a U.S. person who receives a distribution of a QEF's previously taxed income must recognize a currency exchange gain or loss equal to the difference between:

(i) The dollar value of the actual distribution as determined using the spot rate for the date of the distribution and

---

[39] Code Sec. 959(c).
[40] Code Secs. 986(b)(2) and 989(b)(3).
[41] Code Sec. 986(b)(1).

¶602.04

(ii) The taxpayer's basis in the distribution as determined by the dollar amount at which the taxpayer previously included the earnings in U.S. taxable income.[42]

Such gains are treated as ordinary income.[43]

.05 Foreign Income Taxes

Taxpayers that account for foreign taxes on an accrual basis generally should translate foreign income taxes accrued into U.S. dollars at the average exchange rate for the tax year to which the taxes relate. However, the spot rate (the exchange rate on the date of payment) applies to (i) foreign taxes actually paid more than two years from the close of such tax year, (ii) foreign taxes paid in a tax year prior to the year to which they relate, and (iii) foreign taxes paid in a hyperinflationary currency. In addition, any adjustment to the amount of the taxes is translated using the spot rate when the adjusted taxes are paid to the foreign country. In the case of any refund or credit of foreign taxes, taxpayers must use the spot rate when the original payment of the foreign taxes was made.[44]

An accrual basis taxpayer may elect to translate foreign income taxes denominated in a nonfunctional currency using the spot rate when accrued.[45] Consequently, a taxpayer may be able to increase the amount of foreign income taxes paid.

Consider the following two examples involving a C corporation with a branch operation in a foreign country.

> **Example 6.7:** USAco is an accrual-basis, calendar-year U.S. C corporation that has a branch in a foreign country where the franc (F) is the local currency. During the current year, USAco remits F1 million of foreign income taxes on both June 30 and September 30. In closing its books for the year, USAco estimates that it owes an additional F1 million of foreign income taxes for the year. The franc was worth $0.10 on June 30, $0.12 on September 30, $0.13 on December 31 and had an average value during the year of $0.11. Therefore, USAco's creditable foreign income taxes are $330,000, computed as follows:

Date	U.S. Dollars	Converting Francs to U.S. Dollars (average exchange rate)
June 30	110,000	(F1 million × $0.11)
September 30	110,000	(F1 million × $0.11)
December 31	110,000	(F1 million × $0.11)
Total	330,000	

---

[42] Code Sec. 986(c)(1).

[43] Code Sec. 986(c)(1).

[44] Code Sec. 986(a). However, the IRS has the authority to issue regulations that would allow these foreign tax payments to be translated into U.S. dollar amounts using an average exchange rate for a specified period.

[45] Code Sec. 986(a)(1)(D).

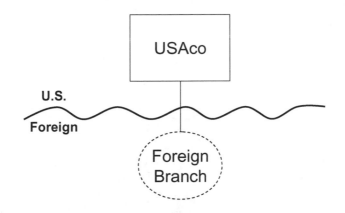

However, if USAco elects to translate foreign income taxes paid on an accrual basis using the spot rate on the foreign income tax accrual date, USAco's creditable foreign income taxes are $350,000, computed as follows:

Date	U.S. Dollars	Converting Francs to U.S. Dollars (spot rate)
June 30	100,000	(F1 million × $0.10)
September 30	120,000	(F1 million × $0.12)
December 31	130,000	(F1 million × $0.13)
Total	350,000	

Here, the election resulted in an additional $20,000 of creditable foreign income taxes.

However, the election must be made with caution because if, for example, an election were made for a branch in a foreign country constituting a QBU and the functional currency of that QBU depreciated in value relative to the U.S. dollar, a taxpayer would have fewer creditable foreign income taxes.

Example 6.8: USAco is an accrual-basis, calendar-year U.S. C corporation that has a branch in a foreign country where the franc (F) is the local currency. During the current year, USAco remits F1 million of foreign income taxes on both June 30 and September 30. In closing its books for the year, USAco estimates that it owes an additional F1 million of foreign income taxes for the year. The franc has declined in value such that it was worth $0.13 on June 30, $0.10 on September 30, and $0.09 on December 31, and had an average value during the year of $0.11. Therefore, USAco's creditable foreign income taxes decrease to $320,000, computed as follows:

Date	U.S. Dollars	Converting Francs to U.S. Dollars (spot rate)
June 30	130,000	(F1 million × $0.13)
September 30	100,000	(F1 million × $0.10)
December 31	90,000	(F1 million × $0.09)
Total	320,000	

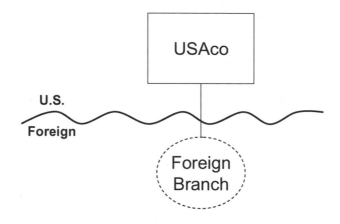

If, however, USAco had not made the election for the branch, USAco would use the average exchange rate for the year of $0.11 and have $330,000 of foreign income taxes paid.

Planning for this election must be carefully evaluated. More specifically, if a currency currently has what would historically be a relatively low value compared to the U.S. dollar, it is likely that that foreign currency may appreciate to the U.S. dollar over time and an election for such a QBU should be made. On the other hand, if the currency currently has a historically high value compared to the U.S. dollar, it is anticipated that that foreign currency may depreciate against the U.S. dollar and making an election would decrease the amount of foreign income taxes paid. Under such a circumstance, the election should not be made.

.06 Hyperinflationary Currencies

Special rules apply to any QBU that would otherwise be required to use a hyperinflationary currency as its functional currency. A hyperinflationary currency is the currency of a foreign country in which there is a cumulative compounded rate of inflation of at least 100% during the 36-month period immediately preceding the first day of the current calendar year.[46] The rates of inflation are generally determined by reference to the consumer price index of the country as listed in the monthly issues of "International Financial Statistics" or a successor publication of the International Monetary Fund.[47]

Hyperinflationary currency creates significant problems with the conventional methods for translating the results of a foreign operation into U.S. dollars. For example, in a hyperinflationary environment, the conventional methods do not provide an accurate comparison of current-year inflated revenues to the costs of prior-year investments in property, plant, and equipment, reducing the dollar value of depreciation deductions.

---

[46] Reg. § 1.985-1(b)(2)(ii)(D).

[47] *Id.* If a country's currency is not listed in such publication, a QBU may use any other reasonable method consistently applied for determining the country's consumer price index.

A QBU that would otherwise be required to use a hyperinflationary currency must use the U.S. dollar as its functional currency and must compute its taxable income (and earnings and profits) using the dollar approximate separate transactions method (the DASTM).[48] The DASTM attempts to mitigate these problems by translating the QBU's taxable income (and earnings and profits) on at least a monthly basis,[49] and by annually recognizing certain unrealized exchange gains and losses.[50] The DASTM is generally applied by preparing an income statement for the QBU in its hyperinflationary currency with certain adjustments (e.g., to conform to U.S. generally accepted accounting principles and tax accounting principles, etc.), converting the adjusted amounts into U.S. dollars and computing and adjusting for DASTM gain or loss.

A QBU that has been required to use the DASTM and the U.S. dollar because its otherwise functional currency was hyperinflationary must use that functional currency once it ceases to be hyperinflationary.[51]

> ***Example 6.9:*** [52] Forco is a corporation incorporated under the laws of Foronia, a country whose local currency, the Foro, has experienced annual inflation rates for the past three years of 29%, 25% and 30%. The cumulative inflation rate for this three-year period is 109.625% [(1.29 × 1.25 × 1.30) − 1.0 = 109.625]. As such, Forco must use the U.S. dollar as its functional currency (and not the Foro) and the DASTM until the Foro ceases to be a hyperinflationary currency.

¶ 603 FOREIGN CURRENCY TRANSACTIONS

.01 Applicable Transactions

Special rules apply for purposes of determining the amount, timing, character, and source of currency exchange gains and losses associated with Code Sec. 988 transactions. Code Sec. 988 transactions include the following:

(i) Dispositions of a nonfunctional currency, and

(ii) The following three categories of transactions where the amount the taxpayer is entitled to receive or required to pay is denominated in a nonfunctional currency:[53]

    (a) *Debt instruments*—This includes transactions where the taxpayer lends or borrows funds through the use of a bond, debenture, note, certificate, or other evidence of indebtedness.

---

[48] Reg. §§ 1.985-1 (b) (2) (ii) (A) and 1.985-3. There are exceptions for foreign corporations other than controlled foreign corporations and certain QBU branches of foreign corporations. Reg. § 1.985-1 (b) (2) (ii) (B).

[49] Reg. § 1.985-3 (b) (3) and (c) (7). The conventional approach is to translate taxable income on an annual basis.

[50] Reg. § 1.985-3 (b) (4) and (d) (1).

[51] Reg. § 1.985-1 (b) (2) (ii) (E). Note that this change can result in the need for certain adjustments. See Reg. § 1.985-5.

[52] *Compare* Reg. § 1.985-1 (b) (2) (ii) (D).

[53] In addition to being denominated in a nonfunctional currency, the amount may also be determined by reference to a nonfunctional currency.

    (b) *Receivables and payables*—This includes transactions where the taxpayer accrues an item of income or expense that will be received or paid at a future date, including a payable or receivable relating to a capital expenditure.

    (c) *Forward, futures, and option contracts*—This includes transactions where the taxpayer enters into a forward contract, futures contract, currency option, or similar financial instrument.[54]

However, Code Sec. 988 transactions do not include any transaction entered into by an individual unless the transaction is related to a business or investment activity[55] and certain transactions between or among a taxpayer and/or QBUs of that taxpayer.[56]

    The entire amount of gain or loss is treated as an exchange gain or loss[57] when arising from either a disposition of functional currency or loss arising from a currency forward, futures, or option contract.[58]

    In contrast, a gain or loss arising from a transaction involving a debt instrument, receivable, or payable is treated as an exchange gain or loss only to the extent it is attributable to a change in exchange rates that occurs between the transaction's booking date and the payment date.[59] For this purpose, the payment date is the date on which payment is made or received,[60] whereas the booking date is the date on which funds are borrowed or lent in the case of a debt instrument[61] or the date on which the item is accrued in the case of a receivable or payable.[62]

    A special rule applies to simplify the accounting for trade receivables and trade payables. If an average exchange rate is consistent with the taxpayer's financial accounting, the taxpayer can elect to use that average exchange rate, based on intervals of one quarter year or less, to both accrue and record the receipt and payment of amounts in satisfaction of trade receivables and payables that are denominated in a nonfunctional currency. For example, a taxpayer may use the average exchange rate for the first quarter to accrue all payables and receivables incurred during the first quarter. The same average rate also would be used to record all payments made and amounts received in satisfaction of payables and receivables during the first quarter.[63]

.02 Tax Consequences

    Amount and timing of exchange gains and losses. The taxation of exchange gains and losses is based on the premise that, for U.S. tax purposes, only

---

[54] Code Sec. 988(c)(1)(A), (B), and (C), and Reg. § 1.988-1(a)(1) and (a)(2). A forward contract is an agreement to buy or sell a given amount of foreign currency on a future date at a specified exchange rate. A futures contract is an agreement to buy or sell foreign currency that is traded on a futures exchange. A currency option gives the holder the right to buy or sell a given amount of currency at a specified exchange rate prior to the contract's expiration date.

[55] Code Sec. 988(e) and Reg. § 1.988-1(a)(9).

[56] Reg. § 1.988-1(a)(10). Code Sec. 988 transactions also do not include either regulated futures contracts or nonequity options, which would be marked to market under Code Sec. 1256 if held on the last day of the taxable year.

[57] Code Sec. 988(c)(1)(C)(i)(II).

[58] Code Sec. 988(b)(3).

[59] Code Sec. 988(b)(1) and (2).

[60] Code Sec. 988(c)(3).

[61] Code Sec. 988(c)(2)(A).

[62] Code Sec. 988(c)(2)(B).

[63] Reg. § 1.988-1(d)(3). A taxpayer cannot change the use of a convention without the consent of the Commissioner once it has been adopted.

¶603.02

U.S. dollars are money. As a consequence, currencies other than the U.S. dollar are treated as "property" that has a tax basis independent of its specific denomination. One implication of this approach is that exchange gains and losses arising from a Code Sec. 988 transaction involving debt instruments, receivables, or payables generally are accounted for separately from the gain or loss on the underlying transaction.[64] For example, if a domestic corporation with the U.S. dollar as its functional currency makes a sale on account that is denominated in a foreign currency, the gross profit from the sale is recognized separately from any exchange gain or loss on the receivable denominated in the foreign currency.

> *Example* **6.10:** USAco is an accrual-basis, domestic corporation with the U.S. dollar as its functional currency. On January 1, USAco makes an export sale denominated in kronor (K). The sales price is K2,000. The foreign customer remits the K2,000 on April 1 and USAco converts the K2,000 into U.S. dollars on April 10. The kronor was worth $1.50 on January 1, $1.45 on April 1, and $1.43 on April 10. Therefore, on January 1, USAco recognizes sales revenues of $3,000 [K2,000 × $1.50]. In addition, because the kronor weakened against the dollar between the booking date of January 1 and the payment date of April 1 ($1.45), USAco realizes an exchange loss on the collection of the receivable. The loss is $100, which represents the difference between the value of the kronor received in payment of $2,900 [K2,000 × $1.45] and USAco's basis in the related account receivable of $3,000 [K2,000 × $1.50].[65] USAco also must recognize an exchange loss upon converting the kronor into dollars. The loss is $40, which represents the difference between the amount realized from the sale of the kronor of $2,860 [K2,000 × $1.43] and USAco's basis in the kronor of $2,900 [K2,000 × $1.45].[66]

Character and source of exchange gains and losses. Exchange gains and losses attributable to a Code Sec. 988 transaction are treated as ordinary income or loss[67] and are sourced by reference to the residence of the taxpayer or the QBU of the taxpayer on whose books the underlying asset, liability, or item of income or expense is properly reflected.[68] For purposes of this source rule, a U.S. resident is any corporation, partnership, trust, or estate that is a U.S person, as well as any individual who has a tax home in the United States.[69] An individual's tax home is his or her regular or principal place of business, provided that he or she is not treated as having a tax home in a foreign country during any period in which his or her abode is in the United States.[70] A foreign resident is any corporation, partnership,

---

[64] Code Sec. 988(a)(1)(A) and Reg. §1.988-1(e). However, the exchange gain or loss realized on transactions involving debt instruments is limited to the total gain or loss realized on the transaction. Reg. §1.988-2(b)(8).

[65] Reg. §1.988-2(c)(2).

[66] Reg. §1.988-2(a)(2)(i).

[67] Code Sec. 988(a)(1)(A). However, a taxpayer can elect to characterize exchange gains or losses on certain identified currency forward, futures, or option contracts as capital gains or losses. Code Sec. 988(a)(1)(B) and Reg. §1.988-3(b).

[68] Code Sec. 988(a)(3)(A). However, any exchange gain or loss realized by a foreign person from the conduct

of a U.S. trade or business is treated as U.S. source income. Reg. §1.988-4(c).

[69] Code Sec. 988(a)(3)(B)(i)(I) and (II).

[70] Code Sec. 911(d)(3) and Reg. §1.911-2(b). An individual's abode is in the United States if that is where his or her economic, social, and personal ties are closest (for example, *see J.T. Lemay,* CA-5, 88-1 USTC ¶9182, 837 F2d 681 (5th Cir. 1988). Aff'g 53 TCM 862, Dec. 43,931(M), TC Memo. 1987-256; *and D.P. Lansdown,* 68 TCM 680, Dec. 50,114(M), TC Memo. 1994-452. Aff'd, 73 F3d 373 (10th Cir. 1995)). An individual who does not have a tax home is treated as a U.S. resident if such individual is a U.S. citizen or resident alien and as a foreign resident if

trust, or estate that is a foreign person, as well as any individual who has a tax home in a foreign country.[71] The residence of any QBU of the taxpayer (e.g., a branch of a domestic corporation) is the country in which the QBU's principal place of business is located.[72]

For purposes of the foreign tax credit limitation, net gains from foreign currency transactions generally are assigned to the passive income category.[73] An exception applies to certain business and hedging transactions, which are assigned to the general limitation category.

.03 Hedging Transactions

A taxpayer can reduce or eliminate the currency exchange risk component of a transaction through the use of a variety of financial instruments, such as currency forward, futures and options contracts.

> **Example 6.11:** On February 1, USAco, a domestic corporation, agrees to pay a Mexican supplier 600,000 pesos on July 1 for the delivery of some raw materials on July 1. Also on February 1, USAco hedges against the currency exchange risk associated with this purchase agreement by entering into a currency forward agreement with a bank to buy 600,000 pesos for $100,000 on July 1. The forward contract effectively eliminates the currency exchange risk component of the purchase agreement by fixing the purchase price of the raw materials in U.S. dollars at $100,000.

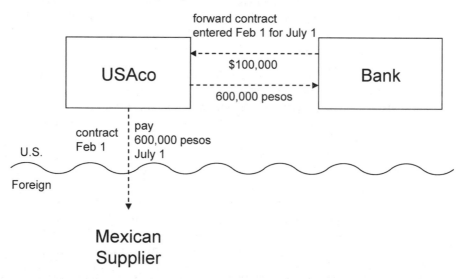

Because there is no currency exchange risk associated with a fully hedged transaction, in certain circumstances a taxpayer is allowed to integrate the accounting for the hedge with the accounting for the underlying hedged transaction. This ap-

---

(Footnote Continued)

such individual is not a U.S. citizen or resident alien. Code Sec. 988(a)(3)(B)(i).

[71] Code Sec. 988(a)(3)(B)(i)(I) and (III).

[72] Code Sec. 988(a)(3)(B)(ii).

[73] Code Secs. 904(d)(2)(A) and (B) and 954(c)(1)(D).

¶603.03

proach reflects the reality that a fully hedged transaction is, in substance, a transaction denominated in the hedge security (in Example 7.9, the U.S. dollar).

A hedge and hedged transaction qualify for integration treatment only if they meet the definitional requirements of a Code Sec. 988 hedging transaction.[74] If these requirements are met, the taxpayer can ignore the nonfunctional currency aspect of the transaction and account for the transaction as if it were denominated in the hedge currency, in which case no exchange gain or loss is recognized. Code Sec. 988 includes the following three categories of hedging transactions:

(i) *Hedged debt instruments*—These include hedges associated with transactions in which the taxpayer lends or borrows funds through the use of a bond, debenture, note, certificate, or other evidence of indebtedness (but not accounts payable, accounts receivable, or similar items of income and expense).[75]

(ii) *Hedged executory contracts for goods and services*—These include hedges involving executory contracts to pay or receive nonfunctional currency in the future with respect to the sale or purchase of property or services in the ordinary course of the taxpayer's business.[76]

(iii) *Hedge for the period between the trade and settlement dates on the purchase or sale of a publicly traded stock or security.*[77]

Example 6.12: [78] USAco is an accrual-basis, calendar year domestic corporation with the dollar as its functional currency. On June 1 of the current year, USAco enters into a contract with a German steel manufacturer to buy steel for 200,000 euros (€) for delivery and payment on November 1. USAco hedges against the currency exchange risk associated with this purchase agreement by purchasing €195,000 on June 1 ($253,500 as the spot price of the euro on June 1 is $1.30) and depositing €195,000 in a separate bank account that will make a €5,000 interest payment on the deposited funds on November 1. On November 1, USAco withdraws the principal and interest of €200,000 from the bank account and makes payment in exchange for delivery of the steel. Assume the euro was worth $1.30 on June 1 and $1.35 on November 1.

The contract to purchase the steel and the simultaneous purchase of euros are part of a single economic transaction. As such, USAco may treat them as an integrated transaction if USAco satisfies certain requirements (e.g., USAco identifies the transaction as a hedged executory contract and deposits the euros in a separate account).[79]

Under this approach, USAco treats the $253,500 paid under the hedge as an amount paid directly for the steel and recognizes *no* gain or loss for the exchange rate fluctuation between June 1 and November 1. USAco treats the €5,000 of interest as part of the hedge[80] and, using the spot rate for the date of

---

[74] Code Sec. 988(d).
[75] Reg. § 1.988-5(a).
[76] Reg. § 1.988-5(b).
[77] Reg. § 1.988-5(c).

[78] Compare Reg. § 1.988-5(b)(4), Example 6(v).
[79] Reg. § 1.988-5(b).
[80] Reg. § 1.988-5(b)(2)(iii)(E).

the interest payment,[81] USAco recognizes interest income of $6,750 [€ 5,000 × $1.35]. However, because the interest is part of the hedge, USAco recognizes *no* exchange gain or loss when the interest is used to purchase the steel. USAco's basis in the steel is $260,250 [$253,500 + $6,750].

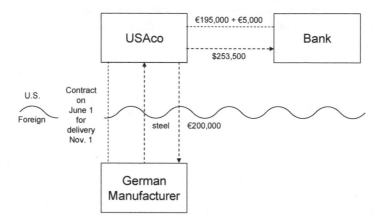

.04 Foreign Currency Transactions for Personal Use

Exchange gains of an individual from the disposition of foreign currency in a personal transaction are not taxable, provided that the gain realized does not exceed $200. Note that the threshold is $200 per transaction, as opposed to cumulative gains of $200 per year. This simplification measure is intended to eliminate the need to compute and report gains arising from exchanges of currency that are small in amount and that are associated with personal and business travel, as well as other nonbusiness activities. The term "personal transaction" refers to any transaction other than one with respect to which properly allocable expenses are deductible as trade or business expenses under Code. Sec. 162 (other than travel expenses in connection with a business trip) or investment expenses under Code Sec. 212. As a result, transactions entered into in connection with business travel are personal transactions under this provision. Exchange gains in excess of $200 will continue to be taxed as before and exchange losses are unaffected by this provision.[82]

---

[81] Reg. § 1.988-2(b)(1).   [82] Code Sec. 988(e).

Chapter 7
Export Benefits

¶ 701 THE EXPORT BENEFITS SAGA

In 1971, Congress enacted the domestic international sales corporation (DISC) provision in an attempt to stimulate U.S. exports. A DISC allowed a U.S. exporter to avoid U.S. tax on a portion of its export profits by allocating those profits to a special type of domestic subsidiary known as a DISC. A DISC was a domestic corporation that was little more than a paper corporation. In the mid-1970s, major trading partners of the United States began complaining that the DISC provisions were an illegal export subsidiary in violation of the General Agreement on Tariffs and Trade (GATT).

Congress tried to end the controversy in 1984 by enacting the foreign sales corporation (FSC) provisions as a replacement for the DISC regime (a vestige of the old DISC, the Interest Charge-DISC, or the IC-DISC, remains). The FSC regime responded to the GATT controversy by requiring U.S. exporters to establish a foreign corporation that performs certain activities abroad in order to obtain a U.S. tax benefit. The magnitude of these foreign activities was typically negligible, however. Therefore, like the DISC, a FSC was little more than a paper corporation. A domestic corporation that established a FSC allocated a portion of its qualified export profits to the FSC and a pre-specified portion of the FSC's profits were exempt from U.S. tax. The net effect of this arrangement was that a portion of a domestic corporation's export profits was permanently excluded from U.S. tax of both the FSC and U.S. shareholder levels.

In 1998, the European Union filed a complaint with the World Trade Organization (WTO) asserting that the FSC regime, like the DISC regime that preceded it, was an illegal export summary in violation of GATT. In 1999, the WTO released its report on the European Union's complaint, ruling that the FSC regime was an illegal export subsidiary and called for its elimination by 2000.

In response to the WTO's ruling, in 2000, the United States enacted into law the FSC Repeal and Extraterritorial Income Exclusion Act of 2000. The extraterritorial income (ETI) exclusion provided U.S. exporters with essentially the same tax benefit as the old FSC regime without even having to form a corporation. As a consequence, the enactment of the ETI exclusion did not put an end to the trade controversy. The WTO ruled that the ETI exclusion is similarly an illegal export subsidiary and called for elimination of the ETI exclusion.

As a result, in the American Jobs Creation Act of 2004 (the "2004 Act"), Congress phased out a repeal of the ETI exclusion while phasing in a domestic production deduction. Although the domestic production activities deduction does not require an export sale, this chapter will discuss the domestic production activities deduction because it replaces an export benefit, the ETI exclusion, and, despite its name, should be able to involve some foreign manufacturing. Nevertheless, as this chapter will show, the current export benefit is the IC-DISC, which has become favored as a result of the lower rate of tax on dividends received from domestic corporations at the 15 percent capital gains rate (through December 31, 2012).[1] In the past several years, Congress has considered eliminating the IC-DISC benefit, but has never passed such legislation.

¶ 702 INTRODUCTION TO THE IC-DISC

.01 Taxation of an IC-DISC and Its Shareholders

The IC-DISC was designed as a means by which a U.S. exporter could borrow funds from the U.S. Treasury. An IC-DISC must be a domestic corporation with a single class of stock that has a minimum par value of $2,500.[2] More importantly, an IC-DISC is not subject to the regular U.S. corporate income tax.[3]

Although the IC-DISC itself is not a taxable entity, the IC-DISC's U.S. shareholders are subject to tax on both actual and deemed dividend distributions from the IC-DISC.[4] The deemed distributions do not include income derived from the first $10 million of the IC-DISC's qualified export receipts each year.[5] Therefore, an IC-DISC allows a U.S. shareholder to defer paying U.S. tax on the income derived from up to $10 million of qualified export receipts each year. The IC-DISC generally may include in the $10 million its most profitable export sales.[6]

If a U.S. shareholder fails to take a dividend at the favorable 15% tax rate, the U.S. shareholder must pay an interest charge on its IC-DISC-related deferred tax liability. That liability equals the difference between the shareholder's tax for the taxable year computed first with, and then without, the accumulated IC-DISC income of the shareholder that has been deferred.[7] Therefore, a U.S. shareholder must continue to pay interest on deferred IC-DISC income until that income is distributed or deemed distributed by the IC-DISC. The interest rate is the current

---

[1] Code Sec. 1(h)(11).
[2] Code Sec. 992(a)(1)(C).
[3] Code Sec. 991.
[4] Code Sec. 995(a) and (b).

[5] Code Sec. 995(b)(1)(E). It is not possible to circumvent the $10 million limitation by creating multiple IC-DISCs. Code Sec. 995(b)(4)(B).
[6] Reg. § 1.995-8(b).
[7] Code Sec. 995(f)(2).

market rate for 52-week Treasury bills.[8] That rate is adjusted annually and applies for the fiscal year ending September 30. The rates for the last several years are as follows:

Year ending September 30	Interest Rate
2000	5.96%[9]
2001	4.41%[10]
2002	2.18%[11]
2003	1.30%[12]
2004	1.60%[13]
2005	3.18%[14]
2006	4.76%[15]
2007	4.87%[16]
2008	2.48%[17]
2009	0.63%[18]
2010	0.34%[19]

IC-DISC shareholders compute the interest charge on Form 8404, Computation of Interest Charge on DISC-Related Deferred Tax Liability (a copy of which is in the Appendix), and the interest is due on the same date as the shareholder's regular tax return, without any extensions.[20] No estimated tax payments are required with respect to the interest charge.[21] If the IC-DISC distributes cash representing all its income (as most do to lock in taxation at only a 15% rate), the interest charge is inapplicable.

Example 7.1: Uncle Sam, a U.S. citizen, wholly owns USAco, a manufacturer of widgets. Due to burgeoning export sales, Uncle Sam forms an IC-DISC that receives a commission on $9 million of qualified export receipts. Should Uncle Sam decide not to distribute the cash representing the commission on $9 million of qualified export receipts (and pay tax at only the 15% capital gains rate on dividends), the IC-DISC would pay an interest charge to the U.S. government based on the difference between the hypothetical amount of tax due if Uncle Sam had received the distribution of the qualified export receipts and Uncle Sam's actual U.S. tax due.

---

[8] Code Sec. 995(f)(4).
[9] Rev. Rul. 2000-52 , 2002-2 CB 516.
[10] Rev. Rul. 2001-56, 2001-2 CB 500.
[11] Rev. Rul. 2002-68, 2002-45 IRB 808.
[12] Rev. Rul. 2003-111, 2003-45 IRB 1009.
[13] Rev. Rul. 2004-99, 2004-44 IRB 720.
[14] Rev. Rul. 2005-70, 2005-45 IRB 919.

[15] Rev. Rul. 2006-54, 2006-45 IRB 834.
[16] Rev. Rul. 2007-64, 2007-45 IRB 953.
[17] Rev. Rul. 2008-51, 2008-47 IRB 1171.
[18] Rev. Rul. 2009-36, 2009-47 IRB 650.
[19] Rev. Rul. 2010-28, 2010-49 IRB 804.
[20] Reg. § 1.995(f)-1(j)(3)(i).
[21] Reg. § 1.995(f)-1(a)(2)(iii).

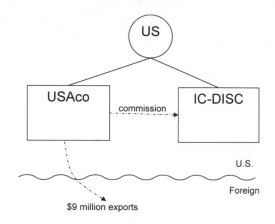

.02 Tests to Qualify as an IC-DISC

To qualify as an IC-DISC, the domestic corporation must pass both a gross receipts and export assets test.

The gross receipts test states that 95 percent of the gross receipts of the IC-DISC must constitute qualified gross receipts.[22] Qualified gross receipts include the following:

(i) Gross receipts from the sale, exchange, or other disposition of export property;

(ii) Gross receipts from the lease or rental of export property for use outside the United States;

(iii) Gross receipts for services that are related in or are subsidiary to any exchange of property;

(iv) Interest on any obligation that is a qualified export asset;

(v) Gross receipts for engineering or architectural services for construction projects located outside the United States; and

(vi) Gross receipts for the managerial services for furtherance of production or other qualified export receipts.

Example 7.2: Uncle Sam, a U.S. citizen, wholly owns USAco, a manufacturer of widgets. Due to burgeoning export sales, Uncle Sam forms an IC-DISC whose only activity results in receiving a commission on $9 million of qualified export receipts. Because 100% of the IC-DISC's gross receipts constitute commissions, the IC-DISC satisfies the gross receipts test.

---

[22] Code Secs. 992(a)(1) and 993(d) and (f).

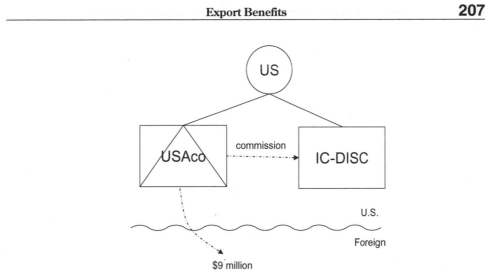

The qualified export assets test states that 95 percent of the assets of the corporation must be qualified export assets.[23] Qualified export assets include the following:

(i) Accounts receivable,

(ii) Temporary investments,

(iii) Export property,

(iv) Assets used primarily in connection with the production of qualified export receipts, and

(v) Loans to producers.

Example 7.3: Uncle Sam, a U.S. citizen, wholly owns USAco, a manufacturer of widgets. Uncle Sam forms an IC-DISC that receives a commission on $9 million of qualified export receipts. The IC-DISC, instead of distributing a dividend to Uncle Sam, loans the cash representing the commission back to USAco. Because loans to producers, such as the widget manufacturing USAco, constitute qualified export assets, 100% of the IC-DISC's assets constitute qualified export assets. Consequently, the IC-DISC passes the qualified export assets test.

---

[23] Code Secs. 992(a)(1)(E) and 993(b).

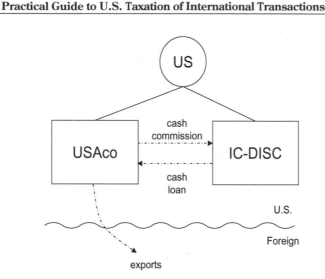

¶ 703 SALES OF EXPORT PROPERTY

Although exporters often think of newly manufactured property as export property, the property can be used equipment or even scrap. There are three requirements for an IC-DISC to receive income from a sale of export property:[24]

(i) The property must be manufactured, produced, grown or extracted in the United States by a person other than the IC-DISC;

(ii) The export property must be held primarily for sale, lease or rental for direct use, consumption or disposition outside the United States; and

(iii) The export property must have a minimum of 50 percent U.S. content.

.01 The Manufacturing Requirement

The IC-DISC may not manufacture the export property. It must be manufactured in the United States by a U.S. person other than the IC-DISC.[25] Generally, the shareholders of a U.S. manufacturing entity will form an IC-DISC to capture export sales. The IC-DISC will typically receive a commission for the export sales (with a corresponding commission deduction by the U.S. manufacturing entity).[26] Property is manufactured within the United States if either (i) 20 percent of its conversion costs are incurred in the United States, (ii) there is a substantial transformation in the United States, or (iii) the operations in the United States are generally considered to constitute manufacturing.[27]

---

[24] Code Sec. 993(c).

[25] Code Sec. 993(c)(1)(A).

[26] Although not as common, occasionally an IC-DISC will be a "buy-sell" IC-DISC, whereby the IC-DISC will actually buy and take title to the export property from the U.S. manufacturing entity before the export sale occurs.

[27] Reg. § 1.993-3(c). The IRS will not rule on whether a product is manufactured. Rev. Proc. 2008-7, 2008-1 IRB 229.

.02 The Destination Test

The export property must satisfy a destination test, which means it must be held for sale, lease or rental in the ordinary course of business for direct use, disposition or consumption outside the United States.[28]

Property satisfies the destination test if it is delivered to a freight forwarder for ultimate shipment abroad.[29] Property also satisfies the destination test if it is sold to a purchaser in the United States, provided the property does not undergo further manufacturing or use by the purchaser prior to export, and the property is shipped to a foreign destination within one year.[30] Under this destination test, what may seemingly be domestic sales could qualify as export sales. The purchasers of an exporter's product will have to provide the exporter with information showing that the product was exported and, if the domestic purchasers cooperate, the IC-DISC can benefit from these sales. The U.S. purchaser should provide the IC-DISC with documentation of ultimate shipment outside the United States, which includes, *inter alia,* a copy of the export bill of lading or the shipper's export declaration.

The law is somewhat vague regarding what constitutes further manufacturing in the United States. In *General Electric Co.,*[31] the Tax Court denied an export benefit, finding that the jet engines General Electric manufactured were subject to further manufacturing and use when they were assembled into Boeing's jet planes to be delivered overseas. However, the Second Circuit Court of Appeals reversed, finding that: (i) the airplane industry recognizes aircraft and engines as legally distinct and separate; and (ii) affixing a completed product to another does not constitute manufacturing or use.[32]

> **Example 7.4:** TireCo, a U.S. corporation, manufactures automobile tires in the United States with U.S. materials. TireCo, through its IC-DISC, sells its tires to Big3co, a Detroit auto manufacturer, which affixes the tires to its new automobiles that are exported to Canada. The IC-DISC can benefit from the sale of its tires to Big3co because the final destination of the automobiles is outside the United States. Furthermore, affixing of tires to automobiles does not appear to be further manufacturing or use.

---

[28] Code Sec. 993(c)(1)(B).

[29] Reg. § 1.993-3(d)(2)(i)(a).

[30] Reg. § 1.993-3(d)(2)(i)(b).

[31] 70 TCM 39, Dec. 50,743(M), TC Memo. 1995-306.

[32] *General Electric Co.,* CA-2, 2001-1 USTC ¶ 50,329, 245 F.3d 149.

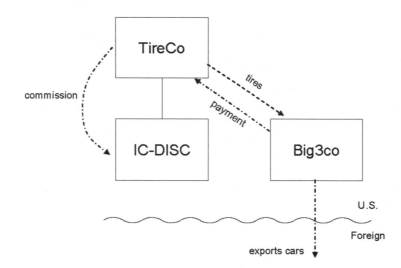

An exporter can receive an IC-DISC benefit on sales to a foreign subsidiary. However, only the amount earned by the IC-DISC (and not its foreign subsidiary) qualifies.

Five types of property are ineligible to be qualified export property.[33] Ineligible property consists of (i) property rented for use by a related party, (ii) intellectual property other than films, tapes, records or computer software, (iii) unprocessed softwood timber, (iv) products, such as oil or coal, for which a depletion deduction is allowable, and (v) property the President designates as being in short supply.

.03 The Maximum of 50 Percent Foreign Content Requirement

No more than 50% of the fair market value of export property may be attributable to the fair market value of articles imported into the United States.[34] The fair market value of the foreign content is determined by the dutiable value of any foreign components.[35]

> **Example 7.5:** Willie, a U.S. citizen, wholly-owns PAPco, a manufacturer of paper products that is a C corporation. Due to burgeoning export sales, Willie forms an IC-DISC that receives commissions on PAPco's sales of $200 per paper product. The materials to manufacture the paper products are wood pulp, which is purchased from companies located in the United States, and kryptonite, which is purchased from a kryptonite mine in Mexico. The dutiable value of the kryptonite is $80 per paper product. Because the majority of the content constitutes materials purchased in the United States, the paper products satisfy the content requirement. However, should the cost of kryptonite ever rise to the extent that it exceeds 50% of the value of the paper products, the paper products would have too much foreign content and would not qualify as export property.

---

[33] Code Sec. 993(c)(2).
[34] Code Sec. 993(c)(1)(C).

[35] Reg. § 1.993-3(e)(4)(i).

¶703.03

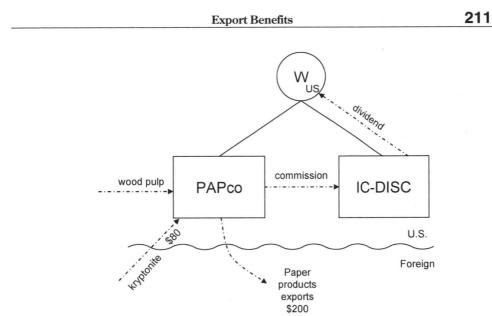

¶ 704 DETERMINING THE IC-DISC BENEFIT

The income of an IC-DISC from sales of export property is in an amount constituting:

- 4 percent of qualified export receipts,[36]
- 50 percent of the combined taxable income,[37] or
- The arm's-length amount determined under the transfer pricing principles of section 482.[38]

As a practical matter, taxpayers rarely use the section 482 transfer pricing method to determine the arm's-length amount of income in the IC-DISC. These methods to determine the IC-DISC's income apply regardless of whether the IC-DISC is a "commission" IC-DISC or a "buy-sell" IC-DISC. The IC-DISC may also add 10 percent of its export promotion expenses to the commission, but the export promotion expenses are typically negligible. Any of these transfer pricing methods for the IC-DISC combined with the 15 percent rate of tax on dividends by domestic corporations to U.S. individual shareholders, creates tax savings from this export benefit.[39]

The qualified export receipts method allocates 4 percent of the qualified export receipts from the export sales to the IC-DISC.

Example 7.6: Uncle Sam, a U.S. citizen, owns USAco, a domestic corporation. USAco has qualifying export sales of $6 million of low margin products through its IC-DISC. Using 4% of the qualified export receipts method, USAco

---

[36] Code Sec. 994(a)(1).
[37] Code Sec. 994(a)(2).
[38] Code Sec. 994(a)(3).

[39] Code Sec. 246(d). C corporations are not tax-advantaged owners of IC-DISCs because the dividends received deduction does not apply to dividends received from an IC-DISC. However, the shareholders of the C corporation can directly own the IC-DISC's shares.

will exclude a commission of $240,000 of gross receipts, resulting in a U.S. tax reduction of $84,000 (35% of $240,000). If USAco's IC-DISC distributed the cash representing this income as a dividend to Uncle Sam, Uncle Sam would pay U.S. tax of $36,000 ($240,000 at the 15% capital gains rate for dividends). As a result, the impact of the 4% of qualified gross receipts method combined with the 15% capital gains rate for dividends is a tax savings of $48,000 ($84,000 less $36,000) with the cash outside of the corporate solution.

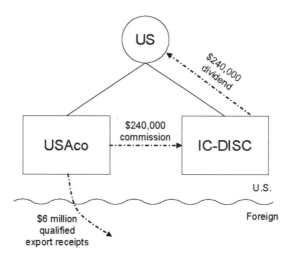

The combined taxable income method allocates 50 percent of the taxable income from the export sales to the IC-DISC.

Example 7.7: Uncle Sam, a U.S. citizen, owns USAco, a domestic corporation. USAco earns $1 million of taxable income from the export of high margin products through its IC-DISC. Using the 50% of combined taxable income method, USAco pays $500,000 as a commission to its IC-DISC and USAco pays tax on only the $500,000 of remaining taxable income, which is $175,000 (35% of $500,000). If the IC-DISC distributes the $500,000 of cash representing the income as a dividend to an individual U.S. shareholder, that $500,000 would be subject to a capital gains tax on dividends of $75,000 (15% of $500,000). Uncle Sam's tax of $75,000 and USAco's tax of $175,000 totals $250,000 and moves the cash out of the corporate solution, which is $100,000 less than the $350,000 if USAco had operated without the IC-DISC.

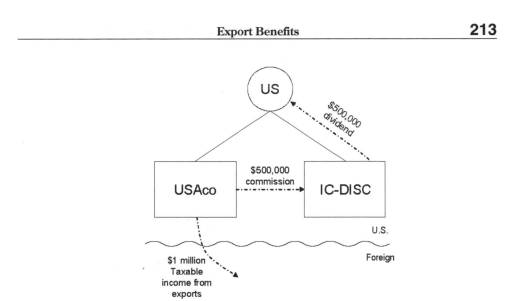

Very few taxpayers determine the IC-DISC's income using the transfer pricing principles of section 482 because IC-DISC's generally have little economic activity and, consequently, lower income under those principles than under the other two methods.

¶ 705 MAXIMIZING THE IC-DISC INCOME

An exporter can use any of the methods described in the previous section to achieve the greatest IC-DISC income possible. The IC-DISC rules permit the use of different methods to different sales based on product lines, recognized industry or trade usage, and even by transaction.[40] In practice, most of the decisions will be between the qualified export receipts and combined taxable income methods. As a simple rule of thumb, the combined taxable income method results in the largest IC-DISC income when exports have a net pre tax margin of 8.7 percent or greater. On the other hand, the qualified export receipts method provides the largest IC-DISC income when the net pre-tax margin is less than 8.7 percent. If the net pre-tax margin on exports is lower than worldwide net pre-tax margins, which often occurs due to the extra shipping and administrative expenses of foreign sales, the marginal costing of combined taxable income may result in the largest commission. Finally, the exporter can maximize the IC-DISC's income by ignoring loss sales.[41]

.01 Grouping

Grouping refers to the exporter's maximizing the IC-DISC's commission by separating high-margin sales from low-margin sales.

Example 7.8: USAco, a domestic corporation, exports domestically produced red and white wines. The annual gross receipts and combined taxable income from these export sales are as follows:

---

[40] Reg. § 1.994-1(c)(7).   [41] Reg. § 1.994-1(e)(1).

	Gross receipts	Combined taxable income	Net pre-tax margin
Red wine	$500,000	$100,000	20%
White wine	$500,000	$20,000	4%
Total export sales	$1,000,000	$120,000	12%

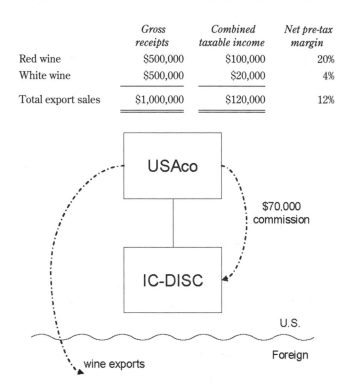

Through product grouping, USAco can use the 50% of combined taxable income method for sales of red wine, which allocates $50,000 [50% of $100,000] to the IC-DISC. At the same time, USAco can use the 4% of qualified export receipts method for sales of white wine, which excludes $20,000 [4% of $500,000]. The total amount of the IC-DISC's income is $70,000.

Exporters have considerable flexibility in grouping. An exporter's product or product line groupings will be accepted if the groupings conform to recognized trade or industry usage or the two-digit major groups (or inferior classifications) of Standard Industrial Classification codes.[42] In addition, within the same taxable year, an exporter can use grouping for one product line and the transaction-by-transaction method for another product line.[43] The availability of specialized software designed to optimize the IC-DISC's income generated by transactional pricing (as well as marginal costing and expense allocations, as discussed below) has greatly enhanced the ability of companies to take advantage of these planning techniques.

.02 Marginal Costing

A second technique for increasing the IC-DISC's income is marginal costing.[44] Under the general rule, combined taxable income equals the excess of the qualified export receipts over the total direct and indirect costs related to exports.[45] If the exporter elects marginal costing, however, only marginal costs are taken into

---

[42] Reg. § 1.994-1(c)(7)(ii).
[43] Reg. § 1.994-1(c)(7)(iii).

[44] Code Sec. 994(b)(2) and Reg. § 1.994-2(c).
[45] Reg. § 1.994-1(c)(3).

account in computing combined taxable income. Therefore, marginal costing allows a taxpayer to increase combined taxable income by the amount of the fixed costs related to export sales. Marginal costs include only the direct material and direct labor costs. All other costs, such as selling, general, and administrative expenses, and interest expense, are ignored for purposes of computing combined taxable income.[46]

An overall profit percentage limitation restricts the combined taxable income of an exporter to an amount equal to full costing combined taxable income from all sales (domestic and foreign) multiplied by the ratio of qualified export receipts to total receipts (domestic and foreign).[47] Because of this limitation, marginal costing is advantageous only when export sales are less profitable than domestic sales.

Example 7.9: USAco, a domestic corporation, exports products through its IC-DISC that constitute export property. During the current year, USAco's results from operations are as follows:

	Export sales	*U.S. sales*	*Total sales*
Sales	$10 million	$15 million	$25 million
Direct material and labor	– 6 million	– 7 million	– 13 million
Marginal costing CTI	$ 4 million	$ 8 million	$12 million
Indirect expenses	– 3 million	– 3 million	– 6 million
Full costing CTI	$ 1 million	$ 5 million	$ 6 million

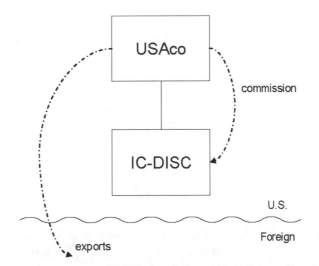

The marginal costing profit margin on export sales of 40% ($4 million ÷ $10 million) exceeds the overall profit percentage of 24% ($6 million ÷ $25 million). Therefore, the overall profit limitation restricts combined taxable income to $2.4 million (24% of $10 million of export sales). Marginal costing that is limited by the overall profit percentage to $2.4 million is still preferable

---

[46] Reg. § 1.994-2(b)(2). [47] Reg. § 1.994-2(b)(3).

to full costing, however, because full costing produces only $1 million of combined taxable income.

.03 Expense Allocations

A third technique for increasing the IC-DISC's income is expense allocations. As discussed above, combined taxable income equals the excess of qualified export receipts over the total costs of the exporter, which includes deductions that are definitely related to export sales (e.g., cost of goods sold) and a ratable portion of any deductions that are not definitely related to any specific class of gross income (e.g., interest expense and selling, general and administrative expenses).[48] Therefore, a taxpayer can increase combined taxable income and, in turn, the amount of its IC-DISC's income, by developing defensible apportionment bases that allocate fewer deductions against qualified export receipts.[49]

¶ 706 IC-DISC COMPREHENSIVE EXAMPLE

USAco, a domestic corporation, manufactures products for sale in the United States and abroad. During the current year, USAco's qualified export receipts are $1,000 and the related cost of goods sold is $600. USAco incurs $275 of administrative expenses related to the qualified export receipts. With respect to domestic sales, USAco's gross receipts are $24,000, the related cost of goods sold is $16,400, and administrative expenses are $4,225. USAco also has overhead expenses of $500 that are related to all of its income. In sum, USAco's results for the year are as follows (before the IC-DISC commission):

	Total receipts	Qualified export receipts	Domestic receipts
Gross receipts	$25,000	$1,000	$24,000
Cost of goods sold (direct material and labor)	(17,000)	(600)	(16,400)
Gross profit	$8,000	$400	$7,600
Administrative expenses	(4,500)	(275)	(4,225)
Overhead expenses	(500)		
Net income	$3,000		

Using gross profit as an apportionment base, USAco apportions $25 of overhead expenses against its qualified export receipts ($500 overhead expenses × [$400 export gross profit / $8,000 total gross profit]). Therefore, USAco's combined taxable income equals $100, computed as follows:

---

[48] Reg. § 1.994-1(c)(6)(iii).

[49] For an example in the context of research and development expenditures, see *St. Jude Medical, Inc.*, CA-8, 94-2 USTC ¶ 50,459, 34 F.3d 1394.

	Combined taxable income
Qualified export receipts	$1,000
Cost of goods sold	(600)
Gross profit	$400
Administrative expenses	(275)
Overhead expenses	(25)
Combined taxable income	$100

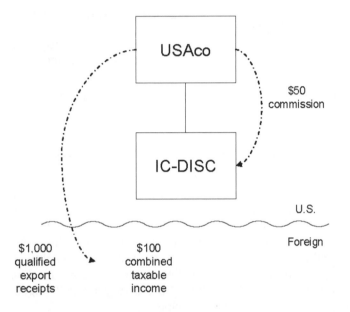

Now assume, for example, that USAco has an IC-DISC. The amount of the IC-DISC's income is $50, which correspondingly reduces USAco's taxable income by $50, which represents the greatest of:

   (i) $40 (4% × $1,000 qualified export receipts), or

   (ii) $50 (50% × $100 combined taxable income).

If marginal costing were elected, the combined taxable income would exclude the administrative expenses and overhead expenses and preliminarily be $400. However, the overall profit percentage of 12% ($3,000 divided by $25,000) on qualified export receipts limits combined taxable income to $120, which still results in a greater commission than either $40 or $50.

¶ 707 DOMESTIC PRODUCTION DEDUCTION

The domestic production deduction equals 9 percent of the lesser of taxable income or qualified production activities income of the taxpayer. Although the domestic production deduction applies to domestic as well as foreign sales, Congress enacted it to replace the extraterritorial income inclusion.

> *Example 7.10:* USman, a U.S. corporation, manufactures widgets. Because the widget manufacturing process comprises entirely U.S.-source components and activities, USman's taxable income of $1 million is the same as its qualified production activities income. Further assume that all other requirements for the domestic production deduction are satisfied. USman should receive a domestic production deduction of $90,000. If this were the taxable year 2009, USman would receive a domestic production deduction of $60,000.

USman

$1 million taxable income

$1 million qualified production activities income

In determining the amount of the deduction, a taxpayer must analyze the following items:

- Domestic production gross receipts,
- Costs allocated to domestic production gross receipts, and
- Total wages on Forms W-2.

Domestic production gross receipts are generally any sale, exchange, or other disposition of qualifying production property that is manufactured, produced, grown, or extracted by the taxpayer in the United States. Once the domestic production gross receipts are determined, allocable costs (the cost of goods sold deduction and other deductions allocable to the receipts) are subtracted from them to determine qualified production activities income. Finally, the domestic production deduction is limited to 50 percent of the taxpayer's W-2 wages paid that are related to domestic production gross receipts.

.01 Determining Domestic Production Gross Receipts

Domestic production gross receipts are generally any sale, exchange, or other disposition of qualifying production property (including, *inter alia,* tangible personal property) that is manufactured, produced, grown, or extracted by the taxpayer "in whole or in significant part within the United States."[50]

> *Example 7.11:* USman, a U.S. corporation, manufactures widgets, which are tangible personal property. Because USman's manufactured products constitute qualifying production property, their sale constitutes domestic production gross receipts.

Definition of "qualifying production property." By using the phrase "in significant part within the United States," Congress has created an ambiguity with respect to how much of the property can be produced outside the United States. Pursuant to regulations issued by the IRS, property is produced "in significant part

---

[50] Code Sec. 199(c)(4)(A)(i)(I).

within the United States" if the production activity in the United States is substantial in nature. A safe harbor states that property is substantial in nature if at least 20 percent of the cost of goods sold of the property is attributed to U.S. activity.[51]

Example **7.12:** USman, a U.S. C corporation, manufactures widgets for sale to customers in the ordinary course of business. USman engages contract manufacturers in Mexico and Canada to manufacture a portion of the widgets. Of the final cost of good sold of widgets, 30% is attributable to Canadian activities, 30% is attributable to Mexican activities, and 40% is attributable to U.S. activities. By incurring more than 20% of the cost of goods sold in the United States (even though U.S. costs are less than half of the cost of goods sold), the U.S. activities constitute a significant part of the manufacturing process, the sale of the widgets constitutes the sale of qualifying production property, and USman has domestic production gross receipts that would qualify for the domestic production deduction.

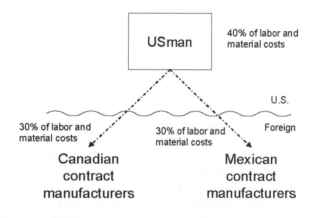

If the 20 percent safe harbor does not apply, there is a facts and circumstances test to determine if the U.S. activity is substantial in nature. However, the use of a previously existing design from the United States with a foreign contract manufacturer does not constitute "substantial" activity in the United States.[52]

Example **7.13:** ResearchCo, a U.S. C corporation, conducts research and development activities. ResearchCo develops designs for the super widget. Instead of licensing the super widget, ResearchCo desires to sell the super widgets itself. Because ResearchCo does not have any manufacturing facilities, ResearchCo engages a contract manufacturer, CANco, a Canadian corporation with manufacturing facilities in Toronto, to manufacture the super widgets by using the design developed by ResearchCo. Although the key economic factor behind the value of the super widget is the design that was previously developed in the United States, engaging a foreign contract manufacturer does not constitute manufacturing by ResearchCo.

---

[51] Reg. § 1.999-3(g).   [52] Reg. § 1.999-3(g)(5)(Ex. 9).

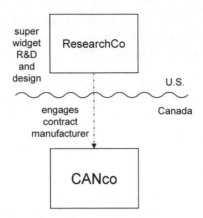

Broad definition of production activity. Qualifying production property also includes the sale of electricity, natural gas, potable water, engineering or architectural services performed in the United States for construction projects located in the United States, musical CDs, software, and the sale or license of a qualified film the taxpayer produces (more than 50 percent of the compensation of which is paid for services that are performed in the United States).[53]

The domestic production deduction even offers a planning opportunity for filmmakers to bring some of their production back to the United States.[54]

Example **7.14:** FilmCo, a U.S. C corporation, is a major motion picture studio. A recent script requires that the track film "Crazylegs" be set in San Francisco. However, wanting to take advantage of decreased production costs, the head of FilmCo, Harold Hecuba, seeks to shoot the movie in Vancouver, Canada. His controller informs him that if his costs of services performed in the United States by actors, production personnel, directors, and producers are at least 50% of compensation costs, the studio's investors will be much happier because the film "Crazylegs" will produce domestic production gross receipts that are eligible for the domestic production deduction. As a result, Harold Hecuba decides to shoot only exterior scenes in Vancouver to satisfy this requirement.

---

[53] Code Sec. 199(c)(4) and (5).   [54] Code Sec. 199(c)(6).

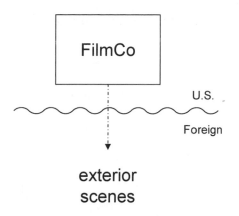

exterior
scenes

.02 Allocable Costs and Qualified Production Gross Income

After determining domestic production gross receipts, the taxpayer arrives at qualified production activities income by subtracting allocable costs—the cost of goods sold deduction and other deductions allocable to these receipts.[55]

Example **7.15:** USman, a U.S. C corporation, manufactures widgets for sale to customers in the ordinary course of business. USman earns domestic production gross receipts of $10 million and incurs $9 million in cost of goods sold and other deductions allocable to those domestic production gross receipts. As a result, this year USman has $1 million of qualified production activities income.

$10 million of domestic
production gross receipts

$9 million of cost of goods
sold and other deductions

Special rules determine costs when the manufacturing of the qualifying production property includes some foreign activity. To maintain the integrity of any cost allocation, any item or service shall be treated as purchased for a cost equal to its value when it enters the United States.[56]

Example **7.16:** USman, a U.S. C corporation, manufactures widgets for sale to customers in the ordinary course of business. A key component of each widget is a pound of the material kronos, which sells at the fair market value in the United States at $10 per pound. In a bankruptcy sale in Mexico, USman purchases a year's supply of kronos for $4 per pound. Because the fair market value of the kronos in the United States is $10 per pound, when determining the U.S. allocable cost of goods sold (as well as whether a significant part of manufacturing occurs in the United States), USman allocates a $10 cost per

---

[55] Code Sec. 199(c)(1)(B) and (2); Prop. Reg. § 1.199-4(c). [56] Code Sec. 199(c)(3)(A).

widget to nondomestic expenses, instead of a $4 cost to determine qualified production activities income.

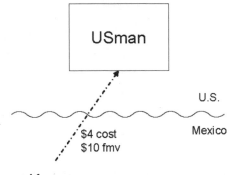

Furthermore, if property is exported for further manufacturing abroad, when the property reenters the United States, the costs of the further manufacturing abroad cannot exceed the difference between the value of the property when exported and the value of the property when it reenters the United States.[57] This rule effectively limits expenses allocable to foreign production activities, which prevents taxpayers from artificially increasing their qualified production activities income.

Example **7.17:** USman, a U.S. C corporation, manufactures widgets for sale to customers in the ordinary course of business. USman conducts a significant part of the manufacturing process within the United States. However, USman exports semifinished widgets with a value of $16 to Mexico for finishing before re-entry into the United States with a value of $25. As a result, the cost allocable to Mexico, regardless of the costs incurred in Mexico, cannot exceed $9 per widget.

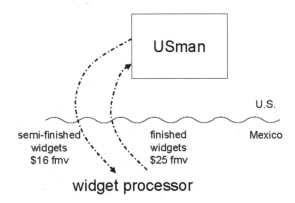

---

[57] Code Sec. 199(c)(3)(B).

¶**707.02**

.03 Deduction Limited to 50 Percent of W-2 Wages

The deduction is limited to 50 percent of the W-2 wages related to the taxpayer's domestic production gross receipts.[58] Apparently, the policy behind tying the maximum deduction to an amount based on W-2 wages is to increase W-2 wages, which presumably are paid to employees in manufacturing jobs.[59]

> *Example* **7.18:** USman, a U.S. C corporation, manufactures widgets for sale to customers in the ordinary course of business. USman's taxable income is the same as its qualified production activities income of $1 million. Although USman is interested in taking a domestic production deduction of $90,000, constituting 9% of $1 million, USman only pays W-2 wages of $120,000 related to domestic production gross receipts. As a result, USman's domestic production deduction is limited to one half of its W-2 wages paid totaling $120,000, which is $60,000. To obtain the full domestic production deduction of $90,000, USman would have to increase its total W-2 wages paid to $180,000.

USAco

$1 million taxable income

$1 million qualified production activities income

$120,000 of W-2 wages related to domestic production gross receipts

The domestic production deduction is also available to S corporations, partnerships, and other passthrough entities, such as single-member limited liability companies, by determining the individual owner's proportionate share of the qualified production activities income of the flow-through entity. Although the deduction is taken by the individual owner, Congress recognized that the wage limitation should be determined at the entity level and the IRS has written regulations relating to the determination of compensation deductions at the individual owner level.[60] Furthermore, when one determines the lesser of taxable income or qualified production activities income for individual owners, adjusted gross income is used instead of taxable income.[61]

---

[58] Code Sec. 199(b).
[59] Conf. Rep. No. 755, 108th Cong., 2d Sess. 11 (2004).

[60] Reg. § 1.999-9(c).
[61] Code Sec. 199(d).

¶ 708 APPENDIX

Betsy Ross, a U.S. citizen, wholly-owns the shares of FLAGco, a U.S. S corporation that manufactures and exports flags. Due to growing exports, Betsy incorporates an IC-DISC effective January 1, 2010, with a capital contribution of $3,000. During the taxable year 2010, FLAGco exports $6 million of flags (the cost of good sold is $5 million and the other expenses allocable to exports are $520,000) and pays a commission to the IC-DISC of $240,000 that the IC-DISC distributes as a dividend through FLAGco to Betsy Ross on December 31, 2010. A Form 4876-A was filed by March 30, 2010 (90 days after the start of the taxable year) electing IC-DISC status for FLAGco IC-DISC. FLAGco IC-DISC must file a Form 1120-IC-DISC, but Betsy does not have to file a Form 8404 because the IC-DISC has distributed all of its income as a dividend as there is not any deferral.

Form **4876-A**
(Rev. December 2009)
Department of the Treasury
Internal Revenue Service

Election To Be Treated as an Interest Charge DISC

OMB No. 1545-0190

Part I   The corporation named below elects to be treated as an interest charge domestic international sales corporation (IC-DISC) for income tax purposes. All of the corporation's shareholders must consent to this election.

Name of corporation			A Employer identification number	
FLAGco IC-DISC			98 : 7654321	

Number, street, and room or suite no. (or P.O. box if mail is not delivered to street address)

B   Principal business classification (see instructions)

City or town, state, and ZIP code
USA

423990 7389 229

D   Name of person who may be called for information: (optional)

C   Tax year of IC-DISC: Must use tax year of shareholder (or shareholder group) with the highest percentage of voting power (see instructions). Enter ending month and day ▶

E   Election is to take effect for the tax year beginning (month, day, year)   **January 1, 2010**

F   Date corporation began doing business   **January 1, 2010**

Telephone number:
( )

G   Name and address (including ZIP code) of each shareholder (or expected shareholder) at the beginning of the tax year the election takes effect and when the election is filed.

		H Number of shares of stock held on— (Complete both columns for each shareholder.)		**I** Identifying number (see instructions)
		First day of year of election	Date consent is made	
1	Betsy Ross	100	100	474-34-7439
2				
3				
4				
5				
6				
7				
8				
9				
10				
Total. Enter total shares for all shareholders (include shares of shareholders listed on any attachments)		100	100	

Under penalties of perjury, I declare that the corporation named above has authorized me to make this election for the corporation to be treated as an IC-DISC and that the statements made are to the best of my knowledge and belief true, correct, and complete.

Signature and Title of Officer ▶   Date

Part II   Shareholders' Consent Statement. Part II may be used instead of attachments. For this election to be valid, each shareholder must sign and date below or attach a separate consent to this form (see instructions).

We, the undersigned shareholders, consent to the election of the corporation named above to be treated as an IC-DISC. Our consent is irrevocable and is binding upon all transferees of our shares in this corporation.

Signature of shareholder and date. (If consent involves transferred shares, attach a schedule showing the name and address of the holder of the shares at the beginning of the tax year and the number of shares for which the consent is made.)

1	Betsy Ross	6	
2		7	
3		8	
4		9	
5		10	

For Paperwork Reduction Act Notice, see page 2.   Cat. No. 62075X   Form **4876-A** (Rev. 12-2009)

¶708

Form **1120-IC-DISC**
(Rev. December 2008)

Department of the Treasury
Internal Revenue Service

Interest Charge Domestic International Sales Corporation Return

▶ See separate instructions.
(Please type or print.)

OMB No. 1545-0938

For calendar year 20 **10** , or tax year beginning _____ , 20_____ , and ending _____ , 20_____.

A Date of IC-DISC election	Name		C Employer identification number
January 1, 2010	FLAGco IC-DISC		98 ⁝ 7654321
	Number, street, and room or suite no. (or P.O. box if mail is not delivered to street address)		D Date incorporated **January 1, 2010**
B Business activity code no. (See instructions.)	City or town, state, and ZIP code		E Total assets (see instructions)
4 2 3 9 9 0	USA		$ 3,000,000

F   Check applicable box(es):   (1) ☑ Initial return   (2) ☐ Final return   (3) ☐ Name change   (4) ☐ Address change   (5) ☐ Amended return

G(1)   Did any corporation, individual, partnership, trust, or estate own, directly or indirectly, 50% or more of the IC-DISC's voting stock at the end of the IC-DISC's tax year? (See section 267(c) for rules of attribution.) . . If "Yes," complete the following schedule. (If a foreign owner, see instructions.)

Yes ☐   No ✓

Name	Identifying number	Address	Voting stock owned	Total assets (corporations only)	Foreign owner	
					Yes	No
Betsy Ross	123-45-6789		100%			✓
			%			

(2)   Enter the following for any corporation listed in G(1) that will report the IC-DISC's income:

Tax year of first corporation	IRS Service Center where return will be filed
Tax year of second corporation	IRS Service Center where return will be filed

H(1)   Check the appropriate box(es) to indicate any intercompany pricing rules that were applied to 25% or more of gross income (line 1 below):

   ☐ 50-50 combined taxable income method   ☑ 4% gross receipts method   ☐ Section 482 method ("arm's length pricing")

(2)   Check here ☐ if the marginal costing rules under section 994(b)(2) were applied in figuring the combined taxable income for any transactions.

All Computations Must Reflect Intercompany Pricing Rules If Used (Section 994)
See separate Schedule P (Form 1120-IC-DISC).

Taxable Income

1	Gross income. Enter amount from Schedule B, line 4, column (e)	1	240,000
2	Cost of goods sold from Schedule A, line 8	2	
3	Total income. Subtract line 2 from line 1	3	240,000
4	Deductions. Enter amount from Schedule E, line 3	4	
5	Taxable income before net operating loss deduction and dividends-received deduction. Subtract line 4 from line 3	5	240,000
6a	Net operating loss deduction (attach schedule) **6a**		
b	Dividends-received deduction from Schedule C, line 9 . . . . . . **6b**		
c	Add lines 6a and 6b	6c	
7	**Taxable income.** Subtract line 6c from line 5	7	240,000
8	Refundable credit for federal tax paid on fuels (attach Form 4136)	8	

Sign Here ▶

Under penalties of perjury, I declare that I have examined this return, including accompanying schedules and statements, and to the best of my knowledge and belief, it is true, correct, and complete. Declaration of preparer (other than taxpayer) is based on all information of which preparer has any knowledge.

Signature of officer	Date	Title

Paid Preparer's Use Only	Preparer's signature ▶	Date	Check if self-employed ☐	Preparer's SSN or PTIN
	Firm's name (or yours if self-employed), address, and ZIP code ▶		EIN ⁝	
			Phone no. ( )	

For Privacy Act and Paperwork Reduction Act Notice, see instructions.   Cat. No. 11473P   Form **1120-IC-DISC** (Rev. 12-2008)

Form 1120-IC-DISC (Rev. 12-2008) Page **2**

Schedule A	Cost of Goods Sold (see instructions)		

If the intercompany pricing rules of section 994 are used, reflect **actual** purchases from a related supplier at the transfer price determined under such rules. See separate Schedule P (Form 1120-IC-DISC).

1	Inventory at beginning of the year	**1**	
2	Purchases	**2**	
3	Cost of labor	**3**	
4	Additional section 263A costs (attach schedule)	**4**	
5	Other costs (attach schedule)	**5**	
6	**Total.** Add lines 1 through 5	**6**	
7	Inventory at end of the year	**7**	
8	**Cost of goods sold.** Subtract line 7 from line 6. Enter here and on line 2, page 1	**8**	

9a Check all methods used for valuing closing inventory: *(i)* ☐ Cost as described in Regulations section 1.471-3

  (ii) ☐ Lower of cost or market as described in Regulations section 1.471-4

  (iii) ☐ Other (Specify method used and attach explanation.) ▶ ---

b Check if there was a writedown of "subnormal" goods as described in Regulations section 1.471-2(c) . . . . ▶ ☐

c Check if the LIFO inventory method was adopted this tax year for any goods. (If checked, attach Form 970.) . ▶ ☐

d If the LIFO inventory method was used for this tax year, enter percentage (or amounts) of closing inventory computed under LIFO **9d**

e If property is produced or acquired for resale, do the rules of section 263A apply to the corporation? . . ☐ Yes ☐ No

f Was there any change in determining quantities, cost, or valuations between the opening and closing inventory? (If "Yes," attach explanation.) ☐ Yes ☐ No

Schedule B	Gross Income (see instructions)				

(a) Type of receipts	Commission sales		(d) Other receipts	(e) Total (add columns (c) and (d))
	(b) Gross receipts	(c) Commission		
1 Qualified export receipts from sale of export property—				
a To unrelated purchasers:				
(i) Direct foreign sales		240,000		240,000
(ii) Foreign sales through a related foreign entity				
(iii) Persons in the United States (other than an unrelated IC-DISC)				
(iv) An unrelated IC-DISC				
b To related purchasers:				
(i) Direct foreign sales				
(ii) Persons in the United States . . .				
c Total				240,000
2 Other qualified export receipts:				
a Leasing or renting of export property . .				
b Services related and subsidiary to a qualified export sale or lease				
c Engineering and architectural services .				
d Export management services				
e Qualified dividends (Schedule C, line 15)				
f Interest on producer's loans				
g Other interest (attach schedule)				
h Capital gain net income (attach Schedule D (Form 1120))				
i Net gain or (loss) from Part II, Form 4797 (attach Form 4797)				
j Other (attach schedule)				
k Total				
3 Nonqualified gross receipts:				
a Ultimate use in United States				
b Exports subsidized by the U.S. Government				
c Certain direct or indirect sales or leases for use by the U.S. Government				
d Sales to other IC-DISCs in the same controlled group				
e Nonqualified dividends (Schedule C, line 16)				
f Other (attach schedule)				
g Total				
4 **Total.** Add lines 1c, 2k, 3g, column (e). Enter here and on line 1, page 1				240,000

Form **1120-IC-DISC** (Rev. 12-2008)

Form 1120-IC-DISC (Rev. 12-2008)   Page **3**

Schedule C   **Dividends and Dividends-Received Deduction** (see instructions)

		(a) Dividends received	(b) %	(c) Dividends–received deduction: ((a) × (b))
1	Dividends from less-than-20%-owned domestic corporations (other than debt-financed stock)		70	
2	Dividends from 20%-or-more-owned domestic corporations (other than debt-financed stock)		80	
3	Dividends on debt-financed stock of domestic and foreign corporations (section 246A)		see instructions	
4	Dividends on certain preferred stock of less-than-20%-owned public utilities		42	
5	Dividends on certain preferred stock of 20%-or-more-owned public utilities		48	
6	Dividends from less-than-20%-owned foreign corporations		70	
7	Dividends from 20%-or-more-owned foreign corporations		80	
8	Dividends from wholly owned foreign subsidiaries (section 245(b)) . . .		100	
9	**Total.** Add lines 1 through 8. See instructions for limitation			
10	Dividends from foreign corporations not included on lines 3, 6, 7, or 8 . . .			
11	Income from controlled foreign corporations under subpart F (attach Form(s) 5471)			
12	IC-DISC and former DISC dividends not included on lines 1, 2, or 3 (section 246(d))			
13	Other dividends			
14	**Total dividends.** Add lines 1 through 13, column (a)			
15	Qualified dividends. Enter here and on Schedule B, line 2e, column (d)			
16	Nonqualified dividends. Subtract line 15 from line 14. Enter here and on Schedule B, line 3e, column (d)			

Schedule E   **Deductions** (Before completing, see **Limitations on Deductions** in the instructions.)

1	Export promotion expenses:		
a	Market studies	1a	
b	Advertising	1b	
c	Depreciation (attach Form 4562)	1c	
d	Salaries and wages	1d	
e	Rents	1e	
f	Sales commissions	1f	
g	Warehousing	1g	
h	Freight (excluding insurance)	1h	
i	Compensation of officers	1i	
j	Repairs and maintenance	1j	
k	Pension, profit-sharing, etc., plans	1k	
l	Employee benefit programs	1l	
m	Other (list):		
	....	1m	
n	**Total.** Add lines 1a through 1m	1n	
2	Other expenses not deducted on line 1:		
a	Bad debts	2a	
b	Taxes and licenses	2b	
c	Interest	2c	
d	Contributions	2d	
e	Freight	2e	
f	Freight insurance	2f	
g	Other (list):		
	....	2g	
h	**Total.** Add lines 2a through 2g	2h	
3	**Total deductions.** Add lines 1n and 2h. Enter here and on line 4, page 1	3	

Form **1120-IC-DISC** (Rev. 12-2008)

¶708

Form 1120-IC-DISC (Rev. 12-2008) Page **4**

Schedule J	Deemed and Actual Distributions and Deferred DISC Income for the Tax Year	

Part I—Deemed Distributions Under Section 995(b)(1) (see instructions)

1	Gross interest derived during the tax year from producer's loans (section 995(b)(1)(A)) . . .	**1**	
2	Gain recognized on the sale or exchange of section 995(b)(1)(B) property (attach schedule)	**2**	
3	Gain recognized on the sale or exchange of section 995(b)(1)(C) property (attach schedule)	**3**	
4	50% of taxable income attributable to military property (section 995(b)(1)(D)) (attach schedule)	**4**	
5	Taxable income from line 7, Part II, below	**5**	
6	Taxable income of the IC-DISC (from line 7, page 1)	**6**	
7	Add lines 1 through 5	**7**	
8	Subtract line 7 from line 6	**8**	
9	If you have shareholders that are C corporations, enter one-seventeenth of line 8 (.0588235 times line 8)	**9**	
10	International boycott income (see instructions)	**10**	
11	Illegal bribes and other payments	**11**	
	Note: *Separate computations for lines 12–23 are required for shareholders that are C corporations and shareholders that are **not** C corporations. Complete lines 12, 14, 15, 17a, 18, 20, and 22 for shareholders that are **not** C corporations. Complete lines 13, 14, 16, 17b, 19, 21, and 23 for shareholders that **are** C corporations.*		
12	Add lines 7, 10, and 11	**12**	
13	Add lines 7, 9, 10, and 11	**13**	
14	Earnings and profits for the tax year (attach schedule)	**14**	
15	Enter the smaller of line 12 or 14	**15**	
16	Enter the smaller of line 13 or 14	**16**	
17	Foreign investment attributable to producer's loans (attach schedule):		
a	For shareholders other than C corporations	**17a**	
b	For shareholders that are C corporations	**17b**	
18	Add lines 15 and 17a	**18**	
19	Add lines 16 and 17b	**19**	
20	Enter percentage of stock owned by shareholders other than C corporations	**20**	%
21	Enter percentage of stock owned by shareholders that are C corporations	**21**	%
22	Multiply line 18 by line 20 (Allocate to shareholders other than C corporations)	**22**	
23	Multiply line 19 by line 21 (Allocate to C corporation shareholders)	**23**	
24	**Total deemed distributions under section 995(b)(1) for all shareholders.** Add lines 22 and 23	**24**	

Part II—Section 995(b)(1)(E) Taxable Income (see instructions)

1	Total qualified export receipts (see instructions)	**1**	
2	Statutory maximum	**2**	$10,000,000
3	Controlled group member's portion of the statutory maximum	**3**	
4	Enter smaller of **(a)** 1 or **(b)** number of days in tax year divided by 365 (or 366) (see instructions)	**4**	
5	Proration. Multiply line 2 or 3, whichever is applicable, by line 4	**5**	
6	Excess qualified export receipts. Subtract line 5 from line 1. (If line 5 exceeds line 1, enter -0- here and on line 7 below.)	**6**	
7	Taxable income attributable to line 6 receipts. Enter here and on line 5 of Part I above . .	**7**	

Part III—Deemed Distributions Under Section 995(b)(2) (see instructions)

1	Annual installment of distribution attributable to revocation of election in an earlier year . . .	**1**	
2	Annual installment of distribution attributable to not qualifying as a DISC or IC-DISC in an earlier year	**2**	
3	**Total deemed distributions under section 995(b)(2).** Add lines 1 and 2	**3**	

Part IV—Actual Distributions (see instructions)

1	Distributions to meet qualification requirements under section 992(c) (attach computation) . .		**1**	
2	Other actual distributions		**2**	240,000
3	**Total.** Add lines 1 and 2		**3**	240,000
4	Amount on line 3 treated as distributed from:			
a	Previously taxed income	**4a**		
b	Accumulated IC-DISC income (including IC-DISC income of the current year)	**4b**	240,000	
c	Other earnings and profits	**4c**		
d	Other	**4d**		

Part V—Deferred DISC Income Under Section 995(f)(3) (see instructions)

1	Accumulated IC-DISC income (for periods after 1984) at end of computation year	**1**	
2	Distributions-in-excess-of-income for the tax year following the computation year to which line 1 applies	**2**	
3	Deferred DISC income under section 995(f)(3). Subtract line 2 from line 1	**3**	

Form **1120-IC-DISC** (Rev. 12-2008)

Form 1120-IC-DISC (Rev. 12-2008)   Page **5**

Schedule L	**Balance Sheets per Books**	**(a)** Beginning of tax year	**(b)** End of tax year
	1 Qualified export assets:		
	a Working capital (cash and necessary temporary investments)	3,000	3,000
	b Funds awaiting investment (cash in U.S. banks in excess of working capital needs) in other qualified export assets		
	c Export-Import Bank obligations		
	d Trade receivables (accounts and notes receivable)		
	Less allowance for bad debts	( )	( )
Assets	**e** Export property (net) (including inventory and qualified property held for lease)		
	f Producer's loans		
	g Investment in related foreign export corporations		
	h Depreciable assets		
	Less accumulated depreciation	( )	( )
	i Other (attach schedule)		
	2 Nonqualified assets (net) (list):		
	3 **Total assets.** Combine lines 1a through 2	3,000	3,000
	4 Accounts payable		
	5 Other current liabilities (attach schedule)		
	6 Mortgages, notes, bonds payable in 1 year or more		
Liabilities and Shareholders' Equity	**7** Other liabilities (attach schedule)		
	8 Capital stock	3,000	3,000
	9 Additional paid-in capital		
	10 Other earnings and profits		
	11 Previously taxed income (section 996(f)(2))		
	12 Accumulated pre-1985 DISC income (see instructions)		
	13 Accumulated IC-DISC income (see instructions)		
	14 Less cost of treasury stock	( )	( )
	15 Total liabilities and shareholders' equity	3,000	3,000

Schedule M-1	**Reconciliation of Income per Books With Income per Return**		
1 Net income (loss) per books . .	240,000	**6** Income recorded on books this year not included on this return (itemize):	
2 Excess of capital losses over capital gains		....	
3 Taxable income not recorded on books this year (itemize):		**7** Deductions on this return not charged against book income this year (itemize):	
4 Expenses recorded on books this year and not deducted on this return (itemize):		....	
....		**8** Add lines 6 and 7	0
5 Add lines 1 through 4	240,000	**9** Income (line 5, page 1)—line 5 less line 8	240,000

Schedule M-2	**Analysis of Other Earnings and Profits (Line 10, Schedule L)**		
1 Balance at beginning of year . .	0	**5** Distributions to qualify under section 992(c)	
2 Increases (itemize): 240,000		**6** Other decreases (itemize): distribution	
	240,000		(240,000)
3 Add lines 1 and 2	240,000	**7** Add lines 4 through 6	
4 Deficit in earnings and profits . .		**8** Balance at end of year (line 3 less line 7)	0

Schedule M-3	**Analysis of Previously Taxed Income (Line 11, Schedule L)**		
1 Balance at beginning of year . .	0	**5** Deficit in earnings and profits	
2 Deemed distributions under section 995(b)		**6** Distributions to qualify under section 992(c)	
3 Other increases (itemize):		**7** Other decreases (itemize):	
....		**8** Add lines 5 through 7	
4 Add lines 1 through 3		**9** Balance at end of year (line 4 less line 8)	0

Schedule M-4	**Analysis of Accumulated IC-DISC Income (Line 13, Schedule L)**		
1 Balance at beginning of year . .	0	**6** Distributions to qualify under section 992(c)	240,000
2 Increases (itemize): .... commissions	240,000	**7** Distributions upon disqualification (sec. 995(b)(2))	
		8 Other decreases (itemize):	
3 Add lines 1 and 2	240,000		
4 Deficit in earnings and profits . .		**9** Add lines 4 through 8	240,000
5 Redemptions under section 996(d)		**10** Balance at end of year (line 3 less line 9)	0

Form **1120-IC-DISC** (Rev. 12-2008)

Schedule N	**Export Gross Receipts of the IC-DISC and Related U.S. Persons** (see instructions)

1 See page 16 of the instructions and enter the product code and percentage of total export gross receipts for **(a)** the largest and **(b)** 2nd largest product or service sold or provided by the IC-DISC:

(a) Code **229** Percentage of total **100** %   **(b)** Code   Percentage of total   %

2 Export gross receipts for the current tax year

(a) Export gross receipts of the IC-DISC	Export gross receipts of related U.S. persons	
	(b) Related IC-DISCs	(c) All other related U.S. persons
		6,000,000

3 If item 2(b) or 2(c) is completed, complete the following (if more space is needed, attach a schedule following the format below):

(a) IC-DISCs in Your Controlled Group

Name	Address	Identifying number

(b) All Other Related U.S. Persons in Your Controlled Group

Name	Address	Identifying number
FLAGco	USA	76-5432198
Betsy Ross	USA	474-34-7439

Schedule O	**Other Information** (see instructions)

		Yes	No
1	See page 15 of the instructions and enter the main:		
a	Business activity ▶ 423990 .... **b** Product or service ▶ 229		
2a	Did 95% or more of the IC-DISC's gross receipts for the tax year consist of qualified export receipts (defined in section 993(a))?	✓	
b	Did the adjusted basis of the IC-DISC's qualified export assets (as defined in section 993(b)) at the end of the tax year equal or exceed 95% of the sum of the adjusted basis of all the IC-DISC's assets at the end of the tax year?	✓	
c	If **a** or **b** is "No," did the IC-DISC make a pro rata distribution of property as defined in section 992(c)? . .		✓
3	Did the IC-DISC have more than one class of stock at any time during the tax year?		✓
4	Was the par or stated value of the IC-DISC's stock at least $2,500 on each day of the tax year (for a new corporation, this means on the last day for making an election to be an IC-DISC and for each later day)? . .	✓	
5	Did the IC-DISC keep separate books and records?	✓	
6a	Does the IC-DISC or any member of the IC-DISC's controlled group (as defined in section 993(a)(3)) have operations in or related to any country (or with the government, a company, or a national of that country) associated with carrying out the boycott of Israel that is on the list kept by the Secretary of the Treasury under section 999(a)(3)?		✓
b	Did the IC-DISC or any member of the controlled group of which the IC-DISC is a member have operations in any unlisted country that the IC-DISC knows or has reason to know requires participation in or cooperation with an international boycott against Israel?		✓
c	Did the IC-DISC or any member of the controlled group of which the IC-DISC is a member have operations in any country that the IC-DISC knows or has reason to know requires participation in or cooperation with an international boycott other than the boycott of Israel?		✓
	If the answer to any of the questions in 6 is "Yes," see instructions and **Form 5713,** International Boycott Report.		
7	Enter the amount of tax-exempt interest income received or accrued during the tax year ▶ $ _____		

Note: *If the IC-DISC, at any time during the tax year, had assets or operated a business in a foreign country or U.S. possession, it may be required to attach* **Schedule N (Form 1120),** *Foreign Operations of U.S. Corporations, to this return. See Schedule N for details.*

Form **1120-IC-DISC** (Rev. 12-2008)

SCHEDULE K
(Form 1120-IC-DISC)

Department of the Treasury
Internal Revenue Service

Shareholder's Statement of IC-DISC Distributions—2010

For calendar year 2010 or tax year

beginning ___January 1___, 2010, ending ___December 31___, 20 ___10___

(Complete for each shareholder. See instructions on back of Copy C.)

OMB No. 1545-0938

COPY A—Attach to Form 1120-IC-DISC

Part I   Taxable Distributions

1	Deemed distributions: **a** Under section 995(b)(1)	1a	
	b Annual installment under section 995(b)(2)	1b	
	c Total. Add lines 1a and 1b	1c	
2	Actual taxable distributions	2	240,000
3	**Total taxable distributions.** Add line 1c and line 2. Enter here and in Section A or B below .	3	240,000

Section A—C Corporations

4a	Part of line 3 above entitled to section 243 dividends-received deduction .	4a	
b	Part of line 3 above **not** entitled to section 243 dividends-received deduction . .	4b	

Section B—Shareholders Other Than C Corporations

5	Amount of taxable dividends included on line 3	5	240,000

Part II   Nontaxable Distributions

6	Actual distributions from previously taxed income and accumulated pre-1985 DISC income .	6	
7	Other actual nontaxable distributions	7	
8	**Total nontaxable distributions.** Add lines 6 and 7	8	

Part III   Other Information

9	Accumulated IC-DISC income attributable to stock sold during the year . . .	9	
10	Deferred DISC income. See instructions	10	

Shareholder's name, identifying number, and address (including ZIP code)

Name, employer identification number, and address (including ZIP code) of IC-DISC, former DISC, or former IC-DISC

Betsy Ross
123-45-6789
239 Arch Street
Philadelphia, PA 19106

For Paperwork Reduction Act Notice, see the instructions for Form 1120-IC-DISC.   Cat. No. 11474A   **Schedule K (Form 1120-IC-DISC) 2010**

¶708

SCHEDULE P	**Intercompany Transfer Price or Commission**	
(Form 1120-IC-DISC)	Attach a separate schedule for each transaction or group of transactions to which the intercompany pricing rules under section 994(a)(1) and (2) are applied.	OMB No. 1545-0938
(Rev. December 2008) Department of the Treasury Internal Revenue Service	For the calendar year 20 <u>10</u>, or fiscal year beginning_____, 20___, and ending_____ , 20__ For amount reported on line _____ , Schedule _____ , Form 1120-IC-DISC	

Name as shown on Form 1120-IC-DISC	Employer identification number	
FLAGco IC-DISC	98 ┆ 7654321	

Identify product or product line reported on this schedule. (Also, enter the Principal Business Activity code number, if used.) (See instructions.)

7389

This schedule is for a (check one):

Single transaction . . . . . . ☐
Group of transactions . . . . . ☑

Part I IC-DISC Taxable Income

SECTION A—Combined Taxable Income

Section A-1—If marginal costing is not used

1	Gross receipts from transaction between IC-DISC (or related supplier) and third party			**1**	6,000,000
2	Less costs and expenses allocable to gross receipts from transaction:				
a	Cost of goods sold from property if sold, or depreciation from property if leased	**2a**	5,000,000		
b	Related supplier's expenses allocable to gross receipts from transaction . .	**2b**	520,000		
c	IC-DISC export promotion expenses allocable to gross receipts from transaction	**2c**			
d	Other IC-DISC expenses allocable to gross receipts from transaction . . .	**2d**			
e	Add lines 2a through 2d			**2e**	5,520,000
3	**Combined taxable income.** Subtract line 2e from line 1. If a loss, enter -0-			**3**	480,000

Section A-2—If marginal costing is used

4	Gross receipts from resale by IC-DISC (or sale by related supplier) to third party			**4**	
5	Costs and expenses allocable to gross receipts from sale:				
a	Cost of direct material from property sold	**5a**			
b	Cost of direct labor from property sold	**5b**			
c	IC-DISC export promotion expenses allocable to gross receipts from sales that are claimed as promotional	**5c**			
d	Add lines 5a through 5c			**5d**	
6	Combined taxable income or (loss) before application of overall profit percentage limitation. Subtract line 5d from line 4. If a loss, skip lines 7 through 11 and enter -0- on line 12			**6**	
7	Gross receipts of related supplier and IC-DISC (or controlled group) from all foreign and domestic sales of the product or product line			**7**	
8	Costs and expenses of related supplier and IC-DISC (or controlled group) allocable to gross income from such sales:				
a	Cost of goods sold from property sold	**8a**			
b	Expenses allocable to gross receipts from such sales	**8b**			
c	Add lines 8a and 8b			**8c**	
9	Subtract line 8c from line 7. If a loss, skip lines 10 and 11 and enter -0- on line 12.			**9**	
10	Overall profit percentage. Divide line 9 by line 7. Check if controlled group optional method is used . . . . ▶ ☐			**10**	%
11	Overall profit percentage limitation. Multiply line 4 by line 10			**11**	
12	**Combined taxable income.** Enter the smaller of line 6 or line 11.			**12**	

SECTION B—50-50 Combined Taxable Income Method (Must be used if marginal costing is used. See instructions.)

13	Combined taxable income. Enter amount from line 3 or line 12	**13**	
14	Multiply line 13 by 50% (.50)	**14**	
15	Enter 10% (.10) of IC-DISC export promotion expenses allocable to gross income from transactions that are claimed as export promotion	**15**	
16	Add lines 14 and 15	**16**	
17	**IC-DISC taxable income.** Enter the smaller of line 13 or line 16	**17**	

SECTION C—4% Gross Receipts Method (Cannot be used if marginal costing is used.)

18	Gross receipts from transaction. Enter amount from line 1	**18**	6,000,000
19	Multiply line 18 by 4% (.04)	**19**	240,000
20	Multiply line 2c by 10% (.10)	**20**	
21	Add lines 19 and 20	**21**	240,000
22	Combined taxable income. Enter amount from line 3 or amount computed under special rule. If special rule is applied, check here ☐ . See instructions.	**22**	480,000
23	**IC-DISC taxable income.** Enter the smaller of line 21 or line 22	**23**	240,000

For Paperwork Reduction Act Notice, see the Instructions for Form 1120-IC-DISC.   Cat. No. 11478S   Schedule P (Form 1120-IC-DISC) (Rev. 12-2008)

¶708

Schedule P (Form 1120-IC-DISC) (Rev. 12-2008)   Page **2**

Part II	**Transfer Price From Related Supplier to IC-DISC** (See instructions.)		
24	Gross receipts from transaction. Enter amount from line 1 or line 4, Part I		**24**
25	Less reductions:		
a	IC-DISC taxable income (but not to exceed amount determined in Part I)	25a	
b	IC-DISC export promotion expenses allocable to gross income from transaction	25b	
c	Other IC-DISC expenses allocable to gross income from transaction	25c	
d	Add lines 25a through 25c		25d
26	**Transfer price from related supplier to IC-DISC.** Subtract line 25d from line 24		**26**

Part III	**IC-DISC Commission From Related Supplier** (See instructions.)		
27	IC-DISC taxable income (but not to exceed amount determined in Part I)	**27**	240,000
28	IC-DISC export promotion expenses allocable to gross receipts from transaction	**28**	
29	Other IC-DISC expenses allocable to gross receipts from transaction	**29**	
30	**IC-DISC commission from related supplier.** Add lines 27 through 29	**30**	240,000

Instructions

Section references are to the Internal Revenue Code unless otherwise noted.

Purpose of schedule. Use Schedule P to show the computation of taxable income used in computing (1) the transfer price from a related supplier to an IC-DISC (Part II) or (2) the IC-DISC commission from a related supplier (Part III).

Complete and attach a separate Schedule P to Form 1120-IC-DISC for each transaction or group of transactions to which the intercompany pricing rules of sections 994(a)(1) and (2) are applied.

IC-DISC taxable income. Generally, the intercompany pricing determinations are to be made on a transaction-by-transaction basis. However, the IC-DISC may make an annual election to determine intercompany pricing on the basis of groups consisting of products or product lines. If the group basis is elected, then all transactions for that product or product line must be grouped. Each group is limited to one type of transaction (i.e., sales, leases, or commissions).

A product or product line determination will be accepted if it conforms to either of the following standards: (1) a recognized industry or trade usage or (2) major product groups (or any subclassifications within a major product group) (see *Schedule P (Form 1120-IC-DISC) Codes for Principal Business Activity* on page 13 of the Instructions for Form 1120-IC-DISC). The corporation may choose a product grouping for one product and use the transaction-by-transaction method for another product within the same tax year.

Generally, the computation of taxable income under the intercompany pricing rules will not be permitted to the extent that their application would result in a loss to the related supplier.

Each of the following methods may be applied for sales, leases, and services. See the regulations under section 994.

50-50 combined taxable income method. The transfer price the related supplier charges the IC-DISC, or the related supplier's IC-DISC commission, is the amount that lowers the taxable income the IC-DISC derives from the

transaction to an amount that is no more than the sum of (1) 50% of the IC-DISC's and related supplier's combined taxable income attributable to the qualified export receipts from the transaction and (2) 10% of the IC-DISC's export promotion expenses (as defined in Regulations section 1.994-1(f)) attributable to the qualified export receipts. Do not include in combined taxable income (line 13) the discount amount reflected in receivables (on the sale of export property) that a related supplier transferred to the IC-DISC. See Regulations sections 1.994-1(c)(3) and (6)(v).

See Part I, Section A instructions below if marginal costing rules apply.

4% gross receipts method. The transfer price charged by the related supplier to the IC-DISC or IC-DISC commission from the related supplier is the amount that ensures that the taxable income derived by the IC-DISC from the transaction does not exceed the sum of (1) 4% of the qualified export receipts of the IC-DISC derived from the transaction and (2) 10% of the export promotion expenses (as defined in Regulations section 1.994-1(f)) of the IC-DISC attributable to the qualified export receipts.

Section 482 method. The transfer price the related supplier charged the IC-DISC, or IC-DISC commission from the related supplier, is the amount actually charged, but is subject to the arm's length standard of section 482. Do not complete Schedule P if the section 482 method is used.

Incomplete transactions. For the 50-50 and 4% methods, if the related supplier sells property to the IC-DISC during the year but the IC-DISC does not resell it during the year, the related supplier's transfer price to the IC-DISC must equal the related supplier's cost of goods sold. Do not complete Schedule P for incomplete transactions. The related supplier's transfer price to the IC-DISC must be recomputed for the year in which the IC-DISC resells the property and the transaction must then be reported on Schedule P for that year.

Part I, Section A—Combined Taxable Income. Complete Section A-1 only if marginal costing is not used.

For purposes of line 2d, be sure to include the appropriate apportionment of deductions that are not directly allocable such as interest expenses and stewardship expenses. See Temporary Regulations sections 1.861-11T(f) and 1.861-14T(f) for an explanation of appropriate apportionment.

Complete Section A-2 if marginal costing is used. The marginal costing rules may be used only for sales, or commissions on sales, of property if the 50-50 method is used.

Marginal costing cannot be used for (1) leasing of property, (2) performance of services, or (3) sales of export property that (in the hands of a purchaser related under section 954(d)(3) to the seller) give rise to foreign base company sales income as described in section 954(d) unless, for the purchaser's year in which it resells the property, section 954(b)(3)(A) applies or the income is under the exceptions in section 954(b)(4).

Line 10. The overall profit percentage may be computed under an optional method. See Regulations section 1.994-2(c)(2).

Part I, Section B and Section C. Complete Section B or Section C. You must complete Section B if marginal costing is used.

Line 22. If IC-DISC taxable income on a sale is computed under the 4% method and the IC-DISC chooses to apply the special rule for transfer prices or commissions, check the box in line 22 and attach a separate computation of the limitation on IC-DISC taxable income determined under the special rule and enter the amount on line 22. Under the special rule, a transfer price or commission will not be considered to cause a loss for a related supplier if the IC-DISC's net profit on the sale does not exceed the IC-DISC's and related supplier's net profit percentage on all their sales of the product or product line. See Regulations section 1.994-1(e)(1)(ii) for details.

Reporting Part II and Part III amounts on Form 1120-IC-DISC. If the computed transfer price for sales, leases, or services (Part II) or IC-DISC commission (Part III) is entered on more than one line of Form 1120-IC-DISC, attach an explanation indicating the portion of the total that is applied to each line.

Schedule P (Form 1120-IC-DISC) (Rev. 12-2008)

Chapter 8
Planning for Foreign Operations

¶ 801 INTRODUCTION

This chapter discusses general planning issues with respect to a U.S. company's foreign operations. More specific planning issues are discussed throughout the book. For example, Chapter 4 (¶ 401) discusses strategies for eliminating excess foreign tax credits and planning for dividend repatriations from foreign countries, Chapter 12 (¶ 1201) discusses developing a transfer pricing strategy, and Chapter 7 (¶ 701) discusses techniques for maximizing certain export tax benefits.

¶ 802 EVOLUTION OF A U.S. EXPORTER

.01 Entering a Foreign Market

There are several options available to a U.S. company that wishes to market its products abroad. For example, a U.S. company may initially export its products through independent brokers or distributors. Smaller U.S. exporters, in particular, may find it advantageous to use independent intermediaries to market their goods abroad as the exporters may lack technical expertise regarding foreign markets and international trade. There are costs to such an arrangement, however, including the need to share profits with the intermediary (either through commission costs or reduced sales revenues) and the loss of control over the sales and distribution functions.

As the exporter's sales volume grows and the exporter becomes more familiar with international trade, the exporter may wish to bring the foreign marketing function in-house by having U.S. employees travel abroad in order to identify customers, display inventory, negotiate sales agreements, and provide technical support. Alternatively, the exporter could employ residents of the foreign market to perform these functions.

The next logical step in the progression of a U.S. company's foreign marketing activities is to establish a liaison or branch sales office within the importing country. The activities of a liaison office usually are limited to advertising and promotion, storing or displaying merchandise, market research, and liaising with agents, distributors, and customers. As foreign sales volume increases, however, the U.S. company may wish to have its foreign office also negotiate and close sales agreements and distribute its products. These activities would elevate the status of the foreign operation to that a branch sales office. A foreign presence often is required in the case of export sales of services. For example, an export sale of construction services usually requires that U.S. engineers and technicians travel abroad in order to provide on-site management of the project.

Licensing and franchising are more indirect methods of entering a foreign market. Both provide for a U.S. company that has purchased or developed a patent, trademark, or other intangible licenses that right to a company located in a foreign country. In return, the licensor receives a percentage of the local sales of the licensed or franchised product in the form of a royalty. In essence, licensing and franchising are types of joint venture arrangements that permit a U.S. company to enter a foreign market quickly, but may not produce the same profit margins that are potentially available from more direct forms of exporting. Moreover, the U.S. company may lose some control over the quality and image of its product.

.02 Basic Tax Issues

Export sales. U.S. exporters sell their products through independent distributors will not have a taxable presence within the importing country and, therefore, foreign tax reduction planning is a moot issue. Nevertheless, foreign tax credit planning may still be worthwhile since the U.S. exporter may be subject to foreign taxation in the future and excess foreign tax credits can be carried back one year. One relatively simple strategy is to pass title abroad on export sales, in which case export sales will generate foreign-source income to the extent of the related marketing profits.

A U.S. exporter that sells its products using its own sales force faces the same tax issues (title passage and export benefits) as those faced by companies that export through independent distributors. In addition, the presence of employees in the importing country may expose the U.S. exporter to foreign taxation. As discussed in the next section, whether the U.S. exporter will be subject to host country taxation depends on the internal tax laws of the host country and the provisions of any applicable tax treaties. Typically, the U.S. exporter will be subject to host country taxation only if it has a permanent establishment within the host country.

A U.S. exporter that establishes a foreign sales office must decide whether to structure the foreign sales operation as a branch or a subsidiary. In addition, assuming the sales office constitutes a taxable presence within the host country, the U.S. exporter must determine its taxable income for foreign tax purposes. The profit of a foreign sales office usually is computed based on the fiction that the office is an independent enterprise dealing at arm's length with the U.S. home office. Therefore, the more functions performed and the greater the risks assumed by the foreign sales office, the more profit it should earn (whether this profit is all foreign-source income for purposes of the foreign tax credit limitation is another matter). For example, if the office operates as a buy-sell distributor that assumes inventory risk, credit risk, and warranty risk, then its profit should be greater than a sales office that functions as a mere commission agent that never takes title to the goods.

Table 8.1 summarizes the primary tax issues associated with the different stages of foreign marketing activities.

TABLE 8.1. EXPORT SALES—BASIC TAX ISSUES

Export sales activities	Basic tax issues
Export through independent distributors	• Title passage
	• Export benefits
Export using company salespersons	• Title passage and export benefits
	• Permanent establishment (PE)
Establish foreign sales office	• Title passage, export benefits, and PE
	• Branch versus subsidiary
	• Profit allocable to sales office

Licensing and franchising. A principal tax issue associated with foreign licensing and franchising arrangements is the appropriate foreign withholding tax rate on the U.S. company's royalty income. Most income tax treaties provide for reduced withholding tax rates on royalties derived by a foreign licensor. Typically, the rate is 10% or less and, in some treaties, varies with whether the payment is an industrial royalty (e.g., a payment for the use of a patent, trade secret, or formula), a motion picture or television royalty, or some other type of royalty, such as a payment for the use of a copyright on a book. Table 8.2 presents the royalty withholding tax rates for some of our major trading partners.

TABLE 8.2. TREATY WITHHOLDING TAX RATES ON ROYALTIES DERIVED BY U.S. RESIDENTS[1]

	Treaty withholding rate		
Foreign payer's country of residence	Industrial royalties (know-how)	Motion pictures and television royalties	Copyrights and patents
Canada	0%	10%	0%
China	10%	10%	10%
France	0%	0%	0%
Germany.	0%	30%	0%
Italy	8%	8%	0%/8%
Japan	0%	0%	0%
Mexico . . . . :	10%	10%	10%
United Kingdom	0%	0%	0%

[1] Taken from Table 1 of IRS Publication 515 (March 2011), which is reproduced in its entirety in the appendix to Chapter 13 (¶ 1301).

¶802.02

¶ 803 DETERMINANTS OF HOST COUNTRY TAXATION

A central tax issue for a U.S. exporter is whether its export profits will be subject to foreign taxation. Foreign taxation is an important issue for two reasons. First, complying with foreign tax laws always entails administrative costs. In addition, if the effective rate of foreign taxation exceeds the U.S. rate on the income considered foreign-source income under the U.S. rules, the resulting excess foreign tax credits represent an out-of-pocket tax cost. Whether a U.S. exporter's activities are subject to foreign taxation depends on several factors, including the nature of the taxpayer's activities within the foreign country, the internal tax laws of the foreign country, and the provisions of any income tax treaty between the foreign country and the United States.

As a general rule, most countries assert jurisdiction over all of the income derived from sources within their borders, regardless of the citizenship or residence of the person receiving that income. However, most tax treaties contain a permanent establishment provision under which a U.S. exporter's business profits are exempt from foreign taxation unless those profits are attributable to a permanent establishment located within the foreign country.[2] A permanent establishment includes a fixed place of business (e.g., a sales office), unless the fixed place of business is used solely for auxiliary functions (e.g., purchasing, storing, displaying, or delivering inventory), or activities of a preparatory nature (e.g., collecting information about potential customers).[3] A permanent establishment also exists if employees or other dependent agents habitually exercise in the foreign country an authority to conclude sales contracts in the taxpayer's name.[4] As a consequence, a U.S. exporter that sends executives or salespeople abroad to enter into contracts may create a permanent establishment even if those employees operate out of hotels and thus have no fixed place of business. Employees who limit their activities to auxiliary or preparatory activities, such as collecting information about potential customers, with sales concluded outside the foreign country (i.e., in the United States), will not create a permanent establishment. Marketing products abroad solely through independent foreign brokers or distributors also does not create a permanent establishment.[5]

¶ 804 STRUCTURING THE FOREIGN OPERATION

A U.S. company that establishes a sales, distribution, service, or manufacturing facility abroad can structure that foreign operation as either a branch or a subsidiary. Therefore, a central tax issue in planning for foreign operations is determining the best legal structure.

.01 Branches

An unincorporated foreign branch is simply an extension of the domestic corporation, as opposed to a separate legal entity. Assuming the branch constitutes a permanent establishment, the branch will be subject to foreign country taxation.

---

[2] For example, *see* Article 7(1) of the U.S. Model Income Tax Treaty (¶ 1302.02).

[3] For example, *see* Article 5(1), (2), and (4) of the U.S. Model Income Tax Treaty (¶ 1302.02).

[4] For example, *see* Article 5(5) of the U.S. Model Income Tax Treaty (¶ 1302.02).

[5] For example, *see* Article 5(6) of the U.S. Model Income Tax Treaty (¶ 1302.02).

Branch taxable income usually is determined on the basis of a separate accounting, whereby the branch reports a profit equal to the amount it would have earned if it were an independent enterprise. Foreign countries usually allow a domestic corporation to allocate all direct costs, such as the cost of goods sold abroad, against branch income. The host country also may allow charges against branch income for reasonable allocations of indirect expenses, such as interest expense and home office overhead.

From a U.S. tax perspective, the income derived by a foreign branch may represent foreign-source income earned directly by the domestic corporation. The branch's income is therefore subject to U.S. tax at the regular corporate rates, with a credit allowed for the lesser of the related foreign income taxes or the applicable foreign tax credit limitation. Therefore, the taxpayer may owe a residual U.S. tax on the income of a branch operating in a low-tax foreign jurisdiction, whereas a branch operating in a high-tax foreign jurisdiction may create excess foreign tax credits. However, excess foreign tax credits may result if not all the income taxed by the foreign country is considered foreign-source income under the U.S. rules (e.g., the 50-50 rule for sales of manufactured inventory).

The remittance of branch profits back to the U.S. home office is not a taxable event for U.S. tax purposes, except to the extent it triggers the recognition of a currency exchange gain or loss (see Chapter 6 (¶ 601)). Whether the remittance impacts the domestic corporation's foreign taxes depends on whether the host country has some type of branch profits tax. Most foreign countries impose withholding taxes on dividends paid by a local subsidiary to its U.S. parent. Some countries also have a branch profits tax, which is a withholding-type tax that is imposed on branch remittances.[6]

.02 Subsidiaries

A foreign subsidiary is a corporation organized under the laws of the foreign country and, therefore, is a separate legal entity from its U.S. parent. The subsidiary's earnings are usually subject to foreign country taxation by virtue of its foreign nationality, as well as the source of its income. As with a branch, the subsidiary's taxable income should reflect the amount of income that the subsidiary would earn if it were an independent enterprise. To achieve this result, the U.S. parent corporation must use arm's length transfer prices for intercompany transactions. For example, if a foreign marketing subsidiary purchases inventory from its U.S. parent for resale abroad, the transfer price should equal the sales price on comparable sales involving two unrelated entities.

The United States generally does not tax foreign business profits earned through a foreign subsidiary until the subsidiary distributes those earnings to the U.S. parent corporation as a dividend. This makes it possible for a domestic corporation to defer payment of the residual U.S. tax on the earnings of foreign subsidiaries operating in low-tax foreign jurisdictions.

---

[6] For example, the United States imposes a branch profits tax on the dividend equivalent amounts of U.S. branches of foreign corporations. Code Sec. 884.

Example 8.1: USAco, a domestic corporation, earns $10 million of for-eign-source income through a foreign sales office. Assume the U.S. tax rate is 35% and the foreign tax rate is 20%. If USAco structures the foreign sales office as a branch, the total tax burden on the $10 million of foreign-source income is $3.5 million, consisting of foreign taxes of $2 million [20% × $10 million] and a residual U.S. tax of $1.5 million [$3.5 million pre-credit U.S. tax – $2 million foreign tax credit]. On the other hand, if USAco structures the foreign sales office as a subsidiary, the only current year tax due on the $10 million of foreign-source income is the foreign tax of $2 million [20% × $10 million]. Payment of the $1.5 million residual U.S. tax is postponed until the subsidiary distributes its earnings to USAco in the form of a dividend.

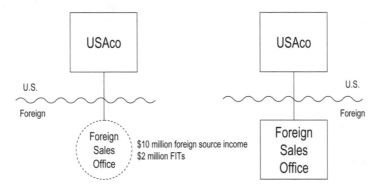

As discussed in Chapter 5 (¶ 501), certain types of unrepatriated income earned through a foreign subsidiary, such as passive investment income, are subject to immediate U.S. taxation.

One disadvantage of deferral is that net operating losses of foreign subsidiaries do not flow-through and offset the U.S. parent corporation's domestic profits. In contrast, a domestic corporation can deduct the losses of a foreign branch. A branch loss recapture rule prevents taxpayers from exploiting this advantage of the branch form by initially operating abroad as a branch and then converting to the subsidiary form when the foreign operation becomes profitable. Under the branch loss recapture rule, a U.S. person must recognize a gain on the incorporation of a foreign branch to the extent it has previously deducted branch losses against its other taxable income.[7]

.03 Branch versus Subsidiary

The choice between the branch and subsidiary forms must take into account not only U.S. and foreign tax laws, but also general business considerations. There is no simple rule that dictates the best structure in all cases. Tax advantages of the subsidiary form include the following:

(i) A subsidiary generally allows a U.S. company to defer the residual U.S. tax on low-tax foreign-source income.

---

[7] Code Sec. 367(a)(3)(C). The branch loss recapture rule is discussed in detail in Chapter 14 (¶ 1401).

(ii) The subsidiary form provides more control over the timing of income recognition, which may be useful in foreign tax credit planning. For example, a U.S. parent in an excess credit position may wish to avoid repatriating the earnings of a highly-taxed foreign subsidiary and, thereby, store excess credits in that subsidiary until they can be used. This option is not available with a branch, because a branch's earnings are always subject to immediate U.S. taxation.

(iii) Local tax incentives, such as a tax holiday, may be available only to a locally incorporated entity.

(iv) The sale of stock in a subsidiary results in a capital gain, which may be exempt from foreign taxation.

(v) The separate legal status of a subsidiary may make it easier to justify management fees and other intercompany charges (such as an allocation of indirect expenses) to foreign tax authorities.

Tax advantages of the branch form include the following:

(i) A domestic corporation can deduct the foreign losses of a branch against its U.S. profits. These losses are recaptured, however, if the branch later incorporates.[8]

(ii) The transfer of assets to a branch is a nontaxable event. In contrast, tax-free transfers of appreciated property to a foreign subsidiary are restricted.[9]

(iii) S corporation shareholders, who are generally individuals, cannot claim a deemed paid credit for foreign taxes incurred by a foreign subsidiary.[10] However, they can claim a direct credit for the foreign taxes, including branch taxes, incurred by a branch. This aspect of a branch form is also advantageous for individuals who are either partners in a U.S. partnership or members of a U.S. limited liability company that is classified as a partnership for U.S. tax purposes.

(iv) There may be no foreign taxes when a branch repatriates its profits, whereas dividends paid by a subsidiary normally attract foreign withholding taxes.

General business factors which should be considered when choosing between the branch and subsidiary form include:

(i) A subsidiary insulates the U.S. parent from legal liability issues in the foreign country.

(ii) A subsidiary may present a better local image to potential customers and employees.

(iii) A branch may be simpler to operate. For example, foreign business registration and financial reporting requirements of a branch may be less onerous than those for an incorporated subsidiary.

---

[8] Code Sec. 367(a)(3)(C).
[9] Code Sec. 367.

[10] Code Sec. 902(a) and 1373(a).

¶804.03

(iv) Foreign laws may require a subsidiary to have outside foreign shareholders or directors.

(v) A subsidiary may make it easier to involve foreign investors in the venture, because a subsidiary can issue additional shares to those foreign investors.

(vi) The use of a branch avoids the minimum capitalization requirements imposed by some countries.

.04 Hybrid Entities

A hybrid entity is a legal entity whose characterization for U.S. tax purposes is different than that for foreign tax purposes. The typical hybrid is a foreign entity that is considered a corporation for foreign tax purposes, but a branch or partnership for U.S. tax purposes.

Most foreign business entities with at least two members can elect to be treated as a corporation or a partnership, while those entities with only a single member can elect to be treated as a corporation or an unincorporated branch. This regime is now commonly known as "check-the-box" because the entity's owner merely checks the box on a Form 8832 to classify the entity (Form 8832 is reproduced in the Appendix to this chapter). A separate entity must actually exist before checking the box. Federal tax law controls for purposes of determining what constitutes an entity.[11] Although federal law is determinative, the regulatory rules reflect the common law partnership definition of an entity as a group of participants carrying on a trade, business, financial operation, or venture and dividing the profits therefrom.[12] A cost sharing arrangement does not constitute an entity.[13]

About 80 types of foreign business entities listed in Table 8.3 below are excluded from the elective system because the IRS determined that they should be treated as "per se" corporations. However, the regulations grandfathered preexisting classifications of foreign business entities that would otherwise be treated as per se corporations if certain conditions are met. For example, a per se entity that qualified as a partnership under the old regulations (pre-1997) may retain its status as a partnership under certain circumstances.[14] Furthermore, any foreign entity existing before the 1997 effective date of the regulations may retain its prior status if that prior status was relevant on a previously filed return.[15]

---

[11] Reg. §§ 301.7701-1(a)(1) and (a)(3).
[12] Reg. § 301.7701-1(a)(2). These factors are based on the case of *H.M. Luna*, 42 TC 1067, Dec. 26,967.

[13] Reg. §§ 301.7701-1(a)(2) and (c).
[14] Reg. § 301.7701-2(d).
[15] Reg. §§ 301.7701-3(b)(3)(ii) and -3(d).

¶804.04

TABLE 8.3. LIST OF PER SE CORPORATE ENTITIES

American Samoa, Corporation
Argentina, Sociedad Anonima
Australia, Public Limited Company
Austria, Aktiengesellschaft
Barbados, Limited Company
Belgium, Societe Anonyme
Belize, Public Limited Company
Bolivia, Sociedad Anonima
Brazil, Sociedade Anonima
Bulgaria, Aktsionerno Druzhestro
Canada, Corporation and Company
Chile, Sociedad Anonima
People's Republic of China, Gufen Youxian Gongsi
Republic of China (Taiwan), Ku-fen Yu-hsien Kung-szu
Colombia, Sociedad Anonima
Costa Rica, Sociedad Anonima
Cyprus, Public Limited Company
Czech Republic, Akciova Spolecnost
Denmark, Aktieselskab
Ecuador, Sociedad Anonima or Compania Anonima
Egypt, Sharikat Al-Mossahamah
El Salvador, Sociedad Anonima
Estonia, Aktsiaselts
European Union, Societas Europaea
Finland, Julkinen Osakeyhtio/Publikt Aktiebolag
France, Societe Anonyme
Germany, Aktiengesellschaft
Greece, Anonymos Etairia
Guam, Corporation
Guatemala, Sociedad Anonima
Guyana, Public Limited Company
Honduras, Sociedad Anonima
Hong Kong, Public Limited Company
Hungary, Reszvenytarsasag
Iceland, Hlutafelag

India, Public Limited Company
Indonesia, Perseroan Terbuka
Ireland, Public Limited Company
Israel, Public Limited Company
Italy, Societa per Azioni
Jamaica, Public Limited Company
Japan, Kabushiki Kaisha
Kazakstan, Ashyk Aktsionerlik Kogham
Republic of Korea, Chusik Hoesa
Latvia, Akciju Sabiedriba
Liberia, Corporation
Liechtenstein, Aktiengesellschaft
Lithuania, Akeine Bendroves
Luxembourg, Societe Anonyme
Malaysia, Berhad
Malta, Public Limited Company
Mexico, Sociedad Anonima
Morocco, Societe Anonyme
The Netherlands, Naamloze Vennootschap
New Zealand, Limited Company
Nicaragua, Compania Anonima
Nigeria, Public Limited Company
Northern Mariana Islands, Corporation
Norway, Allment Aksjeselskap
Pakistan, Public Limited Company
Panama, Sociedad Anonima
Paraguay, Sociedad Anonima
Peru, Sociedad Anonima
Philippines, Stock Corporation
Poland, Spolka Akcyjna
Portugal, Sociedade Anonima
Puerto Rico, Corporation
Romania, Societe pe Actiuni
Russia, Otkrytoye Aktsionernoy Obshchestvo
Saudi Arabia, Sharikat Al-Mossahamah
Singapore, Public Limited Company
Slovak Republic, Akciova Spolocnost

¶804.04

Slovenia, Delniska Druzba

South Africa, Public Limited Company

Spain, Sociedad Anonima

Surinam, Naamloze Vennootschap

Sweden, Publika Aktiebolag

Switzerland, Aktiengesellschaft

Thailand, Borisat Chamkad (Machachon)

Trinidad and Tobago, Limited Company

Tunisia, Societe Anonyme

Turkey, Anonim Sirket

Ukraine, Aktsionerne Tovaristvo Vidkritogo Tipu

United Kingdom, Public Limited Company

United States Virgin Islands, Corporation

Uruguay, Sociedad Anonima

Venezuela, Sociedad Anonima or Compania Anonima

Three special default rules apply if a foreign eligible entity does not make an election.[16] First, if the foreign entity has two or more owners and at least one owner does not have limited liability, the foreign entity is a partnership. Second, if all the owners have limited liability, the foreign entity is a corporation. Finally, if the foreign entity has only one owner that does not have limited liability, the entity is a branch. An owner of a foreign entity has limited liability if ownership does not result in personal liability. This is purely a matter of the foreign country's local law, and requires a review of the foreign entity's organizational documents.[17] Finally, an election can have an effective date of up to seventy-five days prior to the election date and up to one year after the election date. Once elected, an owner cannot re-elect for five years.[18]

Problems can arise when a U.S. taxpayer checks-the-box by filing a Form 8832 more than 75 days after the desired effective date, typically the date of organization of the foreign entity, which may result in a taxable liquidation.[19] Fortunately, Rev. Proc. 2009-41[20] permits delinquently filed Form 8832 that are both (i) due to reasonable cause and (ii) either the entity has not filed a return for the year with the desired effective date or the return was filed consistent with the desired classification.

Hybrid entities provide the tax advantages of the flow-through entity form (i.e., a branch or partnership), while still providing the U.S. parent corporation with limited liability and a "corporate" presence in the foreign country. For example, an entity that is considered a branch or a partnership for U.S. tax purposes allows foreign losses to flow-through and be deducted by the U.S. parent corporation. In contrast, losses of a foreign subsidiary are not deductible by the U.S. parent corporation. In addition, whereas noncorporate shareholders can not claim a deemed paid foreign tax credit for the foreign income taxes incurred by a foreign

---

[16] Reg. § 301.7701-3(b). A different default rule applies for domestic entities, treating the entity as a partnership if the entity has multiple owners and a branch if the entity has only a single owner.

[17] Reg. § 301.7701-3(b)(2)(ii).

[18] Reg. §§ 301.7701-3(b)(3)(iii) and (iv).

[19] A liquidation pursuant to Code Sec. 331 would result in capital gain and a liquidation by a C corporation of an 80% foreign subsidiary pursuant to Code Sec. 332 would result in a dividend (see ¶ 1402).

[20] 2009-39 IRB 439.

corporation,[21] they can claim a direct credit for the foreign taxes incurred by a foreign branch or partnership.[22]

> ***Example 8.2:*** Uncle Sam, a U.S. citizen, owns a U.S. limited liability company, USAllc. USAllc is going to operate in Country H, a high-tax country, through a private limited company. Assuming USAllc has timely checked-the-box for the private limited company to have "branch status," Uncle Sam will be able to take the tax benefits of a net operating loss of the private limited company and take a direct foreign tax credit for foreign income taxes paid by the private limited company.

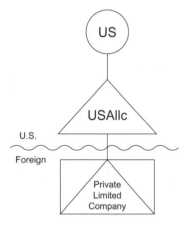

Although hybrid entities have a number of benefits, there are significant tax costs associated with converting an existing foreign subsidiary into a foreign branch or partnership. In particular, "hybridizing" an existing foreign subsidiary is a two-part transaction, involving the inbound liquidation of the foreign corporation, followed by a contribution of those assets to a foreign branch or partnership. Taxpayers must carefully analyze such transactions since inbound repatriating liquidations are subject to a special toll charge tax[23] and an outbound expatriating transfer to a foreign partnership may be subject to a special allocation of income.[24]

.05 Reverse Hybrid Entities

Reverse hybrid entities are treated as corporations by the United States, but as flow-through entities by the foreign countries. From a U.S. perspective, operating as a reverse hybrid offers several tax planning opportunities. A foreign subsidiary generally will allow a U.S. company to defer the residual U.S. tax on foreign profits. Furthermore, a foreign subsidiary offers more control over the timing of income recognition, which is useful in foreign tax credit planning. To take advantage of these opportunities, but avoid local foreign tax, a U.S. company can create a reverse hybrid.

---

[21] Code Sec. 902(a) and 1373(a).
[22] Code Sec. 901(b)(5).

[23] Code Sec. 367(b) and 1248(a). *See* discussion in Chapter 14 (¶ 1401).
[24] Code Sec. 721(c). *See* discussion in Chapter 14 (¶ 1401).

Example 8.3: USAco operates in country L, a low tax country through a flow-through entity, "Limitada," for which it checked the box as "corporate status." Limitada earns $1,000,000 in Country L. Because Country L does not impose any tax on Limitada and does not impose a branch level tax, USAco does not incur any tax in country L on Limitada. Furthermore, there will not be any U.S. tax until the $1,000,000 of earnings are distributed.

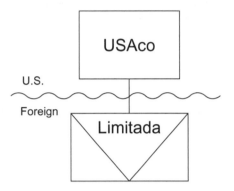

Example 8.4: USAco operates in country L, a low tax country through a flow-through entity, "Limitada," for which it checked the box as "corporate status." In each of its first 5 years, Limitada earns $1,000,000 in Country L, for accumulated earnings of $5,000,000 by the end of year 5. Because Country L does not impose any tax on Limitada and does not impose a branch level tax, USAco does not incur any tax in country L on Limitada. On December 31 of year 5, USAco receives a distribution from Limitada of $1,000,000. USAco pays tax at its U.S. marginal rate on the $1,000,000, but has effectively deferred the U.S. tax for 4 years.

.06 Dual Consolidated Loss Rules

Because the United States treats a corporation as resident of the United States if incorporated in the United States while some foreign countries deem residence based on the location of a corporation's management, a corporation may be resident in two countries. Consider, for example, a U.S. corporation with its management in London. Based on incorporation, the Code treats that corporation as a U.S. corporation and, based on the location of management, the United Kingdom (U.K.) would treat the corporation as a U.K. corporation. As a result, such a corporation may have the opportunity to deduct losses incurred against income earned in both the United Kingdom and the United States.

To prevent such abuse, the dual consolidated loss rules prevent a dual-resident corporation (the DRC) from having its loss reduce U.S. taxable income if the loss is used to offset the income of a foreign affiliate.[25] DRCs include U.S. corporations subject to a foreign country's tax on either a worldwide income or residence basis

---

[25] Code Sec. 1503(d).

and separate units, a term of art that includes foreign branches, partnerships and hybrid entities.[26]

A DRC may not deduct that loss (a "dual consolidated loss") in the United States,[27] unless the DRC elects[28] and annually certifies for five years[29] that the loss will not be used abroad.

> *Example 8.5:* U.S. Parent owns DRC (a corporation incorporated in the United States with its management located in the United Kingdom), which owns UKCo, a U.K. corporation. DRC borrows money from a bank and annually pays interest to the bank. Absent the dual consolidated loss rules, the interest may be deductible against the income of both U.S. Parent and UKCo because DRC is a resident of both countries. However, pursuant to the dual consolidated loss rules, the U.S. Parent-DRC consolidated return may not deduct the interest in the United States unless it elects to not deduct the interest expense in the U.K. and annually certifies that the interest expense was not so deducted.

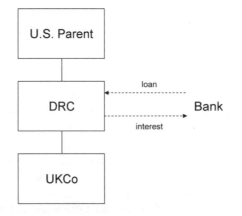

.07 Information Reporting for Foreign Partnerships

Foreign partnerships controlled by U.S. persons have information reporting requirements that are similar to the information reporting rules that have been applied to CFCs. Under these provisions, a U.S. partner that controls a foreign partnership must file an annual information return.[30] A U.S. partner is considered to be in control of a foreign partnership if the U.S. partner holds, directly or indirectly, a greater than 50% interest in the capital, profits, or, to the extent provided in the regulations, deductions or losses of the partnership.[31] Where there is no single controlling partner, but the partnership is controlled by a number of U.S. persons each holding at least a 10% interest in the partnership, similar reporting is required of one or more of the 10% U.S. partners.[32] The penalty for failure to comply with these reporting obligations is $10,000, and may also include a reduction in the

---

[26] Reg. § 1.1503(d)-1(b).
[27] Reg. § 1.1503(d)-4(b).
[28] Reg. § 1.1503(d)-6(d).
[29] Reg. § 1.1503(d)-6(g).

[30] Code Sec. 6038(a).
[31] Code Sec. 6038(e)(3).
[32] Code Sec. 6038(a)(5).

taxpayer's foreign tax credit.[33] In addition to the requirements for U.S. persons that "hold" interests in a controlled foreign partnership, U.S. persons that "acquire" or "dispose" of such interests are also subject to reporting requirements.[34] Moreover, there are reporting requirements for U.S. persons who transfer property to a foreign partnership.[35] This reporting requirement applies only if the U.S. person owns, directly or indirectly, at least a 10% interest in the partnership, or if the fair market value of the property transferred to the foreign partnership during a 12-month period exceeds $100,000.[36] As with the reporting requirements for controlled foreign partnerships, the reporting of contributions to foreign partnerships parallels the reporting of similar transfers to foreign corporations. The penalty for a failure to report a contribution to a foreign partnership equals 10% of the fair market value of the property transferred, as well as gain recognition as if the property had been sold.[37]

The IRS has promulgated regulations implementing the reporting requirements on a Form 8865 for U.S. persons that hold interests in controlled foreign partnerships,[38] U.S. persons that acquire or dispose of an interest in a controlled foreign partnership,[39] and U.S. persons that transfer property to a foreign partnership.[40] A completed Form 8865 is reproduced in its entirety in the Appendix to this chapter.

¶ 805 BASICS OF OUTBOUND TAX PLANNING

Outbound tax planning involves the interplay of the tax laws of two or more countries. From a domestic corporation's perspective, the objective of outbound tax planning is to reduce the U.S. and foreign taxes on foreign-source income. Foreign taxes increase a domestic corporation's total tax costs only to the extent they are not creditable for U.S. tax purposes. Taxpayers can reduce these excess credits either through foreign tax reduction planning or planning that increases the allowable credit for U.S. tax purposes. With respect to U.S. taxes, the United States generally collects any residual U.S. taxes on lightly-taxed foreign-source income. Nevertheless, foreign-source income can give rise to opportunities to defer or even permanently reduce U.S. taxes. These issues are discussed in more detail below.

.01 Export Tax Benefits

Export tax benefits, such as the IC-DISC, are discussed in Chapter 7 (¶ 701).

.02 Operating in Low-Tax Foreign Jurisdictions

The United States generally does not tax foreign business profits earned through a foreign subsidiary until the subsidiary repatriates those earnings through a dividend. Therefore, a U.S. multinational corporation may be able to reduce its total tax costs by shifting income producing assets and activities to a subsidiary

---

[33] Code Sec. 6038(b) and (c).

[34] Code Sec. 6046A.

[35] Code Sec. 6038B(a)(1)(B).

[36] Code Sec. 6038B(b)(1).

[37] Code Sec. 6038B(c). However, the penalty does not apply if the U.S. person can show that the failure to

comply was due to reasonable cause and not to willful neglect. Moreover, the total penalty cannot exceed $100,000 unless the failure is due to intentional disregard of the reporting requirements.

[38] Reg. § 1.6038-3.

[39] Reg. § 1.6046A-1.

[40] Reg. § 1.6038B-2.

located in a low-tax foreign jurisdiction. There are limitations on the tax benefits of this strategy, however. First, shifting income to a lightly-taxed foreign subsidiary does not permanently avoid the residual U.S. tax on lightly-taxed foreign earnings, but instead merely defers those taxes until the subsidiary repatriates its earnings through a dividend distribution. In addition, the eventual repatriation of those earnings may be subject to foreign withholding taxes, which increases the total foreign tax rate on those earnings.

There also are significant constraints on the ability of U.S. multinationals to shift income to lightly-taxed foreign subsidiaries. For example, a domestic parent corporation must use arm's length transfer prices to compute its share of income arising from related party transactions[41] and special penalties may apply if the IRS makes a significant transfer pricing adjustment.[42] Moreover, Congress has enacted a variety of anti-deferral provisions, including the Subpart F and passive foreign investment company provisions (see Chapter 5 (¶ 501)). Under these provisions, certain types of unrepatriated earnings of a foreign corporation, such as passive investment income, are subject to immediate U.S. taxation.

.03 Operating in High-Tax Foreign Jurisdictions

When a U.S. company conducts business in a high-tax foreign jurisdiction, the resulting excess foreign tax credits increase the total tax burden beyond what it would have been if only the United States had taxed the foreign-source income. One strategy for eliminating the excess credits is to increase the proportion of worldwide income that is classified as foreign-source for U.S. tax purposes. For example, by arranging for the passage of title abroad, export sales will generate some foreign-source income. Recharacterizing deductions also is an effective strategy for eliminating excess credits. More specifically, by using alternative apportionment bases for sourcing selling, general, and administrative expenses, a taxpayer may be able to reduce the amount of these deductions allocated and apportioned to foreign-source income.

A second strategy for reducing excess credits is to blend low and high-tax foreign-source income within a single limitation. This allows the excess limitation on the low-tax foreign income to offset the excess credits on the high-tax foreign income. There are currently two categories of income—the passive income limitation category and the general income limitation category.[43] Although this prevents cross-crediting between passive and general category income, cross-crediting is still allowed with respect to the same type of income derived from different foreign countries. Look-through rules make cross-crediting possible with respect to income derived from foreign corporations located in low and high-tax foreign jurisdictions, as long as the underlying earnings are assigned to the same category of income.[44]

A third strategy for eliminating the excess credits on high-tax foreign-source income is foreign tax reduction planning.

---

[41] Code Sec. 482.
[42] Code Sec. 6662. *See* discussion of transactional and net adjustment penalties in Chapter 12 (¶ 1201).

[43] Code Sec. 904(d)(1).
[44] Code Sec. 904(d)(3) and (d)(4).

.04 Foreign Tax Reduction Planning

Many of the techniques that a U.S. taxpayer can use to reduce foreign income taxes are similar to those used to reduce income taxes in a purely domestic context. Examples include realizing income in a form that is taxed at a lower rate (such as a preferential rate for capital gains), deferring the recognition of gross income, and accelerating the recognition of deductions. Other foreign tax reduction techniques are unique to the international context and include taking advantage of local tax incentives, debt financing, transfer pricing, and the use of tax treaties.

Local tax incentives. One way to reduce foreign taxes is to take advantage of the special tax exemptions and holidays that various countries offer as an incentive to locate particular types of operations within their borders. For example, Singapore offers tax breaks for the manufacture of advanced technologies, Puerto Rico grants tax breaks to U.S. companies that establish manufacturing operations in Puerto Rico, Belgium offers tax breaks for financing companies, and Switzerland offer low-tax rates for headquarters companies.

Debt financing. It may be advantageous to finance high-tax foreign subsidiaries in a way that maximizes interest deductions and minimizes dividend payments. The potential advantages of debt financing provided by a U.S. parent include a deduction in the high-tax foreign jurisdiction for interest paid to the U.S. parent, as well as the possibility of lower foreign withholding taxes on interest payments, as opposed to dividend distributions.

Assuming the foreign subsidiary is a CFC, intercompany debt also increases the U.S. parent's foreign tax credit limitation by creating a stream of lightly-taxed foreign-source income. Interest income derived from a CFC by a U.S. shareholder of that CFC is assigned to the passive income category to the extent of the CFC's foreign personal holding company income.[45] Any interest income in excess of the CFC's foreign personal holding company income is apportioned among the separate income categories other than passive income.[46] In contrast, only a portion of the U.S. parent's incremental interest expense, if any, caused by financing the CFC is allocable against foreign-source income under the asset-based apportionment rule for interest expense.[47] Nevertheless, a special rule (referred to as the "CFC netting rule") may require the U.S. parent to specifically allocate certain interest expense deductions against its foreign-source interest income in computing the foreign tax credit limitation.[48]

To secure the benefits of debt financing, the U.S. parent corporation must ensure that any intercompany payments meant to be interest qualify as such under the host country's tax laws. The rules for determining whether an investment in a local subsidiary is treated as debt and not equity vary from country to country. Some countries employ relatively objective standards (for example, a maximum debt to equity ratio of 3 to 1),[49] while other countries employ more subjective facts

---

[45] Code Sec. 954(b)(5).

[46] Code Sec. 904(d)(3)(C). *See* Reg. § 1.904-5(c)(2)(ii) regarding the applicable apportionment method.

[47] Code Sec. 864(e)(2).

[48] Reg. § 1.861-10.

[49] For example, pursuant to the anti-earnings provision of Code Sec. 163(j), a U.S. subsidiary may not deduct interest paid to a foreign parent, when *inter alia*, the U.S. subsidiary's debt to equity ratio exceeds 1.5 to 1 (see ¶ 1003).

and circumstances standards. To the extent that interest payments are limited by these standards, the taxpayer may wish to consider other methods of repatriating earnings that give rise to a deduction at the foreign subsidiary level, such as royalty payments.

Transfer pricing. By altering its transfer pricing policy, a U.S. multinational corporation may be able to allocate a smaller portion of its worldwide profits to subsidiaries located in high-tax foreign jurisdictions. For example, a U.S. parent can allocate a smaller share of the gross profit from intercompany inventory sales by charging foreign marketing subsidiaries a higher price or paying foreign manufacturing subsidiaries a lower price. Another way to shift income is to charge foreign subsidiaries for the use of U.S.-owned manufacturing and marketing intangibles. If the subsidiary is a CFC, the resulting royalties also provide the U.S. parent with a stream of lightly-taxed foreign-source income that has the same character for foreign tax credit limitation purposes as the underlying earnings of the CFC to which the royalty expense is properly allocable.[50] If a foreign jurisdiction does not allow a deduction for technology charges paid to a parent corporation, the taxpayer should consider using a cost-sharing arrangement (see discussion in Chapter 12 (¶ 1202)). Charging a foreign subsidiary for management services provided by the U.S. home office also reduces the foreign income taxes of the subsidiary.

As discussed in detail in Chapter 12 (¶ 1204), special penalties may apply if the IRS makes a significant transfer pricing adjustment.[51] Therefore, U.S. taxpayers must establish defensible positions for the transfer prices they use through contemporaneous documentation of their transfer pricing methodology or through an advance pricing agreement.

Commission agents and contract manufacturing. Pursuant to the economic principles of transfer pricing, a business entity's profits are determined by the functions it performs, the risk it bears, and the assets that it owns. As a consequence, a U.S. multinational may be able to reduce its foreign tax costs by structuring its foreign operations in a manner that minimizes the transfer of risks, responsibilities, and assets to high-tax foreign subsidiaries. Two strategies for achieving this result are the use of commissionaires (or stripped distributors) and contract manufacturing.

A traditional buy-sell foreign sales subsidiary purchases inventory from its U.S. parent for resale abroad. Such subsidiaries often assume responsibility not only for the advertising and selling functions, but also for inventory risks, credit risks, warranty administration, and technical services. As a result, arm's-length transfer prices allocate a significant portion of the U.S. multinational's total export profit to a foreign sales subsidiary. If the subsidiary is located in a high-tax foreign country, this can worsen the U.S. parent's excess credit problem. In contrast, if the U.S. parent holds title to its goods until their ultimate delivery to the foreign customer, with the foreign subsidiary acting as a mere commission agent for the U.S. parent, the subsidiary would earn a profit equal to an arm's-length commission determined under either a cost-plus approach or a percentage of sales revenue approach. A

---

[50] Code Sec. 904(d)(3)(C) and Reg. § 1.904-5(c)(3).   [51] Code Sec. 6662.

commission agent's profit is lower than that of a buy-sell distributor because the functions performed and risks assumed by such agents are typically limited to selling, compared to the much broader set of functions performed by a buy-sell distributor.

Another technique for minimizing the transfer of functions, risks and assets to a foreign operation is the use of contract manufacturing. The maquiladora operations of U.S. multinationals in Mexico are an example of contract manufacturing. Under this arrangement, a Mexican subsidiary processes materials using equipment owned and leased by the U.S. parent. The U.S. parent also provides the managerial and technical support personnel needed to manage the Mexican operation and usually retains title to the raw materials, which are processed on a contract basis (hence, the name "contract manufacturer"). Historically, maquiladoras earn a profit equal to an arm's-length fee determined under a cost-plus approach.

Tax treaties. Taxpayers also can reduce foreign taxes by making use of permanent establishment provisions and the reduced withholding tax rates provided by tax treaties. Under most tax treaties, a U.S. taxpayer's business profits are not subject to foreign taxation unless it conducts business through a permanent establishment located within the foreign country. A permanent establishment is a branch office, or the presence of dependent agents who habitually conclude sales contracts in the taxpayer's name. Marketing products abroad solely through independent brokers or distributors does not create a permanent establishment. Tax treaties also provide lower withholding tax rates on dividends, interest, and royalties derived from sources within the treaty country. As a consequence, a U.S. parent corporation may be able to reduce foreign withholding taxes by owning its foreign subsidiaries through strategically located holding companies (so-called "treaty shopping"). Chapter 13 (¶ 1302) discusses some of the restrictions on a taxpayer's ability to engage in treaty shopping.

.05 Checking-the-Box and Qualified Dividends for U.S. Individuals

Both checking-the-box and the taxation of qualified dividends to U.S. shareholders at a 15% rate have profoundly impacted the outbound tax planning of closely-held businesses. Typically, these businesses involve U.S. individuals who own foreign corporations in either their individual capacity or through a flow-through entity, such as an LLC, partnership, or S corporation. Previously, these U.S. individuals incurred double taxation on the earnings of their foreign corporations because these U.S. individuals are not entitled to a deemed paid foreign tax credit (see Chapter 4 (¶ 410)).

Example 8.6: Betsy Ross, a U.S. citizen, wholly owns FLAGco, a foreign corporation organized in Country H. In year 1, FLAGco earns net income of $1 million, on which FLAGco pays foreign income taxes of $400,000, leaving $600,000 of earnings and profits. Needing cash to finance a revolution, Betsy Ross takes a $600,000 dividend from FLAGco, which is not subject to a withholding tax under the tax treaty between Country H and the United States. The $600,000 dividend will incur U.S. tax of $90,000 (15% of $600,000). The $400,000 of Country H tax and the $90,000 of U.S. tax create an effective tax rate of 49% on the $1 million of income (the sum of $40,000 plus $90,000 divided by $1 million).

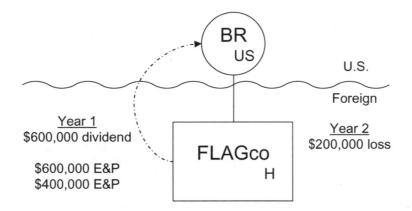

In year 2, FLAGco incurs a net operating loss of $200,000. Because FLAGco is a foreign corporation, Betsy Ross does not get the tax benefit of using the loss against her other income on her U.S. return.

If, however, Betsy Ross had checked-the-box for FLAGco to be a disregarded entity in year 1, Betsy Ross would be treated as receiving $1 million of income on which she pays $400,000 of foreign income taxes to Country H. Her pre-credit U.S. tax would be $350,000 (35% of $1 million), which she would eliminate by taking a direct foreign tax credit of $350,000 of the $400,000 of foreign income taxes paid. Her effective tax rate would be reduced to 40% ($400,000 of foreign income taxes on $1 million of income) and she would have $50,000 of excess foreign tax credits that she could credit against her pre-credit U.S. tax liability from any other foreign-source income.

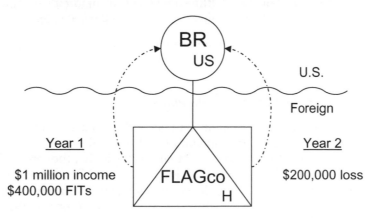

In year 2, the $200,000 of losses flow-through to Betsy Ross for her to use against other income on her U.S. return. Even though Betsy Ross has checked-the-box for FLAGco to be a disregarded entity for U.S. tax purposes only,

¶805.05

FLAGco maintains corporate status and limited liability under corporate law in the United States and Country H.

In the alternative to checking-the-box for flow-through treatment, some U.S. individuals have taken advantage of the reduced 15% rate on qualified dividends received from a foreign corporation.[52] This 15% rate, which essentially treats the dividend as a capital gain, applies only to dividends paid by foreign corporations in treaty countries. In low-tax treaty countries, the preferred strategy is to not check-the-box, have the foreign corporation pay the lower corporate tax, and distribute a dividend to the U.S. individual who pays tax at only a 15% rate.

> **Example 8.7:** Betsy Ross, a U.S. citizen, owns BRITco, a corporation incorporated in the United Kingdom, which has a treaty with the United States. BRITco earns $400,000 on which it pays $80,000 of foreign income taxes. BRITco distributes a $320,000 cash dividend to Betsy Ross, who pays U.S. tax of $48,000 (15% of $320,000).

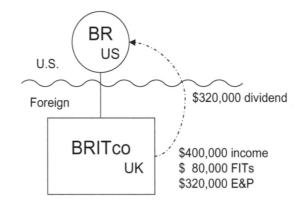

The effective rate of tax is 32% (the sum of $80,000 of foreign income taxes paid by BRITco and $48,000 of U.S. taxes divided by $400,000 of income).

Dividends received from foreign corporations incorporated in non-treaty countries or from a passive foreign investment company do not qualify for the 15% tax rate.

.06 Operating in Tax Haven Jursidictions

U.S. taxpayers can achieve significant tax and nontax benefits from the use of tax haven related strategies. Each nation typically provides a definition of the term "tax haven." Although it may vary, a common factor is that the foreign jurisdiction imposes an income tax that is lower than the tax imposed by the home country. For example, in France, a tax haven is described as a country having a"privileged tax system," which is any country which levies a tax, equal to or less than two-thirds the tax France imposes.[53] The term tax haven, if applied literally, could include countries such as the United States, which does not tax interest earned by nonresi-

---

[52] Code Sec. 1(h)(11).   [53] Code General des Impots Art. 238 A, paragraph 2.

dent aliens on deposits in U.S. banks. It therefore constitutes a tax haven for those foreign investors who derive interest income from deposits in U.S. banks.

Although Congress has passed laws to limit the use of tax havens and other offshore sites for tax-savings purposes (e.g., Subpart F, Code Sec. 367 and the PFIC provisions), there is no official U.S. definition of the term "tax haven."

In general, there are six principal characteristics of tax havens:

    (i) A tax haven either imposes no income tax or imposes a tax on income that is small in comparison to the tax imposed by the home country.

    (ii) A tax haven often protects the confidentiality of financial and commercial information. In so doing, the tax haven may adopt bank secrecy or similar internal laws that make it a crime to disclose this information to any person.

    (iii) Financial institutions, such as banks, frequently assume a dominant role in the tax haven's trade or commerce, and its residents include those skilled in financial transactions, such as bankers, lawyers, and accountants.

    (iv) A tax haven normally possesses modern communications facilities necessary to the conduct of financial and commercial affairs.

    (v) A tax haven often does not impose currency controls or similar restrictions on foreign nationals.

    (vi) If the tax haven has a treaty network, the haven may offer benefits such as reduced tax rates on income tax by its treaty partners.

Tax haven incentives. A tax haven jurisdiction typically imposes a low or zero rate of tax on all or some class of income. The following list describes the special incentives that selected tax havens generally offer:

    (i) *Countries that impose zero tax*—These are jurisdictions that impose no tax on income, capital gains, gifts, inheritances, estates and trusts. Since these countries do not have treaty networks, they have no obligation to furnish tax information to other jurisdictions. Such countries generally charge an annual formation fee to registered companies. An example of this type of tax haven would be Bermuda.

    (ii) *Countries that impose a low tax rate*—In order to compete with havens that impose a zero rate of tax, these jurisdictions offer a low rate of tax combined with a treaty network. The treaty networks are useful in adding some degree of flexibility to tax planning. An example of this type of tax haven would be Ireland.

    (iii) *Countries that impose no tax on foreign source income*—These tax havens do not impose any tax on income earned from sources outside of the particular jurisdiction. These havens are especially attractive to the transportation industry when, for example, the jurisdiction allows the registration of foreign flagships. An example of this type of tax haven would be Hong Kong.

¶805.06

(iv) *Countries that impose a reduced rate of tax on offshore finance and trade-oriented businesses*—These countries usually impose a minimal or token tax to resident companies that do not conduct business or trade within the haven. An example of this type of tax haven would be the British Virgin Islands.

(v) *Countries that offer special inducements*—In order to attract certain companies, such as holding companies, some jurisdictions offer significant inducements that may include privileged treatment with respect to income taxes, import taxes, customs, duties, etc. An example of this type of tax haven would be Ireland. In order to attract manufacturing facilities to their countries, some jurisdictions, such as Singapore, provide for various tax holidays on profits earned on products manufactured for export.

Non-tax factors. The laws of most countries provide for some degree of confidentiality with respect to banking and other commercial activities. However, most nations will not protect information from a legitimate inquiry initiated by a foreign government, especially if the request is made pursuant to a treaty provision. On the other hand, tax havens with stringent secrecy laws typically refuse to breach their secrecy rules even when serious violations of another nation's law may have occurred. To do otherwise may seriously impair the jurisdiction's tax haven status with those persons who need the element of secrecy to plan their tax strategy.

Many jurisdictions, in order to maintain or improve their competitive position as a tax haven, have enacted legislation providing for criminal sanctions for breach of the secrecy laws. An example is the Cayman Islands. The Cayman Islands, which have had stringent bank secrecy laws since the 1960s when it tightened its common law through statute, passed additional legislation providing for substantial sanctions against persons who either divulged or received confidential banking and commercial information.

Many tax havens have a dual currency control system that distinguishes between residents and nonresidents, and between local currency and foreign currency. Generally, residents are subject to currency controls while nonresidents are only subject to controls placed on the local currency. For currency control purposes, a company which is formed in the tax haven and which is beneficially owned by a resident and which conducts its business outside the haven is generally treated as a nonresident. Therefore, a tax haven company doing business solely in other jurisdictions cannot be subject to the tax haven's currency exchange controls provided it deals in the currency of other countries. These rules facilitate the use of a tax haven by a person wishing to establish a tax haven entity for purposes of doing business in other jurisdictions. The rules also offer the free movement of foreign currency abroad.

A tax haven enjoying a treaty network can provide a most attractive combination in the formation of a multi-national tax strategy. This combination offers increased flexibility in devising plans to reduce tax rates through treaty shopping. Many of the U.S. treaty partners have treaties with tax haven type countries.

¶805.06

Finally, in addition to selecting a particular tax haven for purposes such as low tax, secrecy, banking, currency control, communications, and treaty networks, taxpayers should also consider nontax factors. These factors include economic and political stability, geographic accessibility to markets, the availability of labor, the risk of nationalization of assets, and government cooperation.

¶ 806 FINANCIAL REPORTING IMPLICATIONS OF INTERNATIONAL TAX PLANNING

The globalization of U.S. business has increased the importance of understanding how a U.S. multinational corporation's foreign operations impact the effective tax rate it reports in its financial statements. Virtually all countries tax the income of corporations and, therefore, the profits of a U.S. multinational corporation are typically subject to income taxation in a number of countries. A firm's worldwide effective tax rate provides a convenient metric for capturing the cumulative effect of these various income taxes on the corporation's profitability. For financial reporting purposes, a firm's effective tax rate is computed by dividing its total income tax expense by its pre-tax earnings. For example, if the sum of a U.S. corporation's federal, state and foreign income taxes is $100 million, and its pre-tax earnings is $300 million, the company has an effective tax rate of 33 percent.

When evaluating a U.S. corporation's effective tax rate, the de facto benchmark is the U.S. statutory rate. For large U.S. corporations, the statutory tax rate has been 35 percent since 1993.[54] However, a U.S. company's foreign operations can cause its effective tax rate to diverge from 35 percent. For example, operations in high-tax foreign jurisdictions can give rise to excess foreign tax credits that increase a firm's effective tax rate. Likewise, operations in low-tax foreign jurisdictions can reduce a firm's reported effective tax rate if management intends to permanently reinvest those earnings.

.01 Operations in High-Tax Foreign Jurisdictions

The foreign tax credit limitation prevents U.S. companies operating in high-tax jurisdictions from claiming a credit for foreign taxes in excess of the U.S. statutory tax rate. These excess credits can increase the total tax burden on a U.S. company's foreign earnings beyond what it would have been if only the United States had taxed the income. Excess credits can be carried back one year and carried forward ten years and taken as a credit in a year that the limitation exceeds the amount of creditable foreign taxes.[55] Therefore, excess credits increase the reported effective tax rate only to the extent they cannot be utilized in one of the carryback or carryforward years.[56] The financial statements of U.S. oil companies illustrate the impact of excess credits on the effective tax rate of a U.S. multinational corporation. For example, in its annual report for 2010, Exxon Mobil Corporation reported an effective tax rate of 41% on its worldwide earnings. Oil-producing countries often

---

[54] Code Sec. 11.

[55] Code Sec. 905.

[56] If a company carries back its excess credits, it obtains an immediate tax benefit that is reflected in a lower current year income tax expense. The current year income tax expense is also reduced if the firm expects to

use its excess credits in a carryforward year, in which case the firm establishes a deferred tax asset for the expected future tax benefit of the carryforward. Statement of Financial Accounting Standards No. 109, *Accounting for Income Taxes* (Financial Accounting Standards Board, 1992).

impose special taxes the profits of oil companies. For example, U.S. oil companies derive significant profits from operations in Norway, and Norway imposes a special 50 percent petroleum tax in addition to its general corporate income tax of 28 percent.

.02 Operations in Low-Tax Foreign Jurisdictions

There are also a number of foreign jurisdictions that offer corporate income tax rates that are lower than the U.S. statutory rate of 35 percent, such as Bermuda, Hong Kong, Singapore and Switzerland. Other countries have statutory rates comparable to the U.S. rate, but offer special tax breaks to U.S. multinational corporations that locate new facilities within their borders. Likewise, Ireland offers a 12.5% rate to U.S. multinational companies that locate operations in Ireland. Because the U.S. generally does not tax the foreign profits of a foreign subsidiary until those earnings are remitted to the U.S. parent as a dividend, it is possible to defer payment of the "residual" U.S. tax on low-tax foreign earnings.

For financial reporting purposes, it is presumed that the U.S. parent will eventually repatriate all of a foreign subsidiary's undistributed earnings,[57] in which case the tax savings associated with deferral are accounted for as a temporary difference that has no effect on the firm's reported effective tax rate. However, if sufficient evidence shows that the firm has or will reinvest undistributed foreign earnings "indefinitely," it is not necessary to include the residual U.S tax on undistributed low-tax foreign earnings in the current year's income tax expense. This exception provides U.S. corporations with the ability to treat the benefit of operating in a low-tax foreign jurisdiction as a permanent difference that reduces both the income tax expense and the reported effective tax rate.

The financial statements of U.S. pharmaceutical companies illustrate the impact of operations in low-tax jurisdiction on the effective tax rate of a U.S. multinational corporation. Unlike oil companies, drug companies have some flexibility in terms of where they can locate production activities. The effective tax rates of these pharmaceutical firms indicate that they are taking advantage of this flexibility by locating operations in low-tax foreign jurisdictions. For example, in its 2010 annual report, Pfizer, Inc. reported an effective tax rate of 11.99% on its worldwide earnings.

¶ 807 COMPREHENSIVE EXAMPLE

USAco, a domestic corporation, plans to locate a new factory in either country L or country H. USAco will structure the new facility as a wholly-owned foreign subsidiary, FORco, and finance FORco solely with an equity investment. USAco projects that in FORco's first year of operations, it will generate $10 million of taxable income, all from active foreign manufacturing activities. Assume that the U.S. corporate tax rate is 35%. To simplify the analysis, further assume that USAco's only item of income during the year is that derived from FORco.

---

[57] Accounting Principles Board Opinion No. 23, *Accounting for Income Taxes—Special Areas* (1972).

The total tax rate on FORco earnings will vary significantly, depending on a number of factors, including:

(i) Whether FORco is located in a low-tax or high-tax foreign country,

(ii) The extent to which USAco repatriates FORco's earnings,

(iii) Whether USAco repatriates FORco's earnings through dividend distributions, as opposed to interest, rental or royalty payments, and

(iv) The availability of favorable tax treaty withholding rates on dividends, interest, and other payments made by FORco to USAco.

The effect of these factors is illustrated below by computing the worldwide tax rate on FORco's earnings under a variety of assumptions.

Case 1: Low-tax country/No dividends. Country L has a corporate income tax rate of 25%, which is ten percentage points lower than the U.S. rate. If USAco locates FORco in country L and FORco pays no dividends, the total tax rate on its earnings will be 25%, computed as follows:

Foreign income tax

FORco's taxable income	$10,000,000
Country L income tax rate	×25%
Country L income tax	$2,500,000
Foreign withholding taxes on repatriated earnings	$0
U.S. tax on repatriated earnings	$0
Total taxes [$2,500,000 + $0 + $0]	$2,500,000
Worldwide effective tax rate [$2,500,000 ÷ $10,000,000]	25%

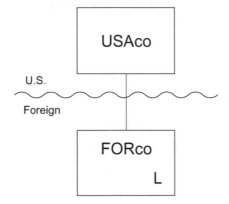

This example illustrates that USAco can reduce the current year worldwide tax rate on the new manufacturing facility below the U.S. tax rate of 35% by locating the factory in L, a low-tax foreign country, without repatriating the foreign earnings, which deters U.S. tax.

¶807

Case 2: Low-tax country/Pays dividend/Tax treaty. Assume that country L has a tax treaty with the United States that provides a 10% withholding tax rate on dividends. If USAco locates FORco in country L and repatriates half of FORco's after-tax earnings through a dividend distribution, the total tax rate on its repatriated and unrepatriated earnings will be 30%, computed as follows:

Foreign income tax

FORco's taxable income	$10,000,000
Country L income tax rate	×25%
Country L income tax	$2,500,000

Foreign withholding taxes on repatriated earnings

FORco's after-tax earnings [$10,000,000 – $2,500,000] . .	$7,500,000
Percentage repatriated through dividend	×50%
Dividend distribution	$3,750,000
Withholding tax rate (per treaty)	×10%
Country L withholding tax	$375,000

U.S. tax on repatriated earnings

Dividend from FORco	$3,750,000
Code Sec. 78 gross-up	+1,250,000
USAco's taxable income	$5,000,000
U.S. tax rate	×35%
Pre-credit U.S. tax	$1,750,000
Foreign tax credit	−1,625,000

Foreign withholding taxes: $375,000

Deemed paid taxes: $2,500,000 × [$3,750,000 ÷ $7,500,000]= $1,250,000

Creditable foreign taxes: [$375,000 + $1,250,000] = $1,625,000

General limitation: $1,750,000 × [$5,000,000 ÷ $5,000,000]= $1,750,000

U.S. income tax	$125,000
Total taxes [$2,500,000 + $375,000 + $125,000]	$3,000,000
Worldwide effective tax rate [$3,000,000 ÷ $10,000,000]	30%

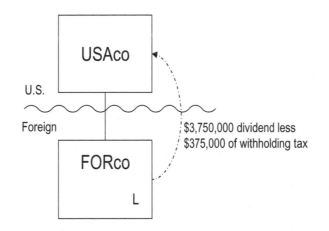

By repatriating half of FORco's earnings through a dividend distribution, USAco increases the worldwide tax rate on FORco's earnings from 25% in Case 1 to 30% in Case 2. The 30% rate is a blended rate, whereby the $5 million of income that USAco recognizes by virtue of the dividend is, in effect, taxed one time at the U.S. rate of 35% and FORco's remaining $5 million of earnings is taxed one time at the country L rate of 25%.

Case 3: Low-tax country/Pays dividend/No tax treaty. An important assumption in Case 2 is that country L had a tax treaty with the United States that provided for a 10% withholding tax rate on dividends. Now assume that there is no tax treaty between the United States and country L and that country L's statutory withholding rate on dividends is 30%. The lack of a favorable treaty withholding rate increases the total tax rate on FORco's repatriated and unrepatriated earnings from 30% in Case 2 to 36.25% in Case 3, computed as follows:

Foreign income tax

FORco's taxable income	$10,000,000
Country L income tax rate	×25%
Country L income tax	$2,500,000

Foreign withholding taxes on repatriated earnings

FORco's after-tax earnings [$10,000,000 − $2,500,000] . .	$7,500,000
Percentage repatriated through dividend	×50%
Dividend distribution	$3,750,000
Withholding tax rate (per statute)	×30%
Country L withholding tax	$1,125,000

U.S. tax on repatriated earnings

Dividend from FORco	$3,750,000
Code Sec. 78 gross-up	+1,250,000

USAco's taxable income	$5,000,000
U.S. tax rate	×35%
Pre-credit U.S. tax	$1,750,000
Foreign tax credit	−1,750,000

Foreign withholding taxes: $1,125,000

Deemed paid taxes: $2,500,000 × [$3,750,000 ÷ $7,500,000]= $1,250,000

Creditable foreign taxes: [$1,125,000 + $1,250,000] = $2,375,000

General limitation: $1,750,000 × [$5,000,000 ÷ $5,000,000]= $1,750,000

U.S. income tax	$0
Total taxes [$2,500,000 + $1,125,000 + $0]	$3,625,000
Worldwide effective tax rate [$3,625,000 ÷ $10,000,000]	36.25%

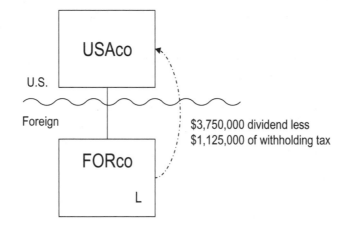

Case 3 shows that if USAco repatriates some of FORco's earnings through a dividend distribution, the availability of a favorable treaty withholding rate on dividends is critical to the ability of USAco to obtain the benefits of lower tax rates abroad.

Case 4: High-tax country/No dividends. Country H has a corporate income tax rate of 45%, which is ten percentage points higher than the U.S. rate. If USAco locates FORco in country H and FORco pays no dividends, the total tax rate on its earnings will be 45%, computed as follows:

Foreign income tax

FORco's taxable income	$10,000,000
Country H income tax rate	×45%
Country H income tax	$4,500,000

Foreign withholding taxes on repatriated earnings	$0
U.S. tax on repatriated earnings	$0
Total taxes [$4,500,000 + $0 + $0]	$4,500,000
Worldwide effective tax rate [$4,500,000 ÷ $10,000,000]	45%

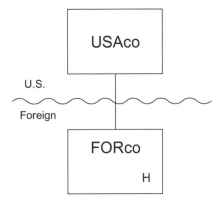

The 45% worldwide tax rate indicates that the total tax rate on USAco new manufacturing facility will exceed the U.S. tax rate of 35% if USAco locates the factory in H, a high-tax foreign country, without repatriating the foreign earnings.

Case 5: High-tax country/Pays dividend/Tax treaty. Assume that country H has a tax treaty with the United States that provides a 10% withholding tax rate on dividends. If USAco locates FORco in country H and repatriates half of FORco's after-tax earnings through a dividend distribution, the total tax rate on its repatriated and unrepatriated earnings will be 47.75%, computed as follows:

Foreign income tax

FORco's taxable income	$10,000,000
Country H income tax rate......................	×45%
Country H income tax	$4,500,000

Foreign withholding taxes on repatriated earnings

FORco's after-tax earnings [$10,000,000 – $4,500,000] ..	$5,500,000
Percentage repatriated through dividend	×50%
Dividend distribution	$2,750,000
Withholding tax rate (per treaty)	×10%
Country H withholding tax	$275,000

U.S. tax on repatriated earnings

Dividend from FORco	$2,750,000
Code Sec. 78 gross-up........................	+2,250,000

USAco's taxable income	$5,000,000
U.S. tax rate	×35%
Pre-credit U.S. tax	$1,750,000
Foreign tax credit	−1,750,000

> Foreign withholding taxes: $275,000
>
> Deemed paid taxes: $4,500,000 × [$2,750,000 ÷ $5,500,000]= $2,250,000
>
> Creditable foreign taxes: [$275,000 + $2,250,000] = $2,525,000
>
> General limitation: $1,750,000 × [$5,000,000 ÷ $5,000,000]= $1,750,000

U.S. income tax	$0
Total taxes [$4,500,000 + $275,000 + $0]	$4,775,000
Worldwide effective tax rate [$4,775,000 ÷ $10,000,000]	47.75%

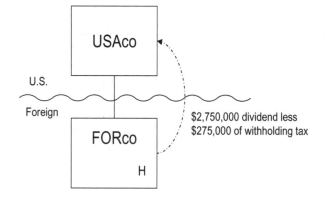

By repatriating half of FORco's earnings through a dividend distribution, USAco increases the worldwide tax rate on FORco's earnings from 45% in Case 4 to 47.75% in Case 5. The foreign withholding tax on the dividend distribution is responsible for the increase in the total tax rate.

Case 6: High-tax country/Pays dividend/No tax treaty. A comparison of Cases 4 and 5 indicates that repatriating half of FORco's earnings through a dividend distribution increases the worldwide tax rate on FORco's earnings from 45% to 47.75%. Now assume that there is no tax treaty between the United States and country H and that country H's statutory withholding rate on dividends is 30%. The lack of a favorable treaty withholding rate further increases the total tax rate on FORco's repatriated and unrepatriated earnings from 47.75% in Case 5 to 53.25% in Case 6, computed as follows:

Foreign income tax

FORco's taxable income	$10,000,000
Country H income tax rate........................	×45%
Country H income tax	$4,500,000

Foreign withholding taxes on repatriated earnings

FORco's after-tax earnings [$10,000,000 – $4,500,000]..	$5,500,000
Percentage repatriated through dividend	×50%
Dividend distribution............................	$2,750,000
Withholding tax rate (per statute)	×30%
Country H withholding tax	$825,000

U.S. tax on repatriated earnings

Dividend from FORco	$2,750,000
Code Sec. 78 gross-up..........................	+2,250,000
USAco's taxable income	$5,000,000
U.S. tax rate...................................	×35%
Pre-credit U.S. tax	$1,750,000
Foreign tax credit	–1,750,000

Foreign withholding taxes: $825,000

Deemed paid taxes: $4,500,000 × [$2,750,000 ÷ $5,500,000]= $2,250,000

Creditable foreign taxes: [$825,000 + $2,250,000] = $3,075,000

General limitation: $1,750,000 × [$5,000,000 ÷ $5,000,000]= $1,750,000

U.S. income tax	$0
Total taxes [$4,500,000 + $825,000 + $0]	$5,325,000
Worldwide effective tax rate [$5,325,000 ÷ $10,000,000]	53.25%

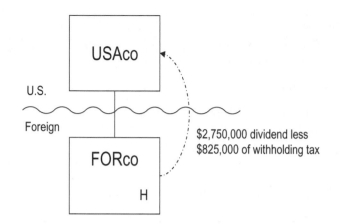

Case 7: High-tax country/Earnings stripping/Tax treaty. If USAco locates FORco in country H, one strategy for reducing the excess credits on FORco's earnings is to engage in earnings stripping, that is, to repatriate FORco's profits through deductible interest, rental, and royalty payments, rather than nondeductible dividend distributions. For example, assume that USAco modifies its plans for FORco, as follows:

   (i) Finance FORco with both debt and equity, such that FORco will pay USAco $3 million of interest each year,

   (ii) Charge FORco an annual royalty of $2 million for the use of USAco's patents and trade secrets, and

   (iii) Eliminate FORco's dividend distribution.

Assume that the applicable tax treaty withholding rate is 0% for both interest and royalties.

As the following computations indicate, debt financing and charges for technology transfers reduces the total tax rate on country H earnings from 47.75% in Case 5 to 40%, computed as follows:

Foreign income tax

FORco's income before interest and royalties	$10,000,000
Interest paid to USAco	– 3,000,000
Royalties paid to USAco	–2,000,000
FORco's taxable income	$5,000,000
Country H income tax rate	×45%
Country H income tax	$2,250,000

Foreign withholding taxes on repatriated earnings

Withholding tax on interest (per treaty)	$0
Withholding tax on royalties (per treaty)	0
Country H withholding taxes	$0

U.S. tax on repatriated earnings

Interest from FORco	$3,000,000
Royalties from FORco	+2,000,000
USAco's taxable income	$5,000,000
U.S. tax rate	×35%
Pre-credit U.S. tax	$1,750,000
Foreign tax credit	–0

Foreign withholding taxes: $0
Deemed paid taxes: $0 (no dividends)

U.S. income tax	$1,750,000
Total taxes [$2,250,000 + $0 + $1,750,000]	$4,000,000
Worldwide effective tax rate [$4,000,000 ÷ $10,000,000]	40%

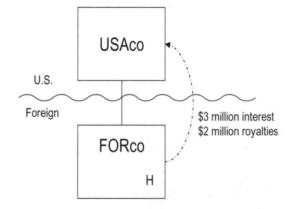

The 40% worldwide tax rate on the country H earnings is a blended rate, whereby the $5 million of interest and royalties paid to USAco are, in effect, taxed one time at the U.S. rate of 35% and the $5 million of unrepatriated earnings is taxed one time at the country H rate of 45%. Therefore, earnings stripping can be an effective method for reducing the worldwide tax rate on the earnings of a highly-taxed foreign subsidiary.

Case 8: Low-tax country/Earnings stripping/Tax treaty. In contrast to the benefits illustrated in Case 7, debt financing and charges for technology transfers will have no effect on FORco's total tax rate if FORco is located in country L (the low-tax country). As in Case 2, where FORco repatriated its earnings through dividend distributions, the worldwide tax rate on FORco's repatriated and unrepatriated earnings is still 30%, computed as follows:

Foreign income tax

FORco's income before interest and royalties	$10,000,000
Interest paid to USAco	− 3,000,000
Royalties paid to USAco	− 2,000,000
FORco's taxable income	$5,000,000
Country L income tax rate	× 25%
Country L income tax	$1,250,000

Foreign withholding taxes on repatriated earnings

Withholding tax on interest (per treaty)	$0
Withholding tax on royalties (per treaty)	0
Country L withholding taxes	$0

U.S. tax on repatriated earnings

Interest from FORco	$3,000,000
Royalties from FORco	+2,000,000
USAco's taxable income	$5,000,000
U.S. tax rate	×35%
Pre-credit U.S. tax	$1,750,000
Foreign tax credit	−0

  Foreign withholding taxes: $0
  Deemed paid taxes: $0 (no dividends)

U.S. income tax	$1,750,000
Total taxes [$1,250,000 + $0 + $1,750,000]	$3,000,000
Worldwide effective tax rate [$3,000,000 ÷ $10,000,000]	30%

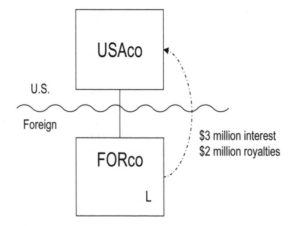

Case 8 shows that earnings stripping from a low-tax country (L) to a higher-tax country (the United States) increases the effective tax rate.

¶807

Case 9: Low-tax country/No dividends/Hybrid entity. Country L has a corporate income tax rate of 25%, which is ten percentage points lower than the U.S. rate. Country L does not impose a branch profits tax. If USAco locates FORco in country L and checks-the-box to treat FORco as a pass through entity, i.e., a branch, USAco is deemed to receive all of FORco's earnings even though FORco does not pay any dividends. The total tax rate on its earnings will be 35%, computed as follows:

Foreign income tax

FORco's taxable income	$10,000,000
Country L income tax rate	×25%
Country L income tax	$2,500,000

Foreign withholding taxes on repatriated earnings $0

U.S. tax on repatriated earnings

Earnings from FORco	$10,000,000
U.S. tax rate	×35%
Pre-credit U.S. tax	$3,500,000
Foreign tax credit	−2,500,000
U.S. income tax	$1,000,000

Total taxes [$2,500,000 + $0 + $1,000,000] $3,500,000

Worldwide effective tax rate [$3,500,000 ÷ $10,000,000] 35%

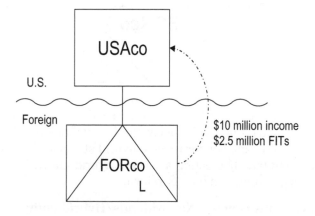

This example illustrates that USAco cannot reduce the current year worldwide tax on the new manufacturing facility below the U.S. tax rate of 35% by locating the factory in L and checking-the-box for hybrid status for FORco in country L. By forming a hybrid in country L, a low tax country, USAco actually loses the opportunity to defer paying U.S. tax.

¶807

Case 10: Low-tax country/No dividends/Reverse hybrid entity. Country L has a corporate income tax rate of 25%, which is ten percentage points lower than the U.S. rate. Country L does not impose a branch profits tax. USAco owns FORlp, a limited partnership in country L (the other partner is a flow-through entity owned by USAco) and checks-the-box for corporate treatment. USAco is not deemed to receive any income because FORco is not treated as a pass through entity. The total tax rate on its earnings will be 25%, computed as follows:

Foreign income tax

FORlp's taxable income	$10,000,000
Country L income tax rate	×25%
Country L income tax	$2,500,000
Foreign withholding taxes on repatriated earnings	$0
U.S. tax on repatriated earnings	$0
Total taxes [$2,500,000 + $0 + $0]	$2,500,000
Worldwide effective tax rate [$2,500,000 ÷ $10,000,000]	25%

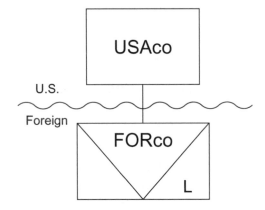

This example illustrates how USAco can reduce the current year worldwide tax rate on the new manufacturing facility below the U.S. tax rate of 35% by locating the factory in L and checking-the-box for reverse hybrid status for FORco in country L, a low-tax foreign country. By creating a reverse hybrid entity, USAco can control the time of reporting earnings on its U.S. return.

Case 11: High-tax country/No dividends/Hybrid entity. Country H has a corporate income tax rate of 45%, which is ten percentage points higher than the U.S. rate. Country H does not impose a branch profits tax. If USAco locates FORco in country H and checks-the-box treating FORco as a pass through entity, i.e., a branch, USAco is deemed to receive all of FORco's earnings even though FORco does not pay any dividends. The total tax rate on its earnings will be 45%, computed as follows:

Foreign income tax

FORco's taxable income	$10,000,000
Country H income tax rate	×45%
Country H income tax	$4,500,000

Foreign withholding taxes on repatriated earnings $0

U.S. tax on repatriated earnings

Earnings from FORco	$10,000,000
U.S. tax rate................................	×35%
Pre-credit U.S. tax	$3,500,000
Foreign tax credit	–3,500,000

Creditable foreign taxes: = $4,500,000

General limitation: $3,500,000 × [$10,000,000 ÷ $10,000,000]= $3,500,000

U.S. income tax	$0

Total taxes [$4,500,000 + $0 + $0] $4,500,000

Worldwide effective tax rate [$4,500,000 ÷ $10,000,000] 45%

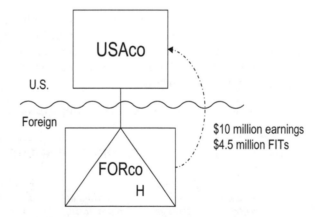

This example illustrates that if USAco locates the factory in H, a high-tax foreign country and checks-the-box for branch treatment, the 45% worldwide tax rate on USAco's new manufacturing facility will exceed the U.S. tax rate of 35%.

Case 12: High-tax country/No dividends/Reverse hybrid entity. USAco owns FORlp, a limited partnership in country H (the other partner is a flow-through entity owned by USAco), which has an income tax rate of 45%, and checks-the-box for corporate treatment. Country H does not impose a branch profits tax. USAco is not deemed to receive any income because FORlp does not make any distributions. The total tax rate on its earnings will be 45%, computed as follows:

¶807

Foreign income tax

FORlp's taxable income	$10,000,000
Country H income tax rate	×45%
Country H income tax	$4,500,000

Foreign withholding taxes on repatriated earnings $0

U.S. tax on repatriated earnings $0

Total taxes [$4,500,000 + $0 + $0] $4,500,000

Worldwide effective tax rate [$4,500,000 ÷ $10,000,000] 45%

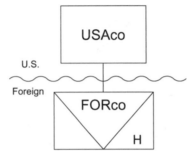

This example illustrates that regardless of the choice of entity in country H, USAco cannot reduce the current year worldwide tax rate on the new manufacturing facility below the country H tax rate of 45% by locating the factory in country H. However, by creating a reverse hybrid entity, USAco can control the time of reporting foreign earnings on its U.S. return.

Summary. Table 8.4 summarizes the results of the twelve case scenarios described above.

TABLE 8.4. COMPREHENSIVE EXAMPLE—SUMMARY

Case	U.S. tax rate	Foreign country tax rate	Percentage of earnings repatriated	Method of repatriating earnings	Foreign withholding tax rate	Current year worldwide effective tax rate
1	35%	25%	None	n.a.	n.a.	25%
2	35%	25%	50%	Dividend	10%	30%
3	35%	25%	50%	Dividend	30%	36.25%
4	35%	45%	None	n.a.	n.a.	45%
5	35%	45%	50%	Dividend	10%	47.75%
6	35%	45%	50%	Dividend	30%	53.25%
7	35%	45%	50%	Interest and royalties	0%	40%

TABLE 8.4. COMPREHENSIVE EXAMPLE—SUMMARY

Case	U.S. tax rate	Foreign country tax rate	Percentage of earnings repatriated	Method of repatriating earnings	Foreign withholding tax rate	Current year worldwide effective tax rate
8	35%	25%	50%	Interest and royalties	0%	30%
9	35%	25%	100%	Pass-through	n.a.	35%
10	35%	25%	None	n.a.	n.a.	25%
11	35%	45%	100%	Pass-through	n.a.	45%
12	35%	45%	None	n.a.	n.a.	45%

¶ 808 SURVEY OF FOREIGN ENTITY CLASSIFICATION

This survey (Tables 8.5, 8.6 and 8.7) lists entities in selected foreign countries, discusses whether the foreign country imposes an entity level tax, describes the treatment for U.S. tax purposes if an election is not made (whether the entity is a per se corporation or has default status as a corporation or flow through entity), and considers the possibility for treatment as a hybrid or reverse hybrid entity. In each listed country, U.S. owners may operate as a sole proprietorship or a branch, which is not treated as a separate entity under the check-the-box rules.

For example, in Hong Kong, the principal business forms are limited liability companies, whether referred to as public or private, partnerships and limited partnerships, branches of foreign companies, and sole proprietors. A public limited liability company is easy to classify because it is the only Hong Kong entity on the per se list.[58] Therefore, the shareholders of a public limited liability company must treat it as a corporation for U.S. tax purposes. As a public limited liability company, it must pay a corporate tax in Hong Kong[59] and does not offer any hybrid planning opportunities.

A private limited liability company is an entity whose creditors are limited to pursuit of the company's assets.[60] As a result, the default rules treat the private limited liability company as a corporation. However, because the private limited liability company pays a Hong Kong corporate income tax,[61] it presents hybrid tax planning opportunities if its shareholders elect partnership or branch classification for U.S. tax purposes. The failure to elect will result in the default rules limiting planning opportunities.

Hong Kong law provides for both partnerships and limited partnerships. Under common law, a partnership constitutes a separate entity.[62] Since each partner is liable for all the debts and obligations of the partnership, the default rules treat the entity as a partnership for U.S. tax purposes. Similarly, the default rules also treat a Hong Kong limited partnership as a partnership because one or more partners have

---

[58] Reg. § 301.7701-2(b)(8); Table 9.3.

[59] Chapter 112, Laws of Hong Kong, Section 41.

[60] Chapter 32, Laws of Hong Kong, Section 4(2)(a).

[61] chapter 112, Laws of Hong Kong, Section 45.

[62] Chapter 112, Laws of Hong Kong, Section 22(1).

unlimited liability. Since Hong Kong taxes a partner's share of partnership income only once,[63] a reverse hybrid entity planning opportunity exists if the partnership's partners elect corporate classification for U.S. purposes. Failure to elect corporate status will result in a loss of this opportunity through partnership classification in both countries.

---

[63] Chapter 112, Laws of Hong Kong, Section 22(1).

TABLE 8.5. CLASSIFICATION OF ENTITIES IN ASIAN COUNTRIES

	Foreign country tax[64]	Status without checking-the-box election	Hybrid or reverse hybrid opportunity
Australia			
Public limited liability company	Yes	Per Se Corp	——
Private limited liability company	Yes	Corporation	Hybrid
Partnership	No	Pass-through	Reverse
Hong Kong			
Public limited liability company	Yes	Per Se Corp	——
Private limited liability company	Yes	Corporation	Hybrid
Partnerships	No	Pass-through	Reverse
Limited partnerships	No	Pass-through	Reverse
Japan			
Joint stock companies(kabushiki kaisha)	Yes	Per Se Corp	——
Limited liability company (yugen kaisha)	Yes	Corporation	Hybrid
Unlimited liability partnership company (gomei kaisha)	Yes	Pass-through	Hybrid
Limited liability partnership company (goshi kaisha)	Yes	Pass-through	Hybrid
General partnership (nin-i kumiai)	No	Pass-through	Hybrid
Silent partnership (tokumei kumiai)	No	Pass-through	Hybrid
Korea			
Stock corporation (chusik hoesa)	Yes	Per Se Corp	——
Limited liability company (yuhan hoesa)	Yes	Corporation	Hybrid
Unlimited membership enterprise (hapmyong hoesa)	No	Pass-through	Reverse
Limited partnership (hapja hoesa)	No	Pass-through	Reverse
Singapore			
Private limited company	Yes	Corporation	Hybrid
Public limited company	Yes	Per Se Corp	——
General partnership	No	Pass-through	Hybrid
Limited partnership	No	Pass-through	Hybrid
Limited liability partnership	No	Pass-through	Hybrid

---

[64] Many of the entities listed as not subject to foreign country tax do contain some type of mechanism, such as withholding to ensure collection of tax on a non-resident's share of income.

¶808

TABLE 8.6. CLASSIFICATION OF ENTITIES IN EUROPE

	Foreign country tax	Status without checking-the-box election	Hybrid or reverse hybrid opportunity
European Union			
Societas Europaea	No	Per Se Corp	——
European Economic Interest Grouping (EEIG)	No	Pass-through	Reverse
Finland			
Public limited company "Oyj" (julkinen osakeyhtio)	Yes	Per Se Corp	——
Limited company "Oy" (osakeyhtio)	Yes	Corporation	Hybrid
Partnership "Ay" (avoin yntio)	No	Pass-through	Reverse
Limited partnership "Ky" (Kommandiittyhtio)	No	Pass-through	Reverse
France			
Joint stock company "SA" (societe anonyme)	Yes	Per Se Corp	——
Limited liability company "SARL" (societe a responsabilite limitee)	Yes	Corporation	Hybrid
Simplified limited liability company "SAS" (societe par actions simplifiee)	Yes	Corporation	Hybrid
General partnership "SNC" (societe en nom collectif)	No	Pass-through	Reverse
Limited partnership "SCS" (societe en commandite simple)	No	Pass-through	Reverse
Partnership limited by shares "SCPA" (societe en commandite par actions)	No	Pass-through	Reverse
Germany			
Limited liability company "GmbH" (Gesellschaft mit beschrankter Haftung)	Yes	Corporation	Hybrid
Stock corporation "AG" (Aktiengesellschaft)	Yes	Per Se Corp	——
General commercial partnership "OHG" (Handelsgesellschaft)	No	Pass-through	Reverse
Limited partnership "KG" (Kommanditgesellschaft)	No	Pass-through	Reverse
Limited partnership with Transferable shares "KgaA" (Kommanditgesellschaft auf Aktien)	No	Pass-through	Reverse
Civil law partnership "GbR" (Gesellschaft burgerlichen Rechts)	No	Pass-through	Reverse
Silent partnership (Stile Gesellschaft)	No	Pass-through	Reverse
Ireland			
Private limited company	Yes	Corporation	Hybrid
Public limited company	Yes	Per Se Corp	——

¶808

	Foreign country tax	*Status without checking-the-box election*	*Hybrid or reverse hybrid opportunity*
General partnership	No	Pass-through	Reverse
Limited partnership	No	Pass-through	Reverse
Italy			
Corporation "SpA" (Societa per Azioni)	Yes	Per Se Corp	——
Limited liability company "SRL" (Societa a Responsabilita Limitata)	Yes	Corporation	Hybrid
General partnership "SNC" (Societa in Nome Collettivo)	No	Pass-through	Reverse
Limited partnership "Sas" (Societa in Accomandita Semplice)	No	Pass-through	Reverse
Limited share partnership "SapA" (Societa in Accomandita per Azioni)	No	Pass-through	Reverse
The Netherlands			
Private limited liability company "BV" (Besloten Vennootschap Mat Beperkte Aansprakelijkheid)	Yes	Corporation	Hybrid
Public limited liability company "NV" (Naamlooze Vennootschap)	Yes	Per Se Corp	——
General partnership "VOF" (Vennootschap Onder Firma)	No	Pass-through	Reverse
Limited partnership "CV" (Commanditaire Vennootschap)	No	Pass-through	Reverse
Switzerland			
Corporation "SA" (Societe Annonyme)	Yes	Per Se Corp	——
Limited liability company "Sarl" (Societe a Responsabilite Limitee)	Yes	Corporation	Hybrid
General partnership (Societe en nom Collectif)	No	Pass-through	Reverse
Limited partnership (Societe en Commandite)	No	Pass-through	Reverse
The United Kingdom			
Private limited company	Yes	Corporation	Hybrid
Public limited company	Yes	Per Se Corp	——
Partnership	No	Flow Through	Reverse
Limited partnership	No	Flow Through	Reverse

TABLE 8.7. CLASSIFICATION OF ENTITIES IN THE AMERICAS

	Foreign country tax	Status without checking-the-box election	Hybrid or reverse hybrid opportunity
Argentina			
Stock corporation (sociedad anonima)	Yes	Per Se Corp	——
Limited liability company (sociedad de responsabilidad limitada)	Yes	Corporation	Hybrid
General partnership (sociedad colectiva)	No	Pass-through	Reverse
Limited partnership (sociedad en comandita)	No	Pass-through	Reverse
Brazil			
Corporation (sociedade anonima)	Yes	Per Se Corp	——
Limited liability company (sociedade limitada)	Yes	Corporation	Hybrid
Partnership (sociedade simples)	No	Pass-through	Reverse
Limited partnership (sociedade em comandita poracoes)	No	Pass-through	Reverse
Silent partnership (sociedade em conta de participacao)	No	Pass-through	Reverse
Canada			
Corporation (federal and provincial)	Yes	Per Se Corp	——
Unlimited Liability Company (ULC)	Yes	Corporation	Hybrid
General partnership	No	Pass-through	Reverse
Limited partnership	No	Pass-through	Reverse
Mexico			
Corporation with fixed capital (sociedad anomima)	Yes	Per Se Corp	——
Corporation with variable capital (sociedad anomima de capital variable)	Yes	Per Se Corp	——
Limited liability company (sociedad responsabilidad limitada)	Yes	Corporation	Hybrid
Limited liability company with variable capital (sociedad responsabilidad limitada de capital variable)	Yes	Corporation	Hybrid
General partnerships (sociedad en nombre colectivo)	No	Pass-through	Reverse
Limited partnership with shares (sociedad en comandita simple)	No	Pass-through	Reverse
Limited partnership without shares (sociedad en comandita por acciones)	No	Pass-through	Reverse
Joint ventures (asociacion en participacion)	No	Pass-through	Reverse

¶808

¶ 809 APPENDIX

On January 1, 2011, Mark Twain, a U.S. citizen, forms the Twain Hong Kong Private Limited Company in Hong Kong. Mark Twain decides to "check-the-box" by filing a Form 8832 and does so on March 15, 2011. Because the election may be retroactive for up to 75 days, Mark Twain chooses to have the election effective January 1, 2011. Pursuant to the IRS's instructions with respect to Form 8832, Twain Hong Kong Private Limited Company had to have an Employer Identification number before its entity classification could be elected. It is insufficient to put "applied for" on the form for the Employer Identification number.

Form **8832** (Rev. January 2011) Department of the Treasury Internal Revenue Service	**Entity Classification Election**	OMB No. 1545-1516

	Name of eligible entity making election **Twain Hong Kong Private Limited Company**	**Employer identification number** 88-8888888
Type or Print	Number, street, and room or suite no. If a P.O. box, see instructions.	
	City or town, state, and ZIP code. If a foreign address, enter city, province or state, postal code and country. Follow the country's practice for entering the postal code. Hong Kong	

▶ Check if: ☐ Address change   ☐ Late classification relief sought under Revenue Procedure 2009-41

Part I   **Election Information**

1   **Type of election** (see instructions):

a   ☑ Initial classification by a newly-formed entity. Skip lines 2a and 2b and go to line 3.
b   ☐ Change in current classification. Go to line 2a.

2a   Has the eligible entity previously filed an entity election that had an effective date within the last 60 months?

☐ **Yes.** Go to line 2b.
☑ **No.** Skip line 2b and go to line 3.

2b   Was the eligible entity's prior election an initial classification election by a newly formed entity that was effective on the date of formation?

☐ **Yes.** Go to line 3.
☐ **No.** Stop here. You generally are not currently eligible to make the election (see instructions).

3   Does the eligible entity have more than one owner?

☐ **Yes.** You can elect to be classified as a partnership or an association taxable as a corporation. Skip line 4 and go to line 5.
☑ **No.** You can elect to be classified as an association taxable as a corporation or to be disregarded as a separate entity. Go to line 4.

4   If the eligible entity has only one owner, provide the following information:

a   Name of owner ▶ Mark Twain
b   Identifying number of owner ▶ 123-45-6789

5   If the eligible entity is owned by one or more affiliated corporations that file a consolidated return, provide the name and employer identification number of the parent corporation:

a   Name of parent corporation ▶
b   Employer identification number ▶

For Paperwork Reduction Act Notice, see instructions.   Cat. No. 22598R   Form **8832** (Rev. 1-2011)

¶809

Part I	**Election Information** (Continued)

6 Type of entity (see instructions):

a   ☐ A domestic eligible entity electing to be classified as an association taxable as a corporation.

b   ☐ A domestic eligible entity electing to be classified as a partnership.

c   ☐ A domestic eligible entity with a single owner electing to be disregarded as a separate entity.

d   ☐ A foreign eligible entity electing to be classified as an association taxable as a corporation.

e   ☐ A foreign eligible entity electing to be classified as a partnership.

f   ☑ A foreign eligible entity with a single owner electing to be disregarded as a separate entity.

7 If the eligible entity is created or organized in a foreign jurisdiction, provide the foreign country of organization ▶   Hong Kong

8 Election is to be effective beginning (month, day, year) (see instructions) . . . . ▶   1/1/2011

9 Name and title of contact person whom the IRS may call for more information	**10** Contact person's telephone number
Mark Twain	573-555-8765

Consent Statement and Signature(s) (see instructions)

Under penalties of perjury, I (we) declare that I (we) consent to the election of the above-named entity to be classified as indicated above, and that I (we) have examined this election and consent statement, and to the best of my (our) knowledge and belief, this election and consent statement are true, correct, and complete. If I am an officer, manager, or member signing for the entity, I further declare under penalties of perjury that I am authorized to make the election on its behalf.

Signature(s)	Date	Title
	March 15, 2011	Member
Mark Twain		

Form **8832** (Rev. 1-2011)

¶809

Form 8832 (Rev. 1-2011)   Page **3**

Part II   **Late Election Relief**

11   Provide the explanation as to why the entity classification election was not filed on time (see instructions).

_____

_____

_____

_____

_____

_____

_____

_____

Under penalties of perjury, I (we) declare that I (we) have examined this election, including accompanying documents, and, to the best of my (our) knowledge and belief, the election contains all the relevant facts relating to the election, and such facts are true, correct, and complete. I (we) further declare that I (we) have personal knowledge of the facts and circumstances related to the election. I (we) further declare that the elements required for relief in Section 4.01 of Revenue Procedure 2009-41 have been satisfied.

Signature(s)	Date	Title

Form **8832** (Rev. 1-2011)

On January 1, 2011, Mark Twain, a U.S. citizen, contributes $15,000,000 U.S. to a Hong Kong private limited company called Twain Hong Kong Private Limited Company. Mark Twain timely files a Form 8832 to check-the-box for the Hong Kong entity.

The chartered accountant in Hong Kong provides you with the following account information in Hong Kong dollars for the year ended December 31, 2011.

Sales:	$25,000,000
Cost of Goods Sold:	$15,000,000
Compensation:	$ 2,000,000
Cash:	$31,400,000
Accounts Payable:	$15,000,000

The average exchange rate is $1.5 U.S. to $1 HK. Twain must prepare a Form 8858 for this foreign disregarded entity.

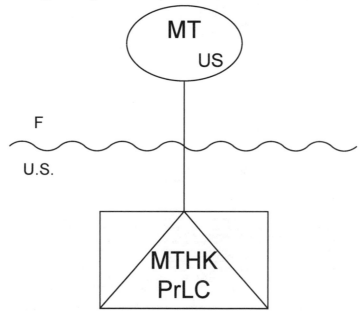

Form **8858**	**Information Return of U.S. Persons With Respect To Foreign Disregarded Entities**	OMB No. 1545-1910
(Rev. December 2008)	▶ See separate instructions.	
Department of the Treasury Internal Revenue Service	Information furnished for the foreign disregarded entity's annual accounting period (see instructions) beginning . . . **Jan 1** , 20 **11** , and ending **Dec 31** , 20 **11**	Attachment Sequence No. **140**

Name of person filing this return	Filer's identifying number
Mark Twain	**123-45-6789**

Number, street, and room or suite no. (or P.O. box number if mail is not delivered to street address)

City or town, state, and ZIP code

Hannibal, MO

Filer's tax year beginning _____ , 20 ____ , and ending _____ , 20 ____

Important: *Fill in all applicable lines and schedules. All information **must** be in English. All amounts **must** be stated in U.S. dollars unless otherwise indicated.*

1a Name and address of foreign disregarded entity	**b** U.S. identifying number, if any
Twain Hong Kong Private Limited Company	**88-8888888**

c Country(ies) under whose laws organized and entity type under local tax law	d Date(s) of organization	e Effective date as foreign disregarded entity
Hong Kong	**1/1/11**	**1/1/11**

f If benefits under a U.S. tax treaty were claimed with respect to income of the foreign disregarded entity, enter the treaty and article number	g Country in which principal business activity is conducted	h Principal business activity	i Functional currency
	Hong Kong	**Sales**	**Hong Kong dollars**

2 Provide the following information for the foreign disregarded entity's accounting period stated above.

a Name, address, and identifying number of branch office or agent (if any) in the United States	b Name and address (including corporate department, if applicable) of person(s) with custody of the books and records of the foreign disregarded entity, and the location of such books and records, if different
	Dave Kong **Hong Kong**

3 For the **tax owner** of the foreign disregarded entity (if different from the filer) provide the following:

a Name and address	b Annual accounting period covered by the return (see instructions)	c U.S. identifying number, if any
	d Country under whose laws organized	e Functional currency

4 For the **direct owner** of the foreign disregarded entity (if different from the tax owner) provide the following:

a Name and address	b Country under whose laws organized	c U.S. identifying number, if any
		d Functional currency

5 Attach an organizational chart that identifies the name, placement, percentage of ownership, tax classification, and country of organization of all entities in the chain of ownership between the tax owner and the foreign disregarded entity, and the chain of ownership between the foreign disregarded entity and each entity in which the foreign disregarded entity has a 10% or more direct or indirect interest. See instructions.

Schedule C | **Income Statement** (see instructions)

Important: *Report all information in functional currency in accordance with U.S. GAAP. Also, report each amount in U.S. dollars translated from functional currency (using GAAP translation rules or the average exchange rate determined under section 989(b)). If the functional currency is the U.S. dollar, complete only the U.S. Dollars column. See instructions for special rules for foreign disregarded entities that use DASTM.*
If you are using the average exchange rate (determined under section 989(b)), check the following box . . . . . ☑

			Functional Currency	U.S. Dollars
1	Gross receipts or sales (net of returns and allowances)	**1**	25,000,000	37,500,000
2	Cost of goods sold	**2**	15,000,000	22,500,000
3	Gross profit (subtract line 2 from line 1)	**3**	10,000,000	15,000,000
4	Other income	**4**		
5	Total income (add lines 3 and 4).	**5**	10,000,000	15,000,000
6	Total deductions	**6**	2,000,000	3,000,000
7	Other adjustments	**7**		
8	Net income (loss) per books	**8**	8,000,000	12,000,000

For Paperwork Reduction Act Notice, see the separate instructions.   Cat. No. 21457L   Form **8858** (Rev. 12-2008)

Schedule C-1 Section 987 Gain or Loss Information

		(a) Amount stated in functional currency of foreign disregarded entity	(b) Amount stated in functional currency of recipient
1	Remittances from the foreign disregarded entity	1 0	
2	Section 987 gain (loss) of recipient	2	

		Yes	No
3	Were all remittances from the foreign disregarded entity treated as made to the direct owner? . . .		
4	Did the tax owner change its method of accounting for section 987 gain or loss with respect to remittances from the foreign disregarded entity during the tax year?		

Schedule F Balance Sheet

Important: *Report all amounts in U.S. dollars computed in functional currency and translated into U.S. dollars in accordance with U.S. GAAP. See instructions for an exception for foreign disregarded entities that use DASTM.*

Assets		(a) Beginning of annual accounting period	(b) End of annual accounting period
1	Cash and other current assets	1		47,100,000
2	Other assets	2		
3	Total assets	3		47,100,000
Liabilities and Owner's Equity			
4	Liabilities	4		22,500,000
5	Owner's equity	5		24,600,000
6	Total liabilities and owner's equity	6		47,100,000

Schedule G Other Information

		Yes	No
1	During the tax year, did the foreign disregarded entity own an interest in any trust?		✓
2	During the tax year, did the foreign disregarded entity own at least a 10% interest, directly or indirectly, in any foreign partnership?		✓
3	*Answer the following question only if the foreign disregarded entity made its election to be treated as disregarded from its owner during the tax year:* Did the tax owner claim a loss with respect to stock or debt of the foreign disregarded entity as a result of the election?		✓
4	*Answer the following question only if the foreign disregarded entity is owned directly or indirectly by a domestic corporation and the foreign disregarded entity incurred a net operating loss for the tax year:* Is the foreign disregarded entity a separate unit as defined in Regulations section 1.1503(d)-1(b)(4)? (If "Yes," see the instructions)		
5	*Answer the following question only if the tax owner of the foreign disregarded entity is a controlled foreign corporation (CFC):* Were there any intracompany transactions between the foreign disregarded entity and the CFC or any other branch of the CFC during the tax year, in which the foreign disregarded entity acted as a manufacturing, selling, or purchasing branch?		

Schedule H Current Earnings and Profits or Taxable Income (see instructions)

Important: *Enter the amounts on lines 1 through 6 in functional currency.*

1	Current year net income or (loss) per foreign books of account	1	8,000,000
2	Total net additions	2	
3	Total net subtractions	3	
4	Current earnings and profits (or taxable income—see instructions) (line 1 plus line 2 minus line 3) .	4	8,000,000
5	DASTM gain or loss (if applicable)	5	
6	Combine lines 4 and 5	6	
7	Current earnings and profits (or taxable income) in U.S. dollars (line 6 translated at the average exchange rate determined under section 989(b) and the related regulations (see instructions)) . .	7	8,000,000
	Enter exchange rate used for line 7 ▶		

Form **8858** (Rev. 12-2008)

On January 1, 2010, Mark Twain, a U.S. citizen, contributes $14,850,000 to a United Kingdom partnership called Brit Partnership. The other 1% partner is Charles Phillip Arthur George, a subject of the United Kingdom, who contributes $150,000 for the remaining 1% interest.

The chartered accountant in Cambridge provides you with the following account information for the year ended December 31, 2010:

Sales:	£25,000,000
Cost of Good Sold:	£15,000,000
Compensation:	£ 2,000,000
Taxes:	£ 2,000,000
Cash:	£16,000,000
Inventory:	£15,000,000
Accounts Payable:	£15,000,000

The British pound was worth $1.50 during each day of 2010.

When filing Form 8865, Mark Twain is a Category 1 filer because he controls a foreign partnership during the year. Twain is not a Category 2 filer because Category 1 filers are excluded from being Category 2 Filers. Twain is a Category 3 filer because he contributed property to the foreign partnership in excess of $100,000 and, in addition, his interest in the foreign partnership is greater than 10% (99%). Twain is a Category 4 filer because he acquired more than 10% of Brit Partnership during the year, but the additional filing requirements of Category 4 (Schedule P) are rendered unnecessary by the Category 3 filings.

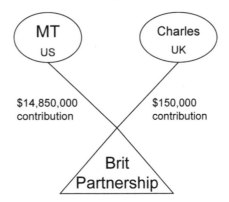

Form **8865**	Return of U.S. Persons With Respect to Certain Foreign Partnerships	OMB No. 1545-1668

► Attach to your tax return. See separate instructions.

2010

Department of the Treasury
Internal Revenue Service

Information furnished for the foreign partnership's tax year
beginning **Jan 1** , 2010 and ending **Dec 31** , 20 **10**

Attachment
Sequence No. **118**

Name of person filing this return

Mark Twain

Filer's identifying number

123-45-6789

Filer's address (if you are not filing this form with your tax return)

A Category of filer (see **Categories of Filers** in the instructions and check applicable box(es)):

1 ☑   2 ☐   3 ☑   4 ☑

B Filer's tax year beginning **Jan 1** , 20 **10** , and ending **Dec 31** , 20 **10**

C Filer's share of liabilities: Nonrecourse $ **22,275,000** Qualified nonrecourse financing $ Other $

D If filer is a member of a consolidated group but not the parent, enter the following information about the parent:

Name   EIN

Address

E Information about certain other partners (see instructions)

(1) Name	(2) Address	(3) Identifying number	(4) Check applicable box(es)		
			Category 1	Category 2	Constructive owner

F1 Name and address of foreign partnership

Brit Partnership
Cambridge, England

2 EIN (if any)

3 Country under whose laws organized
United Kingdom

4 Date of organization	5 Principal place of business	6 Principal business activity code number	7 Principal business activity	8a Functional currency	8b Exchange rate (see instr.)
1/1/10	**United Kingdom**	**423910**	**sporting goods**	**Pound Sterling**	**$1.5 = £1.0**

G Provide the following information for the foreign partnership's tax year:

1 Name, address, and identifying number of agent (if any) in the United States

N/A

2 Check if the foreign partnership must file:
☐ Form 1042   ☐ Form 8804   ☐ Form 1065 or 1065-B
Service Center where Form 1065 or 1065-B is filed:

3 Name and address of foreign partnership's agent in country of organization, if any

Charles Philip Arthur George
Windsor, England

4 Name and address of person(s) with custody of the books and records of the foreign partnership, and the location of such books and records, if different

Charles Philip Arthur George, Windsor, England

5 Were any special allocations made by the foreign partnership? ► ☐ Yes ☑ No

6 Enter the number of Forms 8858, Information Return of U.S. Persons With Respect To Foreign Disregarded Entities, attached to this return (see instructions) ► **0**

7 How is this partnership classified under the law of the country in which it is organized? ► **company**

8 Did the partnership own any separate units within the meaning of Regulations section 1.1503-2(c)(3), (4), or 1.1503(d)-1(b)(4)? ► ☐ Yes ☑ No

9 Does this partnership meet **both** of the following requirements?
- The partnership's total receipts for the tax year were less than $250,000 and
- The value of the partnership's total assets at the end of the tax year was less than $1 million.

If "Yes," **do not** complete Schedules L, M-1, and M-2. ► ☐ Yes ☑ No

Sign Here Only If You Are Filing This Form Separately and Not With Your Tax Return.

Under penalties of perjury, I declare that I have examined this return, including accompanying schedules and statements, and to the best of my knowledge and belief, it is true, correct, and complete. Declaration of preparer (other than general partner or limited liability company member) is based on all information of which preparer has any knowledge.

► Signature of general partner or limited liability company member   ► Date

Paid Preparer Use Only

Print/Type preparer's name	Preparer's signature	Date	Check ☐ if self-employed	PTIN
Firm's name ►			Firm's EIN ►	
Firm's address ►			Phone no.	

Paperwork Reduction Act Notice, see the separate instructions.   Cat. No. 25852A   Form **8865** (2010)

Form 8865 (2010)   Page **2**

Schedule A — **Constructive Ownership of Partnership Interest.** Check the boxes that apply to the filer. If you check box **b,** enter the name, address, and U.S. taxpayer identifying number (if any) of the person(s) whose interest you constructively own. See instructions.

    a ☑ Owns a direct interest   **b** ☐ Owns a constructive interest

Name	Address	Identifying number (if any)	Check if foreign person	Check if direct partner
Mark Twain	1234 Main Street, Hannibal, MO	123-45-6789		✓

Schedule A-1 — **Certain Partners of Foreign Partnership** (see instructions)

Name	Address	Identifying number (if any)	Check if foreign person

Does the partnership have any other foreign person as a direct partner? . . . . ☑ Yes   ☐ No

Schedule A-2 — **Affiliation Schedule.** List all partnerships (foreign or domestic) in which the foreign partnership owns a direct interest or indirectly owns a 10% interest.

Name	Address	EIN (if any)	Total ordinary income or loss	Check if foreign partnership

Schedule B — **Income Statement—Trade or Business Income**

Caution. Include **only** trade or business income and expenses on lines 1a through 22 below. See the instructions for more information.

1a	Gross receipts or sales	**1a**	37,500,000 00		
b	Less returns and allowances	**1b**		**1c**	37,500,000 00
2	Cost of goods sold			**2**	22,500,000 00
3	Gross profit. Subtract line 2 from line 1c			**3**	15,000,000 00
4	Ordinary income (loss) from other partnerships, estates, and trusts (attach statement) . . .			**4**	
5	Net farm profit (loss) (attach Schedule F (Form 1040))			**5**	
6	Net gain (loss) from Form 4797, Part II, line 17 (attach Form 4797)			**6**	
7	Other income (loss) (attach statement)			**7**	
8	**Total income (loss).** Combine lines 3 through 7			**8**	15,000,000 00
9	Salaries and wages (other than to partners) (less employment credits)			**9**	3,000,000 00
10	Guaranteed payments to partners			**10**	
11	Repairs and maintenance			**11**	
12	Bad debts			**12**	
13	Rent			**13**	
14	Taxes and licenses			**14**	
15	Interest			**15**	
16a	Depreciation (if required, attach Form 4562)	**16a**			
b	Less depreciation reported elsewhere on return	**16b**		**16c**	
17	Depletion (**Do not** deduct oil and gas depletion.)			**17**	
18	Retirement plans, etc.			**18**	
19	Employee benefit programs			**19**	
20	Other deductions (attach statement)			**20**	
21	**Total deductions.** Add the amounts shown in the far right column for lines 9 through 20 . .			**21**	3,000,000 00
22	**Ordinary business income (loss)** from trade or business activities. Subtract line 21 from line 8			**22**	12,000,000 00

Income (lines 1a–8), *Deductions* (see instructions for limitations) (lines 9–22)

Form **8865** (2010)

¶809

Form 8865 (2010)   Page **3**

Schedule D	Capital Gains and Losses (Use Schedule D-1 (Form 1065) to list additional transactions for lines 1 and 7)

Part I   Short-Term Capital Gains and Losses—Assets Held One Year or Less

(a) Description of property (Example: 100 shares of "Z" Co.)	**(b)** Date acquired (month, day, year)	**(c)** Date sold (month, day, year)	**(d)** Sales price (see instructions)	**(e)** Cost or other basis (see instructions)	**(f) Gain or (loss)** Subtract (e) from (d)
1					

2	Enter short-term gain or (loss), if any, from Schedule D-1 (Form 1065), line 2	**2**
3	Short-term capital gain from installment sales from Form 6252, line 26 or 37	**3**
4	Short-term capital gain (loss) from like-kind exchanges from Form 8824	**4**
5	Partnership's share of net short-term capital gain (loss), including specially allocated short-term capital gains (losses), from other partnerships, estates, and trusts	**5**
6	**Net short-term capital gain or (loss).** Combine lines 1 through 5 in column (f). Enter here and on Form 8865, Schedule K, line 8 or 11	**6** 0

Part II   Long-Term Capital Gains and Losses—Assets Held More Than One Year

(a) Description of property (Example: 100 shares of "Z" Co.)	**(b)** Date acquired (month, day, year)	**(c)** Date sold (month, day, year)	**(d)** Sales price (see instructions)	**(e)** Cost or other basis (see instructions)	**(f) Gain or (loss)** Subtract (e) from (d)
7					

8	Enter long-term gain or (loss), if any, from Schedule D-1 (Form 1065), line 8	**8**
9	Long-term capital gain from installment sales from Form 6252, line 26 or 37	**9**
10	Long-term capital gain (loss) from like-kind exchanges from Form 8824	**10**
11	Partnership's share of net long-term capital gain (loss), including specially allocated long-term capital gains (losses), from other partnerships, estates, and trusts	**11**
12	Capital gain distributions	**12**
13	**Net long-term capital gain or (loss).** Combine lines 7 through 12 in column (f). Enter here and on Form 8865, Schedule K, line 9a or 11	**13** 0

Form **8865** (2010)

¶809

Form 8865 (2010)   Page **4**

Schedule K		Partners' Distributive Share Items		Total amount	
Income (Loss)	1	Ordinary business income (loss) (page 2, line 22)	1	12,000,000	00
	2	Net rental real estate income (loss) (attach Form 8825)	2		
	3a	Other gross rental income (loss) . . . . ▸ 3a			
	b	Expenses from other rental activities (attach statement) . . . ▸ 3b			
	c	Other net rental income (loss). Subtract line 3b from line 3a	3c		
	4	Guaranteed payments	4		
	5	Interest income	5		
	6	Dividends: a Ordinary dividends	6a		
		b Qualified dividends . . . . . . ▸ 6b			
	7	Royalties	7		
	8	Net short-term capital gain (loss)	8		
	9a	Net long-term capital gain (loss)	9a		
	b	Collectibles (28%) gain (loss) . . . . ▸ 9b			
	c	Unrecaptured section 1250 gain (attach statement) . . . . . ▸ 9c			
	10	Net section 1231 gain (loss) (attach Form 4797)	10		
	11	Other income (loss) (see instructions) Type ▸	11		
Deductions	12	Section 179 deduction (attach Form 4562)	12		
	13a	Contributions	13a		
	b	Investment interest expense	13b		
	c	Section 59(e)(2) expenditures: **(1)** Type ▸ _____ **(2)** Amount ▸	13c(2)		
	d	Other deductions (see instructions) Type ▸	13d		
Self-Employ-ment	14a	Net earnings (loss) from self-employment	14a		
	b	Gross farming or fishing income	14b		
	c	Gross nonfarm income	14c		
Credits	15a	Low-income housing credit (section 42(j)(5))	15a		
	b	Low-income housing credit (other)	15b		
	c	Qualified rehabilitation expenditures (rental real estate) (attach Form 3468)	15c		
	d	Other rental real estate credits (see instructions) Type ▸ _____	15d		
	e	Other rental credits (see instructions) Type ▸ _____	15e		
	f	Other credits (see instructions) Type ▸ _____	15f		
Foreign Transactions	16a	Name of country or U.S. possession ▸ _____			
	b	Gross income from all sources	16b		
	c	Gross income sourced at partner level	16c		
		Foreign gross income sourced at partnership level			
	d	Passive category ▸ _____ e General category ▸ _____ **f** Other (attach statement) ▸	16f		
		Deductions allocated and apportioned at partner level			
	g	Interest expense ▸ _____ h Other . . . . ▸	16h		
		Deductions allocated and apportioned at partnership level to foreign source income			
	i	Passive category ▸ _____ j General category ▸ _____ k Other (attach statement) ▸	16k		
	l	Total foreign taxes (check one): ▸ ☐ Paid ☑ Accrued	16l	3,000,000	00
	m	Reduction in taxes available for credit (attach statement)	16m		
	n	Other foreign tax information (attach statement)			
Alternative Minimum Tax (AMT) Items	17a	Post-1986 depreciation adjustment	17a		
	b	Adjusted gain or loss	17b		
	c	Depletion (other than oil and gas)	17c		
	d	Oil, gas, and geothermal properties—gross income	17d		
	e	Oil, gas, and geothermal properties—deductions	17e		
	f	Other AMT items (attach statement)	17f		
Other Information	18a	Tax-exempt interest income	18a		
	b	Other tax-exempt income	18b		
	c	Nondeductible expenses	18c		
	19a	Distributions of cash and marketable securities	19a		
	b	Distributions of other property	19b		
	20a	Investment income	20a		
	b	Investment expenses	20b		
	c	Other items and amounts (attach statement)			

Form **8865** (2010)

¶809

Form 8865 (2010)   Page **5**

Schedule L	Balance Sheets per Books. (Not required if Item G9, page 1, is answered "Yes.")			
		Beginning of tax year		End of tax year	
	Assets	(a)	(b)	(c)	(d)
1	Cash		15,000,000		24,000,000
2a	Trade notes and accounts receivable				
b	Less allowance for bad debts				
3	Inventories				22,500,000
4	U.S. government obligations				
5	Tax-exempt securities				
6	Other current assets (attach statement)				
7	Mortgage and real estate loans				
8	Other investments (attach statement)				
9a	Buildings and other depreciable assets				
b	Less accumulated depreciation				
10a	Depletable assets				
b	Less accumulated depletion				
11	Land (net of any amortization)				
12a	Intangible assets (amortizable only)				
b	Less accumulated amortization				
13	Other assets (attach statement)				
14	**Total** assets		15,000,000		46,500,000
	Liabilities and Capital				
15	Accounts payable				22,500,000
16	Mortgages, notes, bonds payable in less than 1 year				
17	Other current liabilities (attach statement)				
18	All nonrecourse loans				
19	Mortgages, notes, bonds payable in 1 year or more				
20	Other liabilities (attach statement)				
21	Partners' capital accounts		15,000,000		24,000,000
22	**Total** liabilities and capital		15,000,000		46,500,000

Form **8865** (2010)

¶809

Form 8865 (2010)   Page **6**

Schedule M   Balance Sheets for Interest Allocation

	(a) Beginning of tax year	(b) End of tax year
1 Total U.S. assets		
2 Total foreign assets:		
a Passive category		
b General category		
c Other (attach statement)		

Schedule M-1   Reconciliation of Income (Loss) per Books With Income (Loss) per Return. (Not required if Item G9, page 1, is answered "Yes.")

1 Net income (loss) per books	12,000,000	00
2 Income included on Schedule K, lines 1, 2, 3c, 5, 6a, 7, 8, 9a, 10, and 11 not recorded on books this year (itemize):		
3 Guaranteed payments (other than health insurance)		
4 Expenses recorded on books this year not included on Schedule K, lines 1 through 13d, and 16l (itemize):		
a Depreciation $		
b Travel and entertainment $		
5 Add lines 1 through 4	12,000,000	00
6 Income recorded on books this year not included on Schedule K, lines 1 through 11 (itemize):		
a Tax-exempt interest $		
7 Deductions included on Schedule K, lines 1 through 13d, and 16l not charged against book income this year (itemize):		
a Depreciation $ _____ taxes		
8 Add lines 6 and 7	3,000,000	00
9 Income (loss). Subtract line 8 from line 5	9,000,000	00

Schedule M-2   Analysis of Partners' Capital Accounts. (Not required if Item G9, page 1, is answered "Yes.")

1 Balance at beginning of year	15,000,000	00
2 Capital contributed: a Cash		
b Property		
3 Net income (loss) per books	9,000,000	00
4 Other increases (itemize):		
5 Add lines 1 through 4	7,000,000	00
6 Distributions: a Cash		
b Property		
7 Other decreases (itemize):		
8 Add lines 6 and 7	0	00
9 Balance at end of year. Subtract line 8 from line 5	7,000,000	00

Form **8865** (2010)

Schedule N	Transactions Between Controlled Foreign Partnership and Partners or Other Related Entities

Important: Complete a separate Form 8865 and Schedule N for each controlled foreign partnership. Enter the totals for each type of transaction that occurred between the foreign partnership and the persons listed in columns (a) through (d).

	Transactions of foreign partnership	(a) U.S. person filing this return	(b) Any domestic corporation or partnership controlling or controlled by the U.S. person filing this return	(c) Any other foreign corporation or partnership controlling or controlled by the U.S. person filing this return	(d) Any U.S. person with a 10% or more direct interest in the controlled foreign partnership (other than the U.S. person filing this return)
1	Sales of inventory . . .				
2	Sales of property rights (patents, trademarks, etc.)				
3	Compensation received for technical, managerial, engineering, construction, or like services				
4	Commissions received .				
5	Rents, royalties, and license fees received				
6	Distributions received . .				
7	Interest received . . .				
8	Other				
9	Add lines 1 through 8 . .				
10	Purchases of inventory .	22,500,000			
11	Purchases of tangible property other than inventory				
12	Purchases of property rights (patents, trademarks, etc.)				
13	Compensation paid for technical, managerial, engineering, construction, or like services				
14	Commissions paid . . .				
15	Rents, royalties, and license fees paid				
16	Distributions paid . . .				
17	Interest paid				
18	Other				
19	Add lines 10 through 18 .	22,500,000			
20	Amounts borrowed (enter the maximum loan balance during the year). See instructions				
21	Amounts loaned (enter the maximum loan balance during the year). See instructions				

¶809

Chapter 9

Foreign Persons Investing in the United States

¶ 901 U.S. SYSTEM FOR TAXING FOREIGN PERSONS

.01 Overview

U.S. tax law contains the following two-pronged territorial system for taxing the U.S.-source income of nonresident alien individuals and foreign corporations, also known as, collectively, foreign persons:

(i)   *U.S. trade or business profits*—If a nonresident alien individual or foreign corporation is engaged in a trade or business within the United States, the net amount of income effectively connected with the conduct of that U.S. trade or business is taxed at the regular graduated rates.[1]

(ii) *U.S.-source investment-type income*—If a nonresident alien individual or foreign corporation derives investment-type income from sources within the United States, the gross amount of that income is taxed at a flat rate of 30%.[2] In addition, the person controlling the payment of the income must deduct and withhold U.S. tax at the 30% rate.[3]

There are several major exceptions to the general rules for taxing foreign persons. For example, income tax treaties usually reduce the withholding tax rate on U.S.-source dividend, interest, and royalty income from the statutory rate of 30% to 15% or less. In addition, the United States generally exempts from taxation portfolio interest income.[4] Capital gains also are generally exempt from U.S. taxation,[5] except for gains on the sale of U.S. real property interests, which are taxed in the same manner as income effectively connected with the conduct of a U.S. trade or business.[6] Finally, U.S. branch operations are subject to the branch profits tax and the tax on excess interest.[7]

---

[1] Code Secs. 871(b) and 882(a).
[2] Code Secs. 871(a) and 881(a).
[3] Code Secs. 1441(a) and 1442(a).
[4] Code Secs. 871(h) and 881(c).

[5] Reg. § 1.1441-2(b)(2).
[6] Code Sec. 897(a)(1).
[7] Code Sec. 884.

Chapter 9 discusses the U.S. system for taxing the U.S.-source investment-type income of foreign persons and Chapter 10 (¶ 1001) discusses the U.S. system for taxing a foreign person's income effectively connected with the conduct of a U.S. trade or business.

.02 Impact of U.S. Taxes on Total Tax Costs

The effect of U.S. taxation on a foreign person's total tax costs depends on the type of system which the foreign person's home country employs to mitigate international double taxation. For example, if a foreign person is a citizen or resident of a country that employs a territorial system, then the full amount of any U.S. taxes imposed on the taxpayer's U.S.-source income represents an out-of-pocket cost. In these situations, the foreign person's objective will be to minimize U.S. taxes, since every dollar of U.S. taxes saved reduces the foreign person's total tax costs by a dollar. On the other hand, if a foreign person is a citizen or resident of a country that employs a credit system, then the foreign person's U.S. tax costs may be either partially or fully offset by the tax savings associated with the home country foreign tax credit for U.S. taxes.

Example 9.1: FORco, a foreign corporation, has a branch sales office in the United States. During the current year, FORco's effectively connected income is $100. FORco's home country allows FORco to claim a credit for the U.S. taxes paid on its U.S.-source income. Assuming the U.S. corporate tax rate is 35% and FORco's home country rate is 40%, FORco can claim a credit for all of its U.S. income taxes, as follows.

Home country tax return		U.S. tax return	
Taxable income	$100	Taxable income	$100
Tax rate	× .40	U.S. tax rate	× .35
Pre-credit tax	$ 40	U.S. tax	$ 35
Credit	– 35		
Tax	$ 5		

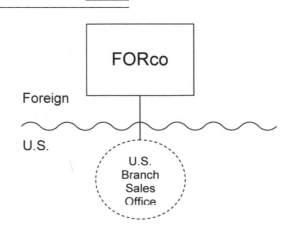

U.S. taxes do not represent an out-of-pocket tax cost in this case. For example, if FORco were able to reduce its U.S. tax from $35 to $34, the U.S. tax savings would be completely offset by an increase in home country taxes from $5 to $6.

In such situations, the foreign person's objective may not be to minimize U.S. taxes, but rather to maintain those taxes at a level which allows a full credit for home country tax purposes.

¶ 902 WITHHOLDING ON U.S.-SOURCE INVESTMENT-TYPE INCOME

.01 Introduction

The United States taxes the gross amount of a foreign person's U.S.-source investment-type income, including dividends, interest, royalties and other "fixed or determinable annual or periodical gains, profits, and income" at a flat rate of 30%.[8] Practitioners refer to this as "FDAP income." The person controlling the payment of the income must deduct and withhold U.S. tax at the 30% rate.[9] Therefore, once the appropriate amount of U.S. tax is withheld, a passive foreign investor generally has no further U.S. tax obligations. Withholding ensures the collection of taxes from passive foreign investors. In order to withhold, the withholding agent must be able to readily ascertain both the tax base and the applicable tax rate. This explains both the gross basis taxation and the use of a flat tax rate because the U.S. withholding agent may not have any way of determining a foreign person's allocable expenses and appropriate tax bracket based on worldwide income.

.02 General Rules

Persons subject to withholding. The following types of foreign persons are subject to U.S. withholding taxes:

(i) Nonresident alien individuals,

(ii) Foreign corporations,

(iii) Foreign partnerships, and

(iv) Foreign estates and trusts.[10]

A nonresident alien is an individual who is neither a citizen nor a resident of the United States.[11] An alien is considered a U.S. resident in any calendar year that he or she meets either the green card test or the substantial presence test.[12] A foreign corporation is a corporation organized or created under the laws of a foreign country or U.S. possession.[13] Likewise, a foreign partnership is a partnership organized or created under the laws of a foreign country or U.S. possession.[14] An estate is foreign if its foreign-source income, other than any income effectively connected with a U.S. trade or business, is not subject to U.S. taxation.[15] A trust is foreign if either no U.S. court is able to exercise primary supervision over the

---

[8] Code Secs. 871(a) and 881(a).

[9] Code Secs. 1441(a) and 1442(a).

[10] Reg. §§ 1.1441-1(a) and 1.1441-3(f) and (g).

[11] Code Sec. 7701(b)(1)(B).

[12] Code Sec. 7701(b)(1)(A). The green card and substantial presence tests are discussed in Chapter 2 (¶ 201).

[13] Code Sec. 7701(a)(5).

[14] Code Sec. 7701(a)(5).

[15] Code Sec. 7701(a)(31)(A).

administration of the trust or no U.S. persons have the authority to control all substantial decisions of the trust.[16]

Income subject to withholding. Withholding is required with respect to any income that meets the following two tests:

    (i) The income is fixed, determinable, annual, or periodic, and

    (ii) The income is derived from sources within the United States.[17]

Fixed, determinable, annual, or periodic income includes dividends, interest (other than original issue discount), rents, royalties, salaries, wages, premiums, annuities, and other forms of compensation.[18] It is immaterial whether the income is received through a series of payments or in a single lump sum. For example, $50,000 in rental income is subject to withholding whether it is paid in ten payments of $5,000 each or in one payment of $50,000.[19] In addition, although original issue discount is specifically exempted from withholding, withholding is required with respect to certain accrued amounts on the sale or exchange of an original issue discount obligation,[20] and on the imputed interest portion of an installment payment.[21]

Allowable deductions. No deductions are allowed for purposes of computing the amount of a foreign person's U.S.-source investment income subject to U.S. withholding taxes.[22]

Applicable tax rate. The statutory withholding rate on a foreign person's U.S.-source investment income generally is 30%.[23] However, special statutory rates apply to the following types of income:

    (i) A 10% withholding rate applies to the amount realized on the disposition of a U.S. real property interest,[24]

    (ii) The applicable withholding rate on a foreign partner's distributive share of a partnership's effectively connected taxable income is the maximum U.S. tax rate applicable to the type of taxpayer (corporate or noncorporate) in question,[25] and

    (iii) A 14% withholding rate applies to scholarships and fellowships received by a nonresident alien individual.[26]

In addition, as discussed later in this chapter, tax treaties often reduce the withholding rate on dividends, interest, and royalties to 15% or less.

Withholding agent responsibilities. Any person having control, receipt, custody, disposal, or payment of an item of U.S.-source investment income to a foreign person is obligated to withhold U.S. tax.[27] Examples of withholding agents include corporations distributing dividends, debtors paying interest, tenants paying rents, and licensees paying royalties. A withholding agent who fails to withhold is

---

[16] Code Sec. 7701(a)(30)(E) and (a)(31)(B).

[17] Code. Sec. 1441(a) and (b). For this purpose, the United States includes the 50 states and the District of Columbia, but not U.S. possessions. Code Sec. 7701(a)(9).

[18] Code. Sec. 1441(b).

[19] Reg. § 1.1441-2(a)(1).

[20] Code Secs. 871(a)(1)(C) and 881(a)(3).

[21] Reg. § 1.1441-2(a)(1) and Code Sec. 483(a).

[22] Reg. §§ 1.871-7(a)(3) and 1.881-2(a)(3).

[23] Code Secs. 1441(a) and 1442(a).

[24] Code Sec. 1445(a).

[25] Code Sec. 1446(b).

[26] Code Sec. 1441(b).

[27] Code Secs. 1441(a) and 1442(a).

¶902.02

liable for the uncollected tax.[28] Therefore, potential withholding agents must care-fully monitor any payments made to foreign persons to ensure that the appropriate amount of tax is being withheld.

As more thoroughly discussed later in this chapter, a U.S. payor ordinarily may rely on a type of Form W-8 or Form W-9 to determine the country of the payee's residence. Therefore, withholding is not required for dividends paid to a payee that has provided a Form W-9 (indicating U.S. status), unless the facts and circum-stances indicate that the payee is a foreign person.[29]

Example **9.2:** USAco, a domestic corporation, is preparing to distribute a dividend. One of USAco's shareholders is Norman Ray Allen (NRA), a nonresi-dent alien individual. NRA provides a Form W-8BEN indicating NRA's foreign status and applicable country under which NRA may be entitled to reduce withholding pursuant to a treaty. Another USAco shareholder is Uncle Sam, a U.S. citizen. Uncle Sam currently resides abroad. To avoid any withholding tax, Uncle Sam must furnish USAco with a Form W-9 indicating that he is a U.S. citizen. Even if Uncle Sam avoids withholding, the dividend is still subject to U.S. taxation by virtue of Uncle Sam's U.S. citizenship and Uncle Sam will report the dividend as income when filing his Form 1040.

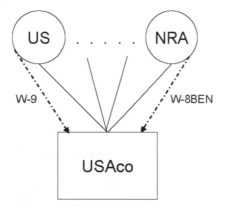

A withholding agent must deposit any taxes withheld with a Federal Reserve bank or an authorized financial institution using a federal tax deposit coupon or through electronic funds transfer.[30] The withholding agent also must file an annual informational return, Form 1042, Annual Withholding Tax Return for U.S. Source Income of Foreign Persons. When filing Form 1042, the withholding agent must attach a separate Form 1042-S, Foreign Person's U.S. Source Income Subject to Withholding, for each foreign payee.[31] A copy of Form 1042-S also must be provided to the payee.[32] (Completed samples of Forms 1042 and 1042-S are included in the Appendix to this chapter.)

---

[28] Code Sec. 1461.
[29] Reg. § 1.1441-1(b)(2)(i).
[30] Reg. § 1.6302-2.

[31] Reg. § 1.1461-2(b). Form 1042 is due by March 15 of the year following the end of the calendar year in which the tax was required to be withheld.
[32] Reg. § 1.1461-2(c).

.03 Exemptions and Special Rules

At first glance, it may appear that the United States imposes a significant tax burden on the U.S.-source investment income of foreign persons given the 30% tax rate and the stringent withholding requirements. According to IRS statistics, however, the effective withholding tax rate on the U.S.-source investment income reported to the IRS in 2007 was only 1.6% (see Table 9.1). This low effective tax rate is due to various exemptions, in particular, the portfolio interest exemption as well as treaty exemptions and reduced treaty withholding rates for interest, dividends, and royalties.

TABLE 9.1. U.S.-SOURCE INCOME PAID TO FOREIGN PERSONS IN 2007

Type of U.S.-source income	Amount (in billions)
Interest	$376.6
Dividends	134.0
Notional principal contract income	68.9
Other	67.0
Total U.S.-source taxable income	$646.5

U.S. withholding taxes	Amount (in billions)
Total income paid to foreign persons (A)	$646.5
Total U.S. tax withholding (B)	$10.2
Effective withholding tax rate (B ÷ A)	1.6%

Source: "Foreign Recipients of U.S. Income, 2007," *IRS Statistics on Income Bulletin,* Winter 2010.

Effectively connected income. Withholding is not required on any U.S.-source income that is effectively connected with the conduct of a U.S. trade or business.[33] Although such income is exempt from withholding, it is subject to U.S. taxes at the regular graduated rates.[34] Interest, dividends, rents and royalties are treated as effectively connected income if the income is derived from assets used in or held for use in the conduct of a U.S. trade or business or if the activities of the U.S. trade or business are a material factor in the realization of the income (also known as the business activities test).[35]

Example 9.3: FORco, a foreign corporation, maintains a distribution branch in the United States. Due to the nature of the business, the branch must typically hold large balances of cash. Temporarily, the large cash balances are not necessary and FORco's branch invests the cash in 90-day notes. Because the notes have a direct relationship to the trade or business of FORco's U.S. branch, the interest on the 90-day notes is derived from an asset

---

[33] Code Sec. 1441(c)(1), Reg. § 1.1441-4(a)(1).
[34] Code Secs. 871(b) and 882(a).

[35] Code Sec. 864(c)(2). *See* discussion in Chapter 10 (¶ 1001).

used in the trade or business. As a result, this interest is effectively connected income and withholding is not required.[36]

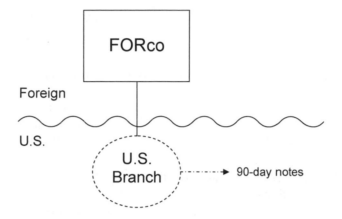

Example **9.4:** FORfund is a foreign corporation that manages portfolios for investing or trading in stocks and bonds worldwide. FORfund has a U.S. office that is engaged in the business of trading in stocks and bonds in the United States. On occasion, U.S. companies, whose shares FORfund owns, will pay a dividend. Also, due to market conditions, the U.S. branch finally sells the shares held for several years at a gain. Because those dividends and the gain are directly related to the business activities of FORfund's U.S. branch, those dividends constitute effectively connected income to FORfund and are exempt from withholding.[37]

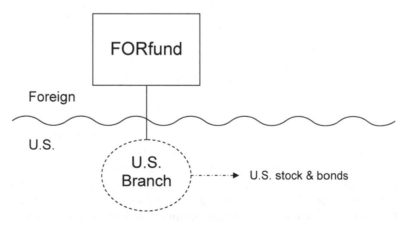

The exemption for effectively connected income also applies to any income received by a foreign partnership or a foreign corporation for the performance of services. However, as discussed below, special rules apply to the effectively connected personal services income of a nonresident alien individual, as well as the effectively connected income of a partnership that is allocable to a foreign partner.

---

[36] Reg. § 1.864-4(c)(2)(iv)(Ex.4).   [37] Reg. § 1.864-4(c)(3)(ii)(Ex.1).

To obtain a withholding exemption for effectively connected income, the foreign person engaged in the U.S. trade or business must submit a Form W-8ECI, Certificate of Foreign Person's Claim for Exemption From Withholding on Income Effectively Connected With the Conduct of a Trade or Business in the United States, to each withholding agent from whom amounts are to be received.[38] A sample of a completed Form W-8ECI is included in the Appendix of this chapter.

Effectively connected personal services income. The withholding exemption for effectively connected income does not apply to the personal services income of a nonresident alien. Instead, the nonresident alien would incur either 30% withholding if the personal services are performed as an independent contractor or wage withholding under Sections 3401 and 3402 if the personal services are performed by an employee.

Example **9.5:** Norman Ray Allen (NRA), a nonresident alien, is engaged by USCo, a U.S. company, to perform personal services in the United States. If NRA is not considered an employee of USCo (and considered an independent contractor), USCo must withhold tax from NRA's wages at a 30% rate. However, if NRA is an employee of USCo, USCo must withhold pursuant to Code Sections 3401 and 3402 as it would withhold for employees who are U.S. citizens or residents.

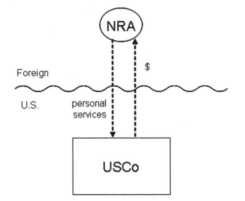

Effectively connected income allocable to a foreign partner. As discussed under the general rules, a partnership must withhold tax on a foreign partner's allocable share of U.S.-source investment income, such as passive dividend and interest income.[39] In addition, a domestic or foreign partnership must withhold income tax at a specified rate on the portion of its effectively connected taxable income which is allocable to a foreign partner.[40] A foreign partner is any partner who is not a U.S. person and, therefore, includes nonresident alien individuals, foreign corporations, foreign partnerships, and foreign trusts or estates.[41] The

---

[38] Reg. § 1.1441-4(a)(2). (Form W-8ECI is reproduced in the appendix to this chapter.)

[39] Reg. § 1.1441-3(f).

[40] Code Sec. 1446(a). This withholding requirement applies regardless of whether any distributions are actually made to such partners. The partnership must file a Form 8804 (Annual Return For Partnership Withholding Tax), Form 8805 (Foreign Partner's Information Statement), and a Form 8813 (Partnership Withholding Tax Payment), complete samples of which are included in the Appendix of this chapter.

[41] Code Sec. 1446(e).

¶902.03

amount of this special withholding tax equals the foreign partner's allocable share of effectively connected taxable income multiplied by the maximum U.S. tax rate applicable to the partner,[42] which is currently 35% for both corporate or noncorporate partners.[43] The partnership must remit this withholding tax through quarterly installment tax payments.[44]

Example **9.6:** T, a U.S. citizen would like to engage in a 50-50 joint venture in the United States with NRA, a nonresident alien. Because a nonresident alien may not be a member of an S corporation, T and NRA form a limited liability company (LLC) that is treated as a partnership for U.S. tax purposes. In year one, the LLC earns $200,000 of taxable income, for which both T and NRA have an allocable share of $100,000 of taxable income. Even if the LLC never distributes any cash to NRA, the LLC must withhold $35,000 of tax on NRA's allocable share [35% × $100,000].

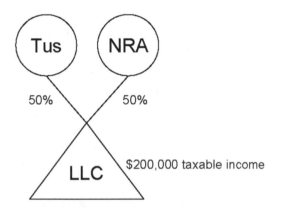

Gains from the sale or exchange of property. Income derived from the sale in the United States of personal property is not subject to withholding. This provision applies to all types of gains, both capital and ordinary. However, its main effect is to exempt from withholding capital gains realized by foreign persons from the sale of U.S. stocks and securities. One rationale for this exemption is the belief that the only way to enforce the taxation of passive foreign investors is through withholding and that withholding on capital gains is not feasible. Taxing the gross amount realized on a sale is unfair if the net gain is small and taxing the net gain may be impractical since the withholding agent may have no way of determining the foreign person's basis in the property.

Example **9.7:** CANtel is a large Canadian telecommunications conglomerate with numerous multi-national subsidiaries, one of which is UStel. UStel has operations in 40 states and gross revenues of $10 billion. CANtel sells at a gain all of its UStel shares to USAco, a domestic corporation. CANtel's capital gain is not subject to tax in the United States.

---

[42] Code Sec. 1446(b).
[43] Code Secs. 1 and 11.
[44] Reg. § 1.1446-3(d)(1)(ii).

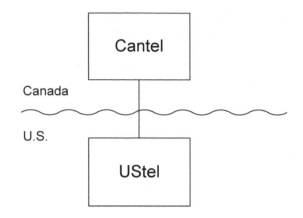

Despite these administrative problems, withholding is required on the following types of gains:[45]

(i) Gains from the disposition of timber, coal, or domestic iron ore with a retained economic interest,[46]

(ii) Gains from the sale or exchange of original issue discount obligations attributable to certain accrued amounts,[47]

(iii) Gains from the sale or exchange of patents, copyrights, secret processes and formulas, goodwill, trademarks, trade brands, franchises, and other like property, to the extent such gains are derived from payments which are contingent on the productivity, use, or disposition of the property,[48] and

(iv) Gains from dispositions of U.S. real property interests.[49]

Portfolio interest exemption. Portfolio interest received by foreign persons is exempt from U.S. withholding tax.[50] Congress enacted the portfolio interest exemption in 1984, partly in recognition of the widespread avoidance of U.S. taxes on portfolio interest. Previously, passive foreign investors were able to avoid U.S. taxation of portfolio interest through treaty exemptions or, in the case of foreign investors from nontreaty countries, treaty shopping.

Generally speaking, portfolio interest is any U.S.-source interest paid or accrued on debt obligations, other than interest effectively connected with the conduct of a U.S. trade or business. However, Congress has enacted various restrictions in order to protect against the unauthorized use of the portfolio interest exemption by U.S. persons.

In the case of registered debt obligations, the exemption applies only if the U.S. withholding agent has received a statement that the beneficial owner of the

---

[45] Code Secs. 1441(b) and 1442(a). Reg. § 1.1441-3(d) discusses the procedures for withholding on gains.

[46] Code Secs. 871(a)(1)(B), 881(a)(2), and 631(b) and (c).

[47] Code Secs. 871(a)(1)(C) and 881(a)(3).

[48] Code Secs. 871(a)(1)(D) and 881(a)(4).

[49] Code Sec. 1445(a).

[50] Code Secs. 1441(c)(9) and 1442(a).

obligation is not a U.S. person.[51] In the case of unregistered (or bearer) debt obligations, the exemption applies only if the following requirements are met:

(i) There are arrangements reasonably designed to ensure that the obligation will be sold (or resold in connection with the original issue) only to a person who is not a U.S. person,

(ii) Interest on the obligation is payable to persons resident only outside the United States and its possessions, and

(iii) There is a statement on the face of the obligation that any U.S. person who holds the obligation will be subject to limitations under the U.S. income tax laws.[52]

In addition, consistent with the principle that the portfolio interest exemption is aimed at passive foreign investors, the following types of foreign lenders do not qualify for the exemption:

(i) *10% shareholders*—Interest received by a 10% shareholder does not qualify for the portfolio interest exemption.[53] In the case of an obligation issued by a corporation, a 10% shareholder is any person who owns, directly or constructively, 10% of more of the combined voting power of all classes of stock of such corporation.[54] In the case of an obligation issued by a partnership, a 10% shareholder is any person who owns 10% of more of the capital or profits interest in such partnership.[55]

(ii) *Foreign banks*—Any interest received by a foreign bank on a loan entered into in the ordinary course of its banking business (other than interest paid on an obligation of the U.S. government) does not qualify for the portfolio interest exemption.[56]

(iii) *Controlled foreign corporations*—Any interest received by a controlled foreign corporation from a related person does not qualify for the portfolio interest exemption.[57]

The portfolio interest exemption does not apply to so-called "contingent interest".[58] The United States taxes gains realized by foreign investors on the disposition of equity interests in U.S. real property.[59] Thus, prior to the enactment of this special rule for contingent interest, shared appreciation mortgages and other hybrid debt instruments were used to obtain debt characterization for what were, in substance, equity investments in U.S. real estate. The contingent interest rules close this loophole by taxing the interest income associated with such hybrid debt instruments. Contingent interest is defined as any interest, the amount of which is determined by reference to one of the following items:

---

[51] Code Secs. 871(h)(2)(B) and 881(c)(2)(B). *See* Code Sec. 871(h)(5) regarding the requirements for this statement; Reg. §§1.871-14(c)(2)(i) and 1.1441-1(e)(1)(ii). *See* ¶1103.

[52] Code Secs. 871(h)(2)(A), 881(c)(2)(A), and 163(f)(2)(B).

[53] Code Secs. 871(h)(3)(A) and 881(c)(3)(B).

[54] Code Secs. 871(h)(3)(B)(i) and (h)(3)(C).

[55] Code Sec. 871(h)(3)(B)(ii).

[56] Code Sec. 881(c)(3)(A).

[57] Code Sec. 881(c)(3)(C). Other special rules apply to portfolio interest received by a controlled foreign corporation (*see* Code Sec. 881(c)(5)).

[58] Code Secs. 871(h)(4) and 881(c)(4).

[59] Code Sec. 897(a)(1).

(i) The receipts, sales, or other cash flows of the debtor or a related person,

(ii) Any income or profits of the debtor or a related person,

(iii) Any change in the value of any property of the debtor or a related person, or

(iv) Any dividend, partnership distribution, or similar payment made by the debtor or a related person.[60]

However, any contingent interest that is exempt under an existing U.S. tax treaty is not subject to the tax on contingent interest.[61]

Other exemptions for interest and dividends. In addition to the portfolio interest exemption, the following types of interest and dividend income also are exempt from the 30% withholding tax:

(i) Interest on bank deposits or amounts held by an insurance company under an agreement to pay interest thereon (the policy is to support U.S. banking and insurance interests),

(ii) For tax years beginning after 2010, the active foreign business percentage of any dividend or interest paid by an 80/20 company that existed prior to 2011 (for tax years beginning before 2011, the active foreign business percentage of any dividend), and

(iii) Income derived by a foreign central bank of issue from banker's acceptances.[62]

Example 9.8: FORco is a corporation organized in a South American country with an unstable banking system and currency. As a result, FORco deposits all its cash reserves in the First National Bank of Florida, a U.S. bank. Although the U.S. bank pays FORco a significant amount of U.S. source interest, no U.S. withholding tax is due.

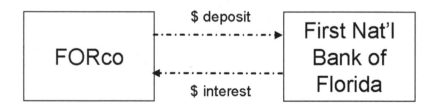

Treaty reductions for dividends, interest, and royalties. Tax treaties usually reduce the 30% statutory withholding tax rate on dividend, interest, and royalty income to 15% or less. These rate reductions and exemptions do not apply, however, if the income is attributable to a permanent establishment that the taxpayer maintains within the United States.[63]

---

[60] Code Sec. 871(h)(4)(A). Various exceptions are provided in Code Sec. 871(h)(4)(C).

[61] Notice 94-39, 1994-1 CB 350.

[62] Code Secs. 871(i) and 881(d).

[63] Generally speaking, a permanent establishment is an office or other fixed place of business (*see* Chapter 13 (¶ 1302) for a more detailed definition).

In the case of dividends, the rate often is lower for controlling shareholders (e.g., a shareholder owning 10% or more of the payer's stock) than for noncontrolling shareholders. For example, under Article 10(2) of the United States Model Income Tax Convention of November 15, 2006 (or the U.S. Model Treaty), the withholding rate on dividends is 5% for a company that directly owns 10% or more of the voting stock of the payer, and 15% for all other shareholders.

Interest and royalties often are exempt from withholding tax.[64] In some treaties, the withholding rate on royalties varies with whether the payment is an industrial royalty (such as a payment for the use of a patent, trade secret, or formula), a motion picture or television royalty, or some other type of royalty (such as a payment for the use of a copyright on a book). The appendix in Chapter 13 (¶ 1305) provides a listing of treaty withholding rates for dividends, interest, and royalties, by country.

Treaty reductions for personal services income. Tax treaties usually provide a variety of tax exemptions for personal services income. For example, under the U.S. Model Treaty, income derived by a nonresident alien individual from employment in the United States is exempt from U.S. taxation if the following requirements are satisfied:

    (i) The employee is present in the United States for 183 days or less,

    (ii) The employee's compensation is paid by, or on behalf of, an employer which is not a U.S. resident, and

    (iii) The compensation is not borne by a permanent establishment or a fixed base that the employer maintains in the United States.[65]

    Example **9.9:** FORco is a company incorporated in country F, which has a treaty with the United States identical to the U.S. Model Treaty. FORco has a sales employee that spends 10 days each year traveling throughout the United States. The sales employee spends no more than a day in any locale and is paid by FORco. The salary of the sales employee is not subject to tax because the sales employee is present in the United States for 183 days or less, the sales employee is paid by FORco (a foreign resident), and the compensation is not borne by a permanent establishment or fixed base that FORco maintains in the United States.

---

[64] For example, *see* Articles 11(1) and 12(1) (¶ 1304.11 and ¶ 1304.12) of the U.S. Model Treaty.

[65] Article 14(2) (¶ 1304.14) of the U.S. Model Treaty.

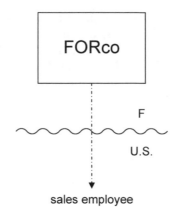

sales employee

Many older treaties contain a separate independent services provision to govern the taxation of personal services income derived by self-employed professionals. However, the current U.S. Model Treaty takes the position that the U.S. taxation of these professionals should occur only if they have a permanent establishment in the United States.[66]

Finally, tax treaties usually contain special rules for specific types of personal services income. For example, under the U.S. Model Treaty, there are special rules governing income derived by crew members of ships and aircraft operated in international traffic,[67] directors' fees,[68] entertainers and athletes,[69] pensions, social security, annuities, alimony and child support,[70] pension funds,[71] government workers,[72] and students and trainees.[73] The Appendix to Chapter 13 (¶ 1305) provides a listing of the treaty provisions governing personal services income, by country.

To obtain a treaty exemption for independent or dependent services, a nonresident alien individual must submit a Form 8233, Exemption from Withholding on Compensation for Independent Personal Services of a Nonresident Alien Individual, to each withholding agent from whom amounts are to be received.[74] (A completed sample of Form 8233 is included in the Appendix to this chapter.)

Election to treat real property income as effectively connected income. A foreign corporation or nonresident alien individual who is a passive investor in a U.S. real property interest may elect to have the U.S.-source income derived from the investment taxed as if it were effectively connected income.[75] This election allows foreign persons to offset the gross income from investments in U.S. real property (e.g., gross rental income) with related deductions (e.g., depreciation, depletion, and interest expense), which are allowable in computing effectively

---

[66] Article 5 of the U.S. Model Treaty of 2006.

[67] For example, *see* Article 14(3) (¶ 1304.14) of the U.S. Model Treaty.

[68] Article 15 (¶ 1304.15) of the U.S. Model Treaty.

[69] For example, *see* Article 16 (¶ 1304.16) of the U.S. Model Treaty.

[70] Article 17 (¶ 1304.17) of the U.S. Model Treaty.

[71] Article 18 (¶ 1304.18) of the U.S. Model Treaty.

[72] For example, *see* Article 19 (¶ 1304.19) of the U.S. Model Treaty.

[73] For example, *see* Article 20 (¶ 1304.20) of the U.S. Model Treaty.

[74] Reg. § 1.1441-4(b)(2).

[75] Code Secs. 871(d)(1) and 882(d)(1).

connected income.[76] The election results in taxation of net income at marginal rates, which may be lower than taxation of gross rents at 30%.

  Example **9.10:** L is a nonresident alien individual. L purchases an office building located in the United States. L does not manage the property, but instead leases the building to unrelated and independent U.S. persons who sublease the property. During the first year of operations, L has rental income of $400,000 and operating expenses (including depreciation and interest expense) of $340,000. Because L's U.S. activities are *de minimis*, L probably is not engaged in a U.S. trade or business. Therefore, under the general rules, L's U.S.-source rental income of $400,000 is subject to withholding tax at a 30% rate. As a consequence, L's U.S. tax would be $120,000 [30% × $400,000], even though L realizes only $60,000 of net income from the U.S. building. On the other hand, if L elects to have its rental income taxed as if it were income effectively connected with a U.S. trade or business, then L's net profit of $60,000 [$400,000 – $340,000] would be subject to a U.S. tax of $21,000 [35% × $60,000].

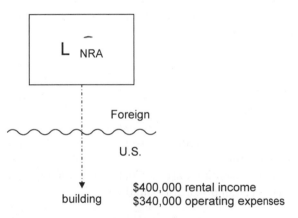

  To qualify for the election, the taxpayer must derive income during the taxable year from real property located within the United States and held for the production of income, including gains from the sale or exchange of real property, rents or royalties from mines, wells, or other natural deposits, and gains from the disposition of timber, coal, or domestic iron ore with a retained economic interest.[77] The election is made when filing the foreign person's return, and applies to all of the taxpayer's income from U.S. real property which would not otherwise be treated as effectively connected income.[78] The election applies for all subsequent taxable years and may be revoked only with the consent of the Commissioner.[79] If the election is revoked, a new election may not be made for five years, unless the Commissioner consents to an early re-election.[80]

---

[76] Reg. §§ 1.873-1(a)(1) and 1.882-4(b)(1).

[77] Code Secs. 871(d)(1) and 882(d)(1).

[78] Reg. § 1.871-10(b)(1).

[79] Code Secs. 871(d)(1) and 882(d)(1). *See* Reg. § 1.871-10(d) regarding the procedures for making and revoking the election.

[80] Code Secs. 871(d)(2) and 882(d)(2).

Foreign governments and international organizations. Income derived by a foreign government from investments in the United States in stocks, bonds, or other domestic securities, financial instruments held in execution of governmental financial or monetary policy, or interest on deposits in U.S. banks, is exempt from U.S. tax.[81] In the case of an international organization, income from investments in the United States in stocks, bonds, or other domestic securities, or from interest on deposits in U.S. banks, is exempt from U.S. tax.[82] The compensation of employees of foreign governments or international organizations also is exempt from U.S. tax under certain conditions.[83] Finally, any income earned by a foreign central bank from obligations of the United States or of any agency or instrumentality thereof, or from interest on bank deposits, is exempt from U.S. tax.[84]

Foreign tax-exempt organizations. A foreign tax-exempt organization is subject to withholding on any receipts of unrelated business taxable income, unless such income is effectively connected with the conduct of a U.S. trade or business.[85] The gross U.S.-source investment income of a foreign private foundation also is subject to withholding taxes, albeit at a reduced rate of 4%.[86] However, if a tax treaty provides an exemption for the specific type of income (e.g., interest income), then the foreign private foundation's income will be exempt.[87]

Social security benefits. Eighty-five percent of the social security benefits received by a nonresident alien individual are subject to the 30% withholding tax.[88]

Gambling winnings. Withholding is not required on proceeds from a wager placed by a nonresident alien individual in gambling on blackjack, baccarat, craps, roulette, or big-6 wheel.[89] Withholding is required on proceeds from horse or dog races occurring in the United States, unless the wager is placed outside the United States.[90] Other gambling winnings are subject to withholding tax if the amount of the winnings exceeds certain dollar thresholds.[91]

Tax on gross transportation income. The U.S.-source gross transportation income of a foreign person is subject to a special 4% tax.[92] Transportation income is income derived from the use or lease of a vessel or aircraft (including any container used in connection with a vessel or aircraft) or from the performance of services directly related to the use of a vessel of aircraft.[93] A foreign person's U.S.-source gross transportation income equals 50% of the income from any transportation that begins in the United States and ends abroad or that begins abroad and ends in the

---

[81] Code Sec. 892(a)(1). This exception does not apply to income derived by a foreign government from the conduct of a commercial activity, either directly or through a controlled commercial entity. Code Sec. 892(a)(2).

[82] Code Sec. 892(b).

[83] Code Sec. 893.

[84] Code Sec. 895. This exception does not apply to an obligation or deposit held for, or used in connection with, the conduct of a commercial activity.

[85] Reg. § 1.1443-1(a).

[86] Reg. § 1.1443-1(b)(1)(i) and Code Sec. 4948(a).

[87] Reg. § 1.1443-1(b)(1)(ii).

[88] Code Sec. 871(a)(3).

[89] Code Secs. 1441(c)(11) and 871(j).

[90] Code Sec. 872(b)(5).

[91] Code Sec. 3402(q).

[92] Code Sec. 887(a).

[93] Code Sec. 863(c)(3).

¶902.03

United States.[94] The 4% tax does not apply to any income effectively connected with the conduct of a U.S. trade or business.[95]

¶ 903 WITHHOLDING PROCEDURES

.01 Introduction

Placing the burden on the U.S. payor to collect the proper withholding tax requires the payor to determine the country of residence and sometimes even the entity status of the payee. Prior to 2001, a domestic corporation that paid a dividend could rely on the address of the payee to determine the country of residence, absent other actual knowledge of residence. Relying on the country of residence created opportunities for abuse by U.S. citizens.

> *Example* **9.11:** USAco is a publicly held U.S. corporation with shareholders located worldwide. Uncle Sam, a U.S. citizen, would prefer not to provide USAco with his social security number because he wants to avoid USAco reporting the payment to the IRS. He hopes that the IRS could not match the payment with his return. Uncle Sam obtains a mailing address in country F, whose treaty with the United States reduces the withholding tax on dividends to 10%. USAco pays a dividend to Uncle Sam. Not having any other knowledge of Uncle Sam's residence, USAco withholds tax at a 10% rate. Uncle Sam does not report any of the dividend on his U.S. return and incurs a tax of only 10%.

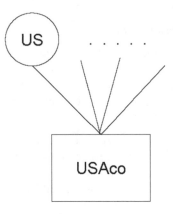

Similarly, residents of foreign countries that did not have a treaty with the United States could try to obtain a mailing address in a treaty country.

> *Example* **9.12:** USAco is a publicly held U.S. corporation that pays dividends to its shareholders worldwide. Norman Ray Allen (NRA) owns shares of USAco and is a resident of Argentina (which does not have an income tax treaty with the United States). NRA obtains a mailing address in

---

[94] Code Sec. 863(c)(2)(A). This rule generally does not apply to transportation income derived from personal services performed by the taxpayer. Code Sec. 863(c)(2)(B).

[95] Code Sec. 887(b)(2). Certain possessions income also is exempt. Code Sec. 887(b)(3).

Germany to try to take advantage of the withholding rates of the tax treaty between the United States and Germany.

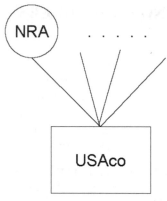

Both of these examples prompted the IRS to issue the withholding regulations that became effective in 2001.

The policy behind these withholding regulations is that reduced withholding tax rates under U.S. income tax treaties are available only to non-U.S. beneficial owners that reside in a treaty country. A U.S. beneficial owner may be subject to back-up withholding at a rate of 28%.[96] A non-U.S. beneficial owner that does not reside in a treaty country should incur withholding at a rate of 30%.[97]

.02 Determining the Beneficial Ownership

The withholding regulations focus on the documentation that the payee must provide to the payor. U.S. persons must provide Form W-9, which contains the U.S. person's taxpayer identification number. A U.S. person's taxpayer identification number is typically the social security number for individuals and the employer identification number for entities.

Foreign persons must file a type of Form W-8. Although there are three different types of Forms W-8,[98] the most common is the Form W-8BEN, Certificate of Foreign Status of Beneficial Owner for United States Tax Withholding, a completed sample of which is included in the Appendix. A foreign person uses a Form W-8BEN to:

   (i) Establish foreign status,

  (ii) Claim beneficial ownership of the income for which the form is furnished,

 (iii) Claim a reduced rate of withholding under an income tax treaty, and

 (iv) Claim exemption from back-up withholding for income that is not subject to withholding under section 1441.

---

[96] Code Secs. 1(c) and 3406(a)(2)(c).

[97] Code Secs. 1441 and 1442.

[98] Other Forms W-8 include Form W-8ECI, Certificate of Foreign Person's Claim for Exemption From Withhold- ing on Income Effectively Connected With the Conduct of a Trade or Business in the United States and Form W-8EXP, Certificate of Foreign Government or Other Foreign Organization for United States Tax Withholding.

Receipt of valid documentation by the payor, such as a Form W-9 or Form W-8BEN (in the absence of actual knowledge that any statements in the form are inaccurate), can be relied on when determining the appropriate withholding.[99]

Example 9.13: Norma Ray Allen (NRA) is a citizen and resident of a European country that has a treaty with the United States identical to the U.S. Model Treaty. NRA is a shareholder of USAco, a U.S. corporation that pays dividends and NRA provides USAco a Form W-8BEN indicating that she is an individual and resident of the European country. Unless USAco has actual knowledge that NRA is not a resident of the European country, USAco can rely on the Form W-8BEN and withhold at the treaty rate.

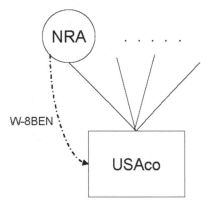

Providing a Form W-8BEN is also important to a foreign corporation that owns stock of a domestic corporation. Most of the tax treaties that the United States has entered provide for reduced withholding on dividends paid by a domestic corporation to a foreign company that has a substantial ownership interest in the domestic payor. For example, the U.S. Model Treaty reduces the withholding tax rate on dividends to only 5% if the foreign owner is a corporation that directly owns at least 10% of the voting stock of the domestic corporation.[100]

Example 9.14: FORco, a corporation organized in country F, owns 10% of USAco. Country F has a treaty with the United States that is identical to the U.S. Model Treaty. If FORco provides a Form W-8BEN indicating that FORco is both a resident of country F and a corporation, USAco should withhold tax on any dividends paid at the special treaty rate of 5% instead of the general treaty rate of 15%.

---

[99] Reg. § 1.1441-1 (b) (2) (vii) (A).

[100] Article 10(2)(a) (¶ 1004.10) of the U.S. Model Treaty.

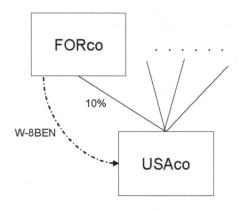

.03 Presumptions in the Absence of Documentation

If a payee fails to provide adequate documentation, such as a Form W-9 or W-8BEN, the payor of income must follow certain presumptions to determine the status of the payee.

The regulations generally presume that a payee is a U.S. person if the withholding agent cannot reliably associate a payment with documentation.[101]

> **Example 9.15:** USAco is a publicly held U.S. corporation with shareholders located worldwide. Uncle Sam, a U.S. citizen, would prefer not to provide USAco with his social security number because he wants to avoid USAco reporting the dividend payment to the IRS, who could match the payment with the income he reports on his Form 1040. Because Uncle Sam has not provided either a Form W-9 or W-8BEN, USAco presumes that Uncle Sam is a U.S. person and back-up withholds tax at a rate of 28%.

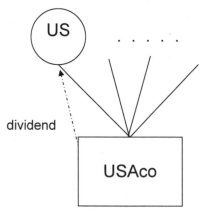

The withholding regulations also provide a presumption to determine the classification of a recipient as an individual or entity. If the payor cannot reliably associate a payment with valid documentation, the payor must presume that the

---

[101] Reg. § 1.1441-1(b)(3)(iii).

payee is an individual, a trust, or an estate based on the payee's name. Otherwise, the payee may be treated as a corporation or a partnership.[102]

.04 Foreign Intermediaries

Income is often paid to foreign recipients through foreign intermediaries. Previously, U.S. payors were often uncertain as to the appropriate withholding rate. To resolve this issue, the withholding regulations provide specific rules for payments to foreign intermediaries.

The withholding regulations differentiate between a qualified intermediary (QI) and a nonqualified intermediary (NQI). A qualified intermediary has qualified and registered with the Internal Revenue Service to be responsible for withholding on payments to the ultimate beneficiaries at the appropriate withholding rate.[103] NQIs must provide the appropriate Forms W-9 and W-8BEN to the payor, who retains responsibility for withholding at the appropriate rate.[104]

¶ 904 TAXATION OF U.S. REAL PROPERTY INTERESTS

.01 Introduction

During the 1970s, U.S. real estate became a popular investment for foreigner investors, in part because the United States generally did not tax foreign investors on any capital gains realized on the sale of U.S. real property interests. This became a domestic political issue, and Congress responded by enacting the Foreign Investment in Real Property Tax Act of 1980 (or FIRPTA), which attempts to equate the tax treatment of real property gains realized by domestic and foreign investors. Under FIRPTA, gains or losses realized by foreign corporations or nonresident alien individuals from any sale, exchange, or other disposition of a U.S. real property interest are taxed in the same manner as income effectively connected with the conduct of a U.S. trade or business.[105] This means that gains from dispositions of U.S. real property interests are taxed at the regular graduated rates, whereas losses are deductible against any other effectively connected income.[106]

> ***Example 9.16:*** NRA is a nonresident alien individual whose only connection with the United States is the ownership of some undeveloped land located in the United States. NRA holds the land as a passive investment. Prior to the enactment of FIRPTA, any gain realized by NRA on the sale of the land would be exempt from U.S. taxation. Under FIRPTA, the United States taxes NRA's gain on the sale of the land in the same manner as income effectively connected with the conduct of a U.S. trade or business, that is, on a net basis and at the regular graduated rates.

---

[102] Reg. § 1.1441-1(b)(3)(ii)(B).

[103] Reg. § 1.1441-1(b)(2)(v).

[104] Reg. § 1.1441-1(b)(2)(vii)(B).

[105] Code Sec. 897(a)(1). In addition, for purposes of computing a nonresident alien individual's alternative minimum tax, the taxable excess amount cannot be less than the individual's net U.S. real property gain for the taxable year. Code Sec. 897(a)(2).

[106] Code Secs. 871(b) and 882(a). However, a loss realized by a nonresident alien individual from the disposition of a U.S. real property interest held for personal use is deductible only if it arises from a fire, storm, or other casualty event. Code Secs. 897(b) and 165(c).

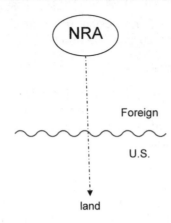

.02 U.S. Real Property Interests

A U.S. real property interest includes interests in any of the following types of property located within the United States:

(i) Land,

(ii) Buildings, including a personal residence,

(iii) Inherently permanent structures other than buildings (e.g., grain bins or broadcasting towers),

(iv) Mines, wells, and other natural deposits,

(v) Growing crops and timber, and

(vi) Personal property associated with the use of real property, such as mining equipment, farming equipment, or a hotel's furniture and fixtures.[107]

For this purpose, an "interest" in real property means any interest, other than an interest solely as a creditor. This includes fee ownership, co-ownership, a leasehold, an option to purchase or lease property, a time-sharing interest, a life estate, remainder, or reversionary interest, and any other direct or indirect right to share in the appreciation in value or proceeds from the sale of real property.[108]

A U.S. real property interest also includes any interest (other than an interest solely as a creditor) in a domestic corporation that was a U.S. real property holding corporation at any time during the five-year period ending on the date of the disposition of such interest or, if shorter, the period the taxpayer held the interest.[109] This provision prevents foreign persons from avoiding the FIRPTA tax by incorporating their U.S. real estate investments and then realizing the resulting gains through stock sales, which ordinarily are exempt from U.S. taxation.[110] A domestic corporation is a U.S. real property holding corporation if the fair market value of its U.S. real property interests equals 50% or more of the fair market value of the sum of the corporation's following interests:

---

[107] Code Sec. 897(c)(1)(A)(i) and Reg. § 1.897-1(b).

[108] Code Sec. 897(c)(6)(A) and Reg. § 1.897-1(d)(2).

[109] Code Sec. 897(c)(1)(A)(ii).

[110] Reg. § 1.1441-2(a)(3).

   (i) U.S. real property interests (including any interest in another U.S. real property holding corporation),

  (ii) Interests in foreign real property, and

 (iii) Any other property of the corporation which is used or held for use in a trade or business.[111]

***Example* 9.17:** NRA is a nonresident alien individual whose only connection with the United States is the ownership of a U.S. corporation, USSub. USSub has cash of $40,000 and a parcel of undeveloped land located in the United States with a fair market value of $60,000. Under FIRPTA, USSub is a U.S. real property holding corporation because over 50% of its fair market value constitutes a U.S. real property interest ($60,000 divided by $100,000 equals 60%). As a result, the United States imposes the FIRPTA tax on NRA's gain on the sale of shares of USSub in the same manner as if NRA had directly owned and sold the parcel of land.

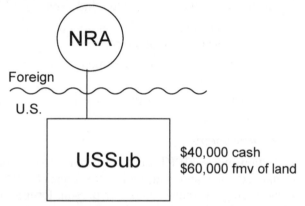

For purposes of determining whether a domestic corporation qualifies as a U.S. real property holding corporation, the domestic corporation is treated as owning a proportionate share of the assets of any other corporation it controls, as well as a proportionate share of the assets of any partnership, trust, or estate, in which it is a partner or beneficiary.[112]

The following types of interests are exempted from the U.S. real property holding corporation taint:

   (i) *Publicly traded corporations*—Stock that is regularly traded on an established securities market generally is not treated as a U.S. real property interest.[113] Without this exception, many major U.S. industrial companies would be treated as U.S. real property holding corporations.

  (ii) *Corporations that have disposed of all U.S. real property interests*—U.S. real property interests do not include an interest in a corporation that has

---

[111] Code Sec. 897(c)(2). For this purpose, a U.S. real property holding corporation includes any interests in a foreign corporation which would qualify as a U.S. real property holding corporation if that foreign corporation were a domestic corporation. Code Sec. 897(c)(4)(A).

[112] Code Sec. 897(c)(4)(B) and (c)(5).

[113] Code Sec. 897(c)(3). An exception applies to a person who owns, directly or constructively, more than 5% of the stock in question. Code Sec. 897(c)(3) and (c)(6)(C).

previously disposed of all of its U.S. real property interests in transactions in which the full amount of gain, if any, was recognized.[114]

(iii) *Domestically controlled real estate investment trusts*—An interest in a real estate investment trust is not a U.S. real property interest if foreign persons directly or indirectly own less than 50% of the value of the stock of the real estate investment trust.[115]

.03 Special Rules for Certain Dispositions

Congress has enacted a variety of special rules in order to apply the FIRPTA tax to the following types of dispositions:

(i) A distribution by a foreign corporation of a U.S. real property interest to its shareholders, either as a dividend, in redemption of stock, or in liquidation,[116]

(ii) A disposition of a U.S. real property interest that would otherwise qualify as a nontaxable transaction (e.g., a like-kind exchange),[117]

(iii) A sale or other disposition of an interest in a partnership, trust, or estate that holds a U.S. real property interest,[118]

(iv) A distribution by a real estate investment trust that holds a U.S. real property interest,[119] and

(v) A transfer of a U.S. real property interest to a foreign corporation as a contribution to capital.[120]

.04 Withholding Requirements

To ensure collection of the FIRPTA tax, any transferee acquiring a U.S. real property interest must deduct and withhold a tax equal to 10% of the amount realized on the disposition.[121] A transferee is any person, foreign or domestic, that acquires a U.S. real property interest by purchase, exchange, gift, or any other type of transfer.[122] The amount realized is the sum of the cash paid or to be paid (excluding interest), the market value of other property transferred or to be transferred, the amount of liabilities assumed by the transferee, and the amount of liabilities to which the transferred property was subject.[123] Withholding requirements also apply to distributions made by a domestic or foreign corporation, partnership, estate, or trust, to the extent the distribution involves a U.S. real property interest, as well as to dispositions of interests in a partnership, trust, or estate that has a U.S. real property interest.[124]

> ***Example 9.18:*** NRA, a citizen of a foreign country, comes to the United States to begin a new job on September 1. NRA immediately purchases a house. However, on October 1, before NRA has become a resident under

---

[114] Code Sec. 897(c)(1)(B).

[115] Code Sec. 897(h)(2) and (h)(4)(B).

[116] Code Sec. 897(d) and Temp. Reg. § 1.897-5T(c).

[117] Code Sec. 897(e) and Temp. Reg. § 1.897-6T.

[118] Code Sec. 897(g).

[119] Code Sec. 897(h)(1) and (h)(3).

[120] Code Sec. 897(j).

[121] Code Sec. 1445(a). A transferee must file Forms 8288 and 8288-A to report and deposit any tax withheld within 20 days of withholding. Reg. § 1.1445-1(c)(1).

[122] Reg. § 1.1445-1(g)(4). Withholding by a transferee who is a foreign person poses a compliance problem.

[123] Reg. § 1.1445-1(g)(5).

[124] Code Sec. 1445(e) and Reg. § 1.1445-5.

either the substantial presence test or the green card test, NRA is fired and leaves the United States. NRA sells the house for $500,000. The purchaser must withhold $50,000 of the sales price as 10% of the gross sales proceeds. If $50,000 exceeds the NRA's ultimate tax due, NRA can file a 1040NR seeking a refund. If NRA's ultimate tax due is greater than $50,000, NRA will owe additional tax.

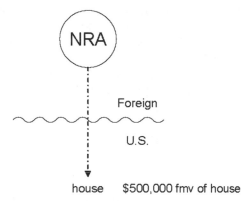

As with withholding taxes in general, a transferee that fails to withhold is liable for any uncollected taxes.[125] Therefore, any transferee of U.S. real property must be careful to determine whether withholding is required. To ease the administrative burden, withholding is not required in the following situations:

(i) The transferee receives an affidavit from the transferor which states, under penalty of perjury, that the transferor is not a foreign person or, in the case of the disposition of an interest in a domestic corporation, that the domestic corporation is not and has not been a U.S. real property holding company,

(ii) The transferee receives a withholding certificate issued by the IRS, which notifies the transferee that no withholding is required,

(iii) The transferee receives a notice from the transferor that no recognition of gain or loss on the transfer is required because a nonrecognition provision applies,

(iv) The transferee acquires the property for use as a personal residence and the purchase price does not exceed $300,000 (compare with the $500,000 price in Example 9.18), or

(v) The transferee acquires stock that is regularly traded on an established securities market.[126]

---

[125] Code Sec. 1461. However, the transferee's liability for a failure to withhold the FIRPTA tax is limited to the transferor's maximum tax liability. Code Sec. 1445(c)(1)(A).

[126] Code Sec. 1445(b) and Reg. § 1.1445-2. An agent of the transferee or transferor, such as a real estate broker or attorney, who has actual knowledge that an affidavit regarding the status of the transferor is false, but fails to notify the transferee that it is false, may be liable for the withholding tax to the extent of the agent's compensation from the transaction. Code Sec. 1445(d) and Reg. § 1.1445-4.

The administrative burden also is eased by a procedure whereby the IRS will issue a withholding certificate that provides for a reduced level of withholding, and a procedure whereby a foreign person may obtain an early refund of any excess withholding taxes.[127]

   Example **9.19:** NRA, a citizen of a foreign country, comes to the United States to begin a new job on September 1. NRA immediately purchases a house. However, on October 1, before NRA has become a resident under either the substantial presence test or the green card test, NRA is fired and leaves the United States. NRA sells the house for $250,000. Because NRA sold the house for less than $300,000, this purchaser need not withhold any of the gross sales proceeds as tax. However, NRA should file a Form 1040NR to report any gain recognized and pay any tax due.

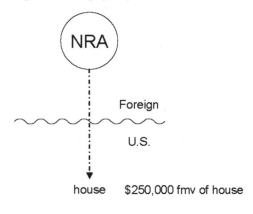

house $250,000 fmv of house

---

[127] Reg. § 1.1445-3.

¶ 905 APPENDIX

USCo, a closely-held C corporation, has Norman Ray Allen (NRA) as one of its owners. NRA is a citizen and resident of the Cayman Islands, which does not have a tax treaty with the United States. USCo declares and pays dividends and withholds the following amounts of tax on the following three dates in 2010:

Date	Dividend	Withholding
March 31, 2010	$10,000	$3,000
June 30, 2010	$ 2,000	$ 600
September 30, 2010	$ 500	$ 150

USAco will complete a Form 1042-S for NRA and transmits to the IRS with a Form 1042-T (along with other Forms 1042-S, if there were any). USAco will file a Form 1042 that compiles all the annual withholding tax information for the IRS. Because the only withholdings were on the payments to NRA, only his withholdings are listed.

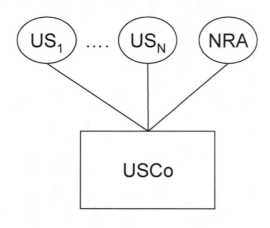

Form **1042-S**	Foreign Person's U.S. Source Income Subject to Withholding				2010	OMB No. 1545-0096
Department of the Treasury Internal Revenue Service		AMENDED			PRO-RATA BASIS REPORTING	Copy A for Internal Revenue Service

1 Income code	2 Gross income	3 Withholding allowances	4 Net income	5 Tax rate	30% .	7 Federal tax withheld	3,750
06	12,500	--		6 Exemption code	--	8 Withholding by other agents	
						9 Total withholding credit	3,750

10 Amount repaid to recipient

11 Withholding agent's EIN ▶	34-5678912		14 Recipient's U.S. TIN, if any ▶	
☐ EIN ☑ QI-EIN			☐ SSN or ITIN ☐ EIN	☐ QI-EIN

12a WITHHOLDING AGENT'S name		15 Recipient's foreign tax identifying number, if any	16 Country code
USCo			CJ

12b Address (number and street)	17 NQI's/FLOW-THROUGH ENTITY'S name	18 Country code

12c Additional address line (room or suite no.)	19a NQI's/Entity's address (number and street)

	19b Additional address line (room or suite no.)

12d City or town, province or state, country, ZIP or foreign postal code	19c City or town, province or state, country, ZIP or foreign postal code
Las Vegas, NV	Cayman Islands

13a RECIPIENT'S name	13b Recipient code	20 NQI's/Entity's U.S. TIN, if any ▶
Norman Ray Allen	01	

13c Address (number and street)	21 PAYER'S name and TIN (if different from withholding agent's)

13d Additional address line (room or suite no.)	22 Recipient account number (optional)

13e City or town, province or state, country, ZIP or foreign postal code	23 State income tax withheld	24 Payer's state tax no.	25 Name of state
Georgetown, Grand Cayman	--	--	

For Privacy Act and Paperwork Reduction Act Notice, see page 17 of the separate instructions.   Cat. No. 11386R   Form **1042-S** (2010)

¶905

DO NOT STAPLE

Form **1042-T** Department of the Treasury Internal Revenue Service	**Annual Summary and Transmittal of Forms 1042-S**	OMB No. 1545-0096 20**10**

Name of withholding agent	Employer identification number
USCo	34-5678912

Number, street, and room or suite no.

City or town, province or state, and country (including postal code)

Las Vegas, NV

If you are an intermediary (see Form 1042 instructions), check if you are a: ☐ QI/Withholding foreign partnership or trust
☐ NQI/Flow-through entity

1a Type of paper Forms 1042-S attached (check only **one** box): ☑ Original ☐ Amended
Also check here if pro-rata (see instructions) ▶ ☐

b Number of paper Forms 1042-S attached ▶ _____1_____

2a Total gross income on all paper Forms 1042-S (box 2) attached . . . . $ _____12,500_____

b Total federal tax withheld on all paper Forms 1042-S (box 9) attached . . . . $ _____3,750_____

Caution: *If you have already filed a Form 1042 and an attached Form 1042-S causes the gross income or tax withheld information shown on your previously filed Form 1042 to change, you must file an amended Form 1042. See the instructions below.*

If this is your FINAL return, enter an "X" here (see instructions) . ▶ ☒

Please return this entire page to the Internal Revenue Service.

Sign Here	Under penalties of perjury, I declare that I have examined this return and accompanying documents, and to the best of my knowledge and belief, they are true, correct, and complete.			
▶	Your signature	Title	Date	Daytime phone number

Instructions

Purpose of form. Use this form to transmit paper Forms 1042-S, Foreign Person's U.S. Source Income Subject to Withholding, to the Internal Revenue Service. Use a separate Form 1042-T to transmit each type of Form 1042-S (see the instructions for line 1a).

⚠ **CAUTION** *If you file 250 or more Forms 1042-S, you are required to submit them electronically. You also can use this method to submit less than 250 Forms 1042-S. If you submit Forms 1042-S electronically, do not use Form 1042-T. See Pub. 1187 for information on filing electronically.*

Use of this form to transmit paper Forms 1042-S does not affect your obligation to file Form 1042, Annual Withholding Tax Return for U.S. Source Income of Foreign Persons.

If you have not yet filed a Form 1042 for 2010, you may send in more than one Form 1042-T to submit paper Forms 1042-S prior to filing your Form 1042. You may submit amended Forms 1042-S even though changes reflect differences in gross income and tax withheld information of Forms 1042-S previously submitted with a Form 1042-T.

If you have already filed a Form 1042 for 2010 and an attached Form 1042-S caused the gross income or tax withheld information previously reported on line 62a or 62b of your Form 1042 to change, you must file an amended Form 1042.

Where and when to file. File Form 1042-T (and Copy A of the paper Forms 1042-S being transmitted) with the Ogden Service Center, P.O. Box 409101, Ogden, UT 84409, by March 15, 2011. Send the forms in a flat mailing (not folded).

Identifying information at top of form. The name, address, and EIN of the withholding agent or intermediary on this form must be the same as those you enter on Forms 1042 and 1042-S. See the instructions for Form 1042 for definitions of withholding agent and intermediary.

Line 1a. You must file a separate Form 1042-T for each type of paper Form 1042-S you are transmitting. Check only the Original or Amended box. If you are filing pro-rata Forms 1042-S (see Form 1042-S instructions), also check the pro-rata box. As a result, there are four possible types of Form 1042-S that may be transmitted:

- Original
- Amended
- Original pro-rata
- Amended pro-rata

Each type would be transmitted with a separate Form 1042-T. For example, you would transmit only original Forms 1042-S with one Form 1042-T and only amended Forms 1042-S with another Form 1042-T.

Line 2a. Enter the total of the gross income amounts shown on the Forms 1042-S (box 2) being transmitted with this Form 1042-T.

Line 2b. Enter the total of the federal tax withheld amounts shown on the Forms 1042-S (box 9) being transmitted with this Form 1042-T.

Final return. If you will not be required to file Forms 1042-S in the future (on paper or electronically), enter an "X" in the "FINAL return" box.

Paperwork Reduction Act Notice. The time needed to complete and file this form will vary depending on individual circumstances. The estimated average time is 12 minutes.

For more information and the Privacy Act and Paperwork Reduction Act Notice, see Form 1042-S.   Cat. No. 28848W   Form **1042-T** (2010)

Form **1042**		Annual Withholding Tax Return for		OMB No. 1545-0096
Department of the Treasury Internal Revenue Service		**U.S. Source Income of Foreign Persons** ▶ See instructions.		2010

If this is an amended return, check here . . . . ▶ ☐

Name of withholding agent	Employer identification number	For IRS Use Only	
USCo	34-5678912	CC	FD
Number, street, and room or suite no. (if a P.O. box, see instructions)		RD	FF
		CAF	FP
City or town, province or state, and country (including postal code)		CR	I
Las Vegas, NV		EDC	SIC

If you will not be liable for returns in the future, check here ▶ ☐   Enter date final income paid ▶ _____

Check here if you made quarter-monthly deposits using the 90% rule (see **Deposit Requirements** in the instructions) . . . . . ▶ ☐

Check if you are a: QI/Withholding foreign partnership or trust ☐   NQI/Flow-through entity ☐   (See instructions.)

Record of Federal Tax Liability (Do not show federal tax deposits here.)

Line No.	Period ending		Tax liability for period (including any taxes assumed on Form(s) 1000)	Line No.	Period ending		Tax liability for period (including any taxes assumed on Form(s) 1000)	Line No.	Period ending		Tax liability for period (including any taxes assumed on Form(s) 1000)
1		7		21		7		41		7	
2	Jan.	15		22	May	15		42	Sept.	15	
3		22		23		22		43		22	
4		31		24		31		44		30	150
5	Jan. total			25	May total			45	Sept. total		150
6		7		26		7		46		7	
7	Feb.	15		27	June	15		47	Oct.	15	
8		22		28		22		48		22	
9		28		29		30	600	49		31	
10	Feb. total			30	June total		600	50	Oct. total		
11		7		31		7		51		7	
12	Mar.	15		32	July	15		52	Nov.	15	
13		22		33		22		53		22	
14		31	3,000	34		31		54		30	
15	Mar. total		3,000	35	July total			55	Nov. total		
16		7		36		7		56		7	
17	Apr.	15		37	Aug.	15		57	Dec.	15	
18		22		38		22		58		22	
19		30		39		31		59		31	
20	Apr. total			40	Aug. total			60	Dec. total		

61	No. of Forms 1042-S filed: **a** On paper _____1_____ **b** Electronically _____		
62	For all Form(s) 1042-S and 1000: **a** Gross income paid 12,500 **b** Taxes withheld or assumed 3.750		
63a	Total tax liability (add monthly total lines from above) . . .	63a	3,750
b	Adjustments (see page 4)	63b	
c	Total **net tax** liability (combine lines 63a and 63b) . . . . ▶	63c	3,750
64	Total paid by federal tax deposit coupons or by electronic funds transfer (or with a request for an extension of time to file) for 2010	64	3,750
65	Enter overpayment applied as a credit from 2009 Form 1042 .	65	
66	Credit for amounts withheld by other withholding agents (see page 4)	66	
67	**Total payments.** Add lines 64 through 66 . . . . ▶	67	3,750
68	If line 63c is larger than line 67, enter **balance due** here	68	
69	If line 67 is larger than line 63c, enter **overpayment** here	69	
70	Penalty for failure to deposit tax when due. Also include on line 68 or line 69 (see page 4) .	70	
71	Apply overpayment on line 69 to (check one): ☐ **Credit on 2011 Form 1042** or ☐ **Refund**		

Third Party Designee	Do you want to allow another person to discuss this return with the IRS (see page 4)? ☐ Yes. Complete the following. ☐ No		
	Designee's name ▶	Phone no. ▶	Personal identification number (PIN)

Sign Here — Under penalties of perjury, I declare that I have examined this return, including accompanying schedules and statements, and to the best of my knowledge and belief, it is true, correct, and complete. Declaration of preparer (other than withholding agent) is based on all information of which preparer has any knowledge.

Your signature ▶	Date	Capacity in which acting ▶
		Daytime phone number ▶

Paid Preparer Use Only	Print/Type preparer's name	Preparer's signature	Date	Check ☐ if self-employed	PTIN
	Firm's name ▶			Firm's EIN ▶	
	Firm's address ▶			Phone no.	

For Privacy Act and Paperwork Reduction Act Notice, see the instructions.   Cat. No. 11384V   Form **1042** (2010)

Uncle Sam, a U.S. citizen, and Norman Ray Allen (NRA), a resident of the Cayman Islands, each own 50% of U.S. Partnership. During 2010, U.S. Partnership earns $100,000 of ordinary income each quarter for annual ordinary income of $400,000. NRA's share of the ordinary income is $50,000 per quarter, which would result in quarterly withholding at a top 35% rate of $17,500. U.S. Partnership would tender a Form 8813 with the quarterly withholding, issue a Form 8805 to NRA (with a copy to the IRS) that details the annual withholding, and file an annual return with respect to the amount of annual withholdings to the IRS on a Form 8804. The attached Form 8813 is for the first quarter of 2010.

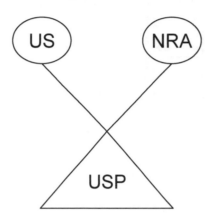

Form **8813**

(Rev. December 2008)

Department of the Treasury
Internal Revenue Service

Partnership Withholding Tax Payment Voucher (Section 1446)

▶ See separate Instructions for Forms 8804, 8805, and 8813.

OMB No. 1545-1119

For calendar year **2010** , or tax year beginning _____ , 20 ____ , and ending _____ , 20 ____

1 Partnership's U.S. employer identification number	2 Amount of this payment
98 : 7654321	$ **17,500**

3 PARTNERSHIP'S name, address, (number, street, and room or suite no.), city, state, and ZIP code. If a P.O. box or foreign address, see instructions.

U.S. Partnership
Anytown, USA

Mail this voucher with a check or money order payable to the "United States Treasury." Write the partnership's employer identification number, tax year, and "Form 8813" on the check or money order.

▶ **Do not staple or attach this voucher to your payment.**

▶ **Do not send cash.**

▶ **If you have applied the provisions of Regulations section 1.1446-6, attach all required Forms 8804-C and computations (see instructions).**

For Paperwork Reduction Act Notice, see separate Instructions for Forms 8804, 8805, and 8813.   Cat. No. 10681H   Form **8813** (Rev. 12-2008)

Form **8805**

Department of the Treasury
Internal Revenue Service

Foreign Partner's Information Statement
of Section 1446 Withholding Tax

▶ **See separate Instructions for Forms 8804, 8805, and 8813.**

For partnership's calendar year 2010, or tax year beginning _____, 2010, and ending _____, 20___

OMB No. 1545-1119

2010

Copy A for Internal Revenue Service
Attach to Form 8804.

1a Foreign partner's name	b U.S. identifying number	5a Name of partnership	b U.S. EIN

NRA

U.S. Partnership

c Address (if a foreign address, see instructions)

c Address (if a foreign address, see instructions)

Georgetown, Grand Cayman
Cayman Islands

Anytown, USA

2 Account number assigned by partnership (if any)

6 Withholding agent's name. If partnership is also the withholding agent, enter "SAME" and do not complete line 7.

3 Type of partner (specify— see instructions) ▶ **Individual**

4 Country code of partner (enter two-letter code; see instructions)

CJ

7 Withholding agent's U.S. employer identification number

8a	Check if the partnership identified on line 5a owns an interest in one or more partnerships	☐
b	Check if any of the partnership's effectively connected taxable income (ECTI) is exempt from U.S. tax for the partner identified on line 1a	☐
9	Partnership's ECTI allocable to partner for the tax year (see instructions)	9	200,000	00
10	Total tax credit allowed to partner under section 1446 (see instructions). **Individual and corporate partners:** Claim this amount as a credit against your U.S. income tax on Form 1040NR, 1120-F, etc.	10	70,000	00

Schedule T—Beneficiary Information (see instructions)

11a Name of beneficiary

c Address (if a foreign address, see instructions)

b U.S. identifying number of beneficiary

12	Amount of ECTI on line 9 to be included in the beneficiary's gross income (see instructions) . . .	12
13	Amount of tax credit on line 10 that the beneficiary is entitled to claim on its return (see instructions) . .	13

For Paperwork Reduction Act Notice, see separate Instructions for Forms 8804, 8805, and 8813.   Cat. No. 10078E   Form **8805** (2010)

¶905

Form **8804**	**Annual Return for Partnership Withholding Tax (Section 1446)** ► See separate Instructions for Forms 8804, 8805, and 8813. ► Attach Form(s) 8804-C and 8805.	OMB No. 1545-1119

Department of the Treasury
Internal Revenue Service

For calendar year 2010 or tax year beginning _____ , 2010, and ending _____ , 20___

20**10**

Check this box if the partnership keeps its records and books of account outside the United States and Puerto Rico . . . ► ☐

Part I   Partnership

1a Name of partnership	**b** U.S. employer identification number
U.S. Partnership	98-7654321

c Number, street, and room or suite no. If a P.O. box, see instructions.	**For IRS Use Only**	
	CC	FD
	RD	FF
d City, state, and ZIP code. If a foreign address, see instructions.	CAF	FP
Anytown, USA	CR	I
	EDC	

Part II   Withholding Agent

2a Name of withholding agent. If partnership is also the withholding agent, enter "SAME" and do not complete lines 2b, 2c, or 2d.	**b** Withholding agent's U.S. employer identification number
Same	

c Number, street, and room or suite no. If a P.O. box, see instructions.

d City, state, and ZIP code

Part III   Section 1446 Tax Liability and Payments

3a Enter number of foreign partners . . . . ►				
b Enter number of Forms 8805 attached to this Form 8804 . . . . . ►				
c Enter number of Forms 8804-C attached to Forms 8805 . . . . ►				
4 Total effectively connected taxable income allocable to foreign partners (see instructions):				
a Net ordinary income and net short-term capital gain	**4a**	200,000	00	
b Reduction to line 4a for state and local taxes under Regulations section 1.1446-6(c)(1)(iii)	**4b**	(	)	
c Reduction to line 4a for certified foreign partner-level items submitted using Form 8804-C	**4c**	(	)	
d Combine lines 4a, 4b, and 4c	. . . . . .	**4d**	200,000	00
e 28% rate gain allocable to non-corporate partners	**4e**			
f Reduction to line 4e for state and local taxes under Regulations section 1.1446-6(c)(1)(iii)	**4f**	(	)	
g Reduction to line 4e for certified foreign partner-level items submitted using Form 8804-C	**4g**	(	)	
h Combine lines 4e, 4f, and 4g	. . . . .	**4h**	0	00
i Unrecaptured section 1250 gain allocable to non-corporate partners	**4i**			
j Reduction to line 4i for state and local taxes under Regulations section 1.1446-6(c)(1)(iii)	**4j**	(	)	
k Reduction to line 4i for certified foreign partner-level items submitted using Form 8804-C	**4k**	(	)	
l Combine lines 4i, 4j, and 4k	. . .	**4l**	0	00
m Qualified dividend income and net long-term capital gain (including net section 1231 gain) allocable to non-corporate partners . .	**4m**			
n Reduction to line 4m for state and local taxes under Regulations section 1.1446-6(c)(1)(iii)	**4n**	(	)	
o Reduction to line 4m for certified foreign partner-level items submitted using Form 8804-C	**4o**	(	)	
p Combine lines 4m, 4n, and 4o	. . . . .	**4p**	0	00

For Paperwork Reduction Act Notice, see separate instructions for Forms 8804, 8805, and 8813.   Cat. No. 10077T   Form **8804** (2010)

5	Gross section 1446 tax liability:				
a	Multiply line 4d by 35% (.35)	5a	70,000	00	
b	Multiply line 4h by 28% (.28)	5b			
c	Multiply line 4l by 25% (.25)	5c			
d	Multiply line 4p by 15% (.15)	5d			
e	Add lines 5a through 5d		5e	70,000	00

6a	Payments of section 1446 tax made by the partnership identified on line 1a during its tax year (or with a request for an extension of time to file) and amount credited from 2009 Form 8804	6a	70,000	00	
b	Section 1446 tax paid or withheld by another partnership in which the partnership identified on line 1a was a partner during the tax year (attach Form(s) 1042-S or 8805)	6b			
c	Section 1445(a) or 1445(e)(1) tax withheld from or paid by the partnership identified on line 1a during the tax year for a disposition of a U.S. real property interest. Attach Form(s) 1042-S or 8288-A. See the instructions	6c			

7	**Total payments.** Add lines 6a through 6c	7	70,000	00
8	Estimated tax penalty (see instructions). Check if Schedule A (Form 8804) is attached ☐	8		
9	Add lines 5e and 8	9	70,000	00
10	**Balance due.** If line 7 is smaller than line 9, enter balance due. Attach a check or money order for the full amount payable to the "United States Treasury." Write the partnership's U.S. employer identification number, tax year, and Form 8804 on it	10		
11	**Overpayment.** If line 7 is more than line 9, enter amount overpaid	11		
12	Amount of line 11 you want **refunded to you** ▶	12		
13	Amount of line 11 you want **credited to next year's Form 8804**	13		

Sign Here

Under penalties of perjury, I declare that I have examined this return, including accompanying schedules and statements, and to the best of my knowledge and belief, it is true, correct, and complete. Declaration of preparer (other than general partner, limited liability company member, or withholding agent) is based on all information of which preparer has any knowledge.

▶ Signature of general partner, limited liability company member, or withholding agent | Title | Date

Paid Preparer Use Only

Print/Type preparer's name	Preparer's signature	Date	Check ☐ if self-employed	PTIN
Firm's name ▶			Firm's EIN ▶	
Firm's address ▶			Phone no.	

Form **8804** (2010)

¶905

Kris Kringle, a merry old soul who is a resident of Finland, works in the United States as an independent contractor and makes personal appearances at various locations during the Christmas season. Although Kris has a U.S. trade or business in the United States, Kris is exempt from tax under the independent services article of the U.S.-Finland Tax Treaty. Kris must provide a Form 8233 with respect to each of his various engagements.

Form **8233** (Rev. March 2009) Department of the Treasury Internal Revenue Service	**Exemption From Withholding on Compensation for Independent (and Certain Dependent) Personal Services of a Nonresident Alien Individual** ► See separate instructions.	OMB No. 1545-0795
Who Should Use This Form? Note: For definitions of terms used in this section and detailed instructions on required withholding forms for each type of income, see **Definitions** on pages 1 and 2 of the instructions.	**IF** you are a nonresident alien individual who is receiving . . .	**THEN,** if you are the beneficial owner of that income, use this form to claim . . .
	Compensation for independent personal services performed in the United States	A tax treaty withholding exemption (Independent personal services, Business profits) for part or all of that compensation and/or to claim the daily personal exemption amount.
	Compensation for dependent personal services performed in the United States	A tax treaty withholding exemption for part or all of that compensation. Note: *Do not* use Form 8233 to claim the daily personal exemption amount.
	Noncompensatory scholarship or fellowship income **and** personal services income **from the same withholding agent**	A tax treaty withholding exemption for part or all of **both** types of income.
DO NOT Use This Form. . .	**IF** you are a beneficial owner who is . . .	**INSTEAD,** use . . .
	Receiving compensation for dependent personal services performed in the United States **and** you are **not** claiming a tax treaty withholding exemption for that compensation	Form W-4 (See page 2 of the Instructions for Form 8233 for how to complete Form W-4.)
	Receiving noncompensatory scholarship or fellowship income **and** you are **not** receiving any personal services income **from the same withholding agent**	Form W-8BEN or, if elected by the withholding agent, Form W-4 for the noncompensatory scholarship or fellowship income
	Claiming only foreign status or treaty benefits with respect to income that is **not** compensation for personal services	Form W-8BEN

This exemption is applicable for compensation for calendar year .... , or other tax year beginning .... and ending ....

Part I	**Identification of Beneficial Owner** (See instructions.)		
1 Name of individual who is the beneficial owner Kris Kringle	**2** U.S. taxpayer identifying number 912-25-1225	**3** Foreign tax identifying number, if any (optional)	
4 Permanent residence address (street, apt. or suite no., or rural route). Do not use a P.O. box. 1234 Christmas Lane			
City or town, state or province. Include postal code where appropriate. Rovaniemi		Country (do not abbreviate) Finland	
5 Address in the United States (street, apt. or suite no., or rural route). Do not use a P.O. box. varies			
City or town, state, and ZIP code			

Note: *Citizens of Canada or Mexico are not required to complete lines 7a and 7b.*

6 U.S. visa type H1B	**7a** Country issuing passport USA	**7b** Passport number 1225
8 Date of entry into the United States November 16, 2008	**9a** Current nonimmigrant status	**9b** Date your current nonimmigrant status expires November 1, 2014

10 If you are a foreign student, trainee, professor/teacher, or researcher, check this box . . . . ► ☐
Caution: *See the line 10 instructions for the required additional statement you must attach.*

For Privacy Act and Paperwork Reduction Act Notice, see separate instructions.   Cat. No. 62292K   Form **8233** (Rev. 3-2009)

¶905

Part II **Claim for Tax Treaty Withholding Exemption and/or Personal Exemption Amount**

11 Compensation for independent (and certain dependent) personal services:
a Description of personal services you are providing Taxpayer participates in numerous Christmas activities playing the role of a jolly elderly gentleman who spreads joy

b Total compensation you expect to be paid for these services in this calendar or tax year $ 10,000
12 If compensation is exempt from withholding based on a tax treaty benefit, provide:
a Tax treaty **and treaty article** on which you are basing exemption from withholding U.S.-Finnish Tax Treaty, Article 14

b Total compensation listed on line 11b above that is exempt from tax under this treaty $ 10,000
c Country of permanent residence Finland

Note: *Do not complete lines 13a through 13c unless you also received compensation for personal services **from the same withholding agent.***

13 Noncompensatory scholarship or fellowship income:
a Amount $
b Tax treaty **and treaty article** on which you are basing exemption from withholding

c Total income listed on line 13a above that is exempt from tax under this treaty $
14 Sufficient facts to justify the exemption from withholding claimed on line 12 and/or line 13 (see instructions)
Kris travels from function to function as an independent contractor. His activities are not attributable to any fixed base regularly available to him. His vagabond-like activities cumulate in visiting the homes of many good girls and boys the night before Christmas.

Note: *Lines 15 through 18 are to be completed only for certain independent personal services (see instructions).*

15	Number of personal exemptions claimed ▶	16	How many days will you perform services in the United States during this tax year? ▶
17	Daily personal exemption amount claimed (see instructions) ▶		
18	Total personal exemption amount claimed. Multiply line 16 by line 17 ▶		

Part III **Certification**

Under penalties of perjury, I declare that I have examined the information on this form and to the best of my knowledge and belief it is true, correct, and complete. I further certify under penalties of perjury that:

• I am the beneficial owner (or am authorized to sign for the beneficial owner) of all the income to which this form relates.

• The beneficial owner is not a U.S. person.

• The beneficial owner is a resident of the treaty country listed on line 12a and/or 13b above within the meaning of the income tax treaty between the United States and that country.

Furthermore, I authorize this form to be provided to any withholding agent that has control, receipt, or custody of the income of which I am the beneficial owner or any withholding agent that can disburse or make payments of the income of which I am the beneficial owner.

Sign Here ▶
Signature of beneficial owner (or individual authorized to sign for beneficial owner)
Date

Part IV **Withholding Agent Acceptance and Certification**

Name	Employer identification number

Address (number and street) (Include apt. or suite no. or P.O. box, if applicable.)

City, state, and ZIP code	Telephone number

Under penalties of perjury, I certify that I have examined this form and any accompanying statements, that I am satisfied that an exemption from withholding is warranted, and that I do not know or have reason to know that the nonresident alien individual is not entitled to the exemption or that the nonresident alien's eligibility for the exemption cannot be readily determined.

Signature of withholding agent ▶
Date ▶

Form **8233** (Rev. 3-2009)

¶905

Norman Ray Allen (NRA), a resident of the Cayman Islands, purchases an apartment building located in the United States. NRA comes to the United States to manage the apartment building where he is responsible for maintenance. On the first day of each month, NRA collects ten rent checks of $1,000 each for a total of $10,000. NRA provides a Form W-8ECI to each tenant to claim that the income is effectively connected with the conduct of a trade or business in the United States so that the tenants do not have to withhold 30%. At the end of 2010, NRA will have to file a Form 1040NR and pay tax on his net rental income.

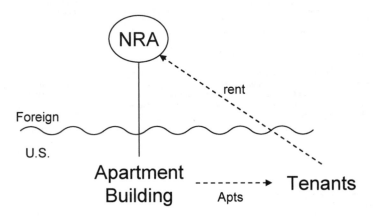

Form **W-8ECI** (Rev. February 2006) Department of the Treasury Internal Revenue Service	**Certificate of Foreign Person's Claim That Income Is Effectively Connected With the Conduct of a Trade or Business in the United States** ► Section references are to the Internal Revenue Code. ► See separate Instructions. ► Give this form to the withholding agent or payer. Do not send to the IRS.	OMB No. 1545-1621

Note: *Persons submitting this form must file an annual U.S. income tax return to report income claimed to be effectively connected with a U.S. trade or business (see instructions).*

Do not use this form for:	Instead, use Form:
● A beneficial owner solely claiming foreign status or treaty benefits	W-8BEN
● A foreign government, international organization, foreign central bank of issue, foreign tax-exempt organization, foreign private foundation, or government of a U.S. possession claiming the applicability of section(s) 115(2), 501(c), 892, 895, or 1443(b) . . .	W-8EXP

Note: *These entities should use Form W-8ECI if they received effectively connected income (e.g., income from commercial activities).*

● A foreign partnership or a foreign trust (unless claiming an exemption from U.S. withholding on income effectively connected with the conduct of a trade or business in the United States)	W-8BEN or W-8IMY
● A person acting as an intermediary	W-8IMY

Note: *See instructions for additional exceptions.*

Part I **Identification of Beneficial Owner** (See instructions.)

1 Name of individual or organization that is the beneficial owner Norman Ray Allen	2 Country of incorporation or organization Cayman Islands

3 Type of entity (check the appropriate box): ☑ Individual ☐ Corporation ☐ Disregarded entity
☐ Partnership ☐ Simple trust ☐ Complex trust ☐ Estate
☐ Government ☐ Grantor trust ☐ Central bank of issue ☐ Tax-exempt organization
☐ Private foundation ☐ International organization

4 Permanent residence address (street, apt. or suite no., or rural route). **Do not use a P.O. box.**
Georgetown, Grand Cayman

City or town, state or province. Include postal code where appropriate.	Country (do not abbreviate) Cayman Islands

5 Business address in the United States (street, apt. or suite no., or rural route). **Do not use a P.O. box.**
1234 Main Street

City or town, state, and ZIP code
Anytown, USA

6 U.S. taxpayer identification number (required—see instructions) 999-99-9999 ☑ SSN or ITIN ☐ EIN	7 Foreign tax identifying number, if any (optional)

8 Reference number(s) (see instructions)

9 Specify each item of income that is, or is expected to be, received from the payer that is effectively connected with the conduct of a trade or business in the United States (attach statement if necessary) Norman Ray Allen is in his first year of the trade or business of renting the residential real estate located at 1234 Main Street, Anytown, USA. Moreover, when he files his Form 1040NR to pay tax at marginal rates on this rental income, he intends to make a protective election to be treated as a trade or business under Treas. Reg. section 1.871-10. Therefore, withholding on rental payments is inappropriate.

Part II **Certification**

Sign Here

Under penalties of perjury, I declare that I have examined the information on this form and to the best of my knowledge and belief it is true, correct, and complete. I further certify under penalties of perjury that:

● I am the beneficial owner (or I am authorized to sign for the beneficial owner) of all the income to which this form relates,
● The amounts for which this certification is provided are effectively connected with the conduct of a trade or business in the United States and are includible in my gross income (or the beneficial owner's gross income) for the taxable year, and
● The beneficial owner is not a U.S. person.

Furthermore, I authorize this form to be provided to any withholding agent that has control, receipt, or custody of the income of which I am the beneficial owner or any withholding agent that can disburse or make payments of the income of which I am the beneficial owner.

Signature of beneficial owner (or individual authorized to sign for the beneficial owner)	Date (MM-DD-YYYY)	Capacity in which acting

For Paperwork Reduction Act Notice, see separate instructions.   Cat. No. 25045D   Form **W-8ECI** (Rev. 2-2006)

Reijo Salo, a resident of Finland, owns 10,000 shares of MagnaSoft, a U.S. corporation. MagnaSoft declares a $100,000 dividend to Reijo Salo. By providing the Form W-8BEN to MagnaSoft, MagnaSoft will only withhold at a treaty rate on dividends to individuals under the U.S.-Finnish Tax Treaty of 15% (for $15,000 of withholding) instead of the non-treaty rate of 30%.

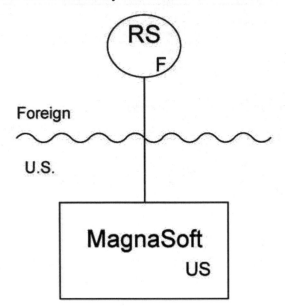

Form **W-8BEN**	**Certificate of Foreign Status of Beneficial Owner**	
(Rev. February 2006)	**for United States Tax Withholding**	OMB No. 1545-1621
Department of the Treasury Internal Revenue Service	▶ Section references are to the Internal Revenue Code. ▶ See separate instructions. ▶ Give this form to the withholding agent or payer. Do not send to the IRS.	

Do not use this form for:	Instead, use Form:
● A U.S. citizen or other U.S. person, including a resident alien individual	W-9
● A person claiming that income is effectively connected with the conduct of a trade or business in the United States	W-8ECI
● A foreign partnership, a foreign simple trust, or a foreign grantor trust (see instructions for exceptions)	W-8ECI or W-8IMY
● A foreign government, international organization, foreign central bank of issue, foreign tax-exempt organization, foreign private foundation, or government of a U.S. possession that received effectively connected income or that is claiming the applicability of section(s) 115(2), 501(c), 892, 895, or 1443(b) (see instructions)	W-8ECI or W-8EXP

Note: *These entities should use Form W-8BEN if they are claiming treaty benefits or are providing the form only to claim they are a foreign person exempt from backup withholding.*

| ● A person acting as an intermediary . . . . | W-8IMY |

Note: *See instructions for additional exceptions.*

Part I   **Identification of Beneficial Owner** (See instructions.)

1 Name of individual or organization that is the beneficial owner	2 Country of incorporation or organization
Reijo Salo	Finland

3   Type of beneficial owner: ☑ Individual   ☐ Corporation   ☐ Disregarded entity   ☐ Partnership   ☐ Simple trust

☐ Grantor trust   ☐ Complex trust   ☐ Estate   ☐ Government   ☐ International organization

☐ Central bank of issue   ☐ Tax-exempt organization   ☐ Private foundation

4   Permanent residence address (street, apt. or suite no., or rural route). **Do not use a P.O. box or in-care-of address.**

4321 Finnish White Wine Way

City or town, state or province. Include postal code where appropriate.	Country (do not abbreviate)
Espoo	Finland

5   Mailing address (if different from above)

City or town, state or province. Include postal code where appropriate.	Country (do not abbreviate)

6 U.S. taxpayer identification number, if required (see instructions)	7 Foreign tax identifying number, if any (optional)
977-77-7777 ☑ SSN or ITIN ☐ EIN	

8   Reference number(s) (see instructions)

Part II   **Claim of Tax Treaty Benefits** (if applicable)

9   I certify that (check all that apply):

a ☑ The beneficial owner is a resident of .... Finland .... within the meaning of the income tax treaty between the United States and that country.

b ☐ If required, the U.S. taxpayer identification number is stated on line 6 (see instructions).

c ☐ The beneficial owner is not an individual, derives the item (or items) of income for which the treaty benefits are claimed, and, if applicable, meets the requirements of the treaty provision dealing with limitation on benefits (see instructions).

d ☐ The beneficial owner is not an individual, is claiming treaty benefits for dividends received from a foreign corporation or interest from a U.S. trade or business of a foreign corporation, and meets qualified resident status (see instructions).

e ☐ The beneficial owner is related to the person obligated to pay the income within the meaning of section 267(b) or 707(b), and will file Form 8833 if the amount subject to withholding received during a calendar year exceeds, in the aggregate, $500,000.

10   **Special rates and conditions** (if applicable—see instructions): The beneficial owner is claiming the provisions of Article ...10... of the treaty identified on line 9a above to claim a ...15... % rate of withholding on (specify type of income): dividends ....

Explain the reasons the beneficial owner meets the terms of the treaty article: The beneficial owner is an individual who is a resident of Finland and, therefore, entitled to the benefits of Article X of the U.S.-Finnish Tax Treaty. ....

Part III   **Notional Principal Contracts**

11 ☐ I have provided or will provide a statement that identifies those notional principal contracts from which the income is **not** effectively connected with the conduct of a trade or business in the United States. I agree to update this statement as required.

Part IV   **Certification**

Under penalties of perjury, I declare that I have examined the information on this form and to the best of my knowledge and belief it is true, correct, and complete. I further certify under penalties of perjury that:

1 I am the beneficial owner (or am authorized to sign for the beneficial owner) of all the income to which this form relates,

2 The beneficial owner is not a U.S. person,

3 The income to which this form relates is (a) not effectively connected with the conduct of a trade or business in the United States, (b) effectively connected but is not subject to tax under an income tax treaty, or (c) the partner's share of a partnership's effectively connected income, **and**

4 For broker transactions or barter exchanges, the beneficial owner is an exempt foreign person as defined in the instructions.

Furthermore, I authorize this form to be provided to any withholding agent that has control, receipt, or custody of the income of which I am the beneficial owner or any withholding agent that can disburse or make payments of the income of which I am the beneficial owner.

Sign Here ▶   _____   _____   _____
     Signature of beneficial owner (or individual authorized to sign for beneficial owner)   Date (MM-DD-YYYY)   Capacity in which acting

For Paperwork Reduction Act Notice, see separate instructions.   Cat. No. 25047Z   Form **W-8BEN** (Rev. 2-2006)

     ✪ *Printed on Recycled Paper*

¶905

Shorty, a resident of the Netherlands, owns real estate known as Blackacre, which is a parcel of land located in Nashville, Tennessee. On February 28, 2010, Shorty sells Blackacre for a price of $1 million to Betsy Ross, a U.S. citizen. Betsy must withhold $100,000, which is 10% of the purchase price of Blackacre. By March 20, 2010, 20 days after the purchase, Betsy must file a Form 8288 with the IRS along with a copy of Form 8288-A (which is also provided to Shorty) and tender the $100,000 of tax withheld.

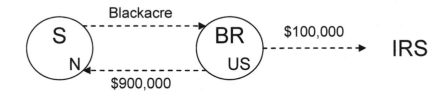

Form **8288**	U.S. Withholding Tax Return for	
(Rev. November 2009)	**Dispositions by Foreign Persons of**	OMB No. 1545-0902
Department of the Treasury Internal Revenue Service	**U.S. Real Property Interests**	

Complete Part I **or** Part II. Also complete and attach Copies A and B of Form(s) 8288-A.
(Attach additional sheets if you need more space.)

Part I   To Be Completed by the Buyer or Other Transferee Required To Withhold Under Section 1445(a)

1 Name of buyer or other transferee responsible for withholding (see page 6)	Identifying number
Betsy Ross	123-41-1234

Street address, apt. or suite no., or rural route. Do not use a P.O. box.
1234 Flag Street

City or town, state, and ZIP code	Phone number (optional)
Boston, MA	( )

2   Description and location of property acquired
Blackacre is located at 1313 21st Avenue South, Nashville, Tennessee 37205

3 Date of transfer	4 Number of Forms 8288-A attached	5 Amount realized on the transfer
February 28, 2010	1	1,000,000

6 Check applicable box.	7 Amount withheld
a Withholding is at 10% . . . . ☑ **b** Withholding is of a reduced amount . . . . ☐	100,000

Part II   To Be Completed by an Entity Subject to the Provisions of Section 1445(e)

1 Name of entity or fiduciary responsible for withholding (see instructions)	Identifying number

Street address, apt. or suite no., or rural route. Do not use a P.O. box.

City or town, state, and ZIP code	Phone number (optional)
	( )

2   Description of U.S. real property interest transferred or distributed

3 Date of transfer	4 Number of Forms 8288-A attached

5 Complete all items that apply.	6 Total amount withheld
a Amount subject to withholding at 35% . . . . _____ **b** Amount subject to withholding at 10% . . . . _____ **c** Amount subject to withholding at reduced rate . . . . . _____ **d** Large trust election to withhold at distribution . . . . ☐	

Sign Here	Under penalties of perjury, I declare that I have examined this return, including accompanying schedules and statements, and to the best of my knowledge and belief, it is true, correct, and complete. Declaration of preparer (other than taxpayer) is based on all information of which preparer has any knowledge.
	▶ _____ Signature of withholding agent, partner, fiduciary, or corporate officer Title (if applicable) Date

Paid Preparer's Use Only	Preparer's signature ▶	Date	Check if self-employed ▶ ☐	Preparer's SSN or PTIN
	Firm's name (or yours if self-employed) and address ▶		EIN ▶	
			ZIP code ▶	

For Privacy Act and Paperwork Reduction Act Notice, see the instructions.   Cat. No. 62260A   Form **8288** (Rev. 11-2009)

¶905

Withholding agent's name, street address, city, state, and ZIP code	1 Date of transfer February 28, 2010	**Statement of Withholding on Dispositions by Foreign Persons of U.S. Real Property Interests**
Betsy Ross 1234 Flag Street Boston, MA	2 Federal income tax withheld 100,000	OMB No. 1545-0902
Withholding agent's Federal identification number 123-41-1234	Identification number of foreign person subject to withholding (see instructions) 966-66-6666	3 Amount realized 1,000,000	4 Gain recognized by foreign corporation	**Copy A For Internal Revenue Service Center**
Name of person subject to withholding Shorty		5 Description of property transferred Blackacre	
Foreign address (number, street, and apt. or suite no.)		6 Person subject to withholding is: An individual ☑ A corporation ☐ Other (specify) ▶	For Privacy Act and Paperwork Reduction Act Notice, see the instructions for Form 8288.
City, province or state, postal code, and country (not U.S.) Amsterdam, The Netherlands		Mailing address of person subject to withholding (if different)	

Form **8288-A** (Rev. 11-2006)   Cat. No. 62261L   **Attach Copies A and B to Form 8288**   Department of the Treasury - Internal Revenue Service

¶905

Judge Aloha, a resident of Ceylon, sells Green Acre, a parcel of land located in Sadstone, Michigan, to Oliver Douglas, a U.S. citizen. Judge Aloha's adjusted basis in Green Acre is $450,000 and the sales price is $500,000, resulting in gain to Judge Aloha of $50,000. Because the tax on the $50,000 gain will be less than the $50,000 withheld under FIRPTA (10% of the purchase price of $500,000), Judge Aloha files a Form 8288-B with the IRS to request a certificate for a reduced amount of withholding at the close.

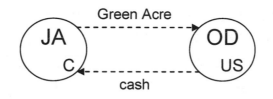

Form **8288-B**
(Rev. November 2006)

Department of the Treasury
Internal Revenue Service

Application for Withholding Certificate for Dispositions by Foreign Persons of U.S. Real Property Interests

OMB No. 1545-1060

▶ **Please type or print.**

1	Name of transferor (attach additional sheets if more than one transferor)	Identification number
	Judge Aloha	**955-55-5555**

Street address, apt. or suite no., or rural route. Do not use a P.O. box.

City, state or province, and country (if not U.S.). Include ZIP code or postal code where appropriate.
Ceylon

2	Name of transferee (attach additional sheets if more than one transferee)	Identification number
	Oliver Douglas	

Street address, apt. or suite no., or rural route. Do not use a P.O. box.

City, state or province, and country (if not U.S.). Include ZIP code or postal code where appropriate.
Hooterville, USA

3   Applicant is: Transferor ☑   Transferee ☐

4a	Name of withholding agent (see instructions)	b	Identification number
	Oliver Douglas		**555-55-5555**
c	Name of estate, trust, or entity (if applicable)	d	Identification number

5	Address where you want withholding certificate sent (street address, apt. or suite no., P.O. box, or rural route number)	Phone number (optional)
		( )

City, state or province, and country (if not U.S.). Include ZIP code or postal code where appropriate.
Hooterville, USA

6   Description of U.S. real property transaction:

a   Date of transfer (month, day, year) (see inst.) ..... **12/25/10**   b   Contract price $ **500,000**

c   Type of interest transferred: ☑ Real property   ☐ Associated personal property
☐ Domestic U.S. real property holding corporation

d   Use of property at time of sale: ☐ Rental or commercial   ☐ Personal   ☐ Other (attach explanation)

e   Adjusted basis $ **450,000**

f   Location and general description of property (for a real property interest), description (for associated personal property), or the class or type and amount of the interest (for an interest in a U.S. real property holding corporation). See instructions.
Green Acre is a parcel of raw land located at 4321 Main Street, Sadstone, MI

g   For the 3 preceding tax years:

(1)   Were U.S. income tax returns filed relating to the U.S. real property interest? . . . .   ☐ Yes   ☑ No
If "Yes," when and where were those returns filed? ▶

(2)   Were U.S. income taxes paid relating to the U.S. real property interest? . . . .   ☐ Yes   ☑ No
If "Yes," enter the amount of tax paid for each year ▶

7   Check the box to indicate the reason a withholding certificate should be issued. See the instructions for information that must be attached to Form 8288-B.

a   ☐ The transferor is exempt from U.S. tax or nonrecognition treatment applies.

b   ☑ The transferor's maximum tax liability is less than the tax required to be withheld.

c   ☐ The special installment sales rules described in section 7 of Rev. Proc. 2000-35 allow reduced withholding.

8   Does the transferor have any unsatisfied withholding liability under section 1445? . . . .   ☐ Yes   ☑ No
See the instructions for information required to be attached.

9   Is this application for a withholding certificate made under section 1445(e)? . . . .   ☐ Yes   ☑ No
If "Yes," check the applicable box in **a** and the applicable box in **b** below.

a   Type of transaction: ☐ 1445(e)(1)   ☐ 1445(e)(2)   ☐ 1445(e)(3)   ☐ 1445(e)(5)   ☐ 1445(e)(6)

b   Applicant is: ☑ Taxpayer   ☐ Other person required to withhold. Specify your title (e.g., trustee) ▶ _____

Under penalties of perjury, I declare that I have examined this application and accompanying attachments, and, to the best of my knowledge and belief, they are true, correct, and complete.

Signature	Title (if applicable)	Date

For Privacy Act and Paperwork Reduction Act Notice, see the instructions.   Cat. No. 10128Z   Form **8288-B** (Rev. 11-2006)

¶905

Chapter 10
Foreign Persons Doing Business in the United States

¶ 1001 TAXATION OF A U.S. TRADE OR BUSINESS

A threshold issue for a foreign company entering the U.S. market is whether the foreign company's U.S. activities are subject to U.S. taxation. As discussed below, the answer to this question depends on both U.S. tax law and the provisions of any income tax treaty between the United States and the foreign company's home country.

.01 *Determinants of U.S. Taxation*

U.S. trade or business. The United States taxes foreign corporations and nonresident alien individuals on the net amount of income effectively connected with the conduct of a trade or business within the United States.[1] Therefore, under the Internal Revenue Code, the existence of a U.S. trade or business is the touchstone of U.S. taxation of a foreign person's business profits. Despite its importance, there is no comprehensive definition of the term "trade or business" in the Code or the Regulations. The relevant case law suggests that a U.S. trade or business exists only if the activities of either the taxpayer or the taxpayer's dependent agents within the United States are considerable, continuous, and regular.[2] This determination is made based on the facts and circumstances of each case.

The conduct of a U.S. trade or business by an independent agent generally is not imputed to the principal.[3] An independent agent is one who is both legally and economically independent of the principal and who is willing to act on behalf of more than one principal. Likewise, the conduct of a U.S. trade or business by a U.S.

---

[1] Code Secs. 871(b) and 882(a). For this purpose, the United States includes the 50 states and the District of Columbia, but not U.S. possessions. Code Sec. 7701(a)(9).

[2] For example, *see I. Balanovski,* CA-2, 56-2 USTC ¶ 9832, 236 F2d 298 (2nd Cir., 1956); *De Amediov,* 34 TC 894, Dec. 24,315. Aff'd, CA-3, 62-1 USTC ¶ 9283, 299 F2d 623 (3rd Cir.1962).

[3] For example, *see British Timken, Ltd.,* 12 TC 880, Dec. 16,992, A. 1949-2 CB 1, and *E. Higgins,* 312 US 212, 1941.

corporation is not imputed to a foreign shareholder, even if the shareholder owns 100% of the stock of the domestic corporation. However, if a partnership, estate, or trust is engaged in a U.S. trade or business, then each partner or beneficiary is considered to be engaged in a U.S. trade or business.[4]

A U.S. trade or business ordinarily includes the performance of personal services in the United States.[5] However, under a *de minimis* rule, the performance of dependent personal services by a nonresident alien individual does not constitute a U.S. trade or business if the following requirements are met:

  (i) the nonresident alien is present in the United States for 90 days or less during the taxable year,

 (ii) the nonresident alien receives no more than $3,000 for his or her U.S. services, and

(iii) the nonresident alien works as an employee or under contract for either a foreign person who is not engaged in a U.S. trade or business or the foreign office of a U.S. person.[6]

Example **10.1:** FORacc is an accounting firm located in country F. FORacc sends a partner to the United States for a brief meeting with management of one of its client's U.S. subsidiaries. Immediately following the half-day meeting, the partner returns to the foreign country. FORacc receives $2,500 from the U.S. subsidiary for attending the meeting. Because the foreign partner was in the United States for 90 days or less, she received less than $3,000 for her U.S. services, and FORacc was not otherwise engaged in a U.S. trade or business, FORacc does not have a U.S. trade or business.

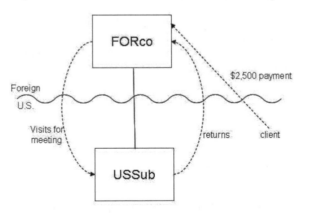

This exception allows nonresident aliens to make short business trips to the United States free of U.S. taxes. As discussed later in this chapter, income tax treaties often contain more generous exemptions which allow for longer stays and increase or eliminate the limitation on earnings for business travelers from treaty countries.

---

[4] Code Sec. 875.
[5] Code Sec. 864(b).

[6] Code Sec. 864(b)(1) and Reg. §1.864-2(b). The compensation of a nonresident alien who meets these requirements is treated as foreign-source income. Code Sec. 861(a)(3).

¶1001.01

In addition to the *de minimis* rule for dependent personal services, the following safe harbor exceptions are provided for foreign persons engaged in the trading of stocks, securities, and certain commodities:[7]

(i) *Broker-dealers*—Trading for the account of another through an independent agent located in the United States does not constitute a U.S. trade or business.[8] This exception does not apply, however, if, at any time during the taxable year, the taxpayer has an office or other fixed place of business in the United States through which, or by the direction of which, the trades are made.[9]

Example **10.2:** Norman Ray Allen (NRA), a nonresident alien, trades lamb chop futures on the Chicago Mercantile Exchange through E.F. Mutton, a brokerage in the United States. Because E.F. Mutton is an independent agent, NRA does not have a U.S. trade or business. However, if NRA's trading volume becomes so large that E.F. Mutton specially designates and reserves an office for NRA, NRA would have a U.S. trade or business.

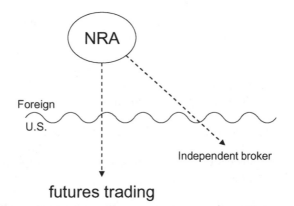

futures trading

(ii) *Trading for own account*—Trading by taxpayers for their own account does not constitute a U.S. trade or business, regardless of whether the trades are made by the taxpayer, the taxpayer's employee, or an independent agent. This exception does not apply to dealers.[10]

Taxpayers whose trading activities do not qualify for one of these safe harbor provisions are not necessarily considered to be engaged in a U.S. trade or business. Instead, that determination is made based on the facts and circumstances of each case.[11]

---

[7] Code Sec. 864(b)(2). These exceptions apply only to commodities of the kind customarily dealt in on an organized commodity exchange (e.g., grain), and then only to transactions of the kind customarily consummated at such an exchange (e.g., futures). Code Sec. 864(b)(2)(B)(iii).

[8] Code Sec. 864(b)(2)(A)(i) and (b)(2)(B)(i). For purposes of this exception, the volume of stock, security, or commodity transactions effected during the taxable year is irrelevant. Reg. § 1.864-2(c)(1).

[9] Code Sec. 864(b)(2)(C).

[10] Code Sec. 864(b)(2)(A)(ii) and (b)(2)(B)(ii).

[11] Reg. § 1.864-2(e).

Permanent establishments. Income tax treaties to which the United States is a party ordinarily contain a provision that exempts a foreign person's business profits from U.S. tax, unless those profits are attributable to a permanent establishment that the taxpayer maintains within the United States.[12] A permanent establishment includes a fixed place of business (e.g., a sales office), unless the fixed place of business is used solely for auxiliary functions (e.g., purchasing, storing, displaying, or delivering inventory) or activities of a preparatory nature (e.g., collecting information about potential customers).[13] A permanent establishment also exists if employees or other dependent agents habitually exercise in the United States an authority to conclude sales contracts in the taxpayer's name.[14] As a consequence, a foreign company that sends executives or salespeople to the United States to enter into contracts may create a permanent establishment even if those employees do not operate out of a formal sales office. Employees who limit their U.S. activities to auxiliary or preparatory functions, with sales concluded in a foreign country, will not create a permanent establishment. Marketing products in the United States solely through independent U.S. brokers or distributors also does not create a permanent establishment.[15]

Tax treaties also usually provide various exemptions for personal services income. These provisions allow nonresident alien individuals to perform personal services within the United States and avoid U.S. taxation as long as their U.S. activities do not exceed a specified level of intensity. A common approach is to exempt income derived by nonresident alien individuals from dependent services performed in the United States if the following requirements are satisfied:

(i)   the employee is present in the United States for 183 days or less,

(ii) the employee's compensation is paid by an employer that is not a U.S. resident, and

(iii) the compensation is not borne by a permanent establishment that the employer maintains in the United States.[16]

Example **10.3:** FORco is a company incorporated in foreign country F, which has a treaty with the United States similar to the U.S. Model Treaty. FORco is in the refrigeration business. Due to the high demand for air conditioning repair services in the United States during the first week of July, FORco sends Norman Ray Allen (NRA), a citizen and resident of country F, to serve customers. During that week, NRA helps repair air conditioning for 15 different customers of FORco. The compensation that FORco pays NRA is $2,000.

---

[12] For example, Article 7(1) (¶ 1304.07) of the United States Model Income Tax Convention of November 15, 2006 (or U.S. Model Treaty).

[13] For example, *see* Article 5(1) and (4) (¶ 1304.05) of the U.S. Model Treaty.

[14] For example, *see* Article 5(5) (¶ 1304.05) of the U.S. Model Treaty.

[15] For example, *see* Article 5(6) (¶ 1304.05) of the U.S. Model Treaty.

[16] For example, *see* Article 14(2) (¶ 1304.14) of the U.S. Model Treaty.

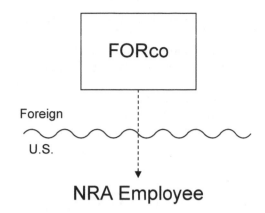

NRA Employee

NRA is not taxed on his $2,000 of compensation for services he performs in the United States pursuant to the Treaty because (i) NRA is in the United States for only 7 days (less than 183 days), (ii) NRA's compensation is paid by FORco, which is not a resident of the United States, and (iii) NRA's compensation is not borne by a permanent establishment or a fixed base that FORco has in the United States.

Some older tax treaties also contain a separate independent personal services article that governs personal services income derived by self-employed professionals, such as accountants, doctors, engineers, and lawyers. Such income ordinarily is exempt from U.S. taxation unless the services are performed in the United States and the income is attributable to an office or other fixed place of business that is located in the United States and is regularly available to the taxpayer for purposes of performing the services. The current U.S. Model Treaty does not contain a separate independent personal services article. Instead, such activities are governed by the general permanent establishment provisions discussed above.

Finally, tax treaties often contain special rules governing personal services income derived by crew members of ships and aircraft operated in international traffic,[17] entertainers and athletes,[18] government workers,[19] and students and trainees.[20] The appendix to Chapter 13 (¶ 1305) provides a listing of the treaty provisions governing personal services income, by country.

Differentiating between the U.S. trade or business and permanent establishment standards. Distinguishing between the Internal Revenue Code standard of a U.S. trade or business and the treaty standard of a permanent establishment is often a matter of degree.

Example **10.4:** FORecq is a foreign corporation that breeds and races thoroughbred horses. FORecq ships a horse, Big Red, to race in the Kentucky Derby. Immediately after winning the Kentucky Derby, FORecq ships Big Red back to the foreign country. FORecq's entering a horse in a single race

---

[17] For example, *see* Article 15(3) (¶ 1304.15) of the U.S. Model Treaty.

[18] For example, *see* Article 16 (¶ 1304.16) of the U.S. Model Treaty.

[19] For example, *see* Article 19 (¶ 1304.19) of the U.S. Model Treaty.

[20] For example, *see* Article 20 (¶ 1304.20) of the U.S. Model Treaty.

¶1001.01

constitutes a U.S. trade or business under the non-treaty standard, and FORecq's winnings would be taxable under Code Sec. 882. However, if FORecq is a resident in a foreign country that has a tax treaty with the United States (similar to the U.S. Model Treaty), the purse is not subject to U.S. tax. FORecq would not be deemed to have a U.S. permanent establishment. If, however, FORecq kept Big Red in the United States to race in the Preakness Stakes and the Belmont Stakes, FORecq may then have a permanent establishment under the treaty standard, and its winnings would be subject to U.S. tax.[21]

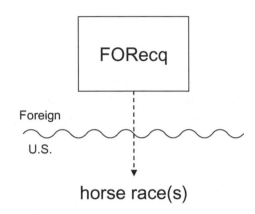

The activities of an independent salesperson typically do not result in either a U.S. trade or business or a permanent establishment for the foreign company principal.[22] However, the activities of dependent salespersons are treated differently, depending on the applicable standard.

   Example 10.5: FORco is a country F corporation that produces widgets. FORco employs a country F citizen and resident that spends three months a year traveling throughout the United States and soliciting widget purchase orders from U.S. customers. The sales employee has the customers sign a purchase order, and then forwards the purchase order to FORco's home office in country F for final approval. Under the non-treaty U.S. trade or business standard, the activities of the sales employee would constitute a trade or business of FORco in the United States. However, if foreign country F had a treaty with the United States similar to the U.S. Model Treaty, FORco would not be subject to U.S. taxes as FORco would not have a permanent establishment in the United States due to the sales employee's lack of final contracting authority.

---

[21] Rev. Rul. 58-63, 1958-1 CB 624; Rev. Rul. 60-249, 1960-2 CB 264.

[22] *Taisei Fire & Marine Ins. Co.*, 104 TC 535, Dec. 50,620. Acq. 1995-20 CB 1.

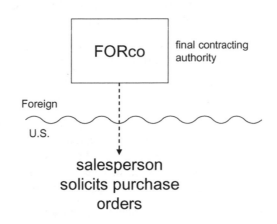

.02 Effectively Connected Income

Overview. A foreign corporation or nonresident alien individual engaged in a U.S. trade or business is subject to U.S. taxation on the income effectively connected with the conduct of that U.S. trade or business.[23] Effectively connected income includes the following five categories of income:

    (i)   certain types of U.S.-source income,[24]

    (ii)   certain types of foreign-source income attributable to a U.S. office,[25]

    (iii)   certain types of deferred income that is recognized in a year that the foreign person is not engaged in a U.S. trade or business, but which would have been effectively connected income if the recognition of the income had not been postponed,[26] and

    (iv)   income from an interest in U.S. real property that a passive foreign investor has elected to treat as effectively connected income.[27]

Categories (i), (ii), and (iii) are discussed in detail below and category (iv) is discussed in Chapter 9 (¶ 904).

U.S.-source income. Effectively connected income includes all of the U.S.-source income of a foreign corporation or nonresident alien individual engaged in a U.S. trade or business, other than U.S. source investment-type income, which ordinarily is subject to the 30% withholding tax.[28] Common examples of such income include income derived by a U.S. branch from the sale of inventory or from providing services.[29]

---

[23] Code Secs. 871(b) and 882(a).

[24] Code Sec. 864(c)(2) and (3).

[25] Code Sec. 864(c)(4).

[26] Code Sec. 864(c)(6) and (7).

[27] Code Secs. 871(d) and 882(d).

[28] Code Sec. 864(c)(3). Chapter 9 (¶ 902) discusses the types of U.S.-source income ordinarily subject to the 30% withholding tax.

[29] Whether the U.S.-source income is actually derived from the taxpayer's U.S. trade or business is irrelevant for this purpose. Reg. § 1.864-4(b). This is known as the force of attraction rule. However, tax treaty provisions regarding permanent establishments usually prohibit the United States from taxing a foreign person's business profits unless those profits are attributable to a permanent establishment. For example, see Article 7(1) (¶ 1304.07) of the U.S. Model Treaty.

U.S.-source dividends, interest, rents, and royalties also are included in effectively connected income if the item of income meets one of the following tests:

(i) *Assets-use test*—The income is derived from assets used in or held for use in, the conduct of the U.S. trade or business.

(ii) *Business-activities test*—The activities of the U.S. trade or business were a material factor in the realization of the income.[30]

Both tests are designed to include in effectively connected income any interest, dividends, rents, and royalties that are in substance business income. Examples include interest income derived from an account or note receivable arising from the trade or business, dividends and interest derived by a dealer in securities, and rents or royalties derived from an active leasing or licensing business.[31]

> *Example* **10.6:** FORco is a foreign corporation that has a U.S. office for purposes of investing in U.S. stocks and bonds. On occasion, those U.S. stocks may pay dividends and the U.S. bonds may pay interest. Because the activities of the U.S. office were a material factor in the realization of the income, that income would be considered effectively connected income to a U.S. trade or business and not fixed, determinable, annual or periodic income.

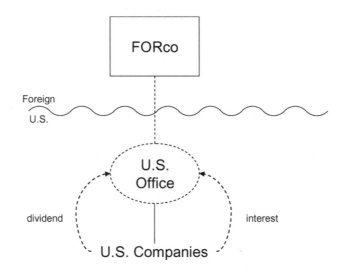

Foreign-source income attributable to a U.S. office. Effectively connected income generally includes only U.S.-source income.[32] However, certain types of foreign-source income are treated as effectively connected income if the foreign person maintains an office or other fixed base in the United States and the U.S. office is a material factor in producing the income and regularly carries on activities

---

[30] Code Sec. 864(c)(2). In determining whether an item of income satisfies either the asset-use and business-activities tests, due regard is given to how the asset or income is reflected in the foreign corporation's books and records. Code Sec. 864(c)(2) and Reg. § 1.864-4(c)(4).

[31] Reg. § 1.864-4(c)(2) and (c)(3). Special rules apply to foreign persons engaged in a banking, financing, or similar business within the United States. Reg. § 1.864-4(c)(5).

[32] Code Sec. 864(c)(4)(A).

of the type that produce such income.[33] This inclusion applies to the following types of foreign-source income:

(i) rents or royalties for the use of any patent, copyright, secret process or formula, goodwill, trademark, trade brand, franchise, or other like property derived from the active conduct of a U.S. trade or business,

(ii) dividend and interest income derived from the active conduct of a banking, financing, or similar business within the United States, or received by a corporation whose principal business is trading in stocks and securities for its own account, and

(iii) gains from the sale or exchange of inventory sold through the U.S. office or other fixed base of business, unless the inventory is sold for use, disposition, or consumption outside the United States and a foreign office materially participates in the sale.[34]

Example **10.7:** EURco is a company incorporated in a European country. EURco has a branch sales office in Chicago staffed with ten sales employees. EURco's Chicago branch purchases widgets in the United States for sales to customers. As the base for EURco's North American operations, EURco's Chicago branch sells widgets to customers in Canada with title passing in Canada. Although all the income from these sales to Canada are foreign source by virtue of the title-passage rules, these sales result in effectively connected income because EURco maintains an office in the United States that is a material factor in producing the income and regularly carries on sales activities that produce such income.

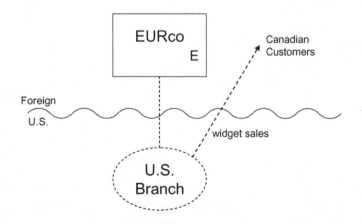

The categories of foreign-source income that are treated as effectively connected income also include economic equivalents of the aforementioned categories of foreign-source income.

---

[33] Code Sec. 864(c)(4)(B).

[34] Code Sec. 864(c)(4)(B). However, effectively connected income does not include any Subpart F income, or any dividend, interest, or royalty income derived from a foreign corporation in which the taxpayer owns directly, indirectly, or constructively more than 50% of the combined voting power of all voting stock. Code Sec. 864(c)(4)(D).

Example 10.8: EURco is a financial services company incorporated in a European country. EURco has a branch office in Chicago staffed with 10 employees. As the base for EURco's North American operations, EURco's Chicago branch accepts and confirms various letters of credit from businesses located in Canada, earning income equivalent to foreign-source interest. This income is equivalent to foreign-source interest that may be treated as effectively connected income. Consequently, the foreign-source interest income earned from accepting or confirming letters of credit is income effectively connected to EURco's U.S. trade or business.

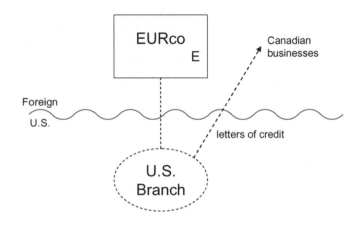

Look-back rules. Generally, only income recognized in the year that the foreign person is engaged in a U.S. trade or business is treated as effectively connected income.[35] However, there are two exceptions that are designed to prevent foreign persons from avoiding the effectively connected income taint by deferring income. Under the first exception, income that is recognized in one taxable year, but is attributable to a disposition of property or the performance of services in a prior taxable year, is treated as effectively connected income if the income would have been effectively connected income in the prior taxable year.[36] An example of such income is a deferred gain from an installment sale of business equipment in the last taxable year in which the foreign person was engaged in a U.S. trade or business. Under the second exception, a gain from the disposition of property that was withdrawn from a U.S. trade or business and is disposed of within 10 years after its withdrawal is treated as effectively connected income if that would have been the treatment had the disposition occurred immediately before the property was withdrawn from the U.S. trade or business.[37]

Example 10.9: EURco is a European media conglomerate that publishes a U.S. newspaper for European nationals living and working in the United States. To print the paper, EURco operates a printing press in the United States at its U.S. offices. EURco decides to terminate the U.S. newspaper and sells the

---

[35] Code Sec. 864(c)(1)(B).
[36] Code Sec. 864(c)(6).

[37] Code Sec. 864(c)(7).

printing press on an installment basis. In future years, even though EURco does not have a U.S. trade or business, EURco must pay U.S. tax on the portion of the installment sale proceeds representing gain because the printing press was sold while EURco had a U.S. trade or business.

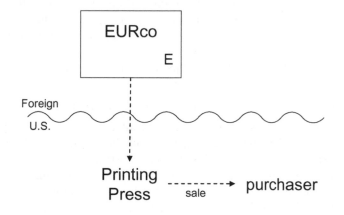

Example 10.10: The facts are the same as in Example 10.9, except that instead of terminating the U.S. newspaper, EURco decides to engage a contract printer to publish the paper and retire the printing press. Several years later, EURco sells the printing press. Even though the printing press is no longer an asset used in a U.S. trade or business, EURco must report effectively connected income from the gain on the sale of the printing press.

Allowable deductions. A foreign corporation or nonresident alien individual engaged in the conduct of a U.S. trade or business can claim the following deductions against its effectively connected gross income:

  (i) expenses, losses, and other deductions that are directly related to effectively connected gross income (e.g., cost of goods sold), as well as a ratable portion of any deductions that are not definitely related to any specific item of gross income (e.g., interest expense),[38]

  (ii) foreign income taxes imposed on either foreign-source effectively connected income or U.S.-source effectively connected income that is subject to foreign taxation by reason of the income's source rather than the taxpayer's citizenship, residence, or domicile,[39]

  (iii) charitable contributions made to U.S. charitable organizations,[40] and

  (iv) in the case of a nonresident alien individual, casualty and theft losses with respect to personal use property located within the United States, and a personal exemption deduction.[41]

---

[38] Reg. §§ 1.873-1(a)(1), 1.882-4(b)(1), and 1.861-8.

[39] Code Secs. 873(a) and 882(c)(1)(A), as modified by Code Sec. 906(b)(1).

[40] Code Secs. 873(b)(2) and 882(c)(1)(B).

[41] Reg. §1.873-1(b)(2)(ii) and (b)(3). Residents of Mexico or Canada may qualify for an additional exemption deduction.

¶1001.02

Special rules under Reg. § 1.882-5 govern the allocation of a foreign corporation's interest expense deduction against effectively connected gross income. Under these rules, the interest expense deduction is generally computed using a three-step process based on the value of the corporation's U.S. assets, its worldwide debt-to-assets ratio, and the liabilities recorded on the books of the U.S. business. These regulations are based on the principle that money is fungible. Therefore, a corporation that operates in two or more countries can artificially allocate borrowings and the related interest expense between the different countries. Consequently, Reg. § 1.882-5 adopts an objective, formulary approach, for computing interest expense deductions, as follows:

(i) Step one: compute the value of the foreign corporation's U.S. assets.

(ii) Step two: compute the total amount of the foreign corporation's U.S. connected liabilities. This is accomplished by multiplying the value of the foreign corporation's U.S. assets (determined in step one) by its worldwide debt-to-asset ratio for the year. The corporation's debt-to-asset ratio equals the total amount of the foreign corporation's worldwide liabilities divided by the total value of its worldwide assets. In lieu of determining its actual ratio, a foreign corporation may elect to use a fixed ratio of 50%, which is increased to 93% in the case of a corporation that is a bank.

(iii) Step three: compare the amount of the foreign corporation's U.S. connected liabilities (determined in step two) to its U.S. booked liabilities, the latter being those liabilities that are properly reflected on the books of the foreign corporation's U.S. trade or business. If the foreign corporation's U.S. booked liabilities exceed its U.S. connected liabilities, the foreign corporation's U.S. interest expense equals the interest accrued on U.S. booked liabilities multiplied by the ratio of U.S. connected liabilities to U.S. booked liabilities. On the other hand, if the foreign corporation's U.S. booked liabilities are less than its U.S. connected liabilities, then the foreign corporation is allowed to increase its interest expense deduction for interest on the excess amount of connected liabilities.[42]

Example 10.11: FORco is a foreign corporation that actively conducts a real estate business in the United States through a U.S. branch. FORco's balance sheet is as follows:

	Value	
U.S. parcel	$100,000	
Foreign parcel	$100,000	

	Amount	Interest Expense
Liability 1 (U.S.)	$40,000	$3,000
Liability 2 (foreign)	$20,000	$1,000

---

[42] Reg. § 1.882-5. In *National Westminster Bank, PLC v. U.S.*, CA-FC, 2008-1 USTC ¶ 50,140 512 F3d 1347, the court ruled that Article 7 of the U.S.-U.K. treaty overrides the formulary approach of Reg. § 1.882-5 insofar as the U.S. branch of a banking corporation is concerned.

¶1001.02

Liability 1 is a booked liability of the U.S. branch and Liability 2 is booked in FORco's home country, F.

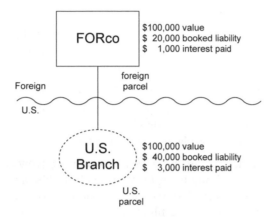

(i) Step One. The total value of U.S. assets is $100,000, the value of the U.S. parcel.

(ii) Step Two. The amount of FORco's U.S. connected liabilities is determined by multiplying $100,000 (the value of U.S. assets determined under Step One) by its debt-to-asset ratio. The debt-to-asset ratio is the amount of FORco's worldwide liabilities divided by the value of FORco's worldwide assets. Adding the two liabilities, the numerator is $60,000 (U.S. liability of $40,000 plus foreign liability of $20,000). The denominator comprises worldwide assets of $200,000 (U.S. parcel of $100,000 plus Foreign parcel of $100,000). The ratio, therefore, is 30% ($60,000 over $200,000), and the amount of U.S. connected liabilities is $30,000 ($100,000 of U.S. assets times 30%).

(iii) Step Three. Because FORco's U.S. booked liabilities ($40,000) exceed the U.S. connected liabilities ($30,000) determined in Step Two, FORco determines its branch's interest deduction by multiplying the interest expense on U.S. booked liabilities ($3,000) times the ratio of U.S. connected liabilities ($30,000) to U.S. booked liabilities ($40,000). As a result, the branch's interest deduction is reduced to $2,250 [$3,000 × ($30,000 ÷ $40,000)].

.03 Applicable Tax Rates

The progressive rate schedules applicable to U.S. persons also apply to the effectively connected income of foreign persons.[43] Therefore, the applicable rates range from 15% to 35% for foreign corporations[44] and 10% to 35% for nonresident alien individuals.[45] For nonresident aliens, the applicable schedules include those for single taxpayers, married individuals filing separately, and surviving spouses.[46]

---

[43] Code Secs. 871(b)(1) and 882(a)(1).
[44] Code Sec. 11.
[45] Code Sec. 1.
[46] Reg. § 1.1-1(a)(1).

Nonresident aliens generally cannot use the head of household or married filing jointly rate schedules.[47]

.04 Foreign Tax Credit

A foreign corporation or nonresident alien individual engaged in a U.S. trade or business can, in lieu of a deduction, claim a credit for any foreign income taxes imposed on the following two types of income:

    (i) foreign-source effectively connected income, and

    (ii) U.S.-source effectively connected income that is subject to foreign taxation by reason of the income's source rather than the taxpayer's citizenship, residence, or place of incorporation.[48]

The credit is allowable only against U.S. taxes on effectively connected income and cannot offset U.S. withholding taxes or the branch profits tax.[49] In addition, only the taxpayer's effectively connected income is taken into account for purposes of computing the foreign tax credit limitation.[50]

.05 Alternative Minimum Tax

The effectively connected income of a foreign corporation or nonresident alien individual is subject to the alternative minimum tax if the taxpayer's tentative minimum tax exceeds the regular tax for the year.[51] A corporate taxpayer's tentative minimum tax equals 20% (in the case of noncorporate taxpayers, a two-tiered rate schedule of 26% and 28% applies) of the taxpayer's alternative minimum taxable income less an exemption amount and is reduced by the alternative minimum foreign tax credit.[52] Alternative minimum taxable income equals a taxpayer's regular taxable income, determined with certain adjustments, and increased by the amount of the taxpayer's tax preferences.[53]

¶ 1002 BRANCH PROFITS TAX

.01 Introduction

Prior to the enactment of the branch profits tax in 1986, there was a substantial disparity between the tax treatment of earnings repatriations from U.S. branch and subsidiary operations. U.S. withholding taxes were imposed on dividend distributions from a U.S. subsidiary, but no shareholder-level U.S. tax was imposed on earnings remittances from a U.S. branch. Therefore, foreign corporations could potentially avoid the shareholder-level U.S. tax on their U.S.-source business profits merely by operating in the United States through a branch rather than a subsidiary.

    ***Example* 10.12:** FORco, a foreign corporation, owns 100% of USAco, a domestic corporation which derives all of its income from U.S. business operations. During its first year of operations, USAco has taxable income of $10 million, and distributes all of its after-tax earnings to FORco as a dividend.

---

[47] Code Secs. 2(b)(3)(A) and 6013(a)(1).

[48] Code Sec. 906(a) and (b)(1). A foreign corporation which receives a dividend from a 10%-or-more-owned foreign corporation also may qualify for a deemed paid foreign tax credit if the dividend income is effectively connected with the recipient's U.S. trade or business.

[49] Code Sec. 906(b)(3) and (7).

[50] Code Sec. 906(b)(2).

[51] Code Secs. 871(b)(1), 882(a)(1), and 55.

[52] Code Sec. 55(b)(1).

[53] Code Sec. 55(b)(2).

Assume the U.S. corporate tax rate is 35% and that the applicable treaty withholding rate for U.S.-source dividends is 5%.

USAco pays $3.5 million of U.S. income tax on its $10 million of taxable income and then distributes a dividend to FORco of $6.5 million [$10 million of taxable income – $3.5 million of U.S. income tax]. The dividend is subject to $325,000 of U.S. withholding tax [$6.5 million dividend × 5% withholding tax rate], which makes the total U.S. tax burden on USAco's repatriated earnings equal to $3,825,000 [$3.5 million of U.S. income tax + $325,000 of U.S. withholding tax].

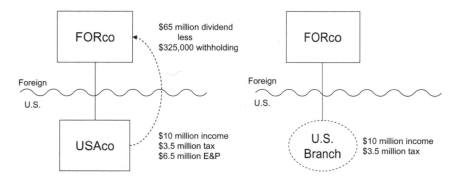

If FORco had structured its U.S. operation as a branch rather than as a subsidiary, it would still pay $3.5 million of U.S. income tax on its $10 million of income effectively connected with the U.S. branch operation. However, ignoring the branch profits tax, the repatriation of branch profits would be an internal fund transfer that would not be subject to U.S. withholding tax. Therefore, without a branch profits tax, FORco would avoid $325,000 of U.S. withholding taxes merely by operating in the United States through a branch rather than a subsidiary.

The branch profits tax better equates the tax treatment of U.S. branch and U.S. subsidiary operations by imposing a tax equal to 30% of a foreign corporation's dividend equivalent amount for the taxable year, subject to treaty reductions.[54] The dividend equivalent amount is an estimate of the amount of U.S. earnings and profits that a U.S. branch remits to its foreign home office during the year. Therefore, similar to the withholding tax imposed on a U.S. subsidiary's dividend distributions, the branch profits tax represents a second layer of U.S. taxes imposed on a foreign corporation's U.S.-source business profits (see Figure 10.1).

---

[54] Code Sec. 884(a).

Figure 10.1 Policy of the branch profits tax

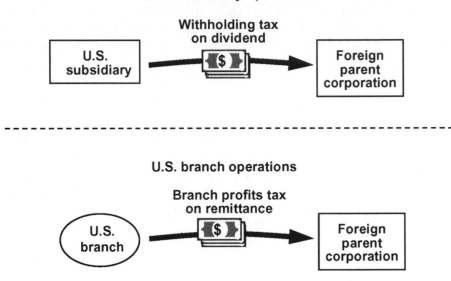

Example 10.13: The facts are the same as in Example 10.12, except now take into account the effects of the branch profits tax. If FORco had structured its U.S. operation as a branch rather than as a subsidiary, it would pay $3.5 million of U.S. income tax on its $10 million of effectively connected income [$10 million × 35% U.S. tax rate]. In addition, assuming the U.S. branch's dividend equivalent amount equals the branch's after-tax earnings of $6.5 million [$10 million of taxable income – $3.5 million of U.S. income taxes], FORco also would be subject to a branch profits tax of $325,000 [$6.5 million dividend equivalent amount × 5% tax rate]. Therefore, the branch profits tax creates a shareholder-level U.S. tax that is equivalent to the U.S. withholding tax imposed on dividends.

The branch profits tax is payable in the same manner as a foreign corporation's regular income tax (see discussion later in this chapter), except that no estimated tax payments are required with respect to the branch profits tax.[55]

.02 Dividend Equivalent Amount

The tax base for the branch profits tax is the dividend equivalent amount, which estimates the amount of U.S. earnings and profits that a branch remits to its foreign home office during the year. Such an estimate must take into account the earnings and profits generated by the U.S. branch during the year, as well as any changes in the branch's accumulated earnings and profits during the year. Consistent with this reasoning, a foreign corporation's dividend equivalent amount for a taxable year is computed using the following two-step procedure:[56]

---

[55] Reg. § 1.884-1(a).   [56] Code Sec. 884(b).

Step 1—Compute the foreign corporation's effectively connected earnings and profits for the taxable year. Effectively connected earnings and profits equals the earnings and profits attributable to income effectively connected with the foreign corporation's U.S. trade or business, before any reductions for dividend distributions, the branch profits tax, or the tax on excess interest.[57]

Step 2—Adjust the effectively connected earnings and profits amount for any changes in the foreign corporation's U.S. net equity during the year. The effectively connected earnings and profits amount from Step 1 is reduced by the amount of any increase in U.S. net equity for the year (but not below zero) and is increased by the amount of any reduction in U.S. net equity for the year.[58] In other words, an increase in U.S. net equity during the year is treated as a reinvestment of earnings and profits in the U.S. branch operation, whereas a reduction in U.S. net equity during the year is treated as a repatriation of earnings and profits, which is similar to a dividend.

Example 10.14: FORco, a foreign corporation, operates a branch sales office in the United States. During its first year of operations, FORco's effectively connected earnings and profits are $250,000 and its U.S. net equity is $500,000 at the beginning of the year and $750,000 at the end of the year. Therefore, FORco's dividend equivalent amount for year 1 is $0, computed as follows:

(A) *Effectively connected earnings and profits*		$250,000
(B) *Increase in U.S. net equity:*		
End of the year U.S. net equity	$750,000	
Beginning of the year U.S. net equity	–$500,000	
Increase in U.S. net equity		$250,000
Dividend equivalent amount [A – B]		None

---

[57] Code Sec. 884(d)(1) and Reg. § 1.884-1(f)(1). A corporation's earnings and profits equals its taxable income, plus or minus various adjustments designed to make earnings and profits a better measure of the corporation's economic income. Examples of common adjustments include federal income taxes, ADS depreciation (Code Sec. 312(k)), and the LIFO recapture amount (Code Sec. 312(n)(4)). Certain types of earnings and profits are excluded from effectively connected earnings and profits (*see* Code Sec. 884(d)(2)).

[58] Code Sec. 884(b). A positive adjustment for a reduction in U.S. net equity for the year cannot exceed an amount equal to the excess of the aggregate amount of effectively connected earnings and profits accumulated in taxable years beginning after December 31, 1986, over the aggregate amount of dividend equivalent amounts from prior taxable years. Code Sec. 884(b)(2)(B). This limitation prevents the taxation of returns of capital.

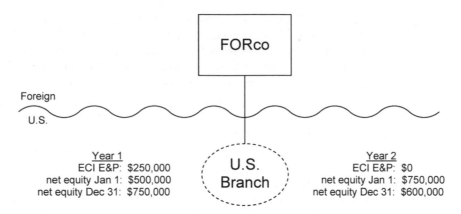

Year 1
ECI E&P: $250,000
net equity Jan 1: $500,000
net equity Dec 31: $750,000

U.S.
Branch

Year 2
ECI E&P: $0
net equity Jan 1: $750,000
net equity Dec 31: $600,000

During year 2, FORco has no effectively connected earnings and profits and its U.S. net equity is $750,000 at the beginning of the year and $600,000 at the end of the year. Therefore, FORco's dividend equivalent amount for year 2 is $150,000, computed as follows:

(A) *Effectively connected earnings and profits* . . . . $ 0

(B) *Decrease in U.S. net equity:*

Beginning of the year U.S. net equity	$750,000	
End of the year U.S. net equity	$600,000	
Decrease in U.S. net equity		$150,000

Dividend equivalent amount [A + B] $150,000

The determination of U.S. net equity is made as of the last day of the foreign corporation's taxable year.[59] U.S. net equity equals the aggregate amount of money and the adjusted basis of the property of the foreign corporation connected with the U.S. trade or business reduced (including below zero) by the amount of liabilities connected with the U.S. trade or business.[60] The amount of U.S.-connected liabilities is determined by applying the same formula used to determine a foreign corporation's interest expense deduction (discussed earlier in this chapter), except that the asset value and liability amounts are based on end of year totals rather than annual averages.[61] Roughly speaking, an asset is considered to be "connected" with a U.S. trade or business to the extent the income produced by the asset or a gain from the disposition of the asset is effectively connected income. Guidance is provided for applying this principle to specific types of assets, such as depreciable property, inventory, installment obligations, accounts receivable, bank deposits, and debt instruments.[62]

Finally, special rules apply to the computation of the branch profits tax for a taxable year in which a termination occurs. A termination includes the incorpora-

---

[59] Reg. § 1.884-1(c)(3).

[60] Code Sec. 884(c).

[61] Reg. §§ 1.884-1(e)(1) and 1.882-5. An election is available whereby the foreign corporation can reduce its

U.S.-connected liabilities by the excess of the formulary amount over a books and records amount. Reg. § 1.884-1(e)(3).

[62] Reg. § 1.884-1(c)(2) and (d).

tion of a branch, the repatriation of all branch assets, a sale of all branch assets, or the liquidation or reorganization of the foreign corporation. The policy behind these provisions is to mimic the tax consequences that the foreign corporation would experience if it had structured its U.S. operations as a subsidiary rather than as a branch.[63]

.03 Treaty Reductions and Exemptions

Some tax treaties provide a specific exemption or rate reduction for the branch profits tax.[64] If the applicable treaty does not provide a specific exemption or rate reduction, the treaty rate for the branch profits tax is the rate that applies to dividends paid to the foreign corporation by a wholly owned domestic corporation.[65]

.04 Taxes on Branch Interest

Branch interest withholding tax. The rationale for the branch profits tax is to place U.S. branch and subsidiary operations on a tax parity. The branch interest withholding tax is designed to further this objective. Under the branch interest withholding tax, any interest paid by a foreign corporation's U.S. branch is treated as if it were paid by a domestic corporation.[66] The effect of this rule is to recharacterize the interest payment as U.S.-source income and thereby subject any interest received by a foreign person from a U.S. branch to the 30% withholding tax which ordinarily applies to U.S.-source interest income.[67] Generally speaking, interest is considered to be "paid by" a U.S. branch if either the underlying liability is designated by the taxpayer as a branch liability or the liability has a particular connection with the branch operation. Examples include a liability that is reflected in the books and records of the U.S. trade or business, a liability secured predominantly by a U.S. asset, or a liability specifically identified by the taxpayer as a liability of the U.S. trade or business.[68]

The branch interest withholding tax is not imposed on interest that qualifies for one of the following withholding tax exemptions (each of which is discussed in Chapter 9 (¶ 902)):[69]

(i) the portfolio interest exemption,[70]

(ii) the exemption for interest paid on a U.S. bank deposit,[71] or

(iii) the exemption for interest income that is effectively connected with the conduct of a U.S. trade or business.[72]

In addition, if the applicable tax treaty provides an exemption or reduced withholding rate for interest income, that treaty relief can be taken into account if the taxpayer satisfies certain requirements.[73]

---

[63] Reg. § 1.884-2 and Temp Reg. § 1.884-2T.

[64] Code Sec. 884(e)(2) and Reg. § 1.884-1(g)(1) and (g)(2). Typically, the reduction is found in the dividend article of a treaty, see, for example, Article 10(8) (¶ 1304.10) of the U.S. Model Treaty.

[65] Code Sec. 884(3)(2)(A)(ii) and Reg. § 1.884-1(g)(4)(i)(A).

[66] Code Sec. 884(f)(1)(A).

[67] Reg. § 1.884-4(a)(1). Unlike the branch profits tax, the branch interest withholding tax is borne by the for-

eign person receiving the interest income, not the foreign corporation making the interest payment.

[68] Reg. § 1.884-4(b).

[69] Reg. § 1.884-4(a)(1).

[70] Code Secs. 871(h) and 881(c).

[71] Code Secs. 871(i)(2)(A) and 881(d).

[72] Code Sec. 1441(c)(1).

[73] Code Sec. 884(f)(3) and Reg. § 1.884-4(b)(8).

Example **10.15:** FORco is a foreign corporation that actively conducts a real estate business through a U.S. branch. The amount of interest expense booked by the U.S. branch and paid to a foreign person is $3,000. However, as determined in Example 10.11, the amount of the interest deduction, pursuant to Reg. § 1.882-5 is reduced to $2,250. The entire amount of interest paid of $3,000 is subject to the branch interest withholding tax.

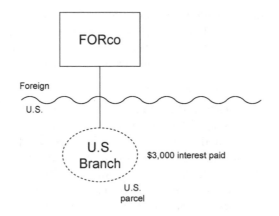

Tax on excess interest. In addition to the branch interest withholding tax, the branch profits tax regime also imposes a tax on excess interest. The idea behind the excess interest tax is that any interest expense that is deductible against the branch's U.S. taxable income also should give rise to an income inclusion, which is analogous to what happens when a U.S. subsidiary corporation makes an interest payment. A foreign corporation's excess interest equals the excess of:

(i) the amount of interest expense that is deducted against the foreign corporation's effectively connected income, over

(ii) the amount of interest deemed paid by the foreign corporation for purposes of the branch interest withholding tax.

Under this provision, on the last day of the foreign corporation's taxable year, the foreign corporation is deemed to have received a payment of interest from a wholly-owned domestic corporation equal to the foreign corporation's excess interest.[74] The effect of this provision is to subject the foreign corporation's excess interest to the 30% withholding tax that ordinarily applies to U.S.-source interest income.[75] However, if a tax treaty with the country of which the foreign corporation is a resident exempts or reduces the withholding rate for interest income, that treaty relief may be taken into account.[76] In all cases, the tax due on excess interest must be reported on the foreign corporation's income tax return and estimated tax payments are required.[77]

---

[74] Code Sec. 884(f)(1)(B) and Reg. § 1.884-4(a)(2). A special exemption applies to interest on deposits with U.S. branches of foreign banks.

[75] Unlike the branch interest withholding tax, the tax on excess interest is borne by the foreign corporation operating the U.S. branch.

[76] Reg. § 1.884-4(c)(3)(i).

[77] Reg. § 1.884-4(a)(2)(iv).

***Example* 10.16:** [78] FORco, a foreign manufacturer of industrial equipment, has a branch sales office in the United States. During the current year, FORco apportions $120,000 of interest expense under Reg. § 1.882-5 against the branch's effectively connected gross income. However, only $100,000 of this amount is considered to be paid by FORco's U.S. branch as a U.S. debt on its books and records for purposes of the branch interest withholding tax. Therefore, FORco has excess interest of $20,000 [$120,000 − $100,000]. FORco's tax on this excess interest is $6,000 [$20,000 of excess interest × 30% statutory withholding rate], assuming a tax treaty does not reduce the withholding rate for interest.

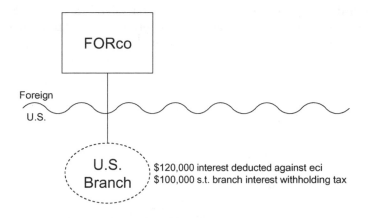

¶ 1003 ANTI-EARNINGS STRIPPING PROVISIONS

.01 What Is Earnings Stripping?

Determining the most tax-efficient way for a foreign parent corporation to repatriate profits from a U.S. subsidiary requires an analysis of both subsidiary-level and parent-level U.S. taxes. At the subsidiary level, the U.S. subsidiary's total taxable income is subject to U.S. taxation at the regular graduated rates. At the foreign parent corporation level, any earnings that are repatriated through a dividend distribution are subject to U.S. withholding taxes at either the 30% statutory rate or a reduced treaty rate. Therefore, the total U.S. tax burden on the earnings of a U.S. subsidiary that are repatriated through a dividend distribution equals the sum of the subsidiary-level corporate income tax and the shareholder-level withholding tax. In contrast to a dividend distribution, repatriating a U.S. subsidiary's earnings through interest payments raises the possibility of both a deduction at the subsidiary level and a lower treaty withholding tax rate at the shareholder level. Therefore, by "stripping" the earnings of a U.S. subsidiary through intercompany interest payments, a foreign parent may be able to reduce or eliminate both levels of U.S. taxation.

---

[78] Compare Reg. § 1.884-4(a)(4), Example 1.

Example 10.17: FORco, a foreign corporation, owns 100% of USAco, a U.S. corporation that derives all of its income from U.S. business operations. During its first year of operations, USAco has taxable income of $10 million. Assume the U.S. corporate tax rate is 35% and that the applicable treaty withholding rate is 5% for dividends and 0% for interest.

Case 1—Repatriate earnings through dividend distribution: Given the 35% U.S. tax rate, USAco pays $3.5 million of U.S. tax on its $10 million of taxable income. As a consequence, if FORco repatriates all of USAco's after-tax earnings through a dividend, FORco would receive a $6.5 million dividend ($10 million of pre-tax earnings – $3.5 million of corporate income tax) and would incur $325,000 of U.S. withholding tax ($6.5 million dividend × 5% treaty withholding rate). Therefore, the total effective U.S. tax on USAco's repatriated profits is 38.25% [($3.5 million of corporate income tax + $325,000 of withholding tax) ÷ $10 million of taxable income].

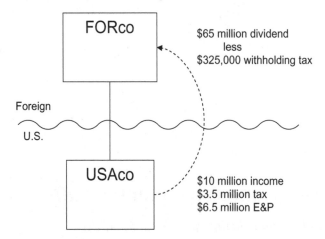

Case 2—Repatriate earnings through interest payments: Now assume that FORco has a bona-fide creditor interest in USAco such that USAco makes annual interest payments of $10 million to FORco. Ignoring the anti-earnings stripping provisions, the $10 million of interest expense would reduce USAco's net taxable income and U.S. tax liability to $0. In addition, FORco is not subject to U.S. withholding taxes on the interest payments because of the treaty exemption. As a consequence, by repatriating USAco's earnings through interest payments rather than a dividend distribution, FORco is able to reduce the total effective U.S. tax rate on USAco's repatriated earning from 38.25% to 0%.

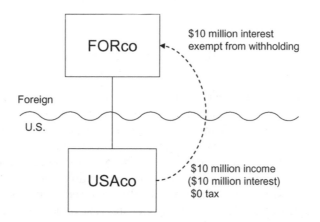

Foreign parent corporations engaging in earnings stripping must ensure that any intercompany payments meant to be interest qualify as such under U.S. tax laws. Historically, the IRS's only alternatives for attacking earnings stripping schemes were to attempt to recharacterize a portion of the U.S. subsidiary's intercompany debt as disguised equity or to argue that the amount of interest paid on the intercompany debt did not represent an arm's-length charge. During the 1980s, Congress became concerned that U.S. tax collections from foreign corporations were not keeping pace with the growth in their U.S. business activities and attributed part of this shortfall to the use of excessive debt by foreign multinationals to finance their U.S. subsidiaries. As a consequence, in 1989 Congress enacted the anti-earnings stripping provisions to attack these schemes.

Before discussing the details of the anti-earnings stripping provisions, it is important to restate a core principle of international tax planning, which is that both U.S. and foreign tax consequences must be considered when analyzing any cross-border transaction. This section considers the efficiency of methods for a foreign parent corporation to repatriate profits from a U.S. subsidiary. Interest payments received by a foreign parent corporation from a U.S. subsidiary are generally subject to taxation in a foreign parent's home country. However, some countries do not tax dividends that its local parent company receives from an operating subsidiary located in another country. Therefore, although interest payments may be the optimal approach for minimizing U.S. taxes, in the case of parent corporations based in selected foreign countries, these U.S. tax savings may be offset by higher foreign taxes.

.02 Calculating the Non-Deductible Interest

The purpose of the Section 163(j) anti-earnings stripping provisions is to limit a U.S. corporation's deductions for interest payments to related foreign lenders whose interest income is exempt from U.S. withholding tax. The calculation of the non-deductible interest requires the following multifaceted analysis:

¶1003.02

(i) The debt-to-equity ratio of the U.S. corporation must exceed 1.5 to 1.[79] The U.S. corporation computes this ratio by comparing the cost basis of the total liabilities to the total assets, less the liabilities.[80]

(ii) The U.S. corporation must have a net interest expense, which is the amount by which its interest expense exceeds its interest income.[81]

(iii) The U.S. corporation must have an excess interest expense, which equals the excess of the U.S. corporation's net interest expense (step (ii)) over 50% of the U.S. corporation's adjusted taxable income.[82] Adjusted taxable income equals a U.S. corporation's taxable income with numerous adjustments designed to produce a better measure of the U.S. corporation's net cash flow from operations before interest income or interest expense. Examples of the required adjustments include adding back to taxable income any net interest expense, net operating losses, depreciation, amortization, and depletion.[83]

(iv) The U.S. corporation must pay or accrue interest to a related person (or its guarantor) who does not pay U.S. tax on the interest income.[84] More specifically, these payments include the following two types of interest:

- *Related-person debt*—Interest paid or accrued by a corporation (directly or indirectly) to a related person that is not subject to U.S. withholding tax.

- *Guaranteed debt*—Interest paid or accrued by the taxpayer to an unrelated person, if a related foreign person or a related tax-exempt entity guarantees the debt, that is not subject to U.S. withholding tax.[85]

For purposes of both related person debt and guaranteed debt, interest that is subject to a reduced rate of U.S. withholding tax under a tax treaty is treated as interest not subject to U.S. tax in proportion to the amount of the treaty reduction. For example, if the statutory withholding rate is 30% and the treaty withholding rate is 10%, then two-thirds of the interest is treated as interest not subject to U.S. tax.[86]

(v) Interest expense is disallowed to the extent of the lower of either excess interest expense (iii) or payments of interest to related parties that do not pay U.S. withholding tax on the interest income (iv).

---

[79] Code Sec. 163(j)(2)(A)(ii). Members of an affiliated group are generally treated as a single corporation. Prop. Reg. § 1.163(j)-5.

[80] Code Sec. 163(j)(2)(C).

[81] Code Sec. 163(j)(6)(B).

[82] Code Sec. 163(j)(2)(B)(i) and (j)(6)(B).

[83] Code Sec. 163(j)(6)(A). Prop. Reg. § 1.163(j)-2(f) lists 21 adjustments.

[84] Code Sec. 163(j)(3)(A). A related person includes any lender that owns more than 50% of the corporate debtor. Code Secs. 163(j)(4) and 267(b). The term of art for the amount in this step is "disqualified interest."

However, the authors have chosen not to use this term of art as the term suggests that the step (iv) amount is not deductible when the non-deductible amount is determined in step (v).

[85] Code Secs. 163(j)(3)(B) and (j)(6)(D)(i). Exceptions apply (i) if the corporation paying the interest owns a controlling interest in the guarantor, or (ii) in any circumstances identified by regulations, where the interest would have been subject to net-basis U.S. taxation if the interest had been paid to the guarantor. Code Sec. 163(j)(6)(D)(ii).

[86] Code Sec. 163(j)(5)(B) and Prop. Reg. § 1.163(j)-4(b).

¶1003.02

Any disallowed interest deductions may be carried forward indefinitely and deducted in a year that the taxpayer has an excess limitation.[87] A taxpayer has an excess limitation in any year that its net interest expense is less than 50% of its adjusted taxable income.[88] In addition, an excess limitation in one year can be carried forward 3 years and used to reduce excess interest expense in a carryforward year.[89]

Example **10.18:** FORco, a foreign corporation, owns 100% of USAco, a domestic corporation that derives all of its income from U.S. business operations. FORco also has a creditor interest in USAco, such that USAco's debt to equity ratio is 2 to 1 and USAco makes annual interest payments of $20 million to FORco. The results from USAco's first year of operations are as follows:

Gross profit . . . . $60 million

Interest income . . . . $ 2 million

Interest expense (paid to FORco) . . . . ($20 million)

Depreciation expense . . . . ($10 million)

Other operating expenses . . . . ($27 million)

Pre-tax income . . . . $ 5 million

Assume the U.S. corporate tax rate is 35% and that the applicable treaty exempts interest income from withholding tax.

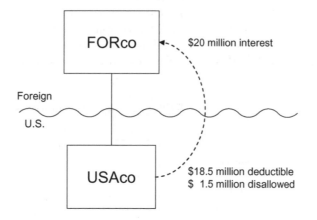

An analysis of the deductibility of interest is as follows:

(i) USAco's debt to equity ratio is 2 to 1, which exceeds 1.5 to 1.

(ii) USAco has a net interest expense of $18 million ($2 million of interest income less $20 million of interest expense).

(iii) USAco's excess interest expense equals its net interest expense of $18 million less 50% of its adjusted taxable income of $33 million ($5 million of pre-tax income + $18 million. of net interest expense + $10

---

[87] Code Sec. 163 (j) (1) (B).   [89] Code Sec. 163 (j) (2) (B) (i) and. (ii).

[88] Code Sec. 163 (j) (2) (B) (iii).

million of depreciation). Therefore, the excess interest expense is $1.5 million [$18 million – (50% × $33 million)].

(iv) The entire amount of interest expense of $20 million is paid to a related party (FORco) that does not pay U.S. withholding tax on the interest income due to the treaty exemption.

(v) The disallowed interest deduction is $1.5 million, which is the lesser of excess interest expense ($1.5 million from (iii)) or the $20 million of interest paid to parties that do not pay U.S. tax on the interest ((iv)). Thus, only $18.5 million of the interest is deductible by USAco. The $1.5 million of disallowed interest can be carried forward and deducted in a year that USAco has an excess limitation.

.03 Timing Restriction on Deductions of U.S. Subsidiaries

Prior to the enactment of Section 267(a)(3), an accrual-basis U.S. subsidiary could deduct an accrued expense for an amount owed to its cash-basis foreign parent, but the foreign parent did not include the amount in income until the subsidiary actually made the payment. Section 267(a)(3) postpones the deduction until the amount due to a related foreign person is actually paid.[90]

> **Example 10.19:** USAco is a U.S. subsidiary of FORco, a country F corporation. USAco is an accrual-basis taxpayer while FORco is a cash-basis taxpayer. In 20Y1, FORco makes a loan to USAco. On December 31, 20Y1, USAco accrues $1 million of interest expense, but USAco does not make the $1 million payment to FORco until 20Y2. Despite being an accrual-basis taxpayer, USAco may not deduct the $1 million of interest expense until 20Y2, which is the year in which FORco recognizes the $1 million of interest income.[91]

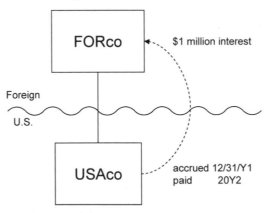

¶ 1004 RETURNS AND PAYMENT OF TAX

A foreign corporation that is engaged in a U.S. trade or business at any time during a taxable year must file Form 1120-F, U.S. Income Tax Return of a Foreign Corporation. This requirement applies even if the foreign corporation has no

---

[90] Reg. § 1.267(a)-3.

[91] Reg. § 1.267(a)-3, and *Tate & Lyle, Inc.*, CA-3, 96-2 USTC ¶ 50,340, 87 F3d 99 (3rd Cir. 1996).

effectively connected income, has no U.S.-source income, or all of the corporation's income is exempt from U.S. tax by reason of a treaty provision.[92] A foreign corporation which is not engaged in a U.S. trade or business but that has income subject to U.S. withholding taxes must also file Form 1120-F, unless its liability for the year is fully satisfied by the withholding tax.[93] (A sample of a completed Form 1120-F is included in the Appendix to this chapter.[94]) A foreign corporation engaged in a U.S. trade or business must make quarterly estimated tax payments of its tax liability.[95] However, no estimated tax payments are required with respect to the branch profits tax.[96]

A nonresident alien individual who is engaged in a U.S. trade or business must file Form 1040NR, U.S. Nonresident Alien Income Tax Return. This requirement applies even if the nonresident alien has no effectively connected income, has no U.S.-source income, or all of its income is exempt from U.S. tax by reason of a treaty provision.[97] A nonresident alien who is not engaged in a U.S. trade or business, but who has income that is subject to U.S. withholding taxes, must also file Form 1040NR, unless his or her liability for the year is fully satisfied by the withholding tax.[98] (A sample of a completed Form 1040NR is included in the Appendix to this chapter.[99]) A nonresident alien whose tax exceeds the amount of any withholding must make estimated tax payments.[100]

Any partnership engaged in a U.S. trade or business, or that has income from U.S. sources, is required to file Form 1065, U.S. Partnership Return of Income, which is an informational return.[101] As discussed in Chapter 9 (¶ 902), the partnership must also withhold on a foreign partner's distributive share of effectively connected income. The partnership must file a Form 8804 (Annual Return For Partnership Withholding Tax), Form 8805 (Foreign Partner's Information Statement), and a Form 8813 (Partnership Withholding Tax Payment). A partnership that is not engaged in a U.S. trade or business and has no U.S.-source income need not file either a Form 1065 or any other type of partnership return.[102]

---

[92] Reg. § 1.6012-2(g)(1)(i). A foreign corporation must timely file a true and accurate Form 1120-F in order to claim a deduction or credit. Reg. § 1.882-4(a)(2). For an example, *see InverWorld Inc.,* 71 TCM 3231, Dec. 51,428(M), TC Memo. 1996-301; *Swallows Holding, Ltd. v. United States,* 515 F.3d 162 (3d Cir. 2008), rev'g 126 TC 96, Dec. 56,417 (2006).

[93] Reg. § 1.6012-2(g)(2).

[94] Form 1120-F is due by the 15th day of the third month following the close of the taxable year if the foreign corporation has a U.S. office, and by the 15th day of the sixth month following the close of the taxable year if the foreign corporation does not have a U.S. office. Reg. § 1.6072-2(a) and (b). However, a foreign corporation can obtain a six-month extension of time for filing Form 1120-F. Reg. § 1.6081-3(a).

[95] Code Sec. 6655.

[96] Reg. § 1.884-1(a).

[97] Reg. § 1.6012-1(b)(1)(i). A nonresident alien individual must timely file a true and accurate Form 1040NR in order to claim a deduction or credit. Reg. § 1.874-1(a).

[98] Reg. § 1.6012-1(b)(2).

[99] Form 1040NR is due by the 15th day of the sixth month following the close of the taxable year, unless the income includes wages subject to withholding, in which case the return is due by the 15th day of the fourth month following the close of the taxable year. Reg. § 1.6072-1(c). A nonresident alien can obtain a six-month extension of time for filing Form 1040NR. Reg. § 1.6081-4(a).

[100] Code Sec. 6654.

[101] Reg. § 1.6031-1(c). Form 1065 generally is due by the 15th day of the fourth month after the close of the partnership's taxable year. Reg. § 1.6031-1(e)(2).

[102] Reg. § 1.6031-1(d)(1).

¶ 1005 APPENDIX

Louis LeBeau is a French national who is a technical consultant on movies produced at Hollywood Studio Company, where LeBeau was provided an office. For his consulting services performed in the United States, Lebeau earns $100,000 during the taxable year. Lebeau is single and is entitled to one exemption. He must file a Form 1040NR as attached.

Form **1040NR**	**U.S. Nonresident Alien Income Tax Return**	OMB No. 1545-0074
Department of the Treasury Internal Revenue Service	For the year January 1–December 31, 2010, or other tax year beginning _____ , 2010, and ending _____ , 20 ___	20**10**

Please print or type.	Your first name and initial Louis	Last name Labeau	Identifying number (see instructions)	
	Present home address (number, street, and apt. no., or rural route). If you have a P.O. box, see instructions.		Check if: ☑ Individual ☐ Estate or Trust	
	City, town or post office, state, and ZIP code. If you have a foreign address, see instructions. Paris			
	Country ▶ France			

Filing Status

Check only one box.

1 ☐ Single resident of Canada or Mexico or single U.S. national   4 ☐ Married resident of South Korea
2 ☑ Other single nonresident alien   5 ☐ Other married nonresident alien
3 ☐ Married resident of Canada or Mexico or married U.S. national   6 ☐ Qualifying widow(er) with dependent child (see instructions)

If you checked box 3 or 4 above, enter the information below.

(i) Spouse's first name and initial	(ii) Spouse's last name	(iii) Spouse's identifying number

Exemptions

7a ☑ **Yourself.** If someone can claim you as a dependent, **do not** check box 7a . . . . . } Boxes checked on 7a and 7b   **1**

b ☐ **Spouse.** Check box 7b only if you checked box 3 or 4 above **and** your spouse **did not** have any U.S. gross income . . . .

If more than four dependents, see instructions.

c **Dependents:** (see instructions)

(1) First name Last name	(2) Dependent's identifying number	(3) Dependent's relationship to you	(4) ✔ if qualifying child for child tax credit (see page 9)
			☐
			☐
			☐
			☐

No. of children on 7c who:
• lived with you
• did not live with you due to divorce or separation
Dependents on 7c not entered above

d Total number of exemptions claimed . . . .   Add numbers on lines above ▶ | **1** |

Income Effectively Connected With U.S. Trade/Business

Attach Form(s) W-2, 1042-S, SSA-1042S, RRB-1042S, and 8288-A here. Also attach Form(s) 1099-R if tax was withheld.

Enclose, but do not attach, any payment.

8	Wages, salaries, tips, etc. Attach Form(s) W-2	8	100,000	00
9a	**Taxable** interest.	9a		
b	**Tax-exempt** interest. **Do not** include on line 9a . . . 9b _____			
10a	Ordinary dividends	10a		
b	Qualified dividends (see instructions) . . . . . 10b _____			
11	Taxable refunds, credits, or offsets of state and local income taxes (see instructions).	11		
12	Scholarship and fellowship grants. Attach Form(s) 1042-S or required statement (see instructions)	12		
13	Business income or (loss). Attach Schedule C or C-EZ (Form 1040)	13		
14	Capital gain or (loss). Attach Schedule D (Form 1040) if required. If not required, check here ☐	14		
15	Other gains or (losses). Attach Form 4797	15		
16a	IRA distributions. . . . 16a _____ 16b Taxable amount (see instructions)	16b		
17a	Pensions and annuities 17a _____ 17b Taxable amount (see instructions)	17b		
18	Rental real estate, royalties, partnerships, trusts, etc. Attach Schedule E (Form 1040)	18		
19	Farm income or (loss). Attach Schedule F (Form 1040)	19		
20	Unemployment compensation	20		
21	Other income. List type and amount (see instructions) _____	21		
22	Total income exempt by a treaty from page 5, Schedule OI, Item L (1)(e) . 22 _____			
23	Combine the amounts in the far right column for lines 8 through 21. This is your **total effectively connected income** . . . . ▶	23	100,000	00

Adjusted Gross Income

24	Educator expenses (see instructions) . . . . 24 ____			
25	Health savings account deduction. Attach Form 8889 . 25 ____			
26	Moving expenses. Attach Form 3903 . . . . 26 ____			
27	One-half of self-employment tax. Attach Schedule SE (Form 1040) 27 ____			
28	Self-employed SEP, SIMPLE, and qualified plans . . . 28 ____			
29	Self-employed health insurance deduction (see instructions) 29 ____			
30	Penalty on early withdrawal of savings . . . . . . 30 ____			
31	Scholarship and fellowship grants excluded . . . . . 31 ____			
32	IRA deduction (see instructions). . . . . 32 ____			
33	Student loan interest deduction (see instructions) . . . 33 ____			
34	Domestic production activities deduction. Attach Form 8903 . 34 ____			
35	Add lines 24 through 34	35		
36	Subtract line 35 from line 23. This is your **adjusted gross income** . . . . . ▶	36	100,000	00

For Disclosure, Privacy Act, and Paperwork Reduction Act Notice, see instructions.   Cat. No. 11364D   Form **1040NR** (2010)

¶**1005**

Form 1040NR (2010)   Page **2**

Tax and Credits	37	Amount from line 36 (adjusted gross income)	37	100,000 00
	38	**Itemized deductions** from page 3, Schedule A, line 17	38	
	39	Subtract line 38 from line 37	39	100,000 00
	40	Exemptions (see instructions)	40	3,500 00
	41	**Taxable income.** Subtract line 40 from line 39. If line 40 is more than line 39, enter -0-	41	96,500 00
	42	**Tax** (see instructions). Check if any tax is from: **a** ☐ Form(s) 8814 **b** ☐ Form 4972	42	20,865 00
	43	**Alternative minimum tax** (see instructions). Attach Form 6251	43	
	44	Add lines 42 and 43 . . . . ▶	44	20,865 00
	45	Foreign tax credit. Attach Form 1116 if required . . .	45		
	46	Credit for child and dependent care expenses. Attach Form 2441	46		
	47	Retirement savings contributions credit. Attach Form 8880	47		
	48	Child tax credit (see instructions) . . . . . . ▶	48		
	49	Residential energy credits. Attach Form 5695	49		
	50	Other credits from Form: **a** ☐ 3800 **b** ☐ 8801 **c** ☐ ____	50		
	51	Add lines 45 through 50. These are your **total credits**	51	
	52	Subtract line 51 from line 44. If line 51 is more than line 44, enter -0-. . . . . ▶	52	20,865 00
Other Taxes	53	Tax on income not effectively connected with a U.S. trade or business from page 4, Schedule NEC, line 15	53	
	54	Self-employment tax. Attach Schedule SE (Form 1040)	54	
	55	Unreported social security and Medicare tax from Form: **a** ☐ 4137 **b** ☐ 8919	55	
	56	Additional tax on IRAs, other qualified retirement plans, etc. Attach Form 5329 if required	56	
	57	Transportation tax (see instructions)	57	
	58	**a** ☐ Schedule H (Form 1040) **b** ☐ Form 5405, line 16	58	
	59	Add lines 52 through 58. This is your **total tax** . . . . ▶	59	20,865 00
Payments	60	Federal income tax withheld from:		
		a Form(s) W-2 or 1099	60a	20,865 00	
		b Form(s) 8805	60b		
		c Form(s) 8288-A	60c		
		d Form(s) 1042-S	60d		
	61	2010 estimated tax payments and amount applied from 2009 return	61		
	62	Additional child tax credit. Attach Form 8812	62		
	63	Amount paid with request for extension to file (see instructions)	63		
	64	Excess social security and tier 1 RRTA tax withheld (see instructions)	64		
	65	Credit for federal tax paid on fuels. Attach Form 4136 . . .	65		
	66	Credits from Form: **a** ☐ 2439 **b** ☐ 8839 **c** ☐ 8801 **d** ☐ 8885	66		
	67	Credit for amount paid with Form 1040-C	67		
	68	Add lines 60a through 67. These are your **total payments** . . . . ▶	68	20,865 00
Refund Direct deposit? See instructions.	69	If line 68 is more than line 59, subtract line 59 from line 68. This is the amount you **overpaid**	69	
	70a	Amount of line 69 you want **refunded to you.** If Form 8888 is attached, check here . ▶ ☐	70a	
		b Routing number ☐☐☐☐☐☐☐☐☐ ▶ **c** Type: ☐ Checking ☐ Savings		
		d Account number ☐☐☐☐☐☐☐☐☐☐☐☐☐☐☐☐☐		
		e If you want your refund check mailed to an address outside the United States not shown on page 1, enter it here.		

	71	Amount of line 69 you want **applied to your 2011 estimated tax** . ▶	71	
Amount You Owe	72	**Amount you owe.** Subtract line 68 from line 59. For details on how to pay, see instructions ▶	72	
	73	Estimated tax penalty (see instructions)	73	

Third Party Designee	Do you want to allow another person to discuss this return with the IRS (see instructions)? ☐ **Yes.** Complete below. ☐ **No** Designee's name ▶ Phone no. ▶ Personal identification number (PIN) ▶ ☐☐☐☐☐
Sign Here Keep a copy of this return for your records.	Under penalties of perjury, I declare that I have examined this return and accompanying schedules and statements, and to the best of my knowledge and belief, they are true, correct, and complete. Declaration of preparer (other than taxpayer) is based on all information of which preparer has any knowledge. ▶ Your signature Date Your occupation in the United States
Paid Preparer Use Only	Print/Type preparer's name Preparer's signature Date Check ☐ if self-employed PTIN Firm's name ▶ Firm's EIN ▶ Firm's address ▶ Phone no.

Form **1040NR** (2010)

¶1005

Schedule A—Itemized Deductions (See instructions.)   07

State and Local Income Taxes	1	State income taxes	**1**	
	2	Local income taxes	**2**	
	3	Add lines 1 and 2	**3**	
Gifts to U.S. Charities		**Caution:** *If you made a gift and received a benefit in return, see instructions.*		
	4	Gifts by cash or check. If you made any gift of $250 or more, see instructions	**4**	
	5	Other than by cash or check. If you made any gift of $250 or more, see instructions. You **must** attach Form 8283 if the amount of your deduction is over $500	**5**	
	6	Carryover from prior year	**6**	
	7	Add lines 4 through 6	**7**	
Casualty and Theft Losses	8	Casualty or theft loss(es). Attach Form 4684. See instructions	**8**	
Job Expenses and Certain Miscellaneous Deductions	9	Unreimbursed employee expenses—job travel, union dues, job education, etc. You **must** attach Form 2106 or Form 2106-EZ if required. See instructions ▶	**9**	
	10	Tax preparation fees	**10**	
	11	Other expenses. See instructions for expenses to deduct here. List type and amount ▶	**11**	
	12	Add lines 9 through 11	**12**	
	13	Enter the amount from Form 1040NR, line 37 **13**		
	14	Multiply line 13 by 2% (.02)	**14**	
	15	Subtract line 14 from line 12. If line 14 is more than line 12, enter -0-	**15**	
Other Miscellaneous Deductions	16	Other—see instructions for expenses to deduct here. List type and amount ▶	**16**	
Total Itemized Deductions	17	Add the amounts in the far right column for lines 3 through 16. Also enter this amount on Form 1040NR, line 38.	**17**	

Form **1040NR** (2010)

¶1005

Form 1040NR (2010)

Page **4**

Schedule NEC—Tax on Income Not Effectively Connected With a U.S. Trade or Business (see instructions)

Enter amount of income under the appropriate rate of tax (see instructions)

Nature of income		(a) 10%	(b) 15%	(c) 30%	(d) Other (specify) %	Other (specify) %
1 Dividends paid by:						
a U.S. corporations	1a					
b Foreign corporations	1b					
2 Interest:						
a Mortgage	2a					
b Paid by foreign corporations	2b					
c Other	2c					
3 Industrial royalties (patents, trademarks, etc.)	3					
4 Motion picture or T.V. copyright royalties	4					
5 Other royalties (copyrights, recording, publishing, etc.)	5					
6 Real property income and natural resources royalties	6					
7 Pensions and annuities	7					
8 Social security benefits	8					
9 Capital gain from line 18 below	9					
10 Gambling—Residents of Canada only. Enter net income in column (c). If zero or less, enter -0-.	10c					
11 Gambling winnings —Residents of countries other than Canada. **Note.** Losses not allowed	11					
12 Other (specify) ▶	12					
13 Add lines 1a through 12 in columns (a) through (d)	13					

14 Multiply line 13 by rate of tax at top of each column **14**

15 Tax on income not effectively connected with a U.S. trade or business. Add columns (a) through (d) of line 14. Enter the total here and on Form 1040NR, line 53 . . . . ▶ **15**

Capital Gains and Losses From Sales or Exchanges of Property

16 (a) Kind of property and description (if necessary, attach statement of descriptive details not shown below)	(b) Date acquired (mo., day, yr.)	(c) Date sold (mo., day, yr.)	(d) Sales price	(e) Cost or other basis	(f) LOSS If (e) is more than (d), subtract (d) from (e)	(g) GAIN If (d) is more than (e), subtract (e) from (d)

17 Add columns (f) and (g) of line 16 . . . . **17** ( )

18 Capital gain. Combine columns (f) and (g) of line 17. Enter the net gain here and on line 9 above (if a loss, enter -0-) ▶ **18**

Enter only the capital gains and losses from property sales or exchanges that are from sources within the United States and not effectively connected with a U.S. business. Do not include a gain or loss on disposing of a U.S. real property interest; report these gains and losses on Schedule D (Form 1040).

Report property sales or exchanges that are effectively connected with a U.S. business on Schedule D (Form 1040), Form 4797, or both.

Form **1040NR** (2010)

Form 1040NR (2010)   Page **5**

Schedule OI — Other Information (see instructions)
Answer all questions

A   Of what country or countries were you a citizen or national during the tax year?   France

B   In what country did you claim residence for tax purposes during the tax year?   France

C   Have you ever applied to be a green card holder (lawful permanent resident) of the United States?.   ☐ **Yes** ☑ **No**

D   Were you ever:
     1. A U.S. citizen?.   ☐ **Yes** ☑ **No**
     2. A green card holder (lawful permanent resident) of the United States?   ☐ **Yes** ☑ **No**
     If you answer "Yes" to 1 or 2, see Pub. 519, chapter 4, to see expatriation rules that may apply to you.

E   If you had a visa on the last day of the tax year, enter your visa type. If you did not have a visa, enter your U.S. immigration status on the last day of the tax year.   **L-1A**

F   Have you ever changed your visa type (nonimmigrant status) or U.S. immigration status?.   ☐ **Yes** ☑ **No**
     If you answered "Yes," indicate the date and nature of the change.   ▶

G   List all dates you entered and left the United States during 2010 (see instructions).
     Note. If you are a resident of Canada or Mexico AND commute to work in the United States at frequent intervals,
     check the box for Canada or Mexico and skip to item H   ☐ Canada   ☐ Mexico

Date entered United States mm/dd/yy	Date departed United States mm/dd/yy	Date entered United States mm/dd/yy	Date departed United States mm/dd/yy
07 / 01 / 10	08 / 31 / 10	/ /	/ /
/ /	/ /	/ /	/ /
/ /	/ /	/ /	/ /
/ /	/ /	/ /	/ /

H   Give number of days (including vacation, nonworkdays, and partial days) you were present in the United States during:
     2008   0   , 2009   0   , and 2010   62   .

I   Did you file a U.S. income tax return for any prior year?   ☐ **Yes** ☑ **No**
     If "Yes," give the latest year and form number you filed.   ▶

J   Are you filing a return for a trust?   ☐ **Yes** ☑ **No**
     If "Yes," did the trust have a U.S. or foreign owner under the grantor trust rules, make a distribution or loan to a
     U.S. person, or receive a contribution from a U.S. person?   ☐ **Yes** ☑ **No**

K   Did you receive total compensation of $250,000 or more during the tax year?   ☐ **Yes** ☑ **No**
     If "Yes," did you use an alternative method to determine the source of this compensation?   ☐ **Yes** ☑ **No**

L   Income Exempt from Tax—If you are claiming exemption from income tax under a U.S. income tax treaty with a
     foreign country, complete 1 and 2 below. See Pub. 901 for more information on tax treaties.
     1. Enter the name of the country, the applicable tax treaty article, the number of months in prior years you claimed the treaty
     benefit, and the amount of exempt income in the columns below. Attach Form 8833 if required (see instructions).

(a) Country	**(b)** Tax treaty article	**(c)** Number of months claimed in prior tax years	**(d)** Amount of exempt income in current tax year

(e) Total. Enter this amount on Form 1040NR, line 22. Do not enter it on line 8 or line 12

2. Were you subject to tax in a foreign country on any of the income shown in 1(d) above?   ☑ **Yes** ☐ **No**

Form **1040NR** (2010)

¶1005

Kingman Private Limited Company is a distributor of foundry manufacturing equipment worldwide and is based in Hong Kong, which is not entitled to the treaty benefits afforded by the U.S.-China Income Tax Treaty. The Company operates in the United States through a sales office headed primarily by Dave Kong. With respect to its U.S. operations, the Company sells $20 million of products and purchased $16 million of products. Kong, who earns an annual salary of $1 million, spends approximately half his time in the United States, where he supervises a staff whose combined wages total $500,000 and incurs advertising expenses of $1 million. For the year, the accounts with respect to the U.S. branch include the following amounts:

Cash (at start of year)	$1 million
Cash (at end of year)	$1 million
Inventory (at start of year)	$2 million (at cost)
Inventory (at end of year)	$2 million (at cost)
Land	$2 million
Booked Liability	$1 million
Retained Earnings (at start of year)	$4 million
Retained Earnings (at end of year)	$4 million
Tax Payments (during the year)	$1 million

The booked liability of $1 million is a bank loan on which the U.S. operations incur simple interest at an annual rate of 5% for $50,000. The Company also incurs simple interest at an annual rate of 5% on its $4 million of non-U.S. booked liabilities.

Kingman Private Limited Company will file a Form 1120-F showing income tax, branch profits tax, and the tax on excess interest. The Company has made estimated tax payments of $1 million.

Form **1120-F**		**U.S. Income Tax Return of a Foreign Corporation**		OMB No. 1545-0126

Department of the Treasury
Internal Revenue Service

For calendar year 2010, or tax year beginning _____, 2010, and ending _____, 20 _____

▶ **See separate instructions.**

2010

Type or Print	Name **Kingman Private Limited Company**	Employer identification number **98-7654321**

Number, street, and room or suite no. (see instructions)

City or town, state and ZIP code, or country (see instructions)
Hong Kong

Check box(es) if:
- ☐ Initial return
- ☐ Name or address change
- ☐ Final return
- ☐ First post-merger return
- ☐ Amended return
- ☐ Schedule M-3 attached
- ☐ Protective return

A Country of incorporation **Hong Kong**

B Foreign country under whose laws the income reported on this return is also subject to tax **NA**

C Date incorporated **1/1/2010**

D (1) Location of corporation's primary books and records (city, province or state, and country) **Hong Kong**

   (2) Principal location of worldwide business **Hong Kong**

   (3) If the corporation maintains an office or place of business in the United States, check here . . . . ▶ ☐

E If the corporation had an agent in the United States at any time during the tax year, enter:

   (1) Type of agent **Sales employee**

   (2) Name **Dave Kong**

   (3) Address **1234 Main Street**
Los Angeles, CA

F See the instructions and enter the corporation's principal:

   (1) Business activity code number ▶ **331500**

   (2) Business activity ▶ **primary metal manufacturing**

   (3) Product or service ▶ **equipment**

G Check method of accounting: (1) ☑ Cash (2) ☐ Accrual

   (3) ☐ Other (specify) ▶

		Yes	No
H	Did the corporation's method of accounting change from the preceding tax year?		✓
	If "Yes," attach an explanation.		
I	Did the corporation's method of determining income change from the preceding tax year?		✓
	If "Yes," attach an explanation.		
J	Did the corporation file a U.S. income tax return for the preceding tax year?		✓
K	(1) At any time during the tax year, was the corporation engaged in a trade or business in the United States?	✓	
	(2) If "Yes," is taxpayer's trade or business within the United States solely the result of a section 897 (FIRPTA) sale or disposition?		✓
L	At any time during the tax year, did the corporation have a permanent establishment in the United States for purposes of any applicable tax treaty between the United States and a foreign country? . . .		✓
	If "Yes," enter the name of the foreign country:		
M	Did the corporation have any transactions with related parties?		✓
	If "Yes," Form 5472 may have to be filed (see instructions).		
	Enter number of Forms 5472 attached ▶		
	Note: Additional information is required on page 2.		

Computation of Tax Due or Overpayment

1	Tax from Section I, line 11, page 2.	**1**			
2	Tax from Section II, Schedule J, line 9, page 4	**2**	637,330	00	
3	Tax from Section III (add lines 6 and 10 on page 5)	**3**	393,801	00	
4	**Total tax.** Add lines 1 through 3			**4**	1,031,131	00
5a	2009 overpayment credited to 2010 . . .	**5a**			
b	2010 estimated tax payments	**5b**	100,000,000	00	
c	Less 2010 refund applied for on Form 4466	**5c**	( )		
d	Combine lines 5a through 5c	**5d**			
e	Tax deposited with Form 7004	**5e**			
f	Credit for tax paid on undistributed capital gains (attach Form 2439). . . .	**5f**			
g	Credit for federal tax on fuels (attach Form 4136). See instructions	**5g**			
h	Refundable credits from Form 3800, line 19c, and Form 8827, line 8c	**5h**			
i	U.S. income tax paid or withheld at source (add line 12, page 2, and amounts from Forms 8288-A and 8805 (attach Forms 8288-A and 8805))	**5i**			
j	Total payments. Add lines 5d through 5i			**5j**	1,000,000	00
6	Estimated tax penalty (see instructions). Check if Form 2220 is attached . . . . ▶ ☐			**6**		
7	**Amount owed.** If line 5j is smaller than the total of lines 4 and 6, enter amount owed			**7**	31,131	00
8a	**Overpayment.** If line 5j is larger than the total of lines 4 and 6, enter amount overpaid			**8a**		
b	Amount of overpayment on line 8a resulting from tax deducted and withheld under Chapter 3 (attach schedule—see instructions)			**8b**		
9	Enter portion of line 8a you want **Credited to 2011 estimated tax** ▶ Refunded ▶			**9**		

Sign Here

Under penalties of perjury, I declare that I have examined this return, including accompanying schedules and statements, and to the best of my knowledge and belief, it is true, correct, and complete. Declaration of preparer (other than taxpayer) is based on all information of which preparer has any knowledge.

▶ Signature of officer   Date   ▶ Title

May the IRS discuss this return with the preparer shown below (see instructions)? ☐ Yes ☐ No

Paid Preparer Use Only	Print/Type preparer's name	Preparer's signature	Date	Check ☐ if self-employed	PTIN
	Firm's name ▶			Firm's EIN ▶	
	Firm's address ▶			Phone no.	

For Paperwork Reduction Act Notice, see separate instructions.   Cat. No. 11470I   Form **1120-F** (2010)

¶1005

Form 1120-F (2010) Page **2**

Additional Information *(continued from page 1)*

		Yes	No
N	Is the corporation a controlled foreign corporation? (See section 957(a) for definition.)		✓
O	Is the corporation a personal service corporation? (See instructions for definition.)		✓
P	Enter tax-exempt interest received or accrued during the tax year (see instructions) ▶ $		
Q	At the end of the tax year, did the corporation own, directly or indirectly, 50% or more of the voting stock of a U.S. corporation? (See section 267(c) for rules of attribution.)		✓
	If "Yes," attach a schedule showing **(1)** name and EIN of such U.S. corporation; **(2)** percentage owned; and **(3)** taxable income or (loss) before NOL and special deductions of such U.S. corporation for the tax year ending with or within your tax year.		
R	If the corporation has an NOL for the tax year and is electing to forego the carryback period, check here ▶ ☐		
S	Enter the available NOL carryover from prior tax years. (Do not reduce it by any deduction on line 30a, page 3.) ▶ $		
T	Is the corporation a subsidiary in a parent-subsidiary controlled group?		✓
	If "Yes," enter the parent corporation's:		
	(1) EIN ▶		
	(2) Name ▶		
U	**(1)** Is the corporation a dealer under section 475?		✓
	(2) Did the corporation mark to market any securities or commodities other than in a dealer capacity?		✓

		Yes	No
V	At the end of the tax year, did any individual, partnership, corporation, estate, or trust own, directly or indirectly, 50% or more of the corporation's voting stock? (See section 267(c) for rules of attribution.)		✓
	If "Yes," attach a schedule showing the name and identifying number. (Do not include any information already entered in item **T**.) Enter percentage owned ▶		
W	Is the corporation taking a position on this return that a U.S. tax treaty overrules or modifies an Internal Revenue law of the United States, thereby causing a reduction of tax?		✓
	If "Yes," the corporation is generally required to complete and attach Form 8833. See Form 8833 for exceptions.		
	Note: *Failure to disclose a treaty-based return position may result in a $10,000 penalty (see section 6712).*		
X	During the tax year, did the corporation own any entity that was disregarded as an entity separate from its owner under Regulations sections 301.7701-2 and 301.7701-3?		✓
	If "Yes," attach a statement listing the name, country under whose laws the entity was organized, and EIN (if any) of each such entity.		
Y	**(1)** Did a partnership allocate to the corporation a distributive share of income from a directly owned partnership interest, any of which is ECI or treated as ECI by the partnership or the partner?		✓
	If "Yes," attach Schedule P. See instructions.		
	(2) During the tax year, did the corporation own at least a 10% interest, directly or indirectly, in any foreign partnership?		✓
	If "Yes," see instructions for required attachment.		
Z	**(1)** Has the corporation made any allocation or reallocation of income based on section 482 and its regulations?		✓
	(2) Has the corporation recognized any interbranch amounts? If "Yes," attach statement (see instructions).		✓
AA	Is the corporation required to file Schedule UTP (Form 1120), Uncertain Tax Position Statement (see instructions)?		✓
	If "Yes," complete and attach Schedule UTP.		

SECTION I— Income From U.S. Sources Not Effectively Connected With the Conduct of a Trade or Business in the United States—Do not report items properly withheld and reported on Form 1042-S. See instructions.

Include below **only** income from U.S. sources that is **not** effectively connected with the conduct of a trade or business in the United States. Do not report items properly withheld and reported on Form 1042-S. Report only items that **(a)** are not correctly withheld at source or **(b)** are not correctly reported on Form 1042-S. The rate of tax on each item of **gross** income listed below is 30% (4% for the gross transportation tax) or such lower rate specified by tax treaty. No deductions are allowed against these types of income. Enter treaty rates where applicable. **If the corporation is claiming a lower treaty rate, also complete item W above.** If multiple treaty rates apply to a type of income (e.g., subsidiary and portfolio dividends or dividends received by disregarded entities), attach a schedule showing the amounts, tax rates, and withholding for each.

Name of treaty country, if any ▶

	(a) Class of income (see instructions)	(b) Gross amount	(c) Rate of tax (%)	(d) Amount of tax liability	(e) Amount of U.S. income tax paid or withheld at the source
1	Interest				
2	Dividends				
3	Rents				
4	Royalties				
5	Annuities				
6	Gains from disposal of timber, coal, or domestic iron ore with a retained economic interest (attach supporting schedule)				
7	Gains from sale or exchange of patents, copyrights, etc.				
8	Fiduciary distributions (attach supporting schedule)				
9	Gross transportation income (attach Schedule V)		4		
10	Other fixed or determinable annual or periodic gains, profits, and income				
11	Total. Enter here and on line 1, page 1 ▶				
12	Total. Enter here and include on line 5i, page 1 ▶				

13 Is the corporation fiscally transparent under the laws of the foreign jurisdiction with respect to any item of income listed above? ☐ Yes ☑ No
  If "Yes," attach a schedule that provides the information requested above with respect to each such item of income.

Form **1120-F** (2010)

Form 1120-F (2010)   Page **3**

SECTION II—Income Effectively Connected With the Conduct of a Trade or Business in the United States (see instructions)

Important: *Fill in all applicable lines and schedules. If you need more space, see* **Assembling the Return** *in the instructions.*

Income	1a	Gross receipts or sales 20,000,000 00 **b** Less returns and allowances — **c** Bal ▶		1c	20,000,000	00
	2	Cost of goods sold (Schedule A, line 8)		2	16,000,000	00
	3	Gross profit (subtract line 2 from line 1c)		3		
	4	Dividends (Schedule C, line 14)		4		
	5	Interest		5		
	6	Gross rents		6		
	7	Gross royalties		7		
	8	Capital gain net income (attach Schedule D (Form 1120))		8		
	9	Net gain or (loss) from Form 4797, Part II, line 17 (attach Form 4797)		9		
	10	Other income (see instructions—attach schedule)		10		
	11	**Total income.** Add lines 3 through 10 ▶		11	4,000,000	00
Deductions (See instructions for limitations on deductions.)	12	Compensation of officers (Schedule E, line 4)		12	500,000	00
	13	Salaries and wages (less employment credits)		13	500,000	00
	14	Repairs and maintenance		14		
	15	Bad debts (for bad debts over $500,000, attach a list of debtors and amounts)		15		
	16	Rents		16		
	17	Taxes and licenses		17		
	18	Interest expense from Schedule I, line 25 (see instructions)		18	125,000	00
	19	Charitable contributions		19		
	20	Depreciation from Form 4562 not claimed on Schedule A or elsewhere on return (attach Form 4562)		20		
	21	Depletion		21		
	22	Advertising		22	1,000,000	00
	23	Pension, profit-sharing, etc., plans		23		
	24	Employee benefit programs		24		
	25	Domestic production activities deduction (attach Form 8903)		25		
	26	Deductions allocated and apportioned to ECI from Schedule H, line 20 (see instructions)		26		
	27	Other deductions (attach schedule)		27		
	28	**Total deductions.** Add lines 12 through 27 ▶		28	2,125,000	00
	29	Taxable income before NOL deduction and special deductions (subtract line 28 from line 11) ▶		29	1,875,000	00
	30	**Less: a** Net operating loss deduction (see instructions)	30a			
		b Special deductions (Schedule C, line 15)	30b			
		c Add lines 30a and 30b		30c		
	31	Taxable income or (loss). Subtract line 30c from line 29		31	1,875,000	00

Schedule A **Cost of Goods Sold** (see instructions)

1	Inventory at beginning of year		1	2,000,000	00
2	Purchases		2	16,000,000	00
3	Cost of labor		3		
4	Additional section 263A costs (attach schedule)		4		
5	Other costs (attach schedule)		5		
6	Add lines 1 through 5		6	18,000,000	00
7	Inventory at end of year		7	2,000,000	00
8	**Cost of goods sold.** Subtract line 7 from line 6. Enter here and on Section II, line 2, above		8	16,000,000	00

9a Check all methods used for valuing closing inventory:

  (1) ☑ Cost as described in Regulations section 1.471-3

  (2) ☐ Lower of cost or market as described in Regulations section 1.471-4

  (3) ☐ Other (Specify method used and attach explanation.) ▶

b Check if there was a writedown of subnormal goods as described in Regulations section 1.471-2(c) ▶ ☐

c Check if the LIFO inventory method was adopted this tax year for any goods (if checked, attach Form 970) ▶ ☐

d If the LIFO inventory method was used for this tax year, enter percentage (or amounts) of closing inventory computed under LIFO | 9d | |

e If property is produced or acquired for resale, do the rules of section 263A apply to the corporation? ☐ Yes ☑ No

f Was there any change in determining quantities, cost, or valuations between opening and closing inventory? ☐ Yes ☑ No
   If "Yes," attach explanation.

Form **1120-F** (2010)

¶1005

SECTION II—Income Effectively Connected With the Conduct of a Trade or Business in the United States (continued)

Schedule C   **Dividends and Special Deductions** (see instructions)

		(a) Dividends received	(b) %	(c) Special deductions: (a) × (b)
1	Dividends from less-than-20%-owned domestic corporations (other than debt-financed stock)		70	
2	Dividends from 20%-or-more-owned domestic corporations (other than debt-financed stock)		80	
3	Dividends on debt-financed stock of domestic and foreign corporations (section 246A)		see instructions	
4	Dividends on certain preferred stock of less-than-20%-owned public utilities		42	
5	Dividends on certain preferred stock of 20%-or-more-owned public utilities .		48	
6	Dividends from less-than-20%-owned foreign corporations		70	
7	Dividends from 20%-or-more-owned foreign corporations		80	
8	**Total.** Add lines 1 through 7. See instructions for limitation			
9	Dividends from foreign corporations not included on lines 3, 6, or 7			
10	Foreign dividend gross-up (section 78)			
11	IC-DISC and former DISC dividends not included on lines 1, 2, or 3 (section 246(d))			
12	Other dividends			
13	Deduction for dividends paid on certain preferred stock of public utilities . .			
14	**Total dividends.** Add lines 1 through 12. Enter here and on line 4, page 3 . .			
15	**Total special deductions.** Add lines 8 and 13. Enter here and on line 30b, page 3 . . . . ▶			NA

Schedule E   **Compensation of Officers** (See instructions for Section II, line 12.)

Note: *Complete Schedule E only if total receipts (line 1a plus lines 4 through 10 of Section II) are $500,000 or more.*

(a) Name of officer	(b) Social security number	(c) Percent of time devoted to business	Percent of corporation stock owned		(f) Amount of compensation
			(d) Common	(e) Preferred	
1a Dave Kong	98-123-4567	50 %	0 %	0 %	500,000
b		%	%	%	
c		%	%	%	
d		%	%	%	
e		%	%	%	
2	Total compensation of officers				500,000
3	Compensation of officers claimed on Schedule A and elsewhere on this return				0
4	Subtract line 3 from line 2. Enter the result here and on line 12, page 3				500,000

Schedule J   **Tax Computation** (see instructions)

1	Check if the corporation is a member of a controlled group (attach Schedule O (Form 1120)) . . . ▶ ☐			
2	Income tax. Check if a qualified personal service corporation (see instructions) . . . . ▶ ☐	2	637,330	00
3	Alternative minimum tax (attach Form 4626)	3		
4	Add lines 2 and 3	4	637,330	00
5a	Foreign tax credit (attach Form 1118)	5a		
b	General business credit (attach Form 3800)	5b		
c	Credit for prior year minimum tax (attach Form 8827)	5c		
d	Bond credits from Form 8912	5d		
6	**Total credits.** Add lines 5a through 5d	6		
7	Subtract line 6 from line 4	7		
8	Other taxes. Check if from: ☐ Form 4255 ☐ Form 8611 ☐ Form 8697 ☐ Form 8866 ☐ Form 8902 ☐ Other (attach schedule) .	8		
9	**Total tax.** Add lines 7 and 8. Enter here and on line 2, page 1	9	637,330	00

Form **1120-F** (2010)

¶1005

SECTION III—Branch Profits Tax and Tax on Excess Interest

Part I—Branch Profits Tax (see instructions)

1	Enter the amount from Section II, line 29	**1**	1,875,000	00
2	Enter total adjustments to line 1 to get effectively connected earnings and profits. (Attach required schedule showing the nature and amount of adjustments.) (See instructions.)	**2**	(637,330	00)
3	Effectively connected earnings and profits. Combine line 1 and line 2	**3**	1,237,670	00
4a	Enter U.S. net equity at the end of the current tax year. (Attach required schedule.)	**4a**	4,000,000	00
b	Enter U.S. net equity at the end of the prior tax year. (Attach required schedule.)	**4b**	4,000,000	00
c	Increase in U.S. net equity. If line 4a is greater than or equal to line 4b, subtract line 4b from line 4a. Enter the result here and skip to line 4e	**4c**		
d	Decrease in U.S. net equity. If line 4b is greater than line 4a, subtract line 4a from line 4b	**4d**		
e	Non-previously taxed accumulated effectively connected earnings and profits. Enter excess, if any, of effectively connected earnings and profits for preceding tax years beginning after 1986 over any dividend equivalent amounts for those tax years	**4e**		
5	Dividend equivalent amount. Subtract line 4c from line 3. If zero or less, enter -0-. If no amount is entered on line 4c, add the lesser of line 4d or line 4e to line 3 and enter the total here	**5**	1,237,670	00
6	**Branch profits tax.** Multiply line 5 by 30% (or lower treaty rate if the corporation is a qualified resident or otherwise qualifies for treaty benefits). Enter here and include on line 3, page 1. (See instructions.) **Also complete item W on page 2**	**6**	371,301	00

Part II—Tax on Excess Interest (see instructions for this Part and for Schedule I (Form 1120-F))

7a	Enter the interest from Section II, line 18	**7a**	125,000	00
b	Enter the inverse of the total amount deferred, capitalized, and disallowed from Schedule I, line 24d (i.e., if line 24d is negative, enter as a positive number; if line 24d is positive, enter as a negative number)	**7b**		
c	Combine lines 7a and 7b (amount must equal Schedule I, line 23)	**7c**	125,000	00
8	**Branch Interest** (see instructions for definition): Enter the sum of Schedule I, line 9, column (c), and Schedule I, line 22. If the interest paid by the foreign corporation's U.S. trade or business was increased because 80% or more of the foreign corporation's assets are U.S. assets, check this box . . . . ▶ ☐	**8**	50,000	00
9a	Excess interest. Subtract line 8 from line 7c. If zero or less, enter -0-	**9a**	75,000	00
b	If the foreign corporation is a bank, enter the excess interest treated as interest on deposits (see instructions for rules for computing this amount). Otherwise, enter -0-.	**9b**		
c	Subtract line 9b from line 9a	**9c**	75,000	00
10	**Tax on excess interest.** Multiply line 9c by 30% or lower treaty rate (if the corporation is a qualified resident or otherwise qualifies for treaty benefits). (See instructions.) Enter here and include on line 3, page 1. **Also complete item W on page 2**	**10**	22,500	00

Part III—Additional Information

		Yes	No
11	Is the corporation claiming a reduction in, or exemption from, the branch profits tax due to:		
a	A complete termination of all U.S. trades or businesses?		✓
b	The tax-free liquidation or reorganization of a foreign corporation?		✓
c	The tax-free incorporation of a U.S. trade or business?		✓
	If **11a** or **11b** applies and the transferee is a domestic corporation, attach Form 8848. If **11c** applies, attach the statement required by Temporary Regulations section 1.884-2T(d)(5).		

¶1005

Form 1120-F (2010)   Page **6**

Note: *Check if completing on ▶*   ☑ U.S. basis or   ☐ Worldwide basis.

Schedule L   **Balance Sheets per Books**

		Beginning of tax year		End of tax year	
Assets		(a)	(b)	(c)	(d)
1	Cash		1,000,000		1,000,000
2a	Trade notes and accounts receivable				
b	Less allowance for bad debts	(	)	(	)
3	Inventories		2,000,000		2,000,000
4	U.S. government obligations				
5	Tax-exempt securities (see instructions)				
6a	Interbranch current assets*				
b	Other current non-U.S. assets*				
c	Other current U.S. assets*				
7	Loans to shareholders				
8	Mortgage and real estate loans				
9a	Other loans and investments—non-U.S. assets*				
b	Other loans and investments—U.S. assets*				
10a	Buildings and other depreciable assets				
b	Less accumulated depreciation	(	)	(	)
11a	Depletable assets				
b	Less accumulated depletion	(	)	(	)
12	Land (net of any amortization)		2,000,000		2,000,000
13a	Intangible assets (amortizable only)				
b	Less accumulated amortization	(	)	(	)
14	Assets held in trust				
15	Other non-current interbranch assets*				
16a	Other non-current non-U.S. assets*				
b	Other non-current U.S. assets*				
17	Total assets		5,000,000		5,000,000
Liabilities					
18	Accounts payable				
19	Mortgages, notes, bonds payable in less than 1 year:				
a	Interbranch liabilities*				
b	Third-party liabilities*				
20	Other current liabilities*				
21	Loans from shareholders				
22	Mortgages, notes, bonds payable in 1 year or more:				
a	Interbranch liabilities*				
b	Third-party liabilities*		1,000,000		1,000,000
23	Liabilities held in trust				
24a	Other interbranch liabilities*				
b	Other third-party liabilities*				
Equity (see instructions)					
25	Capital stock: a Preferred stock				
	b Common stock				
26	Additional paid-in capital				
27	Retained earnings—Appropriated*				
28	Retained earnings—Unappropriated		4,000,000		4,000,000
29	Adjustments to shareholders' equity*				
30	Less cost of treasury stock	(	)	(	)
31	Total liabilities and shareholders' equity		5,000,000		5,000,000

*Attach schedule—see instructions.   Form **1120-F** (2010)

SCHEDULE I (Form 1120-F)	Interest Expense Allocation Under Regulations Section 1.882-5	OMB No. 1545-0126
Department of the Treasury Internal Revenue Service	▶ Attach to Form 1120-F. ▶ See separate instructions.	2010

Name of corporation	Employer identification number
Kingman Private Limited Company	98-7654321

A Check here if the corporation is a foreign bank as defined in Regulations section 1.882-5(c)(4) . . . . ▶ ☐

B This Schedule I is being completed with respect to *(check one):*
   ☑ Adjusted U.S. booked liabilities method under Regs. sec. 1.882-5(d). **Complete lines 1 through 15 and 21 through 25.**
   ☐ Separate currency pools method under Regs. sec. 1.882-5(e). **Complete lines 1 through 9 and 16a through 25.**

Step 1   **Average U.S. Assets for the Tax Year: Regulations Section 1.882-5(b)**

		(a) Set(s) of Books that Give Rise to U.S. Booked Liabilities (see inst.)	(b) Partnership Interests	(c) Set(s) of Books Other than those Described in Columns (a) and (b)	(d) Totals. Add columns (a) through (c)
1	Specify the method used to determine the value of the corporation's U.S. assets on lines 2 through 5 below *(check one):*				
	☑ Adjusted basis method: Regs. sec. 1.882-5(b)(2)(i)				
	☐ Fair market value method: Regs. sec. 1.882-5(b)(2)(ii)				
2	Total assets per books	5,000,000			
3a	Total interbranch assets				
b	Total non-ECI assets under section 864(c)(4)(D)				
c	Total other non-ECI assets				
d	Adjustments for amounts from partnerships and certain disregarded entities included on line 2, column (a) . . .				
e	Adjustments for assets that give rise to direct interest expense allocations under Regs. sec. 1.882-5(a)(1)(ii) . .				
f	Other adjustments to average assets included in line 2 (e.g., mark-to-market differences)				
4	Combine lines 3a through 3f				
5	Total value of U.S. assets for the tax year	5,000,000			5,000,000
	Column (a): Subtract line 4 from line 2.				
	Column (b): Enter total from Schedule P, line 19.				
	Column (c): See instructions for amount to enter.				

Step 2   **U.S.-Connected Liabilities for the Tax Year: Regulations Section 1.882-5(c)**

6	Specify the method used to determine the amounts in Step 2 *(check one):*		
	☐ Actual ratio under Regs. sec. 1.882-5(c)(2). **Complete lines 6a through 6c below.**		
	☑ Fixed ratio under Regs. sec. 1.882-5(c)(4). **Complete line 6d below.**		
a	Average worldwide liabilities		
b	Average worldwide assets		
c	Divide line 6a by line 6b	%	
d	Fixed ratio under Regs. sec. 1.882-5(c)(4). If the corporation is a foreign bank as defined in Regs. sec. 1.882-5(c)(4), enter 95% on line 6d. If the corporation is not a foreign bank or an insurance company, enter 50% on line 6d	50 %	
e	Enter the ratio from line 6c or 6d, as applicable		50 %
7a	U.S.-connected liabilities before Regs. sec. 1.884-1(e)(3) election(s). Multiply line 5, column (d) by line 6e		2,500,000
b	Total amount of U.S. liability reduction under Regs. sec. 1.884-1(e)(3) election(s)		
c	**U.S.-Connected Liabilities.** Subtract line 7b from line 7a . . . . ▶		2,500,000

Step 3   **Interest Expense Paid or Accrued on Average U.S. Booked Liabilities: Regulations Section 1.882-5(d)**

		(a) Set(s) of Books that Give Rise to U.S. Booked Liabilities (see inst.)	(b) Partnership Interests	(c) Totals. Add columns (a) and (b)
8	Total average amount of U.S. booked liabilities as defined in Regs. sec. 1.882-5(d)(2) (see instructions)	1,000,000		1,000,000
	Column (a): Do not include amounts that give rise to directly allocable interest under Regs. sec. 1.882-5(a)(1)(ii) or from partnerships includible in column (b).			
	Column (b): Enter the total from Schedule P, line 17.			
9	Total interest paid or accrued during the tax year on line 8 amount	50,000		50,000
	Column (a): Do not include amounts that give rise to directly allocable interest under Regs. sec. 1.882-5(a)(1)(ii) or from partnerships includible in column (b).			
	Column (b): Enter the total from Schedule P, line 14c.			

Cat. No. 49680W   Schedule I (Form 1120-F) 2010

¶1005

Schedule I (Form 1120-F) 2010   Page **2**

Step 3 (cont.)	**Adjusted U.S. Booked Liabilities Method: Regulations Section 1.882-5(d)**

If line 7c is greater than line 8, column (c), complete lines 10 through 13 below and skip lines 14a and 14b.
If line 7c is less than or equal to line 8, column (c), skip lines 10 through 13 and complete lines 14a and 14b.

10	If the corporation is a foreign bank which is making a current-year election to use the published average 30-day LIBOR (see instructions), check the box on this line, skip lines 10a through 10c, and enter the rate on line 10d . . . . ▶ ☐		
a	Total interest paid or accrued during the tax year on U.S. dollar liabilities that are **not** U.S. booked liabilities included on line 8	**10a**	200,000
b	Average U.S. dollar denominated liabilities that are **not** U.S. booked liabilities included on line 8	**10b**	4,000,000
c	Divide line 10a by line 10b	**10c**	5 %
d	Enter the 30-day LIBOR, if elected under Regs. sec. 1.882-5(d)(5)(ii)(B)	**10d**	%
e	Enter the rate from line 10c or, if elected, the 30-day LIBOR on line 10d	**10e**	5 %
11	**Excess U.S.-connected liabilities.** Subtract line 8 from line 7c . . . . ▶	**11**	1,500,000	00
12	**Excess interest.** Multiply line 10e by line 11 . . . . ▶	**12**	75,000	00
13	Add lines 9, column (c) and 12	**13**	125,000	00
14a	**Scaling ratio.** Divide line 7c by line 8, column (c)	**14a**	%
b	Multiply line 9, column (c) by line 14a. See instructions for hedging amounts	**14b**	
15	**Interest expense allocable to ECI under the adjusted U.S. booked liabilities method.** Enter the result from line 13 or line 14b here and on line 21 . . . . ▶	**15**	125,000	00

Step 3 (cont.)	**Separate Currency Pools Method: Regulations Section 1.882-5(e)**

		(a) U.S. Dollar Denominated	**(b)** Home Country Currency. Specify: ▶	**(c)** Other Currency. Specify: ▶	**(d)** Other Currency. Specify: ▶
16a	**U.S. assets.** Enter the corporation's U.S. assets, using the methodology in Regs. sec. 1.882-5(e)(1)(i). If more columns are needed, attach schedule (see instructions) . . .				
b	Check here if a less than 3% currency election was made . . . . ▶ ☐				
17a	Enter the percentage from line 6e	%	%	%	%
b	**U.S.-connected liabilities.** Multiply line 16a by line 17a, or, if a liability reduction election is made, see instructions . .				
18a	Enter the total interest expense paid or accrued for the tax year with respect to the foreign corporation's worldwide liabilities denominated in that foreign currency (enter in functional currency)				
b	Enter the corporation's average worldwide liabilities (whether interest bearing or not) denominated in that foreign currency (enter in functional currency)				
c	**Borrowing rate:** Divide line 18a by line 18b	%	%	%	%
19	**Interest expense allocation by separate currency pool.** Multiply line 17b by line 18c				
20	**Interest expense allocable to ECI under the separate currency pools method.** Total the amounts on line 19, columns (a) through (d), and amounts from attached schedule, if any, and enter the result here and on line 21				

SUMMARY—Interest Expense Allocation and Deduction under Regulations Section 1.882-5			
21	Amount from line 15 or line 20, as applicable	**21**	125,000	00
22	Enter the corporation's interest expense directly allocable under Regs. sec. 1.882-5(a)(1)(ii). (Include total from Schedule P, line 14b.)	**22**	
23	**Interest expense allocable to ECI under Regs. sec. 1.882-5.** Add lines 21 and 22 . . . . ▶	**23**	125,000	00
24a	Amount of line 23 that is disallowed as a deduction under section 265 or under an income tax treaty (attach schedule—see instructions)	**24a**	(	)
b	Deferred interest expense under section 163(e)(3), 163(j), 267(a)(3), etc. (attach schedule—see instructions)	**24b**	
c	Amount of line 23 that is capitalized under section 263A (attach schedule—see instructions)	**24c**	(	)
d	Combine lines 24a through 24c	**24d**	
25	**Total interest expense deduction under Regs. sec. 1.882-5.** Combine lines 23 and 24d and enter here and on Form 1120F, Section II, line 18. The amount entered on line 25 may not exceed the total interest expense paid or accrued by the foreign corporation . . . . ▶	**25**	125,000	00

Schedule I (Form 1120-F) 2010

SCHEDULES M-1 and M-2 (Form 1120-F) Department of the Treasury Internal Revenue Service	**Reconciliation of Income (Loss) and Analysis of Unappropriated Retained Earnings per Books** ▶ Attach to Form 1120-F.	OMB No. 1545-0126 2010

Name of corporation	Employer identification number
Kingman Private Limited Company	98-7654321

Reconciliation of Income (Loss) per Books With Income per Return

Schedule M-1   Note: Schedule M-3 may be required instead of Schedule M-1—see instructions.

1	Net income (loss) per books	1,875,000	7	Income recorded on books this year not included on this return (itemize):	
2	Federal income tax per books		a	Tax-exempt interest $	
3	Excess of capital losses over capital gains		b	Other (itemize):	
4	Income subject to tax not recorded on books this year (itemize):				
			8	Deductions on this return not charged against book income this year (itemize):	
5	Expenses recorded on books this year not deducted on this return (itemize):		a	Depreciation . . $	
a	Depreciation . . . . $		b	Charitable contributions $	
b	Charitable contributions $		c	Other (itemize):	
c	Travel and entertainment $				
d	Other (itemize):		9	Add lines 7 and 8	
6	Add lines 1 through 5	1,875,000	10	Income—line 6 less line 9	1,875,000

Schedule M-2   Analysis of Unappropriated Retained Earnings per Books

1	Balance at beginning of year	4,000,000	5	Distributions:	a	Cash	1,875,000
2	Net income (loss) per books	1,875,000			b	Stock	
3	Other increases (itemize):				c	Property . . .	
			6	Other decreases (itemize):			
			7	Add lines 5 and 6			
4	Add lines 1, 2, and 3	5,875,000	8	Balance at end of year (line 4 less line 7) .			4,000,000

Who Must File

Generally, any foreign corporation that is required to complete Form 1120-F, Section II must complete Schedules M-1 and M-2 (Form 1120-F). However, under some circumstances, a foreign corporation is required to complete (or may voluntarily complete) Schedule M-3 (Form 1120-F) in lieu of Schedule M-1.

Complete Schedule M-3 in lieu of Schedule M-1 if total assets at the end of the tax year that are reportable on Schedule L are $10 million or more. A corporation filing Form 1120-F that is not required to file Schedule M-3 (Form 1120-F) may voluntarily file Schedule M-3 instead of Schedule M-1. See the Instructions for Schedule M-3 (Form 1120-F) for more information.

Note. If Schedule M-3 is completed in lieu of Schedule M-1, the corporation is still required to complete Schedule M-2.

Do not complete Schedules M-1, M-2, and M-3 if total assets at the end of the tax year (Schedule L, line 17, column (d)) are less than $25,000.

Specific Instructions

Schedule M-1

Line 1. Net income (loss) per books. The foreign corporation must report on line 1 of Schedule M-1 the net income (loss) per the set or sets of books taken into account on Schedule L.

Line 5c. Travel and entertainment expenses. Include any of the following:

• Meal and entertainment expenses not deductible under section 274(n).

• Expenses for the use of an entertainment facility.

• The part of business gifts over $25.

• Expenses of an individual over $2,000 that are allocable to conventions on cruise ships.

• Employee achievement awards over $400.

• The cost of entertainment tickets over face value (also subject to the 50% limit under section 274(n)).

• The cost of skyboxes over the face value of nonluxury box seat tickets.

• The part of luxury water travel expenses not deductible under section 274(m).

• Expenses for travel as a form of education.

• Other nondeductible travel and entertainment expenses.

For more information, see Pub. 542.

Line 7a. Tax-exempt interest. Report any tax-exempt interest received or accrued, including any exempt-interest dividends received as a shareholder in a mutual fund or other regulated investment company. Also report this same amount in item P at the top of page 2 of Form 1120-F.

Schedule M-2

Line 1. Beginning balance of unappropriated retained earnings. Enter the beginning balance of unappropriated retained earnings per the set(s) of books taken into account on Schedule L.

Note. For additional information for Schedule M-2 reporting, see the Instructions for Schedule M-3 (Form 1120-F).

For Paperwork Reduction Act Notice, see the Instructions for Form 1120-F.   Cat. No. 49678K   Schedules M-1 and M-2 (Form 1120-F) 2010

¶1005

Chapter 11

Planning for Foreign-Owned United States Operations

¶ 1101   Introduction
¶ 1102   Evolution of a Foreign-Owned U.S. Business
¶ 1103   Choice of Entity for U.S. Operations
¶ 1104   Basics of Inbound Tax Planning
¶ 1105   Comprehensive Example
¶ 1106   Survey of U.S. Entity Classification

¶ 1101   INTRODUCTION

This chapter discusses general planning issues with respect to foreign-owned U.S. operations. More specific planning issues are discussed throughout this book. For example, Chapter 12 (¶ 1205) discusses transfer pricing strategies to reduce taxable income, Chapter 13 (¶ 1301) discusses the use of tax treaties to avoid double taxation, Chapter 9 (¶ 902) discusses exemptions from the U.S. withholding taxes on investment income, and Chapter 10 (¶ 1001) discusses techniques for reducing effectively connected income from a U.S. trade or business.

¶ 1102   EVOLUTION OF A FOREIGN-OWNED U.S. BUSINESS

.01   Entering the United States

There is a natural progression of market penetration by a foreign company that wishes to market its products in the United States. For example, a foreign company may initially import its products through independent brokers or distributors. Smaller foreign companies, in particular, may find it advantageous to use independent intermediaries to market their goods in the United States since they often lack technical expertise regarding local U.S. markets. There are costs to such an arrangement, however, including the need to share profits with the intermediary (either through commissions or reduced sales revenues), and the loss of control over the sales and distribution functions.

As the foreign company's sales volume grows and the foreign company becomes more familiar with marketing in the United States, the foreign company may wish to bring the U.S. marketing function in-house by having its foreign employees travel to the United States to identify customers, display inventory, negotiate sales agreements, and provide technical support. Alternatively, the foreign company could employ U.S. residents to perform those functions.

¶1102.01

The next logical step in the progression of a foreign company's U.S. marketing activities is to establish a branch sales office in the United States. The activities of a branch sales office would include negotiating and closing sales agreements and distributing the foreign company's products. A United States presence often is required for the import of services. For example, an import of construction services usually requires that foreign engineers and technicians travel to the United States in order to provide on-site management of the project.

In the alternative, licensing and franchising are more indirect methods of entering the United States market. A foreign company that purchases or develops a patent, trademark, or other intangible can license that intangible to a U.S. company. In return, the foreign company receives a percentage of the U.S. sales of the licensed or franchised product in the form of a royalty. In essence, licensing and franchising are types of joint venture arrangements that permit a foreign company to enter the United States quickly, but may not produce the same profit margins that are potentially available from more direct forms of importing. Moreover, the foreign company may lose some control over the quality and image of its product.

.02 Determinants of U.S. Taxation

A central tax issue for a foreign company is whether its activities will be subject to U.S. taxation. Complying with the U.S. tax laws always involves administrative costs and, if the effective rate of U.S. tax affects the foreign company's foreign country rate, any potential excess U.S. taxes paid may represent an out-of-pocket tax cost. Whether a foreign company's activities are subject to U.S. taxation depends on several factors, including the precise nature of the foreign company's activities within the United States, the U.S. laws with respect to that trade or business, and the applicability of any income tax treaty between the foreign company's country and the United States.

As a general rule, the United States asserts jurisdiction over all of the trade or business income derived from sources within its borders, regardless of the citizenship or residence of the person or entity receiving that income. However, most tax treaties contain a permanent establishment article under which a foreign company's business profits are exempt from U.S. taxation unless those profits are attributable to a permanent establishment located within the United States.[1] A permanent establishment includes a fixed place of business (e.g. a sales office), unless the fixed place of business is used solely for auxiliary functions (e.g., purchasing, storing, displaying, or delivering inventory) or activities of a preparatory nature (e.g., collecting information about potential customers).[2] A permanent establishment also exists if employees or other dependent agents habitually exercise in the United States an authority to conclude sales contracts in the foreign company's name.[3] As a consequence, a foreign company that sends executives or salespeople to the United States to enter contracts may create a permanent establishment even if those employees operate out of hotels and do not have a fixed place of business.

---

[1] For example, *see* Article 7(1) (¶ 1004.07) of the U.S. Model Treaty.

[2] For example, *see* Article 5(1), (2), and (4) (¶ 1004.05) of the U.S. Model Treaty.

[3] For example, *see* Article 5(5) (¶ 1004.05) of the U.S. Model Treaty.

Employees who limit their activities to auxiliary or preparatory activities, such as collecting information about potential customers, with sales concluded in the foreign company's country, will not create a permanent establishment. Marketing products in the United States solely through independent U.S. brokers or independent distributors also does not create a permanent establishment.[4]

¶ 1103 CHOICE OF ENTITY FOR U.S. OPERATIONS

A foreign company that establishes a sales, distribution, service, or manufacturing facility in the United States can also structure the U.S. operation as either a branch or a subsidiary. Even if a foreign company forms a limited liability company in the United States, the foreign company will have to choose whether it will treat the limited liability company as a subsidiary or as a branch for tax purposes under the entity classification regulations.[5] The option of forming a domestic hybrid entity or a reverse domestic hybrid entity is also available.

.01 Branches

An unincorporated U.S. branch is simply an extension of the foreign corporation, as opposed to a separate legal entity. Assuming the branch constitutes a U.S. trade or business or a permanent establishment, the branch will be subject to U.S. income taxation. The United States permits a foreign corporation to allocate all direct costs, such as the cost of goods sold abroad, and indirect expenses, such as interest expense and home office overhead, against branch income.

From a U.S. tax perspective, the U.S. branch's income would incur federal tax at rates ranging from 15% to 35%.[6] The branch can take deductions appropriate to the taxed activities, which includes general and administrative expenses calculated on a proportional basis between the branch and its foreign corporate headquarters, assuming that the branch has benefited from these expenditures.[7] A disadvantage is that the branch, as a non-corporate entity, cannot deduct payments for royalties, management fees or interest to its foreign corporation's headquarters.

In lieu of withholding on repatriations (such as dividends), the United States imposes a system of branch taxation on three separate tax bases:

(i) Profits from branch operations that are deemed repatriated from the United States under the branch profits tax rules;[8]

(ii) Interest being paid by the branch to foreign lenders;[9] and

(iii) Excess interest that is apportionable to effectively connected income the foreign corporation does not deem paid by the branch.[10]

Because the repatriation of branch earnings does not involve actual remittances, the foreign corporation would have to segregate its U.S. branch earnings from other earnings.

---

[4] For example, *see* Article 5(6) (¶ 1004.05) of the U.S. Model Treaty.

[5] Reg. § 301.7701-1 through -3.

[6] Code Sec. 11.

[7] Code Sec. 882(c).

[8] Code Sec. 884(b).

[9] Code Sec. 884(f)(1)(A).

[10] Code Sec. 884(f)(1)(B).

If the foreign corporation expects the U.S. operations to lose money the first few years, the branch may permit the U.S. losses to reduce the foreign corporation's taxable income in its country of incorporation.

.02 Subsidiaries

A U.S. subsidiary is a corporation organized under the laws of one of the U.S. states or the District of Columbia. A U.S. subsidiary would incur corporate income tax at rates ranging from 15% to 35%.[11] The foreign corporation and its U.S. subsidiary should allocate a proportional basis of the foreign corporation's general and administrative expenses to reduce the U.S. subsidiary's income. The U.S. subsidiary can deduct payments to the foreign corporation for royalties and interest, which are subject to a withholding tax, and management fees, which do not incur a withholding tax as long as the management fees are for services performed outside the United States. The U.S. subsidiary should also incur a withholding tax when repatriating a cash dividend to the foreign corporation.

Because the U.S. subsidiary is subject to U.S. income taxation, the foreign corporation will want to place all U.S. activities in the U.S. subsidiary to avoid inadvertent treatment of the foreign corporation as a U.S. permanent establishment (or trade or business if there is not an applicable treaty). A permanent establishment that earns effectively connected income in the United States will incur U.S. income tax in addition to the U.S. income tax the U.S. subsidiary will already pay.

More specifically, if the foreign corporation operates in the United States through a U.S. subsidiary, a permanent establishment may inadvertently result from the activities of the foreign corporation's employees in the United States. As a result, the foreign corporation will want to avoid having any of its employees conduct sales at an office of the U.S. subsidiary.

An inadvertent permanent establishment may also result from the foreign corporation giving the contracting authority of an agent to its own employees operating in the United States.[12] Under the agency test, a dependent agent (e.g., an employee) of the foreign corporation may constitute a permanent establishment if the dependent agent has the authority to contract on behalf of the foreign corporation in the United States and the agent habitually exercises that authority. Although the treaty does not define habitual exercise, the exercise of authority to negotiate and enter into contracts once or twice is probably habitual. The more the employee exercises this authority, the more likely the United States would deem it habitual.

In addition to avoiding an inadvertent permanent establishment, a foreign corporation should ensure that its U.S. subsidiary does not have any transfer pricing exposure.[13] Transfer pricing refers to the price that related corporations charge each other for tangible property, intangible property, services and loans. Transfer pricing receives substantial scrutiny from the IRS's International Examiners, who may impose additional tax and a 20% to 40% penalty if prices are not at arm's-length.[14] The best way to avoid transfer pricing adjustments by the IRS to

---

[11] Code Sec. 11.

[12] For example, *see* Article 5(5) (¶ 1004.05) of the U.S. Model Treaty.

[13] Code Sec. 482; Reg. § 1.482.

[14] Code Sec. 6662.

avoid a penalty is to document the pricing practices as required by the regulations[15] or to enter into an advance pricing agreement.[16] In addition to protecting the U.S. subsidiary from a transfer pricing adjustment, foreign corporations should consider transfer pricing as a potential tool in its overall repatriation strategy.

.03 Branch versus Subsidiary

The choice between the branch and subsidiary forms must take into account not only U.S. and foreign tax laws, but also general business considerations. There is no simple rule that dictates the best structure in all cases. Tax advantages of the subsidiary form include the following:

(i) The subsidiary form provides more control over the timing of income recognition of the secondary tax as withholding occurs when dividends are paid instead of the formulary approach of the branch profits tax.

(ii) The sale of stock in a subsidiary is generally exempt from U.S. taxation.

(iii) The separate legal status of a subsidiary makes it easier to justify to the IRS the management fees and other intercompany charges paid to the foreign corporation.

Tax advantages of the branch form include the following:

(i) A foreign corporation can usually deduct the losses of a U.S. branch against its other profits.

(ii) The transfer of assets to a branch is generally a nontaxable event.

General business factors that should be considered when choosing between the branch and the subsidiary form include:

(i) A subsidiary insulates the foreign corporation from legal liability issues in the United States.

(ii) A subsidiary may present a better local image to potential U.S. customers and employees.

(iii) A subsidiary may make it easier to involve U.S. persons in the venture, since it can issue additional shares to those U.S. investors.

(iv) A branch may be simpler to operate. For example, business registration and financial reporting requirements of a branch may be less onerous than those for a U.S. subsidiary.

.04 Domestic Hybrid Entities

A domestic hybrid entity is a legal entity whose characterization for U.S. tax purposes is a pass through entity, but a corporation for foreign tax purposes. With the exception of a U.S. C corporation, which has per se corporate status, all U.S. business entities with at least two members can elect to be treated as a corporation or a partnership, and those entities with only a single member can elect to be treated as a corporation or an unincorporated branch.[17] This regime is now commonly known as "check-the-box" because the entity's owner merely checks the box

---

[15] Reg. § 1.6662-6(b)(2)(iii).

[16] Rev. Proc. 2006-9, IRB 2006-2.

[17] Reg. § 301.7701-3(b)(1).

on a Form 8832 to classify the entity (a sample of a completed Form 8832 is attached to the Appendix to Chapter 8 (¶ 809)). A separate entity must actually exist before checking-the-box. Although federal law is determinative of U.S. tax purposes, the entity must satisfy the rules of its respective state of organization to obtain limited liability. If a domestic entity fails to make an election, the default rules treat the entity as a partnership if the entity has multiple owners or as a branch if the entity has only a single owner.[18]

Congress was concerned about permitting treaty benefits on investment-type income paid by a U.S. corporation through a domestic hybrid entity where

  (i) The foreign country does not treat the investment-type income received by the foreign corporation as income and

  (ii) The income is received by a pass through entity in the United States.

In these situations, Code Sec. 894(c) says that the item of investment-type income is not eligible for reduced treaty rates on withholding.[19]

> **Example 11.1:** FORco is a foreign corporation that owns USAco, a U.S. corporation. FORco contributes both cash and USAco stock to a U.S. limited liability company ("LLC"). The LLC is a domestic hybrid entity because the LLC is a pass through for U.S. tax purposes, but a corporation for foreign country tax purposes. Suppose USAco borrows cash from its owner. For U.S. tax purposes, because the LLC is a pass through entity, the loan is treated as coming from FORco and interest paid by USAco will be treated as passing through the LLC to FORco. However, for foreign country tax purposes the LLC is a corporation that has received a capital contribution and the payment coming from the LLC to FORco is considered a dividend that the foreign country exempts from tax. As a result, the interest payment creates a deduction for USAco and the only tax on the interest payment would be the withholding tax. Barring section 894(c) and the regulations, the withholding tax would be reduced to the treaty rate. However, because section 894(c) and the regulations apply, treaty benefits are not allowed and the appropriate withholding tax rate would be the 30% under U.S. internal law.

---

[18] Reg. § 301.7701-3(b).

[19] Code Sec. 894(c)(1) and (2); Reg. § 1.894-1.

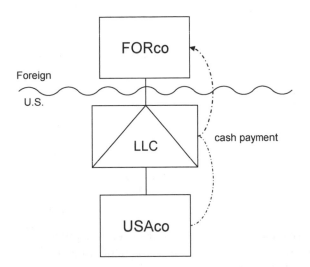

.05 Domestic Reverse Hybrid Entities

Domestic reverse hybrid entities are treated as corporations by the United States, but as pass through entities by the foreign countries. A domestic reverse hybrid entity would be useful to a foreign corporation that wants pass through treatment in its country while avoiding any U.S. repatriation costs in the form of either a withholding tax or a branch tax. A popular form of domestic reverse hybrid entity is a limited partnership for which the foreign owner has filed a Form 8832 that checks-the-box for U.S. corporate tax status.

Example 11.2: FORco operates in country F, where it currently incurs losses and anticipates continuing to incur losses in the near future. FORco considers the United States to be a tremendous market for its products, but wants to limit its liability in the United States. As a result, FORco forms a domestic reverse hybrid entity in the United States (USDRH), which is a corporation for U.S. tax purposes and a limited partnership for country F purposes. FORco can use the income that passes through its U.S. structure against its country F losses. As long as the domestic reverse hybrid entity does not distribute a dividend, neither a withholding tax nor a branch tax would apply.

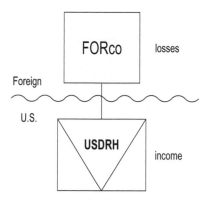

Domestic reverse hybrid entities have been a popular vehicle for "double dip" financing structures, whereby the interest is deductible against the income of both the U.S. subsidiary and the foreign parent.

Example 11.3: FORco, a corporation incorporated in country F, operates in the United States through a U.S. subsidiary, USAco. FORco contributes USAco to a domestic reverse hybrid entity (USDRH), which is a pass through entity for country F tax purposes and a corporation for U.S. tax purposes. USDRH borrows money from a U.S. bank to which USDRH must pay interest. For U.S. tax purposes, USDRH and USAco file a consolidated return, which permits a deduction for the interest payment against the income of USAco. A double dip occurs because the pass through nature of USDRH for country F tax purposes permits FORco to also deduct the interest expense on FORco's country F return.

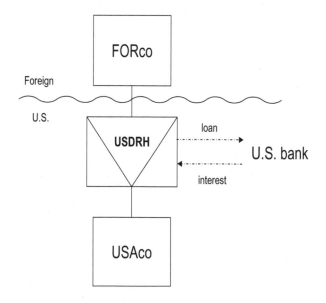

¶1103.05

Due to some abusive financing structures, the IRS has promulgated regulations that recharacterize the interest as a dividend when the domestic reverse hybrid makes a deductible payment to a related foreign owner for which a treaty reduces the withholding tax.

Example 11.4: FORco, a corporation incorporated in country F, operates in the United States through a U.S. subsidiary, USAco. FORco contributes USAco to a domestic reverse hybrid entity (USDRH), which is a pass through entity for country F tax purposes, but a corporation for U.S. tax purposes. For U.S. tax purposes, FORco lends cash to the USDRH, which contributes the cash as equity to USAco. Assume that the treaty between the U.S. and country F exempts interest payments (but not dividends) from withholding. Because USDRH and USAco file a consolidated return in the United States, the USDRH may deduct the interest expense against the operating income of USAco. Before the IRS issued the regulations, the USDRH would not have to incur any withholding tax on the interest payment to FORco under the treaty, while the interest income would not be reported in country F because it is an intracompany transaction. However, the IRS regulations recharacterize the interest payments in this example from interest to dividends, resulting in a withholding tax at the typically higher dividend rate instead of the exemption for interest.[20]

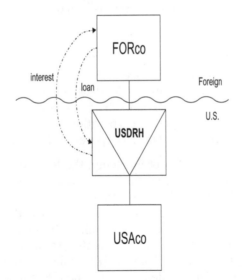

¶ 1104 BASICS OF INBOUND TAX PLANNING

Inbound tax planning involves the interplay of the tax laws of two or more countries. From a foreign corporation's perspective, the objective of inbound tax planning is to reduce the U.S. and foreign taxes on U.S.-source income. U.S. taxes increase a foreign corporation's total tax costs only to the extent they are not creditable for foreign tax purposes.

---

[20] Reg. § 1.894-1(d).

The primary concern of foreign corporations operating in the United States is repatriation—sending money back to the foreign corporation at the lowest possible tax cost. The remainder of this section will focus on methods to repatriate funds.

.01 Dividends

Dividends are the most common method to repatriate funds from a U.S. subsidiary to a foreign corporation. Unlike some other repatriation methods, dividends paid by the U.S. subsidiary are merely the distribution of accumulated earnings and profits to the foreign corporation that do not result in a deduction for the U.S. subsidiary. An advantage of a dividend is that many foreign countries exempt from income the dividends received from other countries, such as the United States.

The primary drawback of a dividend is the withholding tax that an applicable treaty may reduce (but may not exempt) while not providing the U.S. subsidiary a deduction. If the country of the foreign corporation is a territorial country that exempts the dividend from taxation, the withholding tax is non-creditable and represents an out-of-pocket cash cost. If the country of the foreign parent is a credit country with a system comparable to the U.S.'s credit system, the withholding still represents an out-of-pocket cash cost unless the effective U.S. tax rate (U.S. corporate income tax and withholding tax) is less than the tax rate in the country of the foreign corporation.

.02 Debt Financing

It may be advantageous to finance a U.S. subsidiary in a way that maximizes interest deductions and minimizes dividend payments. The potential advantage of debt financing provided to a U.S. subsidiary includes a deduction in the United States for interest paid to the foreign corporation, as well as the possibility of lower withholding tax on interest payments as opposed to dividend distributions.

To secure the benefits of debt financing, the foreign corporation must ensure that any intercompany payments meant to be interest qualify as such under the U.S. tax laws. The rules for determining whether an investment in a U.S. subsidiary is debt and not equity is rarely clear. In addition, the United States imposes the anti-earnings stripping provision[21] that may disallow the deductibility of interest payments. To the extent that interest payments are limited by the anti-earnings stripping provision, the taxpayer may wish to consider other methods of repatriating earnings that give rise to a deduction for the U.S. subsidiary (see ¶ 1003).

.03 Royalties

A foreign corporation choosing to manufacture and/or sell in the United States often makes technology and other intangible assets available to its U.S. subsidiary. These intangibles include patents, copyrights, trademarks, tradenames, unpatented know-how, etc. In return for benefiting from the use of the intangibles, the U.S. subsidiary agrees to pay royalties.

---

[21] Code Sec. 163(j).

¶1104.01

Royalties are a particularly tax efficient means of repatriating funds from a U.S. subsidiary for the use of intangibles. The deduction permitted to the paying U.S. subsidiary will help reduce the U.S. effective tax rate. Furthermore, royalty amounts can be substantial, particularly in light of the super-royalty provision in the last sentence of Section 482. Under this super-royalty provision, a payor of royalties must adjust the amount of royalties from time to time on the basis of the actual profit earned by the U.S. subsidiary and not just on the facts available at the time of the original transfer.

.04 Service Fees

Service fees represent payments a foreign corporation receives for charging its U.S. subsidiary for managerial, administrative, or technical services provided. Service fees paid to a foreign corporation are typically not subject to withholding tax by the United States as long as the services are performed outside the United States. If the services are performed inside the United States, the foreign corporation should be concerned that either (1) withholding should occur at a 30% rate[22] or (2) the foreign corporation will be considered to be engaged in a U.S. trade or business.[23]

The U.S. deduction of the service fee produces potential worldwide tax savings and the payment of the fee may provide a convenient way for the foreign corporation to realize current income, possibly at a cost that is lower than the U.S. income tax savings. More specifically, the service fees paid would reduce the U.S. subsidiary's taxable income while increasing the foreign corporation's income. If the foreign country tax rate on corporate income is lower than the tax rate in the United States, the worldwide effective tax rate will decrease. The worldwide effective tax rate may also decrease even if the tax rate is higher in the country of the foreign corporation if a dividend would otherwise result in a non-creditable U.S. withholding tax.

To determine the amount of service fees the foreign corporation can charge its U.S. subsidiary, the foreign corporation should consider both the direct cost of providing the services and the indirect costs (e.g., an allocation of overhead). A central cost allocation agreement is a formal contract between the parties involved that establishes the services to be performed and the related fees. The challenge is to ensure that the charges for the services provided meet the arm's-length standard of transfer pricing.

.05 Transfer Pricing

By altering its transfer pricing policy, a foreign corporation may be able to allocate a smaller portion of its worldwide profits to its U.S. subsidiary that may incur a withholding tax if repatriated under another method (as well as a smaller amount of taxable income). For example, a foreign corporation can allocate a smaller share of the gross profit from intercompany inventory sales by charging its U.S. subsidiary a higher price. The smaller gross profit will result in smaller

---

[22] Code Sec. 1442.

[23] Code Sec. 882.

earnings and profits. The smaller earnings and profits will result in smaller dividends subject to U.S. withholding tax (see Chapter 12).

Example 11.5: ASIAco is a trading company in an Asian country, where the highest corporate income tax rate is 16%. ASIAco owns USAco, its U.S. subsidiary, which purchases gadgets from ASIAco for resale in the United States. In addition to the U.S. corporate income tax rate at 35%, any dividend distributed by USAco to ASIAco will be subject to a 30% withholding tax, resulting in an effective U.S. tax rate of 54.5% (e.g., after 35 cents of every dollar of income goes to the IRS, an additional 19.5 cents of the remaining 65 cent dividend is withheld). As a result, by aggressively pricing gadgets from ASIAco to USAco, the parties can save 38.5 cents for every dollar subject to the Asian country's tax and not subject to U.S. tax (54.5 cents compared to 16 cents).

Suppose USAco has gross profit of $13 million and operating expenses of $10 million. The Berry Ratio (gross profit over operating expenses) for USAco is 1.3. But suppose that the interquartile range for the comparable profits method is a Berry Ratio of 1.2 to 1.3. By operating at the high end of the Berry Ratio, USAco satisfies the arm's length standard, but may be unnecessarily paying too much U.S. tax. By moving $1 million of gross profit from USAco to ASIAco (in the form of a higher cost of goods sold), the parties will save taxes of approximately $385,000. At the same time, USAco will still be in the interquartile range with a Berry Ratio of 1.2 (gross profit of $12 million over operating expenses of $10 million).

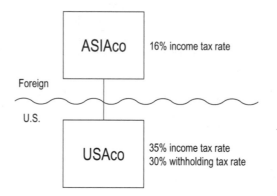

With the exception of dividends, all of the above-mentioned repatriation techniques involve an element of transfer pricing. A foreign corporation may charge no more than an arm's length rate of interest on any loans to its U.S. subsidiary. The foreign corporation may try to shift income by charging its U.S. subsidiary an arm's length royalty for the use of foreign-owned manufacturing and marketing intangibles. In addition, any service fee must be at arm's length. Because transfer pricing is so ingrained in repatriation, transfer pricing is almost always raised by the IRS on audit. Therefore, it is imperative for taxpayers to establish defensible positions for the transfer prices charged through contemporaneous documentation of their transfer pricing methodology or through an advance pricing agreement.

¶1104.05

¶ 1105 COMPREHENSIVE EXAMPLE

FORco, a foreign corporation located in country F, plans to locate a new factory in the United States. FORco will structure the new facility as a wholly-owned U.S. subsidiary, USSub. FORco will finance USSub solely with an equity investment. FORco projects that in USSub's first year of operations, USSub will generate $10 million of taxable income, all from active U.S. manufacturing activities. In conducting this analysis, further assume the following:

   (i) The U.S. corporate tax rate is 35%,

   (ii) FORco's only item of income during the year is that derived from USSub, and

   (iii) Foreign country F taxes its residents on its worldwide income, with the sole exemption for dividends received from corporations outside of country F. Although foreign country F offers a direct credit for income taxes paid in countries outside of foreign country F, a credit is not available for taxes paid to other countries related to dividends received from companies resident in other countries (either the underlying income taxes or any withholding taxes).

The total tax rate on USSub earnings will vary significantly, depending on a number of factors, including:

   (i) Whether foreign country F is a low-tax or high-tax foreign country,

   (ii) Whether FORco repatriates USSub's earnings,

   (iii) Whether FORco repatriates USSub's earnings through dividend distributions, as opposed to interest or royalty payments or higher transfer prices,

   (iv) Whether a favorable tax treaty exists that contains withholding rates on dividends, interest and royalties paid by USSub to FORco, and

   (v) Whether FORco conducts its U.S. operations as a corporation, a domestic hybrid entity or a domestic reverse hybrid entity.

The effect of these factors is illustrated by computing the worldwide tax rate on USSub's earnings under a variety of assumptions.

Case 1: No dividends. If USSub does not pay any dividends, the total tax rate on its earnings will be 35%, computed as follows:

U.S. income tax

USSub's taxable income	$10,000,000
U.S. income tax rate	× 35%
U.S. income tax	$3,500,000
U.S. withholding taxes on repatriated earnings	$0
F tax on repatriated earnings	$0
Total taxes [$3,500,000 + $0 + $0]	$3,500,000
Worldwide effective tax rate [$3,500,000 ÷ $10,000,000]	35%

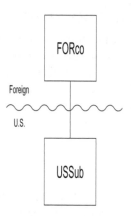

This example illustrates that if USSub does not repatriate any of its earnings to FORco, the worldwide tax rate on the U.S. operations will be the same as the U.S. corporate income tax rate. By not paying any dividends, the worldwide effective tax rate is 35% regardless of whether country F is a high-tax country (a top corporate tax rate above the 35% U.S. corporate tax rate) or a low-tax country (a top corporate tax rate below the 35% U.S. corporate tax rate).

Case 2: Pays dividend/Tax treaty. Assume that country F has a tax treaty with the United States that provides a 10% withholding tax rate on dividends. If FORco repatriates half of USSub's after-tax earnings through a dividend distribution, the total tax rate on USSub's repatriated and unrepatriated earnings will be 38.25%, computed as follows:

U.S. income tax

USSub's taxable income	$10,000,000
U.S. income tax rate	× 35%
U.S. income tax	$3,500,000

U.S. withholding taxes on repatriated earnings

USSub's after-tax earnings [$10,000,000 − $3,500,000]	$6,500,000
Percentage repatriated through dividend	× 50%
Dividend distribution	$3,250,000
Withholding tax rate (per treaty)	× 10%
U.S. withholding tax	$325,000

F tax on repatriated earnings	$0
Total taxes [$3,500,000 + $325,000 + $0]	$3,825,000
Worldwide effective tax rate [$3,825,000 ÷ $10,000,000]	38.25%

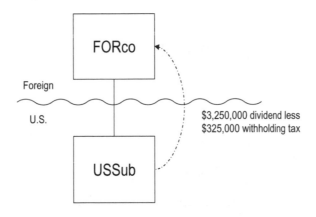

Therefore, by repatriating half of USSub's earnings through a dividend distribution, FORco increases the worldwide tax rate on USSub's earnings from 35% in Case 1 to 38.25% in Case 2. Although foreign country F does not tax the repatriated earnings, (i) the higher worldwide effective tax rate is due to the 10% withholding tax and (ii) due to the country F exemption for dividends, the worldwide effective tax rate does not change regardless of whether foreign country F is a high-tax or low-tax country.

Case 3: Pays dividend/No tax treaty. An important assumption in Case 2 is that country F had a tax treaty with the United States that provided for a 10% withholding tax rate on dividends. Now assume that there is no tax treaty between the United States and country F, such that the U.S.'s statutory withholding rate on dividends of 30% applies. The lack of a favorable treaty withholding rate increases the total tax rate on USSub's repatriated and unrepatriated earnings from 38.25% in Case 2 to 44.75% in Case 3, computed as follows:

U.S. income tax

USSub's taxable income $10,000,000

U.S. income tax rate . . . . × 35%

U.S. income tax $3,500,000

U.S. withholding taxes on repatriated earnings

USSub's after-tax earnings [$10,000,000 – $3,500,000] $6,500,000

Percentage repatriated through dividend . . . . × 50%

Dividend distribution $3,250,000

Withholding tax rate (non-treaty) . . . . × 30%

U.S. withholding tax $975,000

F tax on repatriated earnings $0

Total taxes [$3,500,000 + $975,000,000 + $0] $4,475,000

Worldwide effective tax rate [$4,475,000 ÷ $10,000,000] 44.75%

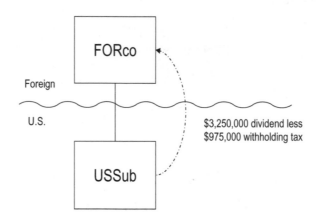

Therefore, assuming FORco repatriates some of USSub's earnings through a dividend distribution, the availability of a favorable treaty withholding rate on dividends is critical to lowering the worldwide effective tax rate. As in Case 1 and Case 2, because country F does not tax dividends received from companies in other countries, the corporate tax rate in country F is irrelevant.

Case 4: Low-tax parent country/No dividends/Higher transfer price. Assume that USSub conducts a transfer pricing study and determines that its Berry Ratio (gross profit over operating expenses) is at the high end of the interquartile range. As part of its repatriation strategy, USSub could increase its transfer price for goods and services paid to FORco by $3,250,000 (half of its previous after-tax income) and still remain in the interquartile range.

U.S. income tax

USSub's previous taxable income	$10,000,000
Additional cost of goods sold	− 3,250,000
USSub's taxable income	$6,750,000
U.S. income tax rate	× 35%
U.S. income tax	$2,362,500

U.S. withholding taxes on repatriated earnings $0

F tax on repatriated earnings

FORco's additional taxable income	$3,250,000
F tax rate	× 25%
F income tax	$812,500

Total taxes [$2,362,500 + $0 + $812,500] $3,175,000

Worldwide effective tax rate [$3,175,000 ÷ $10,000,000] 31.75%

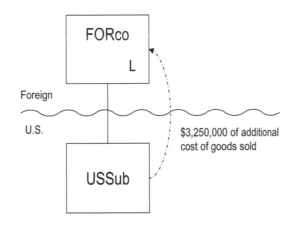

By repatriating $3,250,000 without a withholding tax, USSub has reduced the effective tax rate on the $3,250,000 of repatriated earnings from 35% (the U.S. rate) to 25% (the low-tax rate in foreign country F). When blended with the unrepatriated earnings taxed at the U.S. rate of 35%, the worldwide effective tax rate decreases to 31.75%.

Case 5: High-tax parent country/No dividends/Higher transfer price. Again, assume that USSub conducts a transfer pricing study and determines that its Berry Ratio (gross profit over operating expenses) is at the high end of the interquartile range. As part of its repatriation strategy, USSub could increase its transfer price for goods and services paid to FORco by $3,250,000 (half of its previous after-tax income) and still remain in the interquartile range.

U.S. income tax

USSub's previous taxable income	$10,000,000
Additional cost of goods sold	– 3,250,000
USSub's taxable income	$6,750,000
U.S. income tax rate	× 35%
	$2,362,500
U.S. withholding taxes on repatriated earnings	$0

F tax on repatriated earnings

FORco's additional taxable income	$3,250,000
F tax rate	× 45%
F income tax	$1,462,500

Total taxes [$2,362,500 + $0 + $1,462,500]	$3,825,000
Worldwide effective tax rate [$3,825,000 ÷ $10,000,000]	38.25%

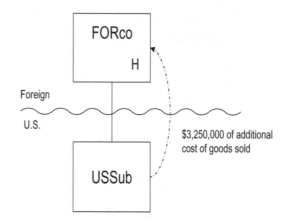

By using transfer pricing techniques to repatriate funds, USSub avoids a U.S. repatriation cost on the $3,250,000. Although the transfer pricing will subject the $3,250,000 to the higher country F corporate tax rate, the lack of a withholding tax provides a worldwide effective tax rate of 38.25%, which is as low as paying dividends with a treaty (Case 2) and lower than paying dividends without a treaty (Case 3), but not as low as not repatriating (Case 1).

Case 6: Low-tax foreign parent/Earnings stripping/Tax treaty. A strategy for reducing the withholding taxes on USSub's earnings is to engage in earnings stripping, that is, to repatriate USSub's profits through deductible interest and royalty payments, rather than nondeductible dividend distributions. For example, assume that FORco, which pays tax at a 25% rate in country F, modifies its plans for USSub, as follows: (i) finance USSub with both debt and equity, such that USSub will pay FORco $2 million of interest each year, (ii) charge USSub an annual royalty of $1.25 million for the use of FORco's patents and trade secrets, and (iii) eliminate USSub's dividend distribution. Further assume that the applicable tax treaty withholding rate is zero percent for both interest and royalties.

As the following computations indicate, debt financing and charges for technology transfers totaling $3.25 million reduce the worldwide effective tax rate on the earnings to 31.75%, computed as follows:

U.S. income tax

USSub's income before interest and royalties	$10,000,000
Interest paid to FORco	− 2,000,000
Royalties paid to FORco	− 1,250,000
USSub's taxable income	$6,750,000
U.S. income tax rate	× 35%
U.S. income tax	$2,362,500

U.S. withholding taxes on repatriated earnings

Withholding tax on interest (per treaty)	$0
Withholding tax on royalties (per treaty)	0
U.S. Withholding taxes	$0

F tax on repatriated earnings

Interest from USSub	$2,000,000
Royalties from USSub	+ 1,250,000
FORco's taxable income	$3,250,000
F tax rate	× 25%
Pre-credit F tax	$812,500
F's credit	– 0
F's income tax	$812,500

Total taxes [$2,362,500 + $0 + $812,500] $3,175,000

Worldwide effective tax rate [$3,175,000 ÷ $10,000,000] 31.75%

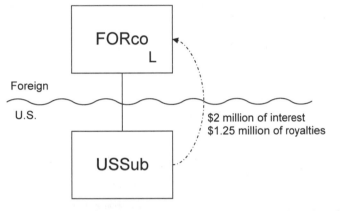

$2 million of interest
$1.25 million of royalties

The 31.75% worldwide effective tax rate on the U.S. earnings is a blended rate, whereby the $3,250,000 of interest and royalties paid to FORco are, in effect, taxed at the F country rate of 25% and the unrepatriated U.S. earnings are taxed at the U.S. rate of 35%. This Case 6 has the same result as when FORco, a low-tax foreign parent, increases its transfer prices (Case 4), which are the two cases with the lowest worldwide effective tax rates of the cases in which FORco is in a low-tax country.

Case 7: High-tax foreign parent/Earnings stripping/Tax treaty. Assume the same facts as in Case 6 (interest of $2 million and royalties of $1.25 million), except that country F is a high-tax country with a tax rate of 45%. As the following computations indicate, debt financing and charges for technology transfers reduce the total tax rate on country F earnings to 38.25%, computed as follows:

U.S. income tax

USSub's income before interest and royalties	$10,000,000
Interest paid to FORco	– 2,000,000
Royalties paid to FORco	– 1,250,000
USSub's taxable income	$6,750,000
U.S. income tax rate	× 35%
U.S. income tax	$2,362,500

U.S. withholding taxes on repatriated earnings

Withholding tax on interest (per treaty)	$0
Withholding tax on royalties (per treaty)	0
U.S. Withholding taxes	$0

F tax on repatriated earnings

Interest from USSub	$2,000,000
Royalties from USSub	+ 1,250,000
FORco's taxable income	$3,250,000
F tax rate	× 45%
Pre-credit F tax	$1,462,500
F's credit	– 0
F's income tax	$1,462,500

Total taxes [$2,362,500 + $0 + $1,462,500]	$3,825,000
Worldwide effective tax rate [$3,825,000 ÷ $10,000,000]	38.25%

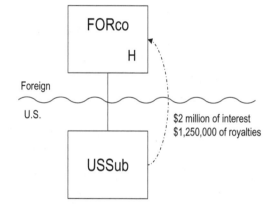

Again, the 38.25% worldwide tax rate on USAco's earnings is a blended rate, whereby the $3,250,000 of interest and royalties paid to FORco are, in effect, taxed at the foreign country F rate of 45% and the unpatriated earnings are taxed at the U.S. rate of 35%. This is the same result as when FORco, a high-tax foreign parent, increases its transfer pricing (Case 5). These two cases result in the lowest worldwide effective tax rate (38.25%) of the cases in which FORco is in a high-tax country and repatriates.

Case 8: Low-tax foreign parent/No dividends/Domestic reverse hybrid. The United States has a corporate income tax rate of 35%, which is 10 percentage points higher than the country F rate of 25%. FORco owns a domestic reverse hybrid entity (USDRH), a limited partnership[24] in the United States and checks-the-box for U.S. corporate tax treatment. For U.S. tax purposes, FORco is not deemed

---

[24] For this case and other cases involving partnerships, we will assume that FORco has formed a flow-through entity, such as an LLC, to be the other partner.

to receive any income because USDRH is not treated as a pass through entity and USDRH does not pay dividends. FORco does not have a country F tax liability because the U.S. taxes constitute a credit that eliminate country F taxes. The total tax rate on USDRH's earnings will be 35% computed as follows:

U.S. income tax

USDRH's taxable income	$10,000,000
U.S. income tax rate	× 35%
U.S. income tax	$3,500,000

U.S. withholding taxes on repatriated earnings	$0

F tax on earnings

Earnings from USDRH	$10,000,000
F tax rate	× 25%
Pre-credit F tax	$2,500,000
F's credit	− 2,500,000
U.S. income tax: $3,500,000	
F income tax	$0

Total taxes [$3,500,000 + $0 + $0]	$3,500,000

Worldwide effective tax rate [$3,500,000 ÷ $10,000,000]	35%

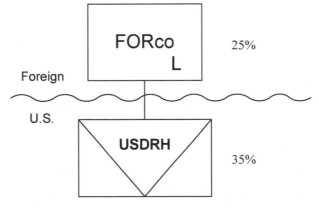

This example illustrates that regardless of whether the U.S. entity is a corporation under a state's corporate law or a domestic reverse hybrid entity by virtue of checking-the-box, the worldwide effective tax rate remains 35% as long as (i) the U.S. entity does not distribute any dividends and (ii) the country F tax rate is less than the U.S. tax rate.

¶1105

Case 9: Low-tax foreign parent/Pays dividend/Tax treaty/Domestic reverse hybrid. The United States has a corporate income tax rate of 35%, which is 10 percentage points higher than the country F rate of 25%. FORco owns USDRH, a limited partnership in the United States and checks-the-box for U.S. corporate tax treatment. USDRH distributes a $3,250,000 dividend that is subject to withholding tax at a 10% treaty rate, but the dividend does not constitute income to FORco and the U.S. withholding tax is not creditable in country F. Instead, FORco reports $10 million of operating income on which the country F credit for U.S. income taxes paid will eliminate. The worldwide effective tax rate on all its earnings will be 38.25%, computed as follows:

U.S. income tax

USDRH's taxable income	$10,000,000
U.S. income tax rate	× 35%
U.S. income tax	$3,500,000

U.S. withholding taxes on repatriated earnings

USDRH's after-tax earnings [$10,000,000 – $3,500,000]	$6,500,000
Percentage repatriated through dividend	× 50%
Dividend distribution	$3,250,000
Withholding tax rate (per treaty)	× 10%
U.S. withholding tax	$325,000

F tax on earnings

Earnings from USDRH	$10,000,000
F tax rate	× 25%
Pre-credit F tax	$2,500,000
F's credit	– 2,500,000

U.S. income tax: $3,500,000

F income tax	$0
Total taxes [$3,500,000 + $325,000 + $0]	$3,825,000
Worldwide effective tax rate [$3,825,000 ÷ $10,000,000]	38.25%

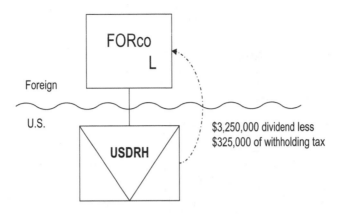

This example illustrates how FORco increases its worldwide effective tax rate above the U.S. tax rate of 35% by using a domestic reverse hybrid entity and repatriating. By creating a domestic reverse hybrid entity, FORco controls the timing of the U.S. withholding taxes on repatriated earnings at a treaty rate of 10%, but incurs a slight increase of the worldwide effective tax rate because the U.S. withholding taxes are not creditable.

Case 10: Low-tax foreign parent/Pays dividend/No treaty/Domestic reverse hybrid. The United States has a corporate income tax rate of 35%, which is 10 percentage points higher than the country F rate of 25%. FORco owns USDRH, a limited partnership in the United States and checks-the-box for U.S. corporate tax treatment. USDRH distributes a dividend that is subject to U.S. withholding tax at a 30% non-treaty rate, but the $3,250,000 dividend does not constitute income to FORco and the U.S. withholding tax is not creditable in country F. Instead, FORco reports $10 million of operating income on which the country F credit for U.S. income taxes paid will eliminate. The worldwide effective tax rate on all its earnings will be 44.75%, computed as follows:

U.S. income tax

USDRH's taxable income	$10,000,000
U.S. income tax	× 35%
	$3,500,000

U.S. withholding taxes on repatriated earnings

USDRH's after-tax earnings [$10,000,000 – $3,500,000]	$6,500,000
Percentage repatriated through dividend	× 50%
Dividend distribution	$3,250,000
Withholding tax rate (non-treaty)	× 30%
U.S. withholding tax	$975,000

F tax on earnings

Earnings from USDRH	$10,000,000
F tax rate	× 25%

Pre-credit F tax	$2,500,000
F's credit	– 2,500,000
U.S. income tax: $3,500,000	
F income tax	$0

Total taxes [$3,500,000 + $975,000 + $0] $4,475,000

Worldwide effective tax rate [$4,475,000 ÷ $10,000,000] 44.75%

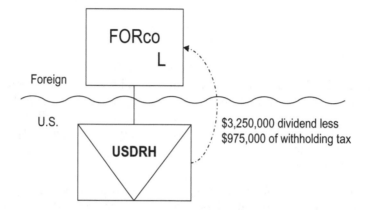

This example illustrates how FORco increases its worldwide effective tax rate above the U.S. tax rate of 35% by using a domestic reverse hybrid entity and repatriating. By creating a domestic reverse hybrid entity, FORco can control the timing of the U.S. withholding taxes on repatriated earnings but is subject to higher U.S. withholding taxes at the non-treaty rate of 30%, which increases the worldwide effective tax rate to 44.75%. Case 10 results in the highest worldwide effective tax rate of the cases in which FORco is in a low-tax country.

Case 11: High-tax foreign parent/No dividends/Domestic reverse hybrid. The United States has a corporate income tax rate of 35%, which is 10 percentage points lower than the country F rate of 45%. FORco owns USDRH, a limited partnership in the United States and checks-the-box for U.S. corporate tax treatment. For U.S. tax purposes, FORco is not deemed to receive any income because USDRH is not treated as a pass through entity and USDRH does not pay dividends. FORco does pay tax on $10 million of operating income in country F on which the country F credit for U.S. income taxes paid should reduce. The total tax rate on USDRH's earnings will be 45%, computed as follows:

U.S. income tax

USDRH's taxable income	$10,000,000
U.S. income tax	× 35%
	$3,500,000

U.S. withholding taxes on repatriated earnings $0

F tax on earnings

Earnings from USDRH	$10,000,000
F tax rate	× 45%
Pre-credit F tax	$4,500,000
F's credit	– 3,500,000

U.S. income tax: $3,500,000

F income tax	$1,000,000
Total taxes [$3,500,000 + $0 + $1,000,000]	$4,500,000
Worldwide effective tax rate [$4,500,000 ÷ $10,000,000]	45%

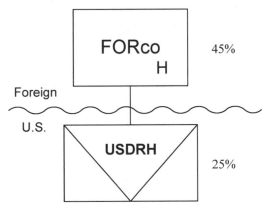

This example illustrates how the worldwide effective tax rate increases to 45% due to the use of a domestic reverse hybrid entity. Although FORco can control the timing of the U.S. withholding tax, all the operating income passes through to FORco in a high tax country.

Case 12: High-tax foreign parent/Pays dividend/Tax treaty/Domestic reverse hybrid. The United States has a corporate income tax rate of 35%, which is 10 percentage points lower than the country F rate of 45%. FORco owns USDRH, a limited partnership in the United States and checks-the-box for corporate treatment. USDRH distributes a $3,250,000 dividend that is subject to withholding tax, but the dividend does not constitute income to FORco and the U.S. withholding tax is not creditable in country F. Instead, FORco reports $10 million of operating income on which the country F credit for U.S. income taxes paid will reduce. The worldwide effective tax rate on USDRH's earnings increases to 48.25%, computed as follows:

U.S. income tax

USDRH's taxable income	$10,000,000
U.S. income tax rate	× 35%
U.S. income tax	$3,500,000

U.S. withholding taxes on repatriated earnings

USDRH's after-tax earnings [$10,000,000 – $3,500,000]	$6,500,000
Percentage repatriated through dividend	× 50%
Dividend distribution	$3,250,000
Withholding tax rate (per treaty)	× 10%
U.S. withholding tax	$325,000

F tax on earnings

Earnings from USDRH	$10,000,000
F tax rate	× 45%
Pre-credit F tax	$4,500,000
F's credit	– 3,500,000

U.S. income tax: $3,500,000

F income tax	$1,000,000
Total taxes [$3,500,000 + $325,000 + $1,000,000]	$4,825,000
Worldwide effective tax rate [$4,825,000 ÷ $10,000,000]	48.25%

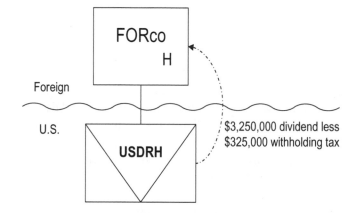

Although this example illustrates that the worldwide effective tax rate is higher due to the distribution of dividends, due to the treaty the rate is only 3.25 percentage points higher than in Case 11.

Case 13: High-tax foreign parent/Pays dividend/No treaty/Domestic reverse hybrid. The United States has a corporate income tax rate of 35%, which is 10 percentage points lower than the country F rate of 45%. FORco owns USDRH, a limited partnership in the United States and checks-the-box for U.S. corporate tax treatment. USDRH distributes a $3,250,000 dividend that is subject to U.S. withholding tax at a 30% non-treaty rate, but the dividend does not constitute income to FORco and the U.S. withholding tax is not creditable in country F. Instead, FORco reports $10 million of operating income on which the country F credit for U.S. income taxes paid will reduce. The total tax rate on USDRH's earnings will be 54.75%, computed as follows:

¶1105

U.S. income tax

USDRH's taxable income	$10,000,000
U.S. income tax rate	× 35%
U.S. income tax	$3,500,000

U.S. withholding taxes on repatriated earnings

USDRH's after-tax earnings [$10,000,000 – $3,500,000]	$6,500,000
Percentage repatriated through dividend	× 50%
Dividend distribution	$3,250,000
Withholding tax rate (non-treaty)	× 30%
U.S. withholding tax	$975,000

F tax on earnings

Earnings from USDRH	$10,000,000
F tax rate	× 45%
Pre-credit F tax	$4,500,000
F's credit	– 3,500,000
U.S. income tax: $3,500,000	
F income tax	$1,000,000

Total taxes [$3,500,000 + $975,000 + $1,000,000]	$5,475,000
Worldwide effective tax rate [$5,475,000 ÷ $10,000,000]	54.75%

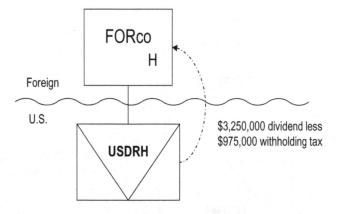

Similar to Case 12, this example illustrates the increase in the worldwide tax rate due to the repatriation. Unlike Case 12, the increase is much greater due to the lack of a treaty and this does not appear to be a tax efficient structure. Case 13 results in the highest worldwide effective tax rate (54.75%) of the cases in which FORco is in a high-tax country.

Case 14: Domestic hybrid/Tax treaty. FORco forms a limited liability company in the United States, which is a domestic hybrid entity (USDH)—a pass through entity for U.S. tax purposes, but a corporation for country F purposes. For U.S. tax purposes, assume that the USDH is a branch that is subject to the branch tax at the treaty rate and the USDH reinvests half of its earnings in the United States. FORco does not report any earnings because any non-reinvested earnings transferred from USDH to FORco are treated as dividends in country F that are exempt from tax. Because the U.S. branch profits tax is not creditable for foreign country F purposes, this $325,000 tax represents an out-of-pocket cost. The total tax rate on the earnings will be 38.25%, computed as follows:

U.S. income tax

USDRH's taxable income	$10,000,000
U.S. income tax	× 35%
	$3,500,000

U.S. branch tax on deemed repatriation

USDRH's after-tax earnings [$10,000,000 – $3,500,000]	$6,500,000
Percentage of earnings reinvested	× 50%
Increase in U.S. net equity	$3,250,000
Dividend equivalent amount [$6,500,000 – $3,250,000]	$3,250,000
Branch tax rate	× 10%
U.S. branch tax	$325,000

F tax on repatriated earnings	$0
Total taxes [$3,500,000 + $325,000 + $0]	$3,825,000
Worldwide effective tax rate [$3,825,000 ÷ $10,000,000]	38.25%

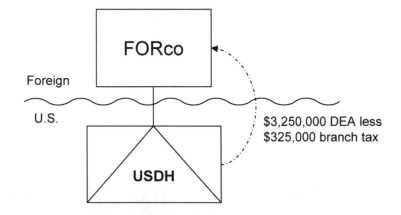

This example shows how the treaty rate of 10% for the branch tax results in a worldwide effective tax rate of 38.25%. Because foreign country F does not tax the repatriated earnings, which it treats as exempt dividends, the worldwide effective tax rate does not change regardless of whether foreign country F is a high-tax or low-tax country.

¶1105

Case 15: Domestic hybrid/No treaty. FORco forms a limited liability company in the United States, which is a USDH—a pass through entity for U.S. tax purposes, but a corporation for country F purposes. For U.S. tax purposes, assume that the USDH is a branch that is subject to the branch tax at the non-treaty rate and the USDH reinvests half of its earnings in the United States. FORco does not report any earnings because any non-reinvested earnings transferred from USDH to FORco are treated as dividends in country F that are exempt from tax under country F law. Because the U.S. branch profits tax is not creditable for foreign country F purposes, this $325,000 tax represents an out-of-pocket cost. The total tax rate on the earnings will be 44.75%, computed as follows:

U.S. income tax

USDRH's taxable income	$10,000,000
U.S. income tax	× 35%
	$3,500,000

U.S. branch tax on deemed repatriation

USDRH's after-tax earnings [$10,000,000 – $3,500,000]	$6,500,000
Percentage of earnings reinvested	× 50%
Increase in U.S. net equity	$3,250,000
Dividend equivalent amount [$6,500,000 – $3,250,000]	$3,250,000
Branch tax rate	× 30%
U.S. branch tax	$975,000

F tax on repatriated earnings	$0
Total taxes [$3,500,000 + $975,000 + $0]	$4,475,000
Worldwide effective tax rate [$4,475,000 ÷ $10,000,000]	44.75%

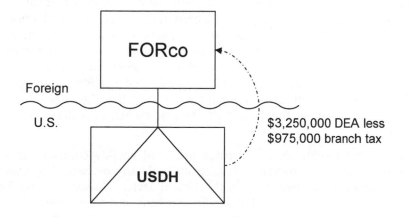

This example illustrates how the use of the hybrid entity without a treaty will result in the higher branch tax and the relatively high worldwide effective tax rate of 44.75%. Because foreign country F does not tax the repatriated earnings, which it treats as exempt dividends, the worldwide effective tax rate does not change regardless of whether foreign country F is a high-tax or low-tax country.

TABLE 11.1. COMPREHENSIVE EXAMPLE—SUMMARY

Case	U.S. tax rate	Country F tax rate	Amount of earnings repatriated	Method of repatriating earnings	U.S. withholding tax rate	Current year worldwide effective tax rate
1	35%	—	None	n.a.	n.a.	35%
2	35%	—	$3,250,000	Dividend	10%	38.25%
3	35%	—	$3,250,000	Dividend	30%	44.75%
4	35%	25%	$3,250,000	Transfer pricing	n.a.	31.75%
5	35%	45%	$3,250,000	Transfer pricing	n.a.	38.25%
6	35%	25%	$3,250,000	Interest and royalties	0%	31.75%
7	35%	45%	$3,250,000	Interest and royalties	0%	38.25%
8	35%	25%	None	n.a.	n.a.	35%
9	35%	25%	$3,250,000	Dividend	10%	38.25%
10	35%	25%	$3,250,000	Dividend	30%	44.75%
11	35%	45%	None	n.a.	n.a.	45%
12	35%	45%	$3,250,000	Dividend	10%	48.25%
13	35%	45%	$3,250,000	Dividend	30%	54.75%
14	35%	—	$3,250,000	Branch	10%	38.25%
15	35%	—	$3,250,000	Branch	30%	44.75%

¶ 1106 SURVEY OF U.S. ENTITY CLASSIFICATION

This survey (Table 11.2) lists common entities in the United States, describes the treatment for U.S. tax purposes if an election is not made (whether the entity is a per se corporation or its default status is a corporation or pass through entity) and considers the possibility for treatment as a domestic hybrid or domestic reverse hybrid entity. Of course, foreign owners may operate as a sole proprietorship or a branch, which is not treated as a separate entity under the check-the-box rules. General partnerships, limited partnerships, and limited liability partnerships are generally pass through entities for foreign tax purposes that the owner may check for corporate treatment in the United States that results in a domestic reverse hybrid entity.

Similarly, if a foreign country treated a limited liability company as a pass through entity, a domestic reverse hybrid entity could also be formed by checking-the-box for corporate tax treatment in the Untied States. However, many foreign countries do not treat the U.S. limited liability company as a pass through entity. As a result, U.S. limited liability companies offer the opportunity to be a domestic hybrid entity by virtue of their pass through status for U.S. tax purposes and their corporate status for foreign country tax purposes. Because U.S. C corporations are per se corporations, they do not offer either domestic hybrid entity or domestic

¶1106

reverse hybrid entity planning opportunities. An S corporation is not appropriate for inbound tax planning because a foreign person may not own an S corporation.[25]

TABLE 11.2. CLASSIFICATION OF U.S. ENTITIES

Entity	Status without checking-the-box election	Hybrid or reverse hybrid opportunity
Corporation	Per Se Corporation	—
General partnership	Pass-through	Reverse
Limited partnership	Pass-through	Reverse
Limited liability partnership	Pass-through	Reverse
Limited liability company	Pass-through	Hybrid or Reverse Hybrid

---

[25] Code Sec. 1361(b).

Chapter 12
Transfer Pricing

¶ 1201 WHAT IS TRANSFER PRICING?

The operating units of a multinational corporation usually engage in a variety of intercompany transactions. For example, a U.S. manufacturer may market its products abroad through foreign marketing subsidiaries. The same U.S. parent corporation also may provide managerial, technical, and administrative services for its subsidiaries. Another common arrangement is for a U.S. parent corporation to license its manufacturing and marketing intangibles to its foreign subsidiaries for commercial exploitation abroad. A "transfer price" must be computed for these controlled transactions in order to satisfy various financial reporting, tax, and other regulatory requirements. Although transfer prices do not affect the combined income of a controlled group of corporations, they do affect how that income is allocated among the group members.

> *Example 12.1:* USAco, a domestic corporation, manufactures small engines for sale both in the United States and abroad. Foreign sales are made through FORco, a wholly owned foreign corporation. On a per-unit basis, USAco's engines cost $600 to manufacture, $100 to market, and sell for $1,000 abroad (see Figure 12.1). Regardless of the transfer price used for sales by USAco to FORco, the combined income from a foreign sale is $300 per engine [$1,000 final sales price – $600 manufacturing cost – $100 selling expense]. However, transfer prices do affect the allocation of that combined profit between USAco and FORco.

Figure 12.1 Transfer pricing example

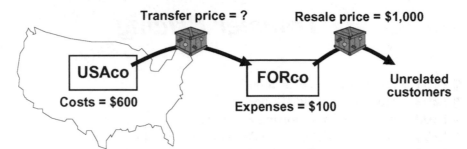

At one extreme, a transfer price of $600 would allocate the combined profit of $300 entirely to FORco, as follows.

Transaction	Effect on USAco	Effect on FORco
Manufacture engine	Production cost = $600	
Controlled sale	Sales revenue = $600	Cost of sales = $600
Foreign selling activities		Selling expense = $100
Sale to foreign customer		Sales revenue = $1,000
	Net profit = $0	Net profit = $300

At the other extreme, a transfer price of $900 would allocate the combined profit of $300 entirely to USAco, as follows.

Transaction	Effect on USAco	Effect on FORco
Manufacture engine	Production cost = $600	
Controlled sale	Sales revenue = $900	Cost of sales = $900
Foreign selling activities		Selling expense = $100
Sale to foreign customer		Sales revenue = $1,000
	Net profit = $300	Net profit = $0

For income tax purposes, multinational corporations must allocate their worldwide profits among the various countries in which they operate. The ideal allocation would permit each country to tax an appropriate portion of the taxpayer's total profit, while avoiding taxation of the same income by more than one country. The mechanism for allocating a multinational's worldwide profits between its U.S. and foreign affiliates is the transfer price used for intercompany transactions. When tax rates vary across countries, transfer pricing can significantly impact the taxpayer's total tax costs.

For example, a U.S. manufacturer may be able to reduce a foreign marketing subsidiary's share of worldwide profits by using higher prices for controlled inventory sales.

Example 12.2: The facts are the same as in Example 12.1. Assume that the U.S. tax rate is 35% and the applicable foreign tax rate is 45%. Given this rate differential, the USAco group can reduce its worldwide taxes by using higher transfer prices for its outbound controlled sales. If a transfer price of $600 is used for a sale by USAco to FORco, the $300 gross profit is allocated entirely to FORco and the total tax on that profit equals the foreign tax of $135

[$300 of income × 45% foreign tax rate]. If a transfer price of $900 is used for the controlled sale, the $300 gross profit is allocated entirely to USAco and the total tax on that profit equals the U.S. tax of $105 [$300 of income × 35% U.S. tax rate].

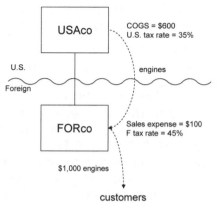

Transfer pricing also is a relevant issue for U.S. companies with operations in low-tax foreign jurisdictions. In these situations, a U.S. parent corporation has an incentive to shift income to its low-tax foreign subsidiary by, for example, using lower transfer prices for its outbound controlled sales. Although shifting income to a low-tax foreign subsidiary does not permanently avoid the residual U.S. tax on those low-taxed foreign earnings, shifting income does defer that tax until the foreign subsidiary repatriates those earnings through a dividend distribution.

***Example* 12.3:** The facts are the same as in Example 12.1. Assume that the U.S. tax rate is 35% and the applicable foreign tax rate is 25%. Given this rate differential, the USAco group can reduce its worldwide taxes by using lower transfer prices for its controlled sale. If a transfer price of $600 is used for a sale by USAco to FORco, the $300 gross profit is allocated entirely to FORco and the total tax on that profit equals $75 [$300 of income × 25% foreign tax rate]. If the transfer price of $900 is used for the controlled sale, the $300 gross profit is allocated entirely to USAco and the total tax on that profit equals the U.S. tax of $105 [$300 of income × 35% U.S. tax rate].

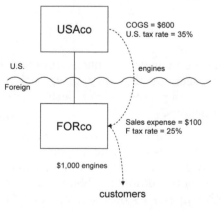

¶1201

In the case of a foreign-owned U.S. corporation, transfer prices affect not only the amount of income reported by the U.S. subsidiary, but can also serve as a method by which the foreign parent company can repatriate cash without paying any dividend withholding taxes. This is particularly important for a foreign parent company that is a resident of a country that does not have an income tax treaty with the United States, in which case the dividend withholding tax rate is 30%.

***Example* 12.4:** HKo is a trading company organized in Hong Kong, which has a corporate tax rate of only 16.5%, and does not have a tax treaty with the United States. HKo's U.S. subsidiary, USDist, purchases widgets from HKo for resale in the United States. In addition to a 35% corporate-level U.S. tax, any dividends paid to HKo are also subject to a shareholder-level U.S. withholding tax of 30%. Thus, the total effective U.S. tax rate on USDist's repatriated earnings is 54.5% (35% + 30% [1 – 35%]). As a result, to the extent HKo can justify charging a higher transfer price on its widget sales to USDist, every dollar of income that is shifted from USDist (54.5% tax rate) to HKo (16.5% tax rate) results in a tax savings of 38¢.

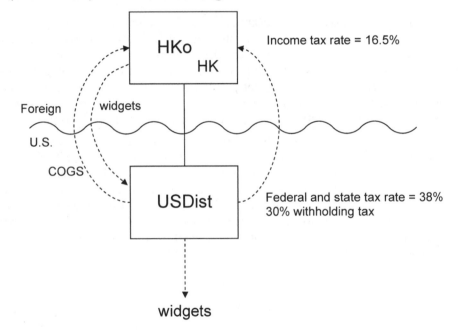

Multinational companies are often surprised by the large number of intercompany transactions that they must analyze. Even relatively simple scenarios for conducting cross-border business may result in numerous intercompany transactions.

***Example* 12.5:** CANco, a Canadian company, manufactures and sells widgets in the United States. Due to increased widget orders from U.S. customers, CANco decides to form a U.S. distribution subsidiary (USSub) to buy and resell widgets. Although USSub does not have any manufacturing functions, USSub employs its own administrative and sales staff while using

CANco's proprietary distribution software. In an effort to ensure that USSub is financially solvent, USSub has payment terms on its trade receivables to CANco of six months (USSub's average collection period is one month). If USSub's customers do not pay, USSub enjoys the use of CANco's collection staff. Finally, USSub uses CANco's storage racks.

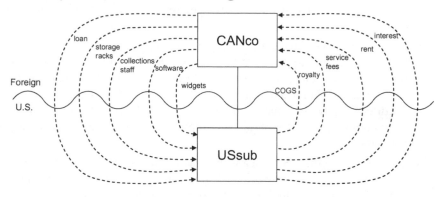

This example illustrates five intercompany transactions for which USSub must pay CANco at arm's length. First, the purchase of widgets constitutes a purchase of tangible property. Second, the use of the distribution software constitutes a transfer of intangible property for which USSub must pay a royalty. Third, the generous payment terms constitute a loan on which USSub must pay an arm's length rate of interest. Fourth, the provision of the collection staff constitutes a service for which USSub must pay an arm's length amount. Fifth, for USSub's use of the storage racks, CANco must be paid an arm's length rental fee.

¶ 1202 TRANSFER PRICING METHODS

.01 Basic Principles

The purpose of Code Sec. 482 is to ensure that taxpayers report and pay tax on their actual share of income arising from controlled transactions.[1] To this end, the Regulations under Code Sec. 482 adopt an arm's length standard for evaluating the appropriateness of a transfer price. Under this standard, a taxpayer should realize a similar amount of income from a controlled transaction as an uncontrolled party would have realized from a similar transaction under similar circumstances.[2]

To arrive at an arm's length result, the taxpayer must select and apply the method that provides the most reliable estimate of an arm's length price.[3] Thus, the primary focus in selecting a transfer pricing method is the reliability of the result, not its theoretical accuracy. The reliability of a pricing method is determined by the degree of comparability between the controlled and uncontrolled transactions, as well as the quality of the data and the assumptions used in the analysis.[4] The principal factors to consider in assessing the comparability of controlled and uncontrolled transactions include the following:[5]

[1] Reg. § 1.482-1(a)(1).
[2] Reg. § 1.482-1(b)(1).
[3] Reg. § 1.482-1(c)(1).
[4] Reg. § 1.482-1(c)(2).
[5] Reg. § 1.482-1(d)(1).

- Functions performed—The functional analysis identifies and compares the economically significant activities undertaken. These activities would include, for example, research and development, manufacturing or production, marketing and distribution, transportation and warehousing, and administrative functions. The theory behind this part of the regulations is that the party performing more functions should receive more of the income.

- Risks assumed—This analysis requires a comparison of the significant risks that could affect the prices to be charged. For example, risk associated with the success or failure of research and development activities, finances (such as fluctuations in foreign currency and interest rates), credit and collection, product liability, and market fluctuation. The theory behind this part of the regulations is that the party assuming more risks should receive greater rewards.

- Contractual terms—Significant contractual terms could affect the economic analysis of two similarly-priced transactions. For example, the quantity of items purchased or sold, the form of consideration (paid in local or foreign currency), the scope of any warranties, the rights to updates or modifications, the duration of the contract, the extent of any collateral transactions between the parties, and the extension of any credit or payment terms may have an economic effect on the transaction.

- Economic conditions and markets—This comparability factor focuses on the economic conditions that could affect the prices to be charged. This includes the similarity of geographic markets, the level of the market (e.g., wholesale or retail), the extent of competition in each market, the economic conditions of the particular industry, and the alternatives realistically available to either party (e.g., manufacture or purchase inventory).

- Nature of the property or services transferred in the transaction—As further discussed later in this chapter, the comparability of property sold or services provided is more relevant to the transaction-based methods than the profit-based methods.

   ***Example* 12.6:** USAco, a U.S. subsidiary of ASIAco, a Japanese parent corporation, purchases televisions from its Japanese parent that USAco markets in the United States. If it were to use one of the transaction-based methods, USAco must compare prices charged for wholesale-level sales of televisions. However, if the taxpayer chooses a profit-based method, such as the comparable profits method, USAco must merely find companies comparable to itself with respect to the type of functions performed and the risks assumed.

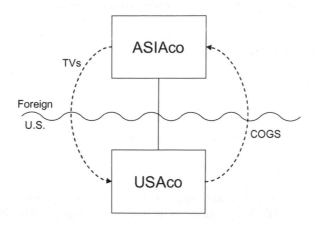

Adjustments must be made for any material differences between the controlled and uncontrolled transactions, assuming the effect of the difference can be ascertained with enough accuracy to improve the reliability of the results.[6]

As a practical matter, comparable transactions often are not readily available for the types of transactions entered into by affiliates of a vertically integrated multinational corporation. For example, inventory sales between affiliated companies often involve component parts and semifinished goods that are unique and are not sold in public markets. As a consequence, the appropriate arm's length price is often ambiguous.

The concept of the arm's length range helps taxpayers deal with uncertainty. Under this provision, a taxpayer may use two or more comparable uncontrolled transactions (of similar comparability and reliability) to establish an arm's length range of prices. If the taxpayer's transfer prices lie within the range, the IRS will not make an adjustment.[7] If the taxpayer's transfer prices lie outside the arm's length range, then the IRS will make an adjustment, generally using either the mean or the median of the range as the benchmark price.[8] Taxpayers also are allowed, under certain circumstances, to satisfy the arm's length requirement by showing that the average result for a multiple-year period is comparable to that of uncontrolled transactions for the same period.[9] The use of multiple-year data helps reduce the effects of short-term variations in prices, such as the effects of an industry business cycle that are unrelated to transfer pricing.

.02 Transfers of Tangible Property

Introduction. A transfer of tangible property is the type of transaction traditionally considered when evaluating a company's transfer pricing practices.

---

[6] Reg. § 1.482-1(d)(2).

[7] Reg. § 1.482-1(e)(1) and (e)(2)(i). All comparable uncontrolled transactions are included in the range if adjustments can be made for all of the material differences between the controlled and uncontrolled transactions. If adjustments cannot be made for all material differences, then the range is limited by statistical techniques, such as restricting the range to those comparable uncontrolled transactions which fall within the 25th and 75th percentiles of the range. Reg. § 1.482-1(e)(2)(iii).

[8] Reg. § 1.482-1(e)(3).

[9] Reg. § 1.482-1(f)(2)(iii).

There are five specified methods for estimating an arm's length charge for transfers of tangible property:

(i) the comparable uncontrolled price method,

(ii) the resale price method,

(iii) the cost plus method,

(iv) the comparable profits method, and

(v) the profit split method.[10]

The taxpayer must select and apply the method that provides the most reliable estimate of an arm's length price.[11] In addition to the five specified methods, the taxpayer also has the option of using an unspecified method. However, an unspecified method can be used only if it provides the most reliable estimate of an arm's length price.[12]

When the transfer involves tangible property with embedded intangibles, such as a controlled sale of inventory where the related seller attaches its trademark to the goods, a separate arm's length charge for the intangible is unnecessary if the purchaser does not acquire the right to exploit the intangible other than in connection with the resale of the property. However, the embedded intangible must be taken into account for purposes of determining the arm's length price for the sale of the related tangible property.[13]

Comparable uncontrolled price method. Under the comparable uncontrolled price (CUP) method, the arm's length price is the price charged for comparable goods in transactions between uncontrolled parties, adjusted for any material differences that exist between the controlled and uncontrolled transactions.[14] The CUP method ordinarily is the most reliable method for estimating an arm's length price if there are only minor differences between the controlled and uncontrolled transactions for which appropriate adjustments can be made.[15]

Example **12.7:** USAco, a domestic corporation, owns 100% of MEXco, a Mexican corporation. USAco manufactures telecommunications equipment at a cost of $500 per unit and sells the equipment to unrelated foreign distributors at a price of $750 per unit. USAco also sells the equipment to MEXco, which then resells the goods to unrelated foreign customers for $850 each. The conditions of USAco's sales to MEXco are substantially equivalent to those of the sales made to unrelated foreign distributors. Because information is available regarding comparable uncontrolled sales, USAco and MEXco should use the CUP method. Under this method, the arm's length price is $750.

---

[10] Reg. § 1.482-3(a).
[11] Reg. § 1.482-1(c)(1).
[12] Reg. § 1.482-3(e)(1).
[13] Reg. § 1.482-3(f).
[14] Reg. § 1.482-3(b)(1) and (b)(2)(ii)(B).
[15] Reg. § 1.482-3(b)(2)(ii)(A).

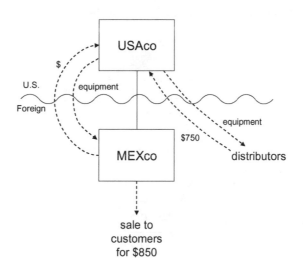

In assessing the comparability of controlled and uncontrolled sales for purposes of the CUP method, the most important factor is product similarity. Other significant factors include the similarity of contractual terms and economic conditions.[16] Because information regarding comparable uncontrolled sales is usually not available, the CUP method is usually difficult to apply in practice.

Resale price method. The type of transaction envisioned by the resale price method is a controlled sale of finished goods followed by the related distributor's resale of the goods to unrelated customers.[17] Under this method, the arm's length price is the resale price charged by the related distributor, reduced by the arm's length gross profit margin for such resales, and adjusted for any material differences that exist between the controlled and uncontrolled transactions. The gross profit margin realized by independent distributors on similar uncontrolled sales provides an estimate of the arm's length gross profit, which is expressed as a percentage of the resale price.[18]

Example **12.8:** USAco, a domestic corporation, owns 100% of CANco, a Canadian corporation. USAco manufactures medical equipment at a cost of $1,000 per unit and sells the equipment to CANco, which resells the goods (without any further processing) to unrelated foreign customers for $1,500 each (see Figure 12.2). Independent foreign distributors typically earn commissions of 10% (expressed as a percentage of the resale price) on the purchase and resale of products comparable to those produced by USAco. Under the resale price method, the arm's length price is $1,350 [$1,500 − (10% × $1,500)].

---

[16] Reg. § 1.482-3(b)(2)(ii)(A).
[17] Reg. § 1.482-3(c)(1).
[18] Reg. § 1.482-3(c)(2) and (c)(3)(ii)(C).

Figure 12.2 Example of resale price method

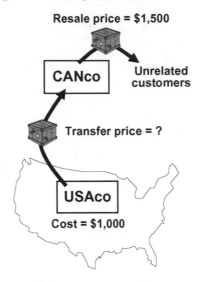

In assessing the comparability of controlled and uncontrolled transactions for purposes of the resale price method, product similarity is less important than under the comparable uncontrolled price method, while the similarity of the functions performed, risks borne, and contractual terms agreed to is relatively more important.[19] Consistency between the accounting methods used to compute the gross profit for the controlled and uncontrolled transactions also is important.[20]

Cost plus method. The type of controlled transaction envisioned by the cost plus method is the manufacture, assembly, or other production of goods that are sold to related parties.[21] Under the cost plus method, the arm's length price is the manufacturing cost incurred by the related manufacturer, increased by the arm's length gross profit markup for such manufacturers and adjusted for any material differences that exist between the controlled and uncontrolled transactions. The gross profit realized by independent manufacturers on similar uncontrolled sales provides an estimate of the arm's length gross profit markup, which is expressed as a percentage of the manufacturing costs.[22]

Example **12.9:** USAco, a domestic corporation, owns 100% of FORco, a foreign corporation. FORco manufactures power tools at a cost of $60 each and sells them to USAco. USAco attaches its trade name to the power tools (which has a significant effect on their resale price) and resells them to unrelated customers in the United States for $100 each (see Figure 12.3). Independent foreign manufacturers producing similar power tools typically earn a gross profit markup of 20%. Under the cost plus method, the arm's length price is $72 [$60 + (20% × $60)].

---

19 Reg. § 1.482-3(c)(3)(ii)(A) and (B).
20 Reg. § 1.482-3(c)(3)(iii)(B).

21 Reg. § 1.482-3(d)(1).
22 Reg. § 1.482-3(d)(2) and (d)(3)(ii)(C).

Figure 12.3 Example of cost plus method

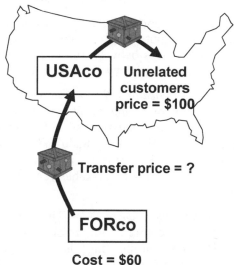

As with the resale price method, in assessing the comparability of controlled and uncontrolled transactions for purposes of the cost plus method, product similarity is less important than under the comparable uncontrolled price method, while the similarity of the functions performed, risks borne, and contractual terms agreed to is relatively more important.[23] Consistency between the accounting methods used to compute the markup for the controlled and uncontrolled transactions also is important.[24]

Comparable profits method. The comparable profits method looks to the profits of uncontrolled entities, rather than the prices used in uncontrolled transactions, to determine an arm's length allocation of profit between two related corporations. Under this method, the profitability of comparable companies is used as a benchmark for determining an arm's length net profit for one of the controlled parties (the "tested party") and then a transfer price is established that leaves the tested party with that amount of net profit.[25]

The methodology for developing an arm's length profit involves the following seven steps:

(1) *Determine the tested party*—The tested party should be the participant in the controlled transaction for which the most reliable data regarding comparable companies can be located. This is likely to be the least complex of the controlled parties and the controlled party that does not own valuable intangible property or unique assets that distinguish it from potential uncontrolled comparable companies.[26]

(2) *Search for comparable companies and obtain their financial data*—The key factors in assessing the comparability of the tested party to comparable

---

[23] Reg. § 1.482-3(d)(3)(ii)(A) and (B).
[24] Reg. § 1.482-3(d)(3)(iii)(B).
[25] Reg. § 1.482-5(b)(1).
[26] Reg. § 1.482-5(b)(2)(i).

companies are the functions performed, risks assumed, and resources employed (e.g., assets used).[27] Another important factor is the consistency between the accounting methods used by the tested and comparable companies to compute their operating profits.[28] Adjustments must be made for any differences between the tested party and the comparable companies that would materially affect the profitability measures used.[29]

(3) *Select a profit level indicator (PLI)*—Examples of PLIs that can be used include the ratio of operating profit to operating assets, the ratio of operating profit to sales, and the ratio of gross profit to operating expenses (also known as the "Berry Ratio"). To enhance the reliability of a PLI, the taxpayer should perform a multiyear analysis which generally should encompass at least the taxable year under review and the two preceding years.[30]

(4) *Develop an arm's length range of PLIs*—The arm's length range of PLIs is the interquartile range (the middle 50%) of the PLIs of the comparable companies. The interquartile range is the range from the 25% to 75% percentile. More specifically, the 25th percentile is the PLI when at least 25% of the results are at or below that PLI. The 75th percentile is the PLI when at least 75% of the results are at or below that PLI.[31]

(5) *Develop an arm's length range of comparable operating profits*—To construct an arm's length range of comparable operating profits, the selected PLI (e.g., the ratio of operating profits to operating assets) for the comparable companies in the arm's length range is applied to the tested party's most narrowly identifiable business activity for which data incorporating the controlled transaction is available (e.g., the operating assets used in the manufacture and sale of inventory).[32]

(6) *Determine if an adjustment must be made*—An adjustment is required if the tested party's reported profit lies outside the arm's length range of comparable operating profits developed in step 5.[33]

(7) *Adjust the transfer price used for the controlled transaction*— If the tested party's reported profit lies outside the arm's length range, an adjustment is made equal to the difference between the tested party's reported profit and the benchmark arm's length profit,[34] such as the mean or the median of the arm's length range of comparable operating profits.[35]

Example 12.10: [36] EURco, a foreign corporation, owns 100% of USAco, a domestic corporation. EURco manufactures consumer products for worldwide

---

[27] Reg. § 1.482-5(c)(2)(ii).

[28] Reg. § 1.482-5(c)(3)(ii).

[29] Reg. § 1.482-5(c)(2)(iv).

[30] Reg. § 1.482-5(b)(4). However, any required adjustments are made on a year-by-year basis. Reg. § 1.482-5(e), Example 2.

[31] Reg. § 1.482-1(e)(2)(C). If, for example, there are eight comparable companies, the range is from an aver-

age between the second and third lowest to an average of the sixth and seventh lowest.

[32] Reg. § 1.482-5(b)(1).

[33] Reg. § 1.482-5(b)(1).

[34] Reg. § 1.482-5(b)(1).

[35] Reg. § 1.482-1(e)(3).

[36] This example is based on Reg. § 1.482-5(e), Example 2.

distribution. USAco imports EURco's finished goods for resale in the United States. USAco's average financial results for the last three years are as follows:

Sales	$50 million
Cost of goods sold	($40 million)
Operating expenses	($ 9 million)
Operating profit	$ 1 million

USAco is selected as the tested party because it engages in activities that are less complex than those of EURco. An analysis of seven comparable uncontrolled U.S. distributors indicates that the ratio of operating profits to sales is the most appropriate PLI. After adjustments have been made to account for material differences between USAco and the uncontrolled distributors, the average ratio of operating profit to sales for each uncontrolled distributor is as follows: 3%, 4%, 4.5%, 5%, 5%, 6%, and 7%.

The arm's length range of PLIs is from 4% to 6% (the interquartile range includes the PLI at which 25% of the results are at or below and 75% of the results are at or below) with the median at 5%. The PLI of operating profits to sales for USAco is only 2% ($1 million of operating profits ÷ $50 million of sales), which is below the low part of the range. Applying these percentages to USAco's sales of $50 million yields an arm's length range of comparable operating profits of $2 million to $3 million with a median of $2.5 million.

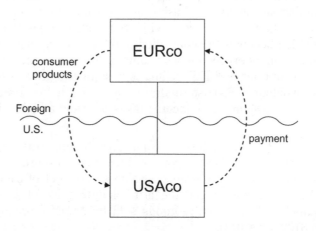

Because USAco's reported operating profit of $1 million lies below the arm's length range, an adjustment is required. The median of the interquartile range of comparable operating profits (i.e., $2.5 million) is determined to be the arm's length profit for USAco. Therefore, the transfer price that USAco pays EURco for its inventory is reduced by $1.5 million, which equals the difference between USAco's reported profit of $1 million and the arm's length profit of $2.5 million. This adjustment increases USAco's U.S. taxable income by $1.5 million per year.

¶1202.02

Profit split method. The profit split method is the most complicated of the specified pricing methods for transfers of tangible property and, therefore, is difficult to apply in practice. The profit split method evaluates whether the allocation of the combined operating profit attributable to a controlled transaction is arm's length by reference to the relative value of each controlled taxpayer's contribution to that combined profit.[37] The relative value of each controlled taxpayer's contribution is determined using either the comparable profit split method or the residual profit split method.

Under the comparable profit split method, the allocation of the combined operating profit between two controlled taxpayers is based on how uncontrolled taxpayers engaged in similar activities under similar circumstances allocate their joint profits.[38] Under the residual profit split method, the comparable profits method is used to estimate and allocate an arm's length profit for the routine contributions made by each controlled taxpayer. Routine contributions ordinarily include contributions of tangible property and services. The residual profit not allocated on the basis of routine contributions is then allocated between the two controlled taxpayers on the basis of the relative value of the intangible property contributed by each party.[39] The difficulty of obtaining this financial data often renders a profit splits method inapplicable.

Ceiling on transfer price for imported goods. There is a statutory ceiling on the transfer prices used for property imported into the United States in a transaction between controlled parties. Examples of such transactions include a U.S. parent corporation purchasing goods from a foreign manufacturing subsidiary, or a U.S. marketing subsidiary purchasing goods from its foreign parent corporation. In such cases, the transfer price used by the controlled purchaser for income tax purposes (which becomes the controlled purchaser's cost basis for computing the gain on resale) cannot exceed the value amount taken into account for purposes of determining custom duties.[40] This ceiling is designed to prevent taxpayers from simultaneously avoiding U.S. custom duties by using a low transfer price for custom purposes and avoiding U.S. income taxes by using a high price for income tax purposes.

Example **12.11:** HKo, a Hong Kong corporation, owns 100% of USDist, a domestic corporation. USDist imports widgets that HKo procures in Asia. For customs purposes, USDist declares a value per widget of $100. As a result, even if USDist determines that the arm's length price of a widget is $120, USDist cannot deduct a cost of goods sold for transfer pricing purposes of more than $100 per widget.

---

[37] Reg. § 1.482-6(a).
[38] Reg. § 1.482-6(c)(2).

[39] Reg. § 1.482-6(c)(3).
[40] Code Sec. 1059A.

¶1202.02

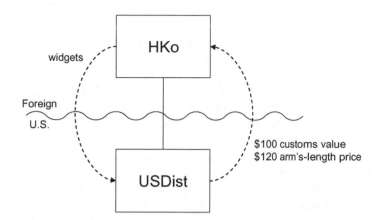

.03 Transfers of Intangible Property

Introduction. For transfer pricing purposes, an "intangible" includes any of the following items:

(i) patents, inventions, formulae, processes, designs, patterns, or know-how,

(ii) copyrights and literary, musical, or artistic compositions,

(iii) trademarks, trade names, or brand names,

(iv) franchises, licenses, or contracts,

(v) methods, programs, systems, procedures, campaigns, surveys, studies, forecasts, estimates, customer lists, or technical data, and

(vi) other similar items.[41]

The owner of an intangible for tax purposes ordinarily is the taxpayer who owns the legally protected right to exploit that intangible.[42] However, if an intangible is not legally protected, the sole consideration in determining ownership for tax purposes is the relative control over the intangible, which is a facts and circumstances test that may focus on economic substance.[43]

There are three specified methods for estimating an arm's length charge for transfers of intangibles:

(i) the comparable uncontrolled transaction method,

(ii) the comparable profits method, and

(iii) the profit split method.[44]

As with the transfer price for transfers of tangible property, the taxpayer must select and apply the method which provides the most reliable estimate of an arm's length price.[45] In addition to the three specified methods, the taxpayer also has the

---

[41] Reg. § 1.482-4(b).

[42] Temp. Reg. § 1.482-4(f)(3)(i).

[43] Reg. § 1.482-4(f)(3)(i)(A). If any other controlled party contributed to the development of the intangible,

the owner must allocate an arm's length compensation to that party. Reg. § 1.482-4(f)(4)(i).

[44] Reg. § 1.482-4(a).

[45] Reg. § 1.482-1(c)(1).

option of using an unspecified method. However, an unspecified method can be used only if it provides the most reliable estimate of an arm's length price.[46]

Comparable uncontrolled transaction method. The comparable uncontrolled transaction method is analogous to the comparable uncontrolled price method used for transfers of tangible property. Therefore, under the comparable uncontrolled transaction method, the arm's length charge for the transfer of an intangible is the amount charged for the same or comparable intangibles in transactions between uncontrolled parties, adjusted for any material differences that exist between the controlled and uncontrolled transactions.[47] In order for the intangibles involved in the uncontrolled transaction to be considered comparable to the intangible involved in the controlled transaction, both intangibles must be used in connection with similar products or processes within the same general industry or market and must have similar profit potential.[48] The comparable uncontrolled transaction method ordinarily is the most reliable method for estimating an arm's length price if there are only minor differences between the controlled and uncontrolled transactions for which reasonably ascertainable adjustments can be made.[49] Because information regarding comparable uncontrolled transactions is usually not available regarding intangible assets such as patents and trademarks, the comparable uncontrolled transaction method often is difficult to apply in practice.[50]

Example **12.12:** USAco, a domestic corporation, is a pharmaceutical company that develops a new drug. USAco licenses the formula to an unrelated pharmaceutical company in California for a royalty of 10% of sales. USAco also licenses the formula to its Canadian production and marketing subsidiary (CANco). If all the comparability factors between the two licenses are identical, CANco should pay USAco a royalty of 10% of sales. However, if the two licenses are not comparable in a manner for which the parties cannot make reasonably ascertainable adjustments, the 10% return on sales royalty is not a comparable uncontrolled transaction.

---

[46] Reg. § 1.482-4(d)(1).

[47] Reg. § 1.482-4(c)(1).

[48] Reg. § 1.482-4(c)(2)(iii)(B)(1).

[49] Reg. § 1.482-4(c)(2)(ii).

[50] *See Veritas Software Corp.*, 133 TC 297, No. 14, Dec. 58,016 (2009), for an example of the use of the comparable uncontrolled transaction method.

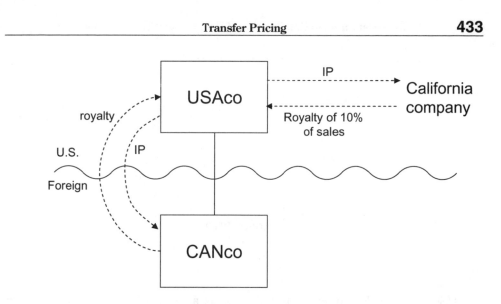

Comparable profits method. The same comparable profits method used to determine arm's length prices for transfers of tangible property also can be used to determine arm's length sales prices or royalty rates for transfers of intangible property.

Example **12.13**: EURpharm, a European pharmaceutical company, owns 100% of USpharm, a domestic corporation. EURpharm develops a pharmaceutical "ColdAway," a cure for the common cold. EURpharm licenses the ColdAway formula with the rights to use the ColdAway trade name in the United States to USpharm. Without considering the appropriate arm's length royalty rate that USpharm must pay EURpharm, USpharm's average financial results for the last three years are as follows:

Sales	$20 million
Cost of goods sold	($12 million)
Operating expenses	($ 2 million)
Operating profit	$ 4 million

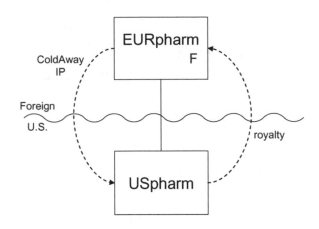

USpharm is selected as the tested party as a result of engaging in relatively routine manufacturing and sales activities, whereas EURpharm engages in a variety of complex activities involving unique and valuable intangibles. Because USpharm is primarily engaged in manufacturing activities, the ratio of operating profits to sales is the most appropriate PLI.

After adjustments have been made to account for material differences between USpharm and a sample of eight comparable companies for which data is available (manufacturers of generic drugs), the average ratio of operating profit to sales for the comparable companies is as follows: 5%, 6%, 8%, 9%, 10%, 15%, 15%, and 18%. Consequently, the arm's length range (the interquartile range) is 7% to 15% (the average of the second and third lowest PLIs and the average of the sixth and seventh lowest PLIs).

USpharm's return on sales is 20% ($4 million of operating profit ÷ by $20 million of sales) and the high profitability is attributable to USpharm's use of EURpharm's intellectual property. Therefore, in order to report a return on sales that is within the arm's-length range of 7% to 15%, USpharm should pay a royalty on sales of between 5% (20% − 5% = 15%) and 13% (20% − 13% = 7%).

As aforementioned, the comparable profits method can be used for tangible property as well as intangible property. The comparable profits method is particularly suitable for multiple transactions between two related parties as they need only conduct one analysis.

> ***Example* 12.14:** USAco is a U.S. pharmaceutical company that develops a drug to soothe mosquito bites. USAco owns a subsidiary in the British Virgin Islands (BVI). USAco provides the formula to BVI and also sells the chemicals used in the formula to BVI. BVI produces the drug and sells the pills back to USAco. As opposed to testing each of the three intercompany transactions in this round-trip scenario (the provision of the formula, the sale of the chemicals, and the purchase of the pill), the parties merely have to provide one comparable profits method analysis for BVI.

¶1202.03

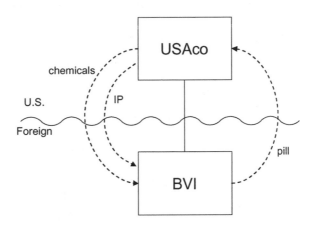

Profit split method. See the discussion of the profit split method under "Transfers of Tangible Property," above.

Commensurate with income requirement. Many U.S. companies have moved operations to foreign countries offering low-cost labor, low tax rates, less government regulation, and new markets. These companies typically transfer manufacturing and marketing intangibles to their foreign subsidiaries. For example, a foreign manufacturing subsidiary might manufacture a good under a license from its domestic parent corporation and then sell its entire output to the parent at a markup. If the foreign subsidiary is located in a low-tax foreign jurisdiction, its U.S. parent will defer U.S. taxes to the extent the intercompany royalty rate understates the economic value of the intangible.

In response to this problem, Congress enacted a requirement that transfer prices for sales or licenses of intangibles must be "commensurate with the income attributable to the intangible."[51] In other words, transfer prices must reflect the actual profit experience realized subsequent to the transfer. To meet this requirement, the original sales price or royalty rate must be adjusted annually to reflect any unanticipated changes in the income actually generated by the intangible.[52] For example, if a new patent leads to a product that turns out to be far more successful than was expected at the time the patent was licensed, the taxpayer must increase the intercompany royalty payments to reflect that unanticipated profitability. A determination in an earlier year that the royalty was arm's length does not preclude the IRS from making an adjustment in a subsequent year.[53]

> *Example* **12.15**: USAco, a pharmaceutical company, licenses the rights to a balm that soothes burns to its British Virgin Islands company (BVI) for what is considered an arm's length royalty rate of 5% of sales. Four years later, an Indian scientist determines that the balm is the key ingredient in his cure for skin cancer. As a result, BVI earns a highly profitable return on sales of

---

[51] Code Sec. 482.
[52] Reg. § 1.482-4(f)(2)(i).

[53] Reg. § 1.482-4(f)(2)(i).

60%. Even though BVI originally agreed to pay what was considered an arm's length royalty to USAco for the balm, the IRS can make an adjustment to reflect the unanticipated profitability.

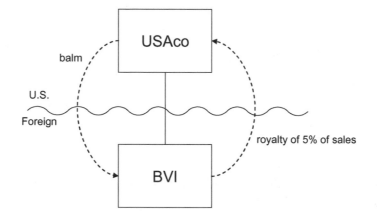

The need to make periodic adjustments places a significant administrative burden on taxpayers. This burden is mitigated somewhat by the following exceptions:

(i) *De minimis exception*—Periodic adjustments are not required if the total profits actually realized by the controlled transferee from the use of the intangible are between 80% and 120% of the profits that were foreseeable when the agreement was entered into and there have been no substantial changes in the functions performed by the transferee since the agreement was executed, except for changes required by unforeseeable events. Other requirements include the existence of a written royalty agreement, and the preparation of contemporaneous supporting documentation. In addition, if the requirements of the *de minimis* exception are met for each of five consecutive taxable years, then no further periodic adjustments are required under any conditions.[54]

(ii) *Extraordinary event exception*—Even if the total profits actually realized by the controlled transferee from the use of the intangible are less than 80% or more than 120% of the profits that were foreseeable when the agreement was entered into, the taxpayer need not make periodic adjustments if the unexpected variation in profits is due to extraordinary events that could not have been reasonably anticipated and are beyond the taxpayer's control. In order to use this exception, all of the requirements of the *de minimis* exception, other than the 80% to 120% test, also must be met.[55]

---

[54] Reg. § 1.482-4(f)(2)(ii)(C)). A slightly different set of requirements applies if the arm's length amount was determined under the comparable uncontrolled transaction method. Reg. § 1.482-4(f)(2)(ii)(B) and (E).

[55] Reg. § 1.482-4(f)(2)(ii)(D).

(iii) *Same intangible exception*—No periodic adjustments are required if the following requirements are met: (i) the same intangible was transferred to an uncontrolled taxpayer under circumstances similar to those of the controlled transaction, (ii) the uncontrolled transaction serves as the basis for the application of the comparable uncontrolled transaction method, and (iii) an arm's length charge is made in the first taxable year of the transfer.[56]

Cost sharing arrangements. One way for controlled parties to avoid the administrative burden and uncertainties associated with transfer pricing for intangibles is to enter into a cost sharing arrangement. For example, a U.S. parent corporation and a foreign subsidiary may agree to equally share the costs of developing a new product. Under such an agreement, the parent might own the rights to manufacture and market the new product in the United States, while the subsidiary might own the rights to manufacture and market the new product abroad. The advantage of a cost sharing arrangement is that the foreign subsidiary's ownership of the foreign rights to the intangible negates the need to have that subsidiary pay a royalty to its U.S. parent. A bona fide cost sharing transaction must allocate intangible development costs in proportion to the reasonably anticipated benefits to each controlled party, which must bear a portion of the costs incurred at each stage of the development of both successful and unsuccessful intangibles.[57]

Example **12.16:** USAco, a maker of sailboat sails, believes that there is a market for a significantly more durable sail than currently exists and anticipates spending $1 million this year on research and development of such a durable sail. USAco believes that 60% of the market for a new durable sail would be in the Caribbean, which is served by its British Virgin Islands subsidiary (BVI). USAco has two alternatives for the taxation of this product intangible. First, USAco may deduct all the R&D expenses for the new product on its U.S. return and license the ultimate product intangible to BVI for a royalty. Second, USAco could enter a cost sharing arrangement with BVI and charge BVI $600,000 (the 60% anticipated share of the market × the $1 million of research and development expenses incurred). By entering into the cost sharing arrangement, BVI would own the Caribbean rights to the new product and not have to pay a royalty in the future for use of that product intangible.

---

[56] Reg. § 1.482-4 (f) (2) (ii) (A).

[57] Reg. § 1.482-7T (a). *See also Veritas Software Corp.*, 133 TC 297, No. 14, Dec. 58,016 (2009); and *Xilinx, Inc.*, CA-9, 2010-1 USTC ¶ 50,302

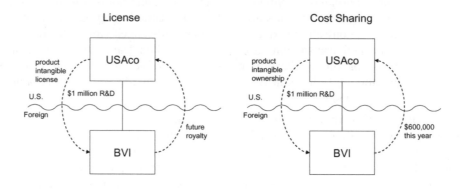

.04 Loans and Advances

Controlled entities generally must charge each other an arm's length rate of interest on any intercompany loans or advances.[58] There is an exception, however, for intercompany trade receivables, which are debts that arise in the ordinary course of business and are not evidenced by a written agreement requiring the payment of interest.[59] If the controlled borrower is located outside the United States, it is not necessary to charge interest on an intercompany trade receivable until the first day of the fourth month following the month in which the receivable arises.[60] If the controlled borrower is located within the United States, the interest-free period extends to the first day of the third month following the month in which the receivable arises.[61] This exception reflects the common business practice of not charging interest on trade receivables.

> **Example 12.17:** USAco, a domestic corporation, owns 100% of ASIAco, a foreign corporation. On November 1, ASIAco purchases $1 million of inventory on account from USAco. The $1 million debt, on which ASIAco pays no interest, is still outstanding on December 31, which is the end of USAco's taxable year. Since the $1 million intercompany trade receivable was outstanding for only two months, USAco does not have to recognize any interest income. However, if the $1 million debt were still outstanding on February 1 of the following year, ASIAco would begin owing USAco interest from that date forward.

---

[58] Reg. § 1.482-2(a)(1)(i).
[59] Reg. § 1.482-2(a)(1)(iii)(A).

[60] Reg. § 1.482-2(a)(1)(iii)(C).
[61] Reg. § 1.482-2(a)(1)(iii)(B).

¶1202.04

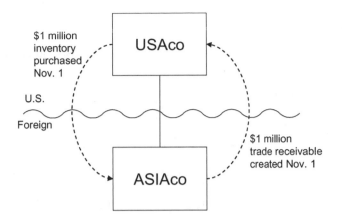

Longer interest-free periods are possible if the controlled lender ordinarily allows unrelated parties a longer interest-free period[62] or if a controlled borrower purchases the goods for resale in a foreign country and the average collection period for its sales is longer than the interest-free period.[63]

Intercompany debt other than a trade receivable generally must bear an arm's length interest charge.[64] To determine the arm's length rate, the taxpayer must consider all relevant factors, including the amount and duration of the loan, the security involved, the credit standing of the borrower, and the interest rate prevailing at the situs of the lender for comparable loans between uncontrolled parties.[65] If an arm's length rate is not readily determinable, the taxpayer can still protect itself against an IRS adjustment by satisfying the requirements of a safe-harbor provision. Under this safe harbor, an interest rate is deemed to be an arm's length rate if the rate is between 100% and 130% of the applicable federal rate.[66] The applicable federal rate is the average interest rate on obligations of the federal government with maturities similar to the term on the intercompany loan.[67]

> **Example 12.18:** EURco, a foreign corporation, owns 100% of USAco, a domestic corporation. During the current year, USAco borrows $1 million from EURco. The loan is denominated in U.S. dollars and has a three-year term. At the time of the loan, the applicable federal rate for a three-year obligation is 8%. Under the safe-harbor provision, an interest rate of between 8% (100% of the applicable federal rate) and 10.4% (130% of the applicable federal rate) is automatically acceptable to the IRS. A rate lower than 8% or higher than 10.4% also can be used if the taxpayer can establish that it is an arm's length rate, taking into account all of the relevant facts and circumstances.

---

[62] Reg. § 1.482-2(a)(1)(iii)(D).
[63] Reg. § 1.482-2(a)(1)(iii)(E).
[64] Reg. § 1.482-2(a)(1)(i).

[65] Reg. § 1.482-2(a)(2)(i).
[66] Reg. § 1.482-2(a)(2)(iii)(B).
[67] Code Sec. 1274(d).

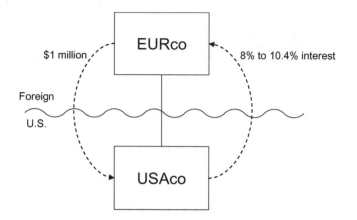

The safe harbor is not available if the intercompany debt is denominated in a foreign currency[68] or if the controlled lender is in the business of making loans to unrelated parties.[69]

A special rule applies if the controlled lender borrows the funds used to make the intercompany loan at the situs of the controlled borrower. In these back-to-back loans, the controlled lender is treated as a mere conduit for the loan entered into with the unrelated lender. Therefore, the arm's length rate on such pass-through loans is assumed to be equal to the rate paid by the controlled lender on the original loan, increased by any associated borrowing costs, unless the taxpayer can establish that a different rate is more appropriate under the general rules.[70]

> **Example 12.19:** USAco, a domestic corporation, owns 100% of GERco, a German corporation. During the current year, USAco borrows $10 million from a German bank at a 10% rate and then relends the funds to GERco. The arm's length rate on the intercompany loan is deemed to be equal to 10% plus any borrowing costs incurred by USAco in securing the original loan. A rate other than 10% also can be used if USAco can establish that such a rate is arm's length, taking into account all of the relevant facts and circumstances.

---

[68] Reg. § 1.482-2(a)(2)(iii)(E).
[69] Reg. § 1.482-2(a)(2)(iii)(D).

[70] Reg. § 1.482-2(a)(2)(ii).

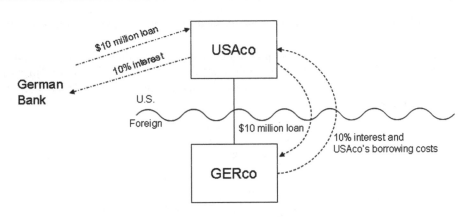

.05 Performance of Services

Generally, an arm's length fee must be charged if one controlled entity performs services for the benefit of, or on behalf of, another controlled entity. However, under a safe-harbor provision known as the services cost method, a charge equal to the total services costs incurred by the controlled entity in providing the service with no markup is deemed to be an arm's length charge.[71] This safe harbor reflects the reality that many intercompany services, such as payroll, human resources and legal, are provided for convenience rather than profit.

The covered services that are eligible for the services cost method include both specified covered services (a listing of back office, support-type services that the IRS identifies in a revenue procedure[72]), and low margin covered services (defined as a markup of 7% or less). To be eligible for the services cost method, the covered services must meet several requirements. First, it must not contribute significantly to key competitive advantages, core capabilities, or fundamental risks of success or failure in one or more trades or business of the controlled group. Second, the taxpayer must maintain adequate books and records. Finally, the covered services must not be an excluded activity, which include: (1) manufacturing; (2) production; (3) extraction, exploration or processing of natural resources; (4) construction; (5) reselling, distribution, acting as a sales or purchasing agent or acting under a commission or other similar arrangement; (6) research, development or experimentation; (7) engineering or scientific; (8) financial transactions, including guarantees; and (9) insurance or reinsurance.[73]

> **Example 12.20:** USsub is a wholly-owned subsidiary of ASIAco, a multinational manufacturing conglomerate. USAco acts as a contract manufacturer for ASIAco, performs all of ASIAco's accounting services, and transports ASIAco's products sold in the United States. USAco must receive an arm's length markup on the costs of providing manufacturing services as manufacturing services are specifically excluded from the services cost method. Assuming that the accounting services do not contribute significantly to the

---

[71] Reg. § 1.482-9(b)(1).
[72] Rev. Proc. 2007-13, IRB 2007-3.

[73] Reg. § 1.482-9(b).

fundamental risks of business success or failure, USAco can merely charge ASIAco the cost of providing these services. If the transportation services have a median comparable markup of 7% or less, USAco does not have to charge a markup. However, if the median comparable markup on the cost of providing these sales agency services exceeds 7%, USAco must charge ASIAco an arm's length markup.

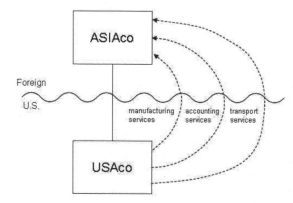

In situations in which the services cost method does not apply, the regulations provide other specific methods to determine the arm's length price. These methods, which are analogous to the methods for the transfers of tangible property, include the following:

(i)   the comparable uncontrolled services price method,[74] which is analogous to the CUP method;

(ii) the gross services margin method,[75] which is analogous to the resale price method;

(iii) the cost of services plus method,[76] which is analogous to the cost plus method;

(iv) the comparable profits method;[77] and

(v)   the profits split method.[78]

***Example* 12.21:** USAco is the wholly-owned U.S. subsidiary of ASIAco, a multinational conglomerate. USAco performs transportation services for ASIAco. USAco also performs transportation services in a functionally identical manner for unrelated companies by charging its costs (direct expenses and an allocation of indirect expenses) plus a 10% markup. Under the cost of services plus method, which is analogous to the cost plus method for tangible property, USAco must charge ASIAco its costs (direct and indirect) plus 10% of those costs for the transportation services.

---

[74] Reg. § 1.482-9(c).
[75] Reg. § 1.482-9(d).
[76] Reg. § 1.482-9(e).

[77] Reg. § 1.482-9(f).
[78] Reg. § 1.482-9(g).

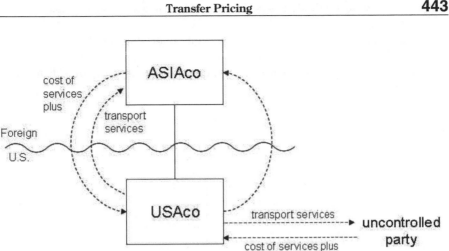

.06 Use of Tangible Property

Intercompany leases of tangible property generally must bear an arm's length rental charge.[79] The arm's length rental is the amount that would have been charged for the use of the same or similar property in a transaction between unrelated parties under similar circumstances. All relevant factors must be considered in determining the arm's length rental, including the period and location of the property's use, the owner's investment in the property, the owner's maintenance expenses, and the type and condition of the property.[80]

A special rule applies if the controlled lessor first leased the property from an unrelated person and then subleased it to the controlled lessee. In such cases, the controlled lessor is treated as a mere conduit for the lease entered into with the unrelated lessor. Therefore, the arm's length rental for such pass-through leases is deemed to be equal to the rental paid by the controlled lessor on the original lease, increased by any associated rental costs (e.g., maintenance, repairs, utilities, and managerial expenses).[81] This rule does not apply if either the controlled lessor or controlled lessee is regularly engaged in the business of leasing the type of property in question to unrelated persons or if the taxpayer establishes a more appropriate rental rate under the general rules.[82]

.07 Correlative Adjustments and Setoffs

When the IRS increases the taxable income of a related party through a transfer pricing adjustment, the IRS will also reduce the income of the related party for U.S. purposes.

> **Example 12.22:** USAco sells machinery to FORco, its foreign subsidiary. The IRS makes a transfer pricing adjustment, increasing the income of USAco on the sale of machinery by $1 million. The IRS will also decrease the income and earnings and profits of FORco by $1 million. The earnings and profits of FORco can affect numerous U.S. tax attributes of USAco, including

---

[79] Reg. § 1.482-2(c)(1).
[80] Reg. § 1.482-2(c)(2)(i).

[81] Reg. § 1.482-2(c)(2)(iii)(A).
[82] Reg. § 1.482-2(c)(2)(iii)(B).

its dividend income, deemed paid foreign tax credits, and Subpart F inclusions. The IRS may also permit USAco to establish an account receivable so that FORco's payment of cash in the amount of the adjustment will not result in additional income to USAco.

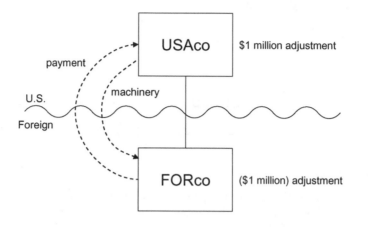

The IRS will generally permit a taxpayer to offset a negative transfer pricing adjustment with a favorable transfer pricing adjustment provided that the adjustments are for the same two related parties.

***Example* 12.23:** USAco sells machinery to FORco, its foreign subsidiary. The IRS makes a transfer pricing adjustment, increasing the income of USAco on the sale of machinery by $1 million. If the IRS also determines that USAco should have paid FORco an additional $600,000 for services, the adjustments are offset for a net adjustment of $400,000. If, however, the IRS makes the adjustment for USAco's sales of machinery to FORco and a negative transfer pricing adjustment for the services received from ASIAco (another of USAco's foreign subsidiaries), USAco would not be able to offset the adjustments.

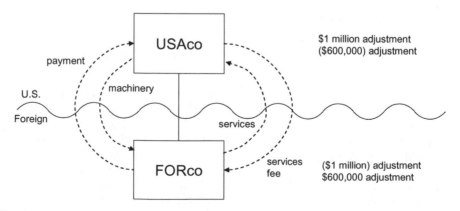

¶ 1203 INFORMATION REPORTING REQUIREMENTS

In order to effectively audit the transfer prices used by a U.S. subsidiary of a foreign corporation, the IRS often must examine the books and records of the foreign parent corporation. As a result, each year certain reporting corporations must (i) file Form 5472, Information Return of a 25% Foreign-Owned U.S. Corporation or a Foreign Corporation Engaged in a U.S. Trade or Business and (ii) maintain certain books and records.[83] A domestic corporation is a reporting corporation if, at any time during the taxable year, 25% or more of its stock, by vote or value, is owned directly or indirectly by one foreign person. A foreign corporation is a reporting corporation if, at any time during the taxable year, the foreign corporation is engaged in a U.S. trade or business and 25% or more of its stock, by vote or value, is owned directly or indirectly by one foreign person.[84] In filing a Form 5472, the reporting corporation must provide information regarding its foreign shareholders, certain other related parties, and the dollar amounts of transactions entered into during the year with foreign related parties.[85] A separate Form 5472 is filed for each foreign or domestic related party with which the reporting corporation engaged in reportable transactions during the year.[86] The practical importance of Form 5472 is that the IRS often uses this form as a starting point for conducting a transfer pricing examination.[87] A completed Form 5472 is included in the Appendix to this chapter.

In addition to filing Form 5472, a reporting corporation also must maintain permanent books and records sufficient to establish the correctness of the reporting corporation's U.S. tax liability, with an emphasis on transactions with related parties.[88] Certain reporting corporations are exempted from these special record maintenance requirements, but still must file Form 5472. These that are exempt include (i) reporting corporations whose U.S. gross receipts are less than $10 million[89] and (ii) reporting corporations whose annual payments to and from foreign related persons with respect to related party transactions are not more than $5 million and are less than 10% of the reporting corporation's U.S. gross income.[90] Any reporting corporation that fails to either file Form 5472 or maintain the requisite records may be subject to an annual penalty of $10,000.[91]

Information reporting also is required with respect to the foreign subsidiaries of domestic corporations.[92] Specifically, each year a U.S. person who owns more than 50% or more of the stock, by vote or value, of a foreign corporation must file a Form 5471, Information Return of U.S. Persons With Respect to Certain Foreign Corporations.[93] In the Form 5471, the U.S. shareholder must provide a wide variety of information regarding the controlled foreign corporation, including the dollar amounts of transactions it entered into with related parties.[94] Any U.S. person who

---

[83] *See generally,* Code Secs. 6038A and 6038C.

[84] Reg. § 1.6038A-1(c).

[85] Reg. § 1.6038A-2(b).

[86] Reg. § 1.6038A-2(a).

[87] *See* Internal Revenue Manual, International Audit Guidelines Handbook, April 1, 2002, 4.61.3.

[88] Reg. § 1.6038A-3(a)(1).

[89] Reg. § 1.6038A-1(h).

[90] Reg. § 1.6038A-1(i).

[91] Reg. § 1.6038A-4(a).

[92] *See generally,* Code Sec. 6038.

[93] Reg. § 1.6038-2(a) and (b).

[94] Reg. § 1.6038-2(f).

fails to furnish the required information may be subject to an annual penalty of $10,000, as well as a reduction in the taxpayer's foreign tax credit.[95] As with Form 5472, the practical importance of Form 5471 is that the IRS often uses this form as a starting point for conducting a transfer pricing examination.[96] A completed Form 5471 is included in the Appendix to Chapter 5 (¶ 504).

¶ 1204 TRANSACTIONAL AND NET ADJUSTMENT PENALTIES

In an attempt to promote more voluntary compliance with the arm's length standard, Congress has enacted two special transfer pricing penalties: the transactional penalty and the net adjustment penalty. Both penalties equal 20% of the tax underpayment related to a transfer pricing adjustment made by the IRS.[97] The transactional penalty applies if the transfer price used by the taxpayer is 200% or more (or 50% or less) of the amount determined under Code Sec. 482 to be the correct amount.[98] The net adjustment penalty applies if the net increase in taxable income for a taxable year as a result of Code Sec. 482 adjustments exceeds the lesser of $5 million or 10% of the taxpayer's gross receipts.[99] Both penalties increase to 40% of the related tax underpayment if the transfer price used by the taxpayer is 400% or more (or 25% or less) of the amount determined under Code Sec. 482 to be the correct amount or if the net adjustment to taxable income exceeds the lesser of $20 million or 20% of the taxpayer's gross receipts.[100]

> *Example* 12.24: FORco is a foreign corporation that manufactures size AAA batteries. FORco sells the AAA batteries to its U.S. distribution subsidiary (USDist) for resale in the United States. During the taxable year, FORco sells 100 million AAA batteries at $1 per battery to USDist. If the IRS determines that the arm's length price is actually 90¢ per battery, the IRS will make a total adjustment of $10 million (10¢ per unit × 100 million units). Assuming a 35% tax rate, this results in $3.5 million of additional U.S. taxes. Because the net adjustment to taxable income of $10 million exceeds $5 million, USDist is subject to a Code Sec. 6662(e) penalty of $700,000 (20% × $3.5 million).

---

[95] Code Sec. 6038(b) and (c).

[96] *See* Internal Revenue Manual, International Audit Guidelines Handbook, May 1, 2006, 4.61.3.4.1.

[97] Code Sec. 6662(a) and (b)(3).

[98] Code Sec. 6662(e)(1)(B)(i).

[99] Code Sec. 6662(e)(1)(B)(ii) and (e)(3)(A).

[100] Code Sec. 6662(h).

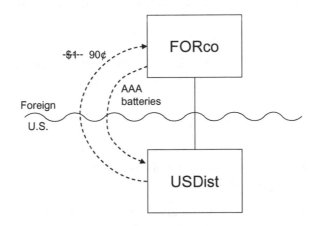

The transactional and net adjustment penalties apply automatically whenever an IRS adjustment exceeds the numerical thresholds. The only way to avoid the penalty in such cases is to satisfy certain safe-harbor requirements. In the case of the transactional penalty, the penalty is waived only if the taxpayer can demonstrate that it had reasonable cause and acted in good faith.[101] In the case of the net adjustment penalty, the reasonable cause and good faith requirements can be met only if the taxpayer can demonstrate, through contemporaneous documentation provided to the IRS within 30 days of a request, that the taxpayer acted reasonably in selecting and applying a transfer pricing method.[102] These added requirements for avoiding the net adjustment penalty are designed to force taxpayers to develop and have waiting for the IRS all of the documentation that the IRS ordinarily would need to review in a transfer pricing examination. In addition to providing protection against the transfer pricing penalty, the documentation may also persuade the IRS that a transfer pricing adjustment is not necessary. The IRS's Large and Mid-Size Business Division (LMSB) has mandated that all LMSB agents should request documentation during audits.[103]

A taxpayer cannot reasonably conclude that the specified method selected provided the most reliable measure of an arm's length result unless the taxpayer has made a reasonable effort to evaluate the potential application of the other specified methods.[104] If the taxpayer used an unspecified method, the taxpayer must demonstrate that none of the specified methods would provide a result that clearly reflected income and that the unspecified method is likely to clearly reflect income.[105]

.01 Preparing Transfer Pricing Documentation

The principal supporting documents that a taxpayer normally must include in its contemporaneous documentation are as follows:

---

[101] Reg. § 1.6662-6(b)(3) and Reg. § 1.6664-4(a).

[102] Code Sec. 6662(e)(3)(B)(i). Documentation is considered contemporaneous if it is in existence when a timely tax return is filed. Reg. § 1.6662-6(d)(2)(iii)(A).

[103] Memorandum for LMSB Executives, Managers, and Agents, January 22, 2003.

[104] Reg. § 1.6662-6(d)(2)(ii).

[105] Reg. § 1.6662-6(d)(3)(ii).

¶1204.01

(i) an overview of the taxpayer's business, including an analysis of the economic and legal factors that affect the pricing of its property and services,

(ii) a description of the organizational structure (including an organization chart) covering all related parties engaged in potentially relevant transactions,

(iii) any documentation explicitly required by the Regulations under Code Sec. 482,

(iv) a description of the pricing method selected and an explanation of why that method was selected,

(v) a description of the alternative methods that were considered and an explanation of why they were not selected,

(vi) a description of the controlled transactions and any internal data used to analyze those transactions,

(vii) a description of the comparables used, how comparability was evaluated, and what adjustments were made,

(viii) an explanation of the economic analyses and projections relied on in developing the pricing method, and

(ix) a general index of the principal and background documents along with a description of the recordkeeping system used for cataloging and accessing those documents.[106]

.02 Information Gathering

The information gathering stage is usually the most time-consuming aspect of preparing transfer pricing documentation. The taxpayer will typically have to interview operational personnel on both sides of the intercompany transaction. In addition, it will also have to obtain relevant financial information, including internal cost accounting and profit margin analysis for the transactions at issue and the latest financial statements for recent years. The taxpayer will have to identify unrelated party transactions, which may be between either two unrelated parties or one of the related parties and an unrelated party.

Example 12.25: USAco sells cheese to FORco, its foreign parent, and wants to apply the comparable uncontrolled price method to determine the appropriate transfer price. USAco has to interview the appropriate personnel to determine the price USAco charges unrelated parties in comparable cheese sales. In addition, USAco also needs to identify, to the extent available, the price charged on comparable sales of cheese by other cheese wholesalers.

---

[106] Reg. § 1.6662-6(d)(2)(iii)(B).

¶1204.02

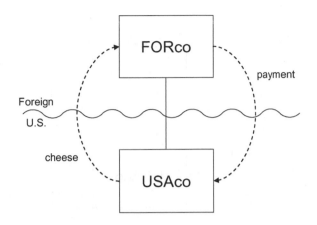

The culmination of the information gathering process is the preparation of a functional analysis. This functional analysis reviews the functions performed and risks assumed by the respective parties, focusing on competition, the market, and other economic factors that may help to determine arm's length pricing.

.03 Identification of the Best Method

The regulations require the taxpayer to apply the "best method" to its intercompany transactions. This requires choosing one of the methods prescribed in the regulations and developing the requisite support for using that method. At the same time, the taxpayer must explain why the other prescribed methods are not applicable. The taxpayer must review accurate and reliable data for application of the method; the degree of comparability between controlled and uncontrolled transactions or companies to which the methods are applied; and the number, magnitude, and accuracy of adjustments required to apply the method.[107]

.04 Economic Analysis

The taxpayer should conduct economic analysis to evaluate the transactional data and obtain information concerning comparable companies from reliable databases.

> **Example 12.26:** USAco, a U.S. subsidiary of ASIAco, a Singapore parent corporation, purchases software from its parent for resale in the United States. USAco wants to apply the comparable profits method to determine the appropriate transfer price. USAco must find companies comparable to itself with respect to the type of functions performed and the risks assumed. As a result, the economist will have to search for potentially comparable companies based, for example, on Form 10-K disclosures made to the Securities and Exchange Commission.

---

[107] Reg. § 1.482-1(d)(2).

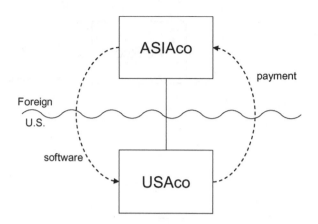

The economic analysis may further compare the financial results of the tested party to the financial results of the comparable transactions or companies. In addition to assuring functional comparability, an economist may also examine financial ratios such as return on costs, return on sales, and return on assets. Where appropriate, an economist may make adjustments for differences in relevant factors.

¶ 1205 DEVELOPING A TRANSFER PRICING STRATEGY

A corporation's transfer pricing strategy is driven, in part, by the need to develop an effective defense against the transactional and net adjustment penalties. The first step in developing a defense against these penalties is to assess the amount of risk associated with the taxpayer's current position. One major determinant of risk is the aggregate dollar value of controlled transactions between U.S. and foreign affiliates. Another major determinant of risk is the relative profitability of U.S. and foreign operations, in particular, the percentage of the taxpayer's worldwide profits that is allocated to low-tax foreign jurisdictions.

As a practical matter, the transactional penalty is likely to arise only if the taxpayer provides for no transfer price.[108] In contrast, any large corporation with a significant volume of cross-border transactions could conceivably exceed the $5 million net adjustment threshold. For example, a company with $100 million of cross-border controlled transactions is potentially subject to the 20% penalty if its transfer prices are off by just 5%.

One strategy to guard against the net adjustment penalty is to demonstrate, through contemporaneous documentation provided to the IRS within 30 days of a request, that the taxpayer acted reasonably in selecting and applying a transfer pricing method. As a consequence, the keys to avoiding the net adjustment penalty are the use of transfer prices that are supported by sufficient documentation and allocating to each affiliate a reasonable profit that reflects the economic realities of the parties' contractual relations. In this regard, reliance on a transfer pricing study

---

[108] For example, if a domestic parent corporation transfers an intangible to a foreign subsidiary and does not provide for any royalty payments, then any price adjustment will exceed the 200% threshold.

done by a professional qualified to conduct such an analysis, such as an attorney, accountant, or economist, is a relevant factor in determining whether the taxpayer selected and applied a transfer pricing method in a reasonable manner.[109] Therefore, a formal transfer pricing study, whether prepared internally by the taxpayer's employees or externally by outside consultants, is an important factor in establishing defensible transfer pricing positions in terms of avoiding a penalty and persuading against an adjustment.

An alternative strategy for avoiding the transactional and net adjustment penalties, as well as an adjustment, is to obtain an advance pricing agreement (or APA). Under the APA procedure, the IRS reviews and agrees to the taxpayer's transfer pricing method before the taxpayer implements it.[110] An APA spells out the factual nature of the related party transactions, an appropriate pricing method, and the expected range of results by applying the agreed-upon method to the transactions. If the taxpayer faithfully applies the agreed-upon methodology, the IRS will not adjust the taxpayer's transfer prices in any future audits. A taxpayer seeking transfer pricing protection in both countries to a transaction may seek a bilateral APA.

Therefore, the advantages of an APA include the certainty of results for the taxpayer, as well as the possibility of reduced record keeping because the taxpayer knows in advance what information the IRS considers to be relevant. The disadvantages include the cost of developing the documentation needed to obtain an APA (including the cost of professionals), as well as the up-front disclosure of information to the IRS. Disclosure may be only a timing issue, however, for large multinational corporations which the IRS routinely audits. Although taxpayers may have some concern that they are disclosing information about their company to potential competitors, the disclosure of the written APAs and any background documents is prohibited.[111]

> ***Example* 12.27:** NORDco, a Nordic company, manufactures widgets and sells them to its U.S. subsidiary (USDist) for resale in the United States. When evaluating USDist's transfer pricing practices, the economist determines in the documentation that USDist should report an arm's length return on sales between 3.1% and 5.3%. Desiring to avoid the expense of annual documentation for the next five years, USDist seeks an APA with the IRS. Subsequently, the IRS and USDist agree that, barring any material changes to the way USDist operates, USDist will annually report a cost of goods sold and, accordingly, a gross profit resulting in a return on sales between 3.1% and 5.3%. Assuming that USDist reports a return on sales within this range, the IRS will not make a transfer pricing adjustment, will not impose a transfer pricing penalty, and will not even audit the transfer pricing issue.

---

[109] Reg. § 1.6662-6(d)(2)(ii)(D).

[110] Rev. Proc. 2006-9, 2006-2 IRB 292, and Announcement 2011-22, IRB 2011-16.

[111] Code Secs. 6103 and 6110.

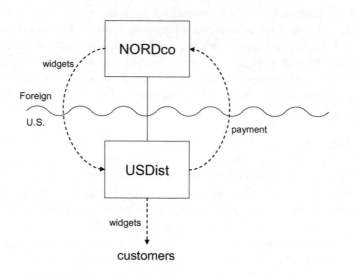

¶ 1206 APPENDIX

USACo, Inc. is 100% owned by ForCo Holdings AB, a holding company resident in Sweden, which is publicly held. ForCo Holdings AB wholly owns ForSub AB, an operating company that is resident in Sweden. USACo, Inc. purchases $20 million of forestry equipment from ForSub AB for distribution to its U.S. customers. In addition, USACo, Inc. pays $1 million to ForCo Holdings AB for management services performed in Sweden. When filing its U.S. Form 1120, USACo, Inc. must attach two Forms 5472 that detail its relationship with both ForCo Holdings AB and ForSub AB as well as identify the related party transactions.

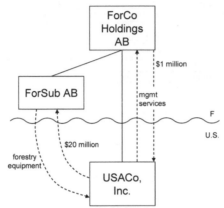

1. USACo, Inc. is a Reporting Corporation.

2. ForCo Holdings AB is a 25% Foreign Shareholder.

3. Both ForCo Holdings AB and ForSub AB are Related Parties to USACo, Inc.

4. Reportable Transactions of USACo, Inc. are its intercompany transactions: $1 million of consideration for management services from ForCo Holdings AB and purchases of $20 million of inventory from ForSub AB.

Form **5472** (Rev. December 2007) Department of the Treasury Internal Revenue Service	**Information Return of a 25% Foreign-Owned U.S. Corporation or a Foreign Corporation Engaged in a U.S. Trade or Business** **(Under Sections 6038A and 6038C of the Internal Revenue Code)** For tax year of the reporting corporation beginning 1/01 ,2010 , and ending 12/31 ,2010 **Note.** *Enter all information in English and money items in U.S. dollars.*	OMB No. 1545-0805

Part I   Reporting Corporation (see instructions). All reporting corporations must complete Part I.

1a Name of reporting corporation USAco, Inc.	**1b** Employer identification number 34 : 5678912

Number, street, and room or suite no. (if a P.O. box, see instructions)	**1c** Total assets
City or town, state, and ZIP code (if a foreign address, see instructions) Chicago, IL 60609	$ 25,000,000

1d Principal business activity ▶	**1e** Principal business activity code ▶

1f Total value of gross payments made or received (see instructions) reported on **this** Form 5472 $ 1,000,000	**1g** Total number of Forms 5472 filed for the tax year 2	**1h** Total value of gross payments made or received (see instructions) reported on **all** Forms 5472 $ 21,000,000

1i Check here if this is a consolidated filing of Form 5472 . . ▶ ☐	**1j** Country of incorporation USA	**1k** Country(ies) under whose laws the reporting corporation files an income tax return as a resident USA	**1l** Principal country(ies) where business is conducted USA

2 Check here if, at any time during the tax year, any foreign person owned, directly or indirectly, at least 50% of **(a)** the total voting power of all classes of the stock of the reporting corporation entitled to vote, or **(b)** the total value of all classes of stock of the reporting corporation . . . . ▶ ☑

Part II   25% Foreign Shareholder (see instructions)

1a Name and address of direct 25% foreign shareholder FORco Holdings AB Stockholm, Sweden	**1b** U.S. identifying number, if any NA

1c Principal country(ies) where business is conducted Sweden	**1d** Country of citizenship, organization, or incorporation Sweden	**1e** Country(ies) under whose laws the direct 25% foreign shareholder files an income tax return as a resident Sweden

2a Name and address of direct 25% foreign shareholder	**2b** U.S. identifying number, if any

2c Principal country(ies) where business is conducted	**2d** Country of citizenship, organization, or incorporation	**2e** Country(ies) under whose laws the direct 25% foreign shareholder files an income tax return as a resident

3a Name and address of ultimate indirect 25% foreign shareholder	**3b** U.S. identifying number, if any

3c Principal country(ies) where business is conducted	**3d** Country of citizenship, organization, or incorporation	**3e** Country(ies) under whose laws the ultimate indirect 25% foreign shareholder files an income tax return as a resident

4a Name and address of ultimate indirect 25% foreign shareholder	**4b** U.S. identifying number, if any

4c Principal country(ies) where business is conducted	**4d** Country of citizenship, organization, or incorporation	**4e** Country(ies) under whose laws the ultimate indirect 25% foreign shareholder files an income tax return as a resident

Part III   Related Party (see instructions)
Check applicable box: Is the related party a ☑ foreign person or ☐ U.S. person?
All reporting corporations must complete this question and the rest of Part III.

1a Name and address of related party FORco Holdings AB Stockholm, Sweden	**1b** U.S. identifying number, if any NA

1c Principal business activity ▶ **offices of other holdings companies**	**1d** Principal business activity code ▶ 55112

1e Relationship—Check boxes that apply: ☑ Related to reporting corporation ☐ Related to 25% foreign shareholder ☑ 25% foreign shareholder

1f Principal country(ies) where business is conducted Sweden	**1g** Country(ies) under whose laws the related party files an income tax return as a resident Sweden

For Paperwork Reduction Act Notice, see page 4.   Cat. No. 49987Y   Form **5472** (Rev. 12-2007)

¶1206

Form 5472 (Rev. 12-2007) Page **2**

Part IV	**Monetary Transactions Between Reporting Corporations and Foreign Related Party** (see instructions)

Caution: *Part IV must be completed if the "foreign person" box is checked in the heading for Part III.*
If estimates are used, check here ▶ ☐

1	Sales of stock in trade (inventory)	1	
2	Sales of tangible property other than stock in trade	2	
3a	Rents received (for other than intangible property rights)	3a	
b	Royalties received (for other than intangible property rights)	3b	
4	Sales, leases, licenses, etc., of intangible property rights (e.g., patents, trademarks, secret formulas) . .	4	
5	Consideration received for technical, managerial, engineering, construction, scientific, or like services . .	5	
6	Commissions received	6	
7	Amounts borrowed (see instructions) **a** Beginning balance _____ **b** Ending balance or monthly average ▶	7b	
8	Interest received	8	
9	Premiums received for insurance or reinsurance	9	
10	Other amounts received (see instructions)	10	
11	**Total.** Combine amounts on lines 1 through 10	11	
12	Purchases of stock in trade (inventory)	12	
13	Purchases of tangible property other than stock in trade	13	
14a	Rents paid (for other than intangible property rights)	14a	
b	Royalties paid (for other than intangible property rights)	14b	
15	Purchases, leases, licenses, etc., of intangible property rights (e.g., patents, trademarks, secret formulas) .	15	
16	Consideration paid for technical, managerial, engineering, construction, scientific, or like services . . .	16	1,000,000
17	Commissions paid	17	
18	Amounts loaned (see instructions) **a** Beginning balance _____ **b** Ending balance or monthly average ▶	18b	
19	Interest paid	19	
20	Premiums paid for insurance or reinsurance	20	
21	Other amounts paid (see instructions)	21	
22	**Total.** Combine amounts on lines 12 through 21	22	1,000,000

Part V	**Nonmonetary and Less-Than-Full Consideration Transactions Between the Reporting Corporation and the Foreign Related Party** (see instructions)

Describe these transactions on an attached separate sheet and check here. ▶ ☐

Part VI	**Additional Information**

All reporting corporations must complete Part VI.

1	Does the reporting corporation import goods from a foreign related party?	☑ Yes ☐ No
2a	If "Yes," is the basis or inventory cost of the goods valued at greater than the customs value of the imported goods?	☐ Yes ☑ No
	If "No," **do not** complete **b** and **c** below.	
b	If "Yes," attach a statement explaining the reason or reasons for such difference.	
c	If the answers to questions 1 and 2a are "Yes," were the documents used to support this treatment of the imported goods in existence and available in the United States at the time of filing Form 5472?	☐ Yes ☐ No

¶1206

Form **5472** (Rev. December 2007) Department of the Treasury Internal Revenue Service	**Information Return of a 25% Foreign-Owned U.S. Corporation** **or a Foreign Corporation Engaged in a U.S. Trade or Business** **(Under Sections 6038A and 6038C of the Internal Revenue Code)** For tax year of the reporting corporation beginning _1/01_ , _2010_ , and ending _12/31_ , _2010_ **Note.** Enter all information in English and money items in U.S. dollars.	OMB No. 1545-0805

Part I   **Reporting Corporation** (see instructions). All reporting corporations must complete Part I.

1a Name of reporting corporation USAco, Inc.	**1b** Employer identification number 34 : 5678912

Number, street, and room or suite no. (if a P.O. box, see instructions)	**1c** Total assets
City or town, state, and ZIP code (if a foreign address, see instructions) Chicago, IL	$ 25,000,000

1d Principal business activity ▶ **Gathering of Forest Products**	**1e** Principal business activity code ▶ 113210

1f Total value of gross payments made or received (see instructions) reported on **this** Form 5472 $ 20,000,000	**1g** Total number of Forms 5472 filed for the tax year 2	**1h** Total value of gross payments made or received (see instructions) reported on **all** Forms 5472 $ 21,000,000

1i Check here if this is a consolidated filing of Form 5472 . . ▶ ☐	**1j** Country of incorporation USA	**1k** Country(ies) under whose laws the reporting corporation files an income tax return as a resident USA	**1l** Principal country(ies) where business is conducted USA

2 Check here if, at any time during the tax year, any foreign person owned, directly or indirectly, at least 50% of **(a)** the total voting power of all classes of the stock of the reporting corporation entitled to vote, or **(b)** the total value of all classes of stock of the reporting corporation . . . . ▶ ☑

Part II   **25% Foreign Shareholder** (see instructions)

1a Name and address of direct 25% foreign shareholder FORco AB Stockholm, Sweden	**1b** U.S. identifying number, if any NA

1c Principal country(ies) where business is conducted Sweden	**1d** Country of citizenship, organization, or incorporation Sweden	**1e** Country(ies) under whose laws the direct 25% foreign shareholder files an income tax return as a resident Sweden

2a Name and address of direct 25% foreign shareholder	**2b** U.S. identifying number, if any

2c Principal country(ies) where business is conducted	**2d** Country of citizenship, organization, or incorporation	**2e** Country(ies) under whose laws the direct 25% foreign shareholder files an income tax return as a resident

3a Name and address of ultimate indirect 25% foreign shareholder	**3b** U.S. identifying number, if any

3c Principal country(ies) where business is conducted	**3d** Country of citizenship, organization, or incorporation	**3e** Country(ies) under whose laws the ultimate indirect 25% foreign shareholder files an income tax return as a resident

4a Name and address of ultimate indirect 25% foreign shareholder	**4b** U.S. identifying number, if any

4c Principal country(ies) where business is conducted	**4d** Country of citizenship, organization, or incorporation	**4e** Country(ies) under whose laws the ultimate indirect 25% foreign shareholder files an income tax return as a resident

Part III   **Related Party** (see instructions)

Check applicable box: Is the related party a ☑ foreign person or ☐ U.S. person?
All reporting corporations must complete this question and the rest of Part III.

1a Name and address of related party ForSub AB Stockholm, Sweden	**1b** U.S. identifying number, if any NA

1c Principal business activity ▶ **Gathering of Forest Products**	**1d** Principal business activity code ▶ 113210

1e Relationship—Check boxes that apply: ☑ Related to reporting corporation   ☐ Related to 25% foreign shareholder   ☑ 25% foreign shareholder

1f Principal country(ies) where business is conducted Sweden	**1g** Country(ies) under whose laws the related party files an income tax return as a resident Sweden

For Paperwork Reduction Act Notice, see page 4.   Cat. No. 49987Y   Form **5472** (Rev. 12-2007)

Part IV	**Monetary Transactions Between Reporting Corporations and Foreign Related Party** (see instructions)

Caution: *Part IV **must** be completed if the "foreign person" box is checked in the heading for Part III.*
If estimates are used, check here ▶ ☐

1	Sales of stock in trade (inventory)	1	
2	Sales of tangible property other than stock in trade	2	
3a	Rents received (for other than intangible property rights)	3a	
b	Royalties received (for other than intangible property rights)	3b	
4	Sales, leases, licenses, etc., of intangible property rights (e.g., patents, trademarks, secret formulas)	4	
5	Consideration received for technical, managerial, engineering, construction, scientific, or like services	5	
6	Commissions received	6	
7	Amounts borrowed (see instructions) **a** Beginning balance _____ **b** Ending balance or monthly average ▶	7b	
8	Interest received	8	
9	Premiums received for insurance or reinsurance	9	
10	Other amounts received (see instructions)	10	
11	**Total.** Combine amounts on lines 1 through 10	11	
12	Purchases of stock in trade (inventory)	12	20,000,000
13	Purchases of tangible property other than stock in trade	13	
14a	Rents paid (for other than intangible property rights)	14a	
b	Royalties paid (for other than intangible property rights)	14b	
15	Purchases, leases, licenses, etc., of intangible property rights (e.g., patents, trademarks, secret formulas)	15	
16	Consideration paid for technical, managerial, engineering, construction, scientific, or like services	16	
17	Commissions paid	17	
18	Amounts loaned (see instructions) **a** Beginning balance _____ **b** Ending balance or monthly average ▶	18b	
19	Interest paid	19	
20	Premiums paid for insurance or reinsurance	20	
21	Other amounts paid (see instructions)	21	
22	**Total.** Combine amounts on lines 12 through 21	22	20,000,000

Part V	**Nonmonetary and Less-Than-Full Consideration Transactions Between the Reporting Corporation and the Foreign Related Party** (see instructions)

Describe these transactions on an attached separate sheet and check here. ▶ ☐

Part VI	**Additional Information**

All reporting corporations must complete Part VI.

1   Does the reporting corporation import goods from a foreign related party?   ☑ Yes ☐ No

2a   If "Yes," is the basis or inventory cost of the goods valued at greater than the customs value of the imported goods?   ☐ Yes ☑ No
If "No," **do not** complete **b** and **c** below.

b   If "Yes," attach a statement explaining the reason or reasons for such difference.

c   If the answers to questions 1 and 2a are "Yes," were the documents used to support this treatment of the imported goods in existence and available in the United States at the time of filing Form 5472?   ☐ Yes ☐ No

Chapter 13
Tax Treaties

¶ 1301 INTRODUCTION

The major purpose of an income tax treaty is to mitigate international double taxation through tax reductions or exemptions on certain types of income derived by residents of one treaty country from sources within the other treaty country. Because tax treaties often substantially modify U.S. and foreign tax consequences, the relevant treaty must be considered in order to fully analyze the income tax consequences of any outbound or inbound transaction. In addition to treaties governing income taxes, the United States has also entered into bilateral tax treaties governing social security taxes, estate and gift taxes, and international shipping and aircraft.

The United States currently has income tax treaties with approximately 60 countries, including most of our major trading partners. Table 13.1 presents the list of foreign countries with which an income tax treaty is currently in force.

TABLE 13.1. COUNTRIES WITH WHICH THE UNITED STATES HAS INCOME TAX TREATIES IN FORCE[a]

Australia	Hungary	Pakistan
Austria	Iceland	Philippines
Bangladesh	India	Poland
Barbados	Indonesia	Portugal
Belgium	Ireland	Romania
Bulgaria	Israel	Russia
Canada	Italy	Slovak Republic
China, Peoples Republic of[b]	Jamaica	Slovenia
	Japan	South Africa
Commonwealth of Independent States[c]	Kazakstan	Spain
	Korea	Sri Lanka
Cyprus	Latvia	Sweden
Czech Republic	Lithuania	Switzerland
Denmark	Luxembourg	Thailand
Egypt	Malta	Trinidad and Tobago
Estonia	Mexico	Tunisia
Finland	Morocco	Turkey
France	Netherlands	Ukraine
Germany	New Zealand	United Kingdom
Greece	Norway	Venezuela

[a]Taken from Table 3 of IRS Pub. No. 515 (March 18, 2011), which is reproduced in its entirety in the appendix to this chapter.

[b]Does not apply to Hong Kong. Notice 97-40, 1997-28 IRB 6.

[c]The members of the Commonwealth of Independent States include: Armenia, Azerbaijan, Belarus, Georgia, Kyrgyzstan, Moldova, Tajikistan, Turkmenistan, and Uzbekistan.

There are several basic treaty provisions, such as permanent establishment provisions and reduced withholding tax rates, that are common to most income tax treaties. In many cases, these provisions are patterned after or similar to the United States Model Income Tax Convention of November 15, 2006 (U.S. Model Treaty), which reflects the traditional baseline negotiating position of the United States in establishing income tax treaties with other countries. Because the U.S. Model Treaty reflects the general pattern of most treaties, it is used as the reference point for the following discussion of typical treaty provisions. Keep in mind, however, that each tax treaty is separately negotiated and therefore is unique. As a consequence, to determine the impact of treaty provisions in any specific situation, one must consult the applicable treaty.

In most foreign countries, a treaty provision will supercede the foreign country's domestic law. The term "treaty override" describes legislation that conflicts with an earlier enacted treaty. The supremacy clause of the U.S. Constitution treats

¶1301

treaties and federal legislation equally. Consequently, if a treaty provision conflicts with legislation, whichever is later enacted will prevail.[1]

¶ 1302 COMMON TREATY PROVISIONS

.01 Definition of Resident

The tax exemptions and reductions that treaties provide are available only to a resident of one of the treaty countries, as determined under the country's internal laws. Income derived by a partnership or other pass-through entity is treated as derived by a resident of a treaty country to the extent the income is treated, under the internal laws of that country, as taxable to a person that qualifies as a resident of that treaty country. Under the U.S. Model Treaty, a resident is any person who, under a country's internal laws, is subject to taxation by reason of domicile, residence, citizenship, place of management, place of incorporation, or other criterion of a similar nature.[2] A resident does not include a person who is subject to tax in the country only with respect to income derived from sources in that country.

Because each country has its own unique definition of residence, a person may qualify as a resident in more than one country. For example, a foreign national who qualifies as a U.S. resident under the substantial presence test pursuant to U.S. tax law may simultaneously qualify as a resident of a foreign country under its definition of residency. To resolve this issue, the United States has included tie-breaker provisions in many of its income tax treaties. Tie-breaker rules are hierarchical in nature, such that a subordinate rule is considered only if the superordinate rule fails to resolve the issue. For example, Article 4(3) of the U.S. Model Treaty provides the following tie-breaker rules for individuals:

(i) The taxpayer is a resident of the country in which he or she has available a permanent home.

(ii) If the taxpayer has a permanent home available in both countries, the taxpayer is a resident of the country in which his or her personal and economic relations are closer (center of vital interests).

(iii) If the country in which the taxpayer's center of vital interests cannot be determined or if the taxpayer does not have a permanent home available to him or her in either country, the taxpayer is a resident of the country in which he or she has a habitual abode.

(iv) If the taxpayer has a habitual abode in both countries or in neither country, the taxpayer is a resident of the country in which he or she is a citizen.

(v) If the taxpayer is a citizen of both countries or of neither country, the competent authorities of the two countries will settle the matter by mutual agreement.

Tie-breaker rules also are provided for corporations and other types of entities.[3]

***Example* 13.1:** Ray Allen is a citizen and resident of country F, which has a tax treaty with the United States identical to the U.S. Model Treaty. Ray

---

[1] *Reid v. Covert,* SCt, 354 US 1, 77 SCt 1222, 18 (1956). *See also* Code Sec. 894(a) and 7852(d).

[2] Article 4(1) (¶ 1304.04) of the U.S. Model Treaty.
[3] Article 4 (¶ 1304.04) of the U.S. Model Treaty.

Allen owns FORco, a company incorporated in country F that is opening a branch office in the United States. Ray is divorced and maintains an apartment in country F, where he spends every other weekend visiting his children. Ray's first wife, who kept their house in their divorce, has never left country F. Ray becomes a U.S. resident alien under the substantial presence test as a result of managing FORco's U.S. branch. In the United States, Ray owns a condominium where he lives with his second wife.

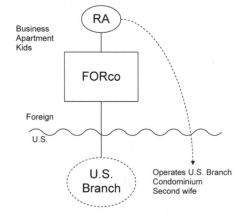

Because Ray Allen is considered a resident of both the United States and country F, we must analyze the Treaty tie-breaker procedures to determine which country has primary taxing jurisdiction. With an apartment in country F and a condominium in the United States, he has a permanent home available in both countries. With his children and the home office in country F, as opposed to his place of business and his second wife in the United States, Ray Allen does not have a center of vital interests in either country. Furthermore, because he regularly spends time in both countries, he arguably has a habitual abode in both. As a result, under the Treaty tie-breakers, Ray Allen should be considered a resident of country F because he is a citizen of country F.

There is an exception to the principle that residence determines the availability of treaty benefits. Under so-called savings clause provisions, a treaty country saves the right to tax its own citizens as though the treaty did not exist.[4] For example, under Article 11(1) of the income tax treaty between the United States and the United Kingdom, interest received by U.K. residents is exempt from U.S. taxation. However, under Article 1(4) of that treaty, the United States reserves the right to tax the payee if a U.K. resident also is a U.S. citizen. As a consequence, the treaty does not impede the right of the United States to tax the worldwide income of U.S. citizens.

.02 Business Profits and Permanent Establishments

A central tax issue for any company exporting its goods or services is whether it is subject to taxation by the importing country. Many countries assert jurisdiction over all of the income derived from sources within their borders, regardless of the citizenship or residence of the person receiving that income. This approach has its

---

[4] Article 1(4) (¶ 1304.01) of the U.S. Model Treaty.

limits, however. For example, if the exporter's marketing activities within the importing country are *de minimis* (e.g., a company salesperson makes a few sales calls), the administrative costs of collecting the tax on those activities may exceed the related tax revenues. Moreover, a policy of imposing unreasonable compliance costs on foreign companies may inhibit a country's ability to benefit from international trade. These concerns have led countries to include permanent establishment provisions in their income tax treaties.

Under a permanent establishment provision, the business profits of a resident of one treaty country are exempt from taxation by the other treaty country unless those profits are attributable to a permanent establishment located within the host country.[5] A permanent establishment includes a fixed place of business, such as a place of management, a branch, an office, a factory, a workshop, or a mine, well, quarry, or other place of natural resource extraction.[6] A fixed base of business does not constitute a permanent establishment if that fixed place of business is used solely for auxiliary functions (e.g., purchasing, storing, displaying, or delivering inventory) or for activities of a preparatory nature (e.g., collecting information about potential customers). In particular, a permanent establishment does not include the following:

1. the use of facilities solely for the purpose of storage, display or delivery of goods or merchandise belonging to the foreign corporation;

2. the maintenance of a stock of goods or merchandise belonging to the foreign corporation solely for the purpose of storage, display or delivery;

3. the maintenance of a stock of goods or merchandise belonging to the foreign corporation solely for the purpose of processing by another enterprise;

4. the maintenance of a fixed place of business solely for the purpose of purchasing goods or merchandise, or of collecting information, for the foreign corporation;

5. the maintenance of a fixed place of business solely for the purpose of carrying on, for the foreign corporation, any other activity of a preparatory or auxiliary character (e.g., collecting information about potential customers);

6. the maintenance of a fixed place of business solely for any combination of the activities mentioned above, provided that the overall activity of the fixed place of business resulting from this combination is of a preparatory or auxiliary character.[7]

In addition, a building or construction site is a permanent establishment only if it continues for more than a specified length of time.[8]

---

[5] Article 7(1) (¶ 1304.07) of the U.S. Model Treaty. A special exemption applies to the business profits of taxpayers that operate or rent ships, aircraft, or containers used in international traffic. Under Article 8 ¶ 1304.05 of the U.S. Model Treaty, such income generally is taxable only by the taxpayer's home country.

[6] Article 5(1) and (2) (¶ 1304.05) of the U.S. Model Treaty.

[7] Article 5(4) (¶ 1304.05) of the U.S. Model Treaty.

[8] Article 5(3) (¶ 1304.05) of the U.S. Model Treaty.

A permanent establishment also exists if employees or other dependent agents habitually exercise in the host country an authority to conclude sales contracts in the taxpayer's name.[9] As a consequence, an exporter that sends executives or salespeople abroad to enter into contracts may create a permanent establishment even if those employees do not operate out of a formal sales office. Employees who limit their activities to auxiliary or preparatory functions, such as collecting information about potential customers, with sales concluded in the home country, will not create a permanent establishment. Marketing products abroad solely through independent brokers or distributors also does not create a permanent establishment, regardless of whether these independent agents conclude sales contracts in the exporter's name.[10] In addition, the mere presence within the importing country of a locally incorporated subsidiary does not create a permanent establishment for a parent company incorporated in another country.[11]

Example **13.2:** USAco, a domestic corporation, markets its products abroad by mailing catalogs to potential foreign customers, who then mail orders back to USAco's home office in the United States. Under the U.S. Model Treaty, the mere solicitation of orders through the mail does not constitute a permanent establishment. Therefore, USAco's export profits are not subject to foreign taxation.

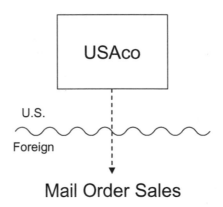

USAco

U.S.

Foreign

Mail Order Sales

Example **13.3:** The facts are the same as in Example 15.2, except now assume that USAco decides to expand its foreign marketing activities by leasing retail store space in a major foreign city in order to display its goods and keep an inventory from which to fill foreign orders. Under the U.S. Model Treaty, USAco's business profits would still not be subject to foreign taxation as long as USAco does not conclude any sales through its foreign office. This may be possible in theory, but as a practical matter, significant foreign sales may make it burdensome to conclude sales in this manner. If USAco's employees start concluding sales at the foreign office, USAco would have a permanent establishment in the importing country.

---

[9] Article 5(5) (¶ 1304.05) of the U.S. Model Treaty.   [11] Article 5(7) (¶ 1304.05) of the U.S. Model Treaty.
[10] Article 5(6) (¶ 1304.05) of the U.S. Model Treaty.

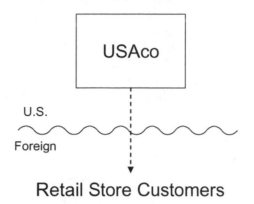

If a resident of one treaty country has a permanent establishment in the other treaty country, the importing country may tax the taxpayer's business profits, but only to the extent those business profits are attributable to the permanent establishment.[12] The portion of an exporter's business profits that is attributable to a permanent establishment is computed based on the fiction that the permanent establishment is a distinct and independent enterprise dealing at arm's length with the home office.[13] Therefore, the more functions performed and the greater the risks assumed by the permanent establishment, the more income it should earn. In making this determination, the taxpayer can allocate all direct costs, such as the cost of goods sold, against the permanent establishment's income. The taxpayer also can make a reasonable allocation of indirect expenses, such as general and administrative expenses, research and development expenses, and interest expense, against the permanent establishment's income.[14]

.03 Personal Services Income

Treaty provisions covering personal services compensation are similar to the permanent establishment clauses covering business profits in that they create a higher threshold of activity for host country taxation. Generally, when an employee who is a resident of one treaty country derives income from services performed in the other treaty country, that income is usually taxable by the host country.[15] However, the employee's income is exempt from taxation by the host country if the following requirements are satisfied:

(i) the employee is present in the host country for 183 days or less,

(ii) the employee's compensation is paid by, or on behalf of, an employer which is not a resident of the host country, and

(iii) the compensation is not borne by a permanent establishment or a fixed base which the employer has in the host country.[16]

---

[12] Article 7(1) (¶ 1304.07) of the U.S. Model Treaty.
[13] Article 7(2) (¶ 1304.07) of the U.S. Model Treaty.
[14] Article 7(3) (¶ 1304.07) of the U.S. Model Treaty.

[15] Article 14(1) (¶ 1304.14) of the U.S. Model Treaty.
[16] Article 14(2) (¶ 1304.14) of the U.S. Model Treaty.

Example **13.4:** FORco is a corporation organized in country F, which has a treaty with the United States identical to the U.S. Model Treaty. FORco is in the refrigeration business. Due to the high demand for air conditioning repair services in the United States the first week of July, FORco sends Norman Ray Allen ("NRA"), a citizen and resident of country F, to serve customers. During that week, NRA helps repair air conditioning for 15 different customers of FORco. The compensation that FORco pays him is $2,000.

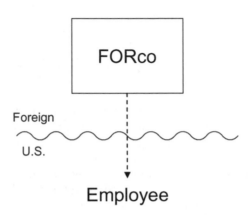

NRA is not taxed on his $2,000 of compensation for services he performs in the United States pursuant to the applicable treaty because (i) NRA is in the United States for only 7 days (less than 183 days), (ii) his compensation is paid by FORco, which is not a resident of the United States, and (iii) his compensation is not borne by a permanent establishment or a fixed base that FORco has in the United States.

Some older tax treaties contain a separate independent services provision that governs the taxation of personal services income derived by self-employed professionals, such as accountants, doctors, engineers, and lawyers. Such income is exempt from host country taxation unless the services are performed in the host country and the income is attributable to an office or other fixed base of business that is located in the host country and is regularly available to the taxpayer for purposes of performing the services. This provision allows self-employed professionals to provide services abroad without local taxation as long as they do not maintain an office or other fixed base of business within the host country. However, due to an emerging global consensus that little difference exists between a fixed base of business and a permanent establishment, the U.S. Model Treaty and more recent treaties do not contain a separate independent personal services article.

Finally, tax treaties usually contain special rules for specific types of personal services income. For example, under the U.S. Model Treaty, there are special rules governing income derived by crew members of ships and aircraft operated in

¶1302.03

international traffic,[17] directors' fees,[18] entertainers and athletes,[19] pensions, social security, annuities, alimony and child support,[20] pension funds,[21] government workers,[22] and students and trainees.[23] A summary of the treaty provisions governing compensation for personal services can be found in the appendix to this chapter.

.04 Dividends, Interest, and Royalties

Like the United States, most foreign countries impose flat rate withholding taxes on dividend, interest, and royalty income derived by offshore investors from sources within the country's borders. As an example, the U.S. statutory withholding tax rate is 30% for both nonresident alien individuals and foreign corporations.[24] However, most tax treaties provide for reduced withholding tax rates, as long as the dividend, interest, or royalty income is not attributable to a permanent establishment of the taxpayer that is located within the host country.

In the case of dividends, the rate often is lower for controlling shareholders (e.g., a corporate shareholder owning 10% or more of the payer's stock) than for noncontrolling shareholders. For example, under the U.S. Model Treaty, the withholding rate on dividends is 5% for a company that directly owns 10% or more of the voting stock of the payer, and 15% for all other shareholders. The U.S. treaties with numerous countries provide for a 0% withholding tax rate for dividends paid by a subsidiary to its parent corporation. Table 13.2 presents the dividend withholding tax rates for selected countries.[25]

TABLE 13.2. TREATY WITHHOLDING TAX RATES ON DIVIDENDS PAID BY U.S. CORPORATIONS[a]

Payee's country of residence	*Type of shareholder*	
	Controlling	*Noncontrolling*
Canada	5%	15%
China	10%	10%
France	0%/5%	15%
Germany	0%/5%	15%
Italy	5%	15%
Japan	0%/5%	10%
Mexico	0%/5%	10%
Netherlands	0%/5%	15%
United Kingdom	0%/5%	15%

[a]Taken from Table 1 of IRS Pub. No. 515 (Mar. 18, 2011), which is reproduced in its entirety in the appendix to this chapter.

Example 13.5: USAco is owned 40% by FORco (a corporation incorporated in country F), 40% by Norman Ray Allen (NRA, a citizen and resident of country F) and 20% by Kong (a citizen and resident of Hong Kong). Country F has a treaty with the United States identical to the U.S. Model Treaty. Hong

---

[17] Article 14(3) (¶ 1304.14) of the U.S. Model Treaty.
[18] Article 15 (¶ 1304.15) of the U.S. Model Treaty.
[19] Article 16 (¶ 1304.16) of the U.S. Model Treaty.
[20] Article 17 (¶ 1304.17) of the U.S. Model Treaty.
[21] Article 18 (¶ 1304.18) of the U.S. Model Treaty.

[22] Article 19 (¶ 1304.19) of the U.S. Model Treaty.
[23] Article 20 (¶ 1304.20) of the U.S. Model Treaty.
[24] Code Secs. 871(a) and 881(a).
[25] Article 10(2) (¶ 1304.10) of the U.S. Model Treaty.

Kong does not have a tax treaty with the United States. When USAco pays dividends to it shareholders, USAco will withhold 5% of the dividends paid to FORco because FORco is a controlling company pursuant to the Treaty, 15% to NRA because NRA is an individual resident of a treaty country, and the statutory rate of 30% to Kong because he is not a resident of a treaty country.

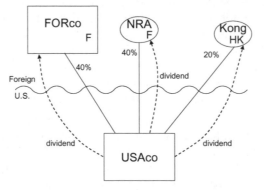

Tax treaties also usually reduce the withholding tax rate on interest to 15% or less. Under the U.S. Model Treaty, interest is exempt from withholding tax.[26] Table 13.3 presents the interest withholding tax rates for selected countries.

TABLE 13.3. TREATY WITHHOLDING TAX RATES ON INTEREST PAID BY U.S. PERSONS[a]

Payee's country of residence	Treaty withholding rate (general)
Canada	0%
China	10%
France	0%
Germany	0%
Italy	10%
Japan	10%
Mexico	15%
Netherlands	0%
United Kingdom	0%

[a]Taken from Table 1 of IRS Pub. No. 515 (March 18, 2011), which is reproduced in its entirety in the appendix to this chapter.

***Example* 13.6:** USAco is owned 40% by FORco (a corporation organized in country F), 40% by Norman Ray Allen (NRA, a citizen and resident of country F) and 20% by Kong (a citizen and resident of Hong Kong). Country F has a treaty with the United States identical to the U.S. Model Treaty. FORco and Kong have also loaned money to USAco. Pursuant to the U.S. Model Treaty, the interest paid by USAco to FORco is exempt from tax. However,

[26] Article 11(1) (¶ 1304.11) of the U.S. Model Treaty. When interest is paid by one related party to another, the treaty exemption applies only to an arm's-length amount of interest. Article 11(5) of the U.S. Model Treaty.

¶1302.04

because Kong is a resident of Hong Kong, a non-treaty country, USAco must withhold the statutory rate of 30% from the interest income.

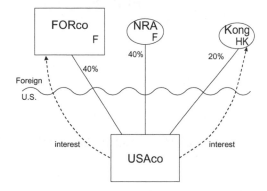

Most tax treaties also provide for lower withholding tax rates on royalties. Typically, the rate is 10% or less. Under the U.S. Model Treaty, all royalties are exempt from withholding.[27] A royalty is any payment for the use of, or the right to use, the following:

(i) any copyright of literary, artistic, or scientific work (but not including motion pictures, or films or tapes used for television or radio broadcasting),

(ii) any patent, trademark, design, model, plan, secret formula or process, or other like right or property,

(iii) any information concerning industrial, commercial, or scientific experience, or

(iv) any gains derived from the disposition of any right or property described in (i) through (iii), where the proceeds are contingent upon the future productivity, use, or disposition of that property.[28]

***Example* 13.7:** FORco is a foreign company incorporated in country F, which has a tax treaty with the United States identical to the U.S. Model Treaty. FORco licenses the manufacturing process for the super-widget to unrelated licensees in the United States. Assuming that FORco is entitled to the benefits of the Treaty, the licensees do not have to withhold on the royalty payments to FORco.

---

[27] Article 12(1) (¶ 1304.12) of the U.S. Model Treaty. When a royalty is paid by one related party to another, the treaty exemption applies only to the arm's-length royalty amount. Article 12(4) of the U.S. Model Treaty.

[28] Article 12(2) (¶ 1304.12) of the U.S. Model Treaty.

¶1302.04

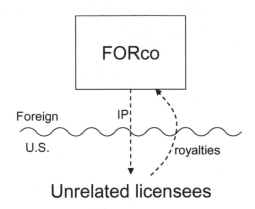

Table 13.4 presents the royalty withholding tax rates for selected countries.

TABLE 13.4. TREATY WITHHOLDING TAX RATES ON ROYALTIES PAID BY U.S. PERSONS[a]			
	Type of royalty		
Payee's country of residence	*Patents*	*Film and TV*	*Copyrights*
Canada	0%	10%	0%
China	10%	10%	10%
France	0%	0%	0%
Germany	0%	30%	0%
Italy	8%	8%	0%
Japan	0%	0%	0%
Mexico	10%	10%	10%
Netherlands	0%	30%	0%
United Kingdom	0%	0%	0%

[a]Taken from Table 1 of IRS Pub. No. 515 (Mar. 18, 2011), which is reproduced in its entirety in the appendix to this chapter.

A full listing of the treaty withholding rates for dividends, interest, and royalties can be found in the appendix to this chapter.

.05 Gains from the Disposition of Property

Under the U.S. Model Treaty, gains from the disposition of property, such as capital gains on the sale of stocks and securities, generally are taxable only by the country in which the seller resides.[29]

> **Example 13.8:** Bridgerock is a foreign corporation organized in country F, which has a tax treaty with the United States identical to the U.S. Model Treaty. Bridgerock owns all the shares of its U.S. subsidiary, Firerock. When Bridgerock sells the Firerock shares to a purchaser, the Treaty does not permit the United States to tax the gain.

---

[29] Article 13(6) (1304.13) of the U.S. Model Treaty.

¶1302.05

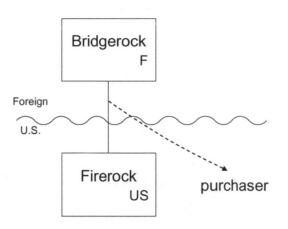

However, the U.S. Model Treaty permits taxation of gains arising from the disposition of real property, including gains from the disposition of shares of a corporation that has significant real property holdings, and gains from the disposition of interests in a partnership, trust, or estate to the extent attributable to real property situated in a contracting state.[30] The U.S. Model Treaty also permits the taxation of gains arising from the disposition of personal property, such as inventory, that are attributable to a permanent establishment.[31]

.06 Income from Real Property

Tax treaties typically do not provide tax exemptions or reductions for income from real property. Therefore, both the home and the host country maintain the right to tax real property income, which includes income from agriculture and forestry.[32] This rule applies to real property rental income,[33] as well as gains from the sale of real property.[34]

> **Example 13.9:** Uncle Sam, a U.S. citizen and resident, owns appreciated real estate in country F, a country that has a tax treaty with the United States identical to the U.S. Model Treaty. Uncle Sam sells the appreciated real estate for substantial gain. Country F can tax that gain and, if it does, Uncle Sam may claim a credit against his U.S. tax liability for the country F income tax paid.

---

[30] Article 13(1) and (2) (¶ 1304.13) of the U.S. Model Treaty.

[31] Article 13(2)(c) (¶ 1304.13) of the U.S. Model Treaty.

[32] Article 6(1) (¶ 1304.06) of the U.S. Model Treaty.

[33] Article 6(3) (¶ 1304.06) of the U.S. Model Treaty.

[34] Article 13(1) and (2) (¶ 1304.13) of the U.S. Model Treaty.

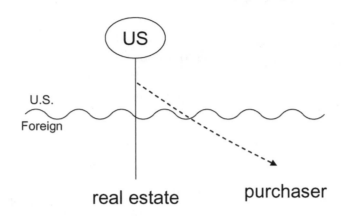

If the real property income of a resident of one treaty country is taxed by the other treaty country, that taxpayer can elect to have its income taxed on a net basis at the normal graduated rates applicable to business profits, rather than having its income taxed on a gross basis through flat rate withholding taxes.[35] This election allows a taxpayer who owns rental property to offset the gross rental income with the related rental expenses, such as depreciation, interest, insurance, and maintenance expenses.

.07 Associated Enterprises Provisions

An associated enterprise treaty provision allows the United States and its treaty partners to allocate profits between two related business enterprises as if their financial relations were those of independent business enterprises. Treating related businesses as independent businesses resembles the arm's-length standard used to allocate income pursuant to Code Sec. 482.

> **Example 13.10:** USAco, a domestic corporation, sells copper tubing to FORco, a wholly-owned country F subsidiary, at a price of $100 per tube. USAco sells the same tubing to independent distributors in country F at a price of $120 per tube. The U.S. and country F have entered a treaty with an associated enterprises provision identical to the U.S. Model Treaty.[36] As a result, the IRS can make a transfer pricing adjustment, increasing the price on tube sold from USAco to FORco to $120 per tube.

---

[35] Article 6(5) (¶ 1304.06) of the U.S. Model Treaty. Code Secs. 871(d) and 882(d) allow nonresident aliens and foreign corporations to make similar elections with respect to their U.S. real property interests.

[36] Article 9 (¶ 1304.09) of the U.S. Model Treaty.

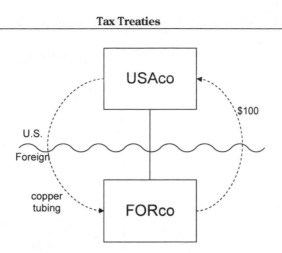

.08 Anti-treaty Shopping Provisions (Limitation on Benefits)

Because tax treaties provide lower withholding tax rates on dividend, interest, and royalty income, a multinational corporation may be able to reduce its foreign withholding taxes by owning its subsidiaries through strategically located holding companies. This practice is known as "treaty shopping."

Example **13.11**: USAco is a domestic corporation with a subsidiary in country X. The treaty between the United States and X provides a 15% withholding rate for dividends paid to a controlling shareholder. In contrast, the withholding rate on dividends is 5% under the treaty between the United States and country Z, and 0% under the treaty between countries Z and X. Country Z further exempts foreign dividends from Z's income tax. Therefore, USAco may be able to reduce the withholding tax rate on earnings repatriated from its country X subsidiary from 15% to 5% by interposing a Z holding company between itself and the X subsidiary.

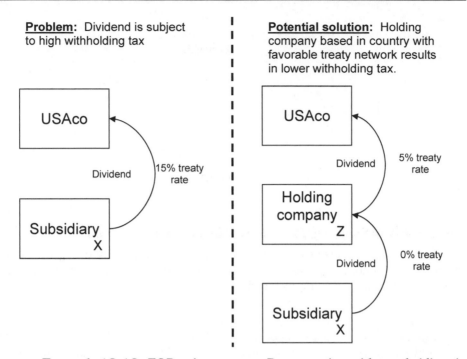

Problem: Dividend is subject to high withholding tax

Potential solution: Holding company based in country with favorable treaty network results in lower withholding tax.

Example 13.12: FORco is a country B corporation with a subsidiary in the United States. Country B does not have an income tax treaty with the United States. Therefore, the U.S. withholding tax rate on any dividends received by FORco from its U.S. subsidiary is 30%. In contrast, the withholding tax rate on dividends is 0% under the treaty between the United States and country C, and 10% under the treaty between countries C and B. Country C further exempts dividends from C's income tax. Therefore, FORco may be able to reduce the withholding tax rate on dividend distributions from its U.S. subsidiary from 30% to 10% by interposing a country C holding company between itself and the U.S. subsidiary.

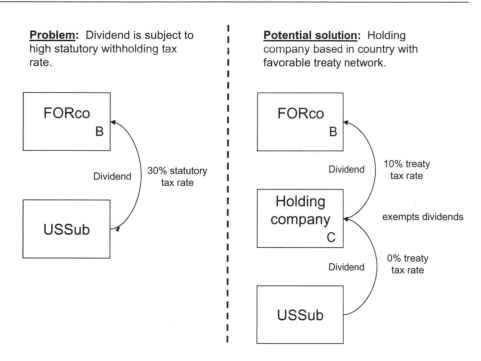

Anti-treaty shopping provisions are formally known as limitation on benefits (or LOB) provisions. The principal target of a LOB provision is a corporation that is organized in a treaty country by a resident of a non-treaty country merely to obtain the benefits of that country's income tax treaty. A limitation on benefits provision denies such corporations the benefits of the treaty. Therefore, even if a corporation qualifies as a resident of the treaty country, that corporation is not entitled to treaty benefits unless it also satisfies the requirements of the treaty's LOB provision. For example, under the limitation on benefits provision found in Article 22 of the U.S. Model Treaty, a corporation that is a resident of a treaty country generally is entitled to treaty benefits only if the corporation meets one of the following additional requirements: (i) the corporation's shares are regularly traded on a recognized stock exchange (i.e., the corporation is a publicly traded company),[37] (ii) the corporation is a subsidiary of a publicly traded corporation,[38] (iii) the corporation meets both a stock ownership test and a base erosion test,[39] or (iv) the corporation earns income that is related to an active trade or business.[40] Each of the four tests is discussed below in more detail.

Shares publicly traded. A corporation is entitled to treaty benefits if both its principal class of shares is publicly traded on a recognized stock exchange and either (a) its principal class of shares is primarily traded on an exchange in its country of residence or (b) the company's primary place of management and

---

[37] Article 22(2)(c)(i) (¶ 1304.22) of the U.S. Model Treaty.

[38] Article 22(2)(c)(ii) (¶ 1304.22) of the U.S. Model Treaty.

[39] Article 22(2)(e) (¶ 1304.22) of the U.S. Model Treaty.

[40] Article 22(3) (¶ 1304.22) of the U.S. Model Treaty.

control is in its country of residence.[41] The principal shares are the common shares of the company that constitute the majority of the voting power and value of the company. If no single class qualifies, then principal class of shares means the class that in the aggregate represents the majority of the voting power and value. Although the recognized stock exchange for foreign country purposes will vary by treaty, the recognized stock exchanges in the United States constitute the NASDAQ system, any stock exchange registered with the U.S. Securities and Exchange Commission as a national securities exchange, and any other exchange agreed upon by the United States and the foreign country.[42]

Example **13.13:** Foreign PubliCo is a foreign corporation whose principal class of shares regularly trade on a recognized stock exchange in country F, which has a tax treaty with the United States identical to the U.S. Model Treaty. Foreign PubliCo, a resident of country F, owns all the shares of USSub. USSub pays a dividend to Foreign PubliCo. Because Foreign PubliCo's shares are primarily and regularly traded on a recognized stock exchange in country F, the dividend Foreign PubliCo receives from USSub is subject to withholding at only the 5% treaty rate.

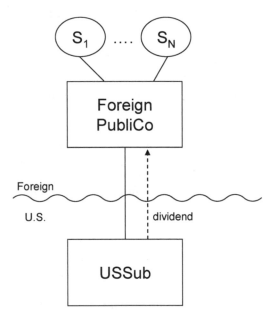

Subsidiary of publicly-traded corporation. A corporation is entitled to treaty benefits if over 50% of its shares are owned by five or fewer corporations entitled to treaty benefits. This test considers both direct and indirect owners.

Example **13.14:** Foreign PubliCo is a foreign corporation whose principal class of shares regularly trade on a recognized stock exchange in country F, which has a tax treaty with the United States identical to the U.S. Model

---

[41] Article 22(2)(c)(i) (¶ 1304.22) of the U.S. Model Treaty.

[42] Article 22(5)(a) (¶ 1304.22) of the U.S. Model Treaty.

Treaty. Foreign PubliCo, a resident of country F, owns all the shares of ForSub, which owns all the shares of USSub. USSub pays a dividend to ForSub. Although ForSub is not publicly traded, because Foreign PubliCo's shares are primarily and regularly traded on a recognized stock exchange in foreign country F and Foreign PubliCo owns all the shares of ForSub, the dividend ForSub receives is subject to withholding at only the 5% treaty rate.

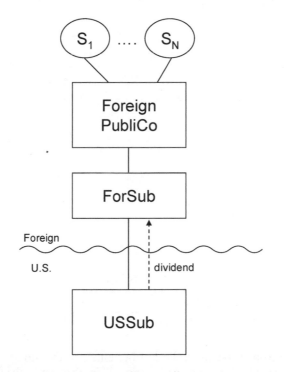

Stock ownership/base erosion test(s). A corporation qualifies for treaty benefits under this test if both at least 50% of the corporation's stock is owned by residents who are entitled to treaty benefits (the stock ownership test) and less than 50% of the corporation's gross income is used to make deductible payments to persons who are not residents of either treaty country (the base erosion test).[43]

Example **13.15:** Frank is a resident of country F, which has a tax treaty with the United States identical to the U.S. Model Treaty. Norman Ray Allen (NRA) is a resident of a country that does not have a treaty with the United States. Frank and NRA each own 50% of ForCo, a corporation organized in country F. ForCo owns all the shares of USCo, a domestic corporation. USCo pays a dividend to ForCo, which earns approximately $50,000 of gross income, before paying a salary to NRA of $20,000. Because at least 50% of the shares are owned by Frank and less than 50% of ForCo's gross income results in deductible payments to nonresidents of treaty countries, ForCo is entitled to

---

[43] Article 22(2)(e) (¶ 1304.22) of the U.S. Model Treaty.

treaty benefits. As a result, the dividend from USCo to ForCo is subject to withholding tax at the 5% treaty rate.

However, the dividend would not be entitled to treaty benefits and withholding would occur at the non-treaty rate of 30% if either: (i) NRA received a salary of $30,000 (over 50% of the gross income of USCo), or (ii) Frank owned less than 50% of the shares of ForCo.

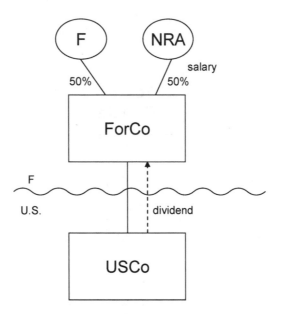

Active trade or business. Treaty benefits are extended to residents that do not otherwise qualify, but who are engaged in the active conduct of a trade or business in their country of residence. For this test, the benefits will extend only to income derived in connection with or incidental to that trade or business and only if that trade or business is substantial in relation to activities of that business in other countries. The substantiality test requires that the trade or business in the resident country is not merely a small portion of the income-generating activity in the source country.

✴ *Example* **13.16:** Norman Ray Allen (NRA), a nonresident alien, wants to acquire USCo, a U.S. manufacturing company, that annually has $10 billion of active business income. Because the country in which NRA resides does not have a treaty with the United States, a 30% non-treaty withholding rate would apply to any dividends paid by USCo. Absent the substantiality requirement, NRA could take advantage of treaty benefits by acquiring USCo through ForCo (a corporation that is a resident of country F, which has a tax treaty with the United States identical to the U.S. Model Treaty) and then arranging for ForCo to have an outlet in country F that sells a relatively miniscule amount of manufactured products for $100,000 of active business income.

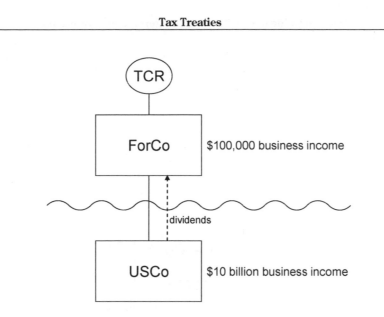

Derivative benefits. Although not in the U.S. Model Treaty, some of the recent treaties concluded with major U.S. trading partners reduce withholding tax rates on payments to corporations that satisfy the derivative benefits test. The policy behind the derivative benefits test is that treaty shopping does not occur when an intermediary receiving a payment is owned by a corporation in another country entitled to treaty benefits. For example, the U.S.-Canadian Treaty permits treaty rates on withholding when paid to a corporation that has a 90% controlling ownership interest by persons who (i) are residents in countries that have a comprehensive income tax treaty with the United States or Canada and will be entitled to the same kind of benefits under that treaty, (ii) would be qualified persons or otherwise eligible for treaty benefits if they were residents of the United States or Canada, (iii) would be entitled to a rate of tax in the other treaty country on the relevant income that is at least as low as the tax rate on the treaty, and (iv) less than 50% of the company's gross income was paid directly or indirectly to persons who are not residents of either country.

Example **13.17:** UKCo is publicly traded on the London Stock Exchange and, if UKCo directly owned USCo, UKCo would be entitled to the benefit of a 5% withholding rate under the U.K.-U.S. Tax Treaty. However, UKCo prefers to operate in North America through a Canadian holding company ("CanCo"). CanCo does not make deductible payments to anyone outside of Canada. Even though CanCo does not satisfy any of the aforementioned limitation of benefits provisions, CanCo is entitled to derivative benefits under the U.S.-Canadian Tax Treaty. Therefore, a dividend from USCo to CanCo would be entitled to the preferential 5% U.S.-Canadian Tax Treaty withholding rate.

¶1302.08

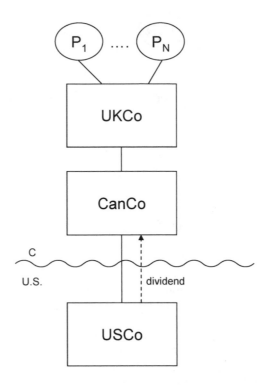

Case law and statutory provisions. In addition to the anti-treaty shopping provisions contained in treaties, the IRS has sought to disallow treaty benefits obtained through the use of intermediary entities by invoking the judicial doctrine of substance over form. The seminal case in this area is *Aiken Industries, Inc. v. Comm'r*,[44] in which the IRS successfully denied treaty benefits that the taxpayer attempted to obtain through the use of a back-to-back loan arrangement.

In addition, Code Sec. 7701(l) gives the IRS the authority to disregard the existence of an intermediary or conduit entity with respect to treaty shopping that results in the avoidance of U.S. taxes. A multi-party financing arrangement is subject to recharacterization if a related intermediate entity participates in a back-to-back loan arrangement as part of a plan to avoid U.S. withholding taxes. These rules also apply to certain unrelated intermediaries, back-to-back leases, and licenses, but do not apply to equity investments or debt guarantees.[45]

The availability of reduced U.S. withholding tax under an income tax treaty for payments to hybrid entities is further limited by Code Sec. 894(c). Specifically, a foreign person is not entitled to a reduced rate of withholding tax under a tax treaty on an item of income derived through a partnership (or other fiscally transparent entity) if all of the following apply: (i) the income item is not treated by the treaty

---

[44] 56 TC 925, Dec. 30,912, A. 1972-2 CB 1. *See also Northern Ind. Pub. Serv. Co.,* 105 TC 341, Dec. 50,979.

Aff'd, CA-7, 97-1 USTC ¶ 50,474, 115 F3d 506 (7th Cir., 1997).

[45] Reg. § 1.881-3.

¶1302.08

partner as an item of income to such foreign person, (ii) the foreign country does not impose tax on a distribution of the item by the U.S. entity to the foreign person, and (iii) the treaty does not contain a provision addressing the applicability of the treaty in the case of an item of income derived through a partnership.[46] Congress enacted Code Sec. 894(c) to primarily prevent the use of a tax planning strategy in which a U.S. limited liability company was interposed between a foreign parent corporation and its U.S. subsidiary.

.09 Non-Discrimination Provisions

Tax treaties generally include non-discrimination provisions, which are designed to prevent a treaty country from imposing a tax on residents of the other treaty country that is more burdensome than the tax imposed under the same circumstances on its own residents. The U.S. Model Treaty specifically prohibits numerous types of discrimination. Examples include imposing a more burdensome tax on a permanent establishment of a foreign corporation than on a U.S. establishment carrying on the same activities, discriminating with respect to personal allowances or deductions based on family status, discriminating with respect to deductions for interest and royalty payments, and imposing a more burdensome tax on a U.S. corporation owned by foreign investors than on a similarly situated U.S. corporation owned by U.S. shareholders.[47]

> **Example 13.18:** FORco, a country Y parent corporation, owns all of the stock of USsub. USsub competes in the U.S. steel market with USAco, a domestic corporation wholly-owned by U.S. citizens. In order to protect the U.S. steel industry, Congress enacts legislation increasing the rate of income tax on all steel wholesalers that are foreign-owned from 35% to 45%. Subsequently, the U.S. and country Y enter into a treaty that contains an anti-discrimination provision identical to the U.S. Model Treaty, which includes a paragraph prohibiting tax discrimination based on capital ownership. As a result, USsub is exempt from the 45% rate, and will pay tax at the same 35% rate as USAco.

.10 Mutual Agreement Procedure

Tax treaties provide a mutual agreement procedure by which a resident of a treaty country can request assistance from the competent authority of that country in obtaining relief from actions of one or both treaty countries that the taxpayer believes are inconsistent with the treaty.[48] The competent authority is the governmental office that administers tax treaties. For example, if one or both treaty countries makes an adjustment to the intercompany transfer prices used by affiliated companies located within their respective countries, both countries might tax the same item of income. In such cases, the taxpayer may wish to seek relief from double taxation by petitioning the appropriate competent authority. Assuming the taxpayer's objections are justified, the competent authority of one treaty country is empowered to resolve the case by mutual agreement with the competent authority of the other treaty country. Other situations in which the taxpayer may wish to seek

---

[46] Code Sec. 894(c) and Temp. Reg. § 1.894-1(a) and (b).

[47] Article 24 (¶ 1304.24) of the U.S. Model Treaty.

[48] Article 25(1) and (2) (¶ 1304.25) of the U.S. Model Treaty.

this mutual agreement procedure include conflicts regarding the proper characterization of an item of income, the application of a source-of-income rule, or the meaning of a term.[49] The various methods by which a U.S. taxpayer can request competent authority assistance are described in Chapter 16 (¶ 1607).

   Example **13.19:** USAco is a subsidiary of EURco. USAco buys widgets from EURco for $200 and resells them in the United States for $210. The IRS argues that the arm's-length price for the intercompany widget sales is $180 and assesses additional tax on USAco. As a consequence, EURco recognizes $200 on gross income with respect to each widget sale, but USAco claims a cost of goods sold deduction of only $180. to obtain relief, either USAco or EURco can petition their respective competent authority.

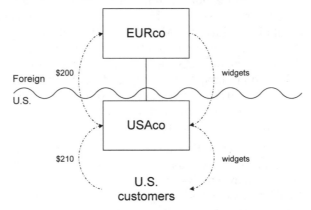

.11 Exchanges of Information

   In addition to the mutual agreement procedures outlined above, tax treaties also provide for exchanges of information regarding taxpayers as a mechanism for enhancing compliance with respect to international transactions. Under the U.S. Model Treaty, the competent authorities of the two treaty countries shall exchange such information as is necessary for enforcing provisions of the tax treaty, as well as the internal laws of the two countries concerning taxes covered by the treaty.[50] For example, the two treaty countries might share information regarding a taxpayer that both countries are auditing. Another example is an exchange of lists of residents of one treaty country deriving dividend, interest, or royalty income from sources within the other treaty country.

   Example **13.20:** A distributor of candy, USAco is a subsidiary of ASIAco. USAco buys the candy from ASIAco for resale in the United States. The IRS's International Examiner conducts a transfer pricing audit of USAco. After USAco fails to respond to the International Examiner's IDR requesting all agreements between USAco and ASIAco, the International Examiner requests the information from ASIA country's tax authority pursuant to the exchange of information provision in the U.S.-ASIA country tax treaty.

---

[49] Article 25(3) (¶ 1304.25) of the U.S. Model Treaty. The procedures for requesting assistance from U.S. competent authorities are found in Rev. Proc. 2006-54, IRB 2006-38.

[50] Article 26(1) (¶ 1304.26) of the U.S. Model Treaty.

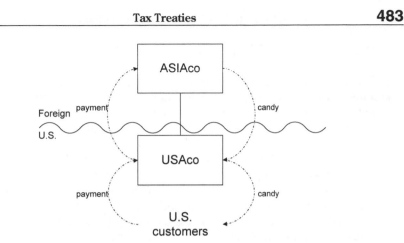

¶ 1303 DISCLOSURE OF TREATY-BASED RETURN POSITIONS

Any taxpayer, U.S. or foreign, that claims the benefits of a treaty by taking a tax return position that is in conflict with the Internal Revenue Code must disclose the position.[51] A tax return position is considered to be in conflict with the Code, and therefore treaty-based, if the U.S. tax liability under the treaty is different from the tax liability that would have to be reported in the absence of a treaty.[52] This reporting requirement is waived in various situations. A taxpayer reports treaty-based positions either by attaching a statement to its return or by using Form 8833 (a sample of a completed Form 8833 is reproduced in the Appendix to this chapter).[53] If a taxpayer fails to report a treaty-based return position, each such failure is subject to a penalty of $1,000, or a penalty of $10,000 in the case of a regular corporation.[54]

The regulations describe the items to be disclosed on a Form 8833. The disclosure statement typically requires six items:

   (i) the name and employer identification number of both the recipient and payor of the income at issue;

   (ii) the type of treaty benefited item and its amount;

   (iii) the facts and an explanation supporting the return position taken;

   (iv) the specific treaty provisions on which the taxpayer bases its claims;

   (v) the Internal Revenue Code provision exempted or reduced; and

   (vi) an explanation of any applicable limitations on benefits provisions.

The disclosure regulations specify a non-exclusive list of treaty benefits that must always be disclosed.[55] The regulations also waive various treaty benefits from disclosure, but specify that if an issue is not on the wavier list, the issue must be disclosed.[56]

---

[51] Code Sec. 6114.

[52] Reg. § 301.6114-1(a)(2)(i).

[53] Reg. § 301.6114-1(d) and Announcement 93-63, IRB 1993-16, 11.

[54] Code Sec. 6712.

[55] Reg. § 301.6114-1(b).

[56] Reg. § 301.6114-1(c).

.01 Specific Disclosure Requirements

The regulations require disclosure of reduced withholding taxes on some payments to related persons. Examples include interest, dividend, rents, and royalties that a U.S. person pays to a related foreign person who is entitled to reduced rates to a withholding tax under a treaty and the payment exceeds $500,000.[57]

Example 13.21: USSub, a domestic corporation, is a subsidiary of FORco, a corporation organized in a country which has a tax treaty with the United States that is identical to the U.S. Model Treaty. USSub pays a $1 million dividend to FORco and withholds $50,000 pursuant to the treaty withholding rate on dividends of 5%. The $1 million dividend must be disclosed to the IRS on a Form 8833.

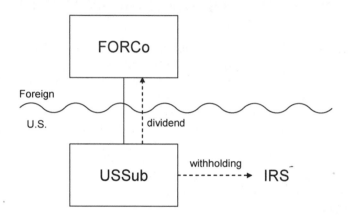

Foreign persons claiming exemption from U.S. tax because their trade or business does not constitute a permanent establishment under a treaty also must disclose that position.[58]

Example 13.22: FORco sells zinc to customers in the United States. FORco's only U.S. presence is a warehouse which FORco uses solely to store and deliver zinc. Without a tax treaty, FORco's sales in the United States combined with a U.S. warehouse would constitute carrying on a trade or business in the United States that would be subject to U.S. income tax. However, FORco is a resident of a country that has a treaty with the United States, under which a permanent establishment does not include a warehouse used solely to store and deliver the taxpayer's own goods. Although FORco is not subject to tax in the United States under the treaty, FORco must file a return disclosing the treaty position.

---

[57] Reg. § 301.6114-1(b)(4). For this purpose, a related foreign person includes a CFC in which the U.S. payer is a 10% or more U.S. shareholder, a foreign corporation controlled by the U.S. payer, a 25% or more foreign shareholder of the U.S. payer, or a foreign related party. This rule applies even though the foreign recipient may not otherwise have to file a U.S. income tax return.

[58] Reg. § 301.6114-1(b)(5)(i).

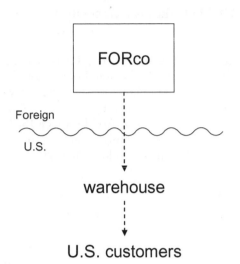

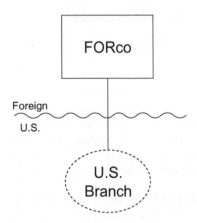

A foreign corporation operating in the United States through a branch may be subject to the Code Sec. 884 branch profits tax. Some treaties provide exemptions or rate reductions for a branch profits tax. Any foreign corporation claiming such an exemption or reduction must disclose this position.[59]

Example 13.23: FORco, a country F corporation, sells paper to customers in the United States through its U.S. branch, which constitutes a permanent establishment under the tax treaty between the United States and country X. The treaty reduces the branch profits tax from 30% to 5%. FORco must disclose the reduced branch profits tax on its Form 1120F.

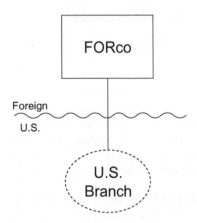

To the extent that a treaty may alter the sourcing of an item of income, a taxpayer must disclose this alteration.[60]

---

[59] Reg. § 301.6114-1(b)(3).   [60] Reg. § 301.6114-1(b)(6).

¶1303.01

Example **13.24:** FORco is a corporation organized in country F, which has a treaty with the United States identical to the U.S. Model Treaty. FORco owns all the shares of USAco. Norman Ray Allen (NRA), a citizen and resident of country F, is the President of FORco. NRA is also on the Board of Directors of USAco, the U.S. subsidiary of FORco. Four times a year, NRA travels to the United States for the Board of Director meetings, for which he receives a total fee of $20,000. Although personal services income is sourced in the United States under Code Sec. 861(a)(3), Article 16 (¶ 1304.16) of the U.S. Model Treaty re-sources the income as foreign source. Due to the Treaty re-sourcing the item of income, NRA must disclose this alteration, although he will not have to pay any U.S. tax.

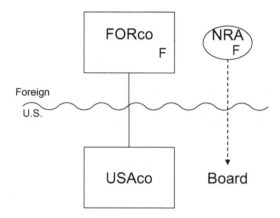

.02 Waiver of Disclosure Requirements

The disclosure regulations provide an exclusive list of issues that do not have to be disclosed.

In contrast to payments in excess of $500,000 to related parties, payments of interest, dividends, rents or royalties by a U.S. person to an unrelated party are not subject to disclosure other than the withholding compliance procedures described in Chapter 9 (¶ 903). As a result, an unrelated foreign recipient of U.S. source investment-type income will not have a filing obligation, unless the taxpayer is engaged in a trade or business within the United States.

Example **13.25:** FORco is a resident of a country that has a tax treaty with the United States that is identical to the U.S. Model Treaty. FORco owns less than 1% of USCo, a domestic corporation which pays FORco a $2 million dividend. The dividend is subject to withholding tax at the 15% treaty rate. Because FORco's percentage ownership of USCo is not high enough for FORco to be considered a related party, disclosure to the IRS is specifically waived.

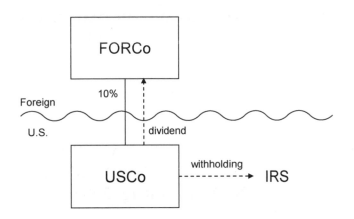

The disclosure requirements also do not apply to a U.S. withholding agent. These withholding agents already have reporting obligations in that they must file Forms 1042 and 1042S and do not have any further obligations with respect to reduced withholding pursuant to a treaty.[61]

No reporting is required when the treaty benefit is based on residency in a treaty partner country due to the tie-breaker rules in the treaty when the individual receives, in the aggregate, amounts less than $100,000.[62] For example, suppose an individual is considered both a resident of the United States under the green card test and a resident of a treaty partner due to that treaty partner's internal laws. If, pursuant to the tie-breaker provisions in that treaty, the individual is classified a resident of the treaty partner, he or she does not have to file a U.S. return.

Nonresident aliens and foreign corporations may occasionally desire to make a protective tax return filing to avoid any penalties and to ensure that the statute of limitations begins to run. This would occur in a situation where it is uncertain whether the foreign corporation has a filing requirement.

---

[61] Reg. § 301.6114-1(c)(5). [62] Reg. § 301.6114-1(c)(2).

¶ 1304 UNITED STATES MODEL INCOME TAX CONVENTION OF NOVEMBER 15, 2006

UNITED STATES MODEL
INCOME TAX CONVENTION OF
NOVEMBER 15, 2006

**CONVENTION BETWEEN
THE GOVERNMENT OF THE UNITED STATES OF AMERICA
AND THE GOVERNMENT OF -------
FOR THE AVOIDANCE OF DOUBLE TAXATION
AND THE PREVENTION OF FISCAL EVASION
WITH RESPECT TO TAXES ON INCOME**

The Government of the United States of America and the Government of -----, desiring to conclude a Convention for the avoidance of double taxation and the prevention of fiscal evasion with respect to taxes on income, have agreed as follows:

2006 U.S. Model
Income Tax Convention

- 2 -

Article 1

GENERAL SCOPE

1.   This Convention shall apply only to persons who are residents of one or both of the Contracting States, except as otherwise provided in the Convention.

2.   This Convention shall not restrict in any manner any benefit now or hereafter accorded:

    a)   by the laws of either Contracting State; or

    b)   by any other agreement to which the Contracting States are parties.

3.   a)   Notwithstanding the provisions of subparagraph b) of paragraph 2 of this Article:

        i)   for purposes of paragraph 3 of Article XXII (Consultation) of the General Agreement on Trade in Services, the Contracting States agree that any question arising as to the interpretation or application of this Convention and, in particular, whether a taxation measure is within the scope of this Convention, shall be determined exclusively in accordance with the provisions of Article 25 (Mutual Agreement Procedure) of this Convention; and

        ii)   the provisions of Article XVII of the General Agreement on Trade in Services shall not apply to a taxation measure unless the competent authorities agree that the measure is not within the scope of Article 24 (Non-Discrimination) of this Convention.

    b)   For the purposes of this paragraph, a "measure" is a law, regulation, rule, procedure, decision, administrative action, or any similar provision or action.

4.   Except to the extent provided in paragraph 5, this Convention shall not affect the taxation by a Contracting State of its residents (as determined under Article 4 (Resident)) and its citizens. Notwithstanding the other provisions of this Convention, a former citizen or former long-term resident of a Contracting State may, for the period of ten years following the loss of such status, be taxed in accordance with the laws of that Contracting State.

5.   The provisions of paragraph 4 shall not affect:

    a)   the benefits conferred by a Contracting State under paragraph 2 of Article 9 (Associated Enterprises), paragraphs 1 b), 2, and 5 of Article 17 (Pensions, Social Security, Annuities, Alimony, and Child Support), paragraphs 1 and 4 of Article 18 (Pension Funds), and Articles 23 (Relief From Double Taxation), 24 (Non-Discrimination), and 25 (Mutual Agreement Procedure); and

2006 U.S. Model
Income Tax Convention

- 3 -

b)   the benefits conferred by a Contracting State under paragraph 2 of Article 18 (Pension Funds), Articles 19 (Government Service), 20 (Students and Trainees), and 27 (Members of Diplomatic Missions and Consular Posts), upon individuals who are neither citizens of, nor have been admitted for permanent residence in, that State.

6.   An item of income, profit or gain derived through an entity that is fiscally transparent under the laws of either Contracting State shall be considered to be derived by a resident of a State to the extent that the item is treated for purposes of the taxation law of such Contracting State as the income, profit or gain of a resident.

2006 U.S. Model
Income Tax Convention

- 4 -

Article 2

TAXES COVERED

1. This Convention shall apply to taxes on income imposed on behalf of a Contracting State irrespective of the manner in which they are levied.

2. There shall be regarded as taxes on income all taxes imposed on total income, or on elements of income, including taxes on gains from the alienation of property.

3. The existing taxes to which this Convention shall apply are:

a) in the case of ------:

b) in the case of the United States: the Federal income taxes imposed by the Internal Revenue Code (but excluding social security and unemployment taxes), and the Federal excise taxes imposed with respect to private foundations.

4. This Convention shall apply also to any identical or substantially similar taxes that are imposed after the date of signature of the Convention in addition to, or in place of, the existing taxes. The competent authorities of the Contracting States shall notify each other of any changes that have been made in their respective taxation or other laws that significantly affect their obligations under this Convention.

2006 U.S. Model
Income Tax Convention

- 5 -

Article 3

GENERAL DEFINITIONS

1.   For the purposes of this Convention, unless the context otherwise requires:

a)   the term "person" includes an individual, an estate, a trust, a partnership, a company, and any other body of persons;

b)   the term "company" means any body corporate or any entity that is treated as a body corporate for tax purposes according to the laws of the state in which it is organized;

c)   the terms "enterprise of a Contracting State" and "enterprise of the other Contracting State" mean respectively an enterprise carried on by a resident of a Contracting State, and an enterprise carried on by a resident of the other Contracting State; the terms also include an enterprise carried on by a resident of a Contracting State through an entity that is treated as fiscally transparent in that Contracting State;

d)   the term "enterprise" applies to the carrying on of any business;

e)   the term "business" includes the performance of professional services and of other activities of an independent character;

f)   the term "international traffic" means any transport by a ship or aircraft, except when such transport is solely between places in a Contracting State;

g)   the term "competent authority" means:

　　i)   in -----, --------------------------; and

　　ii)   in the United States: the Secretary of the Treasury or his delegate;

h)   the term "--------" means ;

i)   the term "United States" means the United States of America, and includes the states thereof and the District of Columbia; such term also includes the territorial sea thereof and the sea bed and subsoil of the submarine areas adjacent to that territorial sea, over which the United States exercises sovereign rights in accordance with international law; the term, however, does not include Puerto Rico, the Virgin Islands, Guam or any other United States possession or territory;

2006 U.S. Model
Income Tax Convention

- 6 -

j)   the term "national" of a Contracting State means:

   i)   any individual possessing the nationality or citizenship of that State; and

   ii)   any legal person, partnership or association deriving its status as such from the laws in force in that State;

k)   the term "pension fund" means any person established in a Contracting State that is:

   i)   generally exempt from income taxation in that State; and

   ii)   operated principally either:

      A)   to administer or provide pension or retirement benefits; or

      B)   to earn income for the benefit of one or more persons described in clause A).

2.   As regards the application of the Convention at any time by a Contracting State any term not defined therein shall, unless the context otherwise requires, or the competent authorities agree to a common meaning pursuant to the provisions of Article 25 (Mutual Agreement Procedure), have the meaning which it has at that time under the law of that State for the purposes of the taxes to which the Convention applies, any meaning under the applicable tax laws of that State prevailing over a meaning given to the term under other laws of that State.

- 7 -

Article 4

RESIDENT

1.   For the purposes of this Convention, the term "resident of a Contracting State" means any person who, under the laws of that State, is liable to tax therein by reason of his domicile, residence, citizenship, place of management, place of incorporation, or any other criterion of a similar nature, and also includes that State and any political subdivision or local authority thereof. This term, however, does not include any person who is liable to tax in that State in respect only of income from sources in that State or of profits attributable to a permanent establishment in that State.

2.   The term "resident of a Contracting State" includes:

a)   a pension fund established in that State; and

b)   an organization that is established and maintained in that State exclusively for religious, charitable, scientific, artistic, cultural, or educational purposes,

notwithstanding that all or part of its income or gains may be exempt from tax under the domestic law of that State.

3.   Where, by reason of the provisions of paragraph 1, an individual is a resident of both Contracting States, then his status shall be determined as follows:

a)   he shall be deemed to be a resident only of the State in which he has a permanent home available to him; if he has a permanent home available to him in both States, he shall be deemed to be a resident only of the State with which his personal and economic relations are closer (center of vital interests);

b)   if the State in which he has his center of vital interests cannot be determined, or if he does not have a permanent home available to him in either State, he shall be deemed to be a resident only of the State in which he has an habitual abode;

c)   if he has an habitual abode in both States or in neither of them, he shall be deemed to be a resident only of the State of which he is a national;

d)   if he is a national of both States or of neither of them, the competent authorities of the Contracting States shall endeavor to settle the question by mutual agreement.

- 8 -

4.   Where by reason of the provisions of paragraph 1 a company is a resident of both Contracting States, then if it is created or organized under the laws of one of the Contracting States or a political subdivision thereof, but not under the laws of the other Contracting State or a political subdivision thereof, such company shall be deemed to be a resident of the first-mentioned Contracting State. In all other cases involving dual resident companies, the competent authorities of the Contracting States shall endeavor to determine the mode of application of the Convention to such company. If the competent authorities do not reach such an agreement, that company will not be treated as a resident of either Contracting State for purposes of its claiming any benefits provided by the Convention.

5.   Where by reason of the provisions of paragraphs 1 and 2 of this Article a person other than an individual or a company is a resident of both Contracting States, the competent authorities of the Contracting States shall by mutual agreement endeavor to determine the mode of application of this Convention to that person.

- 9 -

Article 5

PERMANENT ESTABLISHMENT

1.   For the purposes of this Convention, the term "permanent establishment" means a fixed place of business through which the business of an enterprise is wholly or partly carried on.

2.   The term "permanent establishment" includes especially:

    a)   a place of management;

    b)   a branch;

    c)   an office;

    d)   a factory;

    e)   a workshop; and

    f)   a mine, an oil or gas well, a quarry, or any other place of extraction of natural resources.

3.   A building site or construction or installation project, or an installation or drilling rig or ship used for the exploration of natural resources, constitutes a permanent establishment only if it lasts, or the exploration activity continues for more than twelve months.

4.   Notwithstanding the preceding provisions of this Article, the term "permanent establishment" shall be deemed not to include:

    a)   the use of facilities solely for the purpose of storage, display or delivery of goods or merchandise belonging to the enterprise;

    b)   the maintenance of a stock of goods or merchandise belonging to the enterprise solely for the purpose of storage, display or delivery;

    c)   the maintenance of a stock of goods or merchandise belonging to the enterprise solely for the purpose of processing by another enterprise;

    d)   the maintenance of a fixed place of business solely for the purpose of purchasing goods or merchandise, or of collecting information, for the enterprise;

    e)   the maintenance of a fixed place of business solely for the purpose of carrying on, for the enterprise, any other activity of a preparatory or auxiliary character;

- 10 -

f)   the maintenance of a fixed place of business solely for any combination of the activities mentioned in subparagraphs a) through e), provided that the overall activity of the fixed place of business resulting from this combination is of a preparatory or auxiliary character.

5.   Notwithstanding the provisions of paragraphs 1 and 2, where a person -- other than an agent of an independent status to whom paragraph 6 applies -- is acting on behalf of an enterprise and has and habitually exercises in a Contracting State an authority to conclude contracts that are binding on the enterprise, that enterprise shall be deemed to have a permanent establishment in that State in respect of any activities that the person undertakes for the enterprise, unless the activities of such person are limited to those mentioned in paragraph 4 that, if exercised through a fixed place of business, would not make this fixed place of business a permanent establishment under the provisions of that paragraph.

6.   An enterprise shall not be deemed to have a permanent establishment in a Contracting State merely because it carries on business in that State through a broker, general commission agent, or any other agent of an independent status, provided that such persons are acting in the ordinary course of their business as independent agents.

7.   The fact that a company that is a resident of a Contracting State controls or is controlled by a company that is a resident of the other Contracting State, or that carries on business in that other State (whether through a permanent establishment or otherwise), shall not be taken into account in determining whether either company has a permanent establishment in that other State.

¶1304

- 11 -

Article 6

INCOME FROM REAL PROPERTY

1.   Income derived by a resident of a Contracting State from real property, including income from agriculture or forestry, situated in the other Contracting State may be taxed in that other State.

2.   The term "real property" shall have the meaning which it has under the law of the Contracting State in which the property in question is situated. The term shall in any case include property accessory to real property (including livestock and equipment used in agriculture and forestry), rights to which the provisions of general law respecting landed property apply, usufruct of real property and rights to variable or fixed payments as consideration for the working of, or the right to work, mineral deposits, sources and other natural resources. Ships and aircraft shall not be regarded as real property.

3.   The provisions of paragraph 1 shall apply to income derived from the direct use, letting, or use in any other form of real property.

4.   The provisions of paragraphs 1 and 3 shall also apply to the income from real property of an enterprise.

5.   A resident of a Contracting State who is liable to tax in the other Contracting State on income from real property situated in the other Contracting State may elect for any taxable year to compute the tax on such income on a net basis as if such income were business profits attributable to a permanent establishment in such other State. Any such election shall be binding for the taxable year of the election and all subsequent taxable years unless the competent authority of the Contracting State in which the property is situated agrees to terminate the election.

¶1304

- 12 -

Article 7

BUSINESS PROFITS

1.   The profits of an enterprise of a Contracting State shall be taxable only in that State unless the enterprise carries on business in the other Contracting State through a permanent establishment situated therein. If the enterprise carries on business as aforesaid, the profits of the enterprise may be taxed in the other State but only so much of them as are attributable to that permanent establishment.

2.   Subject to the provisions of paragraph 3, where an enterprise of a Contracting State carries on business in the other Contracting State through a permanent establishment situated therein, there shall in each Contracting State be attributed to that permanent establishment the profits that it might be expected to make if it were a distinct and independent enterprise engaged in the same or similar activities under the same or similar conditions. For this purpose, the profits to be attributed to the permanent establishment shall include only the profits derived from the assets used, risks assumed and activities performed by the permanent establishment.

3.   In determining the profits of a permanent establishment, there shall be allowed as deductions expenses that are incurred for the purposes of the permanent establishment, including executive and general administrative expenses so incurred, whether in the State in which the permanent establishment is situated or elsewhere.*

4.   No profits shall be attributed to a permanent establishment by reason of the mere purchase by that permanent establishment of goods or merchandise for the enterprise.

---

*   Protocol or Notes should include the following language:

It is understood that the business profits to be attributed to a permanent establishment shall include only the profits derived from the assets used, risks assumed and activities performed by the permanent establishment. The principles of the OECD Transfer Pricing Guidelines will apply for purposes of determining the profits attributable to a permanent establishment, taking into account the different economic and legal circumstances of a single entity. Accordingly, any of the methods described therein as acceptable methods for determining an arm's length result may be used to determine the income of a permanent establishment so long as those methods are applied in accordance with the Guidelines. In particular, in determining the amount of attributable profits, the permanent establishment shall be treated as having the same amount of capital that it would need to support its activities if it were a distinct and separate enterprise engaged in the same or similar activities. With respect to financial institutions other than insurance companies, a Contracting State may determine the amount of capital to be attributed to a permanent establishment by allocating the institution's total equity between its various offices on the basis of the proportion of the financial institution's risk-weighted assets attributable to each of them. In the case of an insurance company, there shall be attributed to a permanent establishment not only premiums earned through the permanent establishment, but that portion of the insurance company's overall investment income from reserves and surplus that supports the risks assumed by the permanent establishment.

2006 U.S. Model
Income Tax Convention

- 13 -

5.   For the purposes of the preceding paragraphs, the profits to be attributed to the permanent establishment shall be determined by the same method year by year unless there is good and sufficient reason to the contrary.

6.   Where profits include items of income that are dealt with separately in other Articles of the Convention, then the provisions of those Articles shall not be affected by the provisions of this Article.

7.   In applying this Article, paragraph 6 of Article 10 (Dividends), paragraph 4 of Article 11 (Interest), paragraph 3 of Article 12 (Royalties), paragraph 3 of Article 13 (Gains) and paragraph 2 of Article 21 (Other Income), any income or gain attributable to a permanent establishment during its existence is taxable in the Contracting State where such permanent establishment is situated even if the payments are deferred until such permanent establishment has ceased to exist.

¶1304

2006 U.S. Model
Income Tax Convention

- 14 -

Article 8

SHIPPING AND AIR TRANSPORT

1.　　Profits of an enterprise of a Contracting State from the operation of ships or aircraft in international traffic shall be taxable only in that State.

2.　　For purposes of this Article, profits from the operation of ships or aircraft include, but are not limited to:

　　a)　　profits from the rental of ships or aircraft on a full (time or voyage) basis;

　　b)　　profits from the rental on a bareboat basis of ships or aircraft if the rental income is incidental to profits from the operation of ships or aircraft in international traffic; and

　　c)　　profits from the rental on a bareboat basis of ships or aircraft if such ships or aircraft are operated in international traffic by the lessee.

Profits derived by an enterprise from the inland transport of property or passengers within either Contracting State shall be treated as profits from the operation of ships or aircraft in international traffic if such transport is undertaken as part of international traffic.

3.　　Profits of an enterprise of a Contracting State from the use, maintenance, or rental of containers (including trailers, barges, and related equipment for the transport of containers) shall be taxable only in that Contracting State, except to the extent that those containers are used for transport solely between places within the other Contracting State.

4.　　The provisions of paragraphs 1 and 3 shall also apply to profits from participation in a pool, a joint business, or an international operating agency.

2006 U.S. Model
Income Tax Convention

- 15 -

Article 9

ASSOCIATED ENTERPRISES

1.   Where:

a)   an enterprise of a Contracting State participates directly or indirectly in the management, control or capital of an enterprise of the other Contracting State; or

b)   the same persons participate directly or indirectly in the management, control, or capital of an enterprise of a Contracting State and an enterprise of the other Contracting State,

and in either case conditions are made or imposed between the two enterprises in their commercial or financial relations that differ from those that would be made between independent enterprises, then any profits that, but for those conditions, would have accrued to one of the enterprises, but by reason of those conditions have not so accrued, may be included in the profits of that enterprise and taxed accordingly.

2.   Where a Contracting State includes in the profits of an enterprise of that State, and taxes accordingly, profits on which an enterprise of the other Contracting State has been charged to tax in that other State, and the other Contracting State agrees that the profits so included are profits that would have accrued to the enterprise of the first-mentioned State if the conditions made between the two enterprises had been those that would have been made between independent enterprises, then that other State shall make an appropriate adjustment to the amount of the tax charged therein on those profits. In determining such adjustment, due regard shall be had to the other provisions of this Convention and the competent authorities of the Contracting States shall if necessary consult each other.

- 16 -

Article 10

DIVIDENDS

1.   Dividends paid by a company that is a resident of a Contracting State to a resident of the other Contracting State may be taxed in that other State.

2.   However, such dividends may also be taxed in the Contracting State of which the company paying the dividends is a resident and according to the laws of that State, but if the dividends are beneficially owned by a resident of the other Contracting State, except as otherwise provided, the tax so charged shall not exceed:

> a)   5 percent of the gross amount of the dividends if the beneficial owner is a company that owns directly at least 10 percent of the voting stock of the company paying the dividends;

> b)   15 percent of the gross amount of the dividends in all other cases.

This paragraph shall not affect the taxation of the company in respect of the profits out of which the dividends are paid.

3.   Notwithstanding paragraph 2, dividends shall not be taxed in the Contracting State of which the company paying the dividends is a resident if:

> a)   the beneficial owner of the dividends is a pension fund that is a resident of the other Contracting State; and

> b)   such dividends are not derived from the carrying on of a trade or business by the pension fund or through an associated enterprise.

4.   a)   Subparagraph a) of paragraph 2 shall not apply in the case of dividends paid by a U.S. Regulated Investment Company (RIC) or a U.S. Real Estate Investment Trust (REIT). In the case of dividends paid by a RIC, subparagraph b) of paragraph 2 and paragraph 3 shall apply. In the case of dividends paid by a REIT, subparagraph b) of paragraph 2 and paragraph 3 shall apply only if:

>> i)   the beneficial owner of the dividends is an individual or pension fund, in either case holding an interest of not more than 10 percent in the REIT;

>> ii)   the dividends are paid with respect to a class of stock that is publicly traded and the beneficial owner of the dividends is a person holding an interest of not more than 5 percent of any class of the REIT's stock; or

- 17 -

    iii)   the beneficial owner of the dividends is a person holding an interest of not more than 10 percent in the REIT and the REIT is diversified.

    b)   For purposes of this paragraph, a REIT shall be "diversified" if the value of no single interest in real property exceeds 10 percent of its total interests in real property. For the purposes of this rule, foreclosure property shall not be considered an interest in real property. Where a REIT holds an interest in a partnership, it shall be treated as owning directly a proportion of the partnership's interests in real property corresponding to its interest in the partnership.

5.   For purposes of this Article, the term "dividends" means income from shares or other rights, not being debt-claims, participating in profits, as well as income that is subjected to the same taxation treatment as income from shares under the laws of the State of which the payer is a resident.

6.   The provisions of paragraphs 2 through 4 shall not apply if the beneficial owner of the dividends, being a resident of a Contracting State, carries on business in the other Contracting State, of which the payer is a resident, through a permanent establishment situated therein, and the holding in respect of which the dividends are paid is effectively connected with such permanent establishment. In such case the provisions of Article 7 (Business Profits) shall apply.

7.   A Contracting State may not impose any tax on dividends paid by a resident of the other State, except insofar as the dividends are paid to a resident of the first-mentioned State or the dividends are attributable to a permanent establishment, nor may it impose tax on a corporation's undistributed profits, except as provided in paragraph 8, even if the dividends paid or the undistributed profits consist wholly or partly of profits or income arising in that State.

8.   a)   A company that is a resident of one of the States and that has a permanent establishment in the other State or that is subject to tax in the other State on a net basis on its income that may be taxed in the other State under Article 6 (Income from Real Property) or under paragraph 1 of Article 13 (Gains) may be subject in that other State to a tax in addition to the tax allowable under the other provisions of this Convention.

    b)   Such tax, however, may be imposed:

        i)   on only the portion of the business profits of the company attributable to the permanent establishment and the portion of the income referred to in subparagraph a) that is subject to tax under Article 6 or under paragraph 1 of Article 13 that, in the case of the United States, represents the dividend equivalent amount of such profits or income and, in the case of -------, is an amount that is analogous to the dividend equivalent amount; and

        ii)   at a rate not in excess of the rate specified in paragraph 2 a).

2006 U.S. Model
Income Tax Convention

- 18 -

Article 11

INTEREST

1.   Interest arising in a Contracting State and beneficially owned by a resident of the other Contracting State may be taxed only in that other State.

2.   Notwithstanding the provisions of paragraph 1:

    a)   interest arising in ---------- that is determined with reference to receipts, sales, income, profits or other cash flow of the debtor or a related person, to any change in the value of any property of the debtor or a related person or to any dividend, partnership distribution or similar payment made by the debtor or a related person may be taxed in the Contracting State in which it arises, and according to the laws of that State, but if the beneficial owner is a resident of the other Contracting State, the interest may be taxed at a rate not exceeding 15 percent of the gross amount of the interest;

    b)   interest arising in the United States that is contingent interest of a type that does not qualify as portfolio interest under United States law may be taxed by the United States but, if the beneficial owner of the interest is a resident of ----------, the interest may be taxed at a rate not exceeding 15 percent of the gross amount of the interest; and

    c)   interest that is an excess inclusion with respect to a residual interest in a real estate mortgage investment conduit may be taxed by each State in accordance with its domestic law.

3.   The term "interest" as used in this Article means income from debt-claims of every kind, whether or not secured by mortgage, and whether or not carrying a right to participate in the debtor's profits, and in particular, income from government securities and income from bonds or debentures, including premiums or prizes attaching to such securities, bonds or debentures, and all other income that is subjected to the same taxation treatment as income from money lent by the taxation law of the Contracting State in which the income arises. Income dealt with in Article 10 (Dividends) and penalty charges for late payment shall not be regarded as interest for the purposes of this Convention.

4.   The provisions of paragraphs 1 and 2 shall not apply if the beneficial owner of the interest, being a resident of a Contracting State, carries on business in the other Contracting State, in which the interest arises, through a permanent establishment situated therein, and the debt-claim in respect of which the interest is paid is effectively connected with such permanent establishment. In such case the provisions of Article 7 (Business Profits) shall apply.

2006 U.S. Model
Income Tax Convention

- 19 -

5.   Where, by reason of a special relationship between the payer and the beneficial owner or between both of them and some other person, the amount of the interest, having regard to the debt-claim for which it is paid, exceeds the amount which would have been agreed upon by the payer and the beneficial owner in the absence of such relationship, the provisions of this Article shall apply only to the last-mentioned amount. In such case the excess part of the payments shall remain taxable according to the laws of each State, due regard being had to the other provisions of this Convention.

2006 U.S. Model
Income Tax Convention

- 20 -

Article 12

ROYALTIES

1.   Royalties arising in a Contracting State and beneficially owned by a resident of the other Contracting State may be taxed only in that other State.

2.   The term "royalties" as used in this Article means:

a)   payments of any kind received as a consideration for the use of, or the right to use, any copyright of literary, artistic, scientific or other work (including cinematographic films), any patent, trademark, design or model, plan, secret formula or process, or for information concerning industrial, commercial or scientific experience; and

b)   gain derived from the alienation of any property described in subparagraph a), to the extent that such gain is contingent on the productivity, use, or disposition of the property.

3.   The provisions of paragraph 1 shall not apply if the beneficial owner of the royalties, being a resident of a Contracting State, carries on business in the other Contracting State through a permanent establishment situated therein and the right or property in respect of which the royalties are paid is effectively connected with such permanent establishment. In such case the provisions of Article 7 (Business Profits) shall apply.

4.   Where, by reason of a special relationship between the payer and the beneficial owner or between both of them and some other person, the amount of the royalties, having regard to the use, right, or information for which they are paid, exceeds the amount which would have been agreed upon by the payer and the beneficial owner in the absence of such relationship, the provisions of this Article shall apply only to the last-mentioned amount. In such case the excess part of the payments shall remain taxable according to the laws of each Contracting State, due regard being had to the other provisions of the Convention.

- 21 -

Article 13

GAINS

1.   Gains derived by a resident of a Contracting State that are attributable to the alienation of real property situated in the other Contracting State may be taxed in that other State.

2.   For the purposes of this Article the term "real property situated in the other Contracting State" shall include:

    a)   real property referred to in Article 6 (Income from Real Property);

    b)   where that other State is the United States, a United States real property interest; and

    c)   where that other State is ------,

        i)   shares, including rights to acquire shares, other than shares in which there is regular trading on a stock exchange, deriving their value or the greater part of their value directly or indirectly from real property referred to in subparagraph a) of this paragraph situated in --------; and

        ii)   an interest in a partnership or trust to the extent that the assets of the partnership or trust consist of real property situated in --------, or of shares referred to in clause i) of this sub-paragraph.

3.   Gains from the alienation of movable property forming part of the business property of a permanent establishment that an enterprise of a Contracting State has in the other Contracting State, including such gains from the alienation of such a permanent establishment (alone or with the whole enterprise), may be taxed in that other State.

4.   Gains derived by an enterprise of a Contracting State from the alienation of ships or aircraft operated or used in international traffic or personal property pertaining to the operation or use of such ships or aircraft shall be taxable only in that State.

5.   Gains derived by an enterprise of a Contracting State from the alienation of containers (including trailers, barges and related equipment for the transport of containers) used for the transport of goods or merchandise shall be taxable only in that State, unless those containers are used for transport solely between places within the other Contracting State.

6.   Gains from the alienation of any property other than property referred to in paragraphs 1 through 5 shall be taxable only in the Contracting State of which the alienator is a resident.

2006 U.S. Model
Income Tax Convention

- 22 -

Article 14

INCOME FROM EMPLOYMENT

1. Subject to the provisions of Articles 15 (Directors' Fees), 17 (Pensions, Social Security, Annuities, Alimony, and Child Support) and 19 (Government Service), salaries, wages, and other similar remuneration derived by a resident of a Contracting State in respect of an employment shall be taxable only in that State unless the employment is exercised in the other Contracting State. If the employment is so exercised, such remuneration as is derived therefrom may be taxed in that other State.

2. Notwithstanding the provisions of paragraph 1, remuneration derived by a resident of a Contracting State in respect of an employment exercised in the other Contracting State shall be taxable only in the first-mentioned State if:

    a)   the recipient is present in the other State for a period or periods not exceeding in the aggregate 183 days in any twelve month period commencing or ending in the taxable year concerned;

    b)   the remuneration is paid by, or on behalf of, an employer who is not a resident of the other State; and

    c)   the remuneration is not borne by a permanent establishment which the employer has in the other State.

3. Notwithstanding the preceding provisions of this Article, remuneration described in paragraph 1 that is derived by a resident of a Contracting State in respect of an employment as a member of the regular complement of a ship or aircraft operated in international traffic shall be taxable only in that State.

2006 U.S. Model
Income Tax Convention

- 23 -

Article 15

DIRECTORS' FEES

Directors' fees and other compensation derived by a resident of a Contracting State for services rendered in the other Contracting State in his capacity as a member of the board of directors of a company that is a resident of the other Contracting State may be taxed in that other Contracting State.

2006 U.S. Model
Income Tax Convention

- 24 -

Article 16

ENTERTAINERS AND SPORTSMEN

1.   Income derived by a resident of a Contracting State as an entertainer, such as a theater, motion picture, radio, or television artiste, or a musician, or as a sportsman, from his personal activities as such exercised in the other Contracting State, which income would be exempt from tax in that other Contracting State under the provisions of Articles 7 (Business Profits) and 14 (Income from Employment) may be taxed in that other State, except where the amount of the gross receipts derived by such entertainer or sportsman, including expenses reimbursed to him or borne on his behalf, from such activities does not exceed twenty thousand United States dollars ($20,000) or its equivalent in ---------- for the taxable year of the payment.

2.   Where income in respect of activities exercised by an entertainer or a sportsman in his capacity as such accrues not to the entertainer or sportsman himself but to another person, that income, notwithstanding the provisions of Article 7 (Business Profits) or 14 (Income from Employment), may be taxed in the Contracting State in which the activities of the entertainer or sportsman are exercised unless the contract pursuant to which the personal activities are performed allows that other person to designate the individual who is to perform the personal activities.

2006 U.S. Model
Income Tax Convention

- 25 -

Article 17

**PENSIONS, SOCIAL SECURITY, ANNUITIES,
ALIMONY, AND CHILD SUPPORT**

1.   a)   Pensions and other similar remuneration beneficially owned by a resident of a Contracting State shall be taxable only in that State.

   b)   Notwithstanding subparagraph a), the amount of any such pension or remuneration arising in a Contracting State that, when received, would be exempt from taxation in that State if the beneficial owner were a resident thereof shall be exempt from taxation in the Contracting State of which the beneficial owner is a resident.

2.   Notwithstanding the provisions of paragraph 1, payments made by a Contracting State under provisions of the social security or similar legislation of that State to a resident of the other Contracting State or to a citizen of the United States shall be taxable only in the first-mentioned State.

3.   Annuities derived and beneficially owned by an individual resident of a Contracting State shall be taxable only in that State. The term "annuities" as used in this paragraph means a stated sum paid periodically at stated times during a specified number of years, or for life, under an obligation to make the payments in return for adequate and full consideration (other than services rendered).

4.   Alimony paid by a resident of a Contracting State to a resident of the other Contracting State shall be taxable only in that other State. The term "alimony" as used in this paragraph means periodic payments made pursuant to a written separation agreement or a decree of divorce, separate maintenance, or compulsory support, which payments are taxable to the recipient under the laws of the State of which he is a resident.

5.   Periodic payments, not dealt with in paragraph 4, for the support of a child made pursuant to a written separation agreement or a decree of divorce, separate maintenance, or compulsory support, paid by a resident of a Contracting State to a resident of the other Contracting State, shall be exempt from tax in both Contracting States.

- 26 -

Article 18

PENSION FUNDS

1.   Where an individual who is a resident of one of the States is a member or beneficiary of, or participant in, a pension fund that is a resident of the other State, income earned by the pension fund may be taxed as income of that individual only when, and, subject to the provisions of paragraph 1 of Article 17 (Pensions, Social Security, Annuities, Alimony and Child Support), to the extent that, it is paid to, or for the benefit of, that individual from the pension fund (and not transferred to another pension fund in that other State).

2.   Where an individual who is a member or beneficiary of, or participant in, a pension fund that is a resident of one of the States exercises an employment or self-employment in the other State:

   a)   contributions paid by or on behalf of that individual to the pension fund during the period that he exercises an employment or self-employment in the other State shall be deductible (or excludible) in computing his taxable income in that other State; and

   b)   any benefits accrued under the pension fund, or contributions made to the pension fund by or on behalf of the individual's employer, during that period shall not be treated as part of the employee's taxable income and any such contributions shall be allowed as a deduction in computing the taxable income of his employer in that other State.

The relief available under this paragraph shall not exceed the relief that would be allowed by the other State to residents of that State for contributions to, or benefits accrued under, a pension plan established in that State.

3.   The provisions of paragraph 2 of this Article shall not apply unless:

   a)   contributions by or on behalf of the individual, or by or on behalf of the individual's employer, to the pension fund (or to another similar pension fund for which the first-mentioned pension fund was substituted) were made before the individual began to exercise an employment or self-employment in the other State; and

   b)   the competent authority of the other State has agreed that the pension fund generally corresponds to a pension fund established in that other State.

4.   a)   Where a citizen of the United States who is a resident of ------ exercises an employment in ------- the income from which is taxable in -------, the contribution is borne by an employer who is a resident of ------- or by a permanent establishment situated in -----, and the individual is a member or beneficiary of, or participant in, a pension plan established in ------,

2006 U.S. Model
Income Tax Convention

- 27 -

i)   contributions paid by or on behalf of that individual to the pension fund during the period that he exercises the employment in --------, and that are attributable to the employment, shall be deductible (or excludible) in computing his taxable income in the United States; and

ii)   any benefits accrued under the pension fund, or contributions made to the pension fund by or on behalf of the individual's employer, during that period, and that are attributable to the employment, shall not be treated as part of the employee's taxable income in computing his taxable income in the United States.

b)   The relief available under this paragraph shall not exceed the lesser of:

i)   the relief that would be allowed by the United States to its residents for contributions to, or benefits accrued under, a generally corresponding pension plan established in the United States; and

ii)   the amount of contributions or benefits that qualify for tax relief in --------.

c)   For purposes of determining an individual's eligibility to participate in and receive tax benefits with respect to a pension plan established in the United States, contributions made to, or benefits accrued under, a pension plan established in ------ shall be treated as contributions or benefits under a generally corresponding pension plan established in the United States to the extent relief is available to the individual under this paragraph.

d)   This paragraph shall not apply unless the competent authority of the United States has agreed that the pension plan generally corresponds to a pension plan established in the United States.

- 28 -

Article 19

GOVERNMENT SERVICE

1.   Notwithstanding the provisions of Articles 14 (Income from Employment), 15 (Directors' Fees), 16 (Entertainers and Sportsmen) and 20 (Students and Trainees):

a)   Salaries, wages and other remuneration, other than a pension, paid to an individual in respect of services rendered to a Contracting State or a political subdivision or local authority thereof shall, subject to the provisions of subparagraph b), be taxable only in that State;

b)   such remuneration, however, shall be taxable only in the other Contracting State if the services are rendered in that State and the individual is a resident of that State who:

i)   is a national of that State; or

ii)   did not become a resident of that State solely for the purpose of rendering the services.

2.   Notwithstanding the provisions of paragraph 1 of Article 17 (Pensions, Social Security, Annuities, Alimony, and Child Support):

a)   any pension and other similar remuneration paid by, or out of funds created by, a Contracting State or a political subdivision or a local authority thereof to an individual in respect of services rendered to that State or subdivision or authority (other than a payment to which paragraph 2 of Article 17 applies) shall, subject to the provisions of subparagraph b), be taxable only in that State;

b)   such pension, however, shall be taxable only in the other Contracting State if the individual is a resident of, and a national of, that State.

3.   The provisions of Articles 14 (Income from Employment), 15 (Directors' Fees), 16 (Entertainers and Sportsmen) and 17 (Pensions, Social Security, Annuities, Alimony, and Child Support) shall apply to salaries, wages and other remuneration, and to pensions, in respect of services rendered in connection with a business carried on by a Contracting State or a political subdivision or a local authority thereof.

¶1304

- 29 -

Article 20

STUDENTS AND TRAINEES

1.   Payments, other than compensation for personal services, received by a student or business trainee who is, or was immediately before visiting a Contracting State, a resident of the other Contracting State, and who is present in the first-mentioned State for the purpose of his full-time education or for his full-time training, shall not be taxed in that State, provided that such payments arise outside that State, and are for the purpose of his maintenance, education or training. The exemption from tax provided by this paragraph shall apply to a business trainee only for a period of time not exceeding one year from the date the business trainee first arrives in the first-mentioned Contracting State for the purpose of training.

2.   A student or business trainee within the meaning of paragraph 1 shall be exempt from tax by the Contracting State in which the individual is temporarily present with respect to income from personal services in an aggregate amount equal to $9,000 or its equivalent in [   ] annually. The competent authorities shall, every five years, adjust the amount provided in this subparagraph to the extent necessary to take into account changes in the U.S. personal exemption and the standard deduction.

3.   For purposes of this Article, a business trainee is an individual:

a)   who is temporarily in a Contracting State for the purpose of securing training required to qualify the individual to practice a profession or professional specialty; or

b)   who is temporarily in a Contracting State as an employee of, or under contract with, a resident of the other Contracting State, for the primary purpose of acquiring technical, professional, or business experience from a person other than that resident of the other Contracting State (or a person related to such resident of the other Contracting State).

2006 U.S. Model
Income Tax Convention

- 30 -

Article 21

OTHER INCOME

1. Items of income beneficially owned by a resident of a Contracting State, wherever arising, not dealt with in the foregoing Articles of this Convention shall be taxable only in that State.

2. The provisions of paragraph 1 shall not apply to income, other than income from real property as defined in paragraph 2 of Article 6 (Income from Real Property), if the beneficial owner of the income, being a resident of a Contracting State, carries on business in the other Contracting State through a permanent establishment situated therein and the income is attributable to such permanent establishment. In such case the provisions of Article 7 (Business Profits) shall apply.

2006 U.S. Model
Income Tax Convention

- 31 -

Article 22

LIMITATION ON BENEFITS

1.   Except as otherwise provided in this Article, a resident of a Contracting State shall not be entitled to the benefits of this Convention otherwise accorded to residents of a Contracting State unless such resident is a "qualified person" as defined in paragraph 2.

2.   A resident of a Contracting State shall be a qualified person for a taxable year if the resident is:

    a)   an individual;

    b)   a Contracting State, or a political subdivision or local authority thereof;

    c)   a company, if:

        i)   the principal class of its shares (and any disproportionate class of shares) is regularly traded on one or more recognized stock exchanges, and either:

            A)   its principal class of shares is primarily traded on one or more recognized stock exchanges located in the Contracting State of which the company is a resident; or

            B)   the company's primary place of management and control is in the Contracting State of which it is a resident; or

        ii)   at least 50 percent of the aggregate vote and value of the shares (and at least 50 percent of any disproportionate class of shares) in the company is owned directly or indirectly by five or fewer companies entitled to benefits under clause i) of this subparagraph, provided that, in the case of indirect ownership, each intermediate owner is a resident of either Contracting State;

    d)   a person described in paragraph 2 of Article 4 of this Convention, provided that, in the case of a person described in subparagraph a) of that paragraph, more than 50 percent of the person's beneficiaries, members or participants are individuals resident in either Contracting State; or

    e)   a person other than an individual, if:

¶1304

- 32 -

i)   on at least half the days of the taxable year, persons who are residents of that Contracting State and that are entitled to the benefits of this Convention under subparagraph a), subparagraph b), clause i) of subparagraph c), or subparagraph d) of this paragraph own, directly or indirectly, shares or other beneficial interests representing at least 50 percent of the aggregate voting power and value (and at least 50 percent of any disproportionate class of shares) of the person, provided that, in the case of indirect ownership, each intermediate owner is a resident of that Contracting State, and

ii)   less than 50 percent of the person's gross income for the taxable year, as determined in the person's State of residence, is paid or accrued, directly or indirectly, to persons who are not residents of either Contracting State entitled to the benefits of this Convention under subparagraph a), subparagraph b), clause i) of subparagraph c), or subparagraph d) of this paragraph in the form of payments that are deductible for purposes of the taxes covered by this Convention in the person's State of residence (but not including arm's length payments in the ordinary course of business for services or tangible property).

3.   a)   A resident of a Contracting State will be entitled to benefits of the Convention with respect to an item of income derived from the other State, regardless of whether the resident is a qualified person, if the resident is engaged in the active conduct of a trade or business in the first-mentioned State (other than the business of making or managing investments for the resident's own account, unless these activities are banking, insurance or securities activities carried on by a bank, insurance company or registered securities dealer), and the income derived from the other Contracting State is derived in connection with, or is incidental to, that trade or business.

b)   If a resident of a Contracting State derives an item of income from a trade or business activity conducted by that resident in the other Contracting State, or derives an item of income arising in the other Contracting State from a related person, the conditions described in subparagraph a) shall be considered to be satisfied with respect to such item only if the trade or business activity carried on by the resident in the first-mentioned Contracting State is substantial in relation to the trade or business activity carried on by the resident or such person in the other Contracting State. Whether a trade or business activity is substantial for the purposes of this paragraph will be determined based on all the facts and circumstances.

- 33 -

c)   For purposes of applying this paragraph, activities conducted by persons connected to a person shall be deemed to be conducted by such person. A person shall be connected to another if one possesses at least 50 percent of the beneficial interest in the other (or, in the case of a company, at least 50 percent of the aggregate vote and value of the company's shares or of the beneficial equity interest in the company) or another person possesses at least 50 percent of the beneficial interest (or, in the case of a company, at least 50 percent of the aggregate vote and value of the company's shares or of the beneficial equity interest in the company) in each person. In any case, a person shall be considered to be connected to another if, based on all the relevant facts and circumstances, one has control of the other or both are under the control of the same person or persons.

4.   If a resident of a Contracting State is neither a qualified person pursuant to the provisions of paragraph 2 nor entitled to benefits with respect to an item of income under paragraph 3 of this Article the competent authority of the other Contracting State may, nevertheless, grant the benefits of this Convention, or benefits with respect to a specific item of income, if it determines that the establishment, acquisition or maintenance of such person and the conduct of its operations did not have as one of its principal purposes the obtaining of benefits under this Convention.

5.   For purposes of this Article:

a)   the term "recognized stock exchange" means:

i)   the NASDAQ System owned by the National Association of Securities Dealers, Inc. and any stock exchange registered with the U.S. Securities and Exchange Commission as a national securities exchange under the U.S. Securities Exchange Act of 1934;

ii)   stock exchanges of -------; and

iii)   any other stock exchange agreed upon by the competent authorities;

b)   the term "principal class of shares" means the ordinary or common shares of the company, provided that such class of shares represents the majority of the voting power and value of the company. If no single class of ordinary or common shares represents the majority of the aggregate voting power and value of the company, the "principal class of shares" are those classes that in the aggregate represent a majority of the aggregate voting power and value of the company

c)   the term "disproportionate class of shares" means any class of shares of a company resident in one of the Contracting States that entitles the shareholder to disproportionately higher participation, through dividends, redemption payments or otherwise, in the earnings generated in the other State by particular assets or activities of the company; and

- 34 -

d)   a company's "primary place of management and control" will be in the Contracting State of which it is a resident only if executive officers and senior management employees exercise day-to-day responsibility for more of the strategic, financial and operational policy decision making for the company (including its direct and indirect subsidiaries) in that State than in any other state and the staff of such persons conduct more of the day-to-day activities necessary for preparing and making those decisions in that State than in any other state.

2006 U.S. Model
Income Tax Convention

- 35 -

Article 23

RELIEF FROM DOUBLE TAXATION

1.   In the case of -------, double taxation will be relieved as follows:

2.   In accordance with the provisions and subject to the limitations of the law of the United States (as it may be amended from time to time without changing the general principle hereof), the United States shall allow to a resident or citizen of the United States as a credit against the United States tax on income applicable to residents and citizens:

    a)   the income tax paid or accrued to ------ by or on behalf of such resident or citizen; and

    b)   in the case of a United States company owning at least 10 percent of the voting stock of a company that is a resident of -------- and from which the United States company receives dividends, the income tax paid or accrued to ------- by or on behalf of the payer with respect to the profits out of which the dividends are paid.

For the purposes of this paragraph, the taxes referred to in paragraphs 3 a) and 4 of Article 2 (Taxes Covered) shall be considered income taxes.

3.   For the purposes of applying paragraph 2 of this Article, an item of gross income, as determined under the laws of the United States, derived by a resident of the United States that, under this Convention, may be taxed in ----- shall be deemed to be income from sources in -----.

4.   Where a United States citizen is a resident of -------:

    a)   with respect to items of income that under the provisions of this Convention are exempt from United States tax or that are subject to a reduced rate of United States tax when derived by a resident of ------ who is not a United States citizen, ------- shall allow as a credit against -------- tax, only the tax paid, if any, that the United States may impose under the provisions of this Convention, other than taxes that may be imposed solely by reason of citizenship under the saving clause of paragraph 4 of Article 1 (General Scope);

    b)   for purposes of applying paragraph 2 to compute United States tax on those items of income referred to in subparagraph a), the United States shall allow as a credit against United States tax the income tax paid to -------- after the credit referred to in subparagraph a); the credit so allowed shall not reduce the portion of the United States tax that is creditable against the ----------- tax in accordance with subparagraph a); and

    c)   for the exclusive purpose of relieving double taxation in the United States under subparagraph b), items of income referred to in subparagraph a) shall be deemed to arise in ------- to the extent necessary to avoid double taxation of such income under subparagraph b).

- 36 -

Article 24

NON-DISCRIMINATION

1.   Nationals of a Contracting State shall not be subjected in the other Contracting State to any taxation or any requirement connected therewith that is more burdensome than the taxation and connected requirements to which nationals of that other State in the same circumstances, in particular with respect to residence, are or may be subjected. This provision shall also apply to persons who are not residents of one or both of the Contracting States. However, for the purposes of United States taxation, United States nationals who are subject to tax on a worldwide basis are not in the same circumstances as nationals of --------- who are not residents of the United States.

2.   The taxation on a permanent establishment that an enterprise of a Contracting State has in the other Contracting State shall not be less favorably levied in that other State than the taxation levied on enterprises of that other State carrying on the same activities.

3.   The provisions of paragraphs 1 and 2 shall not be construed as obliging a Contracting State to grant to residents of the other Contracting State any personal allowances, reliefs, and reductions for taxation purposes on account of civil status or family responsibilities that it grants to its own residents.

4.   Except where the provisions of paragraph 1 of Article 9 (Associated Enterprises), paragraph 5 of Article 11 (Interest), or paragraph 4 of Article 12 (Royalties) apply, interest, royalties, and other disbursements paid by a resident of a Contracting State to a resident of the other Contracting State shall, for the purpose of determining the taxable profits of the first-mentioned resident, be deductible under the same conditions as if they had been paid to a resident of the first-mentioned State. Similarly, any debts of a resident of a Contracting State to a resident of the other Contracting State shall, for the purpose of determining the taxable capital of the first-mentioned resident, be deductible under the same conditions as if they had been contracted to a resident of the first-mentioned State.

5.   Enterprises of a Contracting State, the capital of which is wholly or partly owned or controlled, directly or indirectly, by one or more residents of the other Contracting State, shall not be subjected in the first-mentioned State to any taxation or any requirement connected therewith that is more burdensome than the taxation and connected requirements to which other similar enterprises of the first-mentioned State are or may be subjected.

6.   Nothing in this Article shall be construed as preventing either Contracting State from imposing a tax as described in paragraph 8 of Article 10 (Dividends).

7.   The provisions of this Article shall, notwithstanding the provisions of Article 2 (Taxes Covered), apply to taxes of every kind and description imposed by a Contracting State or a political subdivision or local authority thereof.

- 37 -

Article 25

MUTUAL AGREEMENT PROCEDURE

1.   Where a person considers that the actions of one or both of the Contracting States result or will result for such person in taxation not in accordance with the provisions of this Convention, it may, irrespective of the remedies provided by the domestic law of those States, and the time limits prescribed in such laws for presenting claims for refund, present its case to the competent authority of either Contracting State.

2.   The competent authority shall endeavor, if the objection appears to it to be justified and if it is not itself able to arrive at a satisfactory solution, to resolve the case by mutual agreement with the competent authority of the other Contracting State, with a view to the avoidance of taxation which is not in accordance with the Convention. Any agreement reached shall be implemented notwithstanding any time limits or other procedural limitations in the domestic law of the Contracting States. Assessment and collection procedures shall be suspended during the period that any mutual agreement proceeding is pending.

3.   The competent authorities of the Contracting States shall endeavor to resolve by mutual agreement any difficulties or doubts arising as to the interpretation or application of the Convention. They also may consult together for the elimination of double taxation in cases not provided for in the Convention. In particular the competent authorities of the Contracting States may agree:

a)   to the same attribution of income, deductions, credits, or allowances of an enterprise of a Contracting State to its permanent establishment situated in the other Contracting State;

b)   to the same allocation of income, deductions, credits, or allowances between persons;

c)   to the settlement of conflicting application of the Convention, including conflicts regarding:

i)   the characterization of particular items of income;

ii)   the characterization of persons;

iii)   the application of source rules with respect to particular items of income;

iv)   the meaning of any term used in the Convention;

v)   the timing of particular items of income;

¶1304

- 38 -

d)   to advance pricing arrangements; and

e)   to the application of the provisions of domestic law regarding penalties, fines, and interest in a manner consistent with the purposes of the Convention.

4.   The competent authorities also may agree to increases in any specific dollar amounts referred to in the Convention to reflect economic or monetary developments.

5.   The competent authorities of the Contracting States may communicate with each other directly, including through a joint commission, for the purpose of reaching an agreement in the sense of the preceding paragraphs.

- 39 -

Article 26

EXCHANGE OF INFORMATION AND ADMINISTRATIVE ASSISTANCE

1.   The competent authorities of the Contracting States shall exchange such information as may be relevant for carrying out the provisions of this Convention or of the domestic laws of the Contracting States concerning taxes of every kind imposed by a Contracting State to the extent that the taxation thereunder is not contrary to the Convention, including information relating to the assessment or collection of, the enforcement or prosecution in respect of, or the determination of appeals in relation to, such taxes. The exchange of information is not restricted by paragraph 1 of Article 1 (General Scope) or Article 2 (Taxes Covered).

2.   Any information received under this Article by a Contracting State shall be treated as secret in the same manner as information obtained under the domestic laws of that State and shall be disclosed only to persons or authorities (including courts and administrative bodies) involved in the assessment, collection, or administration of, the enforcement or prosecution in respect of, or the determination of appeals in relation to, the taxes referred to above, or the oversight of such functions. Such persons or authorities shall use the information only for such purposes. They may disclose the information in public court proceedings or in judicial decisions.

3.   In no case shall the provisions of the preceding paragraphs be construed so as to impose on a Contracting State the obligation:

   a)   to carry out administrative measures at variance with the laws and administrative practice of that or of the other Contracting State;

   b)   to supply information that is not obtainable under the laws or in the normal course of the administration of that or of the other Contracting State;

   c)   to supply information that would disclose any trade, business, industrial, commercial, or professional secret or trade process, or information the disclosure of which would be contrary to public policy (ordre public).

4.   If information is requested by a Contracting State in accordance with this Article, the other Contracting State shall use its information gathering measures to obtain the requested information, even though that other State may not need such information for its own purposes. The obligation contained in the preceding sentence is subject to the limitations of paragraph 3 but in no case shall such limitation be construed to permit a Contracting State to decline to supply information because it has no domestic interest in such information.

¶1304

2006 U.S. Model
Income Tax Convention

- 40 -

5.   In no case shall the provisions of paragraph 3 be construed to permit a Contracting State to decline to supply information requested by the other Contracting State because the information is held by a bank, other financial institution, nominee or person acting in an agency or a fiduciary capacity or because it relates to ownership interests in a person.

6.   If specifically requested by the competent authority of a Contracting State, the competent authority of the other Contracting State shall provide information under this Article in the form of depositions of witnesses and authenticated copies of unedited original documents (including books, papers, statements, records, accounts, and writings).

7.   Each of the Contracting States shall endeavor to collect on behalf of the other Contracting State such amounts as may be necessary to ensure that relief granted by the Convention from taxation imposed by that other State does not inure to the benefit of persons not entitled thereto. This paragraph shall not impose upon either of the Contracting States the obligation to carry out administrative measures that would be contrary to its sovereignty, security, or public policy.

8.   The requested State shall allow representatives of the requesting State to enter the requested State to interview individuals and examine books and records with the consent of the persons subject to examination.

8.   The competent authorities of the Contracting States may develop an agreement upon the mode of application of this Article, including agreement to ensure comparable levels of assistance to each of the Contracting States, but in no case will the lack of such agreement relieve a Contracting State of its obligations under this Article.

2006 U.S. Model
Income Tax Convention

- 41 -

Article 27

MEMBERS OF DIPLOMATIC MISSIONS AND CONSULAR POSTS

Nothing in this Convention shall affect the fiscal privileges of members of diplomatic missions or consular posts under the general rules of international law or under the provisions of special agreements.

¶1304

- 42 -

Article 28

ENTRY INTO FORCE

1.   This Convention shall be subject to ratification in accordance with the applicable procedures of each Contracting State, and instruments of ratification will be exchanged as soon thereafter as possible.

2.   This Convention shall enter into force on the date of the exchange of instruments of ratification, and its provisions shall have effect:

> a)   in respect of taxes withheld at source, for amounts paid or credited on or after the first day of the second month next following the date on which the Convention enters into force;

> b)   in respect of other taxes, for taxable periods beginning on or after the first day of January next following the date on which the Convention enters into force.

3.   Notwithstanding paragraph 2, the provisions of Article 26 (Exchange of Information and Administrative Assistance) shall have effect from the date of entry into force of this Convention, without regard to the taxable period to which the matter relates.

- 43 -

Article 29

TERMINATION

This Convention shall remain in force until terminated by a Contracting State. Either Contracting State may terminate the Convention by giving notice of termination to the other Contracting State through diplomatic channels. In such event, the Convention shall cease to have effect:

        a)   in respect of taxes withheld at source, for amounts paid or credited after the expiration of the 6 month period beginning on the date on which notice of termination was given; and

        b)   in respect of other taxes, for taxable periods beginning on or after the expiration of the 6 month period beginning on the date on which notice of termination was given.

IN WITNESS WHEREOF, the undersigned, being duly authorized thereto by their respective Governments, have signed this Convention.

DONE at _____ in duplicate, in the English and ---------- languages, both texts being equally authentic, this __ day of _____, 20_.

FOR THE GOVERNMENT OF   FOR THE GOVERNMENT OF
THE UNITED STATES OF AMERICA: ----------------------

¶ 1305 APPENDIX

FORco is a foreign corporation that is incorporated in country F, a country with which the United States has a tax treaty similar to the U.S. Model Treaty. A publicly-held company on a recognized stock exchange in foreign country F, FORco occasionally sends sales employees to the United States to solicit customers, but the sales employees do not have final contracting authority. These sales employees are FORco's only contacts with the United States. FORco takes the position that it is not subject to U.S. tax because it does not have a permanent establishment in the United States due to the sales employees (dependent agents) not having final contracting authority. FORco files a Form 8833 with the IRS stating that FORco is not subject to U.S. tax.

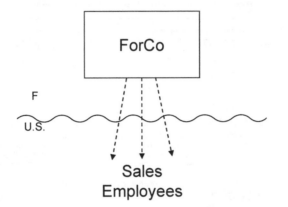

Form **8833** (Rev. August 2006) Department of the Treasury Internal Revenue Service	**Treaty-Based Return Position Disclosure Under Section 6114 or 7701(b)** ▶ Attach to your tax return.	OMB No. 1545-1354

Attach a separate Form 8833 for each treaty-based return position taken. Failure to disclose a treaty-based return position may result in a penalty of $1,000 ($10,000 in the case of a C corporation) (see section 6712).

Name **FORco**	U.S. taxpayer identifying number **98-8888888**

Address in country of residence **Country F**	Address in the United States **NA**

Check one or both of the following boxes as applicable:

● The taxpayer is disclosing a treaty-based return position as required by section 6114 . . . . ▶ ☑

● The taxpayer is a dual-resident taxpayer and is disclosing a treaty-based return position as required by Regulations section 301.7701(b)-7 . . . . ▶ ☐

Check this box if the taxpayer is a U.S. citizen or resident or is incorporated in the United States . . . . ▶ ☐

1 Enter the specific treaty position relied on: **a** Treaty country **Country F** **b** Article(s) **5(5)** **2** List the Internal Revenue Code provision(s) overruled or modified by the treaty-based return position **I.R.C. section 882(a)**	**3** Name, identifying number (if available to the taxpayer), and address in the United States of the payor of the income (if fixed or determinable annual or periodical). See instructions. **NA**

4 List the provision(s) of the limitation on benefits article (if any) in the treaty that the taxpayer relies on to prevent application of that article ▶ **Article 22(2)(c)(i): publicly traded**

5 Explain the treaty-based return position taken. Include a brief summary of the facts on which it is based. Also, list the nature and amount (or a reasonable estimate) of gross receipts, each separate gross payment, each separate gross income item, or other item (as applicable) for which the treaty benefit is claimed **FORco periodically sends sales employees to the United States to solicit a single customer that resulted in approximately $2 million of gross receipts during the taxable year. Although the sales employees may constitute a trade or business in the United States, FORco is entitled to the benefits of the tax treaty between Country F and the United States. More specifically, the treaty only permits the United States to tax a permanent establishment, which FORco does not have, because its sales employees do not have final contracting authority.**

For Paperwork Reduction Act Notice, see page 3.   Cat. No. 14895L   Form **8833** (Rev. 8-2006)

Table 1. **Withholding Tax Rates on Income Other Than Personal Service Income Under Chapter 3, Internal Revenue Code, and Income Tax Treaties—For Withholding in 2011**

Income Code Number		1	2	3	6	7	9
		Interest			Dividends		
Name	Code	Paid by U.S. Obligors— General[dd]	On Real Property Mortgages[dd]	Paid to a Controlling Foreign Corporation[dd]	Paid by U.S. Corporations— General[a,dd]	Qualifying for Direct Dividend Rate[a,dd]	Capital Gains[e,u,dd]
Australia	AS	10 g,k,nn	10 g,k,ee,nn	10 g,k,nn	15 g,mm	5 g,mm,oo	30
Austria	AU	0 g,jj	0 g,ee,jj	0 g,jj	15 g,w	5 g,w	0 g
Bangladesh	BG	10 g,bb,jj	10 g,bb,ee,jj	10 g,bb,jj	15 g,mm	10 b,g,mm	0 g
Barbados	BB	5 g	5 g	5 g	15 g,w	5 b,g,w	0 g
Belgium	BE	0 g,jj	0 g,ee,jj	0 g,jj	15 g,ss,tt	5 g,oo,ss,tt	0 g
Bulgaria	BU	5 g,jj,nn,ss	5 g,ee,jj,nn,ss	5 g,jj,nn,ss	10 g,ss,tt	5 g,ss,tt	0 g
Canada	CA	0 g,jj	0 g,ee,jj	0 g,jj	15 g,mm	5 g,mm	0 r
China, People's Rep. of	CH	10 g	10 g	10 g	10 g	10 g	30
Comm. of Independent States[*]		0 n	30	30	30	30	0 o
Cyprus	CY	10 g	10 g	10 g	15 g	5 b,g	0 g
Czech Republic	EZ	0 g	0 g,ee	0 g	15 g,w	5 b,g,w	0 g
Denmark	DA	0 g,kk	0 g,ee,kk	0 g,kk	15 g,ss,tt	5 g,oo,ss,tt	0 g
Egypt	EG	15 h	30	15 h	15 h	5 b,h	0 h
Estonia	EN	10 g,kk	10 g,ee,kk	10 g,kk	15 g,w	5 b,g,w	0 g
Finland	FI	0 g,kk	0 g,ee,kk	0 g,kk	15 g,ss,tt	5 g,oo,ss,tt	0 g
France	FR	0 g	0 g,ee	0 g	15 g,tt	5 g,oo,tt	0 g
Germany	GM	0 g,jj	0 g,ee,jj	0 g,jj	15 g,ss,tt	5 g,oo,ss,tt	0 g
Greece	GR	0 h	0 h	30	30	30	30
Hungary	HU	0 g	0 g	0 g	15 g	5 b,g	0 g
Iceland	IC	0 g,kk	0 g,ee,kk	0 g,kk	15 g,mm,ss	5 g,mm,ss	0 g
India	IN	15 g,z	15 g,z	15 g,z	25 g,w	15 b,g,w	30
Indonesia	ID	10 g	10 g	10 g	15 g	10 b,g	0 g
Ireland	EI	0 g	0 g,ee	0 g	15 g,mm	5 g,mm	0 g
Israel	IS	17½ z,gg	17½ z,ee,gg	17½ z,gg	25 w,gg	12½ b,w,gg	0 gg
Italy	IT	10 g,yy	10 g,ee,yy	10 g,yy	15 g,mm	5 g,mm	0 g
Jamaica	JM	12½ g	12½ g	12½ g	15 g	10 b,g	0 g
Japan	JA	10 g,qq,rr,ss	10 g,ee,qq,rr,ss	10 g,qq,rr,ss	10 g,qq,ss,tt	5 b,g,qq,ss,tt	0 g
Kazakhstan	KZ	10 g	10 g,ee	10 g	15 g,ff	5 b,g,ff	0 g
Korea, South	KS	12 g	12 g	12 g	15 g	10 b,g	0 g
Latvia	LG	10 g,kk	10 g,ee,kk	10 g,kk	15 g,w	5 b,g,w	0 g
Lithuania	LH	10 g,kk	10 g,ee,kk	10 g,kk	15 g,w	5 b,g,w	0 g
Luxembourg	LU	0 g,k	0 g,ee,k	0 g,k	15 g,w	5 b,g,w	0 g

* Those countries to which the U.S.-U.S.S.R. income tax treaty still applies: Armenia, Azerbaijan, Belarus, Georgia, Kyrgyzstan, Moldova, Tajikistan, Turkmenistan, and Uzbekistan.

Table 1.**Withholding Tax Rates on Income Other Than Personal Service Income Under Chapter 3, Internal Revenue Code, and Income Tax Treaties—For Withholding in 2011**

Income Code Number		10	11	12		13	14
			Royalties				
Name	Code	Equipment	Know-how	Film & TV	Copyrights	Patents	Real Property Income and Natural Resources^{zz}	Pensions and Annuities
Australia	AS	30 u	5 g	5 g	5 g	5 g	30	0 d
Austria	AU	30 u	0 g	10 g	0 g	0 g	30	0
Bangladesh	BG	30 u	10 g	10 g	10 g	10 g	30	0 d,f,q
Barbados	BB	30 u	5 g	5 g	5 g	5 g	30	0 d,f
Belgium	BE	30 u	0 g	0 g	0 g	0 g	30	0 d,f
Bulgaria	BU	30 u	5 g	5 g	5 g	5 g	30	0 d,f
Canada	CA	30 u	0 g	10 g	0 g	0 g	30	15
China, People's Rep. of	CH	10 g,v	10 g	10 g	10 g	10 g	30	0 d,t
Comm. of Independent States		0	0	0	0	0	30	30
Cyprus	CY	30 u	0 g	0 g	0 g	0 g	30	0 d,f
Czech Republic	EZ	10 g	10 g	0 g	0 g	10 g	30	0 d,f
Denmark	DA	30 u	0 g	0 g	0 g	0 g	30	30 c,d,t
Egypt	EG	30 u	30 u	30 u	15 g	15 g	30	0 d,f
Estonia	EN	5 g	10 g	10 g	10 g	10 g	30	0 d,f
Finland	FI	30 u	0 g	0 g	0 g	0 g	30	0 d,f
France	FR	30 u	0 g	0 g	0 g	0 g	30	30
Germany	GM	30 u	0 g	30	0 g	0 g	30	0 d,f
Greece	GR	0 h	30 u	30 u	0 h	0 h	30	0 d
Hungary	HU	30 u	0 g	0 g	0 g	0 g	30	0 d,f
Iceland	IC	30 u	5 g	5 g	0 g,l	0 g	30	0 d
India	IN	10 g	15 g	15 g	15 g	15 g	30	0 d,f
Indonesia	ID	10 g	10 g	10 g	10 g	10 g	30	15 d,f,q
Ireland	EI	30 u	0 g	0 g	0 g	0 g	30	0 d,f
Israel	IS	30 u, gg	30 u, gg	10 gg	10 gg	15 gg	30	0 f
Italy	IT	5 g	8 g	8 g	0 g	8 g	30	0 d,f
Jamaica	JM	30 u	10 g	10 g	10 g	10 g	30	0 d,f,p
Japan	JA	30 u	0 g,qq	0 g,qq	0 g,qq	0 g,qq	30	0 d
Kazakhstan	KZ	10 g	10 g	10 g	10 g	10 g	30	0 d,f
Korea, South	KS	30 u	15 g	10 g	10 g	15 g	30	0 d,f
Latvia	LG	5 g	10 g	10 g	10 g	10 g	30	0 d,f
Lithuania	LH	5 g	10 g	10 g	10 g	10 g	30	0 d,f
Luxembourg	LU	30 u	0 g	0 g	0 g	0 g	30	0 d

¶1305

Table 1.**Withholding Tax Rates on Income Other Than Personal Service Income Under Chapter 3, Internal Revenue Code, and Income Tax Treaties—For Withholding in 2011**

Income Code Number		1	2	3	6	7	9
			Interest		Dividends		
Name	Code	Paid by U.S. Obligors— General[dd]	On Real Property Mortgages[dd]	Paid to a Controlling Foreign Corporation[dd]	Paid by U.S. Corporations— General[a,dd]	Qualifying for Direct Dividend Rate[a,dd]	Capital Gains[e,u,dd]
Malta	MT	10 g,jj	10 g,ee,jj	10 g,jj	15 g,tt	5 g,tt	0 g
Mexico	MX	15 g,hh	15 g,ee,hh	15 g	10 g,mm,pp	5 g,mm,oo,pp	0 g
Morocco	MO	15 g	15 g	15 g	15 g	10 b,g	0 g
Netherlands	NL	0 g	0 g	0 g	15 g,xx	5 b,gg,oo,xx	0
New Zealand	NZ	10 g,jj,nn	10 g,ee,jj,nn	10 g,jj,nn	15 g,tt	5 g,tt	0 g
Norway	NO	0 g	0 g	0 g	15 g	15 g	0 g
Pakistan	PK	30	30	30	30	15 b,h	30
Philippines	RP	15 g	15 g	15 g	25 g	20 b,g	0 g
Poland	PL	0 g	0 g	0 g	15 g	5 b,g	0 g
Portugal	PO	10 h	10 h,ee	10 h	15 h,w	5 b,h,w	0 g
Romania	RO	10 g	10 g	10 g	10 g	10 g	0 g
Russia	RS	0 g	0 g,ee	0 g	10 g,ff	5 b,g,w	0 g
Slovak Republic ...	LO	0 g	0 g,ee	0 g	15 g,w	5 b,g,mm	0 g
Slovenia	SI	5 g	5 g,ee	5 g	15 g,mm	5 b,g,mm	0 g
South Africa	SF	0 g,jj	0 g,ee,jj	0 g,jj	15 g,w	5 g,w	0
Spain	SP	10 g	10 g	10 g	15 g,w	10 b,g,w	0 g
Sri Lanka	CE	10 g,jj	10 g,ee,jj	10 g,jj	15 g,ww	15 g,ww	0 g,uu
Sweden........	SW	0 g	0 g,ee	0 g	15 g,ss,tt	5 b,g,oo,ss,tt	0 g
Switzerland	SZ	0 g,y	0 g,y,ee	0 g,y	15 g,w	5 g,w	0
Thailand	TH	15 g,z	15 g,z,ee	15 g,z	15 g,w	10 g,w	30
Trinidad & Tobago	TD	30	30	30	30	30	30
Tunisia	TS	15 g	15 g	15 g	20 g,w	14 b,g,w	0 g
Turkey	TU	15 g,m,z	15 g,m,z,ee	15 g,m,z	20 g,w	15 g,w	0 g
Ukraine	UP	0 g	0 g,ee	0 g	15 g,ff	5 b,g,ff	0 g
United Kingdom ...	UK	0 g,kk,qq	0 g,ee,kk,qq	0 g,kk,qq	15 g,mm,qq	5 g,mm,oo,qq	0 g
Venezuela	VE	10 g,kk,ll	10 g,ee,kk,ll	10 g,kk,ll	15 g,mm	5 b,g,mm	0 g
Other Countries ...		30	30	30	30	30	30

¶1305

Table 1. **Withholding Tax Rates on Income Other Than Personal Service Income Under Chapter 3, Internal Revenue Code, and Income Tax Treaties—For Withholding in 2011**

Income Code Number		10	11	12			13	14
				Royalties				
Name	Code	Equipment	Know-how	Film & TV	Copyrights	Patents	Real Property Income and Natural Resources ᶻᶻ	Pensions and Annuities
Malta	MT	30 u	10 g	10 g	10 g	10 g	30	0 d,f
Mexico	MX	10 g	10 g	10 g	10 g	10 g	30	0 d
Morocco	MO	30 u	10 g	10 g	10 g	10 g	30	0 d,f
Netherlands	NL	30 u	0 g	30 g	0 g	0 g	30	0 d,f,ii
New Zealand . . .	NZ	30 u	5 g	5 g	5 g	5 g	30	0 d
Norway	NO	30 u	0 g	30 u	0 g	0 g	30	0 d,f
Pakistan	PK	30 u	30 u	30 u	0 g	0 g	30	0 d,j
Philippines	RP	30 u	15 g	15 g	15 g	15 g	30	30 q
Poland	PL	30 u	10 g	10 g	10 g	10 g	30	30
Portugal	PO	10 h	10 h	10 h	10 h	10 h	30	0 d,f
Romania	RO	30 u	15 g	10 g	10 g	15 g	30	0 d,f
Russia	RS	30 u	0 g	0 g	0 g	0 g	30	0 d
Slovak Republic . .	LO	10 g	10 g	0 g	0 g	10 g	30	0 d,f
Slovenia	SI	30 u	5 g	5 g	5 g	5 g	30	0 d,f
South Africa	SF	30 u	0 g	0 g	0 g	0 g	30	15 d,l
Spain	SP	8 g,aa	10 g,aa	8 g,aa	5 g,aa	10 g,aa	30	0 d,f
Sri Lanka	CE	5 g	10 g	10 g	10 g	10 g	30	0 d,t
Sweden	SW	30 u	0 g	0 g	0 g	0 g	30	0 d
Switzerland	SZ	30 u	0 g	30 g,u	0 g	0 g	30	0 d
Thailand	TH	8 g	15 g	5 g	5 g	15 g	30	0 d,f
Trinidad & Tobago	TD	30 u	15 g	30 u	0 g,cc	15	30	0 d,f
Tunisia	TS	10 g	15 g	15 g	15 g	15 g	30	0 f
Turkey	TU	5 g	10 g	10 g	10 g	10 g	30	0 d
Ukraine	UP	30 u	10 g	10 g	10 g	10 g	30	0 d
United Kingdom . .	UK	30 u	0 g,qq	0 g,qq	0 g,qq	0 g,qq	30	0 d,f
Venezuela	VE	5 g	10 g	10 g	10 g	10 g	30	0 d,t
Other Countries . .		30	30	30	30	30	30	30

ᵃ No U.S. tax is imposed on a percentage of any dividend paid by a U.S. corporation that received at least 80% of its gross income from an active foreign business for the 3-year period before the dividend is declared. (see sections 871(i)(2)(B) and 881(d) of the Internal Revenue Code.

ᵇ The reduced rate applies to dividends paid by a subsidiary to a foreign parent corporation that has the required percentage of stock ownership. In some cases, the income of the subsidiary must meet certain requirements (e.g., a certain percentage of its total income must consist of income other than dividends and interest). For Japan, dividends received from a more than 50% owned corporate subsidiary are exempt if certain conditions are met.

ᶜ Generally, if the person was receiving pension distributions before March 31, 2000, the distributions continue to be exempt from U.S. tax.

ᵈ Exemption does not apply to U.S. Government (federal, state, or local) pensions and annuities; a 30% rate applies to these pensions and annuities. For this purpose, railroad retirement tier 2, dual, and supplemental benefits are not considered U.S. Government pensions or annuities. U.S. Government pensions paid to an individual who is both a resident and national of Bangladesh, Belgium, Bulgaria, China, Denmark, Estonia, Finland, Germany, Hungary, Iceland, India, Ireland, Italy, Latvia, Lithuania, Luxembourg, Malta, Mexico, the Netherlands, Portugal, Russia, Slovenia, South Africa, Spain, Switzerland, Thailand, Turkey, the United Kingdom, or Venezuela are exempt from U.S. tax. U.S. Government pensions paid to an individual who is both a resident and citizen of Kazakhstan, New Zealand, or Sweden are exempt from U.S. tax.

ᵉ No withholding is required on capital gains other than those listed earlier under *Capital Gains*, even if the gain is subject to U.S. tax.

ᶠ Includes alimony.

ᵍ The exemption or reduction in rate does not apply if the recipient has a permanent establishment in the United States and the property giving rise to the income is effectively connected with this permanent establishment. Under certain treaties, exemption or reduction in rate also does not apply if the property producing the income is effectively connected with a fixed base in the United States from which the recipient performs independent personal services. Even with the treaty, if the income is not effectively connected with a trade or business in the United States by the recipient, the recipient will be considered as not having a permanent establishment in the United States under Internal Revenue Code section 894(b).

ʰ The exemption or reduction in rate does not apply if the recipient is engaged in a trade or business in the United States through a permanent establishment that is in the United States. However, if the income is not effectively connected with a trade or business in the United States by the recipient, the recipient will be considered as not having a permanent establishment in the United States to apply the reduced treaty rate to that item of income.

ⁱ The rate is 5% for trademarks and any information for rentals of industrial, commercial, or scientific equipment.

¶1305

i Exemption is not available when paid from a fund under an employees' pension or annuity plan, if contributions to it are deductible under U.S. tax laws in determining taxable income of the employer.

k The rate is 15% for interest determined with reference to the profits of the issuer or one of its associated enterprises.

l Annuities purchased while the annuitant was not a resident of the United States are not taxable. The reduced rate applies if the distribution is not subject to a penalty for early withdrawal.

m Contingent interest that does not qualify as portfolio interest is treated as a dividend and is subject to the rate under column 6 or 7.

n The exemption applies only to interest on credits, loans, and other indebtedness connected with the financing of trade between the United States and the C.I.S. member. It does not include interest from the conduct of a general banking business.

o The exemption applies only to gains from the sale or other disposition of property acquired by gift or inheritance.

p The exemption does not apply if the recipient was a resident of the United States when the pension was earned or when the annuity was purchased.

q Annuities paid in return for other than the recipient's services are exempt. For Bangladesh, exemption does not apply to annuity received for services rendered.

r Generally, if the property was owned by the Canadian resident on September 26, 1980, not as part of the business property of a permanent establishment or fixed base in the U.S., the taxable gain is limited to the appreciation after 1984. Capital gains on personal property not belonging to a permanent establishment or fixed base of the taxpayer in the U.S. are exempt.

s The rate for royalties with respect to tangible personal property is 7%.

t Does not apply to annuities. For Denmark, annuities are exempt.

u Depending on the facts, the rate may be determined by either the Business Profits article or the Other Income article.

v Tax imposed on 70% of gross royalties for rentals of industrial, commercial, or scientific equipment.

w The rate in column 6 applies to dividends paid by a regulated investment company (RIC) or a real estate investment trust (REIT). However, that rate applies to dividends paid by a REIT only if the beneficial owner of the dividends is an individual holding less than a 10% interest (25% in the case of Portugal, Spain, and Tunisia) in the REIT.

x Royalties taxed at the 5% or 8% rate are taxed at a 10% rate, unless footnote (g) applies.

y The exemption does not apply to contingent interest that does not qualify as portfolio interest. Generally, this is interest based on receipts, sales, income, or changes in the value of property.

z The rate is 10% if the interest is paid on a loan granted by a bank or similar financial institution. For Thailand, the 10% rate also applies to interest from an arm's length sale on credit of equipment, merchandise, or services.

aa The rate is 8% for copyrights of scientific work.

bb The rate is 5% for interest (a) beneficially owned by a bank or other financial institution (including an insurance company) or (b) paid due to a sale on credit of any industrial, commercial, or scientific equipment, or of any merchandise to an enterprise.

cc The rate is 15% for copyrights of scientific work.

dd Under some treaties, the reduced rates of withholding may not apply to a foreign corporation unless a minimum percentage of its owners are citizens or residents of the United States or the treaty country.

ee Exemption or reduced rate does not apply to an excess inclusion for a residual interest in a real estate mortgage investment conduit (REMIC).

ff The rate in column 6 applies to dividends paid by a regulated investment company (RIC). Dividends paid by a real estate investment trust (REIT) are subject to a 30% rate.

gg The exemption or reduction in rate does not apply if the recipient has a permanent establishment in the United States and the income is effectively connected with this permanent establishment. Instead, tax is not withheld at source and the provisions of Article 8 (Business profits) apply. Additionally, even if the income is not effectively connected with a U.S. permanent establishment, the recipient may choose to treat net interest income as industrial or commercial profits subject to Article 8 of the treaty.

hh The rate is 4.9% for interest derived from (1) loans granted by banks and insurance companies and (2) bonds or securities that are regularly and substantially traded on a recognized securities market. The rate is 10% for interest not described in the preceding sentence and paid (i) by banks or (ii) by the buyer of machinery and equipment to the seller due to a sale on credit.

ii The exemption does not apply if (1) the recipient was a U.S. resident during the 5-year period before the date of payment, (2) the amount was paid for employment performed in the United States, and (3) the amount is not a periodic payment, or is a lump-sum payment in lieu of a right to receive an annuity.

jj The rate is 15% (10% for Bulgaria; 30% for Germany and Switzerland) for contingent interest that does not qualify as portfolio interest. Generally, this is interest based on receipts, sales, income, or changes in the value of property.

kk The rate is 15% for interest determined with reference to (a) receipts, sales, income, profits or other cash flow of the debtor or a related person, (b) any change in the value of any property of the debtor or a related person, or (c) any dividend, partnership distribution, or similar payment made by the debtor or related person.

ll The rate is 4.95% if the interest is beneficially owned by a financial institution (including an insurance company).

mm The rate in column 6 applies to dividends paid by a regulated investment company (RIC) or real estate investment trust (REIT). However, that rate applies to dividends paid by a REIT only if the beneficial owner of the dividends is (a) an individual (or pension fund, in the case of France) holding not more than a 10% interest in the REIT, (b) a person holding not more than 5% of any class of the REIT's stock and the dividends are paid on stock that is publicly traded, or (c) a person holding not more than a 10% interest in the REIT and the REIT is diversified.

nn Interest received by a financial institution is exempt.

oo Dividends received from an 80%-owned corporate subsidiary are exempt if certain conditions are met.

pp Dividends received by a trust, company, or other organization operated exclusively to administer or provide pension, retirement, or other employee benefits generally are exempt if certain conditions are met.

qq Exemption does not apply to amount paid under, or as part of, a conduit arrangement.

rr Interest is exempt if (a) paid to certain financial institutions, or (b) paid on indebtedness from the sale on credit of equipment or merchandise.

ss Amounts paid to a pension fund that are not derived from the carrying on of a business, directly or indirectly, by the fund are exempt. This includes amounts paid by a REIT only if the conditions in footnote tt are met. For Sweden, to be entitled to the exemption, the pension fund must not sell or make a contract to sell the holding from which the dividend is derived within 2 months of the date pension fund acquired the holding.

tt The rate in column 6 applies to dividends paid by a regulated investment company (RIC) or real estate investment trust (REIT). However, that rate applies to dividends paid by a REIT only if the beneficial owner of the dividends is (a) an individual or pension fund holding not more than a 10% interest in the REIT, (b) a person holding not more than 5% of any class of the REIT's stock and the dividends are paid on stock that is publicly traded, or (c) a person holding not more than a 10% interest in the REIT and the REIT is diversified. Dividends paid to a pension fund from a RIC, or a REIT that meets the above conditions, are exempt. For Sweden, the pension fund must also satisfy the requirements in footnote ss.

uu The exemption does not apply to a sale of a U.S. company's stock representing ownership of 50% or more.

vv The rate is 5% for the rental of tangible personal property.

ww The rate applies to dividends paid by a real estate investment trust (REIT) only if the beneficial owner of the dividends is (a) an individual holding less than a 10% interest in the REIT, (b) a person holding not more than 5% of any class of the REIT's stock and the dividends are paid on stock that is publicly traded, or (c) a person holding not more than a 10% interest in the REIT and the REIT is diversified.

xx The rate in column 6 applies to dividends paid by a regulated investment company (RIC) or real estate investment trust (REIT). However, that rate applies to dividends paid by a REIT only if the beneficial owner of the dividends is (a) an individual holding not more than a 25% interest in the REIT (b) a person holding not more than 5% of any class of the REIT's stock and the dividends are paid on stock that is publicly traded, or (c) a person holding not more than a 10% interest in the REIT and the REIT is diversified, or (d) a Dutch beleggingsinstelling.

yy Interest paid or accrued on the sale of goods, merchandise, or services between enterprises is exempt. Interest paid or accrued on the sale on credit of industrial, commercial, or scientific property is exempt.

zz Withholding at a special rate may be required on the disposition of U.S. real property interests. See *U.S. Real Property Interest* earlier in this publication.

¶1305

Table 2. Compensation for Personal Services Performed in United States Exempt from Withholding and U.S. Income Tax Under Income Tax Treaties

Country (1)	Code[1] (2)	Category of Personal Services — Purpose (3)	Maximum Presence in U.S. (4)	Required Employer or Payer (5)	Maximum Amount of Compensation (6)	Treaty Article Citation (7)
Australia	16	Independent personal services[7,22]	183 days	Any contractor	No limit	14
	20	Public entertainment[22]	183 days	Any contractor	$10,000.	17
	17	Dependent personal services[17]	183 days	Any foreign resident	No limit	15
	20	Public entertainment[22]	183 days	Any foreign resident	$10,000.	17
	19	Studying and training: Remittances or allowances[11]	No limit		No limit	20
Austria	16	Independent personal services[7]	No limit	Any contractor	No limit	14
	20	Public entertainment[22]	No limit	Any contractor	$20,000[25]	17
	17	Dependent personal services[17]	183 days	Any foreign resident	No limit	15
	20	Public entertainment[22]	No limit	Any U.S. or foreign resident	$20,000[25]	17
	19	Studying and training: Remittances or allowances	3 years[45]	Any foreign resident	No limit	20
Bangladesh	15	Scholarship or fellowship grant[4]	2 years[45]	Any U.S. or foreign resident[5]	No limit	21(2)
	16	Independent personal services[22]	183 days	Any contractor	No limit	15
	20	Public entertainment[22]	183 days	Any contractor	$10,000[30]	18
	17	Dependent personal services[17]	183 days	Any foreign resident	No limit	16
	20	Public entertainment[22]	No limit	Any contractor	$10,000[30]	18
	18	Teaching or research[4]	2 years	Any U.S. or foreign resident	No limit	21(1)
	19	Remittances or allowances[4]	2 years[45]	Any foreign resident	No limit	21(2)
		Compensation during study or training	2 years[45]	Any U.S. or foreign resident	$8,000 p.a.	21(2)
Barbados	16	Independent personal services[7,8,22]	89 days	Any foreign contractor	No limit	14
			89 days	Any U.S. contractor	$5,000 p.a. or $4,000 p.a.[6]	14
	20	Public entertainment[22]	No limit	Any contractor	$250 per day	17
	17	Dependent personal services[8,17]	183 days	Any foreign resident	$5,000 p.a.	15
	20	Public entertainment[22]	No limit	Any U.S. or foreign resident	$250 per day or $4,000 p.a.[6]	17
	19	Studying and training[23]: Remittances or allowances[11]	No limit		No limit	20
Belgium	16	Independent personal services[53]	183 days	Any foreign resident	No limit	7
	17	Dependent personal services[12,17]	No limit	Any U.S. or foreign resident	No limit	14
	20	Public entertainment	No limit		$20,000 p.a.[25]	16
	18	Teaching[4]	2 years	U.S. educational or research institution	No limit	19(2)
	19	Studying and training[11]	No limit[52]	Any foreign resident	$9,000 p.a.	19(1)(a)
		Compensation during study or training	No limit[52]	Any U.S. or foreign resident	$9,000 p.a.	19(1)(b)
Bulgaria	16	Independent personal services[53]	183 days	Any foreign resident	No limit	7
	17	Dependent personal services[8,17]	No limit	Any U.S. or foreign resident	$15,000 p.a.[25]	14
	20	Public entertainment	No limit		No limit	16
	18	Teaching[4]	2 years	U.S. educational or research institution	No limit	19(2)
	19	Studying and training[11]	No limit[52]	Any foreign resident	No limit	19(1)(a)
		Compensation during study or training	No limit[52]	Any U.S. or foreign resident	$9,000 p.a.	19(1)(b)
Canada	16	Independent personal services[53]	No limit	Any contractor	$15,000 p.a.[25]	VII
	20	Public entertainment	No limit	Any U.S. or foreign resident[19]	$10,000.	XVI
	17	Dependent personal services	183 days	Any foreign resident[19]	No limit[13]	XV
	20	Public entertainment	No limit	Any U.S. or foreign resident	$15,000 p.a.[25]	XVI
	19	Studying and training: Remittances or allowances[11]	No limit[52]	Any foreign resident	No limit	XX

¶1305

Table 2. (Continued)

Country (1)	Code[1] (2)	Category of Personal Services — Purpose (3)	Maximum Presence in U.S. (4)	Required Employer or Payer (5)	Maximum Amount of Compensation (6)	Treaty Article Citation (7)
China, People's Rep. of	15	Scholarship or fellowship grant[15]	No limit	Any U.S. or foreign resident[5]	No limit	20(b)
	16	Independent personal services[39,22]	183 days	Any contractor	No limit	13
	20	Public entertainment[8]	No limit	Any contractor	No limit	16
	17	Dependent personal services[6,17]	183 days	Any foreign resident	No limit	14
	20	Public entertainment[29]	183 days	Any U.S. or foreign resident	No limit	16
	18	Teaching[4]	3 years	U.S. educational or research institute	No limit	19
	19	Studying and training: Remittances or allowances	No limit	Any foreign resident	No limit	20(a)
		Compensation during training or while gaining experience.	No limit	Any U.S. or foreign resident	$5,000 p.a.	20(c)
Commonwealth of Independent States	15	Scholarship or fellowship grant[15]	5 years	Any U.S. or foreign resident.	Limited	VI(1)
	16	Independent personal services[22]	183 days	Any U.S. or foreign contractor	No limit	VI(2)
	17	Dependent personal services	183 days	Any U.S. or foreign resident.	No limit	VI(1)
	18	Teaching[4,20]	2 years	U.S. educational or scientific institution.	No limit	VI(1)
	19	Studying and training: Remittances or allowances.	5 years	Any U.S. or foreign resident.	Limited	VI(1)
		Compensation while gaining experience.	1 year	C.I.S. resident.	No limit[21]	VI(1)
		Compensation under U.S. Government program	1 year	Any U.S. or foreign resident.	No limit	VI(1)
Cyprus	15	Scholarship or fellowship grant[15]	Generally, 5 years	Any U.S. or foreign resident[5]	No limit	21(1)
	16	Independent personal services[7,22]	182 days	Any contractor	No limit	17
	20	Public entertainment[8]	No limit	Any contractor	$500 per day or $5,000 p.a.	19(1)
	17	Dependent personal services[17]	182 days	Any foreign resident	No limit	18
	20	Directors' fees	No limit	U.S. corporation.	No limit[24]	20
		Public entertainment	No limit	Any U.S. or foreign resident.	$500 per day or $5,000 p.a.	19(1)
	19	Studying and training: Remittances or allowances.	Generally, 5 years	Any foreign resident	No limit	21(1)
		Compensation during training	Generally, 5 years	Any U.S. or foreign resident.	$2,000 p.a.	21(1)
		Compensation while gaining experience[2]	1 year	Cyprus resident.	$7,500	21(2)
		Compensation under U.S. Government program	1 year	U.S. Government or its contractor	$10,000	21(3)
Czech Republic	15	Scholarship or fellowship grant[4,15]	5 years	Any U.S. or foreign resident[5]	No limit	21(1)
	16	Independent personal services[22]	183 days	Any contractor	No limit	14
	20	Public entertainment[8]	183 days	Any foreign resident	$20,000 p.a.[30]	18
	17	Dependent personal services[8,17]	183 days	Any foreign resident	No limit	15
	20	Public entertainment	183 days	Any foreign resident	$20,000 p.a.[30]	18
	18	Teaching[35]	2 years	Any U.S. educational or research institution	No limit	21(5)
	19	Studying and training: Remittances and allowances	5 years	Any foreign resident	No limit	21(1)
		Compensation during training	5 years	Any U.S. or foreign resident.	$5,000 p.a.	21(1)
		Compensation while gaining experience[2]	12 consec. mos.	Czech resident	$8,000	21(2)
		Compensation under U.S. Government program	1 year	U.S. Government.	$10,000	21(3)
Denmark	16	Independent personal services[7]	No limit	Any contractor	No limit	14
	20	Public entertainment[20]	No limit	Any contractor	$20,000 p.a.[26]	17
	17	Dependent personal services[22,17]	183 days	Any foreign resident	No limit	15
	20	Public entertainment[22]	183 days	Any foreign resident	$20,000 p.a.[26]	17
	19	Studying and training: Remittances or allowances[4,11]	3 years[48]	Any foreign resident	No limit	20

¶1305

Table 2. (Continued)

Country (1)	Code[1] (2)	Category of Personal Services — Purpose (3)	Maximum Presence in U.S. (4)	Required Employer or Payer (5)	Maximum Amount of Compensation (6)	Treaty Article Citation (7)
Egypt	15	Scholarship or fellowship grant[15]	Generally, 5 years	Any U.S. or foreign resident[5]	No limit	23(1)
	16	Independent personal services[22]	89 days	Any foreign contractor	No limit	15
	20	Public entertainment[22]	No limit	Any contractor	$400 per day.	17
	17	Dependent personal services[16,17]	89 days	Egyptian resident	No limit	16
	20	Public entertainment	No limit	Any U.S. or foreign resident	$400 per day.	17
	18	Teaching[4]	2 years	U.S. educational institution	No limit	22
	19	Studying and training:				
		Remittances or allowances	Generally, 5 years	Any foreign resident	No limit	22(1)
		Compensation during training	Generally, 5 years	U.S. or any foreign resident	$3,000 p.a.	22(1)
		Compensation while gaining experience[2]	12 consec. mos.	Egyptian resident	$7,500	23(2)
		Compensation under U.S. Government program	1 year	U.S. Government or its contractor	$10,000	23(3)
Estonia	15	Scholarship or fellowship grants[4]	5 years	Any U.S. or foreign resident[5]	No limit	20(1)
	16	Independent personal services[22]	183 days	Any contractor	No limit	14
	20	Public entertainment[22]	No limit	Any contractor	$20,000[30]	17
	17	Dependent personal services[8,17]	183 days	Any foreign resident	No limit	15
	20	Public entertainment[22]	No limit	Any U.S. or foreign resident	$20,000[30]	17
	19	Studying and training:[4]				
		Remittances or allowances	5 years	Any foreign resident	No limit	20(1)
		Compensation during training	12 consec. mos.	Estonian resident	$8,000	20(2)
		Compensation while gaining experience[2]	5 years	Other foreign or U.S. resident	$5,000 p.a.	20(1)
			12 consec. mos.	Estonian resident	$8,000	20(2)
	-	Compensation under U.S. Gov't. program	1 year	U.S. Government or its contractor.	$10,000	20(3)
Finland	16	Independent personal services[7,22]	No limit	Any contractor	No limit	14
	20	Public entertainment[22]	No limit	Any contractor	$20,000 p.a.[26]	17
	17	Dependent personal services[17]	183 days	Any foreign resident	No limit	15
	20	Public entertainment	No limit	Any U.S. or foreign resident	$20,000 p.a.[26]	17
	19	Studying and training:				
		Remittances or allowances[11]	No limit	Any foreign resident	No limit	20
France	15	Scholarship or fellowship grant[15]	5 years[43]	Any U.S. or foreign resident[5]	No limit	21(1)
	16	Independent personal services[22]	No limit	Any contractor	No limit	14
	20	Public entertainment[22]	No limit	Any contractor	$10,000[30]	17
	17	Dependent personal services[8,17]	183 days	Any foreign resident	No limit	15
	20	Public entertainment	No limit	Any U.S. or foreign resident	$10,000[30]	17
	18	Teaching[4,44]	2 years[45]	U.S. educational or research institution	No limit	20
	19	Studying and training:				
		Remittances or allowances	5 years[43]	Any foreign resident	No limit	21(1)
		Compensation during study or training	12 consec. mos.	French resident	$8,000	21(2)
		Compensation while gaining experience[2]	5 years[43]	Other foreign or U.S. resident	$5,000 p.a.	21(1)
			12 consec. mos.	French resident	$8,000	21(2)
Germany	15	Scholarship or fellowship grant	No limit	Any U.S. or foreign resident[5]	No limit	20(3)
	16	Independent personal services[33]	183 days	Any foreign resident	No limit	7
	17	Dependent personal services[12,17]	No limit	Any foreign resident	No limit	15
	20	Public entertainment	No limit	Any U.S. or foreign resident	$20,000 p.a.[30]	17
	18	Teaching[4,55]	2 years	U.S. educational or research institution	No limit	20(1)
	19	Studying and training:[11]				
		Remittances or allowances	No limit	Any foreign resident	No limit	20(2)
		Compensation during study or training	4 years	Any U.S. or foreign resident	$9,000 p.a.	20(4)
		Compensation while gaining experience[2]	1 year	Any foreign resident	$10,000[28]	20(5)

¶1305

Table 2. *(Continued)*

Country (1)	Code[1] (2)	Purpose (3)	Maximum Presence in U.S. (4)	Required Employer or Payer (5)	Maximum Amount of Compensation (6)	Treaty Article Citation (7)
Greece	16	Independent personal services[22]	183 days	Greek resident contractor	No limit	X
			183 days	Other foreign or U.S. resident contractor	$10,000	X
	17	Dependent personal services	183 days	Greek resident	No limit	X
			183 days	Other foreign or U.S. resident	$10,000	X
	18	Teaching	3 years	U.S. educational institution	No limit	XII
	19	Studying and training: Remittances or allowances	No limit	Any foreign resident	No limit	XIII
Hungary	16	Independent personal services[7,22]	183 days	Any contractor	No limit	13
	17	Dependent personal services[7]	183 days	Any foreign resident	No limit	14
	18	Teaching[4]	2 years	U.S. educational institution	No limit	17
	19	Studying and training:[23] Remittances or allowances[11]	No limit	Any foreign resident	No limit	18(1)
Iceland	15	Scholarship and fellowship grant	5 years	Any U.S. or foreign resident[5]	No limit	19(1)
	16	Independent personal services[53]			No limit	7
	17	Dependent personal services[8,17]	183 days	Any foreign resident	No limit	14
	20	Public entertainment[17]	No limit	Any U.S. or foreign resident	$20,000 p.a.[25]	16
	19	Studying and training: Remittances or allowances	5 years	Any foreign resident	No limit	19(1)
		Compensation during study or training	5 years	Any U.S. or foreign resident	$9,000 p.a.	19(1)
		Compensation while gaining experience	12 consec. mo.	Any U.S. or foreign resident[2]	$9,000	19(2)
		Compensation under U.S. Government program	1 year	U.S. Government or its contractor	$9,000	19(3)
India	16	Independent personal services[7,8,22]	89 days	Any contractor	No limit	15
	20	Public entertainment[7,22]	89 days	Any contractor	$1,500 p.a.[26]	18
	17	Dependent personal services[17]	183 days	Any foreign resident	No limit	16
	20	Public entertainment[17]	183 days	Any foreign resident	$1,500 p.a.[26]	18
	18	Teaching[4]	2 years	U.S. educational institution	No limit	22
	19	Studying and training: Remittances or allowances	No limit	Any foreign resident[27]	No limit	21(1)
Indonesia	15	Scholarship or fellowship grant[15]	5 years	Any U.S. or foreign resident[5]	No limit	19(1)
	16	Independent personal services[7,22]	119 days	Any contractor	No limit	15
	20	Public entertainment[22]	No limit	Any contractor	$2,000 p.a.[25]	17
	17	Dependent personal services[17]	119 days	Any foreign resident	No limit	16
	20	Public entertainment	No limit	Any U.S. or foreign resident	$2,000 p.a.[25]	17
	18	Teaching[4,24]	2 years	U.S. educational institution	No limit	20
	19	Studying and training: Remittances or allowances	5 years	Any foreign resident	No limit	19(1)
		Compensation during training	5 years	Any foreign or U.S. resident	$2,000 p.a.	19(1)
		Compensation while gaining experience	12 consec. mo.	Any U.S. or foreign resident	$7,500	19(2)
Ireland	16	Independent personal services[7]	No limit	Any contractor	No limit	14
	20	Public entertainment[22]	No limit	Any contractor	$20,000[25]	17
	17	Dependent personal services[17,47]	183 days	Any foreign resident	No limit	15
	20	Public entertainment[22]	No limit	Any U.S. or foreign resident	$20,000[25]	17
	19	Studying and training:[11] Remittances or allowances	1 year[45]	Any foreign resident	No limit	20

¶1305

Table 2. (Continued)

Country (1)	Code[1] (2)	Category of Personal Services — Purpose (3)	Maximum Presence in U.S. (4)	Required Employer or Payer (5)	Maximum Amount of Compensation (6)	Treaty Article Citation (7)
Israel	15	Scholarship or fellowship grant[5]	5 years	Any U.S. or foreign resident[5]	No limit	24(1)
	16	Independent personal services[22]	182 days	Any contractor	No limit	16
	20	Public entertainment[22]	No limit	Any contractor	$400 per day[37]	18
	17	Dependent personal services[16, 17]	182 days	Israeli resident[18]	$400 per day[37]	17
	20	Public entertainment	No limit	Any U.S. or foreign resident	No limit	18
	19	Teaching[39]	2 years	U.S. educational institution	No limit	23
		Studying and training:				
		Remittances or allowances	5 years	Any foreign resident	No limit	24(1)
		Compensation during study or training	5 years	Any U.S. or foreign resident	$3,000 p.a.	24(1)
		Compensation while gaining experience[3]		Israeli resident	$7,500	24(2)
		Compensation under U.S. Government program	1 year	U.S. Government or its contractor	$10,000	24(3)
Italy	16	Independent personal services[7]	No limit	Any contractor	No limit	14(1)
	17	Dependent personal services[8,17]	183 days	Any foreign resident	No limit	15(2)
	20	Public entertainment	90 days	Any U.S. or foreign resident	$20,000 p.a.25	17
	18	Teaching[4]	2 years	Any U.S. or foreign resident	No limit	20
	19	Studying and training: Remittances or allowances	No limit	Any foreign resident	No limit	21
Jamaica	16	Independent personal services[7,22]	89 days	Any foreign contractor	No limit	14
	20	Public entertainment[22]	89 days	Any U.S. contractor	$5,000 p.a.	14
				Any contractor	$400 per day or $5,000 p.a.[6]	
	17	Dependent personal services[17]	183 days	Any foreign resident	$5,000 p.a.	18
	20	Public entertainment	No limit	Any U.S. or foreign resident	$400 per day or $5,000 p.a.[6]	15
	18	Director's fees	No limit	U.S. resident	$400 per day[5]	18
	19	Teaching[4,45]	2 years	U.S. educational institution	No limit	16
		Studying and training:[23]				
		Remittances or allowances[11]	No limit	Any foreign resident	No limit	22
		Compensation during study	12 consec. mo.	Jamaican resident	$7,500 p.a.	21(1)
		Compensation while gaining experience[2]	12 consec. mo.	Jamaican resident	$7,500 p.a.	21(2)
Japan	16	Independent personal services[8, 53]	No limit	Any contractor	$10,000 p.a.25	7
	20	Public entertainment[22]	183 days	Any foreign resident	No limit	16
	17	Dependent personal services[8, 17]	No limit	Any U.S. or foreign resident	$10,000 p.a.25	14
	20	Public entertainment				16
	18	Teaching[4]	2 years	U.S. educational institution	No limit	20
	19	Studying and training: Remittances or allowances	1 year[45]	Any foreign resident	No limit	19
Kazakstan	15	Scholarship or fellowship grant[4,15,41]	5 years[31]	Any U.S. or foreign resident[5]	No limit	19
	16	Independent personal services[7]	183 days	Any contractor	No limit	15
	17	Dependent personal services[17,47]	183 days	Any foreign resident	No limit	16
	19	Studying and training: Remittances or allowances	5 years	Any foreign resident	No limit	19
Korea, South	15	Scholarship or fellowship grant[15]	5 years	Any U.S. or foreign resident[5]	No limit	21(1)
	16	Independent personal services[22]	182 days	Any contractor	$3,000 p.a.	18
	17	Dependent personal services[17]	182 days	Korean resident[18]	$3,000 p.a.	19
	18	Teaching[4]	2 years	U.S. educational institution	No limit	20
	19	Studying and training:				
		Remittances or allowances	5 years	Any foreign resident	No limit	21(1)
		Compensation during training	5 years	Any foreign or U.S. resident	$2,000 p.a.	21(1)
		Compensation while gaining experience[3]	1 year	Korean resident	$5,000	21(2)
		Compensation under U.S. Government program	1 year	U.S. Government or its contractor	$10,000	21(3)

¶1305

Table 2. *(Continued)*

Country (1)	Code[1] (2)	Category of Personal Services — Purpose (3)	Maximum Presence in U.S. (4)	Required Employer or Payer (5)	Maximum Amount of Compensation (6)	Treaty Article Citation (7)
Latvia	15	Scholarship or fellowship grants[4]	5 years	Any U.S. or foreign resident[5]	No limit	20(1)
	16	Independent personal services[2]	183 days	Any contractor	No limit	14
	20	Public entertainment[2,17]	No limit	Any contractor	$20,000[30]	17
	17	Dependent personal services[8,17]	183 days	Any foreign resident	No limit	15
	20	Public entertainment[22]	No limit	Any U.S. or foreign resident	$20,000[30]	17
	19	Studying and training:[4] Remittances or allowances	5 years	Any foreign resident	No limit	20(1)
		Compensation during training	12 consec. mos.	Latvian resident	$8,000	20(2)
		Compensation while gaining experience[2]	5 years	Other foreign or U.S. resident	$5,000 p.a.	20(1)
			12 consec. mos.	Latvian resident	$8,000	20(2)
		Compensation under U.S. Gov't. program	1 year	U.S. Government or its contractor	$10,000	20(3)
Lithuania	15	Scholarship or fellowship grants[4]	5 years	Any U.S. or foreign resident[5]	No limit	20(1)
	16	Independent personal services[2]	183 days	Any contractor	No limit	14
	20	Public entertainment[2,17]	No limit	Any contractor	$20,000[30]	17
	17	Dependent personal services[8,17]	183 days	Any foreign resident	No limit	15
	20	Public entertainment[22]	No limit	Any U.S. or foreign resident	$20,000[30]	17
	19	Studying and training:[4] Remittances or allowances	5 years	Any foreign resident	No limit	20(1)
		Compensation during training	12 consec. mos.	Lithuanian resident	$8,000	20(2)
		Compensation while gaining experience[2]	5 years	Other foreign or U.S. resident	$5,000 p.a.	20(1)
			12 consec. mos.	Lithuanian resident	$8,000	20(2)
		Compensation under U.S. Gov't. program	1 year	U.S. Government or its contractor	$10,000	20(3)
Luxembourg	16	Independent personal services[7]	No limit	Any contractor	No limit	15
	20	Public entertainment[22]	No limit	Any contractor	$10,000[25]	18
	17	Dependent personal services[12,17]	No limit	Any foreign resident	No limit	16
	20	Public entertainment[22]	No limit	Any U.S. or foreign resident	$10,000[25]	18
	18	Teaching[9]	2 years	Any U.S. or foreign resident	No limit	21(2)
	19	Studying and training:[11] Remittances or allowances	2 years[45]	Any U.S. or foreign resident	No limit	21(1)
Malta	16	Independent personal services[53]	183 days	Any foreign resident	No limit	7
	17	Dependent personal services[12,17]	No limit	Any U.S. or foreign resident	No limit	14
	20	Public entertainment		Any U.S. or foreign resident	$20,000 p.a.[25]	16
	19	Studying and training: Remittances or allowances				
Mexico	16	Independent personal services[7,22]	183 days	Any contractor	No limit	14
	20	Public entertainment[22]	No limit	Any contractor	$3,000 p.a.[30]	18
	17	Dependent personal services[17,47]	183 days	Any foreign resident	No limit	15
	20	Public entertainment[22]	No limit	Any U.S. or foreign resident	$3,000 p.a.[30]	18
	19	Studying and training: Remittances and allowances	No limit	Any foreign resident	No limit	21

Table 2. *(Continued)*

Country (1)	Code[1] (2)	Category of Personal Services — Purpose (3)	Maximum Presence in U.S. (4)	Required Employer or Payer (5)	Maximum Amount of Compensation (6)	Treaty Article Citation (7)
Morocco	15	Scholarship or fellowship grant[15]	No limit	Any U.S. or foreign resident[5]	No limit	18
	16	Independent personal services[22]	182 days	Any contractor[13]	$5,000	14
	17	Dependent personal services[7]	182 days	Moroccan resident[13,18]	No limit	15
	19	Studying and training:[5]				
		Remittances or allowances	5 years	Any foreign resident	No limit	18
		Compensation during training	5 years	U.S. or any foreign resident	$2,000 p.a.	18
Netherlands	15	Scholarship or fellowship grant[15,33]	3 years	Any U.S. or foreign resident[5]	No limit	22(2)
	16	Independent personal services[22]	No limit	Any contractor	No limit	15
	20	Public entertainment[2]	No limit	Any foreign resident	$10,000 p.a.[30]	18
	17	Dependent personal services[17,47]	183 days	Any foreign resident	No limit	16
	20	Public entertainment	183 days	Any foreign resident	$10,000 p.a.[30]	18
	18	Teaching[4,34]	2 years	U.S. educational institution	No limit	21(1)
	19	Studying and training:[33]				
		Remittances or allowances	No limit	Any foreign resident	No limit	22(1)
		Compensation while gaining experience.	No limit	Any U.S. or foreign resident.	$2,000 p.a.	22(1)
		Compensation while recipient of scholarship or fellowship grant	3 years	Any U.S. or foreign resident.	$2,000 p.a.[36]	22(2)
New Zealand	16	Independent personal services[53]	183 days	Any foreign resident	No limit	7
	17	Dependent personal services[7]	No limit	Any foreign resident	$10,000[25]	15
	20	Public entertainment[17]				17
	19	Studying and training:				
		Remittances or allowances[11]	No limit	Any foreign resident	No limit	20
Norway	15	Scholarship or fellowship grant[15]	5 years	Any U.S. or foreign resident[5]	No limit	16(1)
	16	Independent personal services[22]	182 days	Any resident contractor	No limit	13
	20	Public entertainment[2]	90 days	Any resident contractor	$10,000 p.a.	13
	17	Dependent personal services[17]	No limit	Norwegian resident[18]	No limit	14
	18	Teaching[4]	2 years	U.S. educational institution	No limit	15
	19	Studying and training:				
		Remittances or allowances	5 years.	Any foreign resident	No limit	16(1)
		Compensation during training.	5 years.	U.S. or any foreign resident.	$2,000 p.a.	16(1)
		Compensation while gaining experience[2]	12 consec. mo.	Norwegian resident	$5,000	16(2)
		Compensation under U.S. Government program	1 year	U.S. Government or its contractor	$10,000	16(3)
Pakistan	15	Scholarship or fellowship grant[15,62,22]	No limit.	Pakistani nonprofit organization	No limit	XIII(1)
	16	Independent personal services[22]	183 days.	Pakistani resident contractor.	No limit	XI
	17	Dependent personal services[6]	183 days.	Pakistani resident	No limit	XI
	18	Teaching	2 years.	U.S. educational institution	No limit	XII
	19	Studying and training:				
		Remittances or allowances	No limit.	Any foreign resident	No limit	XIII(1)
		Compensation during training.	No limit.	U.S. or any foreign resident.	$5,000 p.a.	XIII(1)
		Compensation while gaining experience[2]	1 year	Pakistani resident	$6,000	XIII(2)
		Compensation under U.S. Government program.	No limit.	U.S. Government, its contractor, or any foreign resident employer	$10,000	XIII(3)

¶1305

Table 2. (Continued)

Country (1)	Code[1] (2)	Category of Personal Services — Purpose (3)	Maximum Presence in U.S. (4)	Required Employer or Payer (5)	Maximum Amount of Compensation (6)	Treaty Article Citation (7)
Philippines	15	Scholarship or fellowship grant[15]	5 years	Any U.S. or foreign resident[5]	No limit	22(1)
	16	Independent personal services[22]	89 days	Any foreign contractor	No limit	15
			89 days	Any U.S. contractor	$10,000 p.a.	15
	20	Public entertainment[22]	No limit	Any contractor	$100 per day or $3,000 p.a.	17
	17	Dependent personal services[17]	89 days	Any Philippines resident[18]	No limit	16
	20	Public entertainment	No limit	Any U.S. or foreign resident	$100 per day or $3,000 p.a.	17
	18	Teaching[4,38]	2 years	U.S. educational institution	No limit	21, 22(4)
	19	Studying and training:				
		Remittances or allowances	5 years	Any foreign resident	No limit	22(1)
		Compensation during study	5 years	Any U.S. or foreign resident	$3,000 p.a.	22(1)
		Compensation while gaining experience[2]	12 consec. mo.	Philippines resident	$7,500 p.a.	22(2)
		Compensation under U.S. Government program	1 year	U.S. Government or its contractor	$10,000 p.a.	22(3)
Poland	15	Scholarship or fellowship grant[15]	5 years	Any U.S. or foreign resident[5]	No limit	18(1)
	16	Independent personal services[22]	182 days	Any contractor	No limit	15
	17	Dependent personal services[17]	182 days	Any foreign resident	No limit	16
	18	Teaching[4]	2 years	U.S. educational institution	No limit	17
	19	Studying and training:				
		Remittances or allowances	5 years	Any foreign resident	No limit	18(1)
		Compensation during training	5 years	U.S. or any foreign resident	$2,000 p.a.	18(1)
		Compensation while gaining experience[2]	1 year	Polish resident	$5,000	18(2)
		Government program	1 year	U.S. Government or its contractor	$10,000	18(3)
Portugal	15	Scholarship or fellowship grant[15]	5 years	Any U.S. or foreign resident[5]	No limit	23(1)
	16	Independent personal services[22]	182 days	Any contractor	No limit	15
	20	Public entertainment[2]	No limit	Any contractor	$10,000 p.a.[30]	19
	17	Dependent personal services[2,17]	183 days	Any U.S. or foreign resident	$10,000 p.a.[30]	19
	20	Public entertainment	No limit	U.S. educational or research institution.	No limit	19
	18	Teaching[4,42]	2 years	Any foreign resident	No limit	22
	19	Studying and training:				
		Remittances or allowances	5 years	Any foreign or U.S. resident	$5,000 p.a.	23(1)
		Compensation during training	5 years	Portuguese resident	$8,000	23(2)
		Compensation while gaining experience[2]	12 consec. mos.	Portuguese resident	$8,000	23(2)
Romania	15	Scholarship or fellowship grant[15]	5 years[31]	Any U.S. or foreign resident[5]	No limit	20(1)
	16	Independent personal services[22]	182 days	Any contractor	No limit	14
	20	Public entertainment[2]	90 days	Any contractor	$3,000	14
	17	Dependent personal services[17]	182 days	Romanian resident	$2,999.99	15
	20	Public entertainment	89 days	Romanian resident	No limit	15
	18	Teaching[4]	2 years	U.S. educational institution	No limit	19
	19	Studying and training:				
		Remittances or allowances	5 years	Any foreign resident	No limit	20(1)
		Compensation during training	5 years	U.S. or any foreign resident	$2,000 p.a.	20(1)
		Compensation while gaining experience[2]	1 year	Romanian resident	$5,000	20(2)
		Compensation while under U.S. Government program	1 year	U.S. Government or its contractor	$10,000	20(3)
Russia	15	Scholarship or fellowship grant[4,15,41]	5 years[31]	Any U.S. or foreign resident[5]	No limit	18
	16	Independent personal services[22]	183 days	Any contractor	No limit	13
	17	Dependent personal services[5,17,32]	183 days	Any foreign resident	No limit	14
	19	Studying and training:				
		Remittances and allowances	5 years[31]	Any foreign resident	No limit	18

Publication 515 (2011)

¶1305

Table 2. (Continued)

Country (1)	Code[1] (2)	Category of Personal Services — Purpose (3)	Maximum Presence in U.S. (4)	Required Employer or Payer (5)	Maximum Amount of Compensation (6)	Treaty Article Citation (7)
Slovak Republic	15	Scholarship or fellowship grant[4,15]	5 years	Any U.S. or foreign resident[5]	No limit	21(1)
	16	Independent personal services[22]	183 days	Any contractor	No limit	14
	20	Public entertainment[2]	183 days	Any contractor	$20,000 p.a.[30]	18
	17	Dependent personal services[12,17]	183 days	Any foreign resident	No limit	15
	20	Public entertainment[2]	183 days	Any foreign resident	$20,000 p.a.[30]	18
	18	Teaching[18]	2 years	Any U.S. educational or research institution	No limit	21(5)
	19	Studying and training:[4] Remittances and allowances	5 years	Any foreign resident	No limit	21(1)
		Compensation during training	5 years	Any U.S. or foreign resident	$5,000 p.a.	21(1)
		Compensation while gaining experience[2]	12 consec. mos.	Slovak resident	$8,000	21(2)
		Compensation under U.S. Government program	1 year	U.S. Government	$10,000	21(3)
Slovenia	15	Scholarship or fellowship grant[4]	5 years[10]	Any U.S. or foreign resident[5]	No limit	20(1)
	16	Independent personal services[22]	No limit	Any contractor	No limit	14
	20	Public entertainment[2]	No limit	Any contractor	$15,000 p.a.[51]	17
	17	Dependent personal services[12,17]	183 days	Any U.S. or foreign resident	No limit	15
	20	Public entertainment[2]	No limit	Any U.S. or foreign resident	$15,000 p.a.[51]	17
	18	Teaching or research[4]	2 years[40]	Any U.S. or foreign resident	No limit	20(3)
	19	Studying and training:[4] Remittances or allowances	5 years[10]	Any foreign resident	No limit	20(1)
		Compensation during training	5 years[10]	Any U.S. or foreign resident	$5,000 p.a.	20(1)
		Compensation while gaining experience[2]	12 mo.	Slovenian resident	$8,000	20(2)
So. Africa	16	Independent personal services[7,22]	183 days	Any contractor	No limit	14
	20	Public entertainment[2]	No limit	Any contractor	$7,500[30]	17
	17	Dependent personal services[12,17]	183 days	Any foreign resident	No limit	15
	20	Public entertainment[2]	No limit	Any U.S. or foreign resident	$7,500[30]	17
	19	Studying and training:[11] Remittances or allowances	1 year[65]	Any foreign resident	No limit	20
Spain	15	Scholarship or fellowship grant[4,15]	5 years[10]	Any U.S. or foreign resident[5]	No limit	22(1)
	16	Independent personal services[22]	No limit	Any contractor	No limit	15
	20	Public entertainment[2]	No limit	Any contractor	$10,000 p.a.[30]	19
	17	Dependent personal services[17]	183 days	Any foreign resident	No limit	16
	20	Public entertainment[2]	No limit	Any U.S. or foreign resident	$10,000 p.a.[30]	19
	19	Studying and training:[4] Remittances or allowances	5 years	Any foreign resident	No limit	22(1)
		Compensation during training	5 years	Any U.S. or foreign resident	$5,000 p.a.	22(1)
		Compensation while gaining experience[2]	12 consec. mo.	Spanish resident	$8,000	22(2)
Sri Lanka	16	Independent personal services[7,12]	183 days	Any contractor	No limit	15
	20	Public entertainment[2]	183 days	Any contractor	$6,000 p.a.[51]	18
	17	Dependent personal services[12,17]	183 days	Any foreign resident	No limit	16
	20	Public entertainment[2]	183 days	Any foreign resident	$6,000 p.a.[51]	18
	19	Studying and training: Remittances or allowances[11]	No limit	Any foreign resident	No limit	21(1)
		Compensation while gaining experience[2]	1 year	Sri Lankan resident[19]	$6,000	21(2)
Sweden	16	Independent personal services[7]	No limit	Any contractor	No limit	14
	20	Public entertainment[2]	No limit	Any contractor	$6,000[25]	18
	17	Dependent personal services[12,17]	183 days	Any foreign resident	No limit	15
	20	Public entertainment[2]	No limit	Any U.S. or foreign resident	$6,000[25]	18
	19	Studying and training: Remittances or allowances[11]	No limit	Any foreign resident	No limit	21
Switzerland	16	Independent personal services[7]	No limit	Any contractor	No limit	14
	20	Public entertainment[2]	No limit	Any contractor	$10,000[25]	18
	17	Dependent personal services[12,17]	183 days	Any foreign resident	No limit	15
	20	Public entertainment[2]	No limit	Any U.S. or foreign resident	$10,000[25]	17
	19	Studying and training:[11] Remittances or allowances	No limit	Any foreign resident	No limit	20

¶1305

Table 2. *(Continued)*

Country (1)	Code[1] (2)	Category of Personal Services — Purpose (3)	Maximum Presence in U.S. (4)	Required Employer or Payer (5)	Maximum Amount of Compensation (6)	Treaty Article Citation (7)
Thailand	15	Scholarship or fellowship grant[22]	5 years	Any U.S. or foreign resident[5]	No limit	22(1)
	16	Independent personal services[22]	89 days	Any U.S. resident	$10,000	15
			89 days	Any foreign contractor	No limit[49]	15
	20	Public entertainment[22]	No limit	Any contractor	$100 per day or $3,000 p.a.[48]	19
	17	Dependent personal services[17,47]	183 days	Any foreign resident	No limit	16
	20	Public entertainment[22]	No limit	Any U.S. or foreign resident	$100 per day or $3,000 p.a.[48]	19
	18	Teaching or research[4,38]	2 years	Any U.S. or foreign resident	No limit	23
	19	Studying and training: Remittances or allowances	5 years	Any foreign resident	No limit	22(1)
		Compensation during training	5 years	Any U.S. or foreign resident	$3,000 p.a.	22(1)
		Compensation while gaining experience	12 consec. mos.	Thai resident[2]	$7,500	22(2)
		Compensation while under U.S. Government program	1 year	U.S. Government	$10,000[36]	22(3)
Trinidad and Tobago	15	Scholarship or fellowship grant[15]	5 years	Any U.S. or foreign resident[5]	No limit	19(1)
	16	Independent personal services[14,22]	183 days	Any foreign resident contractor	No limit	17
			183 days	Any U.S. contractor	$3,000[5]	17
	17	Dependent personal services[14]	183 days	Any foreign resident	No limit	17
			183 days	Any U.S. resident	$3,000[5]	17
	18	Teaching[4]	2 years	U.S. educational institution or U.S. Government	No limit	18
	19	Studying and training: Remittances or allowances	5 years	Any foreign resident	No limit	19(1)
		Compensation during training	5 years	U.S. or any foreign resident	$2,000 p.a.[6]	19(1)
		Compensation during professional training	5 years	U.S. or any foreign resident	$5,000 p.a.[6]	19(1)
		Compensation while gaining experience[7]	1 year	Trinidad—Tobago resident	$5,000[6]	19(2)
		Compensation under U.S. Government program	1 year	U.S. Government or its contractor	$10,000[6]	19(3)
Tunisia	15	Scholarship or fellowship grant[11,15]	5 years	Any U.S. or foreign resident[5]	No limit	20
	16	Independent personal services[22]	183 days	U.S. resident contractor	$7,500 p.a.[25]	14
	20	Public entertainment[17]	No limit	Any contractor	$7,500 p.a.[25]	17
	17	Dependent personal services[17]	183 days	Any foreign resident	No limit	15
	20	Public entertainment	No limit	Any U.S. or foreign resident	$7,500 p.a.[25]	17
	19	Studying and training: Remittances or allowances	5 years	Any foreign resident	No limit	20
		Compensation during training	5 years	Any U.S. or foreign resident	$4,000 p.a.	20
Turkey	16	Independent personal services[22,50]	183 days	Any contractor	No limit	14
	20	Public entertainment	No limit	Any contractor	$3,000[46]	17
	17	Dependent personal services[12,17]	183 days	Any U.S. or foreign resident	No limit	15
	20	Public entertainment[22,50]	No limit	Any U.S. or foreign resident	$3,000[46]	17
	18	Teaching or research[4]	2 years	Any foreign resident	No limit	20(2)
	19	Studying and training: Remittances or allowances[11]	5 years	Any foreign resident	No limit	20(1)
Ukraine	15	Scholarship or fellowship grants[41]	5 years[31]	Any U.S. or foreign resident[5]	No limit	20
	16	Independent personal services[3,7]	No limit	Any contractor	No limit	14
	17	Dependent personal services[3,17]	183 days	Any U.S. or foreign resident	No limit	15
	19	Studying and training: Remittances or allowances	5 years[31]	Any foreign resident	No limit	20
United Kingdom	16	Independent personal services[53]	No limit	Any foreign resident	No limit	7
	17	Dependent personal services[12,17]	183 days	Any U.S. or foreign resident	$20,000 p.a.[25]	14
	20	Public entertainment[22]	No limit	U.S. educational institution	No limit	16
	18	Teaching or research[4]	2 years			20A
	19	Studying and training: Remittances or allowances[11]	No limit[52]	Any foreign resident	No limit	20

¶1305

Table 2. (Continued)

Country (1)	Code[1] (2)	Category of Personal Services — Purpose (3)	Maximum Presence in U.S. (4)	Required Employer or Payer (5)	Maximum Amount of Compensation (6)	Treaty Article Citation (7)
Venezuela	15	Scholarship or fellowship grants[4]	5 years[10]	Any U.S. or foreign resident[5]	No limit	21(1)
	16	Independent personal services[7,12]	No limit	Any contractor	No limit	14
	20	Public entertainment[22]	No limit	Any contractor	$6,000[30]	18
	17	Dependent personal services[12,17]	183 days	Any foreign resident	No limit	15
	20	Public entertainment[22]	No limit	Any U.S. or foreign contractor	$6,000[30]	18
	18	Teaching[4]	2 years[40]	Any U.S. or foreign resident.	No limit	21(3)
	19	Studying and training:[4]				
		Remittances or allowances	5 years[10]	Any foreign resident	No limit	21(1)
		Compensation during training	12 mos.	Venezuelan resident	$8,000	21(2)
		Compensation while gaining experience[2]	5 years[10]	Other foreign or U.S. resident.	$5,000 p.a.	21(1)
			12 mos.	Venezuelan resident	$8,000	21(2)

35 Exemption does not apply if the individual either (a) claimed the benefit of Article 21(5) previously, or (b) during the immediately preceding period, claimed the benefit of Article 21(1), (2), or (3).

36 Exemption applies only to compensation for personal services performed in connection with, or incidental to, the individual's study, research, or training.

37 If the compensation exceeds $400 per day, the entertainer may be taxed on the full amount. If the individual receives a fixed amount for more than one performance, the amount is prorated over the number of days the individual performs the services (including rehearsals).

38 Exemption does not apply if during the immediately preceding period, the individual derived any benefits of Article 22(1).

39 Exemption does not apply if during the immediately preceding period, the individual derived any benefits of Article 24(1).

40 The combined period of benefits for teaching cannot exceed 5 tax years.

41 Applies to grants, allowances, and other similar payments received for studying or doing research.

42 Exemption does not apply if the individual either (a) previously claimed the benefit of this Article, or (b) during the immediately preceding period, claimed the benefit of Article 23. The benefits under Articles 22 and 23 cannot be claimed at the same time.

43 The combined period of benefits under Articles 20 and 21(1) cannot exceed 5 years.

44 The exemption does not apply if the individual previously claimed the benefit of this Article.

45 The time limit pertains only to an apprentice or business trainee.

46 Exemption does not apply if gross receipts exceed this amount.

47 Fees paid to a resident of the treaty country for services as a director of a U.S. corporation are subject to U.S. tax, unless the services are performed in the country of residence.

48 Exemption does not apply if gross receipts exceed this amount. Income is fully exempt if visit to the United States is substantially supported by public funds of the treaty country or its political subdivisions or local authorities.

49 A $10,000 limit applies if the expense is borne by a permanent establishment or a fixed base in the United States.

50 This provision does not apply if these activities are substantially supported by a nonprofit organization of the treaty country or by public funds of the treaty country or its political subdivisions or local authorities.

51 Exemption does not apply if gross receipts, including reimbursements, exceed this amount during the year. Income is fully exempt if visit is wholly or mainly supported by public funds of one or both of the treaty countries or their political subdivisions or local authorities.

52 Exemption applies to business apprentice (trainee) only for a period not exceeding 1 year (2 years for Belgium and Bulgaria) from the date of arrival in the United States.

53 Treated as business profits under Article 7(VII) of the treaty.

54 Does not apply to an athlete employed with a team that is in a league with regularly scheduled games in both countries.

55 Exemption does not apply if during the immediately preceding period, the individual claimed the benefit of Article 20(2), (3), or (4).

18 The exemption also applies if the employer is a permanent establishment in the treaty country.

19 Applies also to a participant in a program sponsored by the U.S. government or an international organization.

20 The exemption is also extended to journalists and correspondents who are temporarily in the U.S. for periods not exceeding 2 years and who receive compensation from abroad.

21 Also exempt are amounts of up to $10,000 received from U.S. sources to provide ordinary living expenses. For students, the amount will be less than $10,000, determined on a case-by-case basis.

22 Withholding at 30% may be required because the factors on which the treaty exemption is based may not be determinable until after the close of the tax year. However, see *Withholding agreements*, and *Final payment exemption*, under *Pay for independent personal services*, a n d *Central withholding agreements*, under *Artists and Athletes*, discussed in this publication.

23 A student or trainee may choose to be treated as a U.S. resident for tax purposes. If the choice is made, it may not be revoked without the consent of the U.S. competent authority.

24 Does not apply to amounts received in excess of reasonable fees payable to all directors of the company for attending meetings in the United States.

25 Exemption does not apply if gross receipts (including reimbursements) exceed this amount during the year (or during any 12-month period for Sweden).

26 Exemption does not apply if net income exceeds this amount.

27 Exemption does not apply to payments borne by a permanent establishment in the United States or paid by a U.S. citizen or resident or the federal, state, or local government.

28 Exemption does not apply if compensation exceeds this amount.

29 The exemption applies only to income from activities performed under special cultural exchange programs agreed to by the U.S. and Chinese governments.

30 Exemption does not apply if gross receipts (or compensation for Portugal), including reimbursements, exceed this amount during the year. Income is fully exempt if visit to the United States is substantially supported by public funds of the treaty country or its political subdivisions or local authorities.

31 The 5-year limit pertains only to training or research.

32 Compensation from employment directly connected with a place of business that is not a permanent establishment is exempt if the alien is present in the United States for a period not exceeding 12 consecutive months. Compensation for technical services directly connected with the application of a right or property giving rise to a royalty is exempt if the services are provided as part of a contract granting the use of the right or property.

33 Exemption does not apply if, during the immediately preceding period, the individual claimed the benefits of Article 21.

34 Exemption does not apply if, during the immediately preceding period, the individual claimed the benefits of Article 22.

1 Refers to income code numbers described in this publication and to be reported on Forms 1042-S. Personal services must be performed by a nonresident alien individual who is a resident of the specified treaty country.

2 Applies only if training or experience is received from a person other than the alien's employer.

3 The exemption does not apply to income received for performing services in the United States as an entertainer or a sportsman. However, this income is exempt from U.S. income tax if the visit is (a) substantially supported by public funds of Ukraine, its political subdivisions, or local authorities, or (b) made under a specific arrangement agreed to by the governments of the treaty countries.

4 Does not apply to income for research work primarily for private benefit.

5 Grant must be from a nonprofit organization. In many cases, the exemption applies to amounts from either the U.S. or foreign government. In the case of Indonesia and the Netherlands, the exemption also applies if the amount is awarded under a technical assistance program entered into by the United States or foreign government, or its political subdivisions or local authorities.

6 Reimbursed expenses are not taken into account in figuring any maximum compensation to which the exemption applies. For Trinidad and Tobago, only reimbursed travel expenses are disregarded in figuring maximum compensation.

7 Exemption does not apply to the extent income is attributable to the recipient's fixed U.S. base. For residents of Belgium, Iceland, Korea, and Norway, the fixed base must be maintained for more than 182 days; for residents of Morocco, the fixed base must be maintained for more than 89 days.

8 Does not apply to fees of a foreign director of a U.S. corporation.

9 Does not apply to compensation for research work for other than the U.S. educational institution involved.

10 Applies to any additional period that a full-time student needs to complete the educational requirements as a candidate for a postgraduate or professional degree from a recognized educational institution.

11 Applies only to full-time student or trainee.

12 Fees paid to a resident of the treaty country for services performed in the United States as a director of a U.S. corporation are subject to U.S. tax.

13 Does not apply to compensation paid to public entertainers (actors, artists, musicians, athletes, etc.).

14 Does not apply to compensation paid to public entertainers in excess of $100 a day.

15 Does not apply to payments from the National Institutes of Health under its Visiting Associate Program and Visiting Scientist Program.

16 Exemption applies only if the compensation is subject to tax in the country of residence.

17 The exemption does not apply if the employee's compensation is borne by a permanent establishment or in some cases a fixed base that the employer has in the United States.

¶1305

Table 3.   **List of Tax Treaties** (Updated through December 31, 2011)

Country	Official Text Symbol[1]	General Effective Date	Citation	Applicable Treasury Explanations or Treasury Decision (T.D.)
Australia	TIAS 10773	Dec. 1, 1983	1986-2 C.B. 220	1986-2 C.B. 246
Protocol	TIAS	Jan. 1, 2004		
Austria	TIAS	Jan. 1, 1999		
Bangladesh	TIAS	Jan. 1, 2007		
Barbados	TIAS 11090	Jan. 1, 1984	1991-2 C.B. 436	1991-2 C.B. 466
Protocol	TIAS	Jan. 1, 2005		
Belgium	TIAS	Jan. 1, 2008		
Bulgaria	TIAS	Jan. 1, 2009		
Canada[2]	TIAS 11087	Jan. 1, 1985	1986-2 C.B. 258	1987-2 C.B. 298
Protocol	TIAS	Jan. 1, 2009		
China, People's Republic of	TIAS 12065	Jan. 1, 1987	1988-1 C.B. 414	1988-1 C.B. 447
Commonwealth of Independent States[3]	TIAS 8225	Jan. 1, 1976	1976-2 C.B. 463	1976-2 C.B. 475
Cyprus	TIAS 10965	Jan. 1, 1986	1989-2 C.B. 280	1989-2 C.B. 314
Czech Republic	TIAS	Jan. 1, 1993		
Denmark	TIAS	Jan. 1, 2001		
Protocol	TIAS	Jan. 1, 2008		
Egypt	TIAS 10149	Jan. 1, 1982	1982-1 C.B. 219	1982-1 C.B. 243
Estonia	TIAS	Jan. 1, 2000		
Finland	TIAS 12101	Jan. 1, 1991		
Protocol	TIAS	Jan. 1, 2008		
France	TIAS	Jan. 1, 1996		
Protocol	TIAS	Jan. 1, 2009		
Germany	TIAS	Jan. 1, 1990		
Protocol	TIAS	Jan. 1, 2008		
Greece	TIAS 2902	Jan. 1, 1953	1958-2 C.B. 1054	T.D. 6109, 1954-2 C.B. 638
Hungary	TIAS 9560	Jan. 1, 1980	1980-1 C.B. 333	1980-1 C.B. 354
Iceland	TIAS	Jan. 1, 2009		
India	TIAS	Jan. 1, 1991		
Indonesia	TIAS 11593	Jan. 1, 1990		
Ireland	TIAS	Jan. 1, 1998		
Israel	TIAS	Jan. 1, 1995		
Italy	TIAS	Jan. 1, 2010		
Jamaica	TIAS 10207	Jan. 1, 1982	1982-1 C.B. 257	1982-1 C.B. 291
Japan	TIAS	Jan. 1, 2005		
Kazakhstan	TIAS	Jan. 1, 1996		
Korea, Republic of	TIAS 9506	Jan. 1, 1980	1979-2 C.B. 435	1979-2 C.B. 458
Latvia	TIAS	Jan. 1, 2000		
Lithuania	TIAS	Jan. 1, 2000		
Luxembourg	TIAS	Jan. 1, 2001		
Malta	TIAS	Jan. 1, 2011		
Mexico	TIAS	Jan. 1, 1994		
Protocol	TIAS	Jan. 1, 2004		
Morocco	TIAS 10195	Jan. 1, 1981	1982-2 C.B. 405	1982-2 C.B. 427
Netherlands	TIAS	Jan. 1, 1994		
Protocol	TIAS	Jan. 1, 2005		
New Zealand	TIAS 10772	Nov. 2, 1983	1990-2 C.B. 274	1990-2 C.B. 303
Protocol	TIAS	Jan. 1, 2011		
Norway	TIAS 7474	Jan. 1, 1971	1973-1 C.B. 669	1973-1 C.B. 693
Protocol	TIAS 10205	Jan. 1, 1982	1982-2 C.B. 440	1982-2 C.B. 454

¶1305

Table 3. (continued)

Country	Official Text Symbol[1]	General Effective Date	Citation	Applicable Treasury Explanations or Treasury Decision (T.D.)
Pakistan	TIAS 4232	Jan. 1, 1959	1960-2 C.B. 646	T.D. 6431, 1960-1 C.B. 755
Philippines	TIAS 10417	Jan. 1, 1983	1984-2 C.B. 384	1984-2 C.B. 412
Poland	TIAS 8486	Jan. 1, 1974	1977-1 C.B. 416	1977-1 C.B. 427
Portugal	TIAS	Jan. 1, 1996		
Romania	TIAS 8228	Jan. 1, 1974	1976-2 C.B. 492	1976-2 C.B. 504
Russia	TIAS	Jan. 1, 1994		
Slovak Republic	TIAS	Jan. 1, 1993		
Slovenia	TIAS	Jan. 1, 2002		
South Africa	TIAS	Jan. 1, 1998		
Spain	TIAS	Jan. 1, 1991		
Sri Lanka	TIAS	Jan. 1, 2004		
Sweden	TIAS	Jan. 1, 1996		
Protocol	TIAS	Jan. 1, 2007		
Switzerland	TIAS	Jan. 1, 1998		
Thailand	TIAS	Jan. 1, 1998		
Trinidad and Tobago	TIAS 7047	Jan. 1, 1970	1971-2 C.B. 479	
Tunisia	TIAS	Jan. 1, 1990		
Turkey	TIAS	Jan. 1, 1998		
Ukraine	TIAS	Jan. 1, 2001		
United Kingdom	TIAS	Jan. 1, 2004		
Venezuela	TIAS	Jan. 1, 2000		

[1] (TIAS) — Treaties and Other International Act Series.
[2] Information on the treaty can be found in Publication 597, *Information on the United States-Canada Income Tax Treaty.*
[3] The U.S.-U.S.S.R. income tax treaty applies to the countries of Armenia, Azerbaijan, Belarus, Georgia, Kyrgyzstan, Moldova, Tajikistan, Turkmenistan, and Uzbekistan.

How To Get Tax Help

You can get help with unresolved tax issues, order free publications and forms, ask tax questions, and get information from the IRS in several ways. By selecting the method that is best for you, you will have quick and easy access to tax help.

Contacting your Taxpayer Advocate. The Taxpayer Advocate Service (TAS) is an independent organization within the IRS. We help taxpayers who are experiencing economic harm, such as not being able to provide necessities like housing, transportation, or food; taxpayers who are seeking help in resolving tax problems with the IRS; and those who believe that an IRS system or procedure is not working as it should. Here are seven things every taxpayer should know about TAS:

- The Taxpayer Advocate Service is your voice at the IRS.

- Our service is free, confidential, and tailored to meet your needs.

- You may be eligible for our help if you have tried to resolve your tax problem through normal IRS channels and have gotten nowhere, or you believe an IRS procedure just isn't working as it should.

- We help taxpayers whose problems are causing financial difficulty or significant cost, including the cost of professional representation. This includes businesses as well as individuals.

- Our employees know the IRS and how to navigate it. If you qualify for our help, we'll assign your case to an advocate who will listen to your problem, help you understand what needs to be done to resolve it,

and stay with you every step of the way until your problem is resolved.

- We have at least one local taxpayer advocate in every state, the District of Columbia, and Puerto Rico. You can call your local advocate, whose number is in your phone book, in Pub. 1546, Taxpayer Advocate Service — Your Voice at the IRS, and on our website at *www.irs.gov/advocate*. You can also call our toll-free line at 1-877-777-4778 or TTY/TDD 1-800-829-4059.

- You can learn about your rights and responsibilities as a taxpayer by visiting our online tax toolkit at *www.taxtoolkit.irs.gov*. You can get updates on hot tax topics by visiting our YouTube channel at *www.youtube.com/tasnta* and our Facebook page at *www.facebook.com/YourVoiceAtIRS*, or by following our tweets at *www.twitter.com/YourVoiceAtIRS*.

Low Income Taxpayer Clinics (LITCs). The Low Income Taxpayer Clinic program serves individuals who have a problem with the IRS and whose income is below a certain level. LITCs are independent from the IRS. Most LITCs can provide representation before the IRS or in court on audits, tax collection disputes, and other issues for free or a small fee. If an individual's native language is not English, some clinics can provide multilingual information about taxpayer rights and responsibilities. For more information, see Publication 4134, Low Income Taxpayer Clinic List. This publication is available at IRS.gov, by calling 1-800-TAX-FORM (1-800-829-3676), or at your local IRS office.

Free tax services. Publication 910, IRS Guide to Free Tax Services, is your guide to IRS services and resources. Learn about free tax

information from the IRS, including publications, services, and education and assistance programs. The publication also has an index of over 100 TeleTax topics (recorded tax information) you can listen to on the telephone. The majority of the information and services listed in this publication are available to you free of charge. If there is a fee associated with a resource or service, it is listed in the publication.

Accessible versions of IRS published products are available on request in a variety of alternative formats for people with disabilities.

Free help with your return. Free help in preparing your return is available nationwide from IRS-trained volunteers. The Volunteer Income Tax Assistance (VITA) program is designed to help low-income taxpayers and the Tax Counseling for the Elderly (TCE) program is designed to assist taxpayers age 60 and older with their tax returns. Many VITA sites offer free electronic filing and all volunteers will let you know about credits and deductions you may be entitled to claim. To find the nearest VITA or TCE site, call 1-800-829-1040.

As part of the TCE program, AARP offers the Tax-Aide counseling program. To find the nearest AARP Tax-Aide site, call 1-888-227-7669 or visit AARP's website at *www.aarp.org/money/taxaide*.

For more information on these programs, go to IRS.gov and enter keyword "VITA" in the upper right-hand corner.

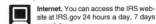 **Internet.** You can access the IRS website at IRS.gov 24 hours a day, 7 days a week to:

- *E-file* your return. Find out about commercial tax preparation and *e-file* services available free to eligible taxpayers.

- Check the status of your 2010 refund. Go to IRS.gov and click on *Where's My Refund*. Wait at least 72 hours after the IRS

¶1305

Chapter 14

Section 367—Outbound, Inbound and Foreign-to-Foreign Transfers

¶ 1401 OUTBOUND TRANSFERS OF PROPERTY TO A FOREIGN CORPORATION

.01 Outbound Toll Charge

In response to changing business conditions, U.S. corporations routinely organize new subsidiaries and merge or liquidate existing subsidiaries. These routine corporate adjustments generally are tax-free transactions, based on the principle that the transactions involve a change in the form of the corporation's investment, not the shareholders' ultimate control of the investment. For example, in a wholly-domestic context, if a domestic corporation transfers appreciated property to a newly-organized subsidiary in exchange for all of the shares of that subsidiary, the gain realized on that exchange is not recognized immediately, but is instead postponed by having the subsidiary take a carryover basis in the property received.[1] However, if the subsidiary is a foreign corporation, then the ultimate disposition of the appreciated property may occur outside the U.S. taxing jurisdiction. As a consequence, transfers of appreciated property to a foreign corporation may represent the U.S. Treasury's last opportunity for taxing the appreciation.

> ***Example 14.1:*** During the current year, USAco (a domestic corporation) organizes EURco, a distribution subsidiary incorporated in a foreign country. USAco then transfers inventory, which has a basis of $1 million and a fair market value of $3 million, to EURco in exchange for all of EURco's shares. Immediately thereafter, EURco sells the inventory to local customers for $3 million. Ignoring Code Sec. 367, USAco's outbound transfer to EURco is not

---

[1] Code Secs. 351(a) and 362.

subject to U.S. tax because it is part of a tax-free incorporation transaction. EURco's gain on the sale of the inventory also is not subject to U.S. taxation because the United States generally does not tax the foreign-source income of foreign corporations. In sum, the $2 million gain is not subject to U.S. tax at either the foreign corporation or the U.S. shareholder level.

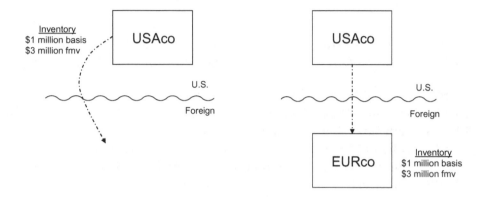

Code Sec. 367 closes this loophole by requiring a U.S. person transferring appreciated property to a foreign corporation to recognize a gain on the transfer. This result is achieved by denying the foreign corporation corporate status,[2] in which case the general rules for taxable exchanges apply.[3]

> ***Example* 14.2:** The facts are the same as in Example 14.1, except now take into account the effects of Code Sec. 367(a). USAco's transfer of inventory to EURco in exchange for all of EURco's shares is treated as a taxable exchange. As a result, USAco recognizes a $2 million gain, which represents the excess of the value of shares received ($3 million) over USAco's basis in the inventory given ($1 million).

The outbound toll charge applies only for purposes of recognizing gains. Such gains are determined on an item-by-item basis, and without offsetting individual losses against individual gains. Transfers of property that produce losses are still generally accorded nonrecognition treatment, assuming the transaction satisfies the requirements of the applicable corporate nonrecognition provision.[4] The character and source of the gain produced by the outbound toll charge is determined as if the transferor had sold the property in a taxable transaction.[5] For example, if the outbound transfer involves inventory that the taxpayer purchased for resale, any resulting gain would be ordinary income sourced under the title passage rule applicable to inventory sales in general.[6] In a similar vein, the U.S. transferor must recapture and recognize as ordinary income any depreciation deductions claimed on depreciable property that was used in the United States.[7] Finally, the U.S.

---

[2] Code Sec. 367(a)(1).

[3] Code Sec. 1001.

[4] Temp. Reg. § 1.367(a)-IT(b)(3)(ii).

[5] Temp. Reg. § 1.367(a)-IT(b)(4)(i)(A).

[6] Reg. § 1.861-7(c).

[7] Temp. Reg. § I.367(a)-4T(b). The U.S. portion of depreciable property used both within and without the United States is determined based on the ratio of the number of months the property was used in the United States to the total number of months the property was used.

transferor's basis in any shares received in an outbound transfer equals the U.S. transferor's basis in the property transferred, increased by the amount of the gain recognized on the transfer.[8]

The types of corporate transactions governed by the Code Sec. 367(a) outbound toll charge provisions include:

(i) *Incorporations*—A U.S. person's contribution of property to a foreign corporation in exchange for shares of the foreign corporation, where immediately after the exchange, the U.S. person controls the foreign corporation.[9]

(ii) *Contributions*—A U.S. person's contributions to the capital of a foreign corporation controlled by the transferors.[10]

(iii) *Reorganizations*—A U.S. person's transfer of shares, securities, or property to a foreign corporation as part of a corporate reorganization.[11]

However, there are numerous special rules that apply to the outbound toll charge, including:

(i) *Active foreign business use exception*—The outbound toll charge does not apply to certain types of property transferred to a foreign corporation for use by that corporation in the active conduct of a trade or business located outside the United States.[12]

(ii) *Branch loss recapture rule*—A U.S. person must recognize a gain on the incorporation of a foreign branch to the extent that U.S. person has previously deducted branch losses against its other taxable income.[13]

(iii) *Deemed royalty regime for intangible property*—An outbound transfer of intangible property is treated as a sale in return for a series of payments that are both received annually over the useful life of the intangible and are contingent upon the productivity, use, or disposition of the intangible.[14]

(iv) *Transfers of stock or securities*—Outbound transfers of stock or securities are subject to special rules, which vary depending on whether the transfer involves stock or securities of a foreign versus a domestic corporation.[15]

These special rules are discussed in the following sections.

.02 Active Foreign Business Use Exception

The outbound toll charge does not apply to property transferred to a foreign corporation if the following requirements are satisfied:

---

[8] Temp. Reg. § 1.367(a)-IT(c)(3)(i)(B).

[9] Code Sec. 367(a)(1), which denies the nonrecognition treatment otherwise provided by Code Sec. 351.

[10] Code Sec. 367(c)(2).

[11] Code Sec. 367(a)(1) and (e)(1), which deny the nonrecognition treatment otherwise provided by Code Secs. 354, 355, 356, and 361.

[12] Code Sec. 367(a)(3)(A).

[13] Code Sec. 367(a)(3)(C).

[14] Code Sec. 367(d).

[15] Code Sec. 367(a)(2) and Reg. § 1.367(a)-3.

    (i) the foreign corporation actively conducts a trade or business;

    (ii) the trade or business is conducted outside the United States; and

    (iii) the foreign corporation uses the property in that trade or business.[16]

In these situations, the policy of allowing companies to make routine corporate adjustments unaffected by taxes is considered more important than the policy of taxing all appreciated property being transferred out of the U.S. taxing jurisdiction. The depreciation recapture rule discussed above still applies, however, and therefore the U.S. transferor still must recapture and recognize as ordinary income any depreciation deductions claimed on depreciable property that was used in the United States.[17]

    Whether a particular transfer satisfies the requirements of the active foreign business use exception is a question of fact.[18] In general, the active conduct of a trade or business requirement is satisfied only if the officers and employees of the transferee or the officers and employees of related entities, if supervised and paid by the transferee, carry out substantial managerial and operational activities.[19] To satisfy the requirement that the business be conducted outside the United States, the primary managerial and operational activities of the trade or business must be conducted abroad and, immediately after the transfer, substantially all of the transferred assets must be located abroad.[20]

    Special rules apply to property that the foreign transferee will lease,[21] property that is expected to be sold in the reasonably foreseeable future other than in the ordinary course of business,[22] working interests in oil and gas property,[23] and compulsory transfers.[24] In addition, certain assets are ineligible for the active foreign business use exception. These tainted assets include the following:

    (i) inventories, including raw materials and supplies, work-in-process, and finished goods,[25]

    (ii) installment obligations, accounts receivable, and similar property,[26]

    (iii) foreign currency or other property denominated in foreign currency, such as an installment obligation, forward contract, or account receivable,[27]

    (iv) intangible property,[28] and

    (v) property that the transferor is leasing at the time of the transfer, with certain exceptions.[29]

---

[16] Code Sec. 367(a)(3)(A). To qualify for this exception, the transferor also must attach Form 926, Return by Transferor of Property to a Foreign Corporation, Foreign Estate or Trust, or Foreign Partnership, to its regular tax return for the year of the transfer. Temp. Reg. § 1.367(a)-2T(a)(2) and Reg. § 1.6038B-1.

[17] Temp. Reg. § 1.367(a)-4T(b).

[18] Temp. Reg. § 1.367(a)-2T(b)(1).

[19] Temp. Reg. § 1.367(a)-2T(b)(3).

[20] Temp. Reg. § 1.367(a)-2T(b)(4).

[21] Temp. Reg. § 1.367(a)-4T(c).

[22] Temp. Reg. § 1.367(a)-4T(d).

[23] Temp. Reg. § 1.367(a)-4T(e).

[24] Temp. Reg. § 1.367(a)-4T(f).

[25] Code Sec. 367(a)(3)(B)(i) and Temp. Reg. §§ 1.367(a)-5T(b).

[26] Code Sec. 367(a)(3)(B)(ii).

[27] Code Sec. 367(a)(3)(B)(iii) and Temp. Reg. § 1.367(a)-5T(d). An exception applies to an obligation that is denominated in the currency of the transferee's country of incorporation and that was acquired in the ordinary course of the business of the transferor that will be carried on by the transferee.

[28] Code Sec. 367(a)(3)(B)(iv).

[29] Code Sec. 367(a)(3)(B)(v) and Temp. Reg. §§ 1.367(a)-5T(f) and 1.367(a)-4T(c).

Example **14.3:** During the current year, USAco (a domestic corporation) organizes MEXco, a manufacturing subsidiary incorporated in Mexico. USAco then transfers inventory and some machinery and equipment to MEXco in exchange for all of MEXco's shares. At the time of the transfer, the basis and the fair market value of the transferred assets are as follows:

	Basis	Fair Market Value
Inventory	$5 million	$7 million
Machinery and equipment	$10 million	$15 million

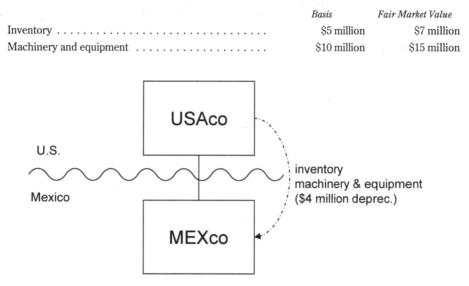

The machinery and equipment were purchased two years ago for $14 million, and USAco took $4 million of depreciation deductions on the machinery prior to the transfer. The machinery was used solely in USAco's U.S. factory.

Assuming MEXco's foreign manufacturing operation satisfies the active foreign business requirements, the outbound transfer does not trigger U.S. taxation of the $1 million of appreciation in the value over the original cost of the machinery and equipment [$15 million fair market value - $14 million original cost]. However, because USAco previously used the machinery and equipment in its U.S. factory, USAco must recognize $4 million of depreciation recapture income. The inventory is a tainted asset and, therefore, USAco must recognize $2 million of gross income [$7 million market value - $5 million basis] on its transfer. In sum, USAco must recognize $6 million of income on the incorporation of MEXco.

The active foreign business use exception will not apply if, at the time the property is transferred, it is reasonably believed that the transferee foreign corporation will soon dispose of the transferred property other than in the ordinary course of business. If the transferee foreign corporation transfers the property to another person as part of the same transaction, the active foreign business use exception will not apply to the initial transfer. Furthermore, any subsequent transfers to a third party in the next six months are presumed to be part of the initial transfer. A

¶1401.02

facts and circumstances test applies to subsequent transfers that occur more than six months after the original transfer.[30]

Example 14.4: USAco, a domestic corporation, organizes CANco, a manufacturing subsidiary incorporated in Canada. USAco transfers machinery purchased last month to CANco in exchange for all of CANco's shares. At the time of the transfer the machinery had a basis of $30 million and a fair market value of $32 million. The machinery was purchased this year for $30 million and has jumped in value due to its suitability for use in the suddenly lucrative oil and gas industry. The machinery has been used solely in USAco's U.S. refinery.

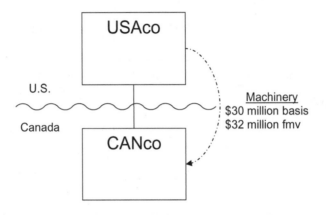

Assuming CANco's foreign manufacturing operations satisfies the active foreign business use exception, the outbound transfer does not trigger the U.S. taxation of the $2 million of appreciation in the value of the machinery [$32 million fair market value minus the $30 million basis]. However, if three months later CANco transfers the machinery to a third party, the subsequent transfer is presumed to be part of the initial transfer and USAco would recognize the $2 million gain. If such a subsequent transfer occurred seven months later, which is more than six months after the initial transfer, a facts and circumstances test would apply to determine whether the subsequent transfer was part of the initial transfer.

In the case of an outbound transfer of assets that is part of a reorganization transaction (e.g., a domestic corporation transferring its assets to a foreign corporation as part of a statutory merger), the active foreign business use exception[31] does not apply unless the U.S. transferor corporation is 80 percent or more owned by five or fewer domestic corporations.[32]

.03 Branch Loss Recapture Rule

A major exception to the active foreign business use exception is the branch loss recapture rule. Under the branch loss recapture rule, a U.S. person must

---

[30] Temp. Reg. § 1.367(a)-2T(c)(1).

[31] Code Sec. 367(a)(3).

[32] Code Sec. 367(a)(5).

recognize gain on the incorporation of a foreign branch to the extent the U.S. person has previously deducted branch losses against its other taxable income. The recaptured income is treated as foreign-source income that has the same character as the related branch losses.[33] The policy behind the branch loss recapture rule is to prevent flowing through losses from a foreign branch before incorporating the foreign branch as a foreign corporation when profits are imminent.

Example **14.5:** Two years ago, USAco (a domestic corporation) established a foreign branch. During its first two years of operations, the branch lost $5 million, which USAco deducted against its other taxable income. If USAco were to incorporate the branch as FORco, USAco may have to recognize $5 million of branch loss recapture income.

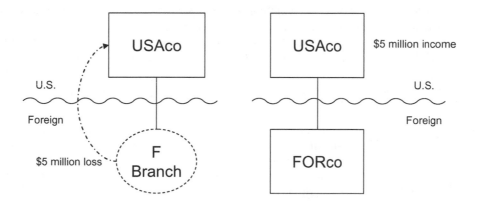

It is not necessary to recapture pre-incorporation losses to the extent those losses are either offset by items of branch income or did not provide the taxpayer with a U.S. tax benefit. Therefore, the pre-incorporation losses are reduced by the following amounts:

(i) any taxable income of the branch recognized prior to incorporation,[34]

(ii) the amount of any foreign-source income that the taxpayer had to recharacterize as U.S.-source in the current or a prior taxable year by reason of the overall foreign loss recapture provisions of the foreign tax credit limitation,[35]

(iii) any gain recognized on the transfer of the branch's appreciated property to the newly organized foreign corporation,[36]

(iv) any branch losses that were part of an expired net operating loss or capital loss carryforward,[37] and

---

[33] Code Sec. 367(a)(3)(C).

[34] Temp. Reg. § 1.367(a)-6T(e)(2).

[35] Temp. Reg. § 1.367(a)-6T(e)(3) and (e)(5). *See* Code Sec. 904(f)(3) regarding the computation of the foreign loss recapture amount. *See also* the discussion of overall foreign losses in Chapter 4 (¶ 406).

[36] Temp. Reg. § 1.367(a)-6T(e)(4). Special rules apply for purposes of computing the creditable gain with respect to intangible property. Temp. Reg. § 1.367(d)-1T(g)(3).

[37] Temp. Reg. §§ 1.367(a)-6T(d)(2) and (d)(3).

¶1401.03

(v) the taxable income equivalent amount of any foreign tax credit carryforwards that expired by reason of the foreign tax credit limitation.[38]

After taking into account these reductions, the remaining branch loss recapture income is further limited to the amount of gain that the taxpayer would have recognized on a taxable sale of the transferred property if each item was sold separately and without offsetting individual losses against individual gains.[39]

.04 Deemed Royalty Regime for Intangible Property

The market value of patents, trademarks, and other intangibles often is highly uncertain, due to the inherent uniqueness of these assets. This uncertainty significantly weakens the deterrent effect of a one-time toll charge imposed at the time of the transfer, since new technologies and products can turn out to be far more successful than originally anticipated. As a consequence, a special deemed royalty regime for intangibles treats an outbound transfer of an intangible as a sale in return for a series of payments that are received annually over the useful life of the intangible and that are contingent on the productivity, use, or disposition of the intangible (similar to a royalty) and are sourced by the location of the intangible's use.[40] This income is characterized as a royalty for purposes of the foreign tax credit limitation.[41]

Example **14.6:** USAco (a domestic corporation) incorporates ASIAco, a manufacturing subsidiary incorporated in a foreign country by transferring a patent to ASIAco in exchange for all of ASIAco's shares. USAco had a zero basis in the patent because it had deducted the related research and development expenditures as these expenditures were incurred.[42]

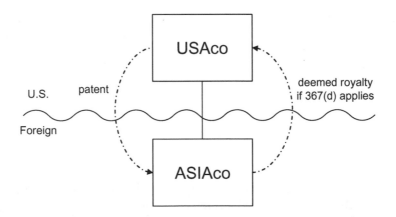

Ignoring Code Sec. 367(d), USAco's outbound transfer to ASIAco is not subject to U.S. tax because it is part of a tax-free incorporation transaction.[43]

---

[38] Temp. Reg. § 1.367(a)-6T(d)(4).

[39] Temp. Reg. §§ 1.367(a)-6T(c)(2) and 1.367(a)-1T(b)(3)(i). Any gain realized on the transfer of foreign goodwill and going concern value is taken into account for purposes of computing this limitation. Temp. Reg. § 1.367(a)-6T(c)(3).

[40] Code Sec. 367(d).

[41] Code Sec. 367(d)(2)(C).

[42] Code Sec. 174.

[43] Code Sec. 351(a).

However, Code Sec. 367(d) recharacterizes the transaction as a sale in return for foreign-source royalty payments received annually over the life of the patent.

The deemed royalty regime applies to a U.S. person's transfer of intangible property to a foreign corporation in exchange for shares of the foreign corporation as part of an incorporation or reorganization transaction.[44] However, the deemed royalty regime does not apply to a domestic subsidiary corporation's distribution of intangible property in complete liquidation to its foreign parent corporation.[45] In addition, a limited exception to the deemed royalty regime is available for transfers of certain operating intangibles (e.g., supply contracts or customer lists) if the U.S. transferor elects to recognize, in the year of the transfer, U.S.-source ordinary income equal to the excess of the intangible's fair market value over its basis.[46]

For purposes of the deemed royalty regime, intangible property includes any patent, invention, formula, process, design, pattern, know-how, copyright, literary, musical, or artistic composition, trademark, trade name, brand name, franchise, license, contract, method, program, system, procedure, campaign, survey, study, forecast, estimate, customer list, technical data, or other similar item.[47] However, foreign goodwill and going concern value are specifically exempted from the deemed royalty requirement[48] and can be transferred to a foreign corporation tax-free as long as the requirements of the active business use exception are satisfied.

The deemed royalty must be an arm's-length amount consistent with the provisions of Code Sec. 482 and the Regulations thereunder.[49] The deemed royalty amount also must be "commensurate with the income attributable to the intangible."[50] In other words, the royalty amounts must reflect the actual profit experience realized subsequent to the outbound transfer. To meet this requirement, the royalty amount must be adjusted annually to reflect any unanticipated changes in the income actually generated by the intangible.[51] For example, if a new patent leads to a product that turns out to be far more successful than was expected at the time the patent was transferred, the taxpayer must increase the amount of the deemed royalty amount to reflect that unanticipated profitability. If, subsequent to the transfer, the foreign transferee disposes of the intangible to an unrelated person, the U.S. transferor must recognize a gain equal to the excess of the intangible's fair market value on the date of the subsequent disposition over its basis on the date of the initial transfer.[52]

[44] Code Sec. 367(d)(1).

[45] However, such transfers generally are subject to the outbound toll charge that governs tangible property. Temp. Reg. § 1.367(a)-5T(e).

[46] Temp. Reg. § 1.367(d)-1T(g)(2).

[47] Code Sec. 367(d)(1) and 936(h)(3)(B).

[48] Temp. Reg. § 1.367(d)-1T(b). A copyright, literary, musical, or artistic composition transferred by the taxpayer whose personal efforts created the property also is exempted from the deemed royalty requirement, but is subject to the outbound toll charge of Code Sec.

367(a)(1). Temp. Reg. §§ 1.367(d)-1T(b) and 1.367(a)-5T(b)(2).

[49] Temp. Reg. § 1.367(d)-1T(c)(1). See Chapter 12 (¶ 1201) for a discussion of transfer pricing methods for intangible property.

[50] Code Sec. 367(d)(2)(A).

[51] Reg. § 1.482-4(f)(2)(i).

[52] Temp. Reg. § 1.367(d)-1T(f). Special rules also apply if, subsequent to the initial transfer of the intangible, the U.S. transferor disposes of the shares of the foreign corporation before the intangible's useful life expires. Temp. Reg. § 1.367(d)-1T(d) and (e).

¶1401.04

To prevent double taxation of the foreign transferee's income, the foreign transferee reduces its earnings and profits by the amount of the deemed royalty amount included in the income of the U.S. transferor. In addition, the deemed royalty is treated as an expense properly allocable to the transferee's gross Subpart F income.[53] The U.S. transferor can establish an account receivable for the deemed royalty amount, in which case any royalty actually paid by the foreign transferee with respect to the intangible is treated as a tax-free payment on account.[54]

In light of the deemed royalty regime, a taxpayer may find it advantageous to structure the transfer of intangible property to a foreign corporation as an actual licensing agreement. One advantage of an actual license is that the foreign transferee ordinarily can deduct an actual royalty payment for foreign tax purposes, whereas the deemed royalty amount is generally not deductible. One potential disadvantage of an actual licensing agreement is that the royalty payments may be subject to foreign withholding taxes, although tax treaties often reduce or exempt the withholding. Even under an actual license, the U.S. transferor still must adjust its royalty income annually to reflect any unanticipated changes in the income actually generated by the intangible.[55]

The deemed royalty regime extends to a partnership's transfer of intangible property. Accordingly, such a transfer will be treated as a sale that generates deemed royalty payments from the foreign transferee to each partner based on the partner's percentage ownership of the partnership.[56] Such payments are considered to be royalty income, must be established on an arm's length basis, and must be commensurate with the annual income attributable to the intangible.

.05 Liquidation of a Domestic Subsidiary into Its Foreign Parent

Under general U.S. tax principles, the complete liquidation of a corporation is a taxable transaction for both the corporation distributing the assets and the shareholders receiving those assets.[57] An exception applies to the liquidation of an 80 percent or more owned subsidiary corporation liquidates into its parent corporation, which is tax-free to both parties.[58] This exception is based, in part, on the premise that any appreciated property not taxed at the time of the liquidation will be subject to corporate-level U.S. taxation when the surviving parent corporation disposes of the property. However, if a domestic subsidiary is liquidating into its foreign parent, the liquidating distribution may represent the U.S. Treasury's last opportunity for taxing appreciation that occurred within the U.S. taxing jurisdiction. As a consequence, the domestic subsidiary must recognize a gain equal to the excess of the distributed property's fair market value over its basis.[59]

---

[53] Temp. Reg. § 1.367(d)-1T(c)(2)(ii).

[54] Temp. Reg. § 1.367(d)-1T(g)(1)(i). If no actual payments are made by the last day of the third taxable year following the year in which the account was established, the account receivable is recharacterized as a contribution to the capital of the foreign corporation, which increases the U.S. transferor's basis in the shares of that foreign corporation. Temp. Reg. § 1.367(d)-1T(g)(1)(ii).

[55] Reg. § 1.482-4(f)(2)(i).

[56] Temp. Reg. § 1.367(a)-IT(c)(3).

[57] The corporation recognizes a gain equal to the excess of the market value of the property distributed over its basis in that property (Code Sec. 336(a)) and the shareholders recognize a gain equal to the excess of the fair market value of the property received over their basis in the corporation's shares (Code Sec. 331(a)).

[58] Code Secs. 332 and 337.

[59] Code Sec. 367(e)(2) and Reg. § 1.367(e)-2(b)(1)(i). Code Sec. 367(a)(1) does not apply to such a liquidation. Reg. § 1.367(e)-2(a)(2).

***Example* 14.7:** FParent, a corporation incorporated in a foreign country, owns all the shares of USSub, a domestic corporation. USSub's assets have a basis of $5 million and a fair market value of $7 million. Despite the profitability of USSub, FParent desires to liquidate USSub to eliminate this business in a manner that is consistent with FParent's world-wide business plan. As a result, FParent liquidates USSub.

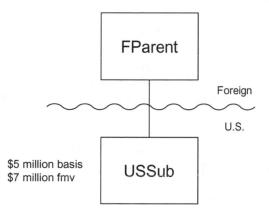

Because this is the last opportunity for the $2 million of appreciation of USSub's assets to be taxed, USSub must recognize $2 million of gain.

Various rules mitigate the effects of the outbound toll charge imposed on the complete liquidation of a domestic subsidiary corporation. First, to the extent the liquidating subsidiary must recognize gains on appreciated property, the liquidating subsidiary also may recognize offsetting losses on depreciated property.[60] Second, the basis of the property distributed to the foreign parent equals the basis of the property in the hands of the domestic subsidiary, increased by the amount of net gain, if any, recognized by the liquidating subsidiary.[61] Finally, the outbound toll charge does not apply to property that remains for use within the United States even though it is now held by a foreign corporation. This U.S.-use exception to the outbound toll charge covers U.S. real property interests, other than shares in a former U.S. real property holding corporation.[62] This U.S.-use exception also covers property used by the foreign corporation in the conduct of a U.S. trade or business, but only if the following requirements are satisfied:

   (i) the foreign corporation is not a CFC,

   (ii) the foreign corporation continues to use the property in the conduct of a U.S. trade or business for 10 years after the distribution (or, in the case of inventory, until the property is disposed), and

---

[60] Reg. §1.367(e)-2(b)(1)(ii). However, losses cannot be recognized on property that the distributing corporation acquired in a nontaxable exchange within five years before the date of liquidation.

[61] Reg. §1.367(e)-2(b)(3)(i).

[62] Reg. §1.367(e)-2(b)(2)(ii). A foreign person's gain on the disposition of a U.S. real property interest is taxed in the same manner as income effectively connected with the conduct of a U.S. trade or business. Code Sec. 897(a)(1).

(iii) the liquidating subsidiary and the foreign corporation file a gain recognition agreement whereby an amended tax return must be filed and back taxes plus interest paid, if requirement (ii) is not satisfied.[63]

.06 Information Reporting for Outbound Transfers

To help the IRS better police outbound transfers, a U.S. person who transfers property to a foreign corporation must attach Form 926, Return by Transferor of Property to a Foreign Corporation, to their regular tax return for the year of the transfer.[64] (A completed Form 926 is reproduced in the Appendix to this chapter.) This reporting requirement applies to outbound transfers of both tangible and intangible property. The penalty for a failure of a U.S. person to properly report a transfer to a foreign corporation equals 10% of the fair market value of the property transferred. However, the penalty does not apply if the U.S. person can show that the failure to comply was due to reasonable cause and not due to willful neglect. Moreover, the total penalty cannot exceed $100,000 unless the failure is due to an intentional disregard of the reporting requirements.[65]

.07 Transfers to Non-Corporate Foreign Entities

If a U.S. person contributes appreciated property to a foreign partnership, the U.S. person will be allocated any gain when the foreign partnership disposes of that appreciated property.[66] In the case of foreign trusts and estates, any transfer of property by a U.S. person to a foreign trust or estate is taxable as a sale or exchange of the property for its fair market value except to the extent provided by regulations.[67] The U.S. person must recognize gain equal to the excess of the property's fair market value over its basis. The gain recognition rule does not apply if the U.S. person is considered to be the owner of the trust under the grantor trust rules.[68]

¶ 1402 INBOUND LIQUIDATION OF A FOREIGN SUBSIDIARY INTO ITS DOMESTIC PARENT

Under general U.S. tax principles, the complete liquidation of a corporation is a taxable transaction for both the corporation distributing the assets and the shareholders receiving those assets.[69] An exception applies to the liquidation of an 80% or more owned subsidiary corporation into its parent corporation, which is tax-free to both parties.[70] This exception is based, in part, on the premise that the United States has already taxed the distributed earnings when they were derived by the subsidiary corporation. This assumption does not hold true, however, with respect to the foreign earnings of a foreign corporation. As a consequence, an inbound liquidating distribution of a foreign subsidiary may represent the U.S. Treasury's only opportunity for subjecting those foreign earnings to the corporate-level U.S. tax.

---

[63] Temp. Reg. § 1.367(e)-2T(b)(2)(i)(B). This exception does not apply to intangible property described in Code Sec. 936(h)(3)(B).

[64] Reg. § 1.6038B-IT(b)(i).

[65] Code Sec. 6038B(c) and Reg. § 1.6038B-1(f).

[66] Code Sec. 704(c). Code Sec. 721(c) empowers the Treasury Department to write regulations dealing with an outbound transfer to a foreign partnership, but the Treasury Department has not written any regulations.

[67] Reg. § 1.864-3.

[68] Code Sec. 684(a).

[69] The corporation recognizes a gain equal to the excess of the fair market value of the property distributed over its basis in that property (Code Sec. 336(a)) and the shareholders recognize a gain equal to the excess of the fair market value of the property received over their basis in the corporation's shares (Code Sec. 331(a)).

[70] Code Secs. 332 and 337.

Example **14.8:** Several years ago, USAco (a domestic corporation) organized AFRIco, a wholly owned subsidiary incorporated in a foreign country. Since its inception, AFRIco has derived $50 million of earnings and profits from foreign manufacturing activities. None of these foreign earnings have been taxed to USAco as a Subpart F inclusion, nor have any of AFRIco's earnings been distributed to USAco as a dividend. Therefore, AFRIco's earnings have not yet been subjected to U.S. taxation at either the foreign subsidiary or domestic parent corporation level. At the end of the current year, AFRIco distributes all of its assets to USAco in complete liquidation.

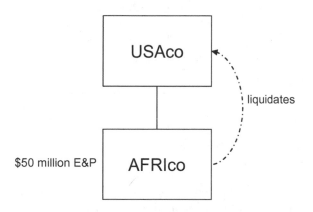

Ignoring Code Sec. 367(b), AFRIco's inbound repatriating liquidation is not subject to U.S. tax because liquidation is part of a tax-free parent-subsidiary liquidation. As a consequence, the $50 million of earnings derived by AFRIco and then transferred to USAco would escape U.S. tax at both the foreign subsidiary and domestic parent corporation levels.

To prevent this result, Code Sec. 367(b) provides that a domestic parent corporation receiving a liquidating distribution from an 80% or more owned foreign subsidiary corporation must include in income all of the subsidiary's earnings and profits attributable to the parent's ownership interest in the liquidating subsidiary.[71] Any gain in excess of the foreign subsidiary's earnings and profits is accorded tax-free treatment.[72] The inclusion in income of a foreign subsidiary's earnings and profits is treated as a cash dividend[73] and, therefore, the domestic parent corporation can claim a deemed paid foreign tax credit for the foreign income taxes related to those earnings and profits.[74] However, the domestic parent corporation does not receive a step-up in basis for the dividend income recognized on the liquidation and takes a carryover basis in the property received in liquidation.[75]

---

[71] Reg. § 1.367(b)-3(b)(3)(i). *See* Reg. § 1.367(b)-2(d) for a definition of earnings and profits for this purpose.

[72] Reg. § 1.367(b)-3(b)(3)(ii)(Exs. 1 and 2) and Code Sec. 332.

[73] Reg. § 1.367(b)-3(b)(3)(i).

[74] Reg. § 1.367(b)-2(e)(4)(Ex. 1) and Code Sec. 902(a).

[75] Reg. § 1.367(b)-3(b)(3)(ii)(Ex. 2) and Code Sec. 334(b).

Example **14.9:** Several years ago, USAco (a domestic corporation) organized FORco, a wholly owned subsidiary incorporated in a foreign country. At the end of the current year, FORco distributes all of its assets to USAco as part of a complete liquidation. On the date of the liquidation, FORco had $3 million of earnings and profits and $1 million of foreign income taxes that have not yet been deemed paid by USAco. Assume the U.S. corporate tax rate is 35%.

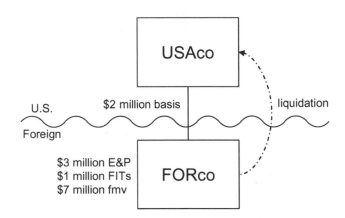

Pursuant to Code Sec. 367(b), USAco recognizes a dividend equal to FORco's earnings and profits of $3 million. Moreover, the $3 million dividend income will carry with it $1 million of deemed paid foreign taxes. Therefore, the pre-credit U.S. tax on the liquidation is $1.4 million [35% U.S. tax rate × ($3 million deemed dividend plus $1 million gross-up)], the deemed paid credit is $1 million, and will reduce USAco's pre-credit U.S. tax of $1.4 million to $400,000. USAco will take a carryover basis in the assets distributed.

¶ 1403 ACQUISITIVE REORGANIZATIONS—BACKGROUND

The acquisition by one corporation of a controlling interest in the stock of another corporation is generally a taxable event. The shareholders of the target corporation recognize gain or loss on the stock sale,[76] and the acquiring corporation takes a basis equal to the amount of cash, debt financing or other consideration paid for the stock.[77] Likewise, the acquisition of a target corporation's assets is generally a taxable event, with the target recognizing corporate-level gains and losses on the asset sale and the acquiring corporation taking a basis equal to market value. If the acquiring corporation uses its own stock as consideration in the stock or asset acquisition, however, the acquisition may qualify as a nontaxable reorganization. The common types of acquisitive reorganizations include the following transactions:

    (i) a statutory merger ("Type A") which may now include foreign corporations;[78]

---

[76] Code Sec. 1001.
[77] Code Sec. 1012.

[78] Code Sec. 368(a)(1)(A); Reg. § 1.368-2(b)(1)((iii)(Ex. 13).

  (ii) an exchange of the shares of the acquiring corporation for the shares of the target corporation ("share-for-share acquisitions," also known as "Type B");[79]

  (iii) an exchange of the shares of the acquiring corporation for the assets of the target corporation ("share-for-asset acquisitions," also known as "Type C");[80]

  (iv) forward triangular mergers;[81] and

  (v) reverse triangular mergers.[82]

Each transaction type must satisfy certain statutory requirements (which vary by transaction type) to qualify as a nontaxable reorganization. Furthermore, any reorganization must satisfy four non-statutory requirements: (1) a continuity of interest requirement; (2) a continuity of business enterprise requirement; (3) a business purpose requirement; and (4) a plan of reorganization requirement.

A transaction that fails to qualify as one of these acquisitive reorganization types is often referred to as a "failed reorganization" and results in a taxable transaction.

These acquisitive reorganizations will not result in U.S. tax to the target corporation's foreign shareholders.[83] Any gain to the foreign shareholders would be foreign-source income (see ¶ 302.06) of a foreign person.

¶ 1404 OUTBOUND TRANSFERS IN AN ACQUISITIVE REORGANIZATION

This section provides a brief introduction to how the United States taxes outbound transfers to a foreign corporation in a transaction that qualifies as a nontaxable acquisitive reorganization, including a Type A statutory merger, Type B share-for-share acquisition, Type C share-for-asset acquisition, forward triangular merger or reverse triangular merger. In general, a transfer of stock or securities by a U.S. person to a foreign corporation in an otherwise nontaxable reorganization is recast as a taxable exchange by Code Sec. 367(a)(1).[84] A limited-interest exception applies, however, if certain requirements are met. The limited-interest exception is based on the premise that when the U.S. persons who are shareholders of the target corporation receive a minority stake in the acquiring foreign corporation, the outbound toll charge should not apply because there is little chance of avoiding U.S. tax. In the case of an outbound transfer of stock or securities of a domestic corporation, the limited-interest exception applies if the following five requirements are met:[85]

  (i) The U.S. transferors receive 50% or less of the shares of the transferee foreign corporation in the exchange;

---

[79] Code Sec. 368(a)(1)(B).

[80] Code Sec. 368(a)(1)(C).

[81] Code Sec. 368(a)(2)(D).

[82] Code Sec. 368(a)(2)(E).

[83] An exception that would result in tax would occur if the target corporation were a U.S. real property holding corporation under the FIRPTA provisions (¶ 904.02).

[84] Reg. § 1.367(a)-3(a).

[85] Reg. § 1.367(a)-3(c). The exception for outbound transfers of stock of a foreign corporation is found in Reg. § 1.367(a)-3(b).

(ii) There is not a control group of U.S. persons with respect to the transferee foreign corporation immediately after the transfer. Under this control group test, U.S. officers, U.S. directors and 5% or greater shareholders of the domestic corporation may not, in the aggregate, own more than 50% of the voting power or value of the transferee foreign corporation immediately after the transfer;

(iii) The transaction satisfies the active trade or business test, which is comprised of two parts, both of which must be satisfied:

- The transferee foreign corporation has engaged in an active trade or business outside the United States for 36 months; and

- At the time of the exchange, neither the transferors nor the transferee foreign corporation intend to discontinue or dispose of the trade or business.

(iv) A U.S. transferor who owns 5% or more of the transferee foreign corporation immediately after the exchange must enter into a five-year gain recognition agreement. Under the gain recognition agreement, the U.S. transferor must recognize any gain deferred on the initial transfer if the transferee foreign corporation disposes of the transferred shares within five years; and

(v) The value of the transferee foreign corporation is, at the time of the exchange, equal to or greater than the value of the domestic corporation.

Example **14.10:** Skipper, a U.S. citizen, wholly-owns and is the only officer of USMinnow, a domestic corporation in the cruise business. In what would otherwise constitute a nontaxable Type B share-for-share acquisition, Skipper exchanges 100% of his shares of USMinnow for 3% of the voting shares of CANwhale, a Canadian corporation, which has operated a cruise business specializing in three-hour tours for years and hopes to continue to do so.

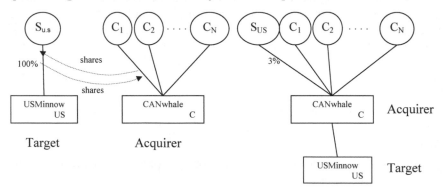

Skipper, who wants to stay in the cruise business, does not recognize gain as a result of satisfying the limited-interest exception as follows:

(i) Skipper receives 50% or less of CANwhale (only 3%);

(ii) As the only shareholder, officer or 5% shareholder of USMinnow, Skipper does not own more than 50% of CANwhale, the transferee foreign corporation, immediately after the transfer (Skipper only owns 3%);

(iii) CANwhale has operated for more than 36 months and neither Skipper nor CANwhale intends to discontinue or dispose of CANwhale's trade or business;

(iv) By acquiring only 3% of CANwhale, Skipper does not need to enter a gain recognition agreement. However, if Skipper acquires between 5% and 50% of CANwhale, he would have to file a five-year gain recognition agreement; and

(v) Considering that CANwhale is a substantially larger company than USMinnow, the value of the transferee foreign corporation is, at the time of the exchange, greater than the value of the domestic corporation.

.01 Outbound Type A Statutory Merger

To qualify as a nontaxable Type A merger, the merger must be pursuant to the corporate laws of the United States, a State, or the District of Columbia[86] and may occur with foreign corporations.[87]

> ***Example* 14.11:** Assume that U.S. Target merges with and into Foreign Acquiror. Further assume that U.S. Target's shares are worth $1 million at the time of the merger and that U.S. Target's U.S. shareholders have $100,000 of basis in their U.S. Target shares and that the U.S. Target shareholders receive Foreign Acquiror shares with a fair market value of $1 million.

> Although the merger occurs with a foreign corporation, the merger qualifies as a Type A merger. Pursuant to the Code Sec. 367(a) outbound toll charge, gain recognition would result by treating Foreign Acquiror as if it were not a corporation. Therefore, unless the limited-interest exception applies, U.S. Target's U.S. shareholders should recognize gain of $900,000 (the $1 million fair market value of Foreign Acquiror's shares less the $100,000 basis in their shares of U.S. Target).

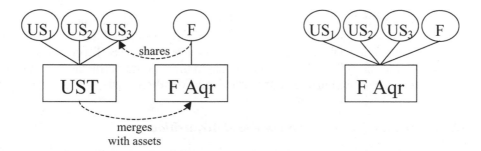

A merger that does not qualify as a Type A merger is taxed as a taxable transfer of the target corporation's assets and liabilities to the acquiring corporation

---

[86] Reg. § 1.368-2(d)(1).

[87] Reg. § 1.368-2(b)(1)(iii)(Ex. 13).

in exchange for the merger consideration, followed by a liquidation of the target corporation.

.02 Outbound Type B Share-For-Share Acquisitions

A Type B share-for-share acquisition is nontaxable as long as there is no consideration other than the voting shares and the acquiring corporation has control of the target corporation immediately after the transaction. The outbound toll charge would apply to treat the foreign corporation as if it were not a corporation and, therefore, result in gain recognition, unless the limited-interest exception applies.

> ***Example* 14.12:** Assume that Foreign Acquiror wishes to acquire U.S. Target. Further assume that U.S. Target's single class of voting shares is worth $1 million. Finally, assume that Foreign Acquiror issues $1 million worth of Foreign Acquiror voting shares to U.S. Target's U.S. shareholders in exchange for their U.S. Target shares. The share exchange should qualify as a Type B acquisition. However, pursuant to the outbound toll charge, gain recognition would result by treating the Foreign Acquiror as if it were not a corporation. Unless the limited-interest exception applies, U.S. Target's U.S. shareholders should recognize gain in the amount of the fair market value of the Foreign Acquiror shares received over their basis in their U.S. Target shares.

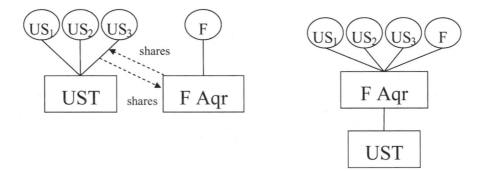

However, if Foreign Acquiror had used any cash as consideration, the solely for voting shares requirement would not be satisfied and the transaction would become a failed reorganization. Consequently, U.S. Target's U.S. shareholders would still recognize capital gain in the amount of the fair market value of the Foreign Acquiror's shares received over their basis in their U.S. target shares.

.03 Outbound Type C Share-For-Asset Acquisitions

A nontaxable Type C acquisition involves the acquisition by a corporation for all or part of its voting shares for substantially all of the properties of the target corporation and the subsequent liquidation of the target corporation. In determining whether the exchange is solely for voting shares, the acquiror's assumption of the target's liabilities is disregarded.

¶1404.02

Example **14.13:** Assume Foreign Acquiror acquires U.S. Target's assets for Foreign Acquiror voting shares. Further assume that U.S. Target subsequently distributes the Foreign Acquiror's shares to its shareholders in liquidation. As a result, the transaction should qualify as a Type C acquisition. However, the Code Sec. 367 outbound toll charge requires U.S. Target's shareholders to recognize gain unless the limited-interest exception applies. Furthermore, any intangibles transferred result in application of the deemed-royalty regime.

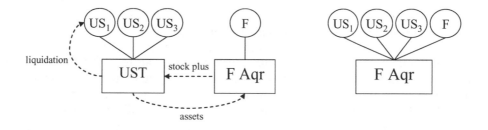

As described above, a Type C acquisition is subject to a solely for voting shares requirement, similar to Type B's solely for voting shares requirement. However, unlike the Type B acquisition rules, the Type C acquisition rules provide for a boot relaxation rule, which allows up to 20% of the consideration to take the form of non-stock consideration. If the boot relaxation rule applies, liabilities assumed are no longer ignored, but are included in the calculation as boot.

.04 Outbound Forward Triangular Mergers

A nontaxable forward triangular merger occurs when an acquiring corporation uses stock of its parent as consideration in a merger in which the target corporation merges into the acquiror, resulting in the acquiror receiving substantially all of the target's assets.[88]

Example **14.14:** Assume that Foreign Parent, a publicly traded corporation, wishes to acquire U.S. Target's business, but does not want to incur the expense of obtaining its own shareholders' approval for a straight merger with U.S. Target. As a result, Foreign Parent forms a wholly-owned subsidiary, U.S. Acquiror, for the purpose of obtaining U.S. Target's business. Finally, assume that U.S. Target merges with and into U.S. Acquiror, with U.S. Target's shareholders receiving Foreign Parent's shares as the merger consideration and with U.S. Acquiror surviving the merger. This transaction should qualify as a forward triangular merger. However, the U.S. Target's U.S. shareholders should recognize gain unless the limited-interest exception applies.

---

[88] Code Sec. 368(a)(2)(D).

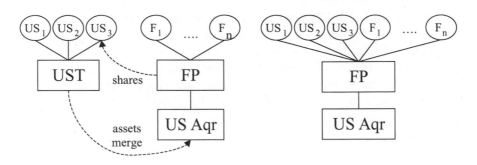

.05 Outbound Reverse Triangular Mergers

A nontaxable reverse triangular merger is similar to a forward triangular merger, except that the surviving entity is the target corporation and not the acquiror. In addition, the parent stock issued as merger consideration must be voting stock and must constitute at least 80% of the merger consideration. Moreover, after the transaction, the surviving target must hold substantially all of its own and the acquiror's properties while former shareholders of the surviving target exchange their shares for shares of the acquiror's parent.

Example **14.15:** Assume that Foreign Parent, a publicly traded-corporation, wishes to acquire U.S. Target's business, but does not want to incur the expense of obtaining its own shareholders' approval for a straight merger of Foreign Parent into U.S. Target (which must survive due to a non-transferrable contract). Further assume that Foreign Parent forms a wholly-owned subsidiary, U.S. Acquiror, as an acquisition vehicle. Finally, assume that U.S. Acquiror merges with and into U.S. Target, with U.S. Target's shareholders receiving Foreign Parent shares as the consideration and with U.S. Target surviving the merger. This merger should qualify as a taxable reverse triangular reorganization.[89] However, the U.S. Target's U.S. shareholders should recognize gain unless the limited-interest exception applies.

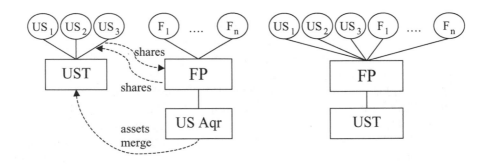

---

[89] Temp.   Reg.   § 1.367(a)-3(d)(1)(ii);   Reg. § 1.368-2(b)(1)(iii)(Ex. 13).

¶ 1405 ANTI-INVERSION PROVISIONS OF CODE SEC. 7874

As aforementioned, Congress enacted Code Sec. 367 to tax shareholders who transfer appreciated shares of U.S. corporations for shares of foreign corporations because these transfers may represent the United States' last opportunity for taxing the appreciation. Despite the fact that the rules provide for an outbound toll charge by deeming the foreign corporation not to be a corporation, beginning in the 1990s, concern arose over whether the rules were detrimental enough to discourage so-called corporate "inversion" transactions.[90]

Example **14.16:** USAco, a publicly held U.S. C corporation, owns FSub, a controlled foreign corporation. HAVENco, a foreign corporation incorporated in a tax haven, is formed and in turn forms a U.S. acquisition corporation, USAcq. In a transaction designed to be what would otherwise be a tax-free forward triangular reorganization,[91] USAco's shareholders receive 100 percent of the shares of HAVENco as USAco merges into USAcq. The resulting structure has the former USAco shareholders now owning all the shares of HAVENco. USAcq, which now operates the business of the former USAco, now owns FSub and distributes FSub's shares to HAVENco. Although USAco will not report any income on the transaction, the former shareholders of USAco should recognize capital gain to the extent that the fair market value of the HAVENco shares received exceeds their basis in the USAco shares.[92] Gain on USAcq's distribution of FSub's shares to HAVENco should be eliminated via foreign tax credits.[93]

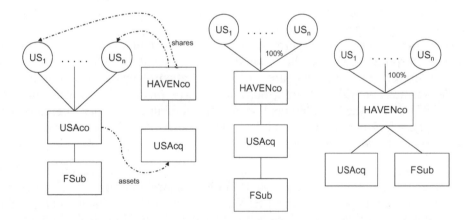

Despite the fact that the transaction results in an outbound toll charge to the former USAco shareholders, the many future tax benefits may be greater than the outbound toll charge, whose rate should be as low as 15 percent.

The USAco assets are now part of USAcq, which is still a U.S. corporation and subject to tax on its worldwide income. The former customers of USAco, who are now customers of USAcq, may not detect this change as the U.S.

---

[90] IRS Notice 94-46.
[91] Code Sec. 368(a)(2)(E).

[92] Code Sec. 367(a).
[93] Code Secs. 902 and 1248.

operations can continue to operate seamlessly. Moreover, USAcq does not own any foreign subsidiaries whose dividends will be subject to U.S. tax before repatriation to HAVENco.

Furthermore, FSub is no longer a CFC. As a result, its income should not result in an inclusion of income for U.S. tax purposes and FSub can invest in assets that produce passive income without ever having to worry about paying U.S. tax.

Finally, assuming that FSub and HAVENco are both incorporated in low-tax rate jurisdictions, there will be little corporate-level tax—United States or foreign—on the earnings of FSub.

This is classic inversion whereby the operations of a U.S. corporation become a subsidiary of a foreign parent. Other techniques by which inversions may be formed include tax-free reincorporations of U.S. corporations as foreign corporations,[94] asset inversions, and other types of share inversions.

The Anti-Inversion Rules. In 2004, Congress enacted the Code Sec. 7874 anti-inversion rules to limit the U.S. tax benefits of corporate inversions by providing different methods of taxation depending on whether the former U.S. shareholders own at least 80 percent of the new foreign corporation or at least 60 percent (but less than 80 percent) of the shares of the new foreign corporation.

More specifically, the anti-inversion rules apply if U.S. shareholders own 80 percent or more (by vote or value) of the shares of the foreign corporation as a result of the inversion transaction and both (i) the U.S. corporation either becomes a subsidiary of a foreign corporation or transfers substantially all its properties to a foreign corporation and (ii) the group does not have substantial business activities in the foreign corporation's country of incorporation compared to the total worldwide business activities of the group. In this type of inversion transaction, Code Sec. 7874 denies the intended tax benefits by deeming the top-tier foreign corporation to be a U.S. corporation for all U.S. tax purposes. A U.S. corporation is subject to tax on its worldwide income.

Example **14.17:** USAco, a publicly held U.S. C corporation, owns FSub, a controlled foreign corporation. HAVENco, a foreign corporation incorporated in a tax haven, is formed and HAVENco forms a U.S. acquisition corporation, USAcq. In a transaction designed to be what would otherwise be a nontaxable triangular merger,[95] USAco's shareholders receive 100 percent of the shares of HAVENco as USAco merges into USAcq. The resulting structure has the former USAco shareholders now owning all the shares of HAVENco. USAcq, which now operates the business of the former USAco, now owns FSub and distributes FSub's shares to HAVENco. Gain on USAcq's distribution of FSub's shares to HAVENco should be eliminated via foreign tax credits.[96]

---

[94] Code Sec. 368(a)(1)(F).
[95] Code Sec. 368(a)(2)(D).

[96] Code Secs. 902 and 1248.

¶1405

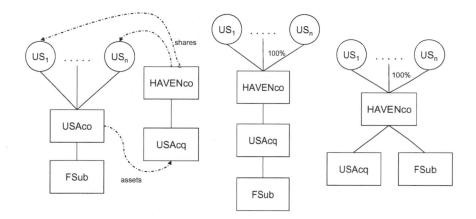

Under the anti-inversion rules, the former USAco shareholders own 80 percent or more of HAVENco and (1) USAco transfers substantially all of its property to HAVENco and (2) the group of HAVENco, USAcq, and FSub does not have substantial business activities in HAVENco's country of incorporation compared to the total worldwide business activities of the group. As a result, HAVENco is treated as if it were a U.S. corporation that will incur tax on its worldwide income (the U.S. shareholders will not have to recognize gain under the outbound toll charge). Finally, passive investment income of FSub may be Subpart F income of FSub, which was and remains a CFC.

If U.S. shareholders own at least 60 percent (but less than 80 percent), by vote or value, of the foreign corporation, Code Sec. 7874 provides that the U.S. tax on any applicable gain may not be offset by any net operating losses or foreign tax credits for ten years following the inversion transaction.

Example **14.18:** USAco, a publicly held U.S. C corporation, owns FSub, a controlled foreign corporation. HAVENco, a foreign corporation incorporated in a tax haven, is formed and HAVENco owns a U.S. acquisition corporation, USAcq. In a transaction designed to be what would otherwise be a nontaxable forward triangular merger,[97] USAco's shareholders receive 60 percent of the shares of HAVENco as USAco merges into USAcq. The resulting structure has the former USAco shareholders now owning 60 percent of the shares of HAVENco. USAcq, which now operates the business of the former USAco, now owns FSub and distributes FSub's shares to HAVENco. USAcq, which is comprised of the operating business of the former USAco, now owns FSub and distributes FSub's shares to HAVENco.

---

[97] Code Sec. 368(a)(2)(D).

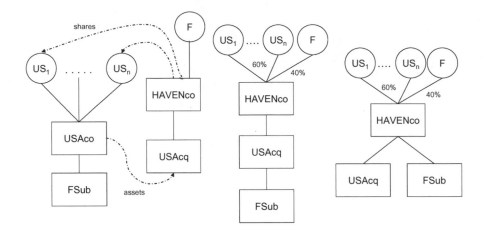

USAcq will recognize gain on the distribution of the FSub shares to the extent their fair market value exceeds basis. Furthermore, the former USAco shareholders should incur the outbound toll charge to the extent that the fair market value of the HAVENco shares received exceeds their basis in the USAco shares.[98] Moreover, because the former USAco shareholders own at least 60 percent (but less than 80 percent) of the shares of HAVENco, all gain recognized may not be reduced via any foreign tax credits or net operating losses over the next 10 years.

Application to U.S. partnerships. Code Sec. 7874's prohibition against using net operating losses or foreign tax credits also applies to inversions where U.S. partners exchange their partnership interests for at least 60 percent of the shares of a new foreign corporation.

Example **14.19:** USLLC, a U.S.-organized limited liability company that is treated as a domestic partnership for U.S. tax purposes, has U.S. citizens as all its members and does not own any valuable intangibles. USLLC owns FSub, a controlled foreign corporation. HAVENco is formed and HAVENco forms a foreign acquisition entity, FORco. In a transaction that is treated as a sale, USLLC's owners receive shares of HAVENco as USLLC merges into FORco. The resulting structure has the former USLLC owners now owning 60 percent of the shares of HAVENco and HAVENco owning FORco. FORco now operates the business of the former USLLC and also owns FSub.

Although USLLC will not report any income on the transaction, the former members of USLLC should recognize gain to the extent that the fair market value of the HAVENco shares received exceeds the basis in the USLLC membership interests relinquished. Because the former USLLC members own at least 60 percent of the shares of HAVENco, any gain recognized pursuant to the outbound toll charge may not be reduced via any foreign tax credits or net operating losses over the next 10 years.

---

[98] Code Sec. 367(a).

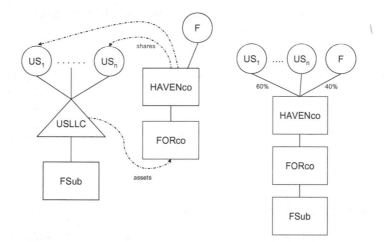

¶ 1406 INBOUND TRANSFERS IN AN ACQUISITIVE REORGANIZATION

This section provides a brief introduction to how the United States taxes inbound transfers from a foreign corporation in a transaction that qualifies as a nontaxable acquisitive reorganization, including a Type A statutory merger, Type B share-for-share acquisition, Type C share-for-asset acquisition, forward triangular merger or reverse triangular merger. The regulations under Code Sec. 367(b) are designed to prevent U.S. shareholders from using inbound reorganizations to avoid U.S. tax on the unrepatriated earnings and profits of a foreign corporation by requiring such shareholders to recognize a deemed dividend equal to an allocable portion of a foreign corporation's earnings and profits.[99]

.01 Inbound Type A Statutory Merger

Pursuant to the relaxed Type A merger rules, a merger may include a foreign corporation.[100] To avoid the loss of the U.S. taxing jurisdiction over a foreign corporation's unrepatriated earnings and profits, the U.S. shareholders of a foreign corporation merged out of existence must include their share of the foreign corporation's earnings and profits as a deemed dividend.[101]

> **Example 14.20:** Assume that Foreign Target merges with and into U.S. Acquiror. Further assume that Foreign Target's shares are worth $1 million at the time of the merger and that Foreign Target's U.S. shareholders have a $100,000 tax basis in their Foreign Target shares. Finally, assume that the consideration received by Foreign Target's shareholders consists of U.S. Acquiror shares with a fair market value of $1 million. Although the merger involves a foreign corporation, it qualifies as a Type A merger.[102] The individual

---

[99] Reg. § 1.367(b)-3.
[100] Reg. § 1.368-2(b)(1)(iii)(Ex. 13).

[101] Reg. § 1.367(b)-3(b)(3).
[102] Reg. § 1.368-2(b)(1)(iii)(Ex. 13).

U.S. shareholders of Foreign Target must include a dividend of the earnings and profits of Foreign Target.[103]

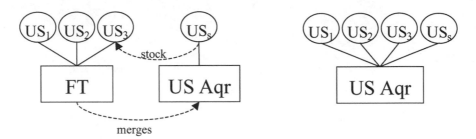

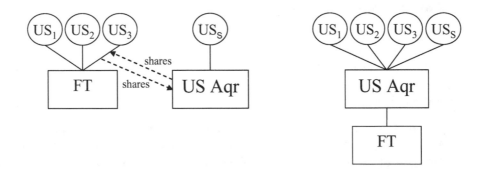

.02 Inbound Type B Share-For-Share Acquisitions

A nontaxable Type B share-for-share acquisition strictly limits the consideration to voting stock of the acquiring corporation and requires that the acquiring corporation has control of the target corporation immediately after the transaction.

Example **14.21:** Assume that U.S. Acquiror wishes to acquire Foreign Target. Further assume that Foreign Target's single class of shares is worth $1 million. Finally, assume that U.S. Acquiror issues $1 million worth of U.S. Acquiror's voting shares to Foreign Target's U.S. shareholders in exchange for their Foreign Target shares. The share-for-share exchange should qualify as a Type B acquisition. Foreign Target's U.S. shareholders should not recognize gain because both (1) they are acquiring property (the U.S. Acquiror's shares) within the U.S. taxing jurisdiction and (2) the earnings of Foreign Target could still come within the U.S. taxing jurisdiction. As a result, the regulations do not require the Foreign Target's shareholders to include the earnings and profits of Foreign Target as a dividend.[104]

However, if U.S. Acquiror used just $1 of cash as consideration, the solely for voting shares requirement would not be satisfied and the transaction would become a failed reorganization. Consequently, Foreign Target's U.S. shareholders would recognize capital gain in the amount of the fair market value of

---

[103] Reg. § 1.367(b)-3(b)(3)(i).   [104] Code Sec. 367(b).

¶1406.02

the U.S. Acquiror's shares received over their basis in their Foreign Target shares.

.03 Inbound Type C Share-For-Asset Acquisitions

A nontaxable Type C acquisition involves the acquisition by a corporation for all or part of its voting shares of substantially all of the properties of the target corporation. To avoid the loss of the U.S. taxing jurisdiction, the U.S. shareholders of a foreign corporation gone out of existence must include their share of the foreign corporation's earnings and profits as a dividend.[105]

> **Example 14.22:** Assume that U.S. Acquiror acquires Foreign Target's assets for U.S. Acquiror's voting shares. Further assume that Foreign Target subsequently distributes the U.S. Acquiror's shares to its U.S. shareholders in liquidation. This transaction should qualify as a Type C acquisition. Depending on the circumstances, any U.S. shareholders of Foreign Target should recognize a dividend to the extent of earnings and profits of the Foreign Target.[106] Even if Foreign Target had significant liabilities incurred in the ordinary course of business, the transaction would still be a good Type C acquisition.

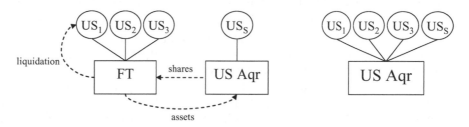

.04 Inbound Forward Triangular Mergers

A nontaxable forward triangular merger occurs when an acquiror uses the shares of its parent as the target merges into the acquiror, resulting in the acquiror receiving substantially all the target's assets.[107] To avoid the loss of the U.S. taxing jurisdiction, the U.S. shareholders of a foreign corporation merged out of existence must include their share of the foreign corporation's earnings and profits as a deemed dividend.[108]

> **Example 14.23:** Assume that U.S. Parent, a publicly-traded domestic corporation, wishes to acquire Foreign Target's business, but does not want to incur the expense of obtaining its shareholders' approval for a straight merger of Foreign Target into U.S. Parent. Further assume that U.S. Parent owns a wholly-owned subsidiary, U.S. Acquiror, for the purpose of obtaining Foreign Target's business. Finally, assume that Foreign Target merges with and into U.S. Acquiror, with Foreign Target's U.S. shareholders receiving U.S. Parent shares as consideration and U.S. Acquiror surviving the merger while obtaining Foreign Target's assets. If the various requirements are satisfied, the transaction would qualify as a forward triangular merger. The individual U.S.

---

[105] Reg. § 1.367(b)-3(b)(3)(ii) (Ex. 5).
[106] Reg. § 1.367(b)-3(b)(3)(i) and (ii) (Ex. 6).

[107] Code Sec. 368(a)(2)(D).
[108] Reg. § 1.367(b)-3(b)(3)(i).

shareholders of Foreign Target must include in income as a dividend the earnings and profits of Foreign Target as a dividend.

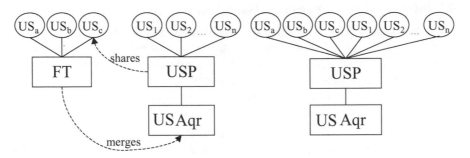

.05 Inbound Reverse Triangular Mergers

A reverse triangular merger is similar to a forward triangular merger, except that the surviving entity is the target and not the acquiror. More specifically, after the transaction, the surviving target holds substantially all of its own and the acquiror's assets and the former shareholders of the surviving target exchange their shares for shares of the acquiror's parent.

Example **14.24:** Assume that U.S. Parent, a publicly-traded corporation, wishes to acquire Foreign Target's business, but does not want to incur the expense of obtaining its shareholders' approval for a straight merger with Foreign Target (which must survive due to a non-transferable contract). Further assume that U.S. Parent forms a wholly-owned subsidiary, U.S. Acquiror, as an acquisition vehicle. Finally, assume that U.S. Acquiror merges with and into Foreign Target, with Foreign Target's shareholders receiving U.S. Parent shares as the merger consideration and with Foreign Target surviving the merger. Because Foreign Target, with its earnings and profits, remains in existence, an income inclusion is unnecessary.[109]

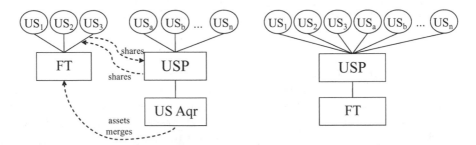

¶ 1407 FOREIGN-TO-FOREIGN TRANSFERS IN AN ACQUISITIVE REORGANIZATION

Provisions similar to those governing inbound and outbound transactions also govern a variety of other exchanges involving transfers of property from one

---

[109] Reg. § 1.367(b)-3(b)(3) only applies when assets of the foreign target are acquired.

foreign corporation to another foreign corporation.[110] The purpose of these provisions is to preserve the ability of the United States to tax both built-in gain on the shares of the foreign corporation tendered and the earnings and profits of a foreign corporation attributable to shares owned by U.S. shareholders. As a result, there is a two-prong analysis. First, to the extent these transactions can be considered an outbound tax-free transaction, the outbound toll charge rules apply. If the outbound toll charge applies, the U.S. shareholders will recognize gain and the analysis ends.[111] If the outbound toll charge does not apply, such as due to the limited-interest exception, then a U.S. shareholder of a CFC (as those phrases are defined in the Subpart F rules), will receive shares of a non-CFC or shares of the CFC in which the U.S. person would not be U.S. shareholder must include the earnings and profits of the foreign target as a dividend.[112]

.01 Foreign-To-Foreign Type A Statutory Merger

Pursuant to the relaxed Type A merger rules, a merger may include foreign corporations.[113] Because this could be considered an outbound tax-free incorporation, the outbound toll charge rules must be analyzed. If the outbound toll charge applies, the analysis ends and the U.S. shareholders will recognize gain.[114] If the outbound toll charge does not apply, such as due to the limited-interest exception, then a U.S. shareholder of a CFC (as those phrases are defined in the Subpart F rules) who receives shares of a non-CFC or shares of a CFC in which the U.S. person would not be a U.S. shareholder must include the earnings and profits of the target as a dividend.[115]

Example 14.25: Assume that Foreign Target merges with and into Foreign Acquiror. Further assume that Foreign Target's shares are worth $1 million at the time of the merger and that Foreign Target's U.S. shareholders have a $100,000 basis in their Foreign Target shares. Finally, assume that the merger consideration received by Foreign Target's shareholders consists of Foreign Acquiror's shares with a fair market value of $1 million. The outbound toll charge rules must be applied to determine if the U.S. shareholders have to recognize built-in gain on their shares of Foreign Target. If there is gain, the analysis ends. If there is not any gain, such as due to the limited-interest exception, further analysis is required. More specifically, if the former Foreign Target would not be a CFC or the individual U.S. shareholders would not be U.S. shareholders (as that phrase is defined in Subpart F), the individual U.S. shareholders must include a dividend to the extent of their share of Foreign Target's earnings and profits.

---

[110] Code Sec. 367(b), and Reg. § 1.367(b)-4.

[111] Reg. § 1.367(a)-3(b)(2).

[112] Reg. § 1.367(b)-1(a).

[113] Reg. § 1.368-2(b)(1)(iii)(Ex. 13).

[114] Reg. § 1.367(a)-3(b)(2).

[115] Reg. § 1.367(b)-1(a).

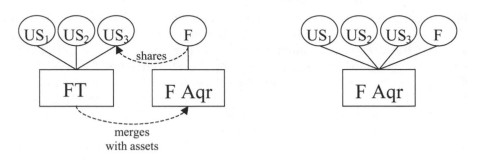

merges
with assets

.02 Foreign-To-Foreign Type B Share-For-Share Acquisitions

A Type B share-for-share acquisition is tax-free as long as the only consideration used is voting stock of the acquiring corporation, and the acquiror has control
of the target immediately after the transaction. Because this could be considered an
outbound tax-free incorporation, the outbound toll charge rules must be analyzed.
If the outbound toll charge applies, the analysis ends and the U.S. shareholders will
recognize gain.[116] If the outbound toll charge does not apply, such as due to the
limited-interest exception, then a U.S. shareholder of a CFC (as those phrases are
defined in the Subpart F rules) who receives shares of a non-CFC or shares of a
CFC in which the U.S. person would not be a U.S. shareholder must include the
earnings and profits of the target as a dividend.[117]

> **Example 14.26:** Skipper, a U.S. citizen, wholly-owns FMinnow, a foreign
> corporation engaged in the shipping business. In what would otherwise consti-
> tute a share-for-share acquisition, Skipper exchanges 100% of his shares of
> FMinnow for 3% of the shares of CANwhale, a publicly-held Canadian corpora-
> tion on the Toronto Stock Exchange. This transaction satisfies the Type B
> rules and the limited-interest exception should apply to avoid the outbound toll
> charge. However, to prevent the loss of the U.S. taxing jurisdiction (Skipper is
> no longer a U.S. shareholder of a CFC), Skipper must include a dividend to the
> extent of FMinnow's earnings and profits.

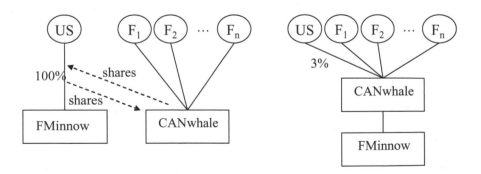

---

[116] Reg. § 1.367(a)-3(b)(2).   [117] Reg. § 1.367(b)-1(a).

¶1407.02

.03 *Foreign-To-Foreign Type C Shares-For-Asset Acquisitions*

As aforementioned, a nontaxable Type C acquisition allows an acquiror, for all or part of its voting shares, to acquire substantially all the assets of the target. Because this could be considered an outbound tax-free incorporation, the outbound toll charge rules must be analyzed. If the outbound toll charge applies, the analysis ends and the U.S. shareholders will recognize gain.[118] If the outbound toll charge does not apply, such as due to the limited-interest exception, then a U.S. shareholder of a CFC (as those phrases are defined in the Subpart F rules) who receives shares of a non-CFC or shares of a CFC in which the U.S. person would not be a U.S. shareholder must include the earnings and profits of the target as a dividend.[119]

> **Example 14.27:** Skipper, a U.S. citizen, wholly-owns FMinnow, a foreign corporation engaged in the shipping business. In what would otherwise constitute a tax-free shares-for-assets acquisition, CANwhale, a publicly-held Canadian corporation traded on the Toronto Stock Exchange, acquires all of FMinnow's assets for 3% of CANwhale's voting shares. Further assume that FMinnow subsequently distributes the CANwhale shares to Skipper in liquidation. As a result, the transaction should qualify as a Type C acquisition. The outbound toll charge rules must be applied to determine if Skipper has to recognize built-in gain on his shares of FMinnow. If there is gain, the analysis ends. If there is not any gain, such as due to the application of the limited-interest exception, further analysis is required. More specifically, because Skipper, who was formerly a U.S. shareholder in a CFC (FMinnow) now owns only 3% of the shares of a non-CFC (CANwhale), Skipper must include the earnings and profits of FMinnow as a dividend.

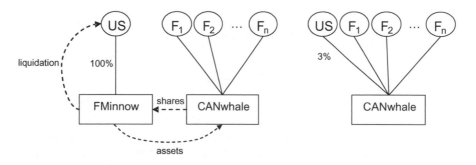

.04 *Foreign-To-Foreign Forward Triangular Mergers*

A nontaxable forward triangular merger occurs when an acquiror uses the shares of its parent as the target merges into the acquiror, resulting in the acquiror receiving substantially all of the target's assets. Because this could be considered an outbound tax-free incorporation, the outbound toll charge rules must be analyzed. If the outbound toll charge applies, the analysis ends and the U.S. shareholders will recognize gain.[120] If the outbound toll charge does not apply, such as due to

---

[118] Reg. § 1.367(a)-3(b)(2).
[119] Reg. § 1.367(b)-1(a).

[120] Reg. § 1.367(a)-3(b)(2).

the limited-interest exception, then a U.S. shareholder of a CFC (as those phrases are defined in the Subpart F rules) who receives shares of a non-CFC or shares of a CFC in which the U.S. person would not be a U.S. shareholder must include the earnings and profits of the target as a dividend.[121]

    Example **14.28:** Assume that Foreign Parent, a foreign corporation, wishes to acquire Foreign Target's business, but does not want to incur the expense of obtaining its shareholders' approval for a straight merger of Foreign Target into Foreign Parent. Further assume that Foreign Parent wholly-owns a subsidiary, Foreign Acquiror, for the purpose of obtaining Foreign Target's business. Finally, assume that Foreign Target merges with and into Foreign Acquiror, with Foreign Target's U.S. shareholders receiving Foreign Parent shares as the merger consideration and Foreign Acquiror surviving the merger while obtaining the assets of Foreign Target. If the various requirements are satisfied, the merger qualifies as a forward triangular reorganization. If this transaction satisfies the limited-interest exception, the outbound toll charge should not apply. Because the transaction is also covered by the inbound rules, the individual U.S. shareholders that are no longer U.S. shareholders of a CFC (Foreign Target) must include a dividend to the extent of their share of the earnings and profits of Foreign Target.[122]

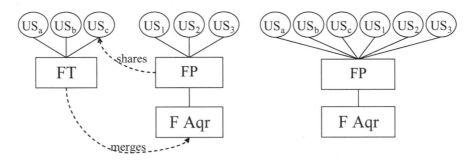

.05 Foreign-To-Foreign Reverse Triangular Mergers

    A nontaxable reverse triangular merger is similar to a forward triangular merger, except that the surviving entity is the target and not the acquiror. More specifically, after the transaction, the surviving target holds substantially all of its own and the acquiror's assets and the former shareholders of the surviving target exchange their shares for shares of the acquiror's parent. Because this could be considered an outbound tax-free reorganization, the outbound toll charge rules must be analyzed. If the outbound toll charge applies, the analysis ends and the U.S. shareholders will recognize gain.[123] If the outbound toll charge does not apply, such as due to the limited-interest exception, then a U.S. shareholder of a CFC (as those phrases are defined in the Subpart F rules) who receives shares of a non-CFC or shares of a CFC in which the U.S. person would not be a U.S. shareholder must include the earnings and profits of the target as a dividend.[124]

---

[121] Reg. § 1.367(b)-1(a).
[122] Reg. § 1.367(a)-3(d)(1)(i).

[123] Reg. § 1.367(a)-3(b)(2).
[124] Reg. § 1.367(b)-1(a).

¶1407.05

Example **14.29:** Assume that Foreign Parent, a publicly-traded foreign corporation, wishes to acquire Foreign Target's business, but does not want to incur the expense of obtaining its shareholders' approval for a straight merger with Foreign Target (which must survive due to a non-transferable contract). Further assume that Foreign Parent forms a wholly-owned subsidiary, Foreign Acquiror, as an acquisition vehicle. Finally, assume that Foreign Acquiror merges with and into Foreign Target, with Foreign Target's shareholders receiving Foreign Parent shares as the merger consideration and with Foreign Target surviving the merger. This transaction could be covered by the outbound rules,[125] but if the transaction satisfies the limited-interest exception, the outbound toll charge should not apply. Because Foreign Target, with its earnings and profits, remains in existence, any dividend inclusion under the inbound rules is unnecessary.[126]

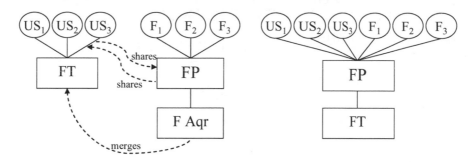

---

[125] Reg. § 1.367(a)-3(d)(1)(ii).

[126] Reg. § 1.367(b)-3(b)(3) only applies if assets of the foreign target are acquired.

¶ 1408 APPENDIX

On January 1, 2010, Mark Twain, a U.S. citizen, contributes $15 million to a newly formed German corporation called WallCo. Twain must prepare a Form 926 that indicates the $15 million contribution.

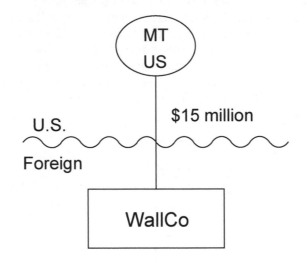

Form **926** (Rev. December 2008) Department of the Treasury Internal Revenue Service	**Return by a U.S. Transferor of Property to a Foreign Corporation** ▶ Attach to your income tax return for the year of the transfer or distribution.	OMB No. 1545-0026 Attachment Sequence No. **128**

Part I   U.S. Transferor Information (see instructions)

Name of transferor	Identifying number (see instructions)
Mark Twain	**123-45-6789**

1 If the transferor was a corporation, complete questions 1a through 1d.

a If the transfer was a section 361(a) or (b) transfer, was the transferor controlled (under section 368(c)) by 5 or fewer domestic corporations? . . . . ☐ Yes ☐ No

b Did the transferor remain in existence after the transfer? . . . . ☐ Yes ☐ No
If not, list the controlling shareholder(s) and their identifying number(s):

Controlling shareholder	Identifying number

c If the transferor was a member of an affiliated group filing a consolidated return, was it the parent corporation? . . . . ☐ Yes ☐ No
If not, list the name and employer identification number (EIN) of the parent corporation:

Name of parent corporation	EIN of parent corporation
N/A	

d Have basis adjustments under section 367(a)(5) been made? . . . . ☐ Yes ☐ No

2 If the transferor was a partner in a partnership that was the actual transferor (but is not treated as such under section 367), complete questions 2a through 2d.
a List the name and EIN of the transferor's partnership:

Name of partnership	EIN of partnership

b Did the partner pick up its pro rata share of gain on the transfer of partnership assets? . . . . ☐ Yes ☐ No
c Is the partner disposing of its **entire** interest in the partnership? . . . . ☐ Yes ☐ No
d Is the partner disposing of an interest in a limited partnership that is regularly traded on an established securities market? . . . . ☐ Yes ☐ No

Part II   Transferee Foreign Corporation Information (see instructions)

3 Name of transferee (foreign corporation)	**4 Identifying number**, if any
WallCo	

5 Address (including country)
Berlin, Gernany

6 Country code of country of incorporation or organization (see instructions)
GM

7 Foreign law characterization (see instructions)
Corporation

8 Is the transferee foreign corporation a controlled foreign corporation? . . . . ☑ Yes ☐ No

For Paperwork Reduction Act Notice, see separate instructions.   Cat. No. 16982D   Form **926** (Rev. 12-2008)

¶1408

| Part III | Information Regarding Transfer of Property (see instructions) | | | | |

Type of property	(a) Date of transfer	(b) Description of property	(c) Fair market value on date of transfer	(d) Cost or other basis	(e) Gain recognized on transfer
Cash	1/1/10		15,000,000		
Stock and securities					
Installment obligations, account receivables or similar property					
Foreign currency or other property denominated in foreign currency					
Inventory					
Assets subject to depreciation recapture (see Temp. Regs. sec. 1.367(a)-4T(b))					
Tangible property used in trade or business not listed under another category					
Intangible property					
Property to be leased (as described in Temp. Regs. sec. 1.367(a)-4T(c))					
Property to be sold (as described in Temp. Regs. sec. 1.367(a)-4T(d))					
Transfers of oil and gas working interests (as described in Temp. Regs. sec. 1.367(a)-4T(e))					
Other property					

Supplemental Information Required To Be Reported (see instructions):

_____
_____
_____
_____
_____

Form **926** (Rev. 12-2008)

¶1408

Form 926 (Rev. 12-2008)   Page **3**

Part IV	**Additional Information Regarding Transfer of Property** (see instructions)

9 Enter the transferor's interest in the foreign transferee corporation before and after the transfer:

(a) Before _____ 0 % **(b)** After _____ 100 %

10 Type of nonrecognition transaction (see instructions) ▶ Section 351 _____

11 Indicate whether any transfer reported in Part III is subject to any of the following:

a	Gain recognition under section 904(f)(3)	☐ Yes	☑ No
b	Gain recognition under section 904(f)(5)(F)	☐ Yes	☑ No
c	Recapture under section 1503(d)	☐ Yes	☑ No
d	Exchange gain under section 987	☐ Yes	☑ No

12 Did this transfer result from a change in the classification of the transferee to that of a foreign corporation? ☐ Yes ☑ No

13 Indicate whether the transferor was required to recognize income under Temporary Regulations sections 1.367(a)-4T through 1.367(a)-6T for any of the following:

a	Tainted property	☐ Yes	☑ No
b	Depreciation recapture	☐ Yes	☑ No
c	Branch loss recapture	☐ Yes	☑ No
d	Any other income recognition provision contained in the above-referenced regulations	☐ Yes	☑ No

14 Did the transferor transfer assets which qualify for the trade or business exception under section 367(a)(3)? ☐ Yes ☑ No

15a Did the transferor transfer foreign goodwill or going concern value as defined in Temporary Regulations section 1.367(a)-1T(d)(5)(iii)? . . . . ☐ Yes ☑ No

b If the answer to line 15a is "Yes," enter the amount of foreign goodwill or going concern value transferred ▶ $ _____

16 Was cash the only property transferred? . . . . ☑ Yes ☐ No

17a Was intangible property (within the meaning of section 936(h)(3)(B)) transferred as a result of the transaction? . . . . ☐ Yes ☑ No

b If "Yes," describe the nature of the rights to the intangible property that was transferred as a result of the transaction:

_____

_____

_____

Form **926** (Rev. 12-2008)

Chapter 15
State Taxation of International Operations

¶ 1501   Overview of State Corporate Income Taxes
¶ 1502   Review of Federal Taxation of Income from Foreign Subsidiaries
¶ 1503   Worldwide Versus Water's-Edge Combined Reporting
¶ 1504   Dividends from Foreign Subsidiaries
¶ 1505   Check-the-Box Foreign Branches
¶ 1506   Treatment of Foreign Income Tax Payments
¶ 1507   State Versus Federal Nexus Standards for Foreign Corporations

¶ 1501 OVERVIEW OF STATE CORPORATE INCOME TAXES

Forty-five states and the District of Columbia impose some type of income-based tax on corporations. Nevada, Ohio, South Dakota, Washington, and Wyoming do not levy a corporate income tax. However, Ohio does impose a gross receipts tax called the *commercial activity tax*, and Washington imposes a gross receipts tax called the *business and occupation tax*. Texas imposes a tax on gross margin, called the *margin tax*.

Most states that impose a corporate income tax use either federal taxable income before the net operating loss and special deductions (federal Form 1120, line 28) or federal taxable income (federal Form 1120, line 30) as the starting place for computing state taxable income. The use of the federal tax base as the starting point eases the administrative burden of computing state taxable income. Despite the broad conformity, each state requires numerous addition and subtraction modifications to arrive at state taxable income. Examples of common addition modifications include interest income received on state and municipal debt obligations, state income taxes, royalties and interest expenses paid to related parties, federal bonus depreciation under Code Sec. 168(k), and the Code Sec. 199 domestic production activities deduction. Examples of common subtraction modifications include interest income received on federal debt obligations, state net operating loss deductions, state dividends-received deductions, and federal Subpart F and Code Sec. 78 gross-up income.

States employ a wide variety of consolidation rules for a group of commonly controlled corporations. A few states require each group member that is taxable in the state to file a return on a separate company basis. About 20 states permit or require a group of commonly controlled corporations to file a consolidated return if certain requirements are met. Roughly another 20 states require members of a unitary business group to compute their taxable income on a combined basis. A unitary business group consists of two or more commonly controlled corporations that are engaged in the same trade or business, as exhibited by such factors as functional integration and centralized management.

To prevent double taxation, corporations that have business activities in two or more states may apportion their income among the taxing states. The multistate corporation uses the apportionment formulas provided by the taxing states to compute an apportionment percentage for each state. These formulas generally reflect the principles embodied in the Uniform Division of Income for Tax Purposes Act (UDITPA), which is a model law for allocating and apportioning income that was promulgated by state tax officials in 1957. Under UDITPA, taxpayers apportion their business income among each taxing state. In contrast, an item of nonbusiness income is specifically allocated to a single state.

The UDITPA distinction between business and nonbusiness income is related to the U.S. constitutional restrictions on the ability of a state to tax an out-of-state corporation. Specifically, the Commerce Clause and Due Process clause limit the ability of states to tax an item of income that has no relationship to the business activity which the corporation conducts in the state. For example, in *Allied-Signal, Inc. v. Division of Taxation*,[1] a Delaware corporation that was taxable in New Jersey and was commercially domiciled in Michigan realized a $211.5 million capital gain from the sale of 20.6% of the stock of ASARCO. The U.S. Supreme Court held that New Jersey could not tax an apportioned percentage of the gain because the taxpayer and ASARCO were "unrelated business enterprises whose activities had nothing to do with the other," and the taxpayer's ownership of the ASARCO stock did not serve an "operational rather than an investment function" in the taxpayer's business. As a consequence, the gain was nonbusiness income which was specifically allocable to the state of commercial domicile.

State formulas for apportioning business income are usually based on the relative amounts of property, payroll, and sales that the corporation has in each taxing state. Each apportionment factor equals the ratio of the corporation's property, payroll, or sales in the state to its property, payroll, or sales everywhere. About 10 states use a formula where the apportionment percentage equals the simple average of the property factor (in-state property ÷ total property), payroll factor (in-state payroll ÷ total payroll), and sales factor (in-state sales ÷ total sales). Many states double-weight the sales factor, and about a dozen states use a formula that includes only a sales factor.

¶ 1502 REVIEW OF FEDERAL TAXATION OF INCOME FROM FOREIGN SUBSIDIARIES

Because states generally use federal taxable income (federal Form 1120, line 28 or 30) as the starting point for computing state taxable income, federal tax law plays an important role in state taxation of a domestic corporation's foreign earnings.

---

[1] 504 U.S. 768 (1992).

The federal government taxes the worldwide taxable income of a domestic corporation,[2] and allows a credit for the foreign income taxes imposed on foreign-source income.[3] On the other hand, the federal government generally does not tax the undistributed earnings and profits of a foreign corporation, even if the foreign corporation is a wholly-owned subsidiary of a domestic corporation.[4] Moreover, foreign corporations are not includible in a federal consolidated return.[5] As a consequence, if a domestic corporation operates abroad through foreign subsidiaries, the foreign earnings of those foreign corporations are generally not subject to U.S. taxation until repatriated to the domestic parent through a dividend distribution. This policy, which is known as *deferral*, is designed to allow U.S. companies to compete in foreign markets on a tax parity with foreign competitors.

A domestic parent corporation's receipt of a dividend distribution from a foreign corporation generally represents the federal government's first opportunity to tax the underlying foreign earnings and profits. Therefore, the domestic corporation generally includes any foreign dividends in its federal taxable income,[6] and is not allowed an offsetting dividends-received deduction.[7] A dividends-received deduction may be available, however, if a 10%-or-more-owned foreign corporation distributes a dividend out of earnings that are attributable to income derived from the conduct of a U.S. trade or business or dividends received from an 80%-or-more-owned domestic corporation.[8]

To mitigate double taxation of a foreign subsidiary's earnings, upon receiving a dividend from a foreign subsidiary, a domestic parent corporation may claim a deemed paid foreign tax credit for the foreign income taxes that a 10%-or-more-owned foreign corporation pays on its earnings.[9] Because the amount of dividend income recognized by a domestic parent corporation is the net of any foreign income taxes paid by a foreign subsidiary, the domestic corporation is implicitly allowed a deduction for those foreign taxes. To prevent a double tax benefit, the domestic corporation must gross up its dividend income by the amount of the deemed paid foreign taxes, which offsets the implicit deduction.[10]

A policy of unrestricted deferral would create an opportunity to avoid U.S. taxes on portable income, such as passive investment income or inventory trading profits, which is easily shifted to a foreign corporation located in a tax haven country. In 1962, Congress attempted to close this loophole by enacting Subpart F (Code Secs. 951–965), which denies deferral to certain types of tainted income earned through a foreign corporation. Subpart F requires a U.S. shareholder of a controlled foreign corporation (CFC) to include in income a deemed dividend equal to a pro rata share of the CFC's Subpart F income.[11] A foreign corporation is a CFC if U.S. shareholders own more than 50% of the stock of the foreign corporation, by vote or value. Examples of Subpart F income include foreign personal holding company income, and foreign base company sales income. Foreign personal hold-

---

[2] Code Sec. 61.
[3] Code Sec. 901.
[4] Code Sec. 881 and 882.
[5] Code Sec. 1504.
[6] Code Sec. 61.

[7] Code Sec. 243.
[8] Code Sec. 245.
[9] Code Sec. 902.
[10] Code Sec. 78.
[11] Code Sec. 951.

ing company income includes dividends, interest, rents, and royalties, whereas foreign base company sales income includes income from the sale of goods which the CFC buys from or sells to a related person, and are neither manufactured nor sold for use in the CFC's country of incorporation.[12]

¶ 1503 WORLDWIDE VERSUS WATER'S-EDGE COMBINED REPORTING

About 20 states require commonly controlled corporations engaged in a unitary business to compute their state taxable income on a combined basis. These states generally take one of two approaches to dealing with unitary group members that are incorporated in a foreign country or conduct most of their business abroad. The first approach is a worldwide combination, under which the combined report includes all members of the unitary business group, regardless of the country in which the group member is incorporated or the country in which the group member conducts business. The second approach is a water's-edge combination, under which the combined report excludes group members that are incorporated in a foreign country or conduct most of their business abroad. A common approach is to exclude a so-called *80/20 company*, which is a corporation whose business activity outside the United States, as measured by some combination of apportionment factors, is 80% or more of the corporation's total business activity.

Requiring a multinational corporation to compute its state taxable income on a worldwide combined reporting basis is controversial for a number of reasons, including: (i) the difficulty of converting books and records maintained under foreign accounting principles and in a foreign currency into a form that is acceptable to the states; (ii) the inability of states to audit books and records located in foreign countries; and (iii) distortions in the property and payroll factors caused by significantly lower wage rates and property values in developing countries. Despite the practical difficulties of apportioning income on a worldwide basis, the constitutionality of requiring a multinational corporation to compute its state taxable income on a worldwide combined basis is firmly established. In *Container Corp. of America v. Franchise Tax Board*,[13] the Supreme Court ruled that California's worldwide combined reporting method was constitutional with respect to a U.S.-based parent corporation and its foreign subsidiaries. In *Barclays Bank plc v. Franchise Tax Board*,[14] the Supreme Court held that California's worldwide combined reporting method was also constitutional with respect to a foreign-based parent corporation and its U.S. subsidiaries. California repealed mandatory worldwide combined reporting in 1988, and permits a unitary group to make a water's-edge election.

Although a water's-edge combination generally reduces the compliance burden, it may also increase the taxpayer member's state tax liability if the unitary group's U.S. operations are more profitable than its foreign operations. The inclusion of a foreign member's profits increases the combined income of the group, whereas the inclusion of the foreign member's property, payroll, and/or sales in the denominators of the apportionment factors generally reduces the state's apportion-

---

[12] Code Sec. 954.

[13] 463 U.S. 159 (1983).

[14] 512 U.S. 298 (1994).

ment percentage. The net effect can be a reduction in state taxable income if the group's foreign operations are less profitable than its U.S. operations, and an increase in state taxable income if the group's foreign operations are more profitable than its U.S. operations.

California, Idaho, Montana and North Dakota require a worldwide combination, but give taxpayers the option to elect a water's-edge combination. Massachusetts, Utah and West Virginia require a water's-edge combination, but give taxpayers the option to elect a worldwide combination. Alaska requires a water's-edge combination, except for oil and gas companies, which must use worldwide combined reporting. The other mandatory combined reporting states, such as Illinois, Michigan and Texas, require a water's-edge combination.

¶ 1504 DIVIDENDS FROM FOREIGN SUBSIDIARIES

.01 Inclusion in Apportionable Income

In states that require or permit water's-edge combined reporting, the state's first opportunity to tax the earnings of a foreign subsidiary arises when the subsidiary pays a dividend to its domestic parent corporation. Assuming the domestic parent and foreign subsidiary are engaged in a unitary business, the dividend is included in the domestic parent's apportionable business income, which means that each state in which the domestic parent is taxable may tax an apportioned percentage of the dividend income. On the other hand, if the business activities of the foreign subsidiary have nothing to do with the business activities of the domestic parent in the taxing state, then the dividends are nonbusiness income that is taxable only in the state in which the domestic parent's headquarters office is located (state of commercial domicile).

In *Mobil Oil Corp. v. Commissioner of Taxes,*[15] the Supreme Court addressed the issue of whether dividends from foreign corporations are business or nonbusiness income. Mobil was a vertically integrated petroleum company that was commercially domiciled in New York. Mobil argued that Vermont could not constitutionally tax the dividends that Mobil received from its foreign subsidiaries because the activities of the foreign subsidiaries were unrelated to Mobil's activities in Vermont, which were limited to marketing petroleum products. Stating that "the linchpin of apportionability in the field of state income taxation is the unitary business principle," the Supreme Court ruled that Vermont could tax an apportioned percentage of the dividends because the foreign subsidiaries were part of the same integrated petroleum enterprise as the business operations conducted in Vermont. In other words, dividends received from unitary subsidiaries are business income. The Court also noted that if the business activities of the foreign subsidiaries had "nothing to do with the activities of the recipient in the taxing state, due process considerations might well preclude apportionability, because there would be no underlying unitary business."

---

[15] 445 U.S. 425 (1980).

.02 Dividends-Received Deductions

In sharp contrast with federal law, most states provide a deduction for dividends received from both domestic and foreign corporations. For example, consistent with how they treat domestic dividends, many states provide a 100 percent deduction for dividends received from an 80-percent-or-more-owned foreign corporation.

In *Kraft General Foods, Inc. v. Department of Revenue*,[16] the Supreme Court ruled that an Iowa law which allowed taxpayers to claim a dividends-received deduction for dividends from domestic, but not foreign, subsidiary corporations was unconstitutional. During the years in question, Iowa conformed to the federal dividends-received deduction. As a consequence, Iowa did not tax dividends received from domestic corporations, but did tax dividends received from foreign corporations unless the dividends represented distributions of U.S. earnings. The Court ruled that the Iowa provision which taxed only dividends paid by foreign corporations out of their foreign earnings facially discriminated against foreign commerce, in violation of the Commerce Clause.

Since the *Kraft* decision, a number of state courts have also struck down dividends-received deduction schemes that favored dividends received from domestic corporations over dividends received from foreign corporations.

In *Dart Industries, Inc. v. Clark*,[17] the Rhode Island Supreme Court ruled the Rhode Island provision which allowed a deduction for dividends from domestic but not foreign subsidiaries was discriminatory in violation of the Commerce Clause. Likewise, in *D.D.I Inc. v. North Dakota*,[18] the North Dakota Supreme Court declared unconstitutional a North Dakota statute that permitted a dividends-received deduction, but only to the extent the dividend payer's income was subject to North Dakota corporate income tax. In *Hutchinson Technology, Inc. v. Commissioner of Revenue*,[19] the Minnesota Supreme Court ruled that a state statute which excluded dividends paid by certain foreign sales corporations from the state's dividends-received deduction was discriminatory in violation of the Commerce Clause. In *Emerson Electric Co. v. Tracy*,[20] the Ohio Supreme Court declared unconstitutional an Ohio statute that permitted a 100% deduction for dividends from domestic subsidiaries, but only an 85% deduction for dividends from foreign subsidiaries. In *Conoco Inc. v. Taxation and Revenue Department*,[21] the New Mexico Supreme Court ruled that the New Mexico scheme under which foreign but not domestic dividends were included in the tax base facially discriminated against foreign commerce, even through the state allowed a taxpayer to include a portion of the dividend-paying foreign subsidiaries' property, payroll, and sales in the denominators of its apportionment factors, thereby reducing the state apportionment percentage.

.03 Dividends-Received Deductions in a Water's-Edge Combined Report

In footnote 23 of its decision in *Kraft*, the Supreme Court stated that:

---

[16] 505 U.S. 71 (1992).

[17] 657 A.2d 1062 (R.I. Sup. Ct., 1995).

[18] 657 N.W.2d 228 (N.D. Sup. Ct., 2003).

[19] 698 N.W.2d 1 (Minn. Sup. Ct., 2005).

[20] 735 N.E.2d 445 (Ohio Sup. Ct., 2000).

[21] 122 N.M. 736 (N.M. Sup. Ct., 1996).

¶1504.02

"If one were to compare the aggregate tax imposed by Iowa on a unitary business which included a subsidiary doing business throughout the United States (including Iowa) with the aggregate tax imposed by Iowa on a unitary business which included a foreign subsidiary doing business abroad, it would be difficult to say that Iowa discriminates against the business with the foreign subsidiary. Iowa would tax an apportioned share of the domestic subsidiary's entire earnings, but would tax only the amount of the foreign subsidiary's earnings paid as a dividend to the parent."

The state supreme courts in several water's-edge combined reporting states have focused on this footnote and ruled that it is constitutionally acceptable to include dividends from foreign subsidiaries in the tax base, while excluding dividends from domestic subsidiaries which are included in the water's-edge combined report.

In *Appeal of Morton Thiokol, Inc.*,[22] the Kansas Supreme Court noted that *Kraft* did not address the taxation of foreign dividends by water's-edge combined reporting states, and that "the aggregate tax imposed by Kansas on a unitary business with a domestic subsidiary would not be less burdensome than that imposed by Kansas on a unitary business with a foreign subsidiary because the income of the domestic subsidiary would be combined, apportioned, and taxed while only the dividend of the foreign subsidiary would be taxed." Likewise, in *E.I. Du Pont de Nemours & Co. v. State Tax Assessor*,[23] the Maine Supreme Judicial Court held that Maine's water's-edge combined reporting method was distinguishable from the Iowa's single-entity reporting method because the income of a domestic subsidiary is included in the Maine combined report. Therefore, taxing dividends paid by foreign but not domestic subsidiaries did not constitute the kind of facial discrimination found in the Iowa system.

Finally, in *General Electric Company, Inc. v. Department of Revenue Administration*,[24] General Electric challenged the constitutionality of a New Hampshire statute that permits a U.S. parent corporation to claim a dividends-received deduction for dividends received from foreign subsidiaries only to the extent the foreign subsidiary has business activity and is subject to tax in New Hampshire. None of General Electric's unitary foreign subsidiaries had business activities in New Hampshire. Thus, General Electric could not claim a dividends-received deduction for the dividends received from those foreign subsidiaries. The New Hampshire Supreme Court ruled that the New Hampshire tax scheme did not discriminate against foreign commerce because both a unitary business with foreign subsidiaries operating in New Hampshire and a unitary business with foreign subsidiaries not operating in New Hampshire are each taxed only one time. Thus, there was no differential treatment that benefits the former and burdens the latter.

.04 Apportionment Factor Relief

The inclusion of dividends received from a foreign subsidiary in the apportionable income of a domestic parent corporation raises the issue of whether the parent's apportionment factors should reflect the foreign subsidiary's property,

---

[22] 864 P.2d 1175 (Kan. Sup. Ct., 1993).

[23] 675 A.2d 82 (Maine Sup Ct., 1996).

[24] No. 2005-668 (N.H. Sup. Ct., Dec. 5, 2006).

payroll, and sales. In his dissent in *Mobil Oil Corp.*, Justice Stevens raised the issue of factor representation, noting that "[u]nless the sales, payroll, and property values connected with the production of income by the payor corporations are added to the denominator of the apportionment formula, the inclusion of earnings attributable to those corporations in the apportionable tax base will inevitably cause Mobil's Vermont income to be overstated."

In *NCR Corp. v. Taxation and Revenue Department*,[25] the New Mexico Court of Appeals rejected the taxpayer's argument that the taxation of dividends received by a domestic parent corporation from its foreign subsidiaries without factor representation resulted in constitutionally impermissible double taxation. Similar arguments made by NCR were also rejected by state supreme courts in Minnesota and South Carolina.[26] Caterpillar, Inc. also litigated the issue of factor representation with respect to dividends received from foreign subsidiaries, and met with limited success. See, for example, *Caterpillar, Inc. v. Commissioner of Revenue*,[27] and *Caterpillar, Inc. v. Department of Revenue Administration*.[28] In *Unisys Corp. v. Commonwealth of Pennsylvania*,[29] the Pennsylvania Supreme Court ruled that factor representation was not constitutionally required because the taxpayer failed to prove that the state was unfairly taxing income earned outside its jurisdiction.

.05 Subpart F Inclusions and Code Sec. 78 Gross-up Income

The rationale for including the Code Sec. 78 gross-up amount in federal taxable income does not apply for state tax purposes because no state allows a deemed paid foreign tax credit for the foreign income taxes paid by a foreign subsidiary. As a consequence, nearly all states provide a subtraction modification or dividends-received deduction for federal Code Sec. 78 gross-up income, in effect, excluding Code Sec. 78 gross-up amounts from state taxation. In *Amerada Hess Corp. v. North Dakota*,[30] the North Dakota Supreme Court ruled that federal Code Sec. 78 gross-up amounts did not qualify as "foreign dividends" under the applicable North Dakota tax statute, and therefore did not qualify for the partial exclusion from income under North Dakota's water's-edge combined unitary reporting method of determining the state corporate income tax.

Consistent with the notion that a Subpart F inclusion is a deemed dividend from a controlled foreign corporation, most states provide a dividends received deduction or subtraction modification for income recognized under Subpart F. A few states, including California, require that the income and apportionment factors of a controlled foreign corporation be included in a water's-edge combined report to the extent of the controlled foreign corporation's Subpart F income.[31] California does not provide a dividends-received deduction for Subpart F income.

---

[25] 856 P.2d 982 (N.M. Ct. App. 1993), cert. denied, 512 U.S. 1245 (1994).

[26] *NCR Corp. v. Commissioner of Revenue*, 438 N.W.2d 86 (Minn. Sup. Ct., 1989), cert. denied, 493 U.S. 848 (1989); *NCR Corp. v. Tax Commission*, 439 S.E.2d 254 (S.C. Sup Ct., 1993), cert. denied, 512 U.S. 1245 (1994).

[27] 568 N.W.2d 695 (Minn. Sup Ct., 1997), cert. denied, 522 U.S. 1112 (1998).

[28] 741 A.2d 56 (N.H. Sup Ct., 1999), cert. denied, 120 S. Ct. 1424 (2000).

[29] 812 A.2d 448 (Pa. Sup. Ct., 2002).

[30] 704 N.W.2d 8 (N.D. Sup. Ct., 2005).

[31] Calif. § 25110.

¶1504.05

¶ 1505 CHECK-THE-BOX FOREIGN BRANCHES

If a domestic corporation operates abroad through an unincorporated foreign branch rather than a separately incorporated subsidiary, the foreign-source income of the branch represents income earned directly by the domestic corporation. Historically, U.S. companies have generally not operated abroad through an unincorporated branch for many reasons, including the desire for limited liability or to have a local corporate presence. Since the check-the-box regulations[32] took effect in 1997, however, it has been possible to organize a foreign entity that is recognized as a separate corporation for foreign tax purposes, but is treated as a disregarded entity or partnership for U.S. tax purposes. States generally conform to the federal check-the-box rules for income tax purposes. Thus, a foreign entity that is a corporation for foreign tax purposes but is a branch or partnership for U.S. federal tax purposes is generally treated as a branch or partnership for state income tax purposes.

In *Manpower Inc. v. Commissioner of Revenue*,[33] a domestic corporation owned 99% of Manpower France S.A.R.L (MPF), a French entity. In 1999, MPF made a federal check-the-box election, which caused the liquidation of a foreign corporation (MPF's previous federal tax status) and a contribution of the distributed assets to a new partnership. For Minnesota tax purposes, income of "foreign corporations and other foreign entities" is not included in apportionable income. The Commissioner argued that when the French subsidiary elected to be classified as a partnership for federal tax purposes, a newly formed partnership was created under U.S. law. The taxpayer argued that, despite the federal check-the-box election, MPF still qualified as a "foreign entity" for Minnesota tax purposes because it was created in France under French law and operated in France. The Minnesota Supreme Court agreed, ruling that the check-the-box election changed the French entity's legal nature but not its nationality. The subsidiary was still a foreign entity, and the only effect of its check-the-box election was to convert it from a foreign corporation to a foreign partnership for federal income tax purposes.

¶ 1506 TREATMENT OF FOREIGN INCOME TAX PAYMENTS

For federal tax purposes, a domestic corporation may claim either a deduction or a credit for foreign income tax payments, but not both.[34] If the taxpayer elects to claim a foreign tax credit, the credit is limited to the portion of the domestic corporation's pre-credit U.S. tax attributable to its foreign source taxable income.[35] A domestic corporation that receives a dividend from a foreign corporation in which it owns at least 10% of the voting stock may also claim a credit for the foreign income taxes paid by the foreign corporation on the earnings from which the dividends were paid.[36] When a domestic corporation claims a deemed paid credit, it must gross up its dividend income by the amount of the deemed paid foreign income taxes.[37]

---

[32] Reg. § 301.7701.
[33] No. A06-468 (Minn. Sup. Ct., Dec. 7, 2006).
[34] Code Secs. 164, 275 and 901.

[35] Code Sec. 904.
[36] Code Sec. 902.
[37] Code Sec. 78.

In contrast to federal law, no state allows a credit for foreign income taxes. However, some states allow a deduction for foreign income taxes, but generally only if a deduction is claimed for federal tax purposes. Because a credit is usually more valuable than a deduction, for federal tax purposes, taxpayers generally elect to claim a foreign tax credit rather than a deduction. A handful of states allow a deduction even if the taxpayer claims the credit for federal tax purposes. Many states, such as California, do not permit a deduction for foreign income taxes, regardless of whether a deduction or a credit is claimed for federal tax purposes.[38]

¶ 1507 STATE VERSUS FEDERAL NEXUS STANDARDS FOR FOREIGN CORPORATIONS

.01 Background Regarding State Nexus Standards

A state has jurisdiction to tax a corporation organized in another state only if the out-of-state corporation's activities within the state are sufficient to create nexus. Historically, states have asserted that virtually any type of in-state business activity creates nexus for an out-of-state corporation. This approach reflects the reality that it is more politically palatable to collect taxes from out-of-state corporations than to raise taxes on in-state business interests. The desire of state lawmakers and tax officials to export the state tax burden is restricted by U.S. Constitutional restrictions and Public Law 86-272 (a federal statute), both of which limit a state's ability to impose a tax obligation on an out-of-state corporation.

In terms of constitutional restrictions on nexus, the Due Process Clause prohibits a state from taxing a company unless there is a "minimal connection" between the company's interstate activities and the taxing state.[39] In addition, the Commerce Clause prohibits a state from enacting laws that unduly burden or otherwise inhibit the free flow of trade among the states. In particular, a state may not tax an out-of-state corporation unless that corporation has a "substantial nexus" with the state.[40]

The landmark case regarding constitutional nexus is *Quill Corp. v. North Dakota*.[41] Quill was a mail-order vendor of office supplies that solicited sales through catalogs mailed to potential customers in North Dakota and made deliveries through common carriers. Quill was incorporated in Delaware and had facilities in California, Georgia, and Illinois. Quill had no office, warehouse, retail outlet, or other facility in North Dakota nor were any Quill employees or representatives physically present in North Dakota. During the years in question, Quill made sales to roughly 3,000 North Dakota customers and was the sixth largest office supply vendor in the state. Under North Dakota law, Quill was required to collect North Dakota sales tax on its mail-order sales to North Dakota residents. Quill challenged the constitutionality of this tax obligation. The Supreme Court held that Quill's economic presence in North Dakota was sufficient to satisfy the Due Process Clause's "minimal connection" requirement. On the other hand, the Court ruled that an economic presence was not, by itself, sufficient to satisfy the Com-

---

[38] Calif. § 24345.

[39] *Mobil Oil Corporation v. Comm'r of Taxes*, 445 U.S. 425 (1980).

[40] *Complete Auto Transit, Inc. v. Brady*, 430 U.S. 274 (1977).

[41] 504 U.S. 298 (1992).

merce Clause's "substantial nexus" requirement. Consistent with its ruling 25 years earlier in *National Bellas Hess, Inc. v. Department of Revenue*,[42] the Court ruled that a substantial nexus exists only if a corporation has a nontrivial physical presence in a state. In other words, the Court ruled that a physical presence is an essential prerequisite to establishing constitutional nexus, at least for sales tax purposes. The *Quill* court did not specifically address the issue of whether the physical presence test also applied for income tax purposes, which remains an ongoing controversy.

In terms of federal statutory restrictions on nexus, in 1959 Congress enacted Public Law 86-272 to provide corporations with a limited safe harbor from the imposition of state income taxes. Specifically, Public Law 86-272 prohibits a state from imposing a "net income tax" on a corporation organized in another state if the corporation's only in-state activity is (i) solicitation of orders by company represent-atives, (ii) for sales of tangible personal property, (iii) which orders are sent outside the state for approval or rejection, and (iv) if approved, are filled by shipment or delivery from a point outside the state. Public Law 86-272 applies only to taxes imposed on net income, and provides no protection against the imposition of a sales tax collection obligation. It also does not protect activities such as leasing tangible personal property, selling services, selling or leasing real estate, or selling or licensing intangibles. Moreover, for businesses that send employees into a state to sell tangible personal property, Public Law 86-272 applies only if those employees strictly limit their in-state activities to the solicitation of orders that are sent outside the state for approval, and if approved, are filled by a shipment or delivery from a point outside the state. Public Law 86-272 does not protect the presence of employ-ees who also perform non-solicitation activities, such as repairs, customer training or technical assistance, within a state.

.02 State Versus Federal Nexus Standards for Foreign Corporations

As discussed above, state income tax nexus generally requires that an out-of-state corporation, including a corporation organized in a foreign country, have both an economic presence and a physical presence of the type not protected by Public Law 86-272. A different nexus standard applies with respect to federal taxation of a foreign corporation. The U.S. has bilateral income tax treaties with about 60 countries. Generally, these treaties include a "permanent establishment" provision, under which the business profits of a foreign corporation that is a resident of a treaty country are exempt from federal income tax, unless the foreign corporation conducts business through a permanent establishment situated in the United States.[43] Treaty permanent establishment provisions are not binding for state nexus purposes, however, because income tax treaties generally do not apply to state taxes.[44]

A permanent establishment generally includes a fixed place of business (e.g., a sales office), or the presence of employees who habitually exercise within the United States an authority to conclude contracts that are binding on the foreign

---

[42] 386 U.S. 753 (1967).

[43] Articles 5 and 7 (¶ 1304.05 and ¶ 1304.07) of the U.S. Model Treaty.

[44] Article 2 (¶ 1304.02) of the U.S. Model Treaty.

corporation. Certain activities are specifically excluded from the definition of a permanent establishment, however, including: (i) using facilities solely for the purpose of storing, displaying or delivering inventory belonging to the taxpayer; (ii) maintaining inventory belonging to the taxpayer solely for the purpose of storage, display or delivery, or processing by another enterprise; and (iii) maintaining a fixed place of business solely for the purpose of purchasing goods or collecting information for the taxpayer, or any other activity of a preparatory or auxiliary character.[45]

As a consequence, it is possible for a foreign (non-U.S.) corporation to have nexus for state but not federal income tax purposes. For example, if a foreign corporation leases warehouse space in a state solely for the purpose of storing and delivering its merchandise to U.S. customers, the physical presence of company-owned inventory would generally create state income tax nexus, but not necessarily federal income tax nexus, because the mere storage of inventory does not constitute a permanent establishment.

---

[45] Article 5 (¶ 1304.05) of the U.S. Model Treaty.

¶1507.02

Chapter 16
International Tax Practice and Procedure

¶ 1601 INTRODUCTION

As the major economies of the world have become global in nature, the frequency and complexity of cross-border transactions have increased significantly. The combination of expense allocation methods and the foreign tax credit limitation has generally resulted in U.S. companies having excess foreign tax credits. Likewise, foreign-owned multinationals with U.S. subsidiaries are subject to a myriad of reporting requirements[1] and provisions with respect to transfer pricing, the deductibility of related party interest[2] and, in turn, the capital structure of their U.S. subsidiaries. While many of the same procedural issues present in audits of domestic businesses are germane, there are other unique problems facing U.S.-based multinationals (outbound investment) as well as U.S. subsidiaries of foreign parent companies (inbound investment).

¶ 1602 ORGANIZATION OF THE INTERNAL REVENUE SERVICE INTERNATIONAL OFFICES

The Office of the Director, International, in Washington, D.C., now only functions as the U.S. Competent Authority.[3] The International Examiners are assigned to the industry groups within the Large Business and International (LB&I) Division.[4]

---

[1] Code Sec. 6038A and 6114.
[2] Code Sec. 163(j).

[3] IRM 4.60.3.1.6.
[4] IRM 4.60.4.

¶ 1603 INTERNATIONAL EXAMINATIONS

Given the extraordinary complexity of the international provisions of the Internal Revenue Code, the importance and involvement of the International Examiner has increased in multinational corporation audits. Recognizing this, the IRS has retrained many of its domestic agents as International Examiners. Whereas previously International Examiners were located only in large metropolitan areas, many audits of corporations in rural areas with international operations now have International Examiners assigned to their audits.

The International Examiners are crucial in any audit involving international issues. Because the international examiners are involved in a complex and sophisticated tax administration, they are specially trained to deal with issues involving controlled foreign corporations, cross-border transfers and reorganizations, transfer pricing, foreign tax credit issues, export benefits, and withholding taxes.[5] Although the International Examiners are assigned to the LB&I Division, they may receive referrals from the Small Business/Self-Employed (SB/SE) Division when international issues arise.[6]

Due to the increased emphasis by the Internal Revenue Service on intercompany transfer pricing, IRS economists are also becoming involved in the audit process. Their role is to identify potential transfer pricing issues early in the examination process as well as assist in gathering factual information in support of the IRS's position.

.01 Coordinated Industry Case Examinations

The IRS established the Coordinated Industry Case Program to provide a team approach to the examination of very large corporate cases that meet specific criteria for size and complexity of audit. This program brings together as one unit for audit purposes the primary taxpayer and all of the taxpayer's effectively controlled corporations and other entities. A Coordinated Industry Case, therefore, will usually involve a large group of closely affiliated, centrally controlled, widely dispersed, and highly diversified business entities. Domestic and foreign corporations, partnerships, joint ventures, syndicates, unincorporated businesses, individual, trusts, estates, foundations, pension and profit sharing trusts and other exempt organizations may be included within the coordinated audit group.[7]

.02 Other Examinations

Where the international taxpayer's examination is not classified as a Coordinated Industry Case, a pre-examination conference may still be held between the taxpayer and the examination team. During this meeting, the taxpayer should meet with the team manager for purposes of providing basic data, establishing the scope and depth of the examination and arranging for computer assistance.[8] The taxpayer will also learn who has been assigned to its audit and may want to begin its own

---

[5] IRM 4.60.4.7.

[6] IRM Exhibits 4.60.5-1 and 4.60.5-2.

[7] IRM 4.45.2.2.2.

[8] The IRS's goals for the pre-audit conference often include reaching an agreement with the taxpayer regarding (i) the lines of communication between the IRS and the taxpayer, (ii) the use of taxpayer resources, such as

office space, (iii) the procedures for providing the IRS with returns of related parties, (iv) the procedures for the taxpayer to present documentation of items that may reduce its tax liability, (v) the procedures for resolving questions regarding the content of IDRs, (vi) the periods of time for submitting and responding to IDRs, and (vii) procedures and timing of the examination of off-site records and facilities.

investigation to better prepare for the audit. Also at this meeting, if not before, taxpayers should agree, preferably in writing,[9] to procedures to be followed during the course of the audit regarding international issues.

.03 LB&I Pre-Filing Agreements

Similar to domestic examinations, international taxpayers may request the examination of specific issues relating to a tax return before the return is filed. If the taxpayer and the IRS are able to resolve the issues prior to the filing of the return, the taxpayer and the IRS may finalize their resolution by executing an LB&I Pre-Filing Agreement.[10]

.04 Industry Issue Focus

LB&I has recently initiated an Industry Issue Focus strategy to coordinate greater national control and consistency over important issues that range across industry lines.[11] Pursuant to this initiative, the International Examiners will identify potential compliance issues through the normal course of an audit. Certain issues are designated as Tier I, II, or III depending on their prevalence across industry lines and their compliance risk. For each issue designated as either a Tier I issue (high strategic importance), a Tier II issue (significant compliance risk), or a Tier III issue (industry risk), the IRS will form an issue management team comprised of personnel from Counsel, Appeals, and other functional areas. This team will provide instructions to the Examiners on how to handle the respective issues. The IRS has announced on its website the Tier I and Tier II issues, but has not designated any issues as Tier III issues. International-oriented Tier I issues include:

(i) § 936 exit strategies—these issues focus on the outbound transfer and transfer pricing issues related to the offshore migration of intangibles from formerly tax-favored Puerto Rican corporations;

(ii) domestic production deduction Code Sec. 199—these issues focus on the allocation of expenses, such as compensation, to and away from qualified production activities income;

(iii) foreign earnings repatriation—these issues focus on the since-repealed one-time dividends received deduction from foreign corporations that expired after September 30, 2006;

(iv) foreign tax credit generators—these issues focus on financial services industry transactions whereby taxpayers eliminate U.S. tax by generating a foreign tax that improperly results in a credit when the underlying business transaction would not ordinarily be subject to foreign tax;

(v) international hybrid instrument transactions—these issues focus on the inconsistent treatment of financial instruments as either debt in the United States and equity in a foreign country or equity in the United States and debt in a foreign country;

(vi) cost-sharing arrangements with buy-in payments—these issues focus on cost-sharing arrangements under the transfer pricing rules when moving intangibles offshore, including the amount of any buy-in payment by a

---

[9] In many IRS areas, there appears to be an objective to have a written audit agreement with every taxpayer under audit.

[10] Rev. Proc. 2009-14, 2009-3 IRB 324.
[11] IRM 4.51.5.

new participant to an existing participant for previously-existing intangibles and the measurement of reasonably anticipated benefits; and

(vii) reporting and withholding on U.S.-source fixed, determinable, annual, or periodic income—these issues focus on the compliance of U.S. withholding agents who make these payments.

International-oriented Tier II issues include:

(i) cost-sharing stock-based compensation—these issues involve the allocation and amount of compensation as a cost to be shared; and

(ii) extraterritorial income exclusion effective date and transition rules—these issues focus on an export benefit that has since been phased out.

The IRS has not announced any international-oriented Tier III issues.

.05 Statute of Limitations

The statute of limitations for the IRS to make an assessment is normally three years,[12] but may be extended to six years due to a 25% understatement of gross income.[13] Moreover, an extension to six years may also occur when amounts attributable to foreign financial assets[14] total more than $5,000 and are not reported on a return.

Example 16.1: USCo, a U.S. company, wholly-owns and, therefore, files a Form 5471 for ForSub, a foreign subsidiary. ForSub earned $35,000 of additional income tax attributable to $100,000 of interest that constituted Subpart F income. USCo failed to report this item of income on the Form 5471 filed with its 2011 return on September 15, 2012. The statute of limitations on the $100,000 of Subpart F interest income is the 6-year statute of limitations, which expires on September 15, 2018.

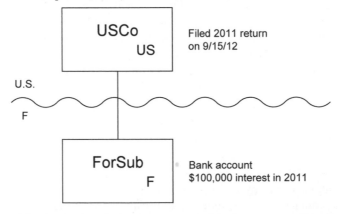

The statute of limitations only begins to run with respect to a tax return when all information reporting that is required to be reported under a number of Code sections[15] has been provided to the IRS.[16] In effect, the entire return is considered not filed, failing to trigger the running of the statute of limitations when a required information reporting schedule is not attached.

---

[12] Code Sec. 6501(a).
[13] Code Sec. 6501(e).
[14] Code Sec. 6038(D).

[15] Code Secs. 1295(b), 1298(f), 6038, 6038(A), 6038(B), 6038(D), 6046, 6046(A) and 6048.
[16] Code Sec. 6501(c)(8).

Example **16.2:** USCo is a U.S. corporation that wholly-owns ForCo, a foreign corporation. USCo files its Form 1120 for 2011 on September 15, 2012 without filing a Form 5471. The 3-year statute of limitations with respect to any item on the return will not begin to run until USCo files a Form 5471.

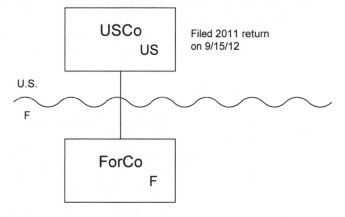

Although the next logical step is to treat this as a failure to file a return, the IRS has not stated whether it would assert the delinquency penalty in these situations.

¶ 1604 IRS PROCEDURAL TOOLS

The primary authority for recordkeeping requirements of an entity potentially liable for U.S. tax is Code Sec. 6001 of the Internal Revenue Code and the related Regulations.[17] The IRS also has the specific authority to examine any books, papers, records, or other data that may be relevant or material to ascertaining the correctness of any return, determining the tax liability of any person, or collecting any tax. Since most taxpayers and other individuals voluntarily produce records and answer questions when requested to do so by the IRS, this authority in itself is normally sufficient to obtain the necessary information.

One of the largest problems for foreign owned U.S. taxpayers is that most foreign corporations do not have records that are in a usable format. Records are often stated in foreign currency and prepared in foreign languages. Therefore, the U.S. taxpayer must spend a large amount of time and money translating and explaining the documents to the IRS.

This problem was confronted in the case of *Nissei Sangyo America, Ltd. v. U.S.*[18] *Nissei* involved the audit of a U.S. subsidiary of a Japanese parent. In response to an IRS summons, the U.S. subsidiary had randomly selected documents relating to the issue under examination and provided full translations. The Japanese parent had also randomly selected and translated documents. In addition,

---

[17] The Regulations may require generally that any person subject to tax under subtitle A of the Code " . . . or any person required to file a return of information with respect to income, shall keep such permanent books or account or records . . . as are sufficient to establish the amount of gross income, deductions, credits, or other matters required to be shown by such person in any return of such tax or information." Reg. § 1.6001-1(a). Additionally, "[t]he director may require any person, by notice served upon him, to make such returns, render such statements, or keep such specific records as will enable the director to determine whether or not such person is liable for tax under subtitle A of the Code." Reg. § 1.6001-1(d).

[18] DC Ill., 95-2 USTC ¶ 50,327. The internal procedures of the IRS require the IRS to request documents, review them and then specify the documents to be translated. Reg. § 1.6038A-3(b)(3)

it translated the subject matter headings or titles of 1,441 pages of Japanese correspondence and prepared English translation keys for the travel expense authorization forms. The IRS demanded that all documents described in the summonses be translated into English, which the company estimated would cost from $850,000 to $1.5 million. The court held that the IRS could not compel the translation of documents that were not relevant to the tax liability or that the IRS already had in its possession.[19] Although this case involved a response to an IRS summons, the translation issue may arise in any type of response to an IRS method to obtain documents.

.01 Information Document Requests

An Information Document Request (IDR) is designed to request information or documents from taxpayers when there are voluminous records to be examined, or when it is desirable to document requests. Requested on Form 4564 (a copy of which is reproduced in the Appendix to this Chapter), an IDR provides the IRS a convenient means to request information and simultaneously yields a permanent record of what was requested, received, and returned to the taxpayer.

An International Examiner in both Coordinated Industry Case and non-Coordinated Industry Case audits will often begin by issuing IDRs for information relevant to the scope of the review. For example, if intercompany purchases or sales of inventory exist, a typical IDR would request a copy of any intercompany pricing agreements as well as any contemporaneous documentation of transfer pricing methodology.[20] As a further example, if the examination involved a foreign tax credit, the International Examiner would generally request copies of the proof of foreign income taxes paid and the allocation and apportionment schedules for the sourcing of deductions.

After reviewing the information gathered from these initial IDRs, the International Examiner will focus on those areas with the largest potential for possible adjustments. As the examination progresses, IDRs generally become more narrow in scope and tend to focus on specific items or transactions.

In addition to this authority, an International Examiner can employ several procedural tools to obtain information beyond that obtained via IDRs. These include on site inspection, summons, designated summons, formal document requests, Code Secs. 6038A and 6038, and exchanges of information under treaties.

.02 On Site Inspections

In addition to IDRs, International Examiners appear to have taken an increased interest in foreign site visits and plant tours over the past few years.[21] While IRS budget constraints and internal administrative requirements may occasionally affect the number or duration of such visits, taxpayers should expect such requests and prepare to respond. The taxpayer should remember that it is a request, not an order, and that any request may be negotiated in terms of choosing the facility to visit (the taxpayer may want to substitute a domestic plant for a foreign plant), the duration of the visit, the timing of the visit, and the number of IRS employees involved. Careful planning of any such trip may result in an opportunity to present,

---

[19] *See* the general summons standard of *M. Powell*, SCt, 64-2 USTC ¶ 9858, 379 US 48, *infra*.

[20] Code Sec. 6662(e)(3)(B)(i)(III).

[21] I.R.M. 4.46.3.10.2 through 4.46.3.10.5.

¶1604.01

in effect, key facts supporting the taxpayer's position. The taxpayer should prepare the plant personnel for the visit. The taxpayer may consider pre-screening the tour to determine if the plant's operations cover processes or procedures relevant to the audit cycle and pre-interviewing all involved personnel to sensitize them to the potential issues. International Examiners have the following instructions for plant tours:[22]

(i) Obtain information about departmental cost sheets or schedules.

(ii) Learn the training requirements of each type of production employee.

(iii) Obtain any records regarding sales to all customers.

(iv) Ascertain the extent of product development performed at the plant.

(v) Interview plant employees. Plant interviews will bring a sense of reality to the case. Interviews should flush out the employee's ability to alter the production process and the technical training each production employee received.

(vi) If the company is a controlled foreign corporation, determine how and to whom it sells its products.

(vii) Obtain all company manuals regarding the operations of the plant.

(viii) Obtain all job descriptions prior to the plant tour.

(ix) Obtain all annual evaluations of the employees to be interviewed.

(x) Obtain all company "programmer" manuals. This manual offers guidance to the programmer to construct the program, so that software can be readily translated and localized.

.03 The Summons Power

To give force and meaning to this general authority to examine, the IRS has been granted the power to compel a taxpayer or any other person to produce records and to testify under oath. This compulsory process is authorization to the IRS to issue an administrative summons.[23] The IRS may summon any person to appear at a time and place named in the summons for the purpose of giving testimony under oath and producing books, papers, records, or other data. The authority to issue summonses has been delegated generally to those agents and other personnel within the IRS who are responsible for the examination of returns, collection of taxes, and investigation of tax offenses.[24] Therefore, International Examiners, Revenue Agents, Tax Auditors, Revenue Officers and Special Agents are all permitted to issue a summons.

When a corporation is under examination, the summons may be directed to either a specific corporate officer or the corporation itself.[25] The summons should indicate the officer's corporate position or title. When a corporation receives a summons, the IRS must serve an officer, director, managing agent or other person authorized to accept service of process on behalf of the corporation.

After service of the summons, the individual serving the summons prepares and signs a certificate of service on the reverse side of the Form 2039 retained by

---

[22] *IRS International Continuing Professional Education materials*, Chicago, Illinois, May 2005; *see also* IRM Exhibit 4.61.3-1.

[23] Code Sec.7602(a)(2).

[24] T.D. 6421, 1959-2 CB 433; Delegation Order No. 4.

[25] IRM 25.5.2.3.

¶1604.03

the IRS. The server enters the date, time, and manner of service on the certificate. The signed certificate of service is evidence in any proceeding to enforce the summons.[26] The date the summons requires for compliance cannot be less than ten days from the date of issuance of the summons.[27]

Scope of the summons power. An IRS summons may be used only for the purposes set forth in Code Sec. 7602. These purposes are the verification, determination and collection of the tax liability of any person. The IRS also has specific authorization to issue summonses for the purpose of investigating any criminal tax offense.[28]

Pursuant to the standards of *United States v. Powell*,[29] to enforce a summons, the IRS must show that:

- There is a legitimate purpose for the investigation;
- The material sought is relevant to that purpose;
- The material sought is not already within the IRS's possession; and
- Those administrative steps that are required by the Internal Revenue Code are followed.

Use of summonses in Tax Court proceedings. The use of administrative summonses by the IRS during Tax Court proceedings has raised objections by taxpayers. The Tax Court discovery rules permitting both parties to obtain relevant information before trial are much more restricted in their scope than the summons power available to the IRS. In certain situations, the Tax Court has held that to allow the IRS in a pending case to use evidence obtained by the issuance of a summons would give the government an unfair advantage over the taxpayer. In effect, such use of the summons would permit the IRS to circumvent the limitations of the Tax Court's discovery rules. Therefore, the Tax Court will issue protective orders to preclude the IRS from using information obtained by such abusive use of an administrative summons.[30] In *Ash v. Commissioner*,[31] the Tax Court set forth guidelines to be followed in determining whether a protective order should be issued when the IRS obtains information during a pending case by means of a summons.

Where Tax Court litigation has commenced and a summons is then issued with regard to the same taxpayer and taxable year involved in the litigation, the Tax Court will issue a protective order to prevent the IRS from using any of the summoned evidence in the litigation.[32] However, the Tax Court will not issue a protective order if the IRS can show that the summons was issued for a sufficient reason that was independent of the pending litigation.

In those cases where the summons is issued before the taxpayer commences litigation by filing a Tax Court petition, no order will be issued with respect to any information obtained as a result of the summons. The Tax Court, in *Ash*, explained that before a petition is filed, the Tax Court has no jurisdiction and there is no basis

---

[26] Code Sec. 7603.

[27] Code Sec. 7605(a). A longer period is required for third-party recordkeeper summonses.

[28] Code Sec. 7602(b).

[29] SCt, 64-2 USTC ¶ 9858, 379 US 48, 85 SCt 248.

[30] Tax Court Rule 103.

[31] 96 TC 459, Dec. 47,221.

[32] The Tax Court issued such an order in *Universal Manufacturing Co.*, 93 TC 589, Dec. 46,154.

for viewing the summons as an attempt to undermine the Tax Court's discovery rules.[33]

Finally, where litigation has commenced, and an administrative summons is issued with regard to a different taxpayer or a different taxable year, the Tax Court in *Ash* normally will not issue a protective order.[34] However, the Tax Court stated a protective order would be issued if the taxpayer could show that the IRS lacked an independent and sufficient reason for the summons.

.04 Designated Summonses

If, after issuing a summons, the IRS does not obtain the desired information, the IRS may consider issuing a designated summons.[35]

A designated summons tolls the running of the statute of limitations during the period in which judicial enforcement proceeding is pending and for either 30 or 120 days thereafter, depending on whether or not the court orders compliance with the summons. The legislative history indicates Congress was concerned that taxpayers made a practice of responding slowly to IRS requests for information without extending the statute of limitations. Congress did not intend to extend the statute of limitations in a large number of cases, but to encourage taxpayers to provide requested information on a timely basis by realizing that the IRS had this tool available. In addition to satisfying the aforementioned *Powell* standards, the internal procedures the IRS personnel have to follow to issue a designated summons are a major impediment to their issuance. A designated summons must be approved by the LB&I Division Commissioner and Division Counsel-LB&I[36] and must be issued at least 60 days before the expiration of the statute of limitations.[37]

> ***Example* 16.3:** A distributor of computers, USAco is a subsidiary of ASIAco. USAco buys computers from ASIAco and resells them in the United States. The IRS's International Examiner conducts a transfer pricing audit of USAco. After USAco fails to respond to the International Examiner's IDR requesting all agreements between USAco and ASIAco, just over 60 days remain on the statute of limitations. USAco will not sign a consent to extend the statute of limitations. Concerned about the possibility that the statute of limitations will expire, the International Examiner issues a designated summons for the agreements. The designated summons tolls the statute of limitations during enforcement proceedings and for a short time thereafter.[38]

---

[33] *Bennett*, ND Tex, 2000-2 USTC ¶ 50,717.

[34] In an earlier case involving this type of situation, the issuance of a protective order was justified by the "compelling facts." *Westreco, Inc.*, 60 TCM 824, Dec. 46,882(M), TC Memo. 1990-501.

[35] Code Sec. 6503(j).

[36] Prop. Reg. § 301.6503(j)-1(c)(1)(i).

[37] Code Sec. 6503(j)(2)(A).

[38] *Derr*, CA-9, 92-2 USTC ¶ 50,369.

¶1604.04

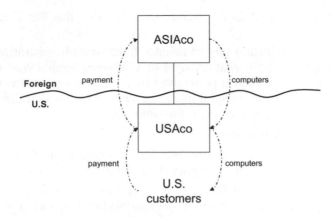

.05 Formal Document Requests

If, through IDRs, the IRS is unable to gather the foreign information it considers necessary to conduct its examination, the IRS may issue a formal document request (FDR). The FDR is not intended to be used as a routine tool at the beginning of an examination, but instead as a mechanism for securing information that could not be obtained through normal IDRs. The rare use of the FDR is indicated by the fact that the IRS does not have a specific form for the FDR. Instead, the IRS will issue a Form 4564 entitled "Information Document Request" with the typed notation "Formal Document Request" (see the Appendix to this chapter). The FDR must be mailed by registered or certified mail and provide:

(i) The time and place for the production of the documentation;

(ii) A statement of the reason the documentation previously produced (if any) is not sufficient;

(iii) A description of the documentation being sought; and

(iv) The consequences to the taxpayer of the failure to produce the documentation described in subparagraph (iii).[39]

If the taxpayer does not furnish the requested information within 90 days of the mailing of the FDR, the taxpayer will be prevented from later introducing the requested documentation. Foreign-based documentation is "any documentation which is outside the United States and which may be relevant or material to the tax treatment of the examined item."[40] Therefore, the IRS has broad authority to request virtually any relevant information as long as the request satisfies the aforementioned *Powell* standards.[41] The purpose of the FDR procedure is to discourage taxpayers from delaying or refusing disclosure of certain foreign-based documentation. To avoid the later exclusion of documents, the taxpayer must substantially comply with the FDR. The FDR is not intended to be used as a routine beginning to an examination, but instead as a mechanism for securing information that could not be obtained through normal request procedures.[42]

---

[39] Code Sec. 982(c)(1).
[40] Code Sec. 982(d).
[41] *Yujuico*, ND Cal, 93-1 USTC ¶ 50,097.

[42] *See* Joint Committee on Taxation, General Explanation of the Tax Equity and Fiscal Responsibility Act of 1982, HR 4961, 97th Cong., 2d Sess. 246-247.

¶1604.05

Whether there has been substantial compliance with an FDR will depend on all the facts and circumstances.[43] For example, if the taxpayer submits nine out of ten requested items and the court believes the missing item is the most substantial, the taxpayer could be found to have failed to comply substantially with the FDR. Accordingly, the taxpayer could be prevented from later introducing the missing documentation.

Any taxpayer that receives an FDR has the right to begin proceedings to quash the request within ninety days after the request was mailed. The standard for quashing a FDR is the same *Powell* standard for quashing a summons.[44] Moreover, the taxpayer may contend, for example, that the information requested is irrelevant, that the requested information is available in the United States, or that reasonable cause exists for the failure to produce or delay in producing the information.

Reasonable cause does not exist where a foreign jurisdiction would impose a civil or criminal penalty on the taxpayer for disclosing the requested documentation.[45] In a proceeding to quash, the IRS has the burden of proof to show the relevance and materiality of the information requested. During the period that a proceeding to quash or any appeal from that proceeding is pending, the statute of limitations is suspended.[46]

The legislative history to Code Sec. 982 specifies that three factors should be considered in determining whether there is reasonable cause for failure to furnish the requested documentation. These factors are: (i) whether the request is reasonable in scope; (ii) whether the requested documents are available within the United States; and (iii) the reasonableness of the requested place of production within the United States.[47]

An example of an unreasonable scope may be a request "for all the books and records and all the supporting documents for all the entries made in such books or records" for a particular foreign entity that is controlled by a taxpayer. However, a request for the general ledger, an analysis of an account, and supporting documents for a particular transaction of such a foreign entity would be reasonable in scope. Moreover, the place of production of records is generally at the taxpayer's place of business or the International Examiner's office. Requesting the production of records in New York City by a taxpayer that is residing in and engages in a trade or business in Los Angeles may be considered unreasonable. The key to the reasonableness of the place for production is that such a place should be mutually convenient to both the taxpayer and the IRS.

.06 Code Secs. 6038A and 6038

Congressional perception that foreign-owned U.S. subsidiaries were not paying their proper share of U.S. tax and the inability of the IRS to obtain foreign-based documentation caused Congress to expand greatly the application of Code Sec. 6038A. The section places the reporting burden for intercompany transactions on the 25 percent or greater foreign-owned corporation with a U.S. subsidiary. The U.S. subsidiary, the "reporting corporation," must furnish certain information annu-

---

[43] *See Good Karma, LLC v. United States*, N.D. IL, 2008-2 USTC ¶ 50,646.

[44] *Yujuico v. United States*, N.D. Cal, 93-1 USTC ¶ 50,097.

[45] Code Sec. 982(e).

[46] Code Sec. 982(e).

[47] Conference Committee Report on P.L. 97-248, The Tax Equity and Fiscal Responsibility Act of 1982.

ally and maintain records necessary to determine the correctness of the intercompany transactions. In addition, the reporting corporation must furnish the required information by filing Form 5472 on an annual basis. A completed Form 5472 is reproduced in the Appendix to Chapter 12 (¶ 1206).

Reg. § 1.6038A-3(a)(1) provides that "[a] reporting corporation must keep the permanent books of account or records as required by section 6001 that are sufficient to establish the correctness of the federal income tax return of the corporation, including information, documents, or records ('records') to the extent they may be relevant to determine the correct U.S. tax treatment of transactions with related parties." Such records may include, for example, cost data, if appropriate, to determine the profit or loss from the transfer pricing of intercompany transactions.

Failure to maintain or timely furnish the required information may result in a penalty of $10,000 for each taxable year in which the failure occurs for each related party.[48] If any failure continues for more than ninety days after notice of the failure to the reporting corporation, an additional penalty of $10,000 per thirty-day period is imposed while the failure continues. Additional penalties can be levied if it is determined the taxpayer fails to maintain records after the ninety-day notification.[49]

More specifically, Code Sec. 6038A(e) allows the IRS to reduce the cost of goods sold when a taxpayer does not obtain its foreign parent's permission to be an agent for the request of certain documents. Within thirty days after a request by the IRS, a foreign-related party must appoint the reporting corporation as its limited agent for service of a summons. Failure to appoint such an agent can result in penalties for noncompliance.[50] In such a case, the LMSB Industry Director in his or her sole discretion shall determine the amount of the relevant deduction or the cost to the reporting corporation.

The IRS is prepared to adhere to Code Sec. 6038A(e) as shown in *Asat, Inc. v. Commissioner*.[51] In *Asat*, the Tax Court literally applied Code Sec. 6038A(e) against the taxpayer, upholding the IRS's reduction to the cost of goods sold. Adhering to the legislative history, the Tax Court further found irrelevant that the foreign parent during the year in issue was not the parent at the time of the audit.

> **Example 16.4:** A distributor of toy dolls, USAco is a subsidiary of ASIAco. USAco buys toy dolls from ASIAco and resells them in the United States. The IRS's International Examiner conducts a transfer pricing audit of USAco. Wanting to obtain documents from ASIAco, the International Examiner requests that ASIAco appoint USAco as its agent for service of a summons. If ASIAco neither appoints USAco as its agent nor provides the pricing data to the International Examiner, the IRS can reduce USAco's cost of goods sold to $0.

---

[48] Reg. § 1.6038A-4(a)(1).
[49] *Id.* Reg. § 1.6038A-4(d)(1).

[50] *Id.* Reg. § 1.6038A-5.
[51] 108 TC 147, Dec. 51,966.

¶1604.06

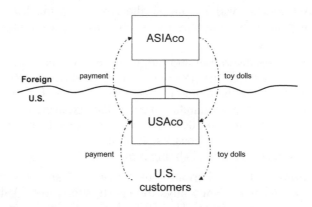

Although there is not the same perception that U.S.-owners of foreign subsidiaries are not paying their proper share of U.S. tax, Code Sec. 6038 places a reporting burden for intercompany transactions on a U.S. owner of a controlled foreign corporation. This information is reported by the U.S. owner filing Form 5471 on an annual basis.

As with Code Sec. 6038A, the failure to maintain or timely furnish the Code Sec. 6038 information may result in a penalty of $10,000 for each taxable year in which the failure occurs.[52] If any failure continues for more than 90 days after notice of the failure, an additional penalty of $10,000 per 30-day period is imposed while the failure continues. The IRS can levy additional penalties if the U.S. owner fails to maintain records after receiving notification. The IRS can further reduce any foreign tax credits taken by the U.S. owner by 10%.[53]

> **Example 16.5:** Uncle Sam, a U.S. citizen, inherits all the shares of FSub, a controlled foreign corporation that is incorporated in Country F. During the taxable year, FSub pays a gross dividend of $100,000, which is reduced by the $10,000 withholding tax imposed by Country F. Although Uncle Sam takes a $10,000 direct foreign tax credit on his return, he never files a Form 5471 for FSub. The IRS can reduce Uncle Sam's foreign tax credit by $1,000.

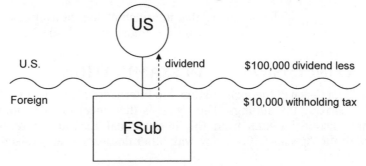

.07 Exchanges of Information Under Tax Treaties

Under the exchange of information provisions of a tax treaty, the IRS can generally request information from a foreign country that is either in the foreign

---

[52] Code Sec. 6038(b).   [53] Code Sec. 6038(c).

country's possession or available under the respective tax laws of that foreign country. These provisions generally do not require the exchange of information that would disclose any trade or business secret.

The IRS exercises discretion and judgment in both requesting and furnishing of information. In general, the IRS will not request information from another country unless: (i) there is a good reason to believe that the information is necessary to determine the tax liability of a specific taxpayer; (ii) the information is not otherwise available to the IRS; and (iii) the IRS is reasonably sure that requested information is in the possession of, or available to, the foreign government from whom the information is being requested.

> **Example 16.6:** A distributor of "Crazylegs" sports shoes, USAco is a subsidiary of ASIAco. USAco buys the sports shoes from ASIAco and resells them in the United States. The IRS's International Examiner conducts a transfer pricing audit of USAco. After USAco fails to respond to the International Examiner's IDR requesting all agreements between USAco and ASIAco, the International Examiner requests the information from ASIA country's tax authority pursuant to the exchange of information provision in the U.S.-ASIA tax treaty.

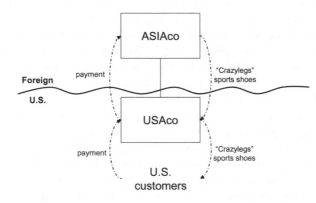

The IRS's internal guidelines require that information sought from another competent authority must specifically describe the information desired and the reason why the information is necessary.[54]

¶ 1605 CONCLUSION OF AN EXAMINATION

At the conclusion of the examination, the International Examiner will prepare a report summarizing the findings. The report is then incorporated into the agent's report. Any disputed issues from the International Examiner's report may be pursued with the Appeals Office along with other domestic issues raised during the examination.

.01 Settling Issues

Certain issues over which there is disagreement may be settled by the team manager under the authority of Code Sec. 7121 to enter closing agreements. This

---

[54] IRM 4.60.1.2.4.2.

authority exists where the Appeals Office has previously approved a settlement agreement involving the same issue in a Coordinated Industry Case in a prior year involving the same taxpayer or a taxpayer directly involved in the taxable transaction.[55]

.02 Accelerated Issue Resolution

Another option available in Coordinated Industry cases for unresolved issues is the accelerated issue resolution (AIR) program. The purpose of this program is to advance the resolution of issues from one tax period to another. Under this program, the taxpayer enters into an AIR agreement that acts as a closing agreement with respect to one or more issues present in a LB&I examination for one or more periods ending before the date of the agreement.[56] Revenue Procedure 94-67 explains the scope and procedure for obtaining an AIR agreement. An AIR agreement may only be entered into for issues that fall under the jurisdiction of the LB&I Industry Director and which relate to other items in another tax period. However, an AIR agreement may not be entered into for transfer pricing transactions or any item designated for litigation by the Office of Chief Counsel.[57] Because the AIR program is voluntary, the taxpayer must submit a written request to the team manager. If the request is denied, the taxpayer does not have a right to appeal the denial.

.03 Early Appeals Referral

If the issue is not within the LB&I team manager's settlement jurisdiction, the taxpayer may elect to use the early appeals referral procedures and have the issue considered by the Appeals Office while the audit work continues in other areas. The IRS has instituted the early referral program for Coordinated Industry Cases in order to expedite the resolution of unagreed issues. Early referral is optional to the taxpayer and is subject to the approval of both the LB&I Industry Director and the Appeals-LB&I Area Manager.[58] Early referral cannot be requested for issues that have been designated for litigation. The early referral request must be submitted in writing, stating the issues and positions involved. If the request is granted, the file is forwarded to the Appeals Office. Similar to an AIR denial, the taxpayer cannot appeal a refusal to grant early referral.

¶ 1606 APPEALS DIVISION OF THE IRS

.01 Protest Requirements

Upon completion of an international examination, the examining office may issue the taxpayer a thirty-day letter proposing a deficiency. The taxpayer may object to any proposed tax adjustments and request a conference with the Appeals Office by filing a protest with the Appeals Office. The taxpayer must formally request the conference by means of a document known as a protest. The protest must be in writing and must include certain elements to meet the requirements of the Appeals Office.[59]

---

[55] IRM 4.45.15.2.1.
[56] Rev. Proc. 94-67, 1994-2 CB 800.
[57] Id.

[58] Rev. Proc. 99-28, 1999-2 CB 109; Code Sec. 7123.
[59] Reg. § 601.106(a)(iii).

.02 Procedure at the Appeals Division

Proceedings before the Appeals Office are informal. Testimony is not taken under oath, although the Appeals Office may require matters alleged to be true to be submitted in the form of affidavits or declarations under the penalties of perjury. The taxpayer or the representative will meet with the Appeals Officer and informally discuss the pros and cons of the various positions taken by the taxpayer and the IRS. Appeals will follow the law and the recognized legal construction in determining facts and applying the law. Appeals will determine the correct amount of the tax with strict impartiality as between the taxpayer and the Government, and without favoritism or discrimination between taxpayers.[60]

Although an Appeals Officer is to maintain a standard of impartiality, he or she must, nevertheless, protect the rights of the IRS and act as an advocate on behalf of the IRS. Therefore, an Appeals Officer can raise a new issue or propose a new theory in support of the examining agent's proposed adjustment. However, an Appeals Officer generally will not do so unless the grounds for raising such new issues are substantial and the effect on the tax liability is material.[61]

.03 Appeals Process for a Coordinated Industry Case

Unlike normal audit and appeal procedures, however, in a Coordinated Industry Case, members of the examination team from LB&I and Appeals personnel are authorized and, in some instances, required to hold a conference before Appeals Office personnel meet with the taxpayer.[62] The purpose of this unique pre-conference is to discuss the issues, the taxpayer's protest and the written rebuttal by the LB&I team members to the protest. Such a conference also serves to identify the need for additional information and development of issues.

Although the examination team is encouraged during this meeting to share its views on the issues, including its assessment of litigating hazards, the parties are specifically instructed that the conference is not to be used as a means for securing a commitment from Appeals that any particular issue should be defended or the manner in which the case should be settled.[63] In substance, despite such intimate discussions of the case, the parties to the pre-conference are reminded that the detached objectivity of Appeals is not to be compromised.

.04 Settlement Agreements

The IRS describes the "Appeals Mission" as one to resolve tax controversies without litigation, on a basis that is fair and impartial to both the government and the taxpayer and in a manner that will enhance voluntary compliance and public confidence in the integrity and efficiency of the IRS.[64] Therefore, the Appeals Officer can split or trade issues where there are substantial uncertainties as to the law, the facts or both. In splitting a "legal issue," the Appeals Officer will ordinarily consider the hazards that would exist if the case were litigated. He or she will weigh the testimony of the proposed witnesses, evaluate the trends that the courts have been following in similar cases, and generally try to predict the outcome of the matter if the case were actually tried. Where a case involves concessions by both

---

[60] Reg. § 601.106(f)(1).
[61] IRM 8.6.1.4.
[62] IRM 8.6.1.2.7.

[63] *Id.*
[64] IRM 8.6.1.3.

¶1606.02

the government and the taxpayer "for purposes of settlement" and where there is substantial uncertainty as to how the courts would interpret and apply the law or what facts the court would find, a settlement is classified as a "mutual concession settlement." No settlement is to be made by Appeals simply on nuisance value.[65]

Where a taxpayer and the Appeals Officer have reached an agreement as to some or all of the issues in controversy, the Appeals Officer will request the taxpayer to sign a Form 870, the same agreement used at the Examination level. However, when neither party with justification is willing to concede in full the unresolved area of disagreement and a resolution of the dispute involves concessions for the purposes of settlement by both parties based on the relative strengths of the opposing positions, a "mutual concession settlement" is reached and a Form 870-AD type of agreement is executed.[66]

The special appeals Form 870-AD differs from the normal Form 870 in several ways. The Form 870-AD agreement contains pledges against reopening that the usual agreement does not contain. Furthermore, the regular 870 becomes effective as a Waiver of Restrictions on Assessment when received by the IRS, whereas the special 870-AD is effective only upon acceptance by or on behalf of the Commissioner of Internal Revenue. Finally, the running of interest is suspended thirty days after a Form 870 is received,[67] whereas with a Form 870-AD, interest is not suspended until thirty days after the government executes the agreement.

¶ 1607 COMPETENT AUTHORITY PROCEDURE

If the taxpayer has been unable to agree with Appeals on an adjustment that results in double taxation, the taxpayer may seek relief through the Competent Authority Procedure. An integral part of all U.S. Income Tax Treaties is a mutual agreement procedure which provides a mechanism for relief from double taxation. The Office of the Director International acts as the U.S. Competent Authority. The Competent Authority's primary objective is to make a reasonable effort to resolve double taxation cases and situations in which U.S. taxpayers have been denied benefits provided for by a treaty.[68] The taxpayer may request the Competent Authority Procedure when the actions of the United States, the treaty country or both will result in taxation that is contrary to provisions of an applicable tax treaty. Revenue Procedure 2006-54[69] explains how to request assistance of the U.S. Competent Authority in resolving conflicts between treaty partners. To the extent a treaty partner proposes an adjustment that appears inconsistent with a treaty provision or would result in double taxation, assistance via the Competent Authority Procedure should be sought as soon as is practical after the issue is developed by the treaty country (Revenue Procedure 2006-54's index, which details specific procedures, is reproduced in the Appendix to this Chapter).

When the IRS proposes adjustments that are inconsistent with a treaty provision or would result in double taxation, the taxpayer is encouraged to seek relief through the Competent Authority Procedure after the IRS determines and communicates the amount of the proposed adjustment to the taxpayer in writing.

---

[65] IRM 8.6.4.1.3.

[66] IRM 8.8.1.1.2.

[67] Code Sec. 6601(c). (Forms 870 and 870-AD are reproduced in the appendix to this chapter.)

[68] IRM 4.60.2.1.

[69] Rev. Proc. 2006-54, IRB 2006-49.

Taxpayers must use the Appeals process to try to resolve the adjustments before pursuing the Competent Authority Procedure. Where it is in the best interests of both parties, the Competent Authority Procedure may begin prior to consideration by the Appeals office. However the U.S. Competent Authority may require the taxpayer to waive the right to the Appeals process at any time during the Competent Authority Procedure.

The opportunities to resolve disputes via the Competent Authority Procedure have increased from the traditional Mutual Agreement Procedure to include the Simultaneous Appeals Procedure and the Accelerated Competent Authority Procedure. All these methods have the potential to resolve disputes of international tax issues in a manner that avoids litigation.

.01 Mutual Agreement Procedure

The Mutual Agreement Procedure (MAP) treaty articles generally apply when the actions of the U.S. or foreign income tax authorities result in taxation not in accordance with the provisions of the applicable treaty.[70] Distribution, apportionment, or allocation under transfer pricing rules may subject a taxpayer to U.S. federal income taxation on income that the taxpayer had attributed to a foreign country. Without an offsetting decrease in income reported to the foreign country, the taxpayer may be subject to double taxation of the same income.

> **Example 16.7:** A widget distributor, USAco is a subsidiary of ASIAco. USAco buys widgets from ASIAco for $100 and resells them in the United States for $105. The IRS argues that the arm's length price from ASIAco to USAco should be $90 and makes an assessment. Because $10 of income (the difference between the $100 ASIAco charged and the $90 the IRS believes is arm's length) is taxed by both the IRS and ASIA's tax administration, USAco and ASIAco can request relief from their respective competent authorities. The competent authorities will negotiate with each other to determine who will tax the $10.

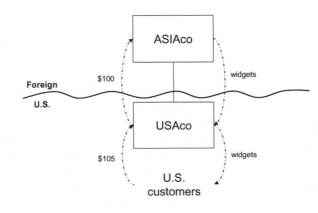

---

70 *Id.* at § 4.01. A small case procedure also exists *Id.* at § 5.01.

¶1607.01

.02 Simultaneous Appeals Procedure

Under the Simultaneous Appeals Procedure (SAP), taxpayers may seek simultaneous Appeals and Competent Authority consideration of an issue.[71] This procedure allows taxpayers to obtain Appeals involvement in a manner consistent with the ensuing Competent Authority Procedure and should reduce the time required to resolve disputes by allowing taxpayers more proactive involvement in the process. By informally approaching the Competent Authority before submitting a formal request, the Competent Authority effectively becomes the taxpayer's advocate. SAP further opens the possibility of developing strategies to explore the view likely to be taken by the other country.

Taxpayers may request SAP with the Competent Authority in three situations:

(i) After Examination has proposed an adjustment with respect to an issue that the taxpayer wishes to submit to the Competent Authority;[72]

(ii) After Examination has issued a 30-day letter, the taxpayer can file a protest, sever the issue, and seek Competent Authority assistance while other issues are referred to or remain at Appeals;[73] or

(iii) After the taxpayer is at Appeals, the taxpayer can request Competent Authority assistance on an issue.[74]

The taxpayer also can request SAP with Appeals after a Competent Authority request is made.[75] Generally, the request will be denied if the U.S. position paper has already been communicated to the foreign Competent Authority. The U.S. Competent Authority also can request the procedure.[76]

SAP is a two-part process. First, the Appeals representative will prepare an Appeals Case Memorandum (ACM) on the issue. The ACM is shared with the Competent Authority representative, but not with the taxpayer. The ACM is a tentative resolution that is considered by the U.S. Competent Authority in preparing the U.S. position paper for presentation to the foreign Competent Authority.[77] Second, the U.S. Competent Authority prepares and presents the U.S. position paper to the foreign Competent Authority. The U.S. Competent Authority meets with the taxpayer to discuss the technical issue to be presented to the foreign Competent Authority and the Appeals representative may be asked to participate. If either the Competent Authorities fail to agree or if the taxpayer does not accept the mutual agreement reached, the taxpayer is allowed to refer the issue to Appeals for further consideration.[78]

.03 Accelerated Competent Authority Procedure

The Accelerated Competent Authority Procedure (ACAP) shortens the time required to complete a case.[79] A taxpayer requesting ACAP assistance with respect to an issue raised by the IRS may request that the Competent Authority resolves the issue for subsequent tax years ending prior to the date of the request for the

---

[71] *Id.* at §8.01.
[72] *Id.* at §8.02(1)(a).
[73] *Id.* at §8.02(1)(b).
[74] *Id.* at §8.02(1)(c).
[75] *Id.* at §8.02(2).
[76] *Id.* at §8.01.

[77] This situation is analogous to the APA process. The Appeals representative will be a team chief, international specialist, or Appeals officer with international experience.
[78] *Id.* at §8.07.
[79] *Id.* at §7.06.

assistance.[80] In such a request, the taxpayer must agree that the inspection of books and/or records under the ACAP will not preclude or impede a later examination or inspection for any period covered in the request; and the IRS need not comply with any procedural restrictions before beginning such an examination or inspection. The U.S. Competent Authority will contact the appropriate LB&I Industry Director to determine whether the issue should be resolved for subsequent tax years. If the director consents, the U.S. Competent Authority will present the request to the foreign Competent Authority.[81]

¶ 1608 CIVIL ACTIONS BY TAXPAYERS

A taxpayer may contest an adverse IRS determination in one of three tribunals. A petition may be filed with the U.S. Tax Court, whereby assessment and collection of the deficiency will be stayed until the Court's decision becomes final. Alternatively, the taxpayer may pay the deficiency including interest and penalties and sue for a refund in a U.S. District Court or the U.S. Court of Federal Claims.[82] A nonresident alien or foreign corporation is not a resident of any U.S. district and may only file a refund suit in the U.S. Court of Federal Claims.

Filing a Petition in the U.S. Tax Court does not require payment of any tax, penalties or interest until the taxpayer's liability has been finally determined. If, on the other hand, the taxpayer sues for a refund in either a U.S. District Court or the U.S. Court of Federal Claims, the taxpayer must initially pay the tax including interest and penalties.

In a suit brought in a U.S. District Court the taxpayer may request that a jury determine factual issues.[83] A jury trial *cannot* be obtained before the U.S. Tax Court or the U.S. Court of Federal Claims. Many factors must be taken into consideration in selecting the forum, including previous rulings on the particular issue by the particular court and whether the issue is one that will affect tax liability for future years.

¶ 1609 UNCERTAIN TAX POSITIONS AND FORM UTP

In an effort to require large taxpayers to disclose uncertain tax positions, which will include many international tax issues, the IRS has promulgated Form UTP. Form UTP will aid the IRS in focusing its examination resources on returns that contain specific uncertain tax positions that are of particular interest or of sufficient magnitude to warrant IRS inquiries. More specifically, the Form UTP requirements expand a taxpayer's obligation to self-report sensitive income tax matters on its tax returns beyond existing requirements for any tax shelters and listed transactions.

Taxpayers who must file Form UTP include the following:

   (i)   Filers of Forms 1120, 1120F, and other corporate forms;

  (ii)   Book value of assets equal to or in excess of $100 million for 2010 and 2011, $50 million for 2012 and 2013, and $10 million thereafter;

 (iii)   A corporation or its related party that receive an audited financial statement that covers all or a portion of the corporation's operations for all or a portion of the tax year; and

 (iv)   The corporation has one or more uncertain tax positions.

---

[80] *Id.*
[81] *Id.*

[82] Judicial Code Sec. 1346; Code Sec. 7422.
[83] 28 U.S.C. Sec. 2402.

Uncertain Tax Positions are either: (i) positions for which a tax reserve must be established in the taxpayer's financial statements under FIN 48 or other accounting standards (e.g., IFRS) or (ii) any position for which a tax reserve has not been recorded because the taxpayer expects to litigate the position. For example, the taxpayer may determine that, if the IRS had full knowledge of the position, there would be a less than 50% chance of settlement and, that if litigated, the taxpayer has a greater than 50% chance of prevailing.

Example **16.8:** USCo has a branch in foreign country F and pays foreign country F taxes. A 1990 Revenue Ruling by the IRS incorrectly states that country F's taxes are not creditable for foreign income tax purposes because, in determining the country F tax, country F does not allow deductions and, therefore, country F's tax fails the net income requirement. USCo's tax director knows that this Revenue Ruling is inapplicable because foreign country F's tax regime allows deductions and, as a result, USCo does not take a tax reserve on its 2011 financial statements with respect to the foreign tax credit position in country F. USCo's tax director realizes that if the IRS knows of USCo taking a foreign tax credit for country F taxes, USCo will be audited on this issue with less than a 50% chance of settlement (due to the existing Revenue Ruling), but if litigated, the Tax Court would agree with USCo. As a result, USCo does not have to report the foreign tax credit position in country F on a Form UTP.

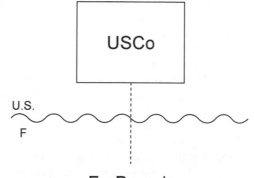

Example **16.9:** USCo sells $10 million of widgets to ForCo, resulting in a return on sale to USCo of $500,000 (5%). USCo's tax director does not conduct a transfer pricing study, but believes that an appropriate return on sale for a company that performs the functions and assumes the risks of USCo would be $600,000 (6%). As a result, USCo's tax director books a reserve with respect to transfer pricing of $35,000 (35% of a potential $100,000 adjustment). USCo's tax director has an uncertain tax position for which USCo must file a Form UTP.

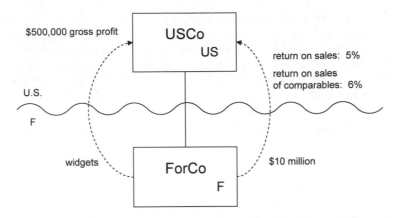

The Form UTP requires the corporation to rank all the tax return positions based on the U.S. federal income tax reserve recorded for the position on the return and state whether a particular UTP results in at least 10% of the total potential tax liability of all UTPs. Tax return positions includes transfer pricing and valuation positions.

The concise description of each UTP must provide "sufficient detail" so that the IRS can identify the tax position and the nature of the issue. A completed Form UTP is attached to the Appendix for this Chapter.

¶ 1610 OFFSHORE INITIATIVE

Although international examinations are primarily conducted within the LB&I Division, the SB/SE Division is responsible for offshore initiatives with respect to individuals. More specifically, the SB/SE Division has jurisdiction for the Report of Foreign Bank and Financial Accounts on TD F 90-22.1 (FBAR), a completed sample of which is reproduced in the Appendix to this chapter. As a result of the Bank Secrecy Act, the Treasury Department has authority to seek information with respect to U.S. persons that control foreign bank accounts.[84] The Treasury Department has delegated this authority for enforcement of these FBAR filings to the IRS.

.01 Potential FBAR Filers

Any U.S. person with financial interest in or signatory authority over a foreign bank account aggregating more than $10,000 at any time during the year must report that account on an FBAR. A foreign bank account does not include an account with a U.S. branch of a foreign bank or a foreign branch of a U.S. bank.[85]

The definition of a U.S. person includes a U.S. citizen, U.S. resident, U.S. partnership, U.S. corporation, U.S. estate, and U.S. trust.[86]

> **Example 16.10:** Bob, a U.S. citizen, is on special assignment during the winter at his condominium in Mexico. For his convenience, Bob opens an account at the Last National Bank of Mexico. At its peak, the account balance is $15,000, but on December 31 the balance is only $8,000. Because its highest balance is above $10,000, Bob must file an FBAR.

---

[84] 31 C.F.R. § 103.56(g).
[85] 31 C.F.R. § 103(o). C.F.R. § 103.24.

[86] 31 C.F.R. § 103.11(z) and (n)(n); IRS Announcement 2010-16, 2010-11 I.R.B. 450.

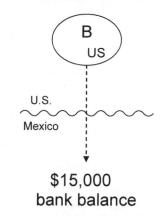

$15,000
bank balance

Multiple accounts are aggregated to determine whether they meet the $10,000 threshold.

Example 16.11: Bob, a U.S. citizen, is on special assignment during the winter at his condominium in Mexico. Bob has two bank accounts in Mexico. The first, at the Hacienda Local Bank, has a peak balance of $2,500 and a year-end balance of $55. The second, at the Last National Bank of Mexico, has a peak balance of $8,000 and a year-end balance of $3,000. Because the aggregate of the peak balances exceed $10,000 ($2,500 plus $8,000 is $10,500), Bob must file an FBAR for the two accounts.

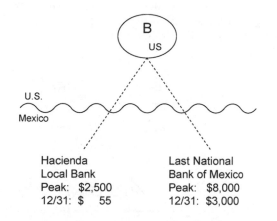

A U.S. person also has to file an FBAR if he or she owns more than 50% of a foreign corporation that has a foreign bank account in excess of $10,000.[87]

Example 16.12: Betsy Ross wholly-owns a European subsidiary called Flag Europa. Flag Europa has a bank account with a dollar equivalence at the Brinker Bank of the Netherlands. Betsy Ross must file an FBAR with respect to Flag Europa's account with the Brinker Bank of the Netherlands.

---

[87] *FBAR Questions and Answers* issued by the IRS on October 22, 2007.

¶**1610.01**

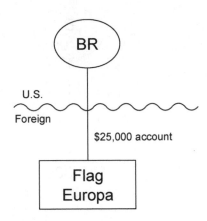

In addition to being U.S. persons that must file FBARs, flow-through[88] entities, such as U.S. partnerships and U.S. S corporations, may result in a U.S. individual having to file an FBAR. More specifically, the U.S. individual would be responsible for filing an FBAR when indirectly owning more than 50% of a foreign corporation.

Example **16.13:** Uncle Sam, a U.S. citizen, is the only U.S. person owning a share (60%) of a U.S. limited partnership. The U.S. limited partnership owns 90% of a foreign corporation (ForCo). Because Uncle Sam's indirect ownership (his interest in the U.S. limited partnership times the U.S. limited partnership's interest in ForCo) is 54%, Uncle Sam's ownership exceeds 50%. Both Uncle Sam and the U.S. limited partnership must file an FBAR for any foreign bank accounts of ForCo in excess of $10,000.

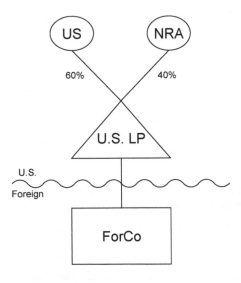

---

[88] *FBAR Questions and Answers* issued by the IRS on October 22, 2007.

A financial account is more than just a bank account. More specifically, the definition includes securities, securities derivatives, mutual funds, deficit cards and prepaid credit accounts.[89]

The FBAR is due June 30th[90] for accounts held the prior taxable year and may not be extended. Also unlike a federal tax return, the FBAR is sent to the IRS Computing Center in Detroit, not the IRS Service Center with which the U.S. person files a return. The various due dates for filing and the different locations may cause confusion for some taxpayers.

> **Example 16.14:** Johnny, a U.S. citizen, has $20,000 in a bank account with the First Bank of Italy. Each year, Johnny files his Form 1040 and his FBAR by April 15. This year, due to some late information from various partnerships in which Johnny owns interests, Johnny extends his tax return and files both his Form 1040 and his FBAR by October 15. Although Johnny's income tax return is timely filed, the FBAR, which had to have been filed by June 30 and for which extension is not allowed, is late.

Failure to file FBARs may result in either civil or criminal penalties.

Civil penalties depend on whether the failure to file was non-willful or willful. A non-willful failure to file results in a penalty that may not exceed $10,000[91] and a trade or business that is merely negligent in failing to file an FBAR incurs a $500 penalty.[92] A willful failure to file can result in a penalty of the greater of $100,000 or half of the balance in the account on June 30 when the FBAR should have been filed.[93]

The normal three-year statute of limitations for income tax cases do not apply to FBAR matters. Instead, the statute of limitations on assessment of civil penalties is six years from the June 30 date that the FBAR was due.[94]

The IRS may also pursue criminal penalties for willful failure to file an FBAR. Those criminal penalties can result in a fine of up to $250,000 and five years of imprisonment.[95]

.02 Penalties for Underpayment Attributable to Undisclosed Foreign Financial Assets

The accuracy related penalty on underpayments[96] was amended to include a penalty for an "undisclosed foreign financial asset understatement." An undisclosed foreign financial asset understatement includes the portion of an underpayment attributable to any transaction involving an undisclosed foreign financial asset. The penalty is 40% of the underpayment due to the lack of disclosure.

Undisclosed foreign financial assets are those assets with respect to required information, which the taxpayer failed to provide, pursuant to:

---

[89] IRS News Release 2007-15.

[90] Timely mailing is not timely filing as Code Sec. 7502(a)(1), which permits timely mailing as timely filing, only applies to filings related to Title 26 of the U.S. Code (the Internal Revenue Code) and the FBAR filing is a Title 31 requirement.

[91] 31 USC section 5321(a)(5)(B). Reasonable cause may be difficult to obtain if the taxpayer files a Form 1040

that inquires about foreign bank accounts and directs the taxpayer to an instruction describing the FBAR.

[92] 31 USC section 5321(a)(6)(A).

[93] 31 USC section 5321(a)(5)(C).

[94] 31 USC section 5321(b)(1).

[95] 31 USC section 5322(a).

[96] Code Sec. 6662.

¶1610.02

  (i) Code Sec. 6038 reporting for foreign corporations and partnerships (Forms 5471, 5472 and 8865);

 (ii) Code Sec. 6038B reporting for transfers to foreign persons (Forms 926, 5471 and 8865);

(iii) Code Sec. 6038D reporting for foreign financial assets held by individuals (Forms 5471 and 8865);

(iv) Code Sec. 6046A reporting for foreign partnership interests (Form 8865);

 (v) Code Sec. 6048 reporting for foreign trusts (Form 3520-A).

Example **16.15:** USCo, a U.S. company, wholly-owns and, therefore, files a Form 5471 for ForSub, a foreign subsidiary. An IRS audit results in $350,000 of additional income tax attributable to $100,000 of interest earned on an unreported bank deposit by ForSub that constituted Subpart F income. USCo is subject to the Code Sec. 6662 accuracy related penalty on underpayments with respect to an undisclosed foreign financial asset understatement.

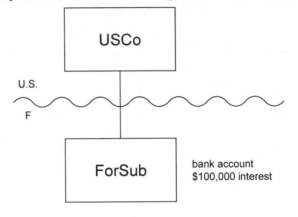

¶ 1611 APPENDIX

Form **870** (Rev. March 1992)	Department of the Treasury — Internal Revenue Service **Waiver of Restrictions on Assessment and Collection of Deficiency in Tax and Acceptance of Overassessment**	Date received by Internal Revenue Service
Names and address of taxpayers *(Number, street, city or town, State, ZIP code)*		Social security or employer identification number

Tax year ended	Tax	Increase (Decrease) in Tax and Penalties			
		Penalties			
	$	$	$	$	$
	$	$	$	$	$
	$	$	$	$	$
	$	$	$	$	$
	$	$	$	$	$
	$	$	$	$	$
	$	$	$	$	$

(For instructions, see back of form)

Consent to Assessment and Collection

    I consent to the immediate assessment and collection of any deficiencies *(increase in tax and penalties)* and accept any overassessment *(decrease in tax and penalties)* shown above, plus any interest provided by law. I understand that by signing this waiver, I will not be able to contest these years in the United States Tax Court, unless additional deficiencies are determined for these years.

YOUR SIGNATURE——▶ HERE		Date
SPOUSE'S SIGNATURE——▶		Date
TAXPAYER'S REPRESENTATIVE HERE ——▶		Date
CORPORATE NAME ——▶		
CORPORATE OFFICER(S) SIGN HERE	Title	Date
	Title	Date

Catalog Number 16894U   Form **870** (Rev. 3-92)

Form **870-AD** (Rev. April 1992)	Department of the Treasury—Internal Revenue Service **Offer to Waive Restrictions on Assessment and Collection of Tax Deficiency and to Accept Overassessment**	
Symbols	Name of Taxpayer	SSN or EIN

Under the provisions of section 6213(d) of the Internal Revenue Code of 1986 (the Code), or corresponding provisions of prior internal revenue laws, the undersigned offers to waive the restrictions provided in section 6213(a) of the Code or corresponding provisions of prior internal revenue laws, and to consent to the assessment and collection of the following deficiencies and additions to tax, if any, with interest as provided by law. The undersigned offers also to accept the following overassessments, if any, as correct. Any waiver or acceptance of an overassessment is subject to any terms and conditions stated below and on the reverse side of this form.

		Deficiencies (Overassessments) and Additions to Tax				
Year Ended	Kind of Tax	Tax				
		$	$	$		
		$	$	$		
		$	$	$		
		$	$	$		
		$	$	$		
		$	$	$		

	Date
Signature of Taxpayer	
Signature of Taxpayer	Date
Signature of Taxpayer's Representative	Date
Corporate Name	Date
By Corporate Officer Title	Date

For Internal Revenue Use Only	Date Accepted for Commissioner	Signature
	Office	Title

Cat. No. 16896Q   **(See Reverse Side)**   Form **870-AD** (Rev. 4-92)

¶1611

This offer must be accepted for the Commissioner of Internal Revenue and will take effect on the date it is accepted. Unless and until it is accepted, it will have no force or effect.

If this offer is accepted, the case will not be reopened by the Commissioner unless there was:

- fraud, malfeasance, concealment or misrepresentation of a material fact
- an important mistake in mathematical calculation
- a deficiency or overassessment resulting from adjustments made under Subchapters C and D of Chapter 63 concerning the tax treatment of partnership and subchapter S items determined at the partnership and corporate level
- an excessive tentative allowance of a carryback provided by law

No claim for refund or credit will be filed or prosecuted by the taxpayer for the years stated on this form, other than for amounts attributed to carrybacks provided by law.

The proper filing of this offer, when accepted, will expedite assessment and billing (or overassessment, credit or refund) by adjusting the tax liability. This offer, when executed and timely submitted, will be considered a claim for refund for the above overassessment(s), if any.

This offer may be executed by the taxpayer's attorney, certified public accountant, or agent provided this is specifically authorized by a power of attorney which, if not previously filed, must accompany this form. If this offer is signed by a person acting in a fiduciary capacity (for example: an executor, administrator, or a trustee) Form 56, Notice Concerning Fiduciary Relationship, must accompany this form, unless previously filed.

If this offer is executed for a year for which a joint return was filed, it must be signed by both spouses unless one spouse, acting under a power of attorney, signs as agent for the other.

If this offer is executed by a corporation, it must be signed with the corporate name followed by the signature and title of the officer(s) authorized to sign. If the offer is accepted, as a condition of acceptance, any signature by or for a corporate officer will be considered a representation by that person and the corporation, to induce reliance, that such signature is binding under law for the corporation to be assessed the deficiencies or receive credit or refund under this agreement. If the corporation later contests the signature as being unauthorized on its behalf, the person who signed may be subject to criminal penalties for representing that he or she had authority to sign this agreement on behalf of the corporation.

Form **870-AD** (Rev. 4-92)

Summons

In the matter of _____

Internal Revenue Service (Division): _____

Industry/Area (name or number): _____

Periods: _____

The Commissioner of Internal Revenue

To: _____

At: _____

You are hereby summoned and required to appear before _____
an officer of the Internal Revenue Service, to give testimony and to bring with you and to produce for examination the following books, records, papers, and other data relating to the tax liability or the collection of the tax liability or for the purpose of inquiring into any offense connected with the administration or enforcement of the internal revenue laws concerning the person identified above for the periods shown.

Do not write in this space

Business address and telephone number of IRS officer before whom you are to appear:

_____

Place and time for appearance at _____

IRS

Department of the Treasury
Internal Revenue Service
www.irs.gov

Form 2039 (Rev. 12-2001)
Catalog Number 21405J

on the _____ day of _____ , _____ at _____ o'clock _____ m.
(year)

Issued under authority of the Internal Revenue Code this _____ day of _____ , _____ ,
(year)

_____   _____
Signature of issuing officer   Title

_____   _____
Signature of approving officer *(if applicable)*   Title

Original — to be kept by IRS

¶1611

Service of Summons, Notice and Recordkeeper Certificates

(Pursuant to section 7603, Internal Revenue Code)

I certify that I served the summons shown on the front of this form on:

Date	Time

How Summons Was Served

1. ❑ I certify that I handed a copy of the summons, which contained the attestation required by § 7603, to the person to whom it was directed.

2. ❑ I certify that I left a copy of the summons, which contained the attestation required by § 7603, at the last and usual place of abode of the person to whom it was directed. I left the copy with the following person (if any): _____

3. ❑ I certify that I sent a copy of the summons, which contained the attestation required by § 7603, by certified or registered mail to the last known address of the person to whom it was directed, that person being a third-party recordkeeper within the meaning of § 7603(b). I sent the summons to the following address: _____

Signature	Title

4. This certificate is made to show compliance with IRC Section 7609. This certificate does not apply to summonses served on any officer or employee of the person to whose liability the summons relates nor to summonses in aid of collection, to determine the identity of a person having a numbered account or similar arrangement, or to determine whether or not records of the business transactions or affairs of an identified person have been made or kept.

I certify that, within 3 days of serving the summons, I gave notice (Part D of Form 2039) to the person named below on the date and in the manner indicated.

Date of giving Notice: _____   Time: _____

Name of Noticee: _____

Address of Noticee (if mailed): _____

How Notice Was Given

❑ I gave notice by certified or registered mail to the last known address of the noticee.

❑ I left the notice at the last and usual place of abode of the noticee. I left the copy with the following person (if any).

❑ I gave notice by handing it to the noticee.

❑ In the absence of a last known address of the noticee, I left the notice with the person summoned.

❑ No notice is required.

Signature	Title

I certify that the period prescribed for beginning a proceeding to quash this summons has expired and that no such proceeding was instituted or that the noticee consents to the examination.

Signature	Title

Form **2039** (Rev. 12-2001)

¶1611

Form **4564** (Rev. September 2006)	Department of the Treasury — Internal Revenue Service **Information Document Request**		Request Number

To: *(Name of Taxpayer and Company Division or Branch)*

Subject
SAIN number	Submitted to:
Dates of Previous Requests *(mmddyyyy)*

Please return Part 2 with listed documents to requester identified below

Description of documents requested

Information Due By_____   At Next Appointment ☐   Mail in ☐

From:

Name and Title of Requester	Employee ID number	Date *(mmddyyyy)*
Office Location		Telephone Number ( )

Catalog Number 23145K   www.irs.gov   Part 1 - Taxpayer's File Copy   Form **4564** (Rev. 9-2006)

FORMAL DOCUMENT REQUEST

Form **4564** (Rev. September 2006)	Department of the Treasury — Internal Revenue Service Information Document Request	Request Number

To: *(Name of Taxpayer and Company Division or Branch)*	Subject	
	SAIN number	Submitted to:
	Dates of Previous Requests *(mmddyyyy)*	

Please return Part 2 with listed documents to requester identified below

Description of documents requested

Information Due By_____	At Next Appointment ☐	Mail In ☐	
From:	Name and Title of Requester	Employee ID number	Date *(mmddyyyy)*
	Office Location		Telephone Number ( )

Catalog Number 23145K	www.irs.gov	Part 1 - Taxpayer's File Copy	Form **4564** (Rev. 9-2006)

¶1611

Rev. Proc. 2006-54

SECTION 1. PURPOSE AND BACKGROUND

.01 Purpose

.02 Background

.03 Changes

SECTION 2. SCOPE

.01 In General

.02 Requests for Assistance

.03 General Process

.04 Failure to Request Assistance

SECTION 3. GENERAL CONDITIONS UNDER WHICH THIS PROCEDURE APPLIES

.01 General

.02 Requirements of a Treaty

.03 Applicable Standards in Allocation Cases

.04 Who Can File Requests for Assistance

.05 Closed Cases

.06 Foreign Initiated Competent Authority Request

.07 Requests Relating to Residence Issues

.08 Determinations Regarding Limitation on Benefits

SECTION 4. PROCEDURES FOR REQUESTING COMPETENT AUTHORITY ASSISTANCE

.01 Time for Filing

.02 Place of Filing

.03 Additional Filing

.04 Form of Request

.05 Information Required

.06 Other Dispute Resolution Programs

.07 Other Documentation

.08 Updates

.09 Conferences

SECTION 5. SMALL CASE PROCEDURE FOR REQUESTING COMPETENT AUTHORITY ASSISTANCE

.01 General

.02 Small Case Standards

.03 Small Case Filing Procedure

SECTION 6. RELIEF REQUESTED FOR FOREIGN INITIATED ADJUSTMENT WITHOUT COMPETENT AUTHORITY INVOLVEMENT

SECTION 7. COORDINATION WITH OTHER ADMINISTRATIVE OR JUDICIAL PROCEEDINGS

¶1611

¶1611

George Washington, a U.S. citizen, has a $20,000 bank account (the U.S. equivalent of British Pounds) in Redcoat Bank of England. George Washington must file a TD F 90-22.1 with the Treasury Department in Detroit by June 30 of the following calendar year.

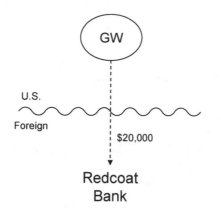

TD F 90-22.1
(Rev. October 2008)
Department of the Treasury
Do not use previous editions of this form after December 31, 2008

REPORT OF FOREIGN BANK AND FINANCIAL ACCOUNTS

Do NOT file with your Federal Tax Return

OMB No. 1545-2038

1 This Report is for Calendar Year Ended 12/31

2 0 1 0

Amended ☐

Part I   Filer Information

2 Type of Filer

a ☑ Individual   b ☐ Partnership   c ☐ Corporation   d ☐ Consolidated   e ☐ Fiduciary or Other—Enter type _____

3 U.S. Taxpayer Identification Number **177-61-7766**	4 Foreign identification (Complete only if item 3 is not applicable.)	5 Individual's Date of Birth MM/DD/YYYY
If filer has no U.S. Identification Number complete Item 4.	a Type: ☐ Passport ☐ Other _____ b Number _____ c Country of Issue _____	**02/22/1732**

6 Last Name or Organization Name **Washington**	7 First Name **George**	8 Middle Initial

9 Address (Number, Street, and Apt. or Suite No.)

3200 Mount Vernon Memorial Highway

10 City **Mt. Vernon**	11 State **VA**	12 Zip/Postal Code **22309**	13 Country **USA**

14 Does the filer have a financial interest in 25 or more financial accounts?

☐ Yes   If "Yes" enter total number of accounts _____

(If "Yes" is checked, do not complete Part II or Part III, but retain records of this information)

☑ No

Part II   Information on Financial Account(s) Owned Separately

15 Maximum value of account during calendar year reported **$20,000**	16 Type of account a ☑ Bank b ☐ Securities c ☐ Other—Enter type below

17 Name of Financial Institution in which account is held

Redcoat Bank of England

18 Account number or other designation **1776**	19 Mailing Address (Number, Street, Suite Number) of financial institution in which account is held **20 Fleet Street**

20 City **London**	21 State, if known	22 Zip/Postal Code, if known	23 Country **United Kingdom**

Signature

44 Filer Signature	45 Filer Title, if not reporting a personal account	46 Date (MM/DD/YYYY)

File this form with: U.S. Department of the Treasury, P.O. Box 32621, Detroit, MI 48232-0621

This form should be used to report a financial interest in, signature authority, or other authority over one or more financial accounts in foreign countries, as required by the Department of the Treasury Regulations (31 CFR 103). No report is required if the aggregate value of the accounts did not exceed $10,000. **See Instructions For Definitions.**

PRIVACY ACT AND PAPERWORK REDUCTION ACT NOTICE

Pursuant to the requirements of Public Law 93-579 (Privacy Act of 1974), notice is hereby given that the authority to collect information on TD F 90-22.1 in accordance with 5 USC 552a (e) is Public Law 91-508; 31 USC 5314; 5 USC 301; 31 CFR 103.

The principal purpose for collecting the information is to assure maintenance of reports where such reports or records have a high degree of usefulness in criminal, tax, or regulatory investigations or proceedings. The information collected may be provided to those officers and employees of any constituent unit of the Department of the Treasury who have a need for the records in the performance of their duties. The records may be referred to any other department or agency of the United States upon the request of the head of such department or agency for use in a criminal, tax, or regulatory investigation or proceeding. The information collected may also be provided to appropriate state, local, and foreign law enforcement and regulatory personnel in the performance of their official duties. Disclosure of this information is mandatory. Civil and criminal penalties, including in certain circumstances a fine of not more than $500,000 and imprisonment of not more than five years, are provided for failure to file a report, supply information, and for filing a false or fraudulent report. Disclosure of the Social Security number is mandatory. The authority to collect is 31 CFR 103. The Social Security number will be used as a means to identify the individual who files the report.

The estimated average burden associated with this collection of information is 20 minutes per respondent or record keeper, depending on individual circumstances. Comments regarding the accuracy of this burden estimate, and suggestions for reducing the burden should be directed to the Internal Revenue Service, Bank Secrecy Act Policy, 5000 Ellin Road C-3-242, Lanham MD 20706.

Cat. No. 12996D   Form **TD F 90-22.1** (Rev. 10-2008)

¶1611

Part II *Continued*—Information on Financial Account(s) Owned Separately		Form TD F 90-22.1
Complete a Separate Block for Each Account Owned Separately		Page Number
This side can be copied as many times as necessary in order to provide information on all accounts.		___ of ___

1 Filing for calendar year ___ ___ ___ ___	3-4 Check appropriate Identification Number ☐ Taxpayer Identification Number ☐ Foreign Identification Number Enter identification number here:	6 Last Name or Organization Name

15 Maximum value of account during calendar year reported		16 Type of account a ☐ Bank b ☐ Securities c ☐ Other—Enter type below
17 Name of Financial Institution in which account is held		
18 Account number or other designation	19 Mailing Address (Number, Street, Suite Number) of financial institution in which account is held	
20 City	21 State, if known	22 Zip/Postal Code, if known	23 Country

15 Maximum value of account during calendar year reported		16 Type of account a ☐ Bank b ☐ Securities c ☐ Other—Enter type below
17 Name of Financial Institution in which account is held		
18 Account number or other designation	19 Mailing Address (Number, Street, Suite Number) of financial institution in which account is held	
20 City	21 State, if known	22 Zip/Postal Code, if known	23 Country

15 Maximum value of account during calendar year reported		16 Type of account a ☐ Bank b ☐ Securities c ☐ Other—Enter type below
17 Name of Financial Institution in which account is held		
18 Account number or other designation	19 Mailing Address (Number, Street, Suite Number) of financial institution in which account is held	
20 City	21 State, if known	22 Zip/Postal Code, if known	23 Country

15 Maximum value of account during calendar year reported		16 Type of account a ☐ Bank b ☐ Securities c ☐ Other—Enter type below
17 Name of Financial Institution in which account is held		
18 Account number or other designation	19 Mailing Address (Number, Street, Suite Number) of financial institution in which account is held	
20 City	21 State, if known	22 Zip/Postal Code, if known	23 Country

15 Maximum value of account during calendar year reported		16 Type of account a ☐ Bank b ☐ Securities c ☐ Other—Enter type below
17 Name of Financial Institution in which account is held		
18 Account number or other designation	19 Mailing Address (Number, Street, Suite Number) of financial institution in which account is held	
20 City	21 State, if known	22 Zip/Postal Code, if known	23 Country

15 Maximum value of account during calendar year reported		16 Type of account a ☐ Bank b ☐ Securities c ☐ Other—Enter type below
17 Name of Financial Institution in which account is held		
18 Account number or other designation	19 Mailing Address (Number, Street, Suite Number) of financial institution in which account is held	
20 City	21 State, if known	22 Zip/Postal Code, if known	23 Country

Form **TD F 90-22.1** (Rev. 10-2008)

¶1611

Part III	Information on Financial Account(s) Owned Jointly	Form TD F 90-22.1

Complete a Separate Block for Each Account Owned Jointly

Page Number ___ of ___

This side can be copied as many times as necessary in order to provide information on all accounts.

1 Filing for calendar year ___ ___ ___ ___	3-4 Check appropriate Identification Number ☐ Taxpayer Identification Number ☐ Foreign Identification Number Enter identification number here:	6 Last Name or Organization Name

15 Maximum value of account during calendar year reported	16 Type of account a ☐ Bank b ☐ Securities c ☐ Other—Enter type below

17 Name of Financial Institution in which account is held

18 Account number or other designation	19 Mailing Address (Number, Street, Suite Number) of financial institution in which account is held		
20 City	21 State, if known	22 Zip/Postal Code, if known	23 Country
24 Number of joint owners for this account	25 Taxpayer Identification Number of principal joint owner, if known. See instructions		
26 Last Name or Organization Name of principal joint owner	27 First Name of principal joint owner, if known		28 Middle initial, if known

29 Address (Number, Street, Suite or Apartment) of principal joint owner, if known

30 City, if known	31 State, if known	32 Zip/Postal Code, if known	33 Country, if known

15 Maximum value of account during calendar year reported	16 Type of account a ☐ Bank b ☐ Securities c ☐ Other—Enter type below

17 Name of Financial Institution in which account is held

18 Account number or other designation	19 Mailing Address (Number, Street, Suite Number) of financial institution in which account is held		
20 City	21 State, if known	22 Zip/Postal Code, if known	23 Country
24 Number of joint owners for this account	25 Taxpayer Identification Number of principal joint owner, if known. See instructions		
26 Last Name or Organization Name of principal joint owner	27 First Name of principal joint owner, if known		28 Middle initial, if known

29 Address (Number, Street, Suite or Apartment) of principal joint owner, if known

30 City, if known	31 State, if known	32 Zip/Postal Code, if known	33 Country, if known

15 Maximum value of account during calendar year reported	16 Type of account a ☐ Bank b ☐ Securities c ☐ Other—Enter type below

17 Name of Financial Institution in which account is held

18 Account number or other designation	19 Mailing Address (Number, Street, Suite Number) of financial institution in which account is held		
20 City	21 State, if known	22 Zip/Postal Code, if known	23 Country
24 Number of joint owners for this account	25 Taxpayer Identification Number of principal joint owner, if known. See instructions		
26 Last Name or Organization Name of principal joint owner	27 First Name of principal joint owner, if known		28 Middle initial, if known

29 Address (Number, Street, Suite or Apartment) of principal joint owner, if known

30 City, if known	31 State, if known	32 Zip/Postal Code, if known	33 Country, if known

Form **TD F 90-22.1** (Rev. 10-2008)

¶1611

Part IV | **Information on Financial Account(s) Where Filer has Signature or Other Authority but No Financial Interest in the Account(s)** | Form TD F 90-22.1

Page Number

___ of ___

Complete a Separate Block for Each Account
This side can be copied as many times as necessary in order to provide information on all accounts.

1 Filing for calendar year	3-4 Check appropriate Identification Number	6 Last Name or Organization Name
___ ___ ___ ___	☐ Taxpayer Identification Number ☐ Foreign Identification Number Enter identification number here:	

15 Maximum value of account during calendar year reported	16 Type of account a ☐ Bank b ☐ Securities c ☐ Other—Enter type below

17 Name of Financial Institution in which account is held

18 Account number or other designation	19 Mailing Address (Number, Street, Suite Number) of financial institution in which account is held

20 City	21 State, if known	22 Zip/Postal Code, if known	23 Country

34 Last Name or Organization Name of Account Owner	35 Taxpayer Identification Number of Account Owner

36 First Name	37 Middle initial	38 Address (Number, Street, and Apt. or Suite No.)

39 City	40 State	41 Zip/Postal Code	42 Country

43 Filer's Title with this Owner

15 Maximum value of account during calendar year reported	16 Type of account a ☐ Bank b ☐ Securities c ☐ Other—Enter type below

17 Name of Financial Institution in which account is held

18 Account number or other designation	19 Mailing Address (Number, Street, Suite Number) of financial institution in which account is held

20 City	21 State, if known	22 Zip/Postal Code, if known	23 Country

34 Last Name or Organization Name of Account Owner	35 Taxpayer Identification Number of Account Owner

36 First Name	37 Middle initial	38 Address (Number, Street, and Apt. or Suite No.)

39 City	40 State	41 Zip/Postal Code	42 Country

43 Filer's Title with this Owner

15 Maximum value of account during calendar year reported	16 Type of account a ☐ Bank b ☐ Securities c ☐ Other—Enter type below

17 Name of Financial Institution in which account is held

18 Account number or other designation	19 Mailing Address (Number, Street, Suite Number) of financial institution in which account is held

20 City	21 State, if known	22 Zip/Postal Code, if known	23 Country

34 Last Name or Organization Name of Account Owner	35 Taxpayer Identification Number of Account Owner

36 First Name	37 Middle initial	38 Address (Number, Street, and Apt. or Suite No.)

39 City	40 State	41 Zip/Postal Code	42 Country

43 Filer's Title with this Owner

Form **TD F 90-22.1** (Rev. 10-2008)

¶1611

Part V	Information on Financial Account(s) Where Corporate Filer Is Filing a Consolidated Report	Form TD F 90-22.1

Complete a Separate Block for Each Account

This side can be copied as many times as necessary in order to provide information on all accounts.

Page Number ___ of ___

1 Filing for calendar year	3-4 Check appropriate Identification Number	6 Last Name or Organization Name
___ ___ ___ ___	☐ Taxpayer Identification Number ☐ Foreign Identification Number Enter identification number here:	

15 Maximum value of account during calendar year reported	16 Type of account a ☐ Bank b ☐ Securities c ☐ Other—Enter type below

17 Name of Financial Institution in which account is held

18 Account number or other designation	19 Mailing Address (Number, Street, Suite Number) of financial institution in which account is held		
20 City	21 State, if known	22 Zip/Postal Code, if known	23 Country
34 Corporate Name of Account Owner			35 Taxpayer Identification Number of Account Owner

38 Address (Number, Street, and Apt. or Suite No.)

39 City	40 State	41 Zip/Postal Code	42 Country

15 Maximum value of account during calendar year reported	16 Type of account a ☐ Bank b ☐ Securities c ☐ Other—Enter type below

17 Name of Financial Institution in which account is held

18 Account number or other designation	19 Mailing Address (Number, Street, Suite Number) of financial institution in which account is held		
20 City	21 State, if known	22 Zip/Postal Code, if known	23 Country
34 Corporate Name of Account Owner			35 Taxpayer Identification Number of Account Owner

38 Address (Number, Street, and Apt. or Suite No.)

39 City	40 State	41 Zip/Postal Code	42 Country

15 Maximum value of account during calendar year reported	16 Type of account a ☐ Bank b ☐ Securities c ☐ Other—Enter type below

17 Name of Financial Institution in which account is held

18 Account number or other designation	19 Mailing Address (Number, Street, Suite Number) of financial institution in which account is held		
20 City	21 State, if known	22 Zip/Postal Code, if known	23 Country
34 Corporate Name of Account Owner			35 Taxpayer Identification Number of Account Owner

38 Address (Number, Street, and Apt. or Suite No.)

39 City	40 State	41 Zip/Postal Code	42 Country

Form **TD F 90-22.1** (Rev. 10-2008)

¶1611

USCo, a U.S. C corporation, wholly-owns ForCo, a foreign corporation. ForCo has $800,000 of accumulated e&p and accumulated foreign taxes paid of $200,000. In 2011, ForCo distributes a dividend of $800,000, which is subject to foreign country F's withholding tax, which is based not on the gross amount of the dividend, but on the amount of the annual income of ForCo at a 10% rate for $30,000. Because of the question over the creditability of the withholding tax as a Section 903 credit for a tax in lieu of an income tax, USCo's tax director books a $30,000 reserve.

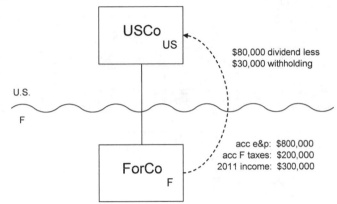

| **SCHEDULE UTP**
(Form 1120)

Department of the Treasury
Internal Revenue Service | **Uncertain Tax Position Statement**

▶ File with Form 1120, 1120-F, 1120-L, or 1120-PC.
▶ See separate instructions. | OMB No. 1545-0123

20**10** |

Name of entity as shown on page 1 of tax return	EIN of entity
USCo	

This Part I, Schedule UTP (Form 1120) is page 1 of 1 Part I pages.

Part I   **Uncertain Tax Positions for the Current Tax Year.** See instructions for how to complete columns (a) through (f). Enter, in Part III, a description for each uncertain tax position (UTP).

Check this box if the corporation was unable to obtain information from related parties sufficient to determine whether a tax position is a UTP (see instructions) ▶ ☐

(a) UTP No.	(b) Primary IRC Section (e.g., "61", "108", etc.)			(c) Timing Codes (check if Permanent, Temporary, or both)		(d) Pass-Through Entity EIN	(e) Major Tax Position	(f) Ranking of Tax Position
1	9	0	3	☑	T	-	☐	1
				P	T	-	☐	
				P	T	-	☐	
				P	T	-	☐	
				P	T	-	☐	
				P	T	-	☐	
				P	T	-	☐	
				P	T	-	☐	
				P	T	-	☐	
				P	T	-	☐	
				P	T	-	☐	
				P	T	-	☐	
				P	T	-	☐	
				P	T	-	☐	
				P	T	-	☐	
				P	T	-	☐	
				P	T	-	☐	
				P	T	-	☐	
				P	T	-	☐	
				P	T	-	☐	

For Paperwork Reduction Act Notice, see the Instructions for Form 1120.   Cat. No. 54658Q   Schedule UTP (Form 1120) 2010

¶1611

Schedule UTP (Form 1120) 2010 Page **2**

Name of entity as shown on page 1 of tax return	EIN of entity
USCo	

This Part II, Schedule UTP (Form 1120) is page ⬛ of ⬛ Part II pages.

Part II Uncertain Tax Positions for Prior Tax Years. Do not complete for 2010.

(a) UTP No.	(b) Primary IRC Section (e.g., "61", "108", etc.)	(c) Timing Codes (check if Permanent, Temporary, or both)	(d) Pass-Through Entity EIN	(e) Major Tax Position	(f) Ranking of Tax Position	(g) Year of Tax Position

Schedule UTP (Form 1120) 2010

¶1611

Name of entity as shown on page 1 of tax return	EIN of entity
USCo	

This Part III, Schedule UTP (Form 1120) is page ___1___ of ___1___ Part III pages.

Part III	**Concise Descriptions of UTPs.** Indicate the corresponding UTP number from Part I, column (a). Use as many Part III pages as necessary (see instructions).

UTP No.	Concise Description of Uncertain Tax Position
1	During 2011, a foreign subsidiary, ForCo, distributed a dividend that was subject to withholding tax, for which the taxpayer took a credit pursuant to Code Sec. 903. The issue is whether the withholding tax constitutes a creditable tax.

¶1611

Index

References are to paragraph (¶) numbers.

References are to paragraph (¶) numbers.

DEE

References are to paragraph (¶) numbers.

References are to paragraph (¶) numbers.

References are to paragraph (¶) numbers.

STA

References are to paragraph (¶) numbers.